Archaeology, History, and Predictive Modeling

Archaeology, History, and Predictive Modeling

Research at Fort Polk
1972–2002

David G. Anderson
and
Steven D. Smith

with contributions by
J. W. Joseph and Mary Beth Reed

The University of Alabama Press
Tuscaloosa and London

Copyright © 2003
The University of Alabama Press
Tuscaloosa, Alabama 35487-0380
All rights reserved
Manufactured in the United States of America

Design: Virginia Horak
Typeface: Times New Roman

∞

The paper on which this book is printed meets the minimum requirements of
American National Standard for Information Science–Permanence of Paper for
Printed Library Materials, ANSI Z39.48-1984.

Library of Congress Cataloging-in-Publication Data

Anderson, David G., 1949–
Archaeology, history, and predictive modeling research at Fort Polk, 1972–2002 /
David G. Anderson and Steven D. Smith; with contributions by
J. W. Joseph and Mary Beth Reed.
p. cm.
Includes bibliographical references and index.
ISBN 0-8173-1270-6 (alk. paper)—ISBN 0-8173-1271-4 (pbk. : alk. paper)
1. Paleo-Indians of North America—Research—Louisiana—Fort Polk. 2. Indians of
North America—Research—Louisiana—Fort Polk. 3. Land settlement patterns,
Prehistoric—Louisiana—Fort Polk. 4. Excavations (Archaeology)—Louisiana—Fort
Polk—Mathematical models. 5. Excavations (Archaeology)—Louisiana—Fort Polk—
Computer simulation. 6. Fort Polk (La.)—Antiquities. I. Smith, Steven D. II. Title.

E78.L8 A53 2003
976.3 ' 6–dc21   2002153959
British Library Cataloguing-in-Publication Data available

For Gator, Charles, Harry, and Jim
And archaeologists too numerous to mention here
Thanks for bringing the past back to life on Fort Polk

Contents

List of Figures

List of Tables

Preface

In compliance with federal mandates, cultural resource investigations have been undertaken on Fort Polk in western Louisiana since the early 1970s. An extensive program of archaeological survey, testing, and large-scale data-recovery excavations has occurred, as well as extensive historic and archival research. More than 125,000 acres of accessible terrain on the installation have been intensively surveyed, and almost 5,000 sites and isolated finds have been recorded. More than 600 of these sites have been intensively tested to evaluate their significance for placement on the National Register of Historic Places. Large-scale archaeological data-recovery excavations have also been undertaken at five sites on the installation: 16VN18, 16VN24 (Big Brushy), 16SA50 (Eagle Hill II), 16VN791, and 16VN794. This research is documented in more than 100 cultural resource management (CRM) reports, which are available for inspection and use at the installation and in a number of libraries.

This volume provides a synthesis of this primary material and includes summaries of local environmental conditions, previous cultural resource investigations, base military history and architecture, pre-1940 history of the area, the prehistoric and historic cultural sequence, predictive models of prehistoric and historic site location, and patterns of historic and prehistoric settlement. The research undertaken at Fort Polk is among the most extensive undertaken in any part of the Southeast, and it shows how archaeologists working in a CRM environment explore the past and offer directions for future research.

Acknowledgments

Syntheses like these require the help and assistance of a great many people to produce, and a major challenge is acknowledging the work of the many fine scholars whose research is being summarized. Over the past 30 years, hundreds of archaeologists have worked at Fort Polk, as crew members or as project directors, making it one of the training grounds of modern southeastern archaeology. Their contributions are summarized and acknowledged in the pages that follow, and to all who have worked on Fort Polk, we owe a debt of thanks.

None of this work would have occurred, however, without the support of a few key individuals responsible for environmental compliance on Fort Polk. In particular, Charles Stagg, Director of the Environmental and Natural Resources Management Division, and Jackie Smith, Chief, Conservation Branch, deserve special thanks for their strong and continuing commitment to cultural resource management (CRM). The primary inspiration, support, and guidance for much of the specific work that has occurred over the past two decades, however, comes from Jim ("Gator") Grafton, Fort Polk's CRM Coordinator. Gator and his assistants, Bob Hayes and Ellen Ibert, have been the heart and soul of the installation's CRM program, and they provided great support in the preparation of this synthesis. Money for CRM work does not fall from the sky but must be programmed and then fought for and, when obtained, used as wisely as possible. James ("Jim") E. Cobb, Headquarters Forces Command Archaeologist, Fort McPherson, Georgia, and the environmental team at Fort Polk named above have all fought the good fight for many years to ensure that a high level of funding has been available for CRM work on Fort Polk. Above and beyond that, their advice and support throughout the preparation of this overview have also been crucial to its completion.

Many others have helped as well. The Ranger Districts of the Kisatchie National Forest surround Fort Polk, and some of its lands are used by the Army. Forest Archeologist Alan Dorian and his staff, particularly Archeologist Geoff Lehmann and Forest Geographic Information System (GIS) Coordinator Lynn Schoelerman, provided advice and tangible help in the form of reports, site data, and GIS-generated information on cultural resources occurring on Forest Service lands. Louisiana's State Historic Preservation Office (SHPO) and the state's Division of Archaeology staff also had a great deal of input into the creation of this overview, as well as in the review of earlier drafts. Those providing assistance included Tom Eubanks (State Archaeologist, 1995–present), Kathleen M. Byrd (State Archaeologist prior to

1995), Staff Archaeologists Philip G. ("Duke") Rivet and Nancy Hawkins in Baton Rouge, Jeff Girard (Northwest Louisiana Regional Archaeologist), and Charles R. ("Chip") McGimsey, Southwest Louisiana Regional Archaeologist. Their advice and assistance, particularly in relaying details about western Louisiana archaeology, are deeply appreciated. The staff of the Western Office of the Advisory Council on Historic Preservation (ACHP) in Denver, Colorado, also provided guidance by meeting with Fort Polk and National Park Service (NPS) staff, reviewing numerous drafts of the present study, and answering a great many questions. Claudia Nissely, director of the western ACHP, and particularly staff historic preservation consultants Lee Keatinge and Alan Stanfill provided extensive assistance and support.

An earlier technical synthesis of cultural resource investigations on Fort Polk, the foundation for the present effort, was completed in 1988 while three contributors to the present volume (Anderson, Joseph, and Reed) were working for Garrow and Associates, Inc., of Atlanta, Georgia. This earlier effort was overseen by Wilfred ("Wil") Husted of the Interagency Archeological Services Division (IASD) of the NPS, which administered the project and provided advice and assistance throughout the course of the work. Mark Barnes, John E. Ehrenhard, and Harry G. Scheele, all with IASD at the time, and Jim Cobb and Constance Ramirez of the Department of the Army also provided advice and assistance to that study.

An updated technical synthesis for Fort Polk was produced in 1999 by the staff of the Technical Assistance and Partnerships division (TAPS) of the Southeast Archeological Center (SEAC). The text for that volume was produced by Anderson, Joseph, Reed, and Smith, the authors of the present study. The final product was guided and greatly shaped by Harry G. Scheele, TAPS staff archaeologist, who has handled all cultural resource contracting for Fort Polk since 1988. Tiffanie Bourassa and Dennis Finch of SEAC provided appreciable help and support in this research by coding site and assemblage data and helping in their analysis and in the assembly of the text and bibliography for the final manuscript.

The current University of Alabama Press volume is an extensively revised and updated version of the 1999 technical synthesis and was largely written by David G. Anderson and Steven D. Smith, who focused on the prehistoric and historic research, respectively. J. W. Joseph and Mary Beth Reed contributed to the historic overviews and research summaries presented in Chapters 7 and 8. Ann Powell and Emily Yates generated the index. The camera-ready manuscript was produced by Virginia Horak. The appearance of the manuscript is in large measure due to her concern with quality control. Finally, John E. Ehrenhard, SEAC's director, deserves special thanks for his support during the preparation of this manuscript.

Other individuals who have helped in the development of this document include Michael Russo, former Louisiana SHPO staff archaeologist and now an NPS archaeologist at SEAC; Greg Heide, also a SEAC archaeologist, who has handled contracts on Fort Polk with Mike Russo and Harry Scheele in recent years; Mary Cleveland, Director, Museum of West Louisiana; Jon L. Gibson, formerly of the Department of Sociology and Anthropology at the University of Southwestern Louisiana and now in enjoyable retirement; Patrick H. Garrow of Garrow and Associates, Inc., who provided advice and guidance throughout the 1988 Historic Preservation Plan project and reviewed the various drafts of that product; Charles E. Cantley, formerly with Commonwealth Associates, Inc., and now with New South Associates, who has directed a number of large-scale projects on Fort Polk; and, above all, the staff of Prentice Thomas and Associates, Inc. (formerly New World Research, Inc.), who have conducted more work at Fort Polk and made more attempts to synthesize the vast amount of data collected there than anyone else down through the years. L. Janice Campbell, Prentice Thomas, James Matthews, and Jim Morehead in particular have provided extensive advice and help over the course of this and the earlier 1988 overview effort. Julie Barnes Smith and Vince Macek prepared some of the graphics that appear in this volume, while Chris Rewerts of the U.S. Army's Construction Engineering Research Laboratory prepared the GIS-based maps.

The staff at the University of Alabama Press deserves our thanks for seeing this volume through to final production. Portions of the environmental descriptions presented in Chapter 6 appeared in somewhat different form in *Archaeology of Eastern North America* and are used here with permission. Art Spiess, the editor of *AENA*, is to be thanked for his assistance. Wayne Boyko and Jeff Irwin of the Fort Bragg Cultural Resource Management Program are to be thanked for allowing us to use Martin Pate's painting of life in the pinelands. Kathy Cummins did a remarkable job of copyediting the manuscript. Finally, Jeff Girard and Chip McGimsey did an excellent job of peer-reviewing the manuscript.

The large numbers of people who have collected cultural resource information on Fort Polk over the past 30 years—that is, the archaeologists and scholars "too numerous to mention" indicated on the dedication page—deserve our particular thanks for compiling a site and assemblage database that is one of the largest and best documented in the southeastern United States. The contributions of these individuals are discussed in the pages that follow. To all of them, this overview is our acknowledgment and tribute to their fine work.

Introduction

O ver the past 35 years, since the passage of the National Historic Preservation Act in 1966, vast quantities of archaeological and historical research have been conducted on public and private lands across the United States. Much of this work remains unknown to all but a handful of specialists, however, even though taken collectively it has helped to revolutionize our understanding of human settlement in our country. The sheer mass of information that has been recovered, however, makes understanding just how much we have learned difficult to comprehend. In this book, archaeological and historical research in a comparatively small area of western Louisiana, on the U.S. Army's Fort Polk military reservation, is summarized. The information that has been recovered and the lessons learned have much to tell us about what went on in this part of western Louisiana and adjacent portions of eastern Texas over the past 13,000 or more years and illustrate how scholars are examining this record.

Fort Polk is the headquarters of the U.S. Army's Joint Readiness Training Center (JRTC) and encompasses approximately 139,000 acres in Vernon, Sabine, and Natchitoches Parishes in west-central Louisiana. Cultural resource management (CRM) activity—mostly archaeological and historical fieldwork—has been conducted almost continuously on Fort Polk since the early 1970s, with the result that the installation has seen more investigations of this kind than any other comparably sized area in Louisiana. Only a very few localities in the entire southeastern United States, in fact, have seen a comparable level of activity. The results of the work at Fort Polk have appeared in more than 100 monographs and shorter length technical studies, most produced in low print runs, which are part of what has come to be known as the gray literature of the CRM world. These reports occupy over 10 feet of linear shelf space and are backed up by several filing cabinets and map drawers of site forms, field notes and photographs, and analysis records, as well as hundreds of boxes of artifacts. Almost 2,700 archaeological sites have been recorded on Fort Polk, an appreciable fraction of the ca. 16,000 currently recorded across the entire state of Louisiana.[1] The result is a vast

---

[1] *In this volume numerous references are made to "sites" and "isolated finds," historic property categories used by the Louisiana Division of Archaeology. Sites are defined by the presence of five or more artifacts in a 20-x-20-m area or where at least one cultural feature is present. An isolated find is defined as no more than four artifacts in a 20-x-20-m*

mass of information that, while superbly maintained by the Army in a state-of-the-art curation facility at the installation and important to documentation of the past human occupation of this part of the Southeast, is all but impossible to examine and understand in its totality.

This volume seeks to correct that situation. In the pages that follow, all of the archaeological and historical investigations undertaken on Fort Polk during the twentieth century, from ca. A.D.1972 to 2002, are summarized. The primary goal of this synthesis is to show how the installation's archaeological and historic record helps us to better understand the human occupation of this part of the Southeast, specifically the western Louisiana area. A complementary goal is to inform the general public about what can be learned from CRM activity. Specific research objectives of this volume are (1) summarizing the archaeological and historical research that has occurred on Fort Polk, including discussing the major findings of each major project; (2) documenting the prehistoric and historic cultural sequence in the area, including identifying diagnostic artifacts used to demarcate individual periods; (3) determining how the landscape in the vicinity of Fort Polk was utilized in the past by resolving what, if any, associations exist between archaeological and historic sites and specific environmental variables, such as distance to water, soil conditions, and so on; (4) documenting patterns of stone tool raw material procurement and use, a primary reason the area appears to have been visited by Native Americans in the past; and (5) documenting land use and economic activities in the area over both the historic and prehistoric eras.

Cultural Resource Management at Fort Polk

Fort Polk is located in the interriverine uplands of west-central Louisiana near the headwaters of the tributaries of three major drainages, the Sabine, the Calcasieu, and the Red Rivers (Figure I.1). The installation consists of two subunits that are in active use by the U.S. Army, the Main Fort to the south, encompassing 105,750.7 acres, and Peason Ridge to the north, encompassing 33,625.1 acres (these acreage figures are derived from the installation Geographic Information System [GIS]). Responsibility for the management of cultural resources on the installation is shared by the U.S.

---

area, with no evidence for cultural features (e.g., Campbell and Weed 1986:6–2). Isolated finds have been systematically recorded by every survey project undertaken on the installation since the 1976–1979 Fort Polk Archaeological Survey program (Servello, ed. 1983) and 2,012 have been recorded to date.

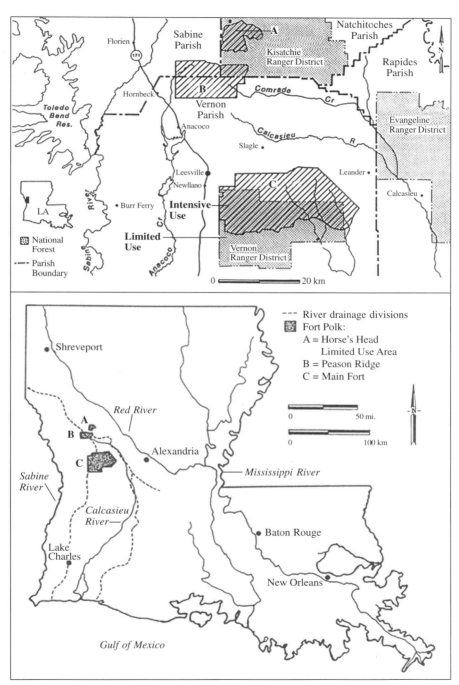

Figure I.1 — The Fort Polk area, west-central Louisiana (from Thomas et al. 1982:2, 47).

Army and the U.S. Forest Service. Approximately 61,000 acres on the Main Fort and all of the land on Peason Ridge are owned and directly controlled by the U.S. Army. The remaining lands on the Main Fort, ca. 45,000 acres, are owned and managed by the U.S. Forest Service, with responsibility for CRM shared by the Army and the U.S. Forest Service.

Approximately 102,000 acres of land on the Kisatchie National Forest are actually used by the Army. Of this total, approximately 45,000 acres are the intensive-use lands in the southern part of the Main Fort and another ca. 45,000 acres are limited-use lands located immediately to the south of these intensive-use lands. The final 12,000 acres are limited-use lands in the Horse's Head Maneuver Area, located to the northeast of Peason Ridge (Figure I.1). U.S. Forest Service land in the vicinity of the Main Fort falls within the Vernon Ranger District of the Kisatchie National Forest, while the Horse's Head Maneuver Area falls within the Kisatchie Ranger District.

On Fort Polk, the Directorate of Engineering and Housing, Environmental and Natural Resources Management Division oversees CRM activity on all installation lands owned by the Army and acts in coordination with the U.S. Forest Service on those lands controlled by that agency. Within the Environmental and Natural Resources Management Division, the Conservation Branch houses the installation Cultural Resource Manager, who is charged with implementing the historic preservation program at Fort Polk. The Cultural Resource Manager's office at the present includes office and lab space, a permanent curation facility meeting federal standards, and a staff that includes the program manager, an assistant, and a curation specialist. Much of the actual archaeological and historical research conducted on the installation has been done through contracts, which over the years have been awarded to a large number of public and private organizations, as summarized in Chapter 2. The National Park Service has assisted Fort Polk in the management of these contracts for approximately 20 years.

An active CRM program has also been operating on the Kisatchie National Forest lands for almost 30 years under the direction of U.S. Forest Service personnel, who have conducted much of the work in-house, using staff archaeologists. As a result, large portions of the intensive- and limited-use lands utilized by Fort Polk have been examined by Forest Service personnel. Although the Army has assumed responsibility for assisting in the inventory and evaluation of historic properties on lands not previously surveyed by the Forest Service, because of the large areas involved and the ongoing activities of each agency, both the Army and the Forest Service continue to conduct survey and evaluation work on these lands, typically as needed for compliance purposes, such as when construction or timber harvesting occurs. Close coordination between the two agencies through the years has resulted in high-quality, standardized data collection and reporting. This volume summarizes work conducted on Army property and U.S. Forest Service lands under intensive use by the Army. Research conducted on other U.S. Forest Service lands in this part of Louisiana is referenced where relevant to an understanding of the archaeology and history of Fort Polk; summarizing the entire Forest Service CRM program in western Louisiana would itself require an extended analysis and synthesis effort that would be to some extent comparable to that required for Fort Polk.

CRM on Fort Polk is thus a partnership between the managing federal agencies, Fort Polk and the U.S. Forest Service, and a number of consulting parties (i.e., other federal and state agencies, Indian tribal groups, and other interested members of the public), all of whom have responsibilities defined by historic preservation legislation. Two major consulting parties for Fort Polk are the Louisiana State Historic Preservation Office (SHPO) and the Advisory Council on Historic Preservation (ACHP).

The SHPO is a state agency established under the terms of the National Historic Preservation Act of 1966 to oversee state activities pursuant to that act. SHPOs also assist federal agencies within their state boundaries in meeting their legal responsibilities, especially under Sections 106 and 110 of the National Historic Preservation Act, as described in the next section. The ACHP is a federal agency, also established by the National Historic Preservation Act, that advises the President and Congress on matters relating to historic preservation and that is responsible for commenting on the appropriateness of treatment/mitigation plans for undertakings that affect historic properties. The ACHP, upon request, also reviews the historic preservation programs of specific federal agencies and installations and makes recommendations as to their effectiveness. In practice, the SHPO assumes the primary responsibility for reviewing federal undertakings for compliance with the National Historic Preservation Act, in coordination with the ACHP.

Cultural resource managers at Fort Polk work closely with the staff of the Louisiana SHPO in Baton Rouge. The SHPO has two divisions, the Division of Archaeology and the Division of Historic Preservation, which administer the implementation of the national historic preservation program in Louisiana. Among the duties of the Division of Archaeology is management of the archaeological site files, which include all of the sites found at Fort Polk. Because most of the historic properties found on Fort Polk to date are archaeological sites, most of the Environmental and Natural Resources Management Division's regular interaction is with staff of the Division of Archaeology.

Why There Is a CRM Program at Fort Polk

The United States has an extensive historic preservation program that has been undertaken, as the National Historic Preservation Act specifically states, "for the inspiration and benefit of the people" (see also Jameson 2000). Two federal laws and their implementing regulations drive most of this activity on Fort Polk: the National Historic Preservation Act of 1966, as amended, and the National Environmental Policy Act of 1969. These laws require federal agencies to inventory, evaluate, assess, and manage historic properties on lands they own or control (Advisory Council on Historic Preservation 1986, 1989).

The National Historic Preservation Act of 1966 established the preservation of significant historic properties as a national policy and created a National Register of Historic Places (NRHP). Historic properties meeting criteria for listing in the National Register may not be adversely affected by federal activities without consideration of mitigation alternatives. Much of the historic preservation program at Fort Polk, accordingly, consists of identifying historic properties, determining whether they are eligible for listing in the NRHP, preserving those properties that meet NRHP criteria or else mitigating adverse effects caused by installation activities when these cannot be avoided, and maintaining the records and collections generated by this activity. More specifically, Section 106 of the National Historic Preservation Act requires federal agency heads to take into account the effects of undertakings on properties included in or eligible for the NRHP. Thus, at Fort Polk, training activities, new construction, and any ground-disturbing activities can be defined as undertakings requiring the assessment of effects to sites eligible for or listed in the National Register. Under Section 110 of the National Historic Preservation Act, agencies are also required to inventory and evaluate, in terms of NRHP significance, all historic properties on their lands. This responsibility constitutes what is called the inventory process, and this is what has driven a great deal of the CRM work that has occurred on Fort Polk. Quite simply, the Army is required to intensively survey its lands for historic properties and to evaluate the resources that are found for NRHP eligibility. In practice, on Fort Polk this has resulted in the archaeological survey of tens of thousands of acres and the location of thousands of sites and isolated finds, plus the testing of hundreds of sites to evaluate their NRHP eligibility.

The National Environmental Policy Act requires federal agencies to incorporate appropriate consideration of the environment in their decision-making process. Further, any major undertaking must be preceded by an Environmental Impact Statement (EIS). Consideration of historic properties is part of an EIS. Specifically, the National Environmental Policy Act requires that the stipulations within Section 106 of the National Historic Preservation Act be included in the development of an EIS. Finally, explicit Army and Department of Defense regulations detail management responsibilities and standards for the treatment of historic properties (AR 200-4; Department of Defense Directive Number 4710.1) and mandate that Army installations identify the likelihood, based on scientific studies, of the presence of significant archaeological and historic properties within their boundaries; describe procedures for complying with federal laws and regulations; and conduct this work in coordination with local, state, and other appropriate federal historic preservation programs. The CRM program undertaken over the past 30 years at Fort Polk occurred because of the Army's efforts to comply with the requirements of the national historic preservation program. Comparable CRM programs, it should be noted, are in place on almost every active federal installation, generating vast amounts of information in need of examination and synthesis.

How This Volume Came About

This book is a revised and updated version of the technical synthesis monograph produced as part of a Historic Preservation Plan (HPP) for Fort Polk completed in 1999. This HPP documented the cultural resources on the installation and outlined procedures for their evaluation and management. Five HPP volumes were produced in hard copy and in electronic form:

Volume 1:   A Cultural Resources Planning Manual/Action Plan for land-management personnel at Fort Polk (Anderson and Smith 1999);

Volume 2:   A Cultural Resources Inventory Primary Data volume containing locational, assemblage, and environmental information for all sites and isolated finds on Fort Polk (Anderson et al. 1999a);

Volume 3:   An Inventory Management Summary listing primary management data on all recorded sites on Fort Polk (Anderson 1999);

Volume 4:   A Technical Synthesis/Overview volume containing knowledge gained through cultural resource investigations undertaken through 1999 on Fort Polk (Anderson et al. 1999b); and

Volume 5:   An Inventory Map volume, with sets of large-scale GIS, U.S.
             Geological Survey, and Army maps detailing the location of
             all sites found to date on the installation, areas where cultural
             resource investigations have occurred, and areas where sites
             are likely to be found (Anderson et al. 1996a).

The five volumes were extensively cross-referenced and were meant to be
used for both planning and research purposes. The contents of all five volumes are maintained in electronic form at Fort Polk and include primary
data on all sites and assemblages found through 1999 on the installation.
These data support the analyses reported here and are available to researchers through the installation's CRM program.

The 1999 HPP Technical Synthesis volume was itself a revision of an
earlier technical synthesis prepared for Fort Polk in the mid-1980s (Anderson et al. 1988; descriptions of the 1988 HPP effort are found in Anderson
1989 and Cobb 1989). The 1988 HPP, like the 1999 study, was a series of
documents that included a technical synthesis (Anderson et al. 1988), a map
volume (Anderson and Macek 1987), a planning manual (Wilson et al. 1988),
and an approximately 2,000-page inventory volume (Anderson et al. 1987).
Both electronic and paper copies of the text and data files for the 1988 HPP
were produced. The 1988 HPP, implemented in coordination with the Louisiana SHPO and the U.S. Forest Service, guided CRM activity on Fort Polk
through the 1990s until the new HPP was finalized in 1999.

The amount of work undertaken on Fort Polk in the years since 1988
was so extensive that by the mid-1990s developing a new technical synthesis and management perspective had become crucial. In 1988, only about
one-third of Fort Polk (ca. 40,000 acres) had been surveyed at some level of
intensity and approximately 1,600 separate archaeological sites and isolated
finds had been recorded. During the next decade, however, more than 50
archaeological survey projects encompassing more than 60,000 acres were
conducted and more than 2,000 new archaeological and historical sites and
isolated finds were recorded. During this same interval more than 500 archaeological sites were intensively tested and two large-scale excavations
were conducted (see Chapter 2).

Coupled with the work on Fort Polk, a great deal of activity has taken
place on nearby Kisatchie National Forest lands, where some 3,400 archaeological sites have been reported. In addition, a great deal of new archaeological, architectural, and historical research has occurred throughout Louisiana and in adjacent states, and regional and national perspectives on both
archaeology, history, and CRM have continued to evolve. To cite just one
example, in 1989 a major cultural resource overview encompassing the Loui-

siana area was completed by the Southwestern District of the U.S. Army Corps of Engineers, offering a broad interpretive perspective that was unavailable when the original Fort Polk HPP was produced (Jeter et al. 1989). Similarly, field and laboratory procedures, site locational/probability models, and interpretations of existing data have changed. Use of Global Positioning Systems to determine site locations was unheard of 15 years ago, for example, but is now a routine part of all survey and testing projects.

The revision of the HPP offered the opportunity to incorporate innovative information-management technologies. Since the early 1990s Fort Polk and the U.S. Army Corps of Engineers Construction Engineering Research Laboratory (USACERL) have been developing a GIS system for the base. Fort Polk's GIS system, developed by Kim Majerus and Chris Rewerts (1994) of USACERL, allows users to create, update, display, analyze, and print maps on a wide range of data layers developed for Fort Polk. In addition, in recent years the U.S. Forest Service has developed its own GIS-based analysis system on the Kisatchie National Forest. A wealth of environmental data has been encoded into these databases, and these data were used in the preparation of the 1999 HPP and this volume.

In compliance with Army regulations mandating periodic HPP revision, in 1993 the Fort Polk Environmental and Natural Resources Management Division asked that the National Park Service prepare an update of the 1988 HPP. A project team was assembled, including David G. Anderson and Harry Scheele of the National Park Service, Steven D. Smith of the South Carolina Institute of Archaeology and Anthropology, Chris Rewerts and Kim Majerus of USACERL, and Alan Dorian, Forest Archeologist for the Kisatchie National Forest. Anderson was a principal author and co-principal investigator (with J. W. Joseph) of the 1988 HPP. Scheele has managed the contracts for almost all of the cultural resource investigations conducted on Fort Polk since the mid-1980s. Smith, in addition to being a principal author of the Louisiana State Comprehensive Archaeological Plan (Smith et al. 1983) and a former staff member of the Louisiana Division of Archaeology, was the principal investigator for a large archaeological survey project on the installation (Abrams et al. 1995) and has recently completed a U.S. Army Legacy demonstration project documenting early historic settlement in the Fort Polk area (Smith 1999). Majerus and Rewerts, as noted above, had developed the GIS data management system now in use on Fort Polk (Majerus and Rewerts 1994). Throughout the project Dorian provided advice and feedback from a U.S. Forest Service perspective and made available site file data and reports from the Kisatchie National Forest's CRM program.

Prior to initiating work, National Park Service personnel prepared a detailed research design describing the work that would be undertaken during the HPP revision (Anderson and Scheele 1993). This document was subsequently reviewed by the Fort Polk Environmental and Natural Resources Management Division, the Kisatchie National Forest Archeologist, the State Archaeologist and other staff members of the Louisiana SHPO, and the western office of the ACHP in Denver. A Programmatic Agreement implementing this work was signed in 1996 by representatives from the Army, Fort Polk, the U.S. Forest Service, the Louisiana SHPO, and the ACHP. All five volumes of the revised HPP were completed in draft form in late 1996 and were submitted to Fort Polk for internal review prior to wider circulation. Formal review by the SHPO and ACHP, as well as a number of authorities on Louisiana archaeology, occurred in 1997 and early 1998. The five volumes, including the technical synthesis, were extensively revised and submitted in final form in 1999.

Because only a small number of copies of the 1999 HPP were produced, a decision was made by the Army and the National Park Service to make the synthesis volume more widely available. The technical synthesis/overview was submitted to the University of Alabama Press for formal publication in late 1999 and, after peer review and extensive revision, was accepted for publication in April 2002. The 30 years of research on and near Fort Polk summarized in the pages that follow are documented in groups of chapters encompassing first the prehistoric and then the historic period occupations in the Fort Polk area. Although this book is a summary of an unusually intensive program of research in a small part of western Louisiana, the approaches used and the results obtained should prove of interest over a much wider area.

Chapter 1

Environmental Setting

This chapter contains a brief environmental overview of the Fort Polk area. Similar environmental summaries have appeared in earlier reports of investigation on Fort Polk, and some of these studies provide great detail on local conditions, including those of specific parts of the installation (e.g., Abrams et al. 1995:7–11; D. Brown 1984; Campbell and Weed 1986:1-1 to 1-12; Cantley et al. 1993a:3–23; Franks 1990a:5–6; Garner 1982; Jetton and Sims 1984; Jones et al. 1997:4–8; Lenzer 1982; Schuldenrein 1984; Servello, ed. 1983:71–76; Sheehan 1982; Williams et al. 1994a:5–13). Likewise, research in nearby areas of Louisiana has provided detailed discussion of the local environmental conditions and how they affected prehistoric use of the landscape and subsequent formation and modification of the archaeological record (e.g., Girard 1998:5–8; McGimsey 1996:31–40, 137–138).

The Regional Setting

The Fort Polk area lies at the southern margin of the Hill physiographic province, in the central Gulf Coastal Plain. The region, sometimes called the Kisatchie Wold (e.g., Kniffen 1968; Welch 1942), is characterized by "(1) uplands in varying degrees of dissection; (2) relatively narrow, flat-floored alluvial valleys; and (3) one or more terraces stepped between the rolling uplands and the valley floors. . . . Deposits which underlie the upland hills and valleys of the study area are well-defined (Anderson 1960; Welch 1942). They comprise: (1) interstratified siltstones and well-cemented to poorly indurated sandstones; (2) friable sands; and (3) gravels, gravelly sands and sandy gravels" (Campbell and Weed 1986:1-3). The Fort consists of two major tracts, the Main Fort to the south, entirely within Vernon Parish, and the Peason Ridge maneuver area to the north, at the intersection of Sabine, Natchitoches, and Vernon Parishes. The two tracts are separated by a distance of about 25 km, between which flows the eastern arm of the Calcasieu River (Figure I.1). In the area of the Main Fort elevations range from 250 to 330 feet, while on Peason Ridge elevations from 300 to 400 feet or more are typical and the terrain is more dissected and irregular. Several higher hills, reaching 450 or more feet, are present in the Peason Ridge area, and Eagle Hill, at 463 feet, is one of the highest points in the immediate region.

Fort Polk lies at or near the headwaters of tributaries flowing into three major drainages, the Sabine, the Calcasieu, and the Red Rivers. The region is part of the Gulf drainage basin, with most flow trending to the south into the Calcasieu and Sabine or to the east and southeast into the combined Red/ Mississippi River system. Modern climate in the Fort Polk area is warm and moist, with average monthly temperatures ranging from the 50s to the 80s Fahrenheit (Lenzer 1982:4-38 to 4-41; NOAA 1975; Schuldenrein 1984:13). Average annual temperature is 66.1 degrees Fahrenheit, and average annual rainfall is about 57 inches. The freeze-free period is approximately 240 days.

Most soil development is assumed to have occurred during the late Pleistocene/early Holocene on underlying Tertiary bedrock units (McCulloh and Heinrich 1999). Compared with the more desiccated Peason Ridge area to the north, the Main Fort area has more floodplain and level to gently sloping terrain, which creates areas with potentially much deeper cultural deposits. Soil profiles in the uplands are typically fairly shallow, deeply weathered Ultisol order soils, whereas lowland soils have developed in deeper profiles. Unfortunately for archaeology, preservation of organic materials such as bone and charcoal is exceedingly poor in most local soil profiles. Throughout the region colluviation rates are high but episodic in character. Close-order soils mapping has been completed over the Fort Polk area, and this information constitutes a data layer within the installation Geographic Information System. The primary soils data have been used to develop measures and maps of slope characteristics, potential depth of cultural deposits, and landform groupings on the installation. The impacts of these environmental characteristics on site location in the past are explored in subsequent chapters.

A number of scholars have examined geomorphological processes operating in the Fort Polk area during the period of human occupation (D. Brown 1984; Foss et al. 1993; Garner 1982; Gunn 1982a, 1984a; Johnson 1990a; Lenzer 1982; Nials and Gunn 1982; Schuldenrein 1984; Servello 1983). Erosional processes are dominated by the effects of continuing stream incision, notably slopewash and colluviation on ridge margins, as well as alluviation in stream valleys. Discontinuous erosional patterning is evident, which reflects broad-scale climatic events over the past 12,000 or so years. Schuldenrein (1984:13) has argued that major periods of slope erosion occurred during early and later Holocene times as a result of moister conditions. During the mid-Holocene Hypsithermal interval from ca. 8000 to 5000 B.P. which was characterized by warm, dry conditions over much of the region, reduced rainfall and hence runoff resulted in lowered slope erosion.

Several pedological investigations have also been conducted in the Fort Polk area in conjunction with archaeological excavations, resulting in detailed descriptions of soil profiles and formation processes for a number of specific locales (e.g., Bianchi 1983; D. Brown 1984; Foss et al. 1993; Garner 1982; Johnson 1990b; Schuldenrein 1984). In conjunction with the data recovery at 16VN794, for example, a series of radiocarbon dates was used to calculate soil deposition rates and a model of landform development and pedogenesis in the immediate site area was proposed (Foss et al. 1993; see chapter 2).

Past and Present Vegetation Communities

At the present, the Fort Polk–Peason Ridge area is dominated by forest, or arboreal, vegetational communities. Longleaf pine is the primary species occurring over the fort area, with major stands of slash pine and oak (Brown 1945). Other tree types present in the uplands include red and post oak, red maple, sweet gum, and sassafras. The relatively narrow bottoms typically feature hardwoods including oak, swamp chestnut, water oak, and sweet gum. Paleoenvironmental analyses, notably palynological and geomorphological investigations (e.g., Delcourt and Delcourt 1983, 1985; Webb et al. 1993; Wright, ed. 1983), have documented broad regional trends in climatic and biotic conditions that would have played an important role in shaping how prehistoric human populations made use of the Fort Polk area. The Pleistocene/Holocene transition over the region was characterized by cool, moist conditions and an increase in deciduous communities, replacing the earlier colder-climate jack-pine/spruce elements. During the mid-Holocene Hypsithermal interval, drier conditions, increased erosion, and some reduction in these communities at the expense of grassland/prairie conditions are indicated; only after ca. 4500 B.P does a return to wetter conditions occur, with the emergence of essential modern vegetational communities.

The alternation of wet and dry conditions, with its concomitant effect on biotic communities, is thought to have played a major role in shaping prehistoric settlement and use of the Fort Polk area. Currently only patchy stands of prairie are present in the Fort Polk area; these are in the vicinity of Anacoco Creek in the northwestern part of Peason Ridge near Eagle Hill. In the past, particularly during the Hypsithermal, this community may have been much more extensive. Gunn (1982a:182–183, 1984a:150–151) has argued that this was likely the case and that the resulting probable decline in local biomass productivity led to a marked decline in human land use: "[I]t seems reasonable to assume that the dry and probably unstable climate resulted in impoverished upland vegetation and degradation of upland soils, including that on Eagle Hill. . . . The dry and unstable climate apparently precluded large populations. . . . Cooler and/or wetter times appear to support [larger] populations" (Gunn 1982a:182–183). With the return to cooler, wetter conditions at the end of the Hypsithermal, greater use of the Fort Polk area would again be expected, an inference matched by the local archaeological record. The basic premise of this model, that broad-scale climatic events were of considerable importance in shaping prehistoric settlement systems, including those encompassing Fort Polk, is highly compelling. As Campbell and Weed (1986:1-12) have correctly noted, however, "sound data linking climate, geomorphic, vegetational, and cultural shifts have not been gathered and synthesized for west central Louisiana."

Archaeological research has contributed directly to our understanding of past environmental conditions in the Fort Polk area. Pollen analyses conducted during the excavations at Eagle Hill II documented a possible replacement of birch-dominated hardwood communities in the Pleistocene with increasingly closed pine forests over the course of the Holocene, although the author of the study emphasized that the sample size and preservational conditions were poor, rendering the interpretation highly tentative at best (Sheehan 1982). Likewise, during the large-scale archaeological investigations at 16VN794, extensive effort was directed to recovering paleosubsistence and paleoenvironmental data (Raymer and Cummings 1993; see Chapter 2). Large quantities of fill from artifact-bearing soil horizons were floated, and the carbonized plant remains that were gathered were used to infer the kinds of tree species and the nature of the vegetational communities present in the site area at various times in the past as far back as 6000 B.P. Pollen and phytolith samples demonstrated the existence of mixed pine-oak forests back to almost 4500 B.P./4000 rcbp, with grasses and herbs in the understory (Cummings 1993:138). The phytolith data suggest relatively moist conditions in the site area over this same interval, with some fluctuation in grass populations. An analysis of charred macroplant remains yielded complementary results regarding the composition of the forest canopy. While preservation of charcoal was generally poor, oak and pine wood charcoal and hickory nutshell fragments were present in site levels dating back to 6800 B.P./6000 rcbp (Raymer 1993a:142–144; see also McGimsey 1996:137).

Lithic Raw Materials

A number of lithic materials of value to prehistoric populations are documented in the Fort Polk area, including sandstone, quartzite, ferruginous concretions, and a number of knappable cryptocrystalline materials such as silicified wood, gravel chert, and opal (Banks 1990:48–51; Heinrich 1983:552–554, 1984:165; Jolly 1982; McGimsey 1996:40–41). These materials occur locally primarily in the Catahoula and overlying Fleming Formations and in gravel deposits in stream beds, for the most part at the southern margins of the Main Fort. In particular, dense lenses of knappable gravels have been reported from the southern part of the Main Fort, where streams have cut into the underlying Miocene Williana Formation (Campbell and Weed 1986:1-4, 1-9; Campbell et al. 1987:15–16) (Figure 1.1). Given extensive land modification during the historic period, particularly erosion-induced alluviation and filling of stream channels, the occurrence of knappable gravels may have been even more extensive during the prehistoric era (Lenzer 1982:4-47 to 4-48).

Relationships between prehistoric site locations and sources of exploitable lithic raw materials have received considerable attention at Fort Polk, and several researchers have argued that the presence of knappable stone was a major factor conditioning prehistoric land use in this area (Campbell and Weed 1986:1-11; Thomas et al. 1982:106–108; see Chapter 3). Indeed, that populations throughout prehistory visited the area to exploit local stone sources is one of the primary conclusions of this volume. That prehistoric populations apparently attached considerable importance to the lithic raw materials occurring in the general area of Fort Polk is not altogether unexpected. Banks (1990:165), in a monumental synthesis of exploitable lithic resources in the south-central part of the United States, noted that the Gulf Coastal Plain west of the Mississippi was largely devoid of knappable stone (Figure 1.2). Indeed, the occurrence of formations where such materials occur in this physiographic province is highly restricted. The Fort Polk area, however, is almost ideally situated for people interested in locating and acquiring knappable stone. The Main Fort area is located at the northern margin of one of the largest sources of knappable chert gravels in the entire region (which extends even farther north than shown in Figure 1.2, to the vicinity of the Main Fort itself), while Peason Ridge lies at the intersection of the exposures of the Catahoula and Fleming Formations, where a number of other knappable materials are found.

Heinrich (1983, 1984) has documented in detail the kinds of lithic raw materials that occur in this general area and that would have been of use to prehistoric populations in a study that drew, in large measure, on archaeological investigations conducted on Fort Polk. Among the materials of which Heinrich provides detailed descriptions are silicified wood, Eagle Hill chert, gravel chert, Fleming gravel chert, Fleming opal, and Catahoula sedimentary quartzite. Silicified or petrified wood from a wide variety of ancient

Figure 1.1 — Chert gravel deposits on the Main Fort at Fort Polk at 16VN403 (top) and 16VN1472 (bottom) (from Cantley and Towler 1984:173; Morehead et al. 1995d:137).

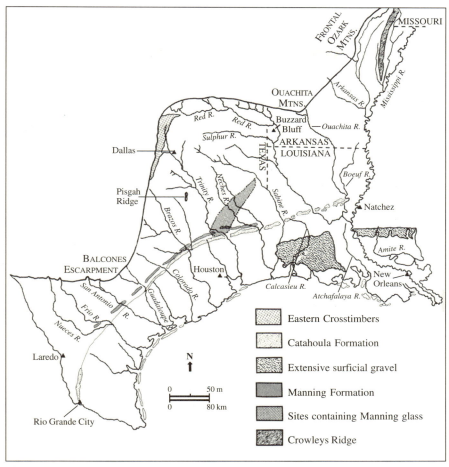

Figure 1.2 — Chert sources in the Trans-Mississippi Gulf Coastal Plain (from Banks 1990:48, courtesy of the author and the Oklahoma Anthropological Society).

species is common in this part of western Louisiana. The most distinctive of these is called fossilized palm wood (*Palmoxylon* sp.), which is characterized by "prominent rod-like structures within the regular grain" (Heinrich 1984:169). The primary outcrops are in the Miocene-age Catahoula and Fleming Formations. Of varying quality, this material was sometimes used by prehistoric populations in the Fort Polk area, although it rarely makes up a high proportion of any given assemblage and tends to be more common on sites on Peason Ridge, near where it outcrops, than on sites on the Main Fort area, where knappable chert gravels are more readily accessible. Petrified wood, when highly silicified, was typically knapped, but at one location on

Peason Ridge a large mallet and an associated anvil stone or very crude core of this material were found at 16VN1696 (Jones et al. 1996a:79–80). A second large petrified wood tool, possibly a chopper, together with a hematite pitted stone, was also found on Peason Ridge at 16VN258 (Mathews et al. 1995:81–82) (Figure 1.3). Use of petrified wood for heavy-duty pounding or chopping functions appears indicated, over and above the more typical pattern of reduction into unifacial and bifacial tool forms.

Eagle Hill chert, named for the locality on Peason Ridge where it is thought to outcrop and where it is fairly common in site assemblages, is described as "massive silicified wood that lacks any visually recognizable relict woody structure" (Heinrich 1984:172). Heinrich further describes the chert as

> a hard, massive, microcrystalline silica. It breaks with a smooth to irregular conchoidal fracture, which reveals a dull to waxy, opaque to translucent chert. It lacks any recognizable relict woody texture. This chert also lacks any visible crystals or grains. . . . The Eagle Hill Chert has a white, earthy cortex that lacks any polished pebble surfaces or associated weathering rinds. . . . [It] has a white to off-white cortex. It varies from a few mm to several cm in thickness. The cortex of an unmodified nodule of Eagle Hill Chert appeared to grade into claystone. . . . [P]oorly preserved, relict woody structures [are] observable only in thin sections [Heinrich 1984:172–173].

Eagle Hill chert is thus an extremely high-quality cryptocrystalline material that is highly uniform in texture. It appears to have been particularly attractive to Paleoindian or Early Archaic populations in the area, supporting arguments advanced by Goodyear (1979) that these populations intentionally sought out the highest-quality materials for their toolkits to facilitate an adaptation based on high mobility and the need for a dependable toolkit when ranging far from raw material sources.

Heinrich (1984:175) describes the gravel cherts that occur widely in the Main Fort area and farther south as the most important and widely utilized knappable lithic raw material in all of Louisiana. These gravel cherts have been described by Heinrich (1984:176) as consisting of

> hard, microcrystalline silica. They possess well-developed pebble surfaces and weathering rinds. Most of these pebbles break along preexisting fractures, forming irregular or flat surfaces unsuitable for the manufacture of artifacts. Enough of the gravel chert breaks with a conchoidal fracture, however, to provide a usable source of

Figure 1.3 — a, b: Petrified wood chopper and hematite pitted stone from 16VN258; c, d: mano and metate from 16VN573; e, f: mano and metate from 16VN1136. The top scale applies to a and b; the bottom scale to c–f (Sources: Campbell et al. 1994a:67; Mathews et al. 1995:82; Morehead et al. 1995a:128).

chert. In some cases, the poor quality and limited size of the chert gravel affected the form of artifacts made from it (Brassieur 1983:253).

The color of the gravel chert varies considerably. Mostly dull, opaque light greys, whites, brownish yellows, dark yellowish browns, and other colors of the [Munsell] 10YR hue dominate the color of this material. Colors ranging from weak red (10YR4/4) to light olive brown have been noted in gravel and artifacts examined. Hues redder than 10R appear to represent colors formed by thermal alteration, because these colors generally are associated with features such as potlids and spalling. The gravel cherts are typically dull and opaque and may contain molds of fossils, pores, or other voids [Heinrich 1984:176].

These gravels are assumed to have been alluvially transported from weathered Paleozoic strata in the Ouachita and other mountains to the north. As noted previously, thick deposits of chert gravel are found near the southern part of the Main Fort on Fort Polk, in the Williana Formation. The vast majority of all flaked stone tools and debitage found on the installation are made of these gravel cherts. Assemblages from sites located at or near the gravels, furthermore, frequently exhibit extensive evidence for the testing and subsequent reduction of these materials (see Chapters 3 and 5). Given the great diversity of diagnostic lithic and ceramic artifacts found on Fort Polk, materials that also tend to occur in small numbers at individual sites, brief visits to exploit these gravel cherts by populations based elsewhere appear to account for much of the local archaeological record.

Fleming gravel chert is a fine-grained black chert whose only known occurrence is in a "ravine tributary of the Sabine River in Vernon Parish" (Heinrich 1984:179). A few artifacts of a black chert have been reported on Fort Polk and may be of this material (Brassieur 1983:252; Jolly 1982:292). Fleming opal is described as "a massive, usually vitreous and translucent material" (Heinrich 1984:179) that can be readily differentiated from local cherts by its lower density and hardness. While this material is knappable, artifacts made of it have not been positively identified at Fort Polk; Heinrich (1984:181) indicates that materials previously identified as Fleming Opal on the installation were, on the basis of petrographic analysis, actually Eagle Hill chert. This conclusion was also generally supported by a neutron activation analysis of chert artifacts found at 16SA50 (Eagle Hill II) by Brown (1982b:180), who notes that "none of the debitage samples studied shows any relationship to the local opal samples. Although visually similar in some cases, they are chemically quite distinct."

Catahoula sedimentary quartzite, also sometimes described as ortho-quartzite, quartz arenite, or silicified sandstone or siltstone, is also found on Peason Ridge, within outcrops of the Catahoula Formation (Heinrich 1984:184). The material is described as

> a very well-cemented sandstone. It breaks through its constituent grains with a rough, hackey fracture. Fractures reveal rough, usu-ally vitreous material, which sparkles with numerous pinpoint re-flections. Scattered grains of opaque black and reddish brown sand seem to "float" in an otherwise translucent matrix. On weathered surfaces, a thin ashy, white cortex occurs. The cortex is less than a millimeter thick and contains distinct grains of sand. Some of the Catahoula Sedimentary Quartzite consists of an opaque and duller material in which distinct grains of sand can be seen. . . .
>
> The Catahoula Sedimentary Quartzite consists of fine to coarse-grained sand cemented by opal. The sand is angular and poorly sorted. Approximately 70 to 90 percent of the sand is quartz, of which half is volcanic quartz. The remaining 10 to 30 percent con-sists of feldspar, volcanic rock fragments, bentonitic clasts, and quartzose rock fragments in variable proportions [Heinrich 1984:182–183].

Artifacts are occasionally found made from this material on Fort Polk; a typical use of the material was for grinding implements like manos and metates, which would have taken advantage of the excellent abrading qual-ity of the grainy surface texture (see Chapter 3).

Paleontological Remains

In 1993 significant Miocene-age fossil-bearing deposits were found on Fort Polk and were the subject of intensive examination in 1994 and 1995 by Dr. Judith A. Schiebout of the Museum of Natural Science, Louisiana State University (M. Jones et al. 1995; Schiebout 1995; Schiebout and Dooley 1995). The fossils were initially found during the excavation of a borrow pit that exposed the Castor Creek Member of the Fleming Formation on the Main Fort. Bone and tooth fragments were noted by personnel from the Cultural Resource Manager's office, including what was later identified as the mandible of a Miocene horse. Dr. Schiebout visited the site on June 24, 1993, and made an initial collection of fossils and fossil-bearing matrix, identifying a number of species of mammals, reptiles, and other organisms.

The significance of the discovery prompted Fort Polk to fund a major multidisciplinary investigation of these remains over the next two years that involved work directed to documenting the fossils within the locality and their paleoenvironmental associations. Coring, thin-sectioning, stable isotope, palynological, paleobotanical, phytolith, and invertebrate and vertebrate paleontological analyses were conducted, documenting the Castor Creek Member in the locality in great detail and generating information on Miocene environmental conditions and paleoecology. Many of the analytical procedures employed, the study demonstrates, could be used to reconstruct environmental conditions in the vicinity of archaeological sites in this part of western Louisiana. The discovery encompasses the oldest terrestrial mammalian faunal remains found to date in Louisiana and has attracted widespread local interest. A popular brochure on the paleontological work and its importance was released in 1995 (Schiebout and Dooley 1995). While bone preservation is almost completely nonexistent in the sandy, well-drained, and acidic soils in the shallow archaeological deposits found and examined to date on Fort Polk, the paleontological study indicates significant fossilized and subfossilized remains are present in the area and should be recorded when encountered during fieldwork.

Blood-residue analyses conducted on projectile points found in the Lake Anacoco area immediately west of Fort Polk produced limited results (there was slight indication that dog blood residue may have been present). This technique offers an alternate means to traditional zooarchaeological or paleontological analyses documenting animal populations exploited by early human populations in the area (McGimsey 1996:121).

Conclusions

Given careful control of geomorphological processes and historic land-modification practices, the environmental associations of archaeological sites can be examined to develop broad pictures of past settlement and land-use practices. Several researchers working on Fort Polk and in the nearby Kisatchie National Forest have attempted to examine these associations, with the ultimate goal of identifying areas that were particularly favorable or unfavorable for past settlement or use (Chapter 3). These researchers have typically examined archaeological site location in relation to soils, drainage, and other landform characteristics. A detailed examination of predictive modeling efforts undertaken on and near Fort Polk is presented in Chapters 3 and 4.

Archaeological research undertaken in this part of Louisiana must above all take into account the extensive changes that have occurred during the historic period. Between the late nineteenth century and the end of the first third of the twentieth century, virtually the entire Fort Polk area was logged over, and a complex array of railroad logging trams was constructed throughout the region (see Chapters 7 and 8). Much of this activity took place at the expense of archaeological sites, which, since they occupy the upper soil horizons, are particularly susceptible to damage by these types of activities. In addition, a certain amount of agricultural land clearing occurred prior to the establishment of the military reservation, with the result that the upper deposits of some sites were also damaged or destroyed. Finally, military use of the area over the past 60 years, particularly tracked-vehicle movement and firing activity, has also resulted in damage to archaeological deposits. These historic land-use practices have combined to alter natural drainage and erosion patterns, affecting the water table and flooding patterns, and this in turn has affected archaeological resources. Erosion-induced alluviation of stream bottoms, for example, is inferred to have covered and hence masked the location of many possible stream-bed gravel/quarry sites (Lenzer 1982:4-48). As we shall see in subsequent chapters, however, a rich archaeological record remains in this part of western Louisiana. As a result of modern cultural resource management practices, the Fort Polk area is one of the few areas in the region where these remains are well protected and where the opportunities exist to examine them carefully.

Chapter 2

Previous Cultural Resource Investigations in the Vicinity of Fort Polk

This chapter provides a brief history and description of the cultural resource investigations undertaken on and near Fort Polk through early A.D. 2002. A listing of these projects is given in Table 2.1, together with summary data on the total acreage investigated or number of sites excavated. As can be seen from the table, almost 5,000 sites and isolated finds have been reported to date on the installation, and 646 of these have received further examination, most in the form of intensive testing. The discussion here focuses primarily on the larger projects that have occurred, including the five major excavation projects at prehistoric sites, for which the work is described at some length. Prehistoric research findings are emphasized in this chapter and in Chapters 3 through 6. The results of investigations at historic sites, briefly noted in this chapter, are summarized in considerable detail in Chapters 7 and 8. The emphasis in this chapter on prehistoric research is related, in part, to the nature of the Fort Polk landscape, on which prehistoric sites and isolated finds outnumber historic sites and isolated finds by almost an order of magnitude. The reasons this is the case are discussed in the pages that follow. Much greater detail about individual projects, of course, can be found in the original documents and in the collections and records curated at Fort Polk and elsewhere.

It must be emphasized that all of the archaeological research that has occurred on Fort Polk is the direct result of federal funding and legal mandates. Prior to 1972, when the first cultural resource management (CRM) work was done, only a handful of sites had been recorded from this part of Louisiana. Indeed, were it not for the federally funded activity that has occurred on Fort Polk, as well as in the nearby Kisatchie National Forest, this part of Louisiana would still be largely unknown and unexplored archaeologically. With the establishment of the Louisiana Regional Archaeology Program in 1989, however, state-supported research carried out in recent years in west-central Louisiana has increased dramatically (e.g., Girard 1998, 2000a; McGimsey 1996). The information gained and lessons learned from the CRM programs conducted on and near Fort Polk have helped shape

Table 2.1 — Cultural resource investigations undertaken on Fort Polk, Louisiana, 1972–2002

Project Name	Date Range	Acres	Sites Examined	Isolates	NRHP *	Location **	Density ***	References
Survey Projects								
Diamond Ore	1972	?	10	0	0	PR	n/a	Gregory and Curry 1972
Fort Polk Archaeological Survey	1976–1979	10,600	352	196	n/a	MF/PR	5.17	Servello, ed. 1983
Bayou Zourie	1980	800	9	10	n/a	MF	2.38	Jolly and Gunn 1981
NWR Sample Survey	1981	8,096	215	133	n/a	MF/PR	4.30	Thomas et al. 1982
MPRC Survey	1985	17,275	339	216	129	MF	3.51	Campbell and Weed 1986
Kisatchie Regional Environmental Management Group (7 projects)	1984–1986	348	n/a	n/a	n/a	MF	n/a	Servello 1985a–e, 1986
Family Housing Area Survey	1987	1,125	18	0	4	MF	1.60	Poplin 1987
NPS Surveys (2 projects)	1987–1988	100	3	1	1	MF	4.00	Husted 1988; Husted and Ehrenhard 1988
Earth Search (17 projects)	1989–1992	4,685	121	78	16	MF/PR	4.25	(See Table 2.2)
Earth Search, Fullerton Area	1993	2,745	20	35	4	MF	2.00	McMakin et al. 1994
R. Christopher Goodwin (19 projects)	1992–1995	12,159	309	280	38	MF/PR	4.84	(See Table 2.3)
Gulf South Research (7 projects)	1994–1996	5,180	94	55	17	MF/PR	2.88	(See Table 2.5)
SCIAA Intensive Survey #1	1993–1994	8,027	154	127	18	MF/PR	3.50	Abrams et al. 1995
New South Associates Survey	1995–1996	14,622	342	414	38	MF	5.17	Cantley et al. 1997
SCIAA Intensive Survey #2	1996–1997	12,538	310	168	76	MF	3.81	Clement et al. 1998
TRC Garrow Associates	1998	6,407	68	79	14	PR	2.29	Ensor et al. 1999
SEAC Surveys (2 projects)	1999	119	4	8	0	MF	10.1	Heide 1999a, 1999b
University of Memphis	1999–2000	4,579	118	90	29	LUA	4.54	Ensor et al. 2001
Panamerican Consultants #1	1999–2000	6,535	27	19	7	LUA	0.70	Saatkamp et al. 2000
Panamerican Consultants #2	2000	4,212	39	22	14	MF/LUA	1.45	Saatkamp et al. 2001
Panamerican Consultants #3	2000–2001	4,862	108	67	17	LUA	3.60	Bundy and Buchner 2002
USFS Surveys on Fort Polk	1977–1996	2,242	30	14	4	MF/PR	1.96	(See Table 2.6)
Totals		127,256	2,690	2,012	426	MF/PR	3.74	

Table 2.1 (cont.) — Cultural resource investigations undertaken on Fort Polk, Louisiana, 1972–2002

Project Name	Date Range	Acres	Sites Examined	Isolates	NRHP *	Location **	Density ***	References
Testing/Excavation Projects								
Fort Polk Archaeological Survey	1976–1979		27			MF/PR		Servello, ed. 1983
Eagle Hill II	1980–1981		1			PR		Gunn and Brown 1982
Eagle Hill Locality Testing	1982–1983		56			PR		Gunn and Kerr, eds. 1984
Commonwealth Associates	1983–1984		39			MF/PR		Cantley and Kern 1984
MPRC Intensive Testing	1986		20			MF		Campbell et al. 1987
Interagency Archeological Services, NPS	1987–1988		1			MF		Husted and Ehrenhard 1988
NWR 16VN791 Data Recovery	1989		1			MF		Campbell et al. 1990
NSA 16VN794 Data Recovery	1991		1			MF		Cantley et al., eds. 1993
PTA Intensive Testing Program (50 projects)	1991–2002		500			MF/PR		(See Table 2.4)
Totals			646					

Exclusion areas:
Peason Ridge Impact Area (GIS), 8,336 acres
Redleg Impact Area (GIS), 4,842 acres
Cantonment Area, 4,000 acres
Area left to survey: none on the Main Fort or Peason Ridge.

*   *Sites potentially eligible for the National Register of Historic Places*
**   *PR = Peason Ridge; FP = Fort Polk; LUA = limited-use area.*
***   *Resource density (sites and isolated finds per 100 acres)*

much of our understanding of past occupation in this area and the research questions currently under examination.

The 1972 Diamond Ore Test Area Survey

The earliest cultural resource investigations undertaken on Fort Polk were conducted in 1972 by Hiram F. Gregory and H. K. Curry (1972) and consisted of a reconnaissance-level walkover survey of unspecified portions of six sections on the eastern end of Peason Ridge, in the proposed Diamond Ore Test Area, Vernon Parish, Louisiana. Fifty person-hours of field time were expended during the survey along roads and compass transects. Attention was directed to areas of exposed ground, and periodic "scratch samples" (the raking away of underbrush) were done in areas of dense underbrush (Gregory and Curry 1972:7). Seven prehistoric and three historic sites were found and described, none of which was considered significant enough to warrant further investigation. The Diamond Ore Test Area was resurveyed in 1977 as part of the Essex Area survey by Servello and his colleagues, who employed shovel testing procedures and found a large number of sites (Servello and Morgan 1983:189–192). The 1972 project was a brief, initial reconnaissance effort and can be judged quite successful by the standards of its time. The project is the only one in which surface survey procedures alone were employed; subsurface testing as a site discovery method has been used on all subsequent projects on the installation.

The 1976–1979 Fort Polk Archaeological Survey Program

From October 1976 through January 1979, an intensive research program was conducted on Fort Polk under the direction of Dr. A. Frank Servello of the University of Southwestern Louisiana: the Fort Polk Archaeological Survey and Cultural Resources Management Program, or FPAS for short. The work included a sample archaeological survey across the entire base for planning and predictive modeling purposes, smaller-scale surveys in proposed development areas, extensive testing at a number of sites, and large-scale excavations at two sites. The research focused on prehistoric sites; historic archaeological sites were recorded in some cases but otherwise saw little investigation. A range of ancillary investigations were also conducted, including studies directed to resolving geomorphological conditions and the identification of local lithic raw materials (e.g., Heinrich 1983; see Chapter 1). The work was reported in a massive 1,156-page monograph that appeared

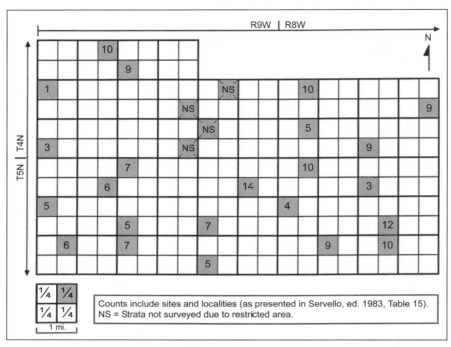

Figure 2.1 — Quarter section random sample survey units on Peason Ridge, FPAS, 1977 (adapted from Servello and Morgan 1983:196).

in two volumes, printed in a large number of copies, that to this date is the largest CRM publication produced at the installation and still among the most accessible (Servello, ed. 1983).

On Peason Ridge, the archaeological survey work included the examination of a randomly selected sample of 27 quarter sections (Figure 2.1), a reexamination of the Essex (Diamond Ore) Test Area, and the intensive archaeological survey of two entire sections in the northwest corner of Peason Ridge in the vicinity of Eagle Hill. A number of sites were also located outside of the designated sample units while the project team worked on the base, and these were examined. On the Main Fort, surveys of specific tracts of land in areas of planned construction were conducted, notably in the Bayou Zourie Area, in two Sewage Treatment Plant Areas, and along the Lookout Road Tank Trail Route. In all, approximately 10,600 acres or just over five percent of the total fort area was examined on the Main Fort and Peason Ridge (Servello, ed. 1983:xiii). A total of 352 archaeological sites and 196 isolated finds were recorded during the FPAS investigations, and the authors estimated that some 10,000 sites and isolated finds were likely present over all of Fort Polk (Servello, ed. 1983:xv); the actual numbers recorded in the years since show this estimate was not far off the mark. The FPAS project marked the first use of extensive subsurface testing to locate archaeological sites, with over 1,500 50-x-50-cm units opened over the course of the investigations and all fill screened through 1/4-inch mesh. A detailed overview of the prehistoric and historic cultural sequence for the immediate region was described (Servello, ed. 1983:19–70, 161–168), providing the first extended review of local archaeological knowledge. Detailed descriptions of prehistoric artifacts were presented (Brassieur 1983; Servello, ed. 1983:329–376), together with an extensive analysis of environmental factors influencing site location (Servello, ed. 1983:71–77, 107–159; see Chapter 3).

Intensive site-mapping, surface-collection, and testing operations were conducted at eight sites in the Eagle Hill area of Peason Ridge: 16SA8 (Eagle Hill I), 16SA50 (Eagle Hill II), 16SA95 (Eagle Hill III), 16SA92 (Eagle Hill IV), 16SA99 (Eagle Hill V), 16SA51 (Eagle Hill VI), 16SA79 (the Observatory site), and 16SA109 (Servello and Bianchi 1983). These examinations provide an extensive body of data on this locality, which appears to have attracted appreciable attention and interest from early human populations in the region, based on the artifacts recovered (Figure 2.2). In fact, the Eagle Hill I site, near the promontory of the same name, appears to have been a focal point for settlement in the Peason Ridge area, particularly during the earlier Archaic and Paleoindian periods: these early groups appear to have been attracted by the prominent landmark. Because the site has been destroyed, the data collected by the FPAS survey (Servello and Bianchi 1983:390–403) may be all that are ever obtained from this location. Intensive surface and subsurface testing was also conducted at nine sites in the Castor Creek Sewage Treatment Facility Area at sites 16VN279–283 and 16VN285–288 (Servello and Morehead 1983). Intensive testing was also conducted at eight sites on the Lookout Road Tank Trail, including 16VN24 (Big Brushy), 16VN77 (Comes Lupi), 16VN79 (Student's), 16VN80 (Little Brushy), 16VN81 (Zerfleischt), 16VN82 (Ribbon), 16VN83, and 16VN125 (Lazy Peons) (Morehead 1983). Large-scale excavations were subsequently conducted at 16VN18 and 16VN24 (Big Brushy) in areas where construction projects were planned (Fredlund 1983; Guderjan and Morehead 1980, 1983). These are two of the five sites that have witnessed large-scale excavation on the installation to date.

THE 16VN18 EXCAVATIONS
Site 16VN18, in the Bayou Zourie survey area, was examined because it was in an area slated for development into family housing units (Figure 2.3). Field investigations were conducted from December 1976 through March 1977 under the direction of Frank Servello and Glen G. Fredlund (Fredlund

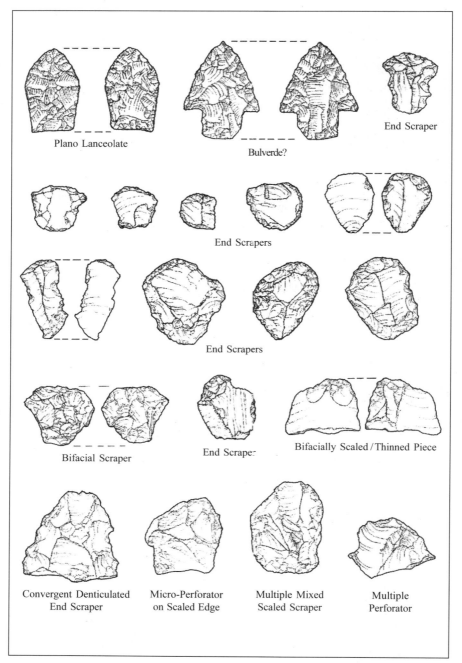

Figure 2.2 — Probable Late Pleistocene/Early Holocene tools, Eagle Hill I site (16SA8), Peason Ridge/Eagle Hill locality (from Servello and Bianchi 1983:394, 395, 402)

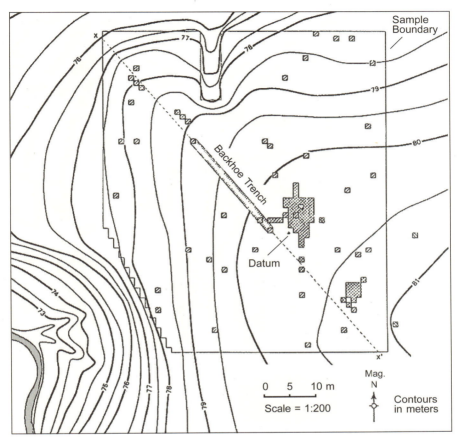

Figure 2.3 — Site 16VN18 contours and excavation units, University of Southwestern Louisiana FPAS excavations (from Fredlund 1983:784).

1983). The site was located along a small tributary of Bayou Zourie in an ecotonal setting dominated by loblolly and oak and between zones characterized by longleaf pine and hardwoods (Figure 2.4). Site 16VN18 was centrally located within this tributary basin near the juncture of two channels. Within the Bayou Zourie survey area a disproportionate number of archaeological sites were found within this loblolly-oak zone, which, although an artifact of modern timbering practices, appears to have been a favored area for prehistoric settlement (Fredlund 1983:780).

A multistage program of field investigations was conducted at 16VN18, consisting of dispersed test pitting followed by the excavation of two block units. First, a 1 percent sample of the total surface area of the scatter, which extended just over 3,000 m², was examined using 1-x-1-m squares. Thirty

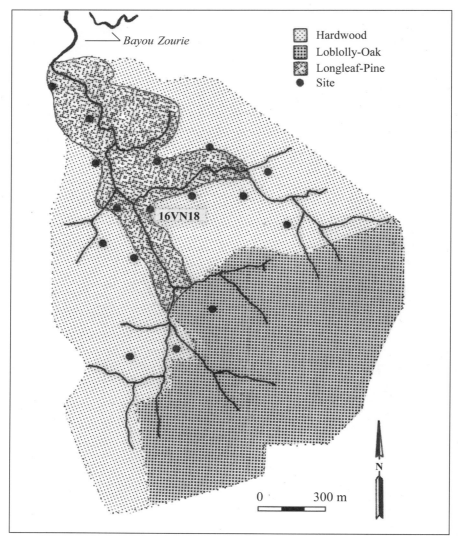

Figure 2.4 — Site 16VN18 local vegetation and drainage conditions (from Fredlund 1983:784).

squares were initially excavated, with each location selected using a simple random sampling procedure. Nine additional 1-x-1-m squares were intuitively placed in site areas left unexamined by the simple random sampling selection procedure. The 39 units were excavated in 10-cm levels, with the fill screened through 1/4-inch mesh; each unit was typically carried to a depth of 80 cm or more. An examination of artifact density revealed three areas of concentration on the site, which were labeled A, B, and C (see Figure 2.5). Eight additional 1-x-1-m test units were opened in these areas: four in A, one in B, and three in C (Fredlund 1983:785). Large numbers of artifacts were observed in Areas B and C. Area B appeared to be fairly late, while evidence for a very early occupation was observed in Area C.

In all, 3,696 artifacts were found during the testing, of which flaked stone (tools and debitage) constituted 99 percent of the total. Some selection for petrified wood was indicated in deeper levels of the test pits, and there was a general tendency for flake size to increase with depth (Fredlund

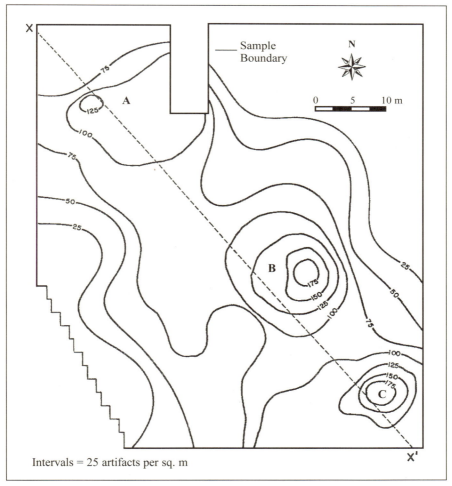

Figure 2.5 — Site 16VN18 total artifact density and site areas A, B, and C (from Fredlund 1983:786).

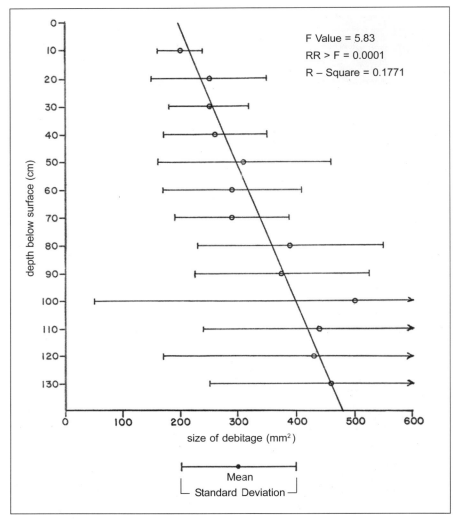

Figure 2.6 — Flake size by depth below surface, 16VN18 (from Fredlund 1983:797).

1983:795–797) (Figure 2.6). Twenty-one projectile points were found during the testing. Small arrow points were found solely in the upper 40 cm, and of a total of five such points, four were in Area B. Three of these could be identified by type: two were Friley points and one was a Perdiz (Fredlund 1983:798). Four Gary points were recovered, one in the 0–40 cm level of Area C, two in the 40–80 cm level of Area B, and one below 80 cm in Area B. Twelve expanding-based projectile points were also found in these units, 10 classified as Ellis, one as an Edgewood, and one as an Evans. Although their location was not reported by type, only one of these forms was found in the 0–40 cm level (in Area C), five came from 40–80 cm in depth (one in Area A and four in Area C), and six came from below 80 cm (one in Area B and five in Area A). A stratigraphic superposition of arrow points and Gary over Ellis points is indicated. A sample of charcoal from levels containing primarily Ellis points produced a date of 3115 ± 615 rcbp (UGa-1877; Fredlund 1983:800) (see Table 6.2 for a listing of all radiocarbon, thermoluminescence, and Oxidized Carbon Ratio [OCR] dates obtained from Fort Polk, with calibrations). Sixteen sand-and-grog-tempered sherds, 15 plain and one incised, were also found in the test units: five from 0–40 cm (all in Area B), 10 from 40–80 cm (one in Area A, seven in Area B, and two in Area C), and one below 80 cm (in Area C) (Fredlund 1983:810). The ceramic distributions indicate fair mixing of the deposits. No cultural features other than one recent privy were identified in the test units and earlier prehistoric features are thought to have eroded and oxidized completely away. The upper level of Area B was interpreted as reflecting late prehistoric probable Caddoan occupation whereas the lower levels of Area C, where the Ellis points occurred, were interpreted as Late Archaic in age (Fredlund 1983:812).

During the second and final phase of the excavations at 16VN18 two block units were excavated, one each in Areas B and C. In all, 40 1-x-1-m squares were opened in the upper part of Area B. Each square was removed in 25-x-25-cm units to provide fine-grained distributional data. The cultural deposits examined in this area were shallow, typically extending no more than 25 cm in depth, and dated primarily to the late prehistoric Caddoan era. In Area C, 10 1-x-1-m units were opened into deeper, presumably Late Archaic levels in 50-x-50-cm quadrants. Overburden to a depth of 80 cm was removed, below which two levels were excavated from 80 to 105 cm and from 105 to 125 cm, respectively. In both blocks all fill was passed through 1/4-inch mesh. On the last day of the excavations a backhoe trench was opened between Areas A and B to explore site geomorphology.

A total of 1,797 artifacts were found in the 40 m² opened in Area B, of which 1,695 were unmodified lithic reduction fragments and 90 were flaked stone tools that included burins, scrapers, perforators, notches, and denticulates (Fredlund 1983:812–813). Only a few nondiagnostic grog- and sand-tempered sherds were recovered; one rim sherd incised with a single line appears to come from a straight-walled jar (Fredlund 1983:809). The distribution of a number of artifact categories was plotted over the excavation block, revealing several possible chipping areas (Fredlund 1983:813–849). Twenty-three bifaces, including one Gary, one Perdiz, and two Friley points, were found in the block; the majority of the remainder of the bifaces are described as "either small fragments or what appear to be Friley points in various production stages" (Fredlund 1983:834). Tool distributions were plotted and examined and refitting analyses were conducted, although no obvious clustering suggesting activity areas was identified (Fredlund 1983:829). A late prehistoric, possibly Caddoan culture extended occupation camp and chipping station was indicated. The low incidence of ceramics, however, suggests a relatively impermanent occupation, perhaps by a male task group.

The excavations in Area C (10 m²) yielded a total of 704 chipped stone artifacts, of which 668 pieces were reduction debris and 36 were tools, mostly retouched flakes (Fredlund 1983:837). Two distinct concentrations of debitage were observed in the southern half of the block in the deeper, Archaic levels, which were thought to reflect differing activities or events (Figure 2.7). Eleven expanding-based projectile points, described as of the "Ellis, Ensor, or Edgewood types," were found, as well as a number of other formal tools, including two adzes or "Clear Fork Gouges" (Fredlund 1983:849). Three possible non–chipped stone tools were found: "two large chunks of poorly cemented local sandstone and one large (8 cm in diameter) cobble" (Fredlund 1983:843). Late Archaic period site use of a relatively uncomplicated nature, associated with lithic raw material reduction activity, was inferred.

Comparative analyses of the assemblages between the two block units indicated more debitage of a smaller size occurred in the Caddoan assemblage in Area B, which also yielded many small retouched flake tools (Fredlund 1983:852–853). Petrified wood was more common in the Late Archaic block, whereas flakes and blades were more common in the late prehistoric Caddoan block. Far fewer cores (n = 5) were observed in Area B than in Area C (n = 10), even though the former area was four times the size of the latter. The figures were attributed to a difference in reduction strategies. The presumed Caddoan occupation in Area B was characterized by a "flake core industry geared to the production of unifacial tools in which one core will produce many tool blanks" (Fredlund 1983:854). The Late Archaic industry in Area C, in contrast, was characterized by what was called a "strategy [that] requires the reduction of many more cobbles to produce the same number of tools" (Fredlund 1983:854). This was supported in an examination of end products; unifacial flakes dominated the later occupation (77 percent of all tools) whereas bifaces dominated the earlier occupation (53 percent of all tools). Additionally, while approximately half of the flake tools in the earlier occupation were made on primary flakes, tools in the later occupation were apparently made exclusively on secondary flakes (Fredlund 1983:855). A change in reduction strategies was inferred that moved from the reduction of single cores or cobbles to individual tools in

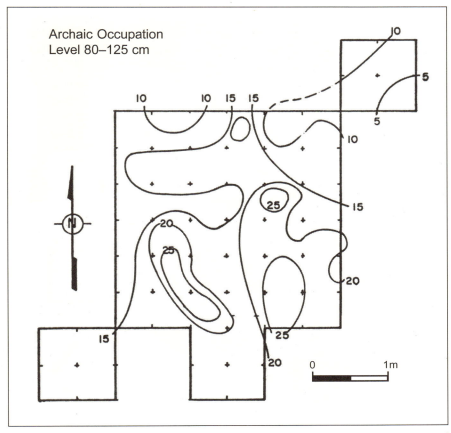

Figure 2.7 — Debitage distributions in the Archaic levels in the block unit opened in Area C, 16VN18 (from Fredlund 1983:838).

the Late Archaic, which left many large cortical and noncortical flakes behind, to the production of multiple tools from a single core in the late prehistoric/Caddoan era, which left more smaller noncortical interior flakes behind. Use of the local pebble cherts in the area appears to have involved one of these two reduction strategies, and this finding is documented in subsequent research on the installation (e.g., Novick 1984:238; see below and Chapter 3).

THE 16VN24 (BIG BRUSHY) EXCAVATIONS

The Big Brushy site, 16VN24, was found in December 1976 during the survey of the Lookout Road Tank Trail (Guderjan and Morehead 1983:862). The site was located on the east side of Big Brushy Creek on a point of land slated for road construction (Figure 2.8). Testing operations were conducted on the site in January 1977, and large-scale excavations were initiated in May of that year. The excavations lasted six weeks and employed a full-time crew of between 20 and 28 people, augmented by volunteers, including the services of an army work detail. The excavations were directed by Frank

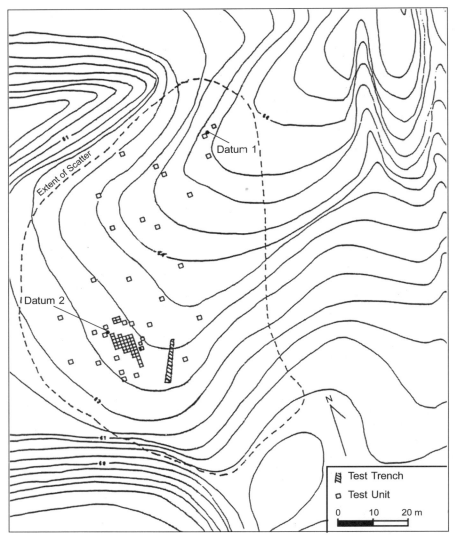

Figure 2.8 — Big Brushy (16VN24) site contours and excavation units, University of Southwestern Louisiana FPAS excavations (from Guderjan and Morehead 1983:863).

Servello, Thomas Bianchi, James R. Morehead, and Thomas H. Guderjan, among whom the latter two assumed responsibility for the final fieldwork and for the subsequent analysis and report preparation (Guderjan and Morehead 1980, 1983). A seemingly logical stratification was observed over the projectile points found in the excavation units, making this site extremely important for resolving the local cultural sequence.

Nearly 5,000 artifacts were recovered from the site's surface in a general collection during the fieldwork, including 5 sherds; 197 unifacial and bifacial tools; 1,757 pieces of unmodified debitage; 134 cores; Alba (n = 1) and Perdiz (n = 1) arrow points; and Angostura-like (n = 1), Dalton (n = 1), San Patrice, *var. St. Johns* (n = 1), Ellis (n = 3), Ensor (n = 1), Gary (n = 2), Marcos (n = 1), Yarbrough (n = 1), and 14 other unidentifiable or unusual dart point types (Guderjan and Morehead 1983:870–872). To examine subsurface deposits over the area, ca. 34 1-x-1-m units were opened, dispersed in an unaligned random sample with one unit selected in each 10-x-10-m area of the site (Guderjan and Morehead 1983:873). Thirty-six contiguous 1-x-1-m units were then opened in a high-density area located during the testing (Figure 2.8; this figure depicts 34 1-x-1-m units located away from the block that apparently made up the random sample). Unit fill was excavated in 10-cm levels and passed through 1/4-inch mesh, with some units opened using 5-cm levels and 1/8-inch mesh. The units in the block were removed in 50-x-50-cm quadrants to provide finer spatial control.

No cultural features were identified, and if any were originally present they are assumed to have eroded away. Large numbers of artifacts were collected, however, including approximately 50,000 pieces of debitage, a range of unifacial and bifacial tool forms, and some 72 nondiagnostic plain sherds with a sandy or "local" paste (Guderjan and Morehead 1980:9, 1983:878, 924). Detailed definitions and summary measurement and stratigraphic data were provided for flaked stone tool categories and the ceramics. Four major occupations were discerned, consisting of assemblages identified with the following periods: Late Paleoindian/Early Archaic (San Patrice culture), Middle Archaic, Late Archaic, and terminal Archaic/Woodland or ceramic prehistoric (Guderjan and Morehead 1983:914–923). A date of 3675 ± 65 rcbp was obtained from the Late Archaic assemblage (UGa-2031; Guderjan and Morehead 1983:917).

Some mixing is evident from the ceramic distributions, rendering placement of individual tools or pieces of debitage somewhat problematic (Figure 2.9). The flaked stone tool descriptions in the report provide useful data on the kinds of artifacts that can occur in Archaic assemblages in this general region, however, and these include chipped celts and celt fragments, end and side scrapers, and crude bifaces (Guderjan and Morehead 1983:885–

	0–10	10–20	20–30	30–40	40–50	50–60	60+
Alba	–	–	1	–	–	–	–
Friley	–	2	–	–	–	–	–
Ellis	1	1	–	1	–	1	–
Evans	–	1	1	–	1	1	–
Gary	1	–	3	2	–	1(?)	–
Thick Stemmed	–	–	–	1	1	–	–
Ensor/Ensor-like	–	1	–	1	–	–	–
Kent	–	1	1	1	2	–	–
Morhiss	–	–	–	1	–	–	–
Lange	–	1	–	1	–	–	–
Yarbrough	–	–	1	2	1	1	–
Williams	–	–	–	2	2	–	–
Edgewood	–	–	–	–	1	–	–
San Patrice	–	–	–	–	–	1	1
Straight Stemmed	–	–	–	–	–	–	1
Ceramics	14	34	8	4	1	4	2

The deeper examples of Ellis (>40 cm), Gary (>30 cm) and Evans (>60 cm) tend to come from the southern and western portions of the deposit, where the later archaeology seems to be deeper.

Figure 2.9 — Projectile point and ceramic distributions by level at the Big Brushy site, 16VN24 (from Guderjan and Morehead 1983:902, 931).

897). A detailed attribute analysis was conducted with a sample of 1,500 pieces of debitage, and the resulting data were explored using factor and cluster analyses (see Guderjan and Morehead 1980:15–25, 1983:931–933). The debitage assemblages in the two earliest occupations were found to be similar, as were the materials in the two latest levels, but considerable differences were evident between these periods (Guderjan and Morehead 1983:931–933). In particular, the earlier assemblages show greater initial core reduction, with more primary decortication flakes, which is a pattern similar to that noted at 16VN18, albeit for earlier periods.

A particularly important aspect of the Big Brushy site excavations was the fair degree of stratification observed in the deposits over the projectile point assemblage. A logical progression was found, moving from arrow points in the upper levels through Archaic dart points in the intermediate levels to San Patrice, and possibly earlier, Paleoindian forms in the lowest levels (Figure 2.9). The site is one of only a very few excavated in the Louisiana area providing evidence for the possible chronological ordering of Archaic dart forms. A San Patrice–Edgewood–Williams–Yarbrough sequence is indicated, with these forms replaced by a group that includes Kent, Ensor, Gary, Evans, and Ellis types, possibly in that rough chronological order (Guderjan and Morehead 1983:902, 913). Similarities with the LaHarpe Aspect sequence from the Yarbrough and Miller sites of northeastern Texas were noted; that is, there was a replacement of expanding stemmed forms by contracting stemmed (i.e., Gary-like) forms, followed by contracting stemmed forms associated with ceramics (Guderjan and Morehead 1983:923; Johnson 1962). The excavations at Big Brushy thus demonstrated early on that information of value to the development of a detailed cultural sequence could be found in the Fort Polk area.

The 1980 Bayou Zourie Terrain Analysis and Settlement Pattern Survey

During May 1980, archaeologists from Environmental and Cultural Services, Inc., conducted a survey and predictive modeling analysis in a ca. 800-acre tract along the Bayou Zourie drainage on the Main Fort (Jolly and Gunn 1981). Using 100-foot shovel testing survey intervals, they found five previously recorded sites, four new sites, and 10 isolated finds (Jolly and Gunn 1981:9, 14). The survey area was subdivided into 196 grid units 400 feet on a side, and seven terrain variables encompassing slope, landform shape, elevation, and drainage were coded for each unit. Principal components and cluster analyses were conducted in an effort to delimit areas that might have a high probability of yielding archaeological sites. A "colluvial/clay interface site model" of prehistoric site location was developed, in which it was predicted that archaeological sites would tend to occur at the interface between the sand/colluvial surface deposits and underlying Miocene clays, where natural seeps would have led to increased biomass productivity, making the area attractive to prehistoric settlement (see also Gunn 1982e:344; Gunn et al. 1982:143; Guy and Gunn 1983). Subsequent tests of this model have yielded ambiguous results, in part because of the difficulty of locating the boundary area (see Chapter 3).

The Eagle Hill II (16SA50) 1980–1981 Excavations

In 1980 and 1981 large-scale excavations were undertaken at Eagle Hill II (16SA50) by the Center for Archaeological Research at the University of Texas at San Antonio (Gunn and Brown, eds. 1982). The site, located 500 m southwest of Eagle Hill, had been previously examined by Servello and Bianchi (1983:404–444), who found it contained relatively undisturbed Paleoindian materials. Their testing had recovered a large number of formal unifacial tools, as well as a well-made Clovis point, at depths of 40 to 50 cm (Figure 2.10). The excavations were undertaken because the site was considered to be seriously threatened by erosion. An intensive preliminary examination of the site area was conducted, which included detailed mapping, the reopening of Servello and Bianchi's old test units to examine the soil profiles, limited new test pitting, and an extensive deep-coring program. Following this, a 6-x-5-m block was opened to culturally sterile subsoil, which was identified by Miocene-age clays that appeared at a depth of approximately 1 m. The fill was carefully removed and screened through 1/8-inch mesh, with artifacts on identified occupation surfaces plotted in three dimensions to an accuracy of approximately 1 cm.

Five more or less distinct occupational episodes were recognized, the upper three being later Archaic/Woodland through late prehistoric in age and the lower two later Paleoindian and Early Archaic in age (Gunn 1982b:6). Three radiocarbon and 11 thermoluminescence determinations were obtained from the site, providing excellent chronological controls on the age of the deposits (Gunn 1984a:164, 1984b:145; Gunn et al. n.d.; McGimsey and van der Koogh 2001:12–13, 137) (see Table 6.1 for a listing of all absolute dates obtained from Fort Polk). Artifact density was fairly low within the block, with 112 tools, 158 sherds, and approximately 4,600 pieces of debitage recovered in the occupational levels (Brown 1982a:263; Gunn 1982a:230–239; Jolly 1982:291). Diagnostic projectile points recovered (n = 6), in stratigraphic order from the base of the deposits, included a possible Paleoindian lanceolate, a Williams, an Edgewood, a Gary, a Friley, and a possible Cuney (Gunn 1982a:230, 239) (Figure 2.11). A distinct occupational hiatus corresponding to much of the Archaic was observed between the upper and lower strata (Gunn 1982c:50–52, 1982d:326–342). The absence of intervening assemblages was attributed to decreased use of the uplands during these periods.

A general climatic model was advanced to explain the trends observed in the archaeological record at Eagle Hill II (Gunn 1982a:182–184, 1982e:344–345; see Chapter 1). During warmer and drier climatic conditions (i.e., such as those inferred to have been present during the Middle Holocene), available biomass/resource productivity would have declined in the uplands around Peason Ridge, leading to decreased use of the area. Cooler and wetter periods, in contrast, were characterized by greater exploitable biomass in the uplands, making them more favorable to human populations. Gunn (1982e:344; Gunn et al. 1982:143) argued that Eagle Hill II was par-

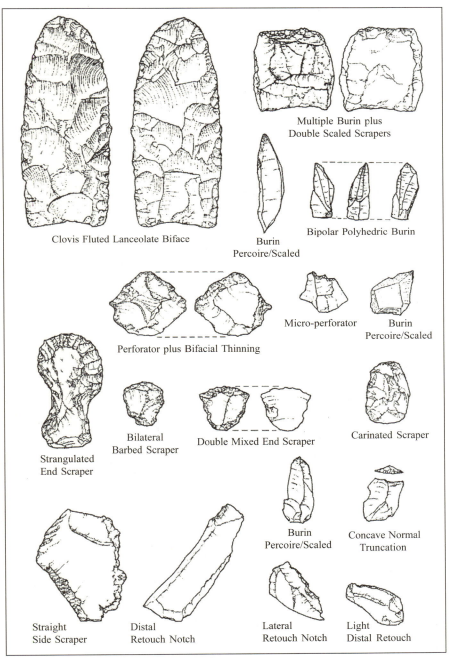

Figure 2.10 — Late Pleistocene/Early Holocene tools at the Eagle Hill II site, 16SA50, Peason Ridge/Eagle Hill locality (from Servello and Bianchi 1983:427, 434, 436, 456).

| Dates | | Soil | Cultural | | Cultural |
B.P.	A.D.–B.C.	Zones	Strata		Chronology
0	2000	———	1.13		Plaquemine
1000	1000	Zone I	1.21	Friley (1) (Ceramic)	Coles Creek Troyville
2000	0	———	2.13	Gary (1)	Tchefuncte
3000	1000		2.31 3.12	Edgewood (1) Williams (1)	
4000	2000	Hiatus			Poverty Point
5000	3000	Deflated			Late Archaic
6000	4000				
7000	5000	———			Middle Archaic
8000	6000		4.12		
9000	7000	Zone II	4.15 4.15	Preceramic	Early Archaic
10000	8000	———	4.17	Paleoindian "Coastview" (1)	——— Dalton
11000	9000	Hiatus			Clovis
12000	10000	———			———
		Zone III			

Figure 2.11 — Cultural stratigraphy at the Eagle Hill II site, 16SA50 (from Gunn 1982b:6).

ticularly favorable for settlement since it lay right at the colluvial/clay interface between the Miocene clay substrate and overlying colluvial sands.

The Eagle Hill II site report is important because a number of innovative analytical procedures were employed for the first time in the Fort Polk area. To determine whether prehistoric ceramics found at the site were made locally or came in from somewhere else, x-ray diffraction, x-ray fluorescence, and neutron activation analyses were conducted on 19 clay samples from the site and the immediately surrounding area, and neutron activation analysis was conducted on 15 sherds from the site assemblage thought to encompass the major technological traditions present (Brown 1982b). Cluster analyses were then conducted to compare the results. Appreciable differences were observed in the elemental signatures of local clay sources, but even so the ceramics were distinctly different, indicating none appeared to have been made using local clay sources (Brown 1982b:166, 173). Four distinct groups of ceramics were recognized, suggesting these analytical procedures can be useful for identifying sherds from differing manufacturing trajectories or geographic areas (see also Steponaitis et al. 1996). Neutron activation analyses were also conducted on 12 pieces of debitage from Eagle Hill II, four pieces of debitage from the nearby Eagle Hill I and III sites, seven samples of opal and petrified wood from sources in the Fort Polk area, and seven samples of chert from sources in Arkansas and Texas (Brown 1982b:174–180). Discriminant function and cluster analyses run on the data identified two main groups in the site assemblage: one visually similar yet chemically distinct from local sources and the other similar to chert sources in central Texas. An unidentified local source for some of the material and a more distant source for the remainder, possibly in Texas, was suggested, although more work was also recommended.

Detailed geochemical, geological, and geomorphological analyses and descriptions of conditions in the immediate site area were also conducted and produced, making the Eagle Hill II depositional matrix one of the most intensively examined and reported on the installation (Garner 1982; Nials and Gunn 1982; Van Note 1982a, 1982b). Only at 16VN794, in fact, have geoarchaeological and paleoenvironmental analyses at a comparable level of sophistication and detail been conducted and reported on Fort Polk (Cantley et al., eds. 1993). A particularly innovative aspect of the Eagle Hill II analysis was the collection of 2,000-cc sediment samples from the southeast corner of each 1-x-1-m square of each major strata/occupational level, together with a single "high resolution environmental column" of fill sampled in 1-cm levels from the surface to the base of the cultural deposits at a depth of about 1 m (Gunn 1982f:143). These samples were used in detailed particle-size analyses (Van Note 1982a:145), including the analysis of larger inclusions such as pebbles (Lopez 1982), to document erosion and down-slope colluvial movement, together with aeolian deposition, as the source of the site sediments. Geochemical analysis, specifically x-ray fluorescence, was also used to examine the site deposits, documenting appreciable downward leaching of iron and clay, which is something not altogether unexpected in the sand-dominated matrix (Van Note 1982b:158). Pollen preservation in the samples was found to be poor, but findings suggested a transition from wetter birch-dominated streamside communities in the deepest (i.e., pre-

sumably Late Pleistocene) levels to open, drier pine forests in the earlier
Holocene, trending to more closed pine forests in the most recent levels
(Sheehan 1982). The role of bioturbation and specifically crayfish burrow-
ing action in the vertical movement of artifacts that was sometimes observed
was also discussed (Nials and Gunn 1982:134). Prehistoric ceramic distributions, for example, indicate some mixing of site deposits (Brown
1982a:267), suggesting difficulties in attributing specific artifacts to specific occupations.

The prehistoric assemblages at Eagle Hill II were intensively examined
and described, primarily by the five occupation levels or periods of site use
that were recognized. The Paleoindian assemblage included a possible lanceolate form and formal tools such as end and side scrapers, burins, and
beaks. A succeeding presumably Early Archaic assemblage, albeit with no
diagnostics, had a number of edge-retouched flake tools. Following a major
erosional hiatus, a dense lithic assemblage with a wide range of tools and
debitage and a Williams point was deposited, followed by two later occupations with a somewhat lower incidence of tool forms and debitage. The lower
of these two later "occupations" (each themselves possibly palimpsests of
two or more periods of site use) had an Edgewood and a Gary point, the
former below the latter stratigraphically. The uppermost occupation had a
Friley and a Cuney point present, the former stratigraphically below the
latter (Gunn 1982a:230–239). Ceramic types present included Coles Creek
Incised (n = 19), Mazique Incised (n = 5), and Evansville Punctated (n = 9),
with no clear stratigraphic relationships evident (Brown 1982a:263–267).

Detailed flake analyses were conducted and then used to identify biface-
reduction areas on all five occupation surfaces (Gunn 1982a:244). Local
versus extralocal lithic raw material use was examined, with results showing the greatest incidence of extralocal raw materials in the third occupation
surface, which also yielded the Williams point (Jolly 1982:298–301). The
lower incidence of extralocal raw material use in the deeper, presumably
Early Archaic and Paleoindian levels was considered surprising, given the
known preference of these early peoples for high-quality materials (e.g.,
Goodyear 1979). In the years since this excavation, however, numerous
Paleoindian San Patrice components have been found on Fort Polk, and appreciable use of local materials is evident in at least some of these occupations. Use-wear analyses of stone tools from the five surfaces suggest the
greatest range of activities occurred in the third (later Archaic) surface, suggesting more extended site use than that which produced the earlier and
later surfaces, whose tools suggested a more limited range of activities (Gunn
1982d:325). Distributional maps were presented for each surface showing
the occurrence of tools, artifact clusters, and possible hearth features (iden-

tified by areas of burned soil) (Gunn 1982d:326–343). These maps reinforce the impression noted earlier that each surface probably represents a palimpsest of several activities or discrete site visits.

No other assemblage on Fort Polk has been examined using as many different analytical approaches. As a result, the Eagle Hill II excavation illustrates what can be learned when a multidisciplinary research approach guides large-scale excavation.

The 1981 New World Research Sample Survey

In 1981, archaeologists from New World Research, Inc., conducted an intensive survey of approximately 8,096 acres on the Main Fort and Peason Ridge with the goal of evaluating and refining existing site locational models (Thomas et al. 1982; see Chapter 3). Approximately 7,441 acres were examined using a stratified random sampling procedure based on major drainage basins and soil associations and employing quarter section (160 acre) sampling units (Thomas et al. 1982:72). Systematic shovel testing or surface inspection (in cleared areas) was conducted, with collection areas placed at 30-m intervals along transects spaced 30 m apart. A total of 49 quarter sections were examined, 13 on Peason Ridge and 36 on the Main Fort (Thomas et al. 1982:54–55) (Figure 2.12). In all, 215 sites and 133 isolated finds were reported. Only 26 prehistoric ceramic fragments and 30 projectile points were found, highlighting the low incidence of diagnostics characterizing archaeological sites in the Fort Polk area. Summary artifactual data for all of the materials obtained from these sites, with definitions or descriptions of the sorting categories used, were presented in a series of appendixes. A geomorphological study was undertaken that included the excavation and documentation of 51 stratigraphic pits and bank sections from across the installation, with samples taken using shovels, posthole diggers, and a small corer (Lenzer 1982). The study marked the first systematic effort to evaluate whether deeply buried archaeological sites occur locally; although none were found, their potential was indicated (Lenzer 1982:4-49).

Data from prehistoric assemblages were used to evaluate Servello's slope element site locational model (Servello 1983) and the colluvial/clay interface site locational model (Jolly and Gunn 1981; see Chapter 3) and to develop a new site locational model for the area (Thomas et al. 1982:77–78, 88–89; see Chapter 3). The prehistoric sites found during the survey were also evaluated using a series of site size/diversity categories, based on the amount of material present and the proportional occurrence of tools (Thomas et al. 1982:98). A relationship between site size and type and distance to

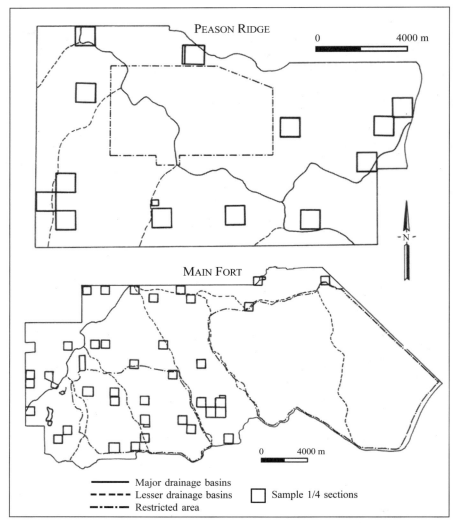

Figure 2.12 — Quarter section survey units, New World Research, Inc., 1981 sample survey (adapted from Thomas et al. 1982:56, 57).

knappable stone source areas was proposed, with larger sites thought to occur closer to exploitable chert gravel deposits. A shift from foraging to collecting strategies from the Archaic to the Woodland era was suggested, since
sites yielding Woodland diagnostics tended to be considerably larger than
those yielding either no diagnostics (i.e., lithic scatters of unknown age) or
else Archaic period diagnostics (Thomas et al. 1982:108–110). All of these
ideas are examined in additional detail in Chapter 3.

Perhaps most important, historic sites and architectural remains on Fort Polk for the first time began to be systematically documented and their assemblages examined (Thomas et al. 1982:115–151; see Chapters 7 and 8). Sixty-one sites predating the military use of the area were recorded, including a number with architectural features such as logging railroad tramlines (n = 28), cattle dipping vats (n = 2), house or farm buildings (n = 7), and cemeteries (n = 1). The remaining historic sites were defined on the basis of artifact scatters and were interpreted as likely temporary work camps or homesteads. *Terminus post* and *ante quem* (i.e., beginning and ending) dates were calculated for each site where artifacts with known manufacturing dates were obtained, and attributes of specific site types like homesteads and temporary work stations were proposed (Thomas et al. 1982:130–136). The collection of turpentine cups and the documentation of tramline locations marked the first attempt to document the timber/turpentine industry on the installation. An examination of historic site locations was conducted in an attempt to develop a predictive model comparable to that for the prehistoric site sample. Although the sample size was low, the authors noted that site location was dictated more by proximity to historic transportation arteries than by drainage or slope conditions (Thomas et al. 1982:138–141). Archaeological examination of several historic sites and the preservation of a sample of World War II–era historic structures were among the management recommendations advanced (Thomas et al. 1982:152–155).

The 1982–1983 Eagle Hill Locality Site-Testing Program of the University of Texas, San Antonio

In 1982 and 1983 the Center for Archaeological Research at the University of Texas, San Antonio, conducted intensive testing operations at 56 sites and isolated finds in two 640-acre sections centered on Eagle Hill on Peason Ridge (Gunn and Kerr 1984a:42; Jolly 1984a:1). On the basis of previous research, the Peason Ridge area was described as having a low site density, and on sites that were found through this program, artifact density was low, diagnostics and other chipped stone tools were infrequent other than for the Paleoindian era, and floral and faunal remains were poorly preserved (Jolly 1984a:5–6). Sites were examined using intuitively or systematically placed 30-cm-diameter shovel tests typically dispersed in linear or cruciform patterns (Figure 2.13), with larger 1-x-1-m units opened at 19 sites (Gunn and Kerr 1984a:42; Jolly 1984b:13). The geomorphology of the area was described in detail, including a discussion of three deep cutbank profiles (D. Brown 1984), and a survey of plant species was undertaken and used to plot

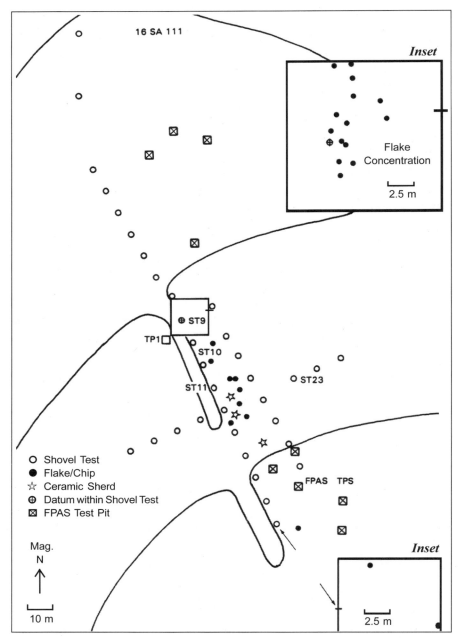

Figure 2.13 — Site 16SA111 test units, 1982/1983 Eagle Hill locality site-testing program, University of Texas, San Antonio, Center for Archaeological Research (from Gunn and Kerr 1984a:98).

vegetational microzones/communities over the study area (Jetton and Sims 1984). A series of analyses were conducted using assemblage and locational information, and these are discussed in greater detail in Chapter 3. An analysis of flake width was conducted, for example, that indicated the assemblages likely derived from late-stage tool manufacture and maintenance, rather than initial reduction (Gunn and Wootan 1984:131).

A series of multivariate analytical procedures were used to examine prehistoric land use over time in the Eagle Hill area. Primary conclusions were that the locality was "a marginal resource area utilized by peoples whose main subsistence was located outside Peason Ridge" (Jolly 1984a:1) and that prehistoric use of the area was "sparse and essentially repetitive" (Gunn and Kerr 1984b:174). The analyses indicated that while most of the sites were small and seemingly uncomplicated, those closest to water typically had small assemblages dominated by scarce extralocal or unusual local materials, those on ridge tops typically had much larger assemblages and were overwhelmingly characterized by abundant or locally available materials, and those on the slopes or interfaces between the two zones were more varied in size but were again dominated by abundant or locally available materials (Kerr 1984:120, 124). The Eagle Hill site itself, however, which yielded dense assemblages prior to its destruction, was apparently an extremely important location, serving "many functions, from lookout to landmark" (Kerr 1984:127) and offering a spectacular view of the ridge areas below (Gunn and Kerr 1984b:171). Settlement in the area appears to have centered on this site at various times in the past, particularly during the late Pleistocene and early Holocene, suggesting some of the limited-activity sites found over the surrounding terrain could have been created by groups located at Eagle Hill, who stayed there for longer periods and conducted a much wider range of activities.

The 1983–1984 Commonwealth Associates Site-Testing Program

From October 1983 through January 1984, archaeologists from Commonwealth Associates, Inc., under the direction of Charles E. Cantley examined 39 sites found during the New World Research 1981 sample survey (Cantley and Kern 1984). Project research focused on identifying the components present on project sites and then using the assemblage data recovered to try to determine the technological organization, geographic scale, and specific mobility strategies employed in the area over time, in part to evaluate the hypothesis raised by New World Research (Thomas et al. 1982:108–110) that a major shift in technological organization occurred at the end of the

Archaic in the area from residentially mobile foraging to more sedentary collector strategies (Cantley and Jackson 1984; see Chapter 3). Systematically placed 50-x-50-cm shovel test units were opened at each site, with larger 1-x-1-m or 1-x-2-m units opened in particularly dense or unusual concentrations; all units were opened using 10-cm levels in an attempt to document vertical stratification (Figure 2.14). All fill was screened through 1/8-inch mesh, and each site was mapped with a transit. Most of these field procedures are still employed on Fort Polk, save for detailed transit map-

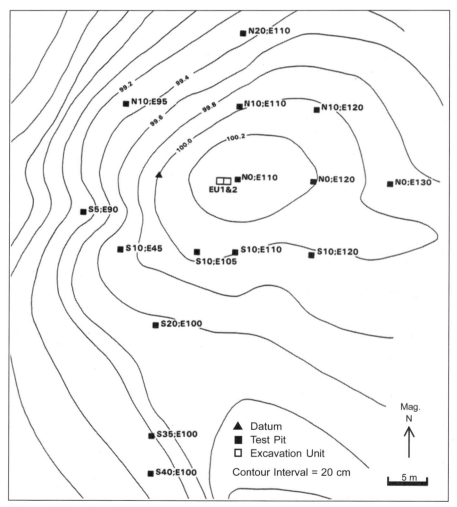

Figure 2.14 — Site 16VN334 test units, 1983/1984 intensive testing program, Commonwealth Associates, Inc. (from Cantley and Towler 1984:155).

ping, which remains uncommon despite the demonstration of its value during this project. In a highly innovative effort to locate deeper deposits, posthole diggers were used to remove fill from the center of each unit until red clays/subsoil was reached. Detailed overviews of the environmental setting (Schuldenrein 1984) and the prehistoric cultural sequence and previous research on the installation (Jackson 1984a, 1984b) were presented. A detailed examination of landownership patterns prior to the establishment of Fort Polk was conducted (Kern 1984a, 1984b), together with an oral-history survey of residents of the area during the pre–World War II era to learn about agriculture and timbering activities (Bernstein 1984); the landownership and oral-history research projects were the first undertaken and reported on the installation.

Detailed artifact analyses were conducted, including a comparative examination of all of the ceramics recovered through that time on the installation (Anderson 1984). Ceramic assemblages from the area were typically quite small and minimally decorated and hence utilitarian in character, suggesting brief or infrequent use of particular locations by small task groups. Most sherds were tempered with grog or sand or some mixture of the two, and identifiable types, which were rare, included wares found in the lower Mississippi Valley, the Red River basin, and east Texas, suggesting visitation by task groups from across the surrounding region. Two lithic-reduction trajectories were identified and described, one involving the reduction of pebbles more or less directly into tools and the other making tools from flakes obtained from these pebbles (Novick 1984:238; see Chapter 3). These reduction strategies are similar to the two identified by Fredlund (1983:854) at 16VN18, although no temporal trends were noted in Novick's analysis. The vast majority of the flakes recovered from the installation appear to derive from the reduction of local chert pebbles, and many of these are fairly small. Only limited evidence for bipolar reduction (one core) was observed in the sample; instead, local pebbles were reduced by freehand percussion (Novick 1984:242).

Perhaps the most important result of the 1983/1984 settlement analysis was the attempt to develop quantitatively based, standardized measures for comparing assemblages, in this case rank size curves of artifact density per shovel test and artifact density by site size (see Chapter 3). An attempt was made to evaluate the project assemblages using Binford's (1980) "forager-collector" model, which equates hunter-gatherer site-assemblage composition to factors such as local and regional resource structure, toolkit and task-specific technological organization, the degree of residential permanence, the frequency and extent of residential movement, and the geographic scale of group mobility (Cantley 1984; Cantley and Jackson 1984; see Chapter 3).

The 1985 Multipurpose Range Complex Survey

In 1985 New World Research, Inc., conducted an intensive, systematic survey of approximately 17,275 acres in the proposed Multipurpose Range Complex (MPRC) centered on the Birds Creek drainage in the middle of the Main Fort and including portions of Whiskey Chitto Creek basin to the west (Campbell and Weed 1986; Figure 2.15). The entire area was examined using systematic shovel testing at 30-m intervals along transects spaced 30 m apart. Shovel tests were 30 to 45 cm in size and typically taken to depths of ca. 40 to 45 cm, and all fill was screened; larger 50-x-50-m and 1-x-1-m units were intuitively opened in a number of locations (Campbell and Weed 1986:6-4). In all, 596 cultural properties were recorded, including 339 sites, 216 isolated finds, 3 cemeteries, 3 turpentine cup concentrations, and 35 railroad tram segments (Campbell and Weed 1986:6-7 to 6-8). Areas excluded from examination were 11 quarter sections previously examined in 1981 during the New World Research Sample Survey (Thomas et al. 1982) and two small impact zone/Explosive Ordnance Disposal areas excluded for safety reasons. The MPRC investigation remains the largest single survey project undertaken on Fort Polk. Detailed appendixes document the individual site artifact assemblages, and the primary records (i.e., site forms, field notes, sketch maps for individual sites) that are curated at Fort Polk provide excellent information on what was done at each site; descriptions of work at individual sites were not provided in the text, however, and this level of reporting was not in fact typical of survey work until the late 1980s locally. Detailed locational/environmental modeling analyses were conducted using the extensive MPRC site sample, resulting in considerable refinement in existing knowledge about the occurrence of cultural resources in the Main Fort area. These predictive modeling and interassemblage comparative analyses and their findings are described in greater detail in Chapter 3. The presentation of a preliminary cultural sequence for the Fort Polk area based primarily on information found on the installation was among the most important results of the survey (Campbell and Weed 1986:9-1 to 9-55; Campbell and Thomas 1989:15–21; see Chapter 6).

Fewer than 100 prehistoric sherds were recovered during the MPRC survey, highlighting the low occurrence of ceramics in the area and providing perhaps the strongest evidence against extended or permanent settlement during the Woodland or later prehistoric periods. As during previous investigations, two major temper groups were identified, dominated by grog or sand/grit, with varying minor inclusions in each (Campbell and Weed 1986:7-7). A few sherds of classic lower Mississippi Valley and Caddoan types were found, and the authors suggested that greater Caddoan use of the

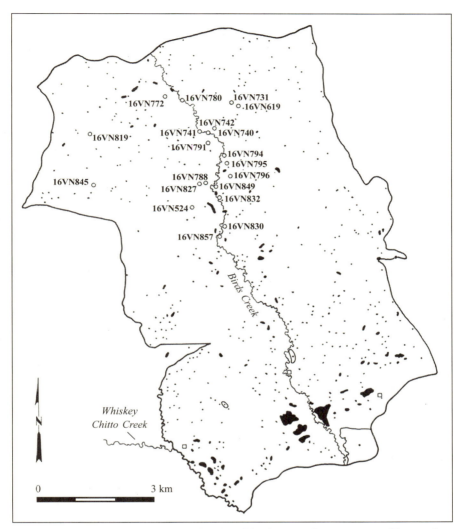

Figure 2.15 — Prehistoric sites and isolated finds, as well as sites tested by number, in the 1985/1986 MPRC New World Research, Inc., survey and testing projects (adapted from Campbell et al. 1987:5, 117).

Peason Ridge area, and greater use of the Main Fort area by peoples from the lower Mississippi Valley, might have occurred, based on the greater occurrence of sand/grit-tempered sherds in the former area and grog-tempered sherds in the latter area (Campbell and Weed 1986:7-17).

Over 19,600 lithic artifacts were also recovered, almost all chipped stone, indicating lithic raw material procurement and reduction were major activities in the area. Expedient use of local pebble cherts was indicated by the recovery of 488 cores and tested cobbles reduced by freehand percussion, with again only limited evidence (n = 1 core) for bipolar reduction activity (Campbell and Weed 1986:7-21). Lithic raw materials described as extralocal made up only a tiny fraction of the total unmodified debitage assemblage (ca. one percent) and included novaculite, palmwood, quartz, quartzite, silicified shell and wood, and Catahoula quartzite; all of the "extralocal" materials save the novaculite, which may have come from southwestern Arkansas, actually occur in western Louisiana, including in the Peason Ridge area (Campbell and Weed 1986:7-24). Some 88 projectile points were recovered, spanning most prehistoric periods (Figure 2.16). An attempt was made to create dart point clusters or groups of related types, and in later years this was formalized with the creation of the Dooley Branch and Birds Creek clusters (Campbell et al. 1990). Numerous blanks and preforms indicating stone tool manufacture were also recovered (Figure 2.17), and again almost all were made from local materials. A small number of groundstone manos (n = 2), basin metates (n = 4), abraders (n = 4), and nutting stones (n = 2) were found. These are artifact categories that occur infrequently on Fort Polk as a whole but whose presence suggests some use of local plant resources, as well as a greater diversity of activities (Campbell and Weed 1986:7-38 to 7-40).

The MPRC report offered an excellent synthesis of the archaeology and history of the Fort Polk area for its time and laid the foundations for the cultural sequence currently employed on the installation (see Chapter 6). A number of general trends about prehistoric settlement were reported in the conclusion to the report, including the following:

1. The large, dense sites which might be base camps or scenes of intensive reoccupation exhibit a strong floodplain orientation with topographic highs in the bottoms and formations at the upland/floodplain juncture being selected for.

2. Sites that appear to be involved in quarrying and initial reduction as well as those that reveal substantial evidence of initial reduction and tool production display a similar [locational] tendency as in 1 above.

3. Dense sites with substantial depth and variable artifact assemblages (e.g., base camps again?) tend to be in proximity to stream ranks 5–6.

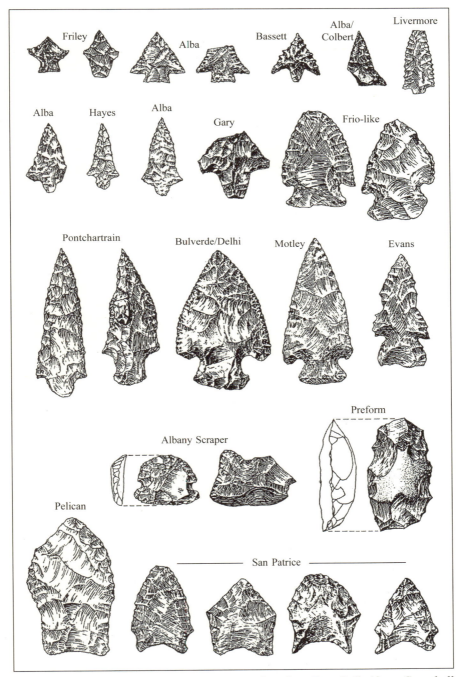

Figure 2.16 — Typical projectile point types found on Fort Polk (from Campbell and Weed 1986:7-28, 7-31, 7-32, 7-34, 7-36; Campbell et al. 1987:102–103).

4. Sites with more than three cores (tested cobbles excluded) and higher frequencies of primary and secondary flakes over tertiary flakes and tools cluster in the southern part of the Main Fort near the Williana outcrop. . . . The most widespread and intensive evidence of initial reduction occurs at sites within easy access of gravels.

5. Of the drainages represented by the MPRC, Paleoindian diagnostics were more frequently found in Birds Creek, but this may reflect nothing more than concentrated coverage because it comprised the largest part of the survey area.

6. It is difficult to pin down trends within any other chronological period, although there does seem to be some evidence to support a variation between settings selected by Woodland Dart Point and Early Arrow Point groups and those inhabited or used by populations affiliated with the later Caddoan components. If this suggestion holds up to further scrutiny, there are three explanations that would be useful to explore: (a) the focus of land use differed between Woodland and Caddoan groups; (b) there was a dramatic shift in affiliation from the Lower Mississippi Valley to the Caddoan cultures west and northwest; (c) the Caddoan components represent intrusions by non-local groups into areas they had not previously inhabited and exploited and which may have still been occupied by local populations that retained strong ties to the Lower Valley [Campbell and Weed 1986:12-11 to 12-12].

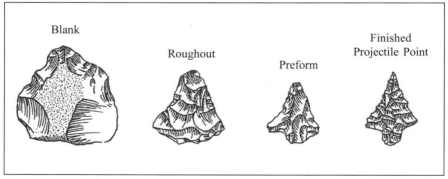

Figure 2.17 — Blanks and preforms from Fort Polk (from Campbell and Weed 1986:7-25).

In addition, the authors suggested that the central portions of tributaries like Birds Creek appeared to have been more intensively used than areas at the headwaters or near their confluence with larger drainages (Campbell and Weed 1986:12-8). These locations would be centrally located, facilitating the exploitation of the entire tributary basin from these settings. The report contains a wealth of inferences that can be examined using larger, regional-scale datasets.

The 1986 Multipurpose Range Complex Intensive Testing Project

In the late spring of 1986 New World Research, Inc., began archaeological site testing and evaluation at 20 sites located in the northern part of the MPRC survey area along and near Birds Creek, where construction was proposed (Figure 2.18). The testing proceeded first with delineation of site boundaries according to the distribution of surface artifacts and using the excavation of 50-x-50-cm units where site boundaries had not been well defined during previous work. This was followed by the excavation of larger 1-x-1-m or 1-x-2-m units in areas of concentration or where features or stratification was suspected. All units were opened using 10-cm arbitrary levels and were taken to subsoil wherever possible or to ca. 120 cm in the case of the 50-x-50-cm tests, in which deeper digging was impractical because of the small size of the unit. A tape and compass were used to disperse test units, which were placed within a standard grid oriented to cardinal directions, and to make detailed sketch maps showing unit placement and major physiographic and cultural features. Permanent datums were established at each site and the horizontal and vertical extent of disturbance was estimated using data from the surface inspection and the test units (Campbell et al. 1987:41–42). The bulk of the report was directed to describing the fieldwork and artifacts found at the project sites and to refining the cultural sequence advanced in the MPRC survey report. Detailed archival record searches were conducted for two farmsteads that were examined, 16VN780 and 16VN788, identifying the ownership of each property by specific families. Large-scale excavations were subsequently conducted at two of the prehistoric sites tested, 16VN791 and 16VN794, as described below (Campbell et al. 1990; Cantley et al., eds. 1993).

A total of 141 prehistoric ceramics and more than 12,500 lithics were recovered, mostly debitage (Campbell et al. 1987:91, 104). The artifact analysis included the calculation of a series of measures to explore the nature of past land use on Fort Polk, including (1) tool-to-debitage ratios, (2) a tool diversity index (the number of tools on a given site divided by the total

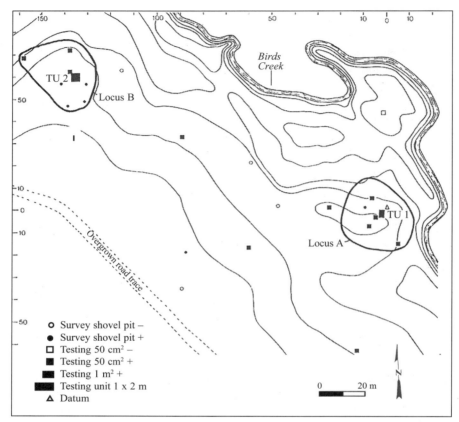

Figure 2.18 — Site 16VN791 map, 1986 New World Research, Inc., intensive testing program, MPRC project area (from Campbell et al. 1987:fig. 1-20).

number possible and the evenness of their distribution, after Pielou [1969]), (3) cortical-to-noncortical flake ratios, and (4) flake size ratios (Campbell et al. 1987:21–22, 92–95). Most of the tested sites were found to have low tool-to-debitage ratios and low diversity measures, suggesting short-term or special-activity areas (Campbell et al. 1987:96). A few sites with higher tool-to-debitage ratios and tool diversity indexes were thought to represent more extended occupation areas, where a greater range of activities appears to have occurred. The large quantities of debitage observed at many sites, coupled with the low incidence of other tool types, led the investigators to initially infer that lithic raw material procurement and reduction was a major if not primary activity behind the formation of many of the site assemblages. To further evaluate this possibility, the distance was calculated from each site to a major known gravel source along Birds Creek, an outcropping of the Citronelle Formation at the southern margins of the Main Fort. No direct relationship was observed between distance and either flake size or incidence of cortex, however (Campbell et al. 1987:97; see also Chapter 3). This led the authors to conclude that a greater range of activities was occurring on most project sites than simply raw material procurement and reduction.

A number of additional observations about prehistoric settlement on Fort Polk were advanced, beyond those noted in the MPRC survey report, notably that prehistoric sites typically

1. occur over a variety of landform types;

2. exhibit discrete concentrations of artifacts;

3. are dominated by lithics, particularly flakes and the by-products of the manufacturing and maintenance stages, but with very few tools;

4. produce few lithic diagnostics;

5. exhibit evidence of reworking and the manufacture of expedient, or "throw-away" tools;

6. lack evidence of midden, features, or structural remains;

7. produce enough potsherds to represent no more than several vessels maximum, if ceramics are present at all; and

8. display a basically utilitarian ceramic assemblage, if ceramics are present at all [Campbell et al. 1987:20].

General overall similarity within the Fort Polk sample, rather than a range of markedly differing site types, was what was indicated to the MPRC testing project team. This in turn was interpreted as representing a broadly similar pattern of land use of the area over much of prehistory involving short-term resource extraction tasks. Use of this part of Louisiana was characterized as including

1. sites associated with raw material exploitation and initial reduction, especially within or near the outcrop area south of the Main Fort;

2. short term camp sites that might have been visited over several
    weeks;

3. sites at which tool maintenance and rejuvenation were taking
    place, probably associated with overnight stops and associated
    hunting and/or possible gathering activities;

4. [sites exhibiting] repeated use of certain locations over a long
    time with little evidence of functional variation [Campbell et
    al. 1987:115].

What has not been found in the Fort Polk area, in contrast, are

1. long-term or even seasonally occupied villages;

2. hamlets, comprised of several households that would be char-
    acterized by traits such as

    a. pottery manufacture suggesting women were in residence
        (i.e., there are no coils and ceramics have not been deter-
        mined to be of local clays—see Gunn and Brown [eds.]
        1982),

    b. intra-site variability in work areas,

    c. structural remains, such as postmolds, features, and hearths,

    d. disposal of the dead on site or in site vicinities;

3. mounds or sites with ceremonial goods, indicating regional cen-
    ters around which either a nucleated or dispersed pattern of
    settlement occurred for any length of time throughout prehis-
    tory [Campbell et al. 1987:115].

Occupation of the area by small, "endemic" populations, or visitation by
groups based outside the area, was inferred. Low local population density
was suggested on the basis of the apparent emergence of pine forests in the
upland areas by ca. 5000 B.P. and the presumed ecological limitations of this
community (Campbell et al. 1987:120).

In summarizing their arguments on the nature of prehistoric land-use
patterns over time on Fort Polk, Campbell and her colleagues concluded
that

Fort Polk is dominated by station camps and short term camps in the absence of more nucleated settlements. Settlement patterns have been explained in terms of a "piney woods" model in which the area was occupied by a small, permanent group of inhabitants whose residences were widely dispersed over the landscape. These indigenous groups are no doubt responsible for the remains of many of the station and short-term camps, assuming their strategies were based on restricted wandering patterns.

Besides the small endemic population, however, we have proposed that Fort Polk was also actively exploited and repeatedly visited by groups whose residential bases were situated outside the area. Moreover, in view of the low floral and faunal potential, it seems clear that the availability of lithics was the major attraction for intrusions into this region from the outside. This hypothesis is supported by a high frequency of sites, dominated by various stages of lithic reduction and the low incidence of sites with tool variability sufficient to assume more permanent settlement. The absence to date of features, structural remains, etc. adds further support [Campbell et al. 1987:130].

The authors also suggested that the Fort Polk archaeological record reflected only a small part of the settlement systems that were in operation at any given time in the past and that many activities occurred elsewhere (Campbell et al. 1987:130).

Kisatchie Regional Environmental Management Group Small-Scale Surveys, 1984–1986

A number of small cultural resource surveys were undertaken on Fort Polk from 1984 through 1986 by archaeologists from the Kisatchie Regional Environmental Management Group, Inc., under the direction of Frank Servello. These investigations included two preliminary sampling surveys in the MPRC (Servello 1984a, 1984b), a survey of a proposed gas transmission line (Servello 1985a), a survey of two proposed firing positions along Sixmile Creek (Servello 1985b), a survey of a firing range in the Zion Hills 3 area (Servello 1985c), and three surveys of artillery firing points in the Slagle 4, 5, and 6 training areas (Servello 1985d, 1985e, 1986). These surveys resulted in the discovery of a small number of sites, primary data for which are included in the reports and collections maintained at Fort Polk.

R. Christopher Goodwin and Associates
Family Housing Area Survey, 1987

In June 1987, archaeologists from R. Christopher Goodwin and Associates, Inc., conducted an intensive archaeological survey of 1,125 acres of terrain in the proposed Family Housing Area in the northwestern part of the Main Fort; they located 18 sites (Poplin 1987). Shovel testing was conducted using screened 30-x-30-cm tests placed at 30-m intervals along transects spaced 30 m apart. When sites were located, shovel tests were opened at 5-m intervals along transects spaced 60 degrees apart and radiating from a central point (Poplin 1987:30). Since coverage decreases with increasing distance from this point, a problem also noted when testing using a cruciform pattern (see the discussion associated with the Earth Search, Inc., investigations below), shovel testing with use of a uniform grid was adopted for all site-delineation work on Fort Polk in the early 1990s to ensure even coverage.

The New World Research site locational model (Thomas et al. 1982) was evaluated, yielding a lower than expected site density (16 sites located vs. 43 expected). The low number of sites was attributed to the project area's unusual location on a major divide between the Calcasieu and the Sabine Rivers; how interriverine divides were used in the general area has been the subject for appreciable research, albeit with somewhat ambiguous results (see Chapter 3). Sites with the greatest artifact densities were found on ridge noses, immediately adjacent to and overlooking watercourses. Transport of small pebbles and their expedient reduction as needed, rather than initial reduction at source areas, were also suggested by a debitage analysis that found high percentages of cortical materials at most project sites (Poplin 1987:79).

Given the widespread occurrence of gravel cherts on the Main Fort area, traditional lithic-reduction models positing an increase in the incidence of interior flakes and a reduction in average flake size with increasing distance from source areas were considered unlikely. The actual situation has proved to be more complex, with appreciable variability evident in installation stone tool and debitage assemblages (see Chapters 3 and 4).

Interagency Archeological Services, National Park Service
Small-Scale Projects, 1987–1988

In October and November of 1987, archaeologists from the National Park Service's Atlanta Interagency Archeological Services office conducted two small archaeological projects on the Main Fort. In the southern part of the main cantonment a ca. 79-acre area was examined and two small prehistoric sites were located, each of which was examined using a cruciform pattern of shovel tests followed by the excavation of a 1-x-1-m test unit (Husted 1988). Both were determined to be low-density lithic scatters. A second survey of a 21-acre area was conducted near the east bank of Whiskey Chitto Creek, locating one prehistoric site, 16VN990, which was intensively tested using four 1-x-1-m, two 50-x-50-cm, and 19 30-x-30-cm tests (Husted and Ehrenhard 1988). More than 1,100 artifacts were recovered at depths of up to 75 cm, including eight plain grog-and-sand-tempered sherds and three projectile points resembling the Alba, Ellis, and Williams types. At least two components were inferred, the upper of Coles Creek or early Caddoan age and the lower dating to the Late Archaic/Woodland period. The presence of extensive, largely undisturbed stratified cultural deposits led to the determination that the site was eligible for inclusion on the NRHP.

1988 Historic Preservation Plan

A detailed synthesis of cultural resource investigations, management procedures, and directions for future CRM work on Fort Polk—a comprehensive Historic Preservation Plan (HPP) for the installation—was produced in 1988 by a team of specialists from Garrow and Associates, Inc. (Anderson and Wilson 1988; Anderson et al. 1989; Cobb 1989; see the Introduction). At the time the 1988 HPP was developed, just over 40,000 acres had been intensively surveyed and 1,657 sites and isolated finds were recorded.

The 1988 HPP consisted of four parts. A technical synthesis volume that was widely distributed provided a detailed summary and overview of the archaeological, architectural, and historical investigations undertaken on Fort Polk through 1987, as well as the findings of appreciable primary research with the data collected during the HPP effort (Anderson et al. 1988). Specific sections of the technical synthesis described the environmental setting, history (including military history and architecture), and prehistory of the area; a review and evaluation of previous cultural resource investigations; descriptions and discussions of previous site locational modeling efforts and the development of a new predictive model for the installation; directions and standards for future research and reporting; and criteria by which sites could be evaluated as eligible or ineligible for inclusion on the National Register of Historic Places (NRHP). The results of research on Fort Polk and on nearby U.S. Forest Service lands were integrated into broader research themes defined at the state and regional levels (e.g., Smith et al. 1983) to aid in the evaluation of NRHP status, which is typically defined in terms of the information a site can add to our understanding of prehistory or history (Butler 1987). The research findings from the 1988 and 1999 HPPs have been incorporated into the present volume.

The other parts of the 1988 HPP were produced in small numbers of copies, since they were intended for internal use and to provide primary supporting data for the technical analyses and management recommendations. A planning manual, designed for land management and planning personnel on Fort Polk, provided a step-by-step guide, with specific recommendations, detailing how CRM activity was to be accomplished on the installation over the next several years (Wilson et al. 1988). A comprehensive cultural resources inventory volume, almost 2,000 pages in length, contained the primary data used to generate the research findings described in the technical synthesis; it included extensive locational, assemblage, component, and environmental data for all of the archaeological and historic sites found on Fort Polk through 1987 (Anderson et al. 1987). An oversized and bound map volume contained information on the location of all known sites and isolated finds on the installation, as well as the probability zones for the 1988 predictive model (Anderson and Macek 1987). This information, compiled prior to the development of the installation Geographic Information System (GIS), was hand-drawn and lettered onto copies of U.S. Geological Survey (USGS) quadrangle sheets and installation Terrain Analysis maps, which had mylar overlays delimiting areas where CRM projects had occurred. Electronic copies of the text and data files for each volume of the 1988 HPP were produced on 3.5-inch floppy disks, but the paper copies of these documents were what researchers and land managers tended to use until the 1999 HPP replaced them (Anderson et al. 1999a).

Earth Search Intensive Surveys, 1989–1992

From the fall of 1989 through the late spring of 1992 archaeologists from Earth Search, Inc., conducted 17 separate small-scale survey projects on Fort Polk. Herschel A. Franks served as the principal investigator for the entire series of projects and additionally was the field director and sole or senior author for most projects, providing a high degree of consistency in the investigations. In all, 4,685 acres were surveyed in project tracts located all over Fort Polk, and 121 sites and 78 isolated finds were documented (Table 2.2). Separate technical appendix volumes containing site forms and location maps were prepared for each study. Survey work proceeded using transects and collection units spaced at 30- and 50-m intervals in High and Low Probability Zones, respectively, as determined using the 1988 HPP pre-

Table 2.2 — Intensive survey projects conducted by Earth Search, Inc., on Fort Polk, Louisiana, 1989–1992

Survey No.	No. Acres	No. Sites	Isolates	NRHP*	Post Location	Resource Density**	References
ES-1	414	8	4	0	PR	2.90	Franks 1990a
ES-2	202	1	2	0	MF	1.49	Franks 1990b
ES-3	194	11	5	2	MF	8.25	Franks 1990c
ES-4	243	8	5	3	MF	5.35	Franks 1990d
ES-5	247	9	2	1	MF	4.45	Franks 1990e
ES-6	240	5	2	0	MF	2.92	Franks and Yakubik 1990a
ES-7	65	1	0	1	MF	1.54	Yakubik and Franks 1990
ES-8	316	9	3	1	MF/PR	3.80	Franks and Yakubik 1990b
ES-9	202	5	2	0	MF/PR	3.47	Franks et al. 1991
ES-10	565	14	12	0	MF	4.60	Franks 1991a
ES-11	96	4	3	0	MF/PR	7.29	Franks and Jones 1991
ES-12	15	0	0	0	MF	0.00	R. Smith 1991
ES-13	371	15	7	3	MF	5.93	Franks 1991b
ES-14	392	6	11	2	PR	4.34	Franks and Rees 1991
ES-15	432	6	7	0	MF	3.01	Franks 1992a
ES-16	274	8	2	1	MF	3.65	Franks 1992b
ES-17	417	11	11	2	MF	5.28	Franks 1992c
Totals	4,685	121	78	16	MF/PR	4.25	

*   *Number of sites potentially eligible for the National Register of Historic Places*
** *Number of sites and isolated finds per 100 acres*

dictive model. Shovel tests were 30-x-30 cm in size and were typically taken to ca. 30 cm in depth. Larger 50-x-50-cm tests were opened on some sites to better determine the depth of deposits. Once sites were located, shovel tests were opened in transects oriented to cardinal directions at closer intervals, with other tests judgmentally placed away from the transects to help delimit boundaries. On small sites all visible artifacts were collected, while on larger sites one or more 2-x-2-m squares were laid out and completely collected and then a general collection of diagnostics and other tools was made over the remaining site area. Sketch maps were made of each site showing the location of major features and excavation units.

The Earth Search projects led to the development of a number of insights about past life on Fort Polk. The project team regularly conducted analyses and research that went above and beyond a strict interpretation of the scope of work. Sites located just outside the survey area were routinely documented. Differences in site discovery rates between projects were explored (Franks 1990d:80), as were attributes of chert quarry sites (Franks and Yakubik 1990b:85–89; see Chapter 3). Chain of title and other archival research was routinely conducted when historic house sites were located, as was done, for example, at the Henry Jeter homestead (16VN1070) (Franks 1990d:84–91; see also Franks 1990e:47, 55). Cemeteries were described in detail, and individuals buried in these cemeteries were tied to local sites or settlements. Artifact assemblages from historic sites were not only described but also analyzed to help provide additional insight into early historic settlement in the area. Descriptions of the work at several major historic sites found during these investigations, including Jetertown (16VN1070), the William Bridges Homestead (16VN1076), the Honor Cryer Homestead (16VN1092), and Fort Polk Cemetery Number 2 (16VN1099), can be found in Chapter 8.

Earth Search, 2,745-Acre Survey

In the summer and fall of 1993 personnel from Earth Search, Inc., conducted an intensive survey of 2,745 acres in the Fullerton area of the Main Fort (McMakin et al. 1994). A total of 20 sites and 35 isolated finds were recorded. Survey work proceeded using the same methods employed during previous Earth Search survey projects on Fort Polk. That is, 30- and 50-m transect intervals were used in High and Low Probability Zones, respectively, as determined from the 1988 HPP predictive model. Importantly, the locations of the probability zones and the individual survey transects were illustrated in the report, documenting the extent of coverage (McMakin et al. 1994:34–36). An assessment of the 1988 HPP predictive model was also conducted (see Chapter 3).

Few historic artifacts or sites were found and recorded (one sherd of ironstone was the only historic artifact collected), although the presence of logging trams and turpentine cup fragments was noted in many areas (McMakin et al. 1994:230). Subsequent investigations in areas around this survey tract indicated many more historic sites were probably present (e.g., Abrams et al. 1995). One home site whose location had been documented in the 1988 HPP inventory and map volumes, in fact, was missed outright. The low site density—one site or isolated find per 49.9 acres—was thought, in part, to be because a large proportion of the project area (ca. 46.6 percent) was in the Low Probability Zone and because the area was owned by commercial timbering interests in the early part of the century (McMakin et al. 1994:227, 229; timber company landownership has also been used in a more recent survey to explain low site-discovery rates [Buchner and Saatkamp 2001:296]).

R. Christopher Goodwin and Associates
Intensive Surveys, 1992–1995

From April 1992 through June 1995, archaeologists from R. Christopher Goodwin and Associates, Inc., conducted 19 separate small-scale survey projects on Fort Polk. Much of the fieldwork and writing for individual projects was handled by Floyd B. Largent or Luis M. Williams, providing a high degree of consistency in the investigations. In all, 12,159 acres were surveyed in project tracts located all over Fort Polk, and 309 sites and 280 isolated finds were documented (Table 2.3). Discovery rates were quite high, averaging 4.84 sites or isolated finds per hundred acres. Considerable differences were noted between tracts located on the Main Fort and Peason Ridge. In most cases a far lower incidence of sites and isolated finds was encountered on Peason Ridge, probably because the area was more remote, being near tributary headwaters rather than along their lower courses.

Separate technical appendix volumes were prepared for each study, containing site forms and location maps. Survey work proceeded using transects

Table 2.3 — Intensive survey projects conducted by R. Christopher Goodwin, Inc., on Fort Polk, Louisiana, 1992-1995

Survey No.	No. Acres	No. Sites	Isolates	NRHP*	Post Location	Resource Density**	References
RCG-1	80	2	1	0	MF	3.75	Largent et al. 1992a
RCG-2	771	22	10	3	MF	4.15	Largent et al. 1992b
RCG-3	358	13	10	0	MF	6.42	Largent et al. 1992c
RCG-4	718	11	23	3	MF	4.74	Largent et al. 1992d
RCG-5	340	1	7	0	PR	2.35	Largent et al. 1992e
RCG-6	924	22	17	4	PR	4.22	Largent et al. 1993a
RCG-7	282	7	7	2	MF	4.96	Largent et al. 1992f
RCG-8/9	665	9	9	1	MF/PR	2.71	Largent et al. 1993b
RCG-10/11	1,962	45	35	9	PR	4.08	Largent et al. 1994b
RCG-12	567	15	13	4	MF	4.94	Largent et al. 1994a
RCG-13	345	6	6	2	MF	3.48	Largent et al. 1993c
RCG-14	985	37	23	4	MF	6.09	Williams et al. 1994a
RCG-15	995	36	45	4	MF	8.14	Williams et al. 1994b
RCG-16	998	35	37	0	MF	7.21	Williams et al. 1995a
RCG-17	1,000	38	20	2	MF	5.80	Williams et al. 1995b
RCG-18	980	10	14	0	PR	2.45	Williams et al. 1994c
RCG-19	189	0	3	0	PR	1.59	Largent et al. 1993d
Totals	12,159	309	280	38		4.84	

*   *Number of sites potentially eligible for the National Register of Historic Places*
**   *Number of sites and isolated finds per 100 acres*

and tests spaced at 30- and 50-m intervals in High and Low Probability Zones, respectively, as determined from the 1988 HPP predictive model. Shovel tests were 30-x-30 cm in size and were typically taken to subsoil, or roughly 50 cm. A least one 50-x-50-cm test was opened at each site to explore stratigraphy. Once sites were located, shovel tests were opened in a grid pattern at 10-m intervals for sites less than 50 m in extent and at 20-m intervals for sites more than 50 m in extent. Testing proceeded until two negative shovel tests were encountered in each direction around lines of positive tests or until topographic conditions (i.e., steep slopes, standing water) precluded the excavation of additional tests. Importantly, boundary definition procedures for isolated finds were the same as those used for sites. That is, when materials were found in subsurface contact, shovel tests were opened in each of the four cardinal directions until two negative tests were reached, adding up to an additional eight tests. Thus, isolated finds encountered during the survey were rigorously evaluated. Finally, surface collection typically entailed 100 percent recovery using a general collection strategy, unless otherwise noted.

Project maps with the locations of individual survey transects were provided with each report, and in smaller parcels the location of each test was illustrated (Figure 2.19). The number and location of shovel tests opened on individual sites were reported and illustrated, and each report also gave the total number of shovel tests opened during the project. Site maps were typically highly detailed, providing useful and accurate information about the location of collection units and showing cultural and natural features, with contours extrapolated from USGS maps and observed field conditions (e.g., Figure 2.20). Transect shovel tests were typically recorded on site maps, aiding in boundary definition. At the end of each volume a detailed appendix was presented, listing artifacts by site, provenience, artifact type, and count, with other descriptive information provided as necessary. Extensive additional information about artifact assemblages was typically provided in the individual site descriptions. Diagnostic projectile points and ceramics were illustrated and temper variation on prehistoric ceramics was noted; for historic artifacts, maker's marks on ceramics and glassware were commonly identified as to age and source.

The project reports contained excellent descriptive information about individual site assemblages and have, in fact, served as a model for reporting in subsequent survey projects on the installation. Site boundaries and internal contents, defined using a grid of shovel tests, are exceptionally well documented and have only rarely required modification during subsequent intensive testing projects. Artifact descriptions in the appendixes are thorough and can be quickly tied to specific proveniences on site maps. The

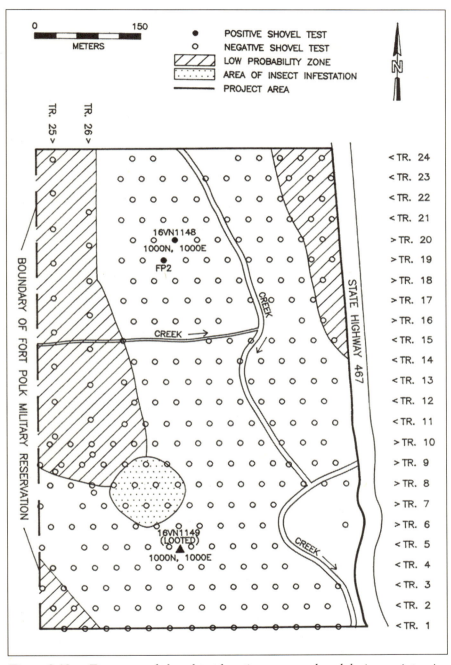

Figure 2.19 — Transect and shovel test location map produced during an intensive survey project by R. Christopher Goodwin and Associates, Inc. (from Largent et al. 1992a:38).

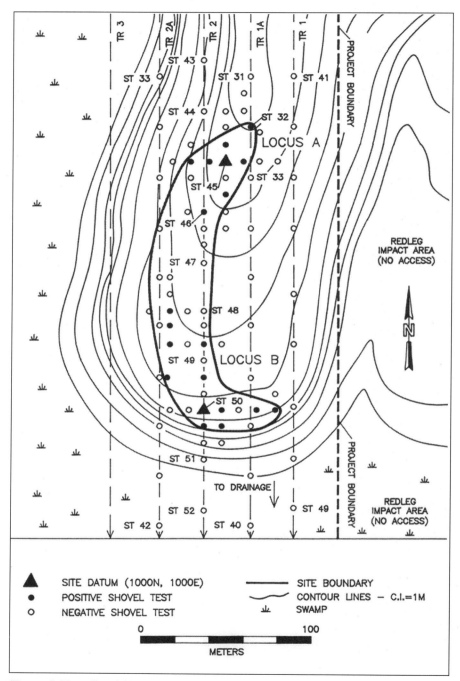

Figure 2.20 — Site 16VN1234 map produced as part of an intensive survey project by R. Christopher Goodwin and Associates, Inc. (from Largent et al. 1993c:50).

project reports are also interesting in that colorful site names were used in some cases (i.e., Banded Skink, Wild Horses, Huckleberry Ridge, Coyote Pup, Big Squirrel). The field team also deserved particular commendation in that an 8.4-gm lump of pure gold, from a melted piece of jewelry, was turned in with the other, more mundane artifacts from a historic farmstead site (Largent et al. 1993a:82). While the reports are excellent descriptive presentations, however, interpretive analyses were rarely undertaken. Thus, although hundreds of sites and isolated finds were examined using grids of shovel tests over the course of the 19 projects, no artifact distribution maps were produced. Archival research was not undertaken when historic sites were located. The conclusions of the reports for projects RCG-14 through RCG-18 did, however, include detailed evaluations of the 1988 HPP predictive model (see Chapter 4). Interpretive analyses and historic archival research, however, were not explicitly called for in the scope of work, although it can be argued that they are important for evaluating site significance (see Conclusions).

16VN791 Data-Recovery Project, New World Research, 1989

In March 1989, archaeologists from New World Research, Inc., under the direction of Prentice Thomas, Jr., conducted large-scale data-recovery excavations at the Beechwood site (16VN791), which yielded stratified deposits spanning the later Paleoindian through Caddoan/Mississippian periods (Campbell et al. 1990) (Figure 2.21). The site is located on a terrace adjacent to and overlooking the western side of the Birds Creek floodplain in the northern part of the Main Fort and had been discovered during the 1985 MPRC survey and then tested in 1986 by New World Research (Campbell et al. 1987). Deeply stratified deposits had been found during the testing in one part of the site, designated Locus A, and 62 m² were opened into these deposits in 1989. Following the establishment of a uniform grid, 26 1-x-1-m units were dispersed over the Locus A area, followed by the excavation of another 36 m². In all, five small blocks were opened, measuring a total of 3, 5, 6, 9, and 17 m² (Figure 2.21). Units were opened in 10-cm and in some cases 5-cm levels, with all fill passed through 1/4-inch mesh. Unit depth ranged up to ca. 1.5 m, although most cultural materials were found in the first meter of deposits. Detailed stratigraphic investigations were undertaken in a largely successful effort to link together the profiles observed in individual test and block units.

A total of 87,160 artifacts were recovered during the 1989 excavations, all prehistoric. This included 232 projectile points and projectile point frag-

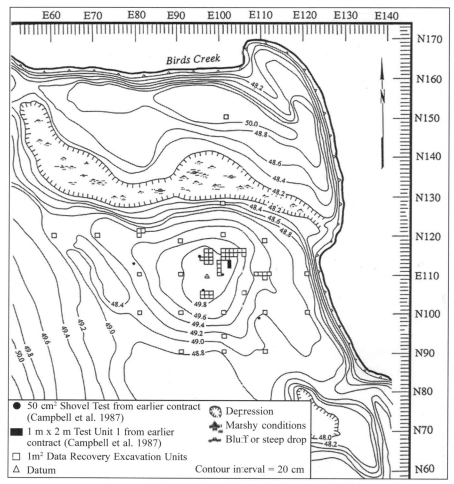

Figure 2.21 — Site 16VN791 map, showing all excavation units (from Campbell et al. 1990:33).

ments, of which over 100 could be identified to specific type. Given the numbers of projectile points found, a major goal of the project was directed toward refining the local projectile point sequence. Struck by the general similarity of point forms co-occurring in the same general levels of each block, the authors intuitively defined four primary clusters and then used statistical analyses to confirm their relative stratigraphic positions. These clusters included the Birds Creek, Dooley Branch, and Williams dart point clusters, plus a fourth cluster consisting of all arrow points. Detailed descriptions of the clusters and individual point types within them are in Chapters 5 and 6. The 16VN791 analysis is noteworthy in that it marks one of the only attempts to simplify the local projectile point sequence and to deal with the bewildering array of type names currently in use in west-central Louisiana. Excellent photographs illustrate the projectile points making up the point clusters. While more explicit analysis of the morphological variability within these clusters has been suggested (Cantley et al. 1993b:258), use of these clusters has become increasingly common in the Fort Polk area in the years since they were defined (Chapters 5 and 6; see also Justice 1987).

Cultural features were rare at 16VN791, as they are everywhere at Fort Polk, with only three observed (Campbell et al. 1990:34, 41). A hearth-like feature extending from 90 to 110 cm below the surface was found in square N116/E103 in Block III, and charcoal from it yielded a radiocarbon determination of 5160 ± 170 rcbp (Beta-33068). The fill contained some 60 pieces of petrified wood, and a heat-damaged Ensor-like point was found in the level just above the feature. The second feature was a cluster of 74 pieces of debitage and an unidentifiable point fragment found at a depth of between 70 and 75 cm in square N114/E95. It was located just above a charcoal sample from general level fill that produced a determination of 2780 ± 140 rcbp (Beta-33070). The third feature was a tight cluster of 12 pieces of chipped stone, including two Ensor-like points, found at about 90 cm below the surface in square N114/E101. Two faint stains that may have been post molds were found nearby, suggesting a possible structure.

A minor San Patrice component was identified, characterized by two San Patrice points and an Albany spokeshave. The primary use of the site area appears to have been during the Late Archaic, however, based on the numbers of Birds Creek and Dooley Branch cluster points present in the blocks (n = 30 and 45, respectively; Campbell et al. 1990:64). Somewhat lesser site use during the subsequent Woodland and Mississippian periods was indicated by a reduced numbers of points. The presence of 145 sherds of a number of distinct types, however, documented use of the site area at a number of times during the later prehistoric era. The vast majority of the sherds were predominantly clay/grog tempered with plain or (due to small size) unidentifiable finishes. Specific types present included one sherd each of Tchefuncte Plain, Marksville Incised, and Baytown Plain, *var. Satartia*, along with an incised sherd that appears to be either Coles Creek Incised, *var. Hardy* or else early Caddoan Davis Incised. In addition, a number of sherds were found with an incised or brushed-incised finish that may be Bossier Brushed or Kiam Incised.

The vast majority of the lithic assemblage consisted of local Citronelle gravels, which outcrop a few miles farther south on Birds Creek near the southern border of the Main Fort. Less than one percent of the assemblage consisted of other materials, including Eagle Hill chert, quartzite, silicified or petrified wood, and Catahoula sandstone. Considerable differences in assemblage diversity were noted between the Birds Creek and Dooley Branch assemblages, with the latter possessing almost twice as many stone tool forms as the former. The upper assemblage—defined as the materials in the upper 20 cm of site deposits, where the Williams cluster, arrow points, and many of the ceramics were found—was also highly diversified. While a range of activities occurred on the site, the low incidence of features suggests visits were comparatively brief and that comparatively few things occurred at any one time. The high incidence of debitage indicates lithic reduction was, however, an important activity for most visitors.

The data from the 16VN791 excavations, coupled with information about projectile point type incidence on Fort Polk contained in the 1988 HPP technical synthesis (Anderson et al. 1988:192), were used to refine the cultural sequence advanced for the Fort Polk area. Specifically, the Late Archaic was subdivided into earlier and later Birds Creek and Dooley Branch phases, while diagnostic artifacts were noted for each period or phase (Campbell et al. 1990:96). One unresolved mystery about the site is the near absence of Gary points in the assemblage, a type that is extremely common elsewhere on the installation. Only one Gary point was found (in Block III). Gary points have an unusual and, to date, unexplained distribution on the installation, being quite common in some areas and seemingly absent in others (Prentice Thomas and Associates, Inc. 1992:101).

The 16VN791 report concluded with an extended examination of the possibility that the deposits were mixed or disturbed, which was done by looking at the vertical distribution of ceramics in the levels. Their distribution indicated that some mixing and downward movement did occur, since sherds occurred at depths up to 80 cm. The fact that 63.7 percent of the sherds came from the 0–20 cm levels and another 25.9 percent came from 20–40 cm levels, however, suggested that this disturbance, which was attributed to trampling and bioturbation, was not particularly dramatic (Campbell et al. 1990:104–109). Disturbance analyses like this should be a routine part of investigations on stratified sites, much in the way refitting studies are used to resolve both horizontal and vertical patterns of movement within assemblages.

16VN794 Data Recovery Project, New South Associates, 1991

From August through October 1991, archaeologists from New South Associates, Inc., under the direction of Charles E. Cantley conducted large-scale data-recovery excavations at site 16VN794, where stratified materials spanning the later Paleoindian through late prehistoric/early historic period were found (Cantley et al., eds. 1993). The site is located on a terrace to the east of and overlooking the Birds Creek floodplain in the northern part of the Main Fort. The site had been discovered during the 1985 MPRC survey and tested in 1986 by archaeologists from New World Research, who documented the presence of two discrete loci with deeply stratified deposits (Campbell et al. 1987). Following vegetation clearing using a small bulldozer, a detailed site map was prepared and a grid laid out (Figure 2.22). Test trenches were placed across each loci: an east-west trench of four 1-x-2-m units in Locus A to the north (Figure 2.23) and a north-south trench of five 1-x-2-m units in Locus B to the south. The units in these trenches were excavated in arbitrary 10-cm levels. Following the completion of the trenches a soil scientist, Dr. John Foss, collected samples from the profiles and, using an auger, from across the site area. The testing demonstrated that artifacts occurred in a logical stratification, albeit with some upward and downward movement, and that the landform had been stable and built up slowly by colluviation since the mid-Holocene.

A large excavation block was then opened in each locus, using 1-m squares for horizontal control and 10-cm arbitrary levels within natural strata as defined by the project soil scientist. All fill was screened through 1/4-inch mesh. Approximately 75 m^3 of fill was excavated in the 55-m^2 block in Locus A and approximately 65 m^3 from the 50-m^2 block in Locus B, both of which were opened to an average depth of about 130 cm. Flotation samples were collected from all features, from each stratum in a vertical column in each block, and from a number of general level proveniences. Pollen and phytolith samples were also taken from 12 proveniences and submitted for analysis. The volume of each sample was recorded in liters and, in all, 733 liters of soil were collected and floated.

Detailed soils and geoarchaeological analyses were undertaken in a largely successful effort to tie recovered artifacts to particular strata and to advance a model of landform development from the late Pleistocene to the present (Foss et al. 1993). Eight radiocarbon dates were obtained from the two blocks, and a fairly straightforward relationship between age and depth was obtained (Figure 2.24; Table 6.1). Six of the dates were on charcoal derived from bulk (40 liter) flotation samples taken from general level fill, while two were from features. Taken together, they indicate that the site deposits had been accumulating slowly for at least 6,000 years, with the bulk of the deposition occurring between 6600 and 3800 B.P./6000 and 3500 rcbp. Sedimentation rates were approximately 2 cm per hundred years in Locus A and 4 cm per hundred years in Locus B, which was about 3 m lower

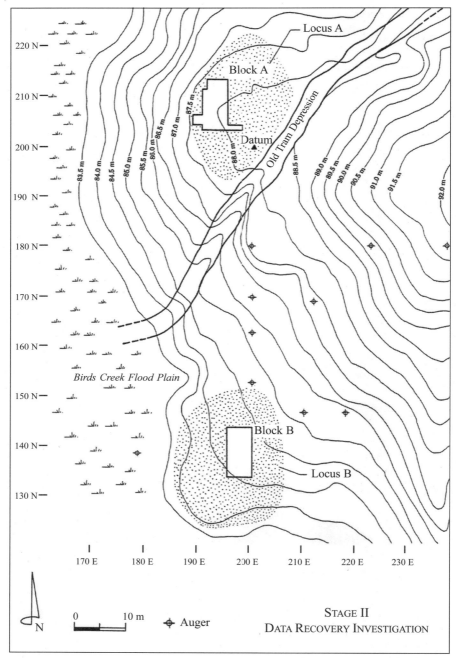

Figure 2.22 — Site 16VN794 map, showing all excavation units (from Cantley and Raymer 1993:61).

Figure 2.23 — Site 16VN794 Locus A excavation block (top) and Feature 6 in Locus B (bottom) (from Cantley and Raymer 1993:65; Raymer 1993b:149).

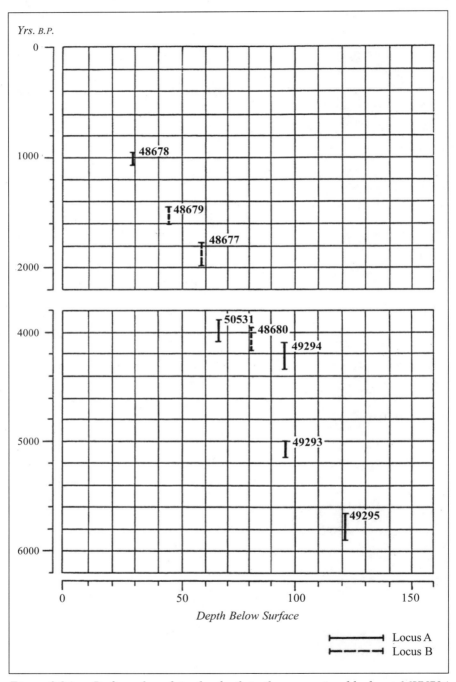

Figure 2.24 — Radiocarbon dates by depth in the excavation blocks at 16VN794 (from Foss et al. 1993:120)

on the terrace and hence likely more susceptible to both alluvial and colluvial deposition. Detailed paleoenvironmental and paleosubsistence research was conducted, employing pollen and phytolith and charred macroplant remains (Cummings 1993; Raymer 1993a; see Chapter 1). The presence of oak and pine charcoal in at least two features suggests use of these woods for fuel, while the presence of hickory and walnut shell in deposits dating back as far as 6600 B.P./6000 rcbp likely points to the consumption of these species.

One possible and six probable cultural features were found during the 16VN794 excavations, all in Locus B (Raymer 1993b). They included five small clusters of burned sandstone that are probably hearth remnants (Features 5, 6, 7, 8, and 10) (Figure 2.23), a well-defined posthole (Feature 4, dated to 1890 ± 110 rcbp; Beta-48677), and a large irregular stain that appeared to be either a hearth or pit (Feature 11, dated to 4030 ± 110 rcbp; Beta-48680). Another five features noted in the field proved upon excavation to be tree roots; charcoal preservation was poor throughout the deposits. Two of the five sandstone clusters (Features 6 and 10) occurred at depths of from 37 to 47 cm, between deposits dated to 1030 ± 50 rcbp and 1520 ± 70 rcbp (Beta-48678, on charcoal from 25 to 33 cm in depth; Beta-48679, on charcoal from 38 to 50 cm in depth). The other three sandstone clusters (Features 5, 7, and 8) occurred at depths of from 48 to 62 cm and appear to be associated with a somewhat older surface, apparently dating to sometime between 1890 ± 110 rcbp (the date for Feature 4, which appears at about 58 cm) and 1520 ± 70 rcbp. Again, as at 16VN791, feature incidence was low, suggesting site use was fairly uncomplicated.

A total of 34,526 lithic and 382 ceramic artifacts were found, including 33,885 pieces of debitage, 218 projectile points and point fragments, 122 bifaces, 140 unifacial tools, 112 cores, and 49 chipped stone adzes. A detailed series of qualitative and quantitative attributes were recorded for each point, tool, and sherd recovered during the project, and these data are included in an appendix to the report. The report appendixes also include detailed information on the location of all artifact categories recovered by provenience, including debitage, together with a series of distribution maps presenting the occurrence of these materials. The 16VN794 excavations are noteworthy in this regard, since this kind of information had been presented only in summary form in previous excavation reports. This standard of data reporting—the inclusion of appendixes detailing all artifacts by provenience—is now required on all field projects conducted on the installation.

Points and bifacial tools were described in the text, with the latter category broken down into subcategories based primarily on shape. In both blocks a more or less logical stratification of projectile point forms was observed, however, enabling a number of inferences to be drawn about the relative ages and co-occurrences of various types (Cantley et al. 1993b:251–258) (Figure 2.25). In particular, it appears that a number of dart point types may have been in use concurrently during the Late Archaic, such as Marcos, Ensor, Edgewood, Williams, Summerfield, and Gary, although different ranges are also indicated for various types.

Woodworking appears to have been a major task on the site, as evidenced by the recovery of a moderate number (n = 49) of chipped stone adzes. Cores, formed for the most part by the detachment of flakes from local gravels, were classified as unidirectional, bidirectional, multidirectional, bipolar, or indeterminate. Unifaces in the assemblage were expediently produced, occurring predominantly on cortical flakes, in part because of the nature of the raw material source (small gravels) and also because the cortex formed a natural backing for easy tool handling. Whole and broken debitage artifacts were examined separately. Broken flakes, which constituted the

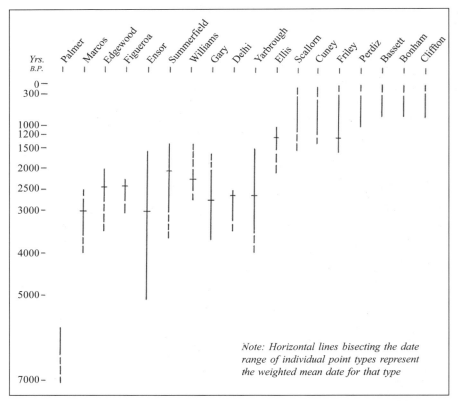

Note: Horizontal lines bisecting the date range of individual point types represent the weighted mean date for that type

Figure 2.25 — Projectile point sequence at 16VN794 (from Cantley et al. 1993b:254).

vast majority of the debitage assemblage, were found to be about evenly divided by count between those with cortex and those on which cortex was lacking. This again appears to be because of the small size of the source materials. Less than one percent of the debitage assemblage derived from nonlocal or exotic materials, and most of this was petrified wood, although a few flakes each of oolitic chert, banded chert, and novaculite were also observed.

A total of 701 whole flakes were found. These were examined by size to explore arguments about the relationship between flake size and age (see Chapter 3). In brief, flake size apparently decreased appreciably with the change from dart to arrow technology, as flake blanks replaced cores (Cantley 1993:188). Additionally, previous work on Fort Polk suggested that the earliest assemblages had somewhat larger flakes, on the average, than those occurring later in the Archaic (Fredlund 1983:fig. 180; Gunn and Wootan 1984; summarized by Cantley 1993:188). This general pattern was observed on the cortical flakes found in both excavation blocks. On noncortical flakes, size was more variable, although the largest flakes were in the deepest levels. Some of this patterning can clearly be attributed to the replacement of darts with arrows, but some of it may also be tied to the gradual exhaustion of high-quality or larger materials at the sources themselves.

Plain finishes and grog tempering dominated the ceramic assemblage, which was thought to represent the remains of no more than 20 or so vessels (Raymer 1993c). The vast majority of the sherds (n = 277, 72.5 percent) had grog tempering, with varying amounts of sand, silt, and other inclusions also noted in many specimens. The only decorated sherds were four examples of Coles Creek Incised, *var. Mott.* Most of the remaining sherds had a sandy paste (n = 93, 24.3 percent) and were assumed to represent a local variant of Goose Creek Plain (Aten 1983:217–219). Twelve sherds of bone-tempered pottery were also found, which is a paste that occurs on Fort Polk in low incidence. The vertical distributions of the sherds in the Locus A block suggest that ceramics with sand-tempered or grog-and-sand-tempered paste may be slightly earlier, on the average, than those with grog tempering alone, although some overlap is evident. The vertical distributions in the Locus B block, in contrast, indicate sandy-paste and grog-tempered pottery co-occur and that, at least here, some of the grog-tempered material was left earlier than the sand-tempered material.

Assemblage analyses indicate that Locus A on the site was briefly used during the Early Archaic period, as represented by the presence of a few corner-notched points that were classified as Palmer points (after Coe 1964:67–70). Also present were a small number of unifacial and bifacial tools, as well as some debitage, including a number of flakes of a high-quality greenish-colored cobble chert that was uncommon in higher levels. Use of high-quality cryptocrystalline materials appears to be a hallmark of early occupations throughout the Southeast, and the presence of this material may be a signature of this selection strategy. A long occupational hiatus appears to have followed, and the site area does not appear to have been used again until the late Middle Archaic or initial Late Archaic, beginning about 5700 B.P./5000 rcbp. Deposition was minimal during the Middle Archaic period, during which the local environment is thought to have been much drier, with upland productivity greatly reduced as the forest canopy was replaced by scrub and grasses (as suggested by Gunn 1982e). With the onset of moister conditions in the Late Archaic, renewed use of the site area occurred. The presence of a number of chipped stone tool forms suggests a range of activities were taking place. Some degree of stratification was evident, enabling the authors to identify separate albeit somewhat intermixed components within the overall assemblage. Use of the Locus A area continued on an intermittent basis throughout the remainder of the prehistoric era.

Use of the Locus B area appears to largely postdate ca. 3500 B.P., although the presence of a Palmer point in level 12 suggests the possibility of earlier components. The water table was reached at about this depth, precluding deeper excavation. Use of this area appears to have been greatest during the Late Archaic, with lesser use in the Woodland and Mississippian eras. Once again, the resolution of individual components was attempted, although some mixing was evident.

Prentice Thomas and Associates, Intensive Site-Testing Program, 1991–2002

Since late 1991 archaeologists from Prentice Thomas and Associates, Inc., have been conducting intensive testing activity on Fort Polk. Through February 2002, 500 sites have been examined and reported in 10 site groups that are referred to using the shorthand code "FP" followed by the project number (i.e., FP-1, FP-2, FP-3, etc.) (Table 2.4). A vast amount of information has been recovered, covering all periods of prehistory and history, and 104 of the sites examined have been determined to be eligible for inclusion on the NRHP. A total of 2,024 m³ of fill have been excavated during this testing, including 7,235 50-x-50-cm and 1,160 1-x-1-m or larger units, for a total area of 2,945.26 m² (Table 2.4). The data from this testing program represent the largest sample of archaeological material collected and reported in a standardized fashion on Fort Polk and, indeed, probably in all of Louisiana. Taken collectively, the area examined and volume of fill vastly ex-

Table 2.4 — Intensive testing projects conducted by Prentice Thomas and Associates, Inc., on Fort Polk, Louisiana, 1991–2002

Survey No.	Sites Tested	50x50 cm*	1x1m **	Area Ex. (m²)	Vol. Ex. (m³)	NRHP ***	Post Location	References
FP-1	10	111	27.00	54.75	n/a	3	PR	P. Thomas & Assoc. 1992
FP-2	10	205	20.00	73.25	41.80	3	PR	Thomas et al. 1992
FP-3	10	226	29.00	85.50	43.05	5	PR	Thomas et al. 1993a
FP-4	10	258	19.00	83.50	48.43	3	MF	Thomas et al. 1993b
FP-5	10	161	25.00	65.25	53.39	7	MF	Thomas et al. 1993c
FP-6	10	172	16.00	59.00	37.27	6	PR	Thomas et al. 1993d
FP-7	10	185	18.00	64.25	44.65	5	MF	Campbell et al. 1994a
FP-8	10	166	15.00	56.75	35.35	0	PR	Thomas et al. 1993e
FP-9	10	204	23.00	74.00	57.62	6	MF	Campbell et al. 1994b
FP-10	10	254	21.00	84.50	45.59	5	MF	Thomas et al. 1994a
FP-11	10	126	22.00	53.50	44.73	4	PR	Thomas et al. 1994b
FP-12	10	172	30.00	73.00	52.46	4	MF	Morehead et al. 1995a
FP-13	10	166	15.00	56.50	45.50	3	MF	Morehead et al. 1995b
FP-14	10	146	13.00	49.50	37.23	2	PR	Morehead et al. 1994
FP-15	10	208	21.00	73.00	54.75	2	MF	Morehead et al. 1995c
FP-16	10	168	22.00	64.00	55.23	2	MF	Meyer et al. 1995a
FP-17	10	144	42.00	78.00	51.80	3	MF	Morehead et al. 1995d
FP-18	10	97	42.00	65.25	50.86	1	MF	Meyer et al. 1996a
FP-19	10	168	19.00	61.00	36.96	1	PR	Mathews et al. 1995
FP-20	10	168	8.00	48.00	30.03	1	PR	Meyer et al. 1995b
FP-21	10	217	21.00	75.25	53.21	2	MF	Morehead et al. 1996a
FP-22	10	187	21.00	67.75	54.19	2	MF	Morehead et al. 1996b
FP-23	10	161	17.00	57.25	41.20	0	MF	Mathews et al. 1996
FP-24	10	192	11.00	59.00	38.60	1	MF	Meyer et al. 1996b
FP-25	10	148	17.00	54.00	38.58	0	MF	Meyer et al. 1997
FP-26	10	151	18.00	55.75	42.58	2	MF	Campbell et al. 1997
FP-27	10	136	24.00	58.00	41.54	2	MF	Mathews et al. 1997
FP-28	10	204	6.00	57.00	31.46	0	PR	Thomas et al. 1997
FP-29	10	141	24.00	59.25	34.99	2	PR	Parrish et al. 1997a
FP-30	10	150	13.00	50.50	41.90	0	PR	Morehead et al. 1997
FP-31	10	53	27.00	40.25	42.88	1	MF	Parrish et al. 1997b
FP-32	10	35	33.00	41.75	35.58	0	MF	Parrish et al. 1997c
FP-33	10	3	38.00	38.75	36.88	1	MF	Parrish et al. 1998
FP-34	10	42	32.00	42.50	36.43	2	MF	Mathews et al. 1998a
FP-35	10	180	23.00	68.00	41.16	2	MF	Thomas et al. 1999a
FP-36	10	154	11.00	43.50	36.50	2	MF	Mathews et al. 1998b
FP-37	10	146	13.00	49.50	34.88	0	MF	Mathews et al. 1998c
FP-38	10	113	39.50	67.75	42.65	2	MF	Thomas et al. 1999b
FP-39	10	45	46.00	57.25	45.48	0	MF	Mathews et al. 1999
FP-40	10	111	22.00	49.75	37.80	0	MF	Morehead et al. 1999a
FP-41	10	189	12.00	59.25	37.95	0	PR	LaHaye et al. 1999a
FP-42	10	151	16.0	53.75	32.12	0	PR	Thomas et al. 1999c
FP-43	10	187	21.00	67.75	45.40	0	LUA	Bourgeois et al. 1999
FP-44	10	183	23.50	44.25	55.73	2	LUA	LaHaye et al. 1999b

Table 2.4 (cont.) — Intensive testing projects conducted by Prentice Thomas and Associates, Inc., on Fort Polk, Louisiana, 1991–2002

Survey No.	Sites Tested	50x50 cm*	1x1 m**	Area Exc. (m²)	Vol. Exc. (m³)	NRHP ***	Post Location	References
FP-45	10	12	40.50	43.50	35.53	2	PR	Morehead et al. 1999b
FP-46	10	105	19.50	45.75	31.28	1	PR	Morehead et al. 2000a
FP-47	10	157	21.00	60.25	31.18	1	PR	Morehead et al. 2000b
FP-48	10	159	22.00	61.75	37.08	6	PR	Campbell et al. 2000
FP-49	10	6	32.25	41.56	42.54	2	MF/LUA	Campbell et al. 2001[†]
FP-50	10	12	49.00	52.20	41.18	3	LUA	Morehead et al. 2002[‡]
Totals	500	7,235	1,160.25	2,945.26	2,024.00	104		

*   In a few cases smaller shovel test units were used (i.e., 30 x 30 cm), and the total number of these units is what is reported.

**   In a few cases larger or smaller units were used (i.e., 0.5 x 2 m, 1 x 2 m), and the area of these units is what is reported.

*** Number of declared sites eligible for the National Register of Historic Places

†   Includes 84 30-x-30 tests

‡   Includes 2 30-x-30 tests

ceed the ca. 359 m² and ca. 300 m³ examined in the five large block unit excavations conducted to date on the installation. The largest of these data-recovery projects was at 16VN794, which encompassed 100 m² in area and ca. 140 m³ of fill. Among the other four projects, 62 m² were opened at 16VN791, 30 m² at Eagle Hill II, 97 m² at 16VN18, and ca. 70 m² at Big Brushy.

Field procedures during the testing included site mapping and the establishment of a grid system using a Brunton compass and tape, followed by the excavation of 50-x-50-cm, 1-x-1-m, and occasionally larger units. Contours on the site maps are interpolated from quadrangle maps and on-site observation and, in many cases, using a hand level and a stadia rod. The site grid is tied in to a permanent datum, and the grid origin (i.e., coordinates N0E0) is always placed well to the southwest of the site so that all units fall within one quadrant. Fieldwork includes a pedestrian reconnaissance of the site area to assess conditions and make surface collections, followed by the excavation of a series of 50-x-50-cm units opened at 10- to 20-m intervals "1) to determine if intact deposits [are] present; 2) to assess the horizontal and vertical extent of the deposits; and 3) to provide information on variation of artifact density across the site area" (Thomas et al. 1997:39). Unit placement is typically judgmental, being based on previous investigations at the site and the results obtained from earlier units opened during the testing itself. Where warranted by either surface conditions or the information gained from the 50-x-50-cm units, larger units are opened in one or more areas. All units are opened in 10-cm levels, and fill is dry screened through 1/4-inch mesh. An average of 5.89 m^2 of area and 4.05 m^3 of fill have been examined per site over the investigations conducted to date.

Testing reports are produced in a standardized format, with chapters devoted to a project introduction, the environment, previous research and culture history, research design and field strategies, and artifact analyses; a chapter devoted to the work and results for each specific site in the 10-site group; and concluding chapters providing interpretations and management recommendations. Appendixes provide information on the occurrence of all artifacts by provenience and on the grid coordinates, results (i.e., positive/negative, artifact data), depth, and volume of each excavation unit opened. The level of description is excellent, and the site maps provide valuable detail on the number, placement, and volume of units, as well as cultural and natural features (Figure 2.26). Work conducted by previous investigators is summarized and the information incorporated into analyses, interpretations, and NRHP eligibility determinations. Archival research is routinely conducted when historic sites are located, in an effort to learn about earlier occupants (e.g., Meyer et al. 1996a:71–72; Morehead et al. 1994:106–108). This work includes consultation of Clerk of Court records in the parish in question, including original survey plat maps, land claims, tax records, successions, deed books, and conveyance records; additionally, census records have also been consulted. The first computerized distributional analyses of artifacts found in systematically dispersed shovel tests conducted on Fort Polk in the past decade came from 16SA73, which was examined during the FP-1 project (Prentice Thomas and Associates, Inc. 1992:47–57). A standardized series of artifact categories has been used from the start, making the data from all 500 sites directly comparable. Importantly, interpretive syntheses are routinely found in each report, recounting the major findings at the tested sites and what they mean in terms of the prehistory and history of the general area.

Almost all of the major advances in our understanding of the cultural sequence in the Fort Polk area since 1990 have come from discoveries made during these intensive testing operations. The reports contain detailed descriptive information on hundreds of sites, and recounting the work at each here is simply not feasible. Instead, the findings from a number of the most significant prehistoric and historic sites are recounted elsewhere in this vol-

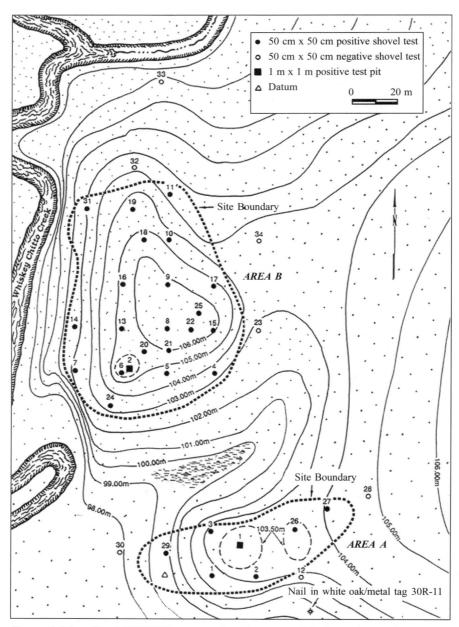

Figure 2.26 — Site 16VN1277 map produced as part of the intensive testing project by Prentice Thomas and Associates, Inc. (from Campbell et al. 1994b:133).

ume. Because the data from these sites were collected and reported in a standardized fashion, they have proven invaluable for comparative analyses and have been used here for that purpose (see Chapter 5).

South Carolina Institute of Archaeology and Anthropology Survey of 8,027 Acres, 1993–1994

From November 1993 through March 1994 personnel from the Cultural Resources Consulting Division of the South Carolina Institute of Archaeology and Anthropology (SCIAA), University of South Carolina, under the direction of Mark Groover, Cynthia Abrams, and Ramona Grunden conducted an intensive survey of 8,027 acres on Fort Polk: 3,880 acres on the Main Fort and 4,147 acres on Peason Ridge (Abrams et al. 1995). A total of 154 sites and 127 isolated finds were recorded, including 106 sites and 76 isolated finds on the Main Fort and 48 sites and 51 isolated finds on Peason Ridge; the totals include revisits to 23 sites for which new data and forms were generated. The fieldwork was conducted using systematically dispersed shovel tests at standard 30- and 50-m transect intervals in High/Indeterminate and Low Probability Zones, respectively, derived from the 1988 HPP predictive model. The survey occurred in the vicinity of Big and Little Brushy Creeks at the eastern end of the Main Fort and in the vicinity of Comrade Creek on the eastern side of Peason Ridge. Site dimensions were determined through systematic excavation of shovel tests at 10-m intervals along transects oriented to cardinal directions around every positive shovel test that was found, in effect creating a gridlike pattern of tests on larger sites (Figure 2.27). A 50-x-50-cm test unit was opened on each site to resolve stratigraphy and document deeper deposits. Each site was discussed in detail in the text, and artifact data from every provenience (including levels within units) were reported in the appendix.

A total of 15,297 artifacts were found, the vast majority prehistoric lithics together with 95 prehistoric ceramics and 213 historic artifacts. Most of the lithics were local gravel cherts, with trace amounts of fossilized palmwood and siltstone. Eighty-seven projectile points were found, from a Clovis base through late prehistoric or early contact-era projectile points; the most common types were Palmillas (n = 9), Gary (n = 6), Ensor (n = 6), and Bonham, Bulverde, Kent, Motley, and San Patrice (n = 5 of each type). A total of 327 other formal stone tools were found, the vast majority bifaces (n = 167) and scrapers (n = 56), with lesser numbers of perforators, spokeshaves, abraders, and hammerstones. Tools were much more commonly found on sites on the Main Fort than on sites on Peason Ridge. Eight Paleoindian sites were

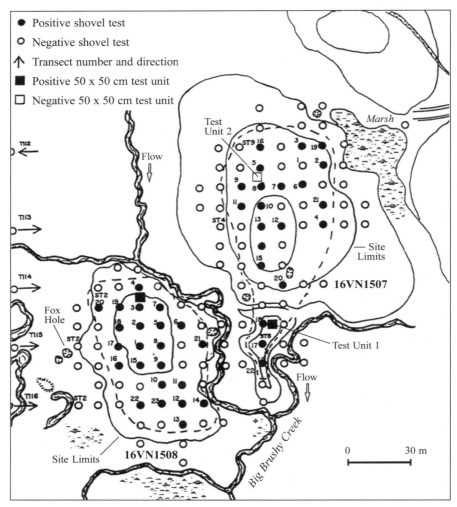

Figure 2.27 — Maps for sites 16VN1507 and 16VN1508 (from Abrams et al. 1995:222).

found on Peason Ridge compared with only two on the Main Fort, and all
appeared to be small special-purpose camps (Clement et al. 1995:426–428).
The differential distribution between the two areas was attributed to an attraction by these earlier peoples for higher points on the landscape, with
distance to water being a secondary consideration. A similar distribution
was observed over Early Archaic components (n = 6, four from Peason Ridge),
which were identified by the presence of side- and corner-notched points
resembling Big Sandy, Palmer, and Kirk forms. Unidentified high-quality
presumably extralocal cherts as well as siltstone were found to be used most

commonly during the Paleoindian and Early Archaic periods; siltstone diagnostics, in fact, were not found in subsequent periods. Based on the number of diagnostic points recovered, the greatest use of both parts of the Fort Polk area occurred during the Middle Archaic and particularly the Late Archaic. Comparatively few Woodland and late prehistoric diagnostic projectile points were found, and those tended to occur primarily on the Main Fort.

The small prehistoric ceramic assemblage recovered was dominated (n = 56, 58.9 percent) by grog-tempered (Baytown-like) plain material or other wares or eroded sherds with a grog paste; only a small number (n = 9, 9.5 percent) of sand-tempered or sandy-paste wares were present, all plain or eroded. Diagnostic ceramics recovered in low incidence included Goose Creek Plain, Coles Creek Incised, *var. Greenhouse*, Dunkin Incised, Marksville Incised, Mazique Incised, *var. Kings Point*, Churupa Punctate, *var. Thornton*, Evansville Punctated, *var. unspecified*, and Marksville Stamped. The low incidence of ceramics was cited as evidence that pottery use was not particularly important locally and that, as a result, Woodland and later occupations were likewise probably fairly brief and limited in scope. The small collection of historic artifacts recovered derived from home or farm sites or else from recent military use of the area; one well-preserved house foundation and debris scatter was recorded at 16VN1374.

Gulf South Research Corporation Intensive Surveys, 1994–1996

From November 1994 through July 1996, archaeologists from Gulf South Research Corporation, Inc., conducted seven separate small-scale survey projects on Fort Polk. Malcolm Shuman served as the principal investigator for the projects, while much of the fieldwork and writing was handled either by Shuman or Dennis Jones. In all, a total of 5,180 acres were surveyed and 94 sites and 55 isolated finds were documented (Table 2.5). Fieldwork and reporting followed the procedures used during the R. Christopher Goodwin and Associates, Inc., survey projects. That is, separate technical appendix volumes containing site forms and location maps were prepared for each study, and survey proceeded using transects and collection units spaced at 30- and 50-m intervals in High and Low Probability Zones, respectively, as determined from the 1988 HPP predictive model. Once sites or isolated finds were located, shovel tests were opened in a grid pattern at 10-m intervals for sites less than 50 m in extent and at 20-m intervals for sites more than 50 m in extent, with at least one 50-x-50-cm test opened at each site to examine stratigraphy. Surface collection typically entailed 100 percent recovery using a general collection strategy, unless otherwise noted. Field teams also

Table 2.5 — Intensive survey projects conducted by Gulf South Research Corporation on Fort Polk, Louisiana, 1994–1996

Survey No.	No. Acres	No. Sites	Isolates	NRHP*	Post Location	Resource Density**	References
GSRI-1	313	2	3	1	PR	1.60	Shuman et al. 1995
GSRI-2	1,930	8	13	1	PR	1.09	Shuman et al. 1996a
GSRI-3	319	5	3	0	PR	2.51	Shuman et al. 1996b
GSRI-4	1,002	15	5	3	MF	2.00	Shuman et al. 1996c
GSRI-5	824	27	7	5	PR	4.13	Jones et al. 1996a
GSRI-6	422	8	15	0	PR	5.45	Jones et al. 1996b
GSRI-7	370	29	9	7	MF	10.27	Jones et al. 1997
Totals	5,180	94	55	17		2.88	

*   *Number of sites potentially eligible for the National Register of Historic Places*
**   *Number of sites and isolated finds per 100 acres*

documented unusual cultural resources, including a historic petroglyph carved into a sandstone boulder from Peason Ridge with the inscription "PHD" and the date "12-20-41" (Jones et al. 1996b:106). Who or what this refers to is unknown, although if the date was misread, it may refer to Pearl Harbor Day. Interestingly, a rusted iron wedge was found nearby with a heavily battered working edge that may have been used to make the inscription.

The location of individual survey transects in each survey area examined was included in the reports. The number and location of shovel tests opened on individual sites were reported and illustrated, and each report also gave the total number of shovel tests opened during the project. Site maps were typically highly detailed, providing accurate information about the location of collection units and cultural and natural features and containing contours extrapolated from USGS maps and observed field conditions (e.g., Figures 2.28 and 2.29). General survey transect shovel tests were recorded on site maps, aiding in boundary definition and reflecting a reporting standard that should be used by all researchers doing survey work. Soil profiles were presented from every site and isolated find examined, which was the first time this level of detail was provided in survey reports from the installation. At the end of each volume a detailed appendix was presented that listed artifacts by site, provenience, artifact type, and count. Archival research was conducted when major historic sites were encountered, as in the case of the Four L Home site (16VN1575; Shuman et al. 1996b:59). Interpretive sections were included in the conclusions of several reports (Jones et al. 1996a:161–162, 1996b:109, 1997:191–192; Shuman et al. 1996c:111).

Site and isolated find density was observed to be much greater on the Main Fort than on Peason Ridge, something attributed to the topographic

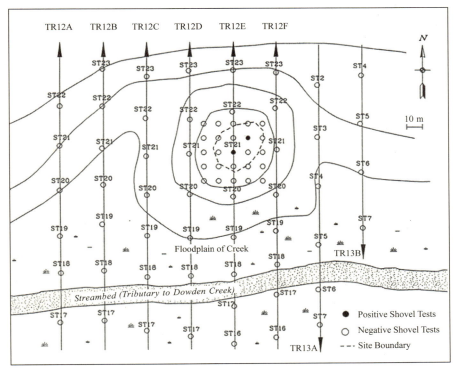

Figure 2.28 — Site 16VN1690 map produced as part of an intensive survey project by Gulf South Research Corporation (from Jones et al. 1997:69).

differences between the two areas (Jones et al. 1996a:164–165). The narrow floodplains and small or ephemeral stream channels that characterize the Peason Ridge area differ markedly from the much broader floodplains of the streams in the Main Fort area, and the latter were assumed to be far more productive in terms of exploitable biomass and hence more attractive to past populations. Even within the Main Fort area, site and isolated find density was observed to be much greater near floodplains than in the more heavily dissected terrain found near the headwaters of small streams (Jones et al. 1997:196).

New South Associates, Survey of 14,622 Acres on the Main Fort, 1995–1996

From October 1995 through July 1996, archaeologists from New South Associates, Inc., under the direction of Charles E. Cantley, conducted an inten-

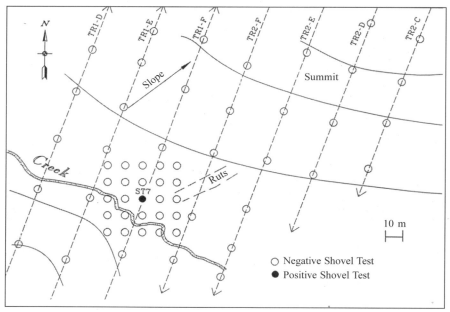

Figure 2.29 — Isolated find shovel test map produced as part of an intensive survey project by Gulf South Research Corporation (from Shuman et al. 1996b:51).

sive survey of 14,622 acres on the Main Fort in Vernon Parish (Cantley et al. 1997). Field methods were the same as those used during the large-scale intensive surveys conducted by SCIAA, R. Christopher Goodwin and Associates, Inc., and Gulf South Research Corporation. That is, systematic shovel testing, using 30-x-30-cm units opened to subsoil, was employed at 30-m transect and collection-unit intervals in High Probability Zones and at 50-m intervals in Low Probability Zones, which were defined using the 1995 predictive model that had just been developed as part of research associated with the revision of the installation HPP and that replaced use of the 1988 predictive model on the installation almost immediately (see Chapter 3). All sites received close-interval shovel testing using a 10- or 15-m grid, depending on whether they were less than or greater than 50 m in extent, coupled with the excavation of a larger 50-x-50-cm unit. At some of the sites, at the discretion of the field director, shovel tests were opened in 10-cm levels in an effort to resolve stratigraphic relationships. The utilization of a 15-m rather than a 20-m grid to delineate large sites was an important modification to earlier survey procedures, since it meant that shovel tests could be placed in between all of the 30-m survey transect tests, resulting in more uniform sampling.

The fieldwork took place on the eastern and west-central portions of the Main Fort, in the Fullerton Maneuver and Zion Hill Training Areas, respectively. The work in the Fullerton Maneuver Area included portions of the basins and main channels of Big, Tenmile, Big Brushy, and Little Brushy Creeks and the East Fork of Sixmile Creek, whereas the work in the Zion Hills Training Area was along both sides of Whiskey Chitto Creek, the largest stream draining the Main Fort area. A total of 342 sites and 413 isolated finds were examined, including revisits to eight sites for which new data and forms were generated. Low-density artifact scatters were found extending almost continuously along the margins of most drainages and particularly along Whiskey Chitto Creek, making resolution of site concentrations and boundaries difficult and requiring the excavation of tens of thousands of site-definition shovel tests (Cantley et al. 1997:806–808). For this reason, close-interval shovel testing using 10- or 15-m intervals was conducted at only 112 of the 342 sites recorded, although judgmental tests were placed on many of the remaining sites to define concentrations. A massive artifact assemblage was recovered, including 143 projectile points and point fragments, 342 prehistoric ceramic fragments, 52,952 pieces of debitage, and 1,784 historic artifacts (Cantley et al. 1997:808–809, 816, 840). Detailed attributes were recorded for much of the assemblage, including the prehistoric stone tools, debitage, and ceramics. This information is presented by artifact and/ or provenience in the appendixes, providing a valuable database for researchers working with collections from the Fort Polk area and a good example for other researchers undertaking these kinds of projects.

The report on the investigations stands as a masterpiece of site description, analysis, and primary data reporting at the survey level; at over 1,000 pages, the two-volume report is second only to the FPAS study in length (cf. Servello, ed. 1983). A number of highly sophisticated analyses were conducted by Cantley and his colleagues, including an evaluation of arguments about the relationship between site size and distance to lithic source areas, which has long been a subject of interest on Fort Polk; an evaluation of the 1995 predictive model; a detailed analysis of the debitage assemblage by size category and reduction stage to examine technological organization and settlement strategies; and an examination of how large site assemblages formed, which demonstrated that many were actually palimpsests of numerous small scatters (Cantley et al. 1997:853; see Chapter 3). The project marked one of the first detailed attempts to understand internal site structure on the installation using survey-level data. It showed the value of close-interval shovel testing in the resolution of individual components or periods of use amid the larger scatter. A detailed biface reduction trajectory was identified, with bifaces measured and described by category (Figure 2.30). While pre-

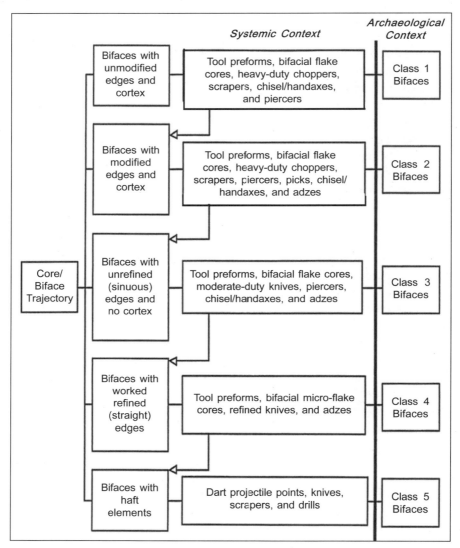

Figure 2.30 — Biface trajectory flow model for the Fort Polk area (from Cantley et al. 1997:811)

historic ceramics were rare, as has been the case in all Fort Polk projects, 44 sherds from the upper part of a Mazique Incised jar were found at one site, 16VN1836. Although it is only about one-third present, this is one of the most complete vessels found to date on the installation (Cantley et al. 1997:837–838). A limited program of geoarchaeological investigations was also conducted in the floodplain of Whiskey Chitto Creek to check for the possibility of buried cultural remains. Three backhoe trenches were opened, and the profiles were recorded, samples of fill screened, and soils retained for specialized analyses, which included OCR dating (Frink 1992, 1994) and detailed description by the project soil scientist, Dr. John Foss (Cantley et al. 1997:796–806) (see Table 6.1 for a listing of the absolute dates). These trenches were from 4 to 5 m long and from 2 to 3 m in depth. No artifacts were found, but the OCR dating of the soil layers indicated that cultural materials could be expected in the first 1.25 m in floodplain areas. Given the small sample size, however, appreciably more work in these areas was recommended.

South Carolina Institute of Archaeology and Anthropology Survey of 12,538 Acres on the Main Fort, 1996–1997

From November 1996 through June 18, 1997, archaeologists from the Cultural Resources Consulting Division of the South Carolina Institute of Archaeology and Anthropology (SCIAA), University of South Carolina, conducted an intensive archaeological survey of 12,538 acres on the Main Fort in Vernon Parish (Clement et al. 1998). The work was directed by Christopher Clement and Ramona Grunden. The survey followed the procedures in place on the installation for several years, with 30- and 50-m transect and collection-unit intervals in respectively High/Indeterminate and Low Probability Zones defined using the 1995 predictive model (see Chapter 4). A total of 308 sites and 172 isolated finds were located and documented. Site boundaries were defined using shovel tests spaced over uniform 10-m and 20-m grids, depending on whether the overall scatter was, respectively, less than or greater than 50 m in extent. Site areas were extensively shovel tested and superbly documented, providing data of great value in the recognition of intrasite component occurrence and function (Figure 2.31). An evaluation of the 1995 installation predictive model was presented, and detailed descriptions of the prehistoric and historic artifacts found were presented, together with innovative comparative analyses of the larger assemblages, as well as of single-component assemblages, to explore variability in quarrying behavior and other aspects of site use (see Chapters 3 and 4).

TRC Garrow Associates, Survey of 6,047 Acres on Peason Ridge, 1998

During the winter and spring of 1998 archaeologists from TRC Garrow Associates, Inc., under the direction of H. Blaine Ensor conducted a 6,047-acre

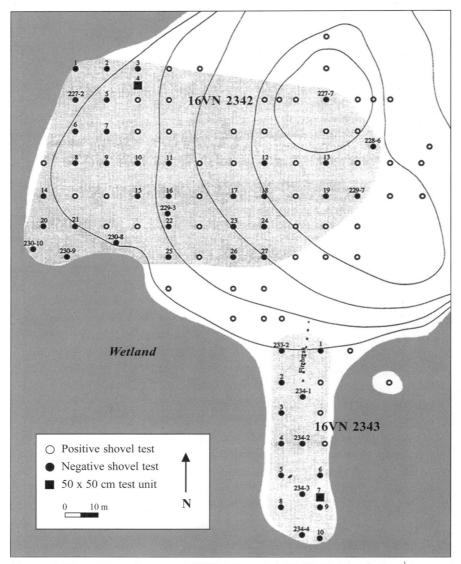

Figure 2.31 — Maps for sites 16VN2342 and 16VN2343 (from Grunden and Clement 1998:75).

survey on Peason Ridge (Ensor et al., eds. 1999). A total of 68 new sites and 79 new isolated finds were located, and five previously recorded sites and isolated finds were revisited. This project marked the completion of survey work on Peason Ridge (i.e., all areas outside of impact zones have now been surveyed). Field procedures were similar to those used in the recent SCIAA

and New South Associates, Inc., projects, except that all sites were systematically shovel tested using a uniform 10-m grid. The resulting data were
used to generate density maps for every site on which more than 20 tests
were opened; this is the first project on Fort Polk in which such analyses
were routinely conducted (Figure 2.32). A comparative analysis of assemblages from 42 sites previously tested on the installation was conducted to
aid in the interpretation and evaluation of sites found during the survey, and
the 1995 predictive model was evaluated with data from the survey (Ezell
and Ensor 1999:340, 367–393; see Chapters 3 and 4).

Only a limited number of the sites (n = 12) and isolated finds (n = 13)
were found to have historic components, and an appreciable number of these
(five sites and nine of the isolated finds) were associated with lumber industry activities (Pietak 1999). These included turpentine cup fragments as well

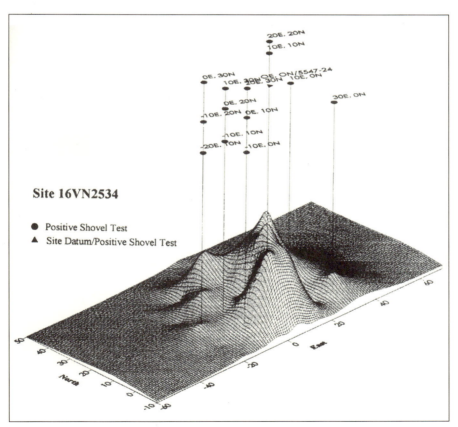

*Figure 2.32 — Site 16VN2534 density plot from the 1998 TRC Garrow Associates,
Inc., survey (from Patton and Ezell 1999:305).*

as bottle glass and ceramics from probable camps. The remaining assemblages appeared to derive primarily from small family farmsteads. The lack of evidence for community buildings such as churches or stores suggested that these sites were fairly isolated. Small samples of prehistoric ceramics (n = 125), stone tools (n = 30), and debitage (n = 1,167) were recovered during the survey (Ezell and Ensor 1999:340, 351, 360). Ceramics were overwhelmingly plain (n = 65), with sand tempering (n = 63) far more common than grog- or grog-and-sand-tempered pastes (Ezell and Ensor 1999:343). One unusual point recovered was the base from a possible Plainview-like lanceolate (Ezell and Ensor 1999:355). The vast majority of the debitage was flakes 1/4 inch in size or smaller, which was attributed to the small size of the gravels available locally (Ezell and Ensor 1999:360–367). Appreciable bifacial reduction was indicated, suggesting the manufacture and reworking of these tool forms.

Southeast Archeological Center, National Park Service Survey Projects, 1999

In 1999, archaeologists from the National Park Service's Southeast Archeological Center conducted two small archaeological projects on the Main Fort (Heide 1999a, 1999b). A proposed 28-mile-long bicycle trail ca. 10 feet in width and located on U.S. Forest Service limited-use lands south of the Main Fort was surveyed using 30-x-30-cm shovel tests opened every 30 m (Heide 1999a). Three sites and seven isolated finds were recorded, all small lithic scatters. A second survey of 84 acres located in the northwest corner of the Main Fort located one new site and one isolated find and reexamined six sites previously recorded in the immediate area; all were prehistoric (Heide 1999b). The reports were noteworthy in that all transect or shovel test locations were delimited on large-scale maps of the project area included in the reports, site delineation proceeded even if the boundaries extended outside the project area (i.e., away from the trail in the case of the first project), and artifact density distribution maps were produced for each site. A low percentage of the survey shovel tests were left undug (ca. 25 percent); in many recent survey projects in which these data are reported on the installation, figures closer to 50 percent are typical (e.g., Ensor et al. 1999:330; Saatkamp et al. 2000:iii, 2001:iii). The artifact density distribution maps and analyses that were conducted help demonstrate that even comparatively small sites may exhibit evidence for multiple activities or periods of site use, reinforcing recent observations advanced by researchers from New South Associates, Inc. (Cantley et al. 1997:877–921).

1999 Historic Preservation Plan

In 1999 an updated HPP was released for Fort Polk. The update included the compilation and synthesis of data from all of the cultural resource investigations conducted on the installation since the 1988 HPP was produced, the development of a new predictive model for the installation, and the presentation of new management procedures and guidelines. Five volumes were produced, as described in the Introduction. These consisted of (1) a planning manual/action plan volume, (2) a cultural resources inventory primary data volume, (3) a cultural resources inventory management summary, (4) a technical synthesis/overview volume, and (5) a map volume. While based on the volumes produced for the 1988 HPP, the contents of the updated volumes had to be extensively revised to accommodate the vast amount of new information produced, as well as the many changes that occurred in fieldwork, reporting, laws and regulations, and in the installation mission itself since the 1980s. A detailed description of the contents of each volume of the 1999 HPP is included in the technical synthesis/overview volume (Anderson et al. 1999b:10–15). The research and synthetic discussions presented in the 1999 HPP Technical Synthesis/Overview are included in this book, albeit appreciably updated and revised given the extensive CRM work ongoing on the installation.

The revised HPP Planning Manual/Action Plan (Anderson and Smith 1999), like its 1988 counterpart, was designed for land management and planning personnel and provides a step-by-step guide, with specific recommendations, as to how cultural resource compliance will be accomplished on Fort Polk. Contents of the planning manual/action plan included the following:

1. A review of relevant federal and agency regulations mandating the CRM program, with reference copies of critical legislation and regulations included in a separate appendix volume.

2. A flow chart by which the compliance process is to be undertaken to inventory, evaluate, and preserve or mitigate project impacts to historic properties.

3. Criteria used to evaluate the NRHP significance of historic properties found at Fort Polk. These were substantially revised from the criteria presented in the 1988 HPP in light of the considerable work done since 1988. These criteria, with justifications, are also presented in the technical synthesis volume.

4. Strategies for preserving and protecting historic properties and proce-
    dures by which they can be implemented. This includes detailed docu-
    mentation explaining how the Special Use Permit from the U.S. Forest
    Service is to be implemented and how coordination with both the For-
    est Service and the Louisiana State Historic Preservation Office (and,
    if and when necessary, the Advisory Council on Historic Preservation)
    is to proceed.

5. Summary data briefly describing the quantity, character, distribution,
    and potential significance of cultural resources/historic properties on
    Fort Polk, presented in the form of maps delimiting areas where sig-
    nificant historic properties are and are not likely to occur. The techni-
    cal analyses documenting and justifying this predictive modeling ef-
    fort are presented at length in the technical synthesis volume, and the
    primary environmental, locational, and archaeological data used to
    generate the model and maps are included in the revised HPP inven-
    tory and map volumes. The inventory also provides an evaluation of
    NRHP significance for every known site on the installation, using one
    of three categories: eligible, not eligible, or potentially eligible.

6. A listing of all actions that might potentially adversely affect historic
    properties on Fort Polk and hence require full compliance action.

7. A listing of routine maintenance activities or upcoming programs that
    do not adversely affect historic properties on Fort Polk and hence do
    not require review by the State Historic Preservation Office or Advi-
    sory Council on Historic Preservation.

8. A description of the professional standards for all cultural resource
    investigations to be undertaken on the base. These indicate the kind of
    work and level of effort that should be accomplished and are intended
    to ensure the consistency and technical excellence of this work. This
    information is also presented in the technical synthesis volume.

9. Procedures for dealing with emergency discovery situations.

10. Procedures for coordination with Native American groups, specifically:
    a. Regarding the effect of installation activities on Native American
        cultural items, to ensure that such items are removed only pursuant
        to a permit issued under Section 4 of the Archeological Resources
        Protection Act of 1979 (ARPA), whose terms shall be developed

consistent with NAGPRA (Native American Graves and Repatriation Act of 1989) and in consultation with appropriate Native American groups, and

b. To ensure that good-faith efforts are made to preserve and protect sites of religious importance on installations, and ensure access to these sites, pursuant to the American Indian Religious Freedom Act of 1978.

11. Procedures for the preservation and protection of historic properties from looting and vandalism, following the provisions of ARPA and NAGPRA and the 1991 Louisiana Unmarked Burial Sites Preservation Act.

12. Standards and guidelines for curation, specifically the treatment of cultural resources/historic properties, reports, collections, and artifact assemblages, including human remains following 36 CFR 79.

Technical documentation for the management recommendations advanced in the planning manual/action plan was provided in the other parts of the 1999 HPP.

The cultural resources inventory primary data and management summary volumes include extensive locational, assemblage, component, environmental, and other data on all archaeological and historic sites reported on Fort Polk through February 1999, providing primary documentation for the analyses and conclusions presented in the 1999 technical synthesis/overview (Anderson 1999; Anderson et al. 1999a, 1999b). Because the complete set of data files in the cultural resources inventory primary data volume encompass over 1,100 pages of text and are extremely cumbersome to use in that format simply by virtue of their size and weight, two solutions were adopted to facilitate the use of this information. First, a compact disk containing the complete contents of the 1999 HPP was included as part of the cultural resources inventory primary data volume. Second, an abbreviated inventory management summary volume was produced providing basic management data on each historic property found on the installation. The information in both inventory volumes is maintained in hard copy and electronic format, using Microsoft Excel spreadsheets as well as more complex databases that can be used on any type of personal computer. It is easily accessible and can be used by researchers and land managers alike.

The map volume, released in 1996, was produced concurrently with the development of a new predictive model for the installation that was finalized in 1995 (see Chapter 4) and the development of a GIS for the installation (Anderson et al. 1996a). Maps in the volume encompass the 1988 and 1995 model resource probability zones, the locations of all archaeological and historic sites and isolated finds, all areas where intensive cultural resource survey has occurred, soil and drainage variables, geological formations, and slope categories, plus a map based on the soils data delimiting the depth of C horizons locally, or the depth to which cultural deposits can be expected on the installation. This information is presented on a series of GIS-generated 1:50,000 and 1:24,000 paper and Mylar maps, corresponding in extent and scale to the installation's Terrain Analysis maps and the 10 USGS 7.5-minute quadrangle sheets that encompass the Fort Polk area, which form base maps for the overlays. All of the data layers are maintained in the installation GIS and updated periodically as new data are developed, allowing users to create, update, display, and analyze data and print maps and other output based on the wide range of data layers that have been developed, including cultural resources. This is a dramatic improvement over the original HPP map volume (Anderson and Macek 1987), which contained information hand-drawn and lettered onto copies of USGS quadrangle sheets and installation Terrain Analysis maps.

University of Memphis Survey of 4,579 Acres in the Rustville Training Area, 1999–2000

Beginning in the late 1990s, the Army began to conduct extensive CRM work south of the Main Fort, on limited-use lands owned by the U.S. Forest Service, who had themselves conducted a number of survey projects in this area (see below). Field procedures were similar to those used in the SCIAA, New South Associates, Inc., and TRC Garrow Associates, Inc., projects, with all sites systematically shovel tested using a uniform 10-m grid and density maps created for every site on which more than 20 tests were opened. A 4,579-acre tract located west of the West Fork of Sixmile Creek was examined in 1999 and 2000, using the 1995 predictive model to define probability zones (Ensor et al. 2001). A total of 118 sites and 90 isolated finds were found, with the prehistoric assemblage including 112 sherds, 462 flaked stone tools, 19,258 pieces of debitage, and 591 pieces of fire-cracked chert. Very few historic sites or artifacts were found, although these were found to increase in the western part of the area, in proximity to the old Fullerton Lumber Mill, which lay just outside the survey tract (Ensor et al. 2001:43; Miller 1997). Detailed debitage and interassemblage analyses were conducted, which indicated that later prehistoric use of the general area included a small number of lithic procurement sites and a much larger number of short-term camps (see Chapter 3).

Panamerican Consultants, Survey of 6,535 Acres on the Main Fort, 1999–2000

An intensive archaeological survey of 6,535 acres located in the northeastern corner of the Main Fort on Fort Polk was conducted by archaeologists from Panamerican Consultants, Inc., in 1999 and 2000 (Saatkamp et al. 2000). Field procedures followed those used in the TRC Garrow Associates, Inc., and University of Memphis projects, with all sites systematically shovel tested using a uniform 10-m grid if the site was less than 50 m across and a 20-m grid if it was larger; artifact density distribution maps were created for every site on which more than 20 tests were opened. A total of 27 sites and 19 isolated finds were documented. A sparse artifact assemblage was recovered, including 13 formal hafted bifaces, 7 bifaces, 13 cores, 4 retouched flakes, 761 pieces of debitage, 1 battered stone, 23 prehistoric sherds, and 155 historic artifacts (Gray and Buchner 2000). Local chert gravels made up the vast majority of the assemblage, with minor quantities of quartzite, petrified wood, and unknown materials observed (Gray and Buchner 2000:75). Detailed historic research was conducted, including an examination of General Land Office land patent reports and other historic landownership maps. This was some of the most innovative historic research undertaken during a large-scale survey project on the installation and a good example for other researchers (Buchner 2000:49–54; see also Kern 1984a, 1984b). The survey found the lowest recovery rate, in terms of numbers of sites and isolated finds per hundred acres, of any large-scale survey undertaken by the Army anywhere on Fort Polk (see Table 2.1). Importantly, the authors sought to understand why this occurred (Buchner and Saatkamp 2000:195–197). On the basis of a comparative analysis, the authors suggested one reason for the low density was that the survey area lay on the northern side of the Main Fort, close to Peason Ridge, where a lower site density occurred. Much of the area had been extensively disturbed by early Army use, specifically heavy-equipment maneuvering and the creation of gravel borrow pits, and these activities were thought to have reduced the site density. It was among the last areas to be surveyed on the installation, in fact, because the extent of disturbance was known to be high. Understanding why major differences in site density occur from area to area and project to project is a critical area for research so that these differences can be controlled for in interpretive analyses and in land-management planning (see Conclusions).

Panamerican Consultants, Survey of 4,212 Acres on the Main Fort and in the Limited-Use Area, 2000

An intensive archaeological survey of 4,212 acres encompassing some 3,150 acres in the northwest corner of the Main Fort and some 1,062 acres in the limited-use area to the south was conducted in the year 2000 by archaeologists from Panamerican Consultants, Inc. (Saatkamp et al. 2001). Field procedures followed those used in all recent survey projects, including the recently completed large-scale survey project by Panamerican Consultants, Inc. (Saatkamp et al. 2000). A total of 39 sites and 22 isolated finds were found, which was again a very low recovery rate for a large-scale survey project on the installation. Because 3,150 acres of this survey were in the same area as the previous survey by Panamerican Consultants—the last area on the Main Fort to be examined because it was known to be extensively disturbed—possible reasons for this low rate were the same as for the earlier survey (Buchner and Saatkamp 2001:288–289; see also Poplin [1987], who encountered only a slightly higher site density in this area, which he explained as a result of the project location being on a major drainage divide [see also Chapter 3]). Another reason advanced was the extensive disturbance and deflation that has occurred in this part of the installation. The low site density may have also been because historic settlement was minimal, possibly because much of the land was controlled by timber companies during the early twentieth century (Buchner and Saatkamp 2001:296; similar reasoning was used to explain why few historic sites were found in an earlier project conducted on the installation [McMakin et al. 1994:227, 229]). The low density may also be because approximately half of the potential shovel test locations were unexcavated (Saatkamp et al. 2001:iii), presumably because of the presence of steep slopes (i.e., greater than a 20-degree slope) or standing water; these locations were excluded from such testing by the scope of work for the project. The portion of the survey in the limited-use area south of the Main Fort (1,062 acres), in contrast, yielded site densities comparable to those found during earlier projects.

Detailed historic research was conducted, including an examination of General Land Office land patent reports and other historic landownership maps (Buchner 2001:58–69). The site and assemblage descriptions and maps are excellent, and artifact density maps were prepared for most sites. Some 3,333 pieces of debitage, 26 ceramic fragments, and 70 flaked stone tools were recovered, plus 291 historic artifacts; the vast majority of the lithics (ca. 94.4 percent) were made from chert gravels, probably from the local Citronelle Formation (Gray 2001:84). Fourteen lithic raw material categories were described, which represents one of the few attempts to examine the variability in worked stone (Gray 2001:72–76; see also Heinrich 1983, 1984). Quartzite and petrified wood and some presumed extralocal raw materials were also present in the assemblage, although in very low incidence; to understand where people who visited Fort Polk came from, determination of the source of such materials will be critical.

Panamerican Consultants, Survey of 4,862 Acres in the Limited-Use Area, 2000–2001

An intensive archaeological survey of 4,862 acres located in the limited-use area south of the Main Fort was conducted by archaeologists from Panamerican Consultants, Inc., in 2000 and 2001 (Bundy and Buchner 2002). Most of the work was conducted in the floodplain and adjacent uplands of the Whiskey Chitto Creek drainage, an area that has in the past produced a high site and artifact density on the Main Fort (e.g., Cantley et al. 1997). Fieldwork followed the same procedures used during earlier projects by this contractor, with analyses including the detailed description of artifacts and the routine production of artifact density distribution maps (see above). A total of 108 sites and 67 isolated finds were found; again, innovative historic research and detailed descriptive and comparative analyses with the site assemblages were conducted to examine landownership patterns, examine intrasite artifact patterning, and evaluate the utility of the 1995 predictive model (Buchner 2002; Bundy 2002a, 2002b). Almost 18,000 artifacts were reported (Bundy 2002a:75), including 53 projectile points and point fragments, 67 bifaces, 402 cores, 16 retouched flakes, 16,414 pieces of debitage, 738 pieces of fire-cracked rock, 95 prehistoric ceramics, and 181 historic artifacts. The prehistoric artifact incidence was comparable to that recovered by New South Associates farther to the north along Whiskey Chitto Creek, although the historic artifact density was appreciably lower, which was attributed to ownership of the land by timber companies (e.g., Bundy 2002b:662; Cantley et al. 1997:808–809, 840; see discussion above).

Kisatchie National Forest Cultural Resource Management Program

An extensive CRM program has also been under way in the Kisatchie National Forest in Louisiana for over two decades. The Forest is spread across six discontinuous Ranger Districts, three of which—Vernon, Evangeline, and Kisatchie—are located immediately to the south, east, and north of Fort

Polk (Figure 2.33). The northern part of the Vernon Ranger District forms the intensive-use lands on the southern part of the Main Fort, while the limited-use lands encompass the southern part of the district. The former Horse's Head Maneuver Area, now no longer under military control or use (although it may be reactivated), lies within the Kisatchie Ranger District just to the north and east of Peason Ridge. Almost all cultural resource investigations on the Forest, typically intensive survey work associated with timber-harvesting activity, are done in-house by U.S. Forest Service staff archaeologists, although some work has been contracted out. A cultural re-

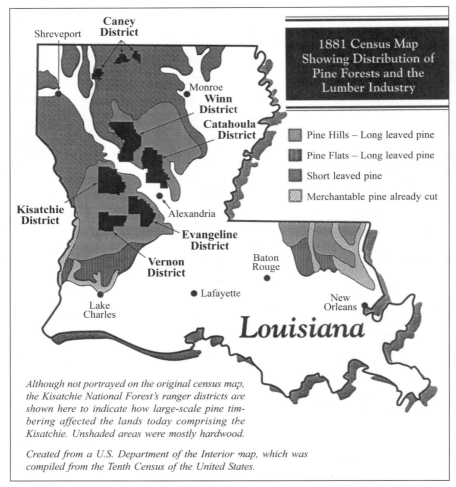

Figure 2.33 — Kisatchie National Forest base map, showing late-nineteenth-century forest conditions (from Burns and Couch 1994:4).

sources overview synthesizing research on the Forest and offering directions for the future was prepared in the early 1980s (Keller 1984). An updated Heritage Preservation Plan for the Forest is currently in preparation.

The CRM program on the Forest is comparable to that on Fort Polk in many ways, particularly in terms of its methods and objectives. U.S. Forest Service archaeologists have conducted extensive predictive modeling analyses in west-central Louisiana and the first broad examination of the occurrence and use of lithic raw materials in the general region (see Chapter 3). The Fort Polk and Forest Service CRM programs have coordinated activity for many years to the mutual benefit of research and management concerns. Through April 2002 approximately 35 percent of the 597,000 acres that make up the Kisatchie National Forest had been surveyed at some level of intensity, with 3,388 sites recorded, 394 of which are classified as potentially eligible for inclusion on the NRHP (Alan Dorian, personal communication, April 17, 2002). All potentially eligible sites are protected and, if threatened, are subject to intensive testing for purposes of NRHP evaluation.

INVESTIGATIONS IN THE KISATCHIE NATIONAL FOREST ON AND NEAR FORT POLK

A listing of survey projects conducted by U.S. Forest Service personnel on land used by Fort Polk is given in Table 2.6. A total of 3,232.6 acres have been surveyed by U.S. Forest Service personnel in the intensive-use lands forming the southern part of the Main Fort in Vernon Parish. In all, 27 sites and nine isolated finds have been documented. Discovery rates average 1.96 sites or isolated finds per hundred acres when two projects tracts that received reconnaissance survey are removed from consideration; comparable site densities have been reported in recent large-scale surveys conducted in this area (Table 2.1). Areas subject to initial reconnaissance-level survey have been resurveyed in recent years or are in the process of being resurveyed.

The first CRM investigations in the Kisatchie National Forest that were conducted on or near Fort Polk date to the mid-1970s (Keller 1984:35–36, 39–40). The first fieldwork on the Vernon Ranger District occurred in 1977, when U.S. Forest Service archaeologists conducted a small 30-acre survey and visited the Fullerton Mill area south of the Main Fort for the first time (Price 1977). During this same project the first work on the Kisatchie Ranger District near Peason Ridge also took place: a revisit to a previously recorded site, 16NA173. The first large-scale survey on the Vernon Ranger District, encompassing 2,000 acres spread over several land-exchange tracts, resulted in the discovery of 18 sites and two isolated finds (Bennett 1982). Soon thereafter a second survey encompassing 680 acres was conducted, locating

Table 2.6 — Intensive survey projects conducted by Kisatchie National Forest personnel on Fort Polk, Louisiana, 1983–1995

Survey No./Yr.	No. Acres	No. Sites	Iso.[†]	NRHP[‡]	Post Location	Density[††]	References
FY 1983*	60	1	1	0	MF	3.33	Johnson 1983
FY 1985	131	2	2	0	MF	3.05	Willingham & Phillips 1987
FY 1986	5	0	1	0	MF	20.00	Phillips & Willingham 1990
FY 1988	75	0	0	0	MF	0.00	Dorian 1988a
FY 1990	25	2	1	0	MF	12.00	Haikey et al. 1991
USFS 92-12	28.6	0	0	0	MF	0.00	Coleman 1992
USFS 92-16*	1,522	2	0	0	MF	0.13	Dorian & Coleman 1992
USFS 93-25	177	0	0	0	MF	0.00	Coleman 1993a
USFS 93-27	382	3	0	0	MF	0.79	Coleman 1993b
USFS 93-31	208	4	1	1	MF	2.40	Coleman 1993c
USFS 94-8	225	9	2	1	MF	4.89	Lehmann 1994a
USFS 94-28	367	3	1	0	MF	1.09	Shreve 1994b
USFS 95-4	27	1	0	1	MF	3.70	Lehmann 1994b
USFS 95-21	591	3	5	1	MF	1.35	Lehmann 1995
Totals	3,232.6	27	9	3	MF	1.11	
	** 2,241.6					** 1.96	

*   Reconnaissance level; resurveyed by Fort Polk
**   Acreage and incidence when reconnaissance-level surveys omitted
†   Number of isolates
‡   Number of sites potentially eligible for the National Register of Historic Places
††   Number of sites and isolated finds per 100 acres

eight new sites (Swanda 1982). In 1978 the first intensive survey on the Kisatchie Ranger District by U.S. Forest Service personnel took place; this was an examination of two small tracts totaling 53 acres plus 2.5 miles of road-construction right-of-way (Prieto et al. 1978).

The 1984 Cultural Resources Overview provided a synthesis of cultural resource investigations on the Kisatchie National Forest. Projects undertaken in each Ranger District were noted, with a brief discussion of results. This summary, besides including the larger projects noted above, provided details on other small projects that took place on the Vernon and Kisatchie Districts from 1977 through 1983, most away from lands owned or used by the Army. The overview identified a number of research concerns to be explored during subsequent work on the Forest (Keller 1984:55–60). For the prehistoric era, these included examining or considering the following:

1. The nature and origins of lithic procurement and utilization strategies in the Kisatchie National Forest . . .

2. The relationship between the cultures of the lower Mississippi Valley as represented by Coles Creek and [those in and north of the Forest area as represented by] the Caddoan culture . . .

3. Location and explanation of salt procurement sites and strategies . . .

4. The nature of the relationship between sites located in the upland pine forests and those occurring in bottomland ecosystems in terms of settlement patterning and seasonality . . .

5. . . . [T]he validity and practicality of utilizing lithic debris as a means of distinguishing cultural affiliation and chronological placement on a technological basis . . .

6. . . . [T]he nature of subsistence among late prehistoric populations . . .

7. [The effect of] modern timber activities . . . on archaeological sites and how . . . these differ from the effect of historic timber harvesting [Keller 1984:55–57].

For the historic period the following questions were proposed:

1. Can the ethnic identities of the various European cultures operating within Louisiana early in the historic period be distinguished archaeologically? . . .

2. How was the Forest environment being utilized during the historic period? . . .

3. Define the nature of the population, culture and operations of the commercial timber operations of the late nineteenth and early twentieth centuries . . .

4. What role did the C.C.C. play in the development of the Kisatchie National Forest? [Keller 1984:59–60].

All of these questions, of course, applied equally to investigations on Fort Polk, and many have received extensive examination over the past two decades.

Cultural resource investigations on the Kisatchie National Forest since the early 1980s have been summarized in a series of annual reports, supplemented with specific reports on individual projects (e.g., Phillips and Haikey 1992; Phillips and Wasson 1989; Phillips and Willingham 1990). The annual reports, besides providing excellent data on the cultural resources work done during the year in question and the historic properties that were found, also typically contain excellent analyses of topics such as lithic raw material occurrence and use in west-central Louisiana or modeling site locations (see Chapter 3). In addition to preparing annual reports, the U.S. Forest Service also produces individual reports on many of its specific projects. These usually document cultural resources inventory and evaluation work on areas slated for activities such as thinning and regeneration cutting (Lehmann 1994a; Shreve 1994a), wildlife viewing areas (Lehmann 1994b), or waterline construction, storm-damage salvage cutting, road or pathway construction, or other activities related to routine operation of the Forest (e.g., Coleman 1993a, 1993b, 1993c) (Table 2.6). The U.S. Forest Service has also from time to time hired outside contractors to handle intensive survey activity when this work exceeded the capabilities of in-house staff (e.g., D. Jones et al. 1994, 1995).

Like Fort Polk, the Kisatchie National Forest also has a GIS system in place that can be used to model site probability zones. Given the long history of effort on this type of research by both agencies, there is a compelling need to coordinate and standardize these analyses. During the development of the 1999 HPP, several meetings were held with U.S. Forest Service personnel to develop procedures for conducting larger-scale analyses, combining data sets from both agencies. Some cultural resources, of course, are virtually unpredictable, which requires that care must always be taken not to take the results of such analyses too literally or to the point that unusual site types might be overlooked.

In 1995, during a survey of 591 acres in the intensive-use area on the Main Fort, for example, U.S. Forest Service Archaeologist Geoffrey Lehmann (1995) observed a light scatter of lithic debitage in the vicinity of two small rock overhangs or shelters found near Bundick Creek. Located on U.S. Forest Service property in the western portion of the Vernon District, the area is well to the south of lands used by Fort Polk, but it serves as an example of a site type that may be present on the installation. Rockshelter sites are extremely rare in Louisiana (this is the first one recorded in the state, according to the report), making this an extremely important site if undisturbed deposits exist. Unfortunately, the overhangs as well as the surrounding ridge line have been extensively disturbed by looters, and the extent of surviving deposits, if any, is unknown.

Conclusions

As can be seen by this review of past work, an impressive body of archaeological research has occurred both on and near Fort Polk over the past three
decades. While it was once possible to note that the Fort Polk area was "one
of the most poorly understood regions in the state" (Campbell and Weed
1986:2-7), this is clearly no longer the case. A great deal of work has been
accomplished and, acre for acre, Fort Polk now stands as one of the most
intensively examined archaeological localities in the United States. Every
accessible acre on the Main Fort and Peason Ridge has, in fact, been intensively surveyed, a record few other large federal installations can match. As
noted in the Introduction, federal installations are charged with locating,
inventorying, and assessing all cultural resources on their grounds, with the
object of preserving and protecting NRHP-eligible sites wherever possible.
This has had a valuable research as well as management payoff, and aspects
of this work, particularly as they relate to predictive modeling and settlement analyses, are examined in subsequent chapters.

Chapter 3

Prehistoric Settlement Analyses and Predictive Modeling in West-Central Louisiana

Over the past 25 years considerable effort has been directed to the development of predictive models of historic and prehistoric site location in the west-central Louisiana area and, coupled with this, to developing an understanding of the nature of past settlement systems. Predictive modeling efforts have taken place primarily in two areas: on Fort Polk proper (e.g., Anderson et al. 1988, 1999b; Campbell and Weed 1986; Servello, ed. 1983; Thomas et al. 1982) and on the Kisatchie National Forest, whose districts largely surround Fort Polk (e.g., Hillman 1980; Johnson 1984a, 1984b; Johnson et al. 1986; Phillips and Willingham 1990; Willingham and Phillips 1987). These analyses have typically employed large datasets, are replicable, and have generated increasingly reliable results. Settlement analyses that have been conducted have explored questions about group technological organization and mobility, site use and site type, lithic raw material procurement and use, and how major sections of the landscape in this part of the region were used over time; these questions have been examined by a great many authors, as detailed in the pages that follow.

While typically focusing on sites of all periods, the general models of site location that have been developed on Fort Polk and in the Kisatchie National Forest tend to be most useful for delimiting where prehistoric sites are located on the landscape, since these make up the overwhelming majority of the sites and isolated finds recorded to date on the installation and in the surrounding region. Predictive modeling activity directed explicitly to historic sites has occurred, however, and a review of this work is presented in Chapter 8. This chapter emphasizes research directed to prehistoric occupations in the area. Predictive models, it should be stressed, are important in both research and resource management. Having accurate information on where sites occur helps us to explore why past peoples made use of the landscape the way they did and allows cultural resource managers to plan projects to minimize impacts to important sites. Accurate predictive models also facilitate the development of appropriate field methods for the detection and documentation of sites. A predictive model of site location was presented in the 1988 Historic Preservation Plan (HPP) for Fort Polk and was improved and updated in 1995 on the basis of the work described in this chapter; the Fort Polk HPP modeling efforts are detailed in Chapter 4.

The Fort Polk Archaeological Survey
Slope Element / Landform Predictive Model

One objective of the Fort Polk Archaeological Survey (FPAS) undertaken in the late 1970s by the University of Southwestern Louisiana was to develop a testable model of site occurrence and density for the Peason Ridge area. Twenty-seven 160-acre quadrats (4,320 acres) from the Peason Ridge landscape were selected using a simple random sampling procedure (Servello and Morgan 1983:194–195) (see Figure 2.1). Four of the quadrats fell within the Peason Ridge Artillery Impact Zone and were not investigated for safety reasons. The area examined, 23 quadrats comprising 3,680 acres, represented approximately 13.2 percent of Peason Ridge. Portions of three major drainages, the Red, the Sabine, and the Calcasieu, lay within the survey area, and roughly 10 quarter section quadrats each (1,600 acres) were surveyed in the Sabine and Red River basins while three quarter section quadrats (480 acres) were examined in the Calcasieu River basin. A total of 115 sites and 51 isolated finds were found in these 23 sample quadrats (Servello and Morgan 1983:198) (Table 3.1).

A series of environmental variables were recorded for each site and isolated find encountered, encompassing elevation, drainage, and landform characteristics (Servello and Morgan 1983:182–203; Servello 1983). While the first two variables were comparatively straightforward and entailed coding elevation and stream rank data (after Strahler 1957, 1964) from U.S. Geological Survey (USGS) quadrangles, the third was much more complex, encompassing larger subregional strata based on underlying geology and more specific landform types based on Ruhe's (1975; Ruhe and Walker 1968) slope element classification system. The Kisatchie Wold, the major landform encompassing Fort Polk, was subdivided into five structural and erosional surfaces based on surficial and underlying geology (Servello 1983). These five strata from north to south were the Horse's Head structural surface, the Peason Ridge structural surface, the Castor erosional surface, the Williana structural surface, and the Bentley erosional surface (Servello 1983:206). Site distributions within these strata were assumed to differ, although since the 23 FPAS sample quadrats all came from the Peason Ridge structural surface, this inference could not be tested. These subregional strata

Table 3.1 — Site and isolated find incidence by landform and drainage basin in the FPAS sample survey tracts from Peason Ridge

Landform Characteristics	Sabine River Drainage			Red River Drainage			Calcasieu River Drainage			Total Sample		
	Total Acreage	No. of Sites/IF	Resource Density*	Total Acreage	No. of Sites/IF	Resource Density*	Total Acreage	No. of Sites/IF	Resource Density*	Total Acreage	No. of Sites/IF	Resource Density*
Summit Slope												
Knoll	33.6	1	2.97	55.7	3	5.39	17.6	1	5.68	106.9	5	4.68
(% of Total)	(2.08)	(1.92)		(3.51)	(3.61)		(3.67)	(3.23)		(2.91)	(3.01)	
Summit	545.6	13	2.38	486.5	24	4.93	230.4	11	4.78	1,262.5	48	3.8
(% of Total)	(33.80)	(25.00)		(30.69)	(28.92)		(48.00)	(35.48)		(34.31)	(28.92)	
Subtotal	579.2	14	2.42	542.2	27	4.98	248	12	4.84	1,369.4	53	3.87
(% of Total)	(35.88)	(26.92)		(34.21)	(32.53)		(51.67)	(38.71)		(37.22)	(31.93)	
Shoulder Slope												
Shoulder	146.4	1	0.68	104.9	0	0	24	0	0	275.3	1	0.36
(% of Total)	(9.07)	(1.92)		(6.62)	(0.00)		(5.00)	(0.00)		(7.48)	(0.60)	
Backslope/Footslope												
Backslope	419.2	17	4.06	374.5	20	5.34	54.4	1	1.83	848.1	38	4.48
(% of Total)	(25.97)	(32.69)		(23.63)	(24.10)		(11.33)	(3.23)		(23.05)	(22.89)	
Footslope	313.6	18	5.74	315.6	33	10.46	60.8	13	21.38	690	64	9.28
(% of Total)	(19.43)	(34.62)		(9.91)	(39.76)		(12.67)	(41.94)		(18.75)	(38.55)	
Subtotal	732.8	35	4.78	690.1	53	7.68	115.2	14	12.15	1,538.1	102	6.63
(% of Total)	(45.39)	(67.31)		(43.54)	(63.86)		(24.00)	(45.16)		(41.80)	(61.45)	

Table 3.1 (cont.) — Site and isolated find incidence by landform and drainage basin in the FPAS sample survey tracts from Peason Ridge

Landform Characteristics	Sabine River Drainage			Red River Drainage			Calcasieu River Drainage			Total Sample		
	Total Acreage	No. of Sites/IF	Resource Density*	Total Acreage	No. of Sites/IF	Resource Density*	Total Acreage	No. of Sites/IF	Resource Density*	Total Acreage	No. of Sites/IF	Resource Density*
Colluvial Toeslope												
Toeslope	52	1	1.92	92	2	2.17	32	4	12.5	176	7	3.98
(% of Total)	(3.22)	(1.92)		(5.80)	(2.41)		(6.67)	(12.90)		(4.78)	(4.22)	
Alluvial Bottom												
Bottom	104	1	0.96	155.8	1	0.64	60.8	1	1.65	320.6	3	0.94
(% of Total)	(6.44)	(1.92)		(9.83)	(1.20)		(12.67)	(3.23)		(8.71)	(1.81)	
Total	1,614.4	52	3.22	1,585	83	5.23	480	31	6.46	3,679.4	166	4.51
(% of Total)	(100.00)	(100.00)		(100.00)	(100.00)		(100.00)	(100.00)		(100.00)	(100.00)	

Data from Servello, ed. 1983:213; Servello and Morgan 1983:198

Sites/IF = Sites and isolated finds
* Sites and isolated finds per 100 acres

have seen little consideration in subsequent analyses, which have focused on finer-grained landform characteristics. The differences observed in prehistoric assemblages from across the larger region, however, such as between sites found on portions of the Main Fort and Peason Ridge, may well ultimately prove to be closely linked to these strata, which have their own characteristic physiography, drainage conditions, and availability of exploitable lithic raw materials.

Below the level of structural and erosional surfaces, Servello (1983:205–209) devised a finer-grained landscape stratification based on the idealized slope development model proposed by Ruhe (1974); this approach has seen considerable use on Fort Polk. Three measurements of surficial topographic conditions were used: (1) element (summit slope, shoulder slope, backslope/footslope, colluvial toeslope, and alluvial bottom categories); (2) subelement (knolls on summits, low gradient summit components, backslope, footslope, toeslope, bottom); and (3) specific underlying soil characteristics. The FPAS analyses addressed variation over the first two measurements; soils data saw minimal consideration, although this measure has since been used extensively as a useful proxy measure of slope and drainage conditions locally, specifically in the 1988 and 1995 HPP predictive modeling analyses (e.g., Anderson et al. 1988, 1999b). In the report, the FPAS data were enumerated by quadrat to show occurrence (site and isolated find) counts, strata acreage, and occurrence density (Servello, ed. 1983:tables 18, 19, and 20).

The analyses demonstrated that archaeological occurrences were not distributed uniformly across the landscape on Peason Ridge. Instead, significant differences in occurrence density (i.e., number of sites and isolated finds per 100 acres) occur among these three drainages, over the total area in each basin, and by landform element and subelement (Table 3.1). Over the entire sample, sites and isolated finds occurred from highest to lowest density on (1) backslopes/footslopes, (2) colluvial toeslopes, (3) summit slopes, (4) alluvial bottoms, and (5) shoulder slopes. The highest density occurred on the footslope subelement of the backslope/footslope element. The lowest densities occurred in alluvial bottoms and on shoulder slopes, a finding replicated in the 1988 HPP predictive modeling analysis (see Chapter 4). Occurrence density varied appreciably from drainage to drainage and was highest in the Calcasieu River drainage, somewhat less in the Red River basin, and lowest in the Sabine drainage (as summarized in Table 3.1). For comparative purposes, the results from the 1981 New World Research sample survey on Peason Ridge, developed in part to test the FPAS model, are presented in Table 3.2. It is apparent from comparison of the density figures that proportionally fewer sites and isolated finds were found by New World Research in the Calcasieu and Red River basins than by the FPAS team. The FPAS

Table 3.2 — Site and isolated find incidence by slope element in the NWR Peason Ridge and Main Fort quadrat random sample

Landform Characteristics	Sabine River Drainage			Red River Drainage			Calcasieu River Drainage			Total Sample		
	Total Acreage	No. of Sites/IF	Resource Density*	Total Acreage	No. of Sites/IF	Resource Density*	Total Acreage	No. of Sites/IF	Resource Density*	Total Acreage	No. of Sites/IF	Resource Density*
Peason Ridge												
Summit	239.3	8	3.34	360	4	1.11	115	3	2.61	714.3	15	2.01
(% of Total)	(23.47)	(61.54)		(42.55)	(36.36)		(71.88)	(75.00)		(35.27)	(53.57)	
Slope	624.2	5	0.8	445	7	1.57	10	0	0	1,079.2	12	1.11
(% of Total)	(61.23)	(38.46)		(52.60)	(63.64)		(6.25)	(0.00)		(53.28)	(42.86)	
Bottom	156	0	0	41	0	0	35	1	2.86	232	1	0.43
(% of Total)	(15.30)	(0.00)		(4.85)	(0.00)		(21.88)	(25.00)		(11.45)	(3.57)	
Total	1,019.5	13	1.28	846	11	1.3	160	4	2.5	2,025.5	28	1.38
(% of Total)	(100.00)	(100.00)		(100.00)	(100.00)		(100.00)	(100.00)		(100.00)	(100.00)	
Main Fort												
Summit	120.6	2	1.66				860.6	27	3.14	981.2	15	1.53
(% of Total)	(16.29)	(11.76)					(18.56)	(24.55)		(18.24)	(53.57)	
Slope	373.5	11	2.95				2,567.7	49	1.91	2,941.2	12	0.41
(% of Total)	(50.45)	(64.71)					(55.37)	(44.55)		(54.69)	(42.86)	
Bottom	246.2	4	1.62				1,209.4	34	2.81	1,455.6	1	0.07
(% of Total)	(33.26)	(23.53)					(26.08)	(30.91)		(27.07)	(3.57)	
Total	740.3	17	2.30				4,637.7	110	2.37	5,378	28	0.52
(% of Total)	(100.00)	(100.00)					(100.00)	(100.00)		(100.00)	(100.00)	

Data from Thomas et al. 1982:81, 91, 95   Sites/IF = Sites and isolated finds   * Sites and isolated finds per 100 acres team appears to have spent far longer in the field and used larger shovel tests (50 x 50 cm as opposed to 30 x 30 cm), however, which likely explains the observed differences. Additionally, the FPAS study examined more acreage and hence may have been more representative. It is noteworthy, however, that the relative resource density for the three major drainages is the same in both surveys. These figures can be used, albeit with caution, to estimate site density in unsurveyed portions of these basins in the general region.

As a first attempt at predictive modeling locally, the FPAS research was noteworthy, and it prompted serious consideration of drainage and landform characteristics in most subsequent analyses. The complex slope element coding they advanced has not proven easy to replicate, however, causing subsequent investigators to adopt much simpler landform stratification systems (Anderson et al. 1988, 1999b; Campbell and Weed 1986:3-4; Ezell and Ensor 1999:340; Thomas et al. 1982:81).

The Colluvial/Clay Interface Site Locational Model

Based on investigations in the Eagle Hill locality of Peason Ridge and Bayou Zourie on the Main Fort, Joel Gunn and his colleagues (Gunn 1982e:344, 1982f:143; Gunn et al. 1982:143; Guy and Gunn 1983; Jolly and Gunn 1981) have suggested that major archaeological sites in this part of Louisiana will tend to occur at the interface between the sand/colluvial surface deposits and the underlying Miocene clays. Natural seeps along this interface would have led to increased biomass productivity, making the area attractive to prehistoric settlement, at least in comparison with surrounding settings. The model has seen only limited testing, with site locational data collected from the Bayou Zourie survey area (Jolly and Gunn 1981) and from the 1981 New World Research sample survey (Thomas et al. 1982:78). These yielded ambiguous results because of the difficulty of locating the colluvial/clay contact zone.

During the Bayou Zourie survey project six sites were found to occur in the high-probability locations predicted by the model, but because the interface was close to the modern floodplain, survey in this area proved extremely difficult: "The colluvial-clay interface along the permanent floodplain presented a sometimes nearly insurmountable obstacle as greenbriar and blackberries engulfed the entire crew" (Jolly and Gunn 1981:12). The analysis concluded with a series of observations about site location in the Bayou Zourie area, notably that (1) upland areas were heavily eroded due to historic disturbance; (2) sites tended to occur on erosional ridge remnants at the junction of stream courses; (3) proximity to water appeared to be a crucial variable, particularly where seepage springs were present; and (4) sites would tend to occur along the colluvial/clay interface only in areas where water was comparatively scarce. Jolly and Gunn (1981:30–33) observed that the model would probably work best in the highly desiccated uplands such as those around Eagle Hill on Peason Ridge; in the lower-lying Bayou Zourie area, the interface was close to large stream channels. Proximity to the clay/colluvial interface was reportedly not found to be a significant factor in site location during the 1981 New World Research sample survey (Thomas et al. 1982:78), although no formal analyses were presented.

The New World Research Slope Element/Drainage Model

During the 1981 New World Research sample survey, a series of locational and environmental variables were recorded over the site assemblage recovered during that project, of which landform category and drainage basin proved the most significant in subsequent analyses. Following an unsuccessful attempt to replicate Servello's (1983) slope element categories (reported in Thomas et al. 1982:77), a new model of prehistoric land use in the Fort Polk area was advanced based on landform type and drainage characteristics, including relative elevation above water, slope, and the occurrence of perennial and intermittent streams. Summit, slope, and bottomland site probability zones were defined, and large-scale maps of these zones were produced for the entire installation that were used to examine the occurrence of prehistoric sites on Peason Ridge and the Main Fort (Thomas et al. 1982:88–89) (Table 3.2). Site locations from the 1981 survey as well as some sites found during the FPAS investigations were plotted on these overlays and the data used to generate predictive statements about site density for specific subareas of the fort by individual drainages and major landform categories (Thomas et al. 1982:84–98). A significantly lower density of sites was observed in the Peason Ridge area than on the Main Fort, and sites on Peason Ridge were observed to occur somewhat randomly over the landscape, at least with respect to slope and drainage (Thomas et al. 1982:90). On the Main Fort, greater numbers of sites than expected were observed on ridge summits and bottomland settings and fewer were found on slopes (Thomas et al. 1982:93). The New World Research slope element/drainage model was used to predict the probable number of sites that would be encountered during the 1985 Multipurpose Range Complex (MPRC) investigation in advance of the survey; the results (n = 552 sites predicted, n = 578 sites actually located, out of 596 total cultural properties recorded) lend credibility to this model (Campbell and Weed 1986:EXEC-5, 6-11). A test of Gunn and Jolly's (Gunn et al. 1982; Jolly and Gunn 1981) clay/colluvial interface model was also attempted, as noted above, and it was suggested that proximity to the interface did not appear to be a particularly significant factor in site location (Thomas et al. 1982:78).

Further evaluation of the slope element/drainage model came during the 17,275-acre MPRC survey and analysis in which the 351 prehistoric sites and isolated finds that were located were classified by (1) the five site size classes advanced by New World Research in 1982 (see below), (2) shovel test artifact density, (3) slope element, (4) stream type, (5) size in square meters, and (6) the size in square meters of the landform the site was on. Importantly, the primary coding data for each site were presented, ensuring analytical replicability (Campbell and Weed 1986:10-3 to 10-9). By slope element, the sites were located in bottoms (n = 87), slopes (n = 168), and summits (n = 95); one site was unreported. Noting that many sites fell close to the upland/floodplain ecotone, an arbitrary 100-m band was drawn following contour lines along bottomland areas—a measure initially developed during a survey conducted just south of Fort Polk on Whiskey Chitto Creek by Campbell et al. (1985)—and site distributions were reexamined. The site distribution, by these revised elements, was bottoms (n = 71), 100-m floodplain/upland junctures (n = 207), slopes (n = 33), and summits (n = 40) (Campbell and Weed 1986:6-14). Differences in bottomland counts between the two analyses reflected revisions made on the basis of field observations (Campbell and Weed 1986:6-13, 6-14). The analysis indicated that a large number of sites were located close to the floodplain margin, a finding reinforced in both the 1988 and 1999 HPP predictive modeling analyses reported below. The High Probability Zones in these more recent models, in fact, employ similar distance-to-water measures or floodplain margins as critical variables.

Analyses of Nearest Water Characteristics

The MPRC survey prehistoric site data were also used to examine site type by the characteristics of the nearest water source (Campbell and Weed 1986:10-18 to 10-35). Using field observations, sites were classified according to whether the nearest water source was ephemeral, intermittent, or perennial. Strong relationships between site density and nearest water source type were indicated. More than three-quarters of the sites near ephemeral streams were reported to have artifact densities averaging less than two artifacts per shovel test, and only one site had an average density greater than 10 artifacts per test (Campbell and Weed 1986:10-18). Sites near intermit-

tent streams likewise had low artifact densities: 91 percent had average artifact densities of less than 10 artifacts per shovel test, and 50 percent had
average densities less than two artifacts per test; only nine percent had artifact densities greater than 10 artifacts per shovel test (Campbell and Weed
1986:10-21). Sites located near intermittent streams, however, tended to be
more varied in assemblage composition and to use more of the immediately
available land surface than those near ephemeral water sources. Finally, sites
near perennial water sources yielded density values and assemblages similar to those found near intermittent water sources, although a tendency toward more substantial deposits was suggested on those sites on which larger
units had been excavated (Campbell and Weed 1986:10-22, 10-23).

The analysis highlights the importance of developing standardized and
replicable measures of environmental conditions. While considered reliable,
the analysis provided no criteria for separating "ephemeral" from "intermittent" water sources, for example, which were categories based on field observations conducted over the course of a several-month survey, and no
summary stream rank data were reported (Campbell and Weed 1986:6-13 to
6-18). Willingham and Phillips (1987:193), working with drainage data from
the Kisatchie National Forest Ranger Districts that occur all around Fort
Polk, have cogently discussed the problems that may be encountered when
documenting water sources in west-central Louisiana: "During the wet season almost any depression along a slope will be carrying some amount of
water and in the dry months many streams carry none at all. To remove some
of the seasonally determined bias of water source selection, the nearest permanent water source in this study is considered to be the nearest drainage,
which appears on USGS topographic maps as a blue (broken or unbroken)
line" (Willingham and Phillips 1987:193). While USGS maps admittedly
"displayed serious errors or lacked detail" about landform and stream data
(Thomas et al. 1982:82), they do offer uniform, replicable information available to all researchers, without the necessity of extended fieldwork or landform mapping/imaging analyses. For this reason watercourse information
used in the 1988 and 1999 HPP predictive modeling analyses was derived
from USGS quadrangles. What the MPRC analysis does indicate, however,
is that finer-grained drainage information, when it can be obtained, is likely
to have considerably better analytical utility.

Site Size / Distance to Exploitable Stone Analyses

The 173 prehistoric archaeological sites found during the 1981 New World
Research survey were divided into five classes, which were based on lithic

artifact frequency and debitage-to-tool ratios. The five site classes were as follows:

(I)   Sites with 1 to 8 artifacts;
(II)   Sites with 9 to 25 artifacts, <15 percent of which are tools;
(III) Sites with 9 to 25 artifacts, >15 percent of which are tools;
(IV)   Sites with 26 to 65 artifacts; and
(V)   Sites with >65 artifacts [Thomas et al. 1982:98].

Presence/absence of ceramics was not considered, because of their low overall incidence (n = 26 sherds). The smaller Class I and II sites were tentatively interpreted as extraction sites or locations, Class III sites as field camps, and Class IV and V sites as possibly representing residential sites or base camps. Class I and II sites were found widely scattered over both the Main Fort and Peason Ridge while the larger sites (Classes III through V) were found exclusively on the Main Fort (Thomas et al. 1982:99). The two largest site classes were observed only within the Calcasieu drainage, while Class III sites were observed within both the Calcasieu and the Sabine drainages on the Main Fort. Site size was considered related in part to proximity to major drainages (with the larger site classes near the larger drainages), since the drainages on the Main Fort were of a higher order than those on Peason Ridge (Thomas et al. 1982:110–111). An attempt by the New World Research team to replicate associations between their site size classes and environmental data using the FPAS site data proved unsuccessful, primarily because many of the FPAS collections were based on intensive testing, rather than survey, and had much larger artifact assemblages (Thomas et al. 1982:111–114).

The authors argued that site size was not necessarily related to permanence of occupation but appeared also to be linked to the occurrence of knappable gravels. The sites yielding the largest numbers of artifacts (Classes IV and V) in their samples tended to occur closest to lithic raw material sources, specifically the massive chert gravel deposits occurring on and to the south of the Main Fort, with the high artifact density thus probably due, at least in part, to raw material procurement activities (Thomas et al. 1982:107–109). This observation received mixed support in subsequent tests of the relationship between site size and distance to knappable stone. In particular, an analysis by archaeologists from Commonwealth Associates, Inc., indicated the model appeared to work better on the Main Fort than on Peason Ridge, where different kinds of lithic raw materials occurred (Cantley 1984:258, 261). During the MPRC survey project analysis, investigators calculated the distance of each site to a major chert gravel source along

Birds Creek; this source is an outcropping of the Citronelle Formation at the southern margins of the Main Fort. No direct relationship was observed between distance to this source and either flake size or incidence of cortex over the project site assemblages, however, leading the authors to conclude that a greater range of activities was occurring on most project sites than simply raw material procurement and reduction (Campbell et al. 1987:97).

How the occurrence of local gravel chert sources influenced prehistoric use of the Fort Polk area continues to interest researchers. An examination of prehistoric assemblage composition in relation to distance to raw material source was conducted by archaeologists from New South Associates, Inc., in the mid-1990s, using data from a large survey project on Fort Polk:

> At the raw material source areas, artifact assemblages are generally dominated by low densities (0 to 0.03 artifacts/acre) of early and intermediate stage bifaces and high proportions of early stage flakes. . . . This artifact pattern is masked in some quarry areas . . . however, by assemblages recovered from compartment stands that contained significant numbers of small staging areas or base camps located along the floodplains within 500 meters of the gravel deposits. Assemblages from these latter site types exhibit higher (0.035 to 0.075) tool densities and have a much higher proportion of late stage bifaces.
>
> From 1,000 meters to 5,000 meters from the gravel deposits, the assemblages reflect a general pattern of low artifact density with similar proportions of early to late stage flakes. In contrast to upland quarry locations, however, these assemblages contain a higher proportion of late and intermediate stage bifaces. Tool discard observed for this occupation zone is consistent with behaviors associated with short-term residential base camps and special purpose camps in which most maintenance activities, such as the replacement of worn-out or broken tools, would be conducted.
>
> At distances of 5,000 meters or more, the assemblage data becomes much more variable with some areas exhibiting very low artifact densities, while others represent relatively high artifact densities. Also, it is at the 5,000 meter mark that flake densities begin to change with a significantly greater representation of late stage flakes in the assemblages. When high artifact densities do occur in this occupation zone, the tool assemblages are usually dominated by late stage bifaces. . . . Overall, the artifact discard pattern observed for this zone suggest[s] that settlement location is more restrictive with certain landforms receiving more attention for reoccu-

pation than others. Also, it is at this distance presumably that the location of occupations become[s] more tethered to resources in the immediate vicinity of the site and less with lithic gravel deposits [Cantley et al. 1997:877].

These studies demonstrate the importance of quantitative analyses using multiple site assemblages to test hypotheses about past land use and that the seemingly undifferentiated lithic scatters on Fort Polk actually encompass appreciable variation. Local land use, it appears, was strongly conditioned both by proximity to watercourses and floodplain areas and by outcrops of lithic raw materials. People apparently did come to this part of west-central Louisiana throughout prehistory to gather lithic raw materials, but they also performed a number of other activities in the process. Tethering of larger and denser sites to lithic raw material sources and to larger drainages is indicated by all of these analyses, although the relationship does not appear to be absolute, since larger and smaller sites can occur both near and away from these source areas (see also Campbell and Weed 1986:12-11; Cantley et al. 1997).

Controlling for Differing Collection Strategies

As part of the 1983/1984 testing program by Commonwealth Associates, Inc., a series of analyses were conducted to evaluate earlier models of prehistoric settlement and land use in the Fort Polk area. Rank size curves of artifact density per shovel test and artifact density by site size were prepared, which is a useful method of standardizing and comparing assemblage data from different sites and projects (Cantley and Schuldenrein 1984:116–122) (Figure 3.1). Breaks in the rank size curve, it was argued, formed an effective method of resolving discrete site categories on the basis of quantitative, not arbitrary or qualitative, selection criteria (Cantley and Schuldenrein 1984:118). Dense sites tended to occur on narrowly circumscribed landforms, which the authors suggested was due to reoccupation of favored loci by numerous groups over time, rather than extended occupation by one or a few groups (Cantley and Schuldenrein 1984:121–122). This conclusion has been reinforced by subsequent intrasite distributional analyses, which show that at least some large and dense sites on the installation were formed through repeated small and presumably short-term visits (Cantley et al. 1997:877–921; see below).

Appreciable differences in site size and assemblage density and diversity and, hence, size class are also closely linked to the level of effort con-

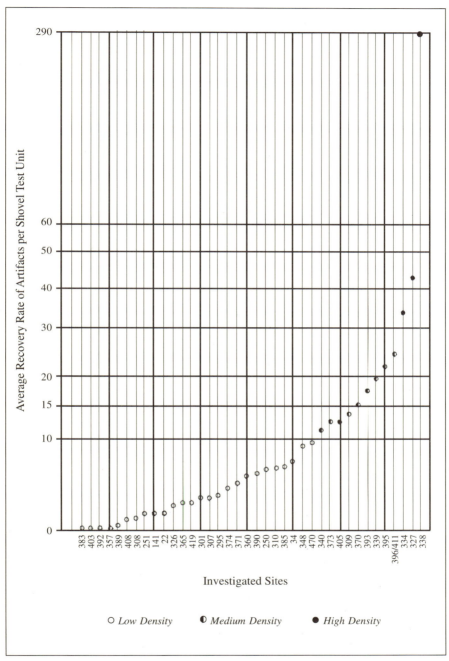

Figure 3.1— Shovel test artifact-density rank-size curve from the Commonwealth Associates, Inc., 1983/1984 site-testing project (from Cantley and Schuldenrein 1984:119).

ducted at individual sites. This was observed in a comparison of the data collected during the New World Research survey that had located the sites with the data obtained from the 1983/1984 Commonwealth Associates, Inc., testing effort (Cantley and Schuldenrein 1984:118–122). Of 36 sites examined by both projects, for example, 23 of those intensively tested were found to be significantly larger, six smaller, and seven essentially the same. Average numbers of artifacts recovered per shovel test from each site were calculated and compared with the 1981 New World Research site size classes, and again this showed appreciable differences. Of 15 New World Research Class I sites examined, for example, defined as sites with from one to eight items in total, six of the 15 sites intensively tested in 1983/1984 yielded an average of more than eight artifacts per shovel test (Cantley and Schuldenrein 1984:117). Artifact density (i.e., number of artifacts per test or per a standardized volume of fill), rather than total number of artifacts, was suggested as an alternative method of examining the variation in local assemblages.

A comparison of artifact density obtained from shovel tests and from larger 50-x-50-cm or 1-x-1-m units was made over a 19-site sample during the New World Research MPRC survey and analysis, with the observation that markedly different density values were obtained by each procedure (Campbell and Weed 1986:10-10 to 10-14), a finding like that noted by the 1983/1984 Commonwealth Associates, Inc., testing program. A comparison of site and landform size with site density yielded somewhat ambiguous results (Campbell and Weed 1986:10-15). In general, high-density sites tended to occur in circumscribed areas, medium-density sites in larger, less circumscribed locales, and low-density sites over a range of landform sizes. While generally supporting Cantley and Schuldenrein's (1984:121–122) observations about the relationship between site size and density in the Fort Polk area, enough contradictory examples were found to argue for caution in the use of these kinds of data and to suggest that effort should be made to standardize data collection procedures to ensure comparable analytical samples (Campbell and Weed 1986:10-16 to 10-18, 12-6).

Differences in recovery strategies between survey and testing work, of course, are appreciable, since in testing, units are typically larger and go much deeper than the shovel tests opened in survey work; at many sites examined during the early years of the cultural resource management (CRM) program at Fort Polk, furthermore, only surface collection occurred or else shovel testing was unsystematic, being limited to one or a few intuitively placed units. These analyses highlight the importance of obtaining complete site samples or, since complete excavation is rarely possible, using statistically representative sampling collection procedures that can generate data useful to a range of analyses and research questions, including accurate estimates about site size and assemblage composition (e.g., Nance and Ball 1986; Shott 1985). Survey work is excellent for locating sites and, when sites are examined using systematic shovel testing in a close-interval grid pattern, assessing boundary definition and intrasite spatial patterning. However, data collection well beyond that occurring at the survey level, these analyses indicate, is essential to accurately sample local assemblages (see also Campbell and Weed 1986:4-20 to 4-22). For this reason, intensive survey work on the installation by the early 1990s had switched to using regularly spaced shovel tests at ca. 30-m intervals in high-probability zones, with site content and boundary definition work routinely making use of even more closely spaced (i.e., 10- or 15-m grid interval) shovel testing; as documented below, even finer intervals should be used in intensive testing and data-recovery work (Cantley et al. 1997:877–892).

The Forager-Collector Continuum: Analyses of Technological Organization and Mobility

A shift from foraging to collecting strategies following the Archaic period in the general west-central Louisiana area was proposed during the 1981 New World Research analysis, since a number of the three largest site classes had ceramics present, suggesting more extended settlement (Thomas et al. 1982:109–110). A model of hunter-gatherer technological organization— the "forager-collector" model—that had been proposed by Lewis R. Binford (1980) was thought to usefully characterize prehistoric assemblage variability observed on Fort Polk. In this model, hunter-gatherer land-use strategies fall between two poles on a spectrum of what he called forager and collector adaptations or technological organizational strategies. Collector adaptations, at one end of the spectrum, tend to occur in patchy environments, which are best exploited by groups radiating out from central base camps and staying at short-term camps as long as necessary to collect resources prior to returning to the home base. The adaptation is known as a collector strategy because task groups go out for extended periods in the collection of resources, which they then bring back to their settlement, which tends to be occupied for fairly lengthy periods. While groups practicing collector strategies do move their base camps, they usually do so only when local resources are depressed or exhausted to the point that the costs of moving are less than those of finding food. The archaeological record of collector groups includes base settlements and extended resource-procurement camps. These adaptations are characterized by highly formalized toolkits made on fine-quality raw material: assemblages that would have been most advantageous during extended resource-procurement forays. Residentially mobile foraging adaptations, in contrast, are those in which people ranged over the landscape, readily and repeatedly moving their residences as food in their immediate area became exhausted. Archaeological assemblages from foraging adaptations are dominated by numerous short-term camps and by what are called expedient assemblages, composed of tools that were casually made, used, and then discarded on an ad hoc or situational basis. Formal, curated tools tend to be rare in such assemblages, as is the use of high-quality lithic material, unless it happens to outcrop locally. While foraging groups may, like collectors, move over large areas, each individual move tends to be fairly limited and typically no greater than necessary to place the residence near undepleted resources (Kelly 1983, 1995; Shott 1986).

In a subsequent critique, Cantley (1984:256–262) suggested that reoccupation, rather than extended settlement, could also explain the observed site densities and that the incidence of ceramics on sites at Fort Polk was so low as to preclude their reliable use as "base camp" indicators (see also Anderson 1984:251). Large, dense sites were found to occur close to major streams in places interpreted as offering the best location from which to exploit the nearby bottomland hardwood forests. Sites containing lower artifact densities tended to occur at higher elevations and farther from major drainages, suggesting limited-activity areas (Cantley 1984:257). Although components ranging from the terminal Paleoindian to the late prehistoric era were identified, no evidence for dramatic changes in land use over time was identified. Likewise, no evidence for extended use or settlement of the Fort Polk area was found and, instead, continuity in land use by small foraging groups or task groups based elsewhere was inferred. Accordingly, the author concluded that a shift from foraging to collecting strategies at the end of the Archaic "must be viewed with skepticism at this time" (Cantley 1984:262). Repeated, low-intensity use of the Fort Polk area over time, probably in short-term visits, was instead indicated (Cantley 1984:262). In the subsequent MPRC analysis (Campbell and Weed 1986), inferences about a forager-to-collector settlement shift at the end of the Archaic were dropped.

The forager-collector model has been repeatedly evaluated with assemblages from the Fort Polk area in recent years; indeed, the model is widely used by prehistoric archaeologists across the Southeast to explore assemblage variability over sites of all periods. During the 1993–1994 South Carolina Institute of Archaeology and Anthropology (SCIAA) large-scale survey project at Fort Polk, lithic data from 14 sites with seemingly single-component Archaic assemblages were used to evaluate the forager-collector model (Clement et al. 1995:422–428) following arguments advanced earlier for the area by Cantley and Jackson (1984:92–93). It was assumed that Peason

Ridge would exhibit more evidence for collector adaptations, since it was characterized by greater topographic and hence ecological variability. Test expectations for foraging and collecting groups were offered, based on work originally advanced by John S. Cable (1982a:148, 1982b; Cantley and Jackson 1984:92–93; see also Clement et al. 1995:423–424), as follows.

Collector strategies should exhibit the following patterns:
1. Bifaces should dominate flake production strategies.
2. Bifaces should exhibit a high degree of reduction and should primarily appear only in a broken state on special purpose sites.
3. As a logical consequence of 1 and 2, debitage should be smaller and less variable in size than in foraging assemblages.
4. Flake tools should also be smaller and less variable in size than in foraging assemblages.
5. Since collector systems are more specialized in the kinds of resources exhibited, flake tools should be less complex and exhibit fewer uses than in foraging systems.

Foraging strategies should manifest the following set of expectations:
1. Flake production strategies should be more variable including higher frequencies of expedient core flake manufacture.
2. Bifaces should be more variable in size and life-history stage as a result of need for raw material conservation.
3. As a logical consequence of 1 and 2, debitage should be larger and more variable in forager systems than in collector systems.
4. Flake tools, by virtue of the more variable flake production techniques, should be more variable in size and larger than in collecting assemblages.
5. Since forager systems are less specialized in their pattern of resource exploitation, flake tools should be responsive to a wider variety of uses and therefore should be more complex and functionally diversified than in collector assemblages [Clement et al. 1995:423–424].

The site assemblages were found to conform to these expectations:

A total of 3278 lithic artifacts were recovered from these sites during the survey, 3197 from the Main Fort and 81 from Peason Ridge. . . . The Main Fort assemblage conforms well to the test expectations for foraging groups presented above (Cable 1982[a]).

Primary, secondary, and tertiary flakes account for 80% of the total assemblage, with secondary flakes being most common at 39% of the assemblage, followed by tertiary and primary flakes. In contrast, these three artifact types account for only 68% of the total artifacts recovered from Peason Ridge. Tertiary flakes are predominant, followed closely by secondary flakes. Primary flakes account for only 7% of the assemblage, indicating that tool maintenance rather than tool production was a more common activity. This suggestion is further indicated by both the high percentage of bifacial thinning flakes at Peason Ridge when compared to the Main Fort (12% and 6% respectively) and the relative frequency of formal tools in the two assemblages (3% at the Main Fort versus 16% at Peason Ridge) [Clement et al. 1995:424].

When the effects of raw material condition and availability were considered, however, the fit of the data with the model was considered more problematic (Clement et al. 1995:426). That is, the observed artifact distributions also appear to be a result of the presence of gravel cherts on the Main Fort and their absence on Peason Ridge. A high incidence of bipolar flaking was noted within the Main Fort assemblages, furthermore, and was attributed to the small size of the source gravels, which necessitated this form of reduction (Clement et al. 1995:426).

Intrasite Spatial Analyses: Long-Term Land Use and Site Structure

A turning point in archaeology in the general region occurred with the analyses associated with the 1995–1996 New South Associates, Inc., large-scale survey (Cantley et al. 1997:877–921). For the first time, detailed intrasite distributional analyses were conducted to evaluate the possibility that most sites in the Fort Polk area were actually palimpsests of numerous small occupations, an observation raised by many earlier researchers but not systematically evaluated until this time (e.g., Anderson et al. 1988:167–170; Campbell et al. 1987:130; Cantley and Schuldenrein 1984:119–122). The intrasite distributional analyses were also used to evaluate the suggestion that site artifact density was to some extent constrained by landform size and shape, with dense sites in some cases reflecting the reoccupation of small, constrained landforms and more diffuse sites reflecting occupations dispersed over larger, more extensive landforms (Cantley and Schuldenrein 1984:122). These expectations were convincingly affirmed by the generation of a series of density maps by level or groups of levels for five sites using data obtained from shovel tests systematically dispersed using a 10-m grid and excavated in 10-cm levels. The results demonstrated that these seemingly undifferentiated lithic scatters actually exhibited an extremely complex internal spatial structure that must be recognized if such sites are to be properly examined and interpreted in the future. At 16VN1811, a small rise 30 x 40 m in extent in a swamp, for example, seven concentrations were delimited at different depths, each with a somewhat different age, size, and extent. At a second and much larger site, 16VN1816, located along a broad finger ridge overlooking a swamp, a number of discrete concentrations were found (Figure 3.2). Similar patterns were observed on the other three locations examined in this manner (e.g., Figure 3.3).

An analysis of concentration size within the five sites that were examined yielded a range from ca. 667 to 987 m^2, or from roughly 29 to 36 m in diameter. These areas are about half again as large as the largest debris scatters from short-term camps used by band-sized groups of ethnographic !Kung San and are appreciably larger (by almost an order of magnitude) than short-term special-purpose extraction sites noted among the Australian Pintupi and the Nunamiut Eskimo (Cantley et al. 1997:906–907). Because the Fort Polk scatters were consistently larger than ethnographic expectations, a simulation analysis was conducted placing varying numbers of !Kung-sized band-level camps on a hypothetical landform and then evaluating the effectiveness of shovel testing at various intervals as a means of resolving the resulting debris scatters. The results, not surprisingly, indicate that shovel test intervals need to be much closer than the 10- or 15-m intervals currently used if intrasite patterning is to be successfully resolved. The analysis also indicated that, given extensive reoccupation on most landforms, the resolution of discrete campsites on high-density sites may be all but impossible, and even on low-density sites complete excavation may be needed.

A major lesson from the intrasite analysis was the demonstration that portions of the vast database of survey-level data collected to date on Fort Polk, specifically the data from the hundreds of sites examined using systematic shovel testing, while admittedly coarse grained, could be used to document appreciable intrasite variation and patterning. The authors also concluded, however, that the detailed resolution of internal site structural and functional information is probably beyond the reach of current survey-level data, given the coarseness of the sampling currently in use that calls for shovel testing at 10- to 20-m intervals. Close-interval shovel test data from smaller, single-component sites would likely yield excellent results, however, and would provide information about the kinds of assemblages/activities that make up the larger and more complex scatters.

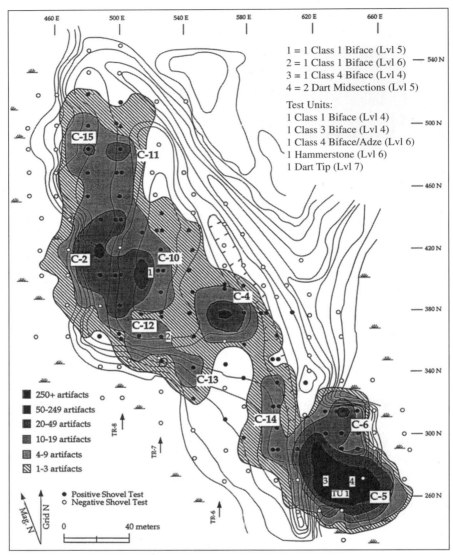

Figure 3.2 — Artifact concentrations from site 16VN1816 (from Cantley et al. 1997:887).

The authors also argued that data-recovery efforts would probably be better directed to small single-component sites, or discrete components that could be spatially differentiated on larger sites, than to the current strategy of small block-unit excavations into the densest parts of heavily reoccupied sites. Optimal field strategies for exploring questions of site structure, it was

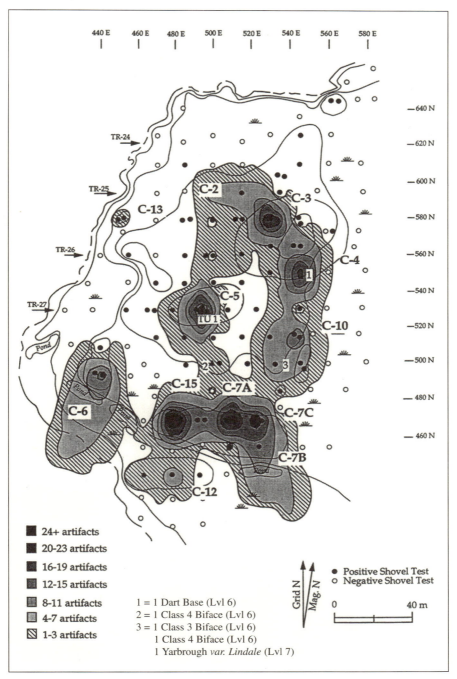

Figure 3.3— Artifact concentrations from site 16VN1820 (from Cantley et al. 1997:893).

suggested, should proceed by the excavation of numerous small units at close intervals, followed by the excavation of much larger block units capable of resolving entire concentrations where these existed (see Cable et al. [1998] for an example from South Carolina of how such fieldwork should proceed). Even total excavation of large areas, however, was considered unlikely to be able to tease out discrete occupations in heavily reoccupied settings (Cantley et al. 1997:921). Such procedures have yet to be attempted on Fort Polk, primarily because no large-scale excavations have occurred since the early 1990s and because current approaches to site testing rely more on the use of a few large test units to delimit stratigraphy and assemblage stratification rather than on the use of numerous smaller units to resolve internal site structure.

The Neutral Zone Model

To explain the seemingly uncomplicated nature of the Fort Polk archaeological record, Campbell and her colleagues (1987:122–130) suggested that the Fort Polk area of west-central Louisiana may have been a neutral zone of sorts, exploited by groups residing elsewhere. They noted that during the early historic era the general area was called the Neutral Ground (Haggard 1945a) and was officially disputed and, hence, left largely unsettled, first by both the Spanish and the French and later by the Spanish and American authorities. Considerable time depth for the existence of such a neutral zone was suggested, possibly extending into Paleoindian times. Facilitating access to the knappable stone that outcropped in the Fort Polk area, a resource presumably of importance to most prehistoric groups living in the larger region, was suggested as the driving force behind the establishment and maintenance of this neutral zone. Gibson (1978a:206) indicated that the lower Sabine River basin immediately to the west may have also been a vacant zone of sorts, suggesting that this neutral zone, if real, may have been geographically fairly extensive.

Other reasons may be advanced to explain the scarcity of permanent or long-term settlements in the general west-central Louisiana area. Rather than a "neutral zone"—an undefended area deliberately maintained as such and outside of the direct control of any one group—it is possible that the area was avoided during much of prehistory because of an overall low resource potential. A good case could be made that, compared with much of the remainder of Louisiana, for example, the Fort Polk area is notably devoid of resources likely to attract and maintain prehistoric populations, notably larger streams and bottomlands. Descriptions from the early historic era reinforce this interpretation; a description of an area just to the north of the fort, written in 1812, noted that the lands were "considerably barren, and of an inferior quality. This tract is rather deficient in good water, and contains more pine than any other wood" (Stoddard 1812:192–193). Following this line of reasoning, it is probable that the Fort Polk area would have been densely populated had it been favorable for prehistoric settlement. Instead, it appears to have been minimally inhabited throughout much of prehistory.

Care must be taken to avoid going too far with such a generalization, of course. During the Late Paleoindian subperiod, for example, considerable use of the area is indicated, given the number of San Patrice sites found in recent years (see Chapters 5 and 6). A mixed hardwood-pine forest is assumed to have been in place at that time, however, which may have made west-central Louisiana more attractive to settlement than during the ensuing Hypsithermal/Middle Archaic period and after, when pine forests began to expand. Likewise, a great many dense Late Archaic Birds Creek and Leander phase assemblages have been found during the intensive testing program in recent years, prompting the suggestion that these sites were produced by groups permanently resident in the area (Thomas et al. 1997:23–24; see Chapter 6). Given the lack of much evidence for archaeological features of any kind on the installation, however, such an assumption will require additional examination.

It is highly unlikely that lithic resources like those occurring in west-central Louisiana were considered important enough to warrant territorial control during much or all of prehistory. Territoriality has been defined as the maintenance of an area through overt defense. As Dyson-Hudson and Smith (1978:23, 25) have noted, "a territorial system is most likely under conditions of high density and predictability of critical resources [when] the costs of exclusive use and defense of an area are outweighed by the benefits gained from this pattern of resource utilization." They further note, however, that "if a resource is so abundant that its availability or rate of capture is not in any way limiting to a population, then there is no benefit to be gained by its defense and territoriality is not expected" (Dyson-Hudson and Smith 1978:25). Given the widespread occurrence of knappable gravels in west-central Louisiana, particularly in stream beds, it is probable that direct control over access would have been difficult or impossible for all but the largest and most complex of prehistoric societies. Only the late prehistoric Caddoan groups to the north and west, who were known for their warlike behavior, may have attempted to regulate use of the area, perhaps in conjunction with the maintenance of hunting territories or buffer zones.

In most hunting-gathering societies, in contrast, lithic raw materials procurement appears to occur in conjunction with normal subsistence pursuits.

As Binford (1979) has argued, lithic raw material procurement in mobile, hunting-gathering societies tends to be embedded in normal group movement patterns. He has suggested that only "very rarely, and then only when things have gone wrong, does one go out into the environment for the express and exclusive purpose of obtaining raw material for tools" (Binford 1979:259). Of course, when stone is unevenly (i.e., patchily) distributed on the landscape, as is the case in this part of the Southeast, provisioning using specialized task groups would be expected, particularly by groups located at greater distances. Prehistoric groups living nearby, perhaps within one to a few hundred kilometers away, thus may have made it a point to visit this part of Louisiana during their normal annual or multiyear ranging to replenish stone before their supplies became exhausted. Groups at greater distances, in contrast, likely relied on direct procurement by specialized task groups or else depended on exchange. In the early historic era the Indians in this general part of Louisiana were known to be traders in stone (Campbell et al. 1987:127; Swanton 1911:272–274, 1946:543; see Chapter 6), and earlier groups may also have engaged in such trade. It is thus likely that lithic raw material sources in the Fort Polk area were accessible to many groups, as the installation's diverse archaeological record suggests, not because the area was a neutral zone, but because it was a largely unoccupied zone that offered few compelling reasons for extended settlement.

The River Causeway / Ridge Causeway Hypotheses

On the basis of the results of an intensive survey in the Horse's Head Maneuver Area just to the north of Peason Ridge, Campbell and her colleagues (1980) argued that prehistoric settlement in west-central Louisiana was primarily along or in close proximity to major drainages (see also Thomas et al. 1982:43). The Horse's Head Maneuver Area is located on the divide between the Sabine and the Red Rivers at a considerable distance from the main channels of these rivers, and an exceedingly low site density was found here. Refinement of what has come to be known as the River Causeway model came as a result of the 1981 sample survey on Fort Polk by New World Research, in which Thomas and his colleagues (1982:43, 110–111) argued that prehistoric settlement in this part of Louisiana was oriented along and shaped by the location of major drainages. Major drainages were considered to be favored resource-exploitation areas and the arteries along which population movement and interaction occurred over the region. The northern part of Fort Polk—the vicinity of the Horse's Head Maneuver Area and possibly the area encompassing Peason Ridge—it was further argued, may have served as a buffer zone separating populations living along the main channel and major tributaries of the Red and Calcasieu Rivers.

An alternative settlement model, the Ridge Causeway hypothesis, was subsequently offered by Guy and Gunn (1983). In their view, while prehistoric settlement was admittedly concentrated along river systems to take advantage of the rich resources to be found there, actual population movement over the region was through the uplands along ridge crests. This pattern characterized seasonal population movements as well as population dispersals that may have occurred during periods of severe resource stress (see also Gunn 1984a:150–154; Jolly 1984a:4–5). The presence of fairly large, dense sites on ridge-crest locations in the Eagle Hill area was thought to confirm the model. This was documented using collections from 56 sites examined during the 1982 University of Texas, San Antonio, testing program (Gunn and Kerr, eds. 1984). The presence of the larger ridge-crest sites was thought to be due to their well-drained conditions, which made for favorable camping, although occupation in these locations was also thought to have been most pronounced during wetter periods in the past, when local biomass and hence subsistence potential would have been greater (Gunn 1984a:152–153).

A 1,125-acre survey on the Main Fort, largely on terrain located on the divide between the Calcasieu and the Sabine Rivers, found few sites (Poplin 1987:61, see Chapter 2), suggesting the Ridge Causeway hypothesis might not be completely viable. A more extensive evaluation of the Ridge Causeway hypothesis appeared in 1996 that was based on impressions of assemblages from 30 sites located in the southeastern portion of Peason Ridge in the so-called Grand Divide between the headwaters of tributaries of the Sabine, Red, and Calcasieu Rivers and tested between 1991 and 1994 during the PTA-11, PTA-19, and PTA-20 projects (Meyer et al. 1995b:103–104). The 30 assemblages were, with a few exceptions, described as low-density lithic scatters and produced some of the lowest numbers of artifacts from any of the sites tested to date on the installation. A few sites were described as having small numbers of sherds and diagnostics from one or more components dating to the San Patrice, Evans, Tchefuncte, Marksville, Coles Creek, and Caddoan cultures. Marksville components were the most common, occurring on three sites, suggesting increased movement during this period. The authors noted that, given the small size of the sites that were found, "the data from the Grand Divide would seem to provide little support for the Ridge Causeway hypothesis" (Meyer et al. 1995b:104). Quantitatively based analyses using numerous assemblages will ultimately prove necessary to determine how prehistoric populations made use of ridge crests and interriverine areas in west-central Louisiana.

While subsequent investigations by U.S. Forest Service personnel have shown that the Horse's Head survey underestimated local site density in the Horse's Head area by a full order of magnitude, the pattern of decreasing site density with increasing distance from major drainages suggested by Campbell and her colleagues has been shown to hold up across the general region (Willingham and Phillips 1987:208–220). This is certainly the case at a more general level—site incidence drops with increasing distance from watercourses of any kind in this part of Louisiana. Most of the predictive modeling research on Fort Polk and U.S. Forest Service districts in west-central Louisiana, as discussed below, has brought together an overwhelming amount of evidence in support of this proposition.

The Piney Woods Model

During the MPRC testing project in the upper Birds Creek drainage in 1986, archaeologists from New World Research suggested that the absence of evidence for permanent settlement in the Fort Polk area was because the resource productivity of the general region was itself low (Campbell et al. 1987:119–130). In their view, the establishment of longleaf pine over much of the area during the Hypsithermal, replacing an earlier mixed deciduous forest, led to a dramatic reduction in the amount of exploitable biomass, making it less attractive for human settlement. While the hardwood canopies of the floodplain areas were acknowledged to be a much richer setting, their importance was considered fairly minimal because these areas made up only a comparatively small part of the landscape. Most sites of the post–Middle Archaic/Hypsithermal era on Fort Polk were interpreted as the remains of special-activity areas and short-term camps left by a small indigenous population, albeit one moving over a very large area, coupled with the remains of temporary camps of peoples from much farther away whose primary purpose in visiting the area was to obtain knappable stone from the dense local gravel deposits. This is perhaps the most widely accepted interpretation in recent years for the seeming sparseness of much of the prehistoric archaeological record on Fort Polk.

The basis for the Piney Woods model derives, in part, from an early study in which it was argued that the Coastal Plain pine barrens "had little subsistence value for the aboriginal inhabitants of the Southeast" (Larson 1980:56). This argument, while intuitively appealing, has been appreciably modified in the area where it was originally formulated, the Coastal Plain of Georgia and the Carolinas (Anderson et al. 1979:22–24; Sassaman and Anderson 1994:149; Stephenson et al. 2002:332–333). While major changes in how interriverine areas were used over time are evident—a considerable reduction in use of the Coastal Plain of Georgia and the Carolinas is indicated following the Early Archaic—it is now known that the major stream terraces and floodplain areas continued to be attractive places for settlement following the emergence and spread of pine forests in the mid-Holocene and that large sites occurred along them throughout the prehistoric era.

While the spread of pine forests over the southeastern Coastal Plain appears to have brought about large-scale population movement and reorganization, no areas were completely abandoned. Instead, populations made increasing use of floodplain areas (Anderson 1996a; Sassaman 1995). The same pattern is likely in the Louisiana Coastal Plain. Franks and Yakubik (1990b:89–90) made essentially the same argument in the Fort Polk area, namely that the local environment, although characterized by extensive pine forests, was not particularly desolate or barren and offered much of value to prehistoric populations. The attractiveness of the pine forest to birds, particularly bobwhite and turkey, and to some mammals was noted. Additionally, the pine forests themselves were shown to be part of a highly diversified environment that included floodplain forests in lower areas and scrub oaks and other hardwoods in more xeric areas. The Piney Woods hypothesis, accordingly, should be qualified to mean that a decreased use of upland areas likely occurred when the early Holocene mixed hardwoods canopy was replaced in the mid-Holocene by stands of the southern evergreen, longleaf pine. One expectation of the revised Piney Woods model that has yet to be realized, however, is that long-term habitation sites might plausibly be expected to occur along the margins of the largest streams in the Fort Polk area, such as along Whiskey Chitto or Birds Creek. As of yet, no such sites have been found, suggesting extended settlement was along even higher-order streams or closer to the mouths of these streams with higher-order drainages.

Patterns of Lithic Raw Material Procurement and Use

USE OF GRAVEL CHERT

Appreciable research has been directed to resolving how prehistoric peoples made use of lithic raw materials found in the west-central Louisiana area. Information collected on Fort Polk has been used for this research, along with data from over the surrounding region, primarily that obtained by researchers working with materials from the Kisatchie National Forest. Exploitation of the extensive chert gravel deposits that occur widely in the vicinity of the Main Fort has received particular attention, as noted previ-

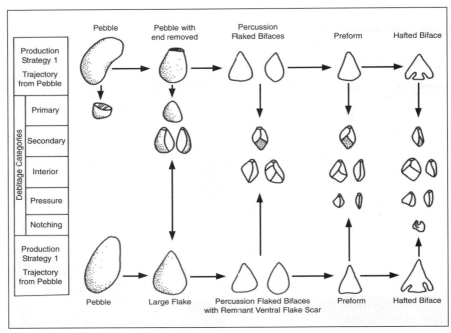

*Figure 3.4 — Lithic reduction trajectories involving the use of pebble cherts ob-
served at sites on Fort Polk (from Novick 1984:239).*

ously in the review of models relating site size to proximity to these sources.
Two major strategies appear to have been employed in the use of these materials, one involving the reduction of chert pebbles more or less directly
into tools and the other involving the reduction of these pebbles into flakes,
which were then made into tools (Novick 1984:238) (Figure 3.4). These
strategies are similar to those identified during the analysis of the 16VN18
excavation assemblage (Fredlund 1983:854), in which a change in reduction strategies over time was inferred from the reduction of cobbles to individual tools in the Late Archaic, which left many large cortical and noncortical
flakes behind, to the production of multiple tools from a single pebble in the
late prehistoric/Caddoan era, which left smaller flakes behind and more
noncortical interior flakes. Similar trends have been inferred in Texas as
being tied to the replacement of dart points by arrow points (Cantley
1993:190–192; Henry et al. 1980; Lynott 1978; Cantley, however, notes that
experimental studies by Peter and McGregor [1987] failed to produce distinctive debitage signatures for the manufacture of the two categories of
artifacts, and he called for appreciably more work on the subject). Most
research in the Fort Polk area involving lithics has been directed to identify-

ing reduction or manufacturing practices (e.g., Cantley et al. 1997:810–816; McGimsey 1996; Novick 1984) or to delimiting possible temporal trends in reduction strategies or patterns of site use by examining variability within and between assemblages.

Dense scatters of chert gravel have been noted at a number of sites on the Main Fort that appear to have functioned as quarry sites during some periods, such as at 16VN646, 16VN652, 16VN687, 16VN692, 16VN738, 16VN739, and 16VN767 (Meyer et al. 1996b:80–82; Thomas et al. 1993b:80–104, 120–145, 1994a:94–121) (see also Chapter 1, Figure 1.1). Quarrying and reduction behavior at sites with major chert gravel deposits and extensive evidence for the testing and initial reduction of this material was explored at some length during the FP-4 project (Table 2.4; Thomas et al. 1993b:156–163). No evidence for mining or excavation was indicated on any of the sites, which is attributed to the common occurrence of gravels on the surface or exposed in erosional channels, tree falls, or stream beds. Quarrying behavior appears to have taken the form of gathering and testing a number of cobbles right at the source area, sometimes followed by the removal of suitable materials to other locations where more extensive reduction occurred. Quarrying areas were thus characterized by a high incidence of tested cobbles and cores with comparatively few flakes detached, as well as large numbers of primary flakes and chunks or shatter fragments. Some of this quarrying activity can be identified to specific time periods. At 16VN675 and 16VN692, for example, assemblages were found exhibiting numerous tools as well as extensive initial-stage reduction debris associated with San Patrice and Sinner components, respectively (Meyer et al. 1995a:144; Thomas et al. 1993b:120–145).

A second site type found at or near source areas, workshop camps, is characterized by both initial- and later-stage reduction debris, as well as a greater incidence and diversity of tool forms (Thomas et al. 1993b:160–163). That is, at a number of sites with gravel deposits, evidence for both quarrying and subsequent reduction activity has been found, suggesting some workshop camps were in close proximity to or right at the source areas. Workshop sites where extensive reduction occurred are characterized by large quantities of cortical material. Sites at increasing distances from the source areas were inferred to be characterized by progressively higher quantities of later-stage reduction debris. Some quantitative analyses of quarry and workshop sites have been conducted. At 16VN753, a large, dense site overlooking a tributary of Birds Creek, for example, reduction assemblages from two differing parts of the site were quantitatively compared to highlight their differences and help interpret the function or activities that were occurring in each area (Meyer et al. 1995a:120–121). In one area, initial quarrying/raw material selection was occurring, while in another evidence for later-stage reduction was evident. The example indicates that the same landform often witnessed different activities, either concurrently or over time, even right at source areas.

A limited test of inferences about quarrying behavior on the Main Fort occurred during the ES-6 project (Table 2.2), a survey-level examination of 16VN403, a site previously interpreted as a quarry (e.g., Thomas et al. 1982:106–107). Franks and Yakubik (1990b:85–87) offered explicit criteria by which quarry sites could be recognized, notably evidence for repeated visits, large amounts of primary debitage from initial reduction activity, and numerous tested and then discarded gravels. To this could be added the presence of worn tools made from materials found in other areas or artifacts of types or styles whose greatest incidence occurs elsewhere in the region. All of these attributes of quarry assemblages have been observed on a number of sites found on Fort Polk in recent years. It is now becoming clear that the gravel deposits in the Fort Polk area were extensively exploited by prehistoric peoples who came from across a wide area or, at least, had ties with peoples over a large area.

Franks and Yakubik (1990b:87–89) advanced an alternative explanation for some of the assemblage variation they believed was present on Fort Polk, which they called the Tethered Resource Hypothesis. Using the results of an earlier analysis by Thomas et al. (1982:108–111) that showed that site assemblage size was to some extent related to distance to gravel sources, they argued that

> [L]onger-term residential sites [should be] concentrated either in or near the area where gravel outcrops are present because workable gravel is a limited resource which is difficult to transport in its natural state. This prediction is testable. To do so, a site typology must be devised that takes into account areal extent, artifact density, and perhaps tool diversity. Larger sites with relatively greater artifact density should be concentrated near the southern portion of the Main Fort. Small sites with low artifact densities, i.e., locations and station camps, should be located at greater distances from gravel outcrops associated with the Williana Formation. The typology to enable the test has not yet been formulated [Franks and Yakubik 1990b:89].

While the assumption that larger residential sites should be located near the major chert sources in the southern part of the Main Fort simply because there are chert sources there cannot be uncritically accepted—the floodplains in this area are, after all, much larger than those in areas farther to the north and hence likely to have been much more attractive to prehistoric populations—the authors are correct in their call for improved site and arti-fact typologies and for more quantitative analyses. These concerns have been explored in a number of comparative analyses, as described in this and sub-sequent chapters.

Lithic raw material procurement activity at quarry and workshop sites on Fort Polk has typically been interpreted as embedded among a much wider range of activities that were occurring among groups occupying por-tions of the regional landscape (i.e., in the general Louisiana area), although not as part of long-term occupations or among groups permanently resident in the immediate area. Instead, many of the archaeological assemblages on the installation are thought to be the remains of transient visits by peoples living elsewhere who came into the area solely to acquire knappable stone; routine tasks such as food collecting and processing and the use of at least temporary shelters, of course, had to have occurred, since people did, after all, have to eat and sleep (e.g., Thomas et al. 1994a:158–162). Typical re-duction activity at gravel source areas included the testing of numerous stones, the discard of those deemed unsuitable, and the collection and transport, sometimes with limited further reduction, of satisfactory materials. There is little evidence at the immediate source areas for the extensive reduction of the gravels into bifaces or preforms for transport elsewhere, although these activities, as well as the manufacture of other tool forms, are observed at a great many sites on the installation, sometimes only a short distance from the area where the materials were obtained.

UNUSUAL REDUCTION STRATEGIES

Most of the small chert gravels found on Fort Polk appear to have been reduced by freehand percussion, with the initial step being the detachment of one or a few flakes to evaluate the material. If discarded without further modification, these pebbles are variously classified as "tested cobbles" or "quarry waste" (after House 1975:67). Even though many of the local chert gravels are small, evidence for bipolar reduction is typically unreported or is stated to be minimal by some investigators (e.g., Novick 1984:242). This opinion is not universal, however. Evidence for bipolar reduction was stated to be "abundant" on sites on the Main Fort by one research team, at least in comparison with its incidence on sites on Peason Ridge (Clement et al. 1995:426), and the occasional reduction of chert gravels using an anvil stone has been noted by other researchers (e.g., Meyer et al. 1995a:144–146). Re-ducing small, rounded, or irregular-shaped gravels using a bipolar hammer-and-anvil procedure produces cores and core fragments that resemble pièces esquillées, although they differ in having a "triangular or quadrilateral cross-section" and are often instead classified as "opposed platform cores . . . reduced on-anvil" (Meyer et al. 1995a:145). A similarity was noted of these artifacts to "fusiform" bipolar cores described by Gagliano (1967a:47) at Avery Island. Whether they are indeed cores or tools used as wedges, punches, or chisels is uncertain. One suggestion was that they may be exhausted cores discarded when their users returned to the raw material source area. Bipolar reduction of chert gravels does appear to have a long history in the Fort Polk area (see also Clement et al. 1995:426).

Another reduction strategy employed at Fort Polk was the reuse of earlier artifacts by later occupants. During the investigations at 16VN804 and 16VN873, for example, evidence was found for Coles Creek/Woodland period use of worked chert from earlier occupations (Morehead et al. 1996b:123–124, 148). The scavenging of earlier materials by later peoples appears to be common in the Southeast; scavenged sites are sometimes called "cultural quarries" (Sassaman and Green 1993:214–224). Reuse is thought to become more common during the Woodland and Mississippian periods, in part because of the increasing cultivation and land clearing that occurred, exposing earlier assemblages and prompting early collector behavior. Furthermore, if use of lithic raw material during earlier periods placed less emphasis on conservation and maximizing the potential of individual pebbles (e.g., as suggested by Fredlund [1983:854] and others), the debris from these assemblages would have provided later peoples with large quantities of material to work with, particularly if they were interested in smaller flakes, as has also been suggested by some analyses.

The occurrence of blades and blade-like flakes was noted in a small number of assemblages on Fort Polk, both on the Main Fort and on Peason Ridge, associated with Paleoindian, San Patrice, Marksville, and Coles Creek occupations (e.g., Meyer et al. 1996a:66–76; Morehead et al. 1995b:125–126; Thomas et al. 1993d:107–117). The function of these tools is uncertain and may have varied from one period to the next. Stone bead production using microdrills obtained from microlithic blade cores created from local gravel cherts has been well documented in later Middle Archaic contexts in the lower Mississippi Alluvial Valley at sites like Watson Brake (J. Johnson 2000), and microblade industries are associated with the Poverty Point culture locally (e.g., Webb 1982), as well as with subsequent periods (J. Johnson 1987:204). At one site on Peason Ridge, 16VN221, microlithic blades were found that resemble materials from Poverty Point period sites, although no diagnostics were associated (Thomas et al. 1993d:115, 180). The production and use of small blade-like flakes or bladelets, bladelet tools, and/or microblade cores—typically chert pebbles with a few small blade-like flakes detached—was also noted at seven sites found on the Main Fort during a large-scale survey (Peterson and Grunden 1998:389–390). While lapidary items that may have been worked by microlithic tools are fairly common in Poverty Point assemblages in eastern Louisiana, such items are almost nonexistent on Fort Polk. A small tubular stone bead 1.5 cm long by 0.5 cm thick was found at 16VN629 near Bayou Zourie on the Main Fort (Thomas et al. 1994a:153), although unfortunately it came from mixed deposits precluding accurate temporal or cultural placement. Poverty Point culture use of the Fort Polk area is suggested by the presence of baked clay balls at a number of sites on the installation. On Fort Polk, microblade technology appears to occur infrequently but in assemblages from across a wide temporal range.

Use of Sandstone

Sandstone from the Catahoula Formation in the Peason Ridge area was sometimes used for grinding implements on Fort Polk and beyond (see Chapter 1). The rough, grainy texture of the material appears to have made an excellent abrading surface. Grinding implements that are presumed to be of local materials have been found at several sites on Fort Polk. A well-defined double basin–shaped metate of sandstone was found at 16VN1136 on the Main Fort, for example, together with a second piece of unmodified sandstone, in levels attributed to a Late Archaic or earlier Woodland occupation (Morehead et al. 1995a:123–127) (see Figure 1.3). A sandstone metate and a petrified wood mano or pestle were found together at 16VN573, and a sandstone rock cluster, possibly a hearth or a raw material cache, was found at 16VN1064; both of these sites are located on the Main Fort (Figure 3.5). A sandstone double basin–shaped metate was found with an associated well-smoothed sandstone mano at 16VN398, near Birds Creek, in levels dated to the Late Archaic or Woodland (Thomas et al. 1994a:67–73), and a crude sandstone metate was found at 16VN1060; these two sites are also on the Main Fort (Morehead et al. 1995b:93) (Figure 3.6). A probable mallet and anvil stone of petrified wood were found during the GSRI-5 project on Peason Ridge (Table 2.5; Jones et al. 1996a:86). Sandstone implements are found on sites throughout the Louisiana area, and the possibility that some of them may have originated in this part of the state must be considered.

Some or all of the sandstone manos and metates found on Fort Polk strongly suggest that they were cached for use in subsequent visits, forming what has been called site furniture. Given the extensive research conducted at Fort Polk to date, however, the number of ground or pecked stone tools that have been found is minimal, adding up to no more than a dozen or so unusual specimens. A similar pattern was observed in an intensive survey

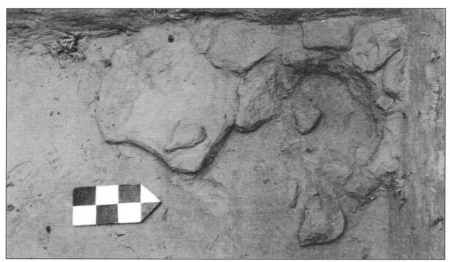

Figure 3.5 — Sandstone mano and metate at 16VN573 (top) and sandstone rock cluster at 140 cm at site 16VN1064 (bottom) (from Campbell et al. 1994a:62; Thomas et al. 1993c:49).

conducted in the Lake Anacoco basin immediately west of Fort Polk, leading to the suggestion that these objects were extensively curated or else alternative technologies were in use, such as wooden mortars and pestles or chipped stone axes or adzes (McGimsey 1996:142). A near absence of

Figure 3.6 — a, Crude sandstone metate (?) from 16VN1060; b, c, sandstone double-basin metate and mano from 16VN398 (from Morehead et al. 1995b:93; Thomas et al. 1994a:73).

hammerstones was also noted, a pattern also observed at Fort Polk, even though suitable materials are available in local stream deposits, leading the author to suggest that wood or antler batons may have instead been used to reduce local materials (McGimsey 1996:142).

USE OF EXTRALOCAL RAW MATERIALS

Lithic artifacts found on Fort Polk are overwhelmingly made on locally available gravel cherts, with lesser quantities of locally occurring petrified wood, quartzite, and opal also found. Extralocal raw materials are extremely uncommon, and probably as a result their description and identification have not been given much research attention. Raw material classification procedures are routinely presented in archaeological reports from the installation, most essentially recapitulating Heinrich's (1983, 1984) pioneering and still unsurpassed classification. A few studies have provided in-depth descriptions of their sorting categories (e.g., Gray 2001:72–76; Gray and Buchner 2000:56–59), and during the Eagle Hill II project neutron activation analyses were conducted comparing debitage from local sites with samples of opal and petrified wood from sources in the Fort Polk area and with cherts from sources in Arkansas and Texas (Brown 1982b:174–180; see Chapter 2). While most material appeared to come from unidentified local sources, a possible origin for some material from central Texas was suggested.

A few lithic artifacts found on Fort Polk do appear to have come from a great distance. A large preform of Edwards Plateau chert was found at 16VN1236 on the Main Fort at a depth of 80 to 90 cm in what are interpreted as Woodland deposits (Campbell et al. 1994b:43–44, 48, 108–109), and two tools made of Edwards Plateau chert were found in San Patrice levels at 16VN259 on Peason Ridge (Mathews et al. 1995:88–95). This material comes from central Texas in the general vicinity of the Colorado River (Banks 1990:58–61) and thus indicates some peoples at Fort Polk either came from or interacted over great distances. Novaculite that presumably came from the Ouachita Mountains of southern Arkansas, cherts from the Edwards Plateau of central Texas, and other unusual and typically unidentifiable/unidentified materials are occasionally reported in assemblages (e.g., Ezell and Ensor 1999:360). More typically lithic raw material variability does not receive much attention in reports, save for when formal tools such as projectile points are made on an unusual material; presumably this is because local materials form the vast majority of assemblages.

The first analysis of lithic raw material incidence over a large part of west-central Louisiana was conducted by Phillips and Haikey (1992:142–163). Using all of the assemblages gathered on the Kisatchie National Forest during FY 1989 from the Vernon, Kisatchie, Evangeline, and Catahoula

Table 3.3 — Incidence of lithic raw materials, by type, on a sample of sites from the Catahoula, Evangeline, Kisatchie, and Vernon Ranger Districts, Kisatchie National Forest, Louisiana

| | Ranger District | | | | |
	Catahoula	Evangeline	Kisatchie	Vernon	Totals
Gravel Chert	1,309	1,749	901	2,569	6,528
(% of Total)	(72.80)	(82.54)	(57.24)	(86.79)	(77.25)
Petrified Wood	64	6	328	14	412
(% of Total)	(3.56)	(0.28)	(20.84)	(0.47)	(4.88)
Catahoula Sedimentary	145	3	146	3	297
Quartzite (% of Total)	(8.06)	(0.14)	(9.28)	(0.10)	(3.51)
Red Jasper	125	181	140	323	769
(% of Total)	(6.95)	(8.54)	(8.89)	(10.91)	(9.10)
Fleming Opal	0	0	2	4	6
(% of Total)	(0.00)	(0.00)	(0.13)	(0.14)	(0.07)
Fleming Chert	4	10	3	3	20
(% of Total)	(0.22)	(0.47)	(0.19)	(0.10)	(0.24)
Banded Chert	69	100	25	39	233
(% of Total)	(3.84)	(4.72)	(1.59)	(1.32)	(2.76)
Quartz	11	11	4	1	27
(% of Total)	(0.61)	(0.52)	(0.25)	(0.03)	(0.32)
Other	71	59	25	4	159
(% of Total)	(3.95)	(2.78)	(1.59)	(0.14)	(1.88)
Totals	1,798	2,119	1,574	2,960	8,451
(% of Total)	(100.00)	(100.00)	(100.00)	(100.00)	(100.00)

Adopted from Phillips and Haikey 1992:142–163

Ranger Districts, they examined the incidence of raw material types by site (Table 3.3). Additionally, they presented maps showing the locations of known outcrops of Catahoula sedimentary quartzite and silicified wood on and near the Kisatchie Ranger District and gravel chert on the Vernon and Evangeline Districts. Gravel cherts were the most common raw material employed. Only in the Kisatchie District near Peason Ridge, where chert gravel deposits are not known, did the incidence drop below an overwhelming majority. Instead, locally available silicified wood appears to have been used as a substitute on occasion. There was a suggestion that Catahoula sedimentary quartzite may have been used primarily during the Early Archaic period, although this possibility was raised more as a hypothesis to be tested. No evidence for the occurrence or use of extralocal raw materials was found over the sample, which is a pattern noted again and again in analyses from the general area, where such materials are extremely rare. The ready availability of local stone may have precluded the need for extralocal materials. The absence of such materials suggests that group ranges may have been circumscribed to the point that these peoples did not intersect other distinctive stone sources or that exchange was either not taking place or did not involve extralocal materials coming into the area.

Given the evidence for repeated use of the Fort Polk area for lithic raw material procurement, it seems unusual that more extralocal material has not been found. Minimally, one would expect groups coming to the area to replenish their stone supplies would discard exhausted tools, which may have included some made of materials from their home range. The sample sizes in the analyses conducted to date are fairly small, however, and analyses examining all of the lithic raw materials from the Forest or these along with the Fort Polk collections, in conjunction with rigorous sourcing studies, would likely prove highly informative about selection practices over time and space. A recent study of raw material preferences conducted in the Lake Anacoco basin immediately west of Fort Polk, for example, suggested a general decrease in the use of petrified wood over time (McGimsey 1996:140).

LITHIC REDUCTION ON PEASON RIDGE
Unlike the Main Fort area, where chert gravels are dense and widespread, lithic raw materials are comparatively scarce on Peason Ridge and include fairly unusual materials like opal, petrified wood, and quartzite (Heinrich 1983, 1984; see Chapter 1). Based on experience gained during the intensive testing program, for example, archaeologists from Prentice Thomas and Associates, Inc., have observed that cores are rare on Peason Ridge in comparison with the Main Fort for all periods save the Paleoindian, when local Eagle Hill chert appears to have been exploited (Meyer et al. 1995b:102–103). Quarry and workshop sites are likewise noted as exceedingly rare, indicating lithic raw material procurement was not a major reason for use of the Peason Ridge area. Finally, extensive reuse and curation of materials was indicated during the San Patrice period, when multiple tools (i.e., tools with more than one working edge) occur, which is a pattern not observed in comparable incidence on the Main Fort. As the authors note, the absence of quarry sites or quarry workshop sites

strongly implies that even if there are small amounts of Citronelle gravel on Peason Ridge, they are highly unlikely to be of workable size. It is seldom clear what the occupants of Peason Ridge were doing, but it is clear that lithic procurement was very rare except for the Paleoindian components around Eagle Hill.

The average component on Peason Ridge has no cores, many small tertiary and/or biface trimming flakes and few formal tools which may or may not include identifiable points. When diagnostics are present and multiple occupations are implicated, it is usually very difficult and often impossible to separate them. Identifiable activities . . . are either hunting or strongly linked to it. . . . Total collections are often smaller than 100 artifacts [Meyer et al. 1995b:103].

Quantitative support for many of these observations, using data generated by the Prentice Thomas and Associates, Inc., intensive testing program, is provided in Chapter 5 and through a series of comparative analyses, as discussed below.

Debitage / Flake Size Analyses

A number of investigators have examined debitage assemblages in the Fort Polk area, sometimes by themselves and in some cases as a part of more complex analyses encompassing some or all of the prehistoric artifact categories recovered. A general tendency for flake size to increase with depth was noted at 16VN18 (Fredlund 1983:795–797). During the site testing conducted in the vicinity of Eagle Hill in 1982, an analysis of flake width was done in which the maximum size of each flake was determined using 5-mm increments and measuring at the widest point parallel to the platform. The assemblages were found to be dominated by small flakes and were considered "tool fabrication and tool maintenance sites not associated with initial reduction of core materials" (Gunn and Wootan 1984:131). A similar trend of increasing flake size with depth was also noted at two sites tested in the Lake Anacoco basin immediately west of Fort Polk (McGimsey 1996:141, 143). This was attributed to increased use of smaller pebbles in later occupations, possibly due to intensive exploitation and gradual exhaustion of larger, more easily located pebbles. Another suggested explanation was decreased exposure of gravel deposits following the mid-Holocene, when reduced erosion and greater ground cover might have made locating exploitable stone more difficult. A shift from bifacial core to flake core technology in the Woodland period after ca. 2000 B.P. has also been suggested (Parry and Clark 1987) but was not considered the reason for the change in flake size in the Lake Anacoco samples, since no other major shifts in flake characteristics were observed. An increase in the incidence of bifacial tool forms during the later Archaic and early ceramic period, in fact, was suggested (McGimsey 1996:141).

A detailed examination of flake morphology was conducted with data gathered during the 1985 MPRC survey project, using more than 5,500 flakes from 59 levels at six tested sites (Gunn and Kerr 1986:7-50, 7-51). Principal component and cluster analyses were undertaken and documented groupings of debitage associated with differing types of site use, such as quarrying activity (i.e., numerous large flakes) and tool production (i.e., a more diversified debitage assemblage), and, apparently, with differing periods in the past. Creating cumulative curves of the debitage from inferred occupation levels was advanced as a simple means of grouping and comparing debitage assemblages (Figure 3.7). During the MPRC testing project, a series of measures were calculated over the assemblage, including (1) tool-to-debitage ratios, (2) a tool diversity index (number of tools on a given site divided by the total number possible and the evenness of their distribution, after Pielou [1969]), (3) ratios of cortical to noncortical flakes, and (4) flake size ratios (Campbell et al. 1987:21–22, 92–95). Most of the tested sites were found to have low tool-to-debitage ratios and low diversity measures, suggesting short-term or special-activity areas (Campbell et al. 1987:96). A few sites with higher tool-to-debitage ratios and tool-diversity indexes were thought to represent more extended occupation areas, where a greater range of activities appears to have occurred. The large quantities of debitage observed at many sites, coupled with the low incidence of other tool types, led the investigators to initially infer that lithic raw material procurement and reduction was a major if not primary activity behind the formation of many of the site assemblages.

The ratio of formal bifacial to unifacial tools (exclusive of projectile points) was examined over all the identified components that had been found during the FP-7, FP-9, and FP-12 testing projects (Table 2.4), and again using the first 20 project assemblages (Campbell et al. 1994a:167–168, 1994b:163–165; Morehead et al. 1995a:199–200, 1996a:195–196). San Patrice and most subsequent Archaic assemblages were found to have a higher incidence of unifaces than bifaces, Woodland assemblages were found to be about equally balanced between the two tool categories, and late prehistoric Caddoan and Mississippian assemblages were dominated by unifaces. Later Woodland Coles Creek assemblages more closely resembled those of earlier Woodland periods. A major period of technological change appears to have

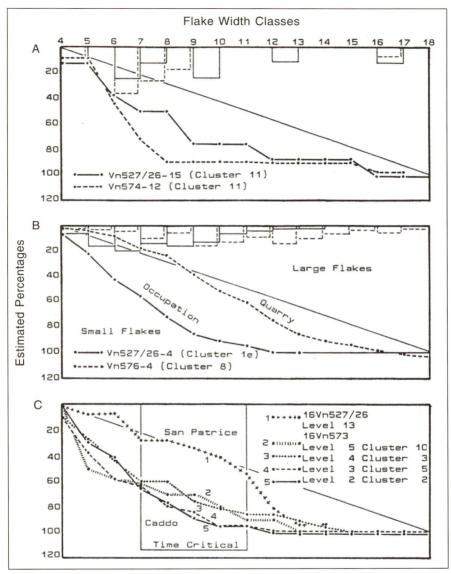

Figure 3.7 — Cumulative debitage curves as a means of documenting site function (from Gunn and Kerr 1986:7–60).

occurred following the later Woodland period. The incidence of formal stone tool types by component found during the first 12 Prentice Thomas and Associates, Inc., testing projects was also examined (Morehead et al. 1995a:200–202). Similarities in toolkit composition between San Patrice and Yarbrough assemblages and between Evans and Sinner assemblages, attributed to the Late Paleoindian/Early Archaic and the Middle Archaic, respectively, were noted. Interestingly, burins and pièces esquillées were observed in a number of Archaic and Woodland components and were not, as sometimes thought, restricted to the Paleoindian or Early Archaic periods. The occurrence of pièces esquillées, as suggested above, may be related to the nature of the predominant local raw material, gravel cherts, which can be reduced using a hammer-and-anvil technique. The authors elsewhere suggested that use of upland areas away from major drainages was primarily for small, short-term special-purpose occupations, probably hunting camps (Thomas et al. 1993d:179–180). These were inferred to be satellite camps to more permanent occupations located elsewhere. Short-term camps, it was argued, tended to occur in a wider variety of microenvironmental settings than more permanent occupations, with less emphasis on factors such as proximity to water (Thomas et al. 1992:119).

During the 16VN794 excavations a sample of 701 whole flakes were examined by size to explore arguments about the relationship between flake size and age (Cantley 1993:188–193). In brief, flake size apparently decreased significantly with the change from dart to arrow technology, as flake blanks replaced cores. This general pattern was observed on the cortical flakes found in both excavation blocks opened at the site. On noncortical flakes, size was more variable, although the largest flakes were in the deepest levels. Some of this patterning can clearly be attributed to the replacement of darts with arrows, but some of it may also be tied to the gradual exhaustion of high-quality or larger materials at the sources themselves.

The debitage collected during the 1995–1996 New South Associates survey project was sorted by size category and reduction stage and was used to examine technological organization and settlement strategies on the installation, with particular reference to the location of gravel chert outcrops (Cantley et al. 1997:853–877). Fairly consistent distributions in flake reduction categories were observed over much of the project area, suggesting an "overall similar organizational structure to the lithic technology" (Cantley et al. 1997:873). A few exceptions were noted, specifically sites with extensive early-stage reduction debris that were assumed to be quarry/workshop areas. When examined carefully, some of these were found to occur in areas of low potential environmental productivity, specifically areas well away from major streams. Such areas were assumed to be less attractive for activities other than lithic raw material procurement; hence the limited nature of the lithic assemblage. A similar pattern was also observed by the authors of the 1996–1997 SCIAA survey, as noted below. Few areas on the Main Fort were found with a high incidence (i.e., greater than 30 percent) of late-stage manufacturing debris, however, suggesting early-stage reduction was nearly ubiquitous in the Main Fort area. Given the close proximity of gravel chert sources, such a utilization strategy is not unexpected.

An extensive debitage assemblage (n = 21,378) was recovered during the 1996–1997 SCIAA survey (Clement and Peterson 1998:414–423). Cortical material was observed on 58 percent of the identifiable debitage, and at least some cobble reduction was noted as occurring at almost every site found during the survey. Evidence for thermal alteration was observed on 26 percent of all debitage, including intentional alteration to improve chipping capability as well as unintentional or accidental fire damage (Clement and Peterson 1998:415).

A detailed comparative analysis was conducted over 52 sites that yielded more than 100 flakes each and on which data derived primarily from excavation as opposed to surface findings; this sample accounted for 57 percent of all the debitage found during the survey (Clement and Peterson 1998:415). Five attributes were examined: "percentage of debitage with cortex . . . percentage of thinning and retouch flakes; percentage of decortication flakes, debitage size, and site landform type" (Clement and Peterson 1998:415). Scatterplots were run comparing a number of these attributes, revealing distinct clusters of sites that were interpreted as likely reflecting similar activities (Clement and Peterson 1998:414–423) (Figure 3.8). Some sites were used almost exclusively for initial reduction activity and may have been quarry/workshop areas. Most sites in the sample had moderate quantities of larger flakes and cortical material, suggesting that initial reduction was embedded amid other activities and occurred on nearly every site to some extent (Clement and Peterson 1998:416–417). Presumed quarry sites had distinctly different flake size distributions. The authors asked an important question: "[W]hy are there some sites in which initial cobble testing and reduction takes place, but not tool production; while at the majority of sites both initial cobble reduction and tool production takes place?" (Clement and Peterson 1998:416). Their answer was, first, that quarry sites tended to be located in upland contexts, while habitation sites tended to occur on floodplain or levee settings and, second, that cobbles were collected intact after minimal testing and were carried about or stockpiled at sites until they were needed for reduction and use (Clement and Peterson 1998:419). An attempt to examine cobble reduction practices and debitage size over time, using data from 45 presumed single-component sites, did not find significant differences from period to period (Clement and Peterson 1998:419–423). Instead, a range of reduction patterns cross-cut sites of differing periods.

A detailed debitage analysis was conducted with materials recovered from a 4,579-acre survey on the Rustville Training area on U.S. Forest Ser-

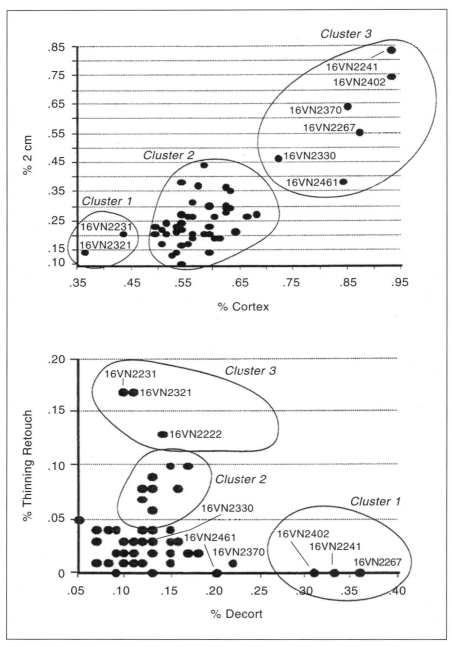

Figure 3.8 — Scatter diagrams of selected sites from the 1996–1997 SCIAA survey by percent of flakes larger than 2 cm vs. percent of cortical flakes (top) and percent of thinning/retouch flakes vs. percent cortical flakes (bottom) (from Clement and Peterson 1998:416).

vice lands south of the Main Fort (Ensor et al. 2001:440–448). The assemblage of 19,850 debitage and fire-cracked rock artifacts recovered from 118 sites and 90 isolated finds in this sample included primary flakes (8 percent), secondary flakes (16 percent), tertiary flakes (13 percent), shatter (5 percent), and fire-cracked pieces (3 percent), with the remainder nondiagnostic fragments. A flake size analysis was conducted using five major groupings by maximum dimension: 1/4 inch or less (79 percent), 3/8 inch (15 percent), 1/2 inch (6 percent), 3/4 inch (less than 1 percent), and 1 inch (less than 1 percent) (Ensor et al. 2001:440). The size distributions implied extensive tool manufacture was occurring, and given the large numbers of bifaces found in the collections this artifact was assumed to be what was being produced.

Finally, during the Lake Anacoco survey, McGimsey (1996:143) found little evidence for the reworking or resharpening of broken or retouched flake tools throughout prehistory, suggesting minimal concern for raw material conservation. Little emphasis on conservation was also observed by Fredlund (1983:854), based on his work at 16VN18, which is not too surprising given the widespread local occurrence of knappable gravels. While some gravel deposits may have been exhausted or rendered less accessible later in prehistory, this does not appear to have caused major changes in technological organization. An increase in the proportion of bifaces and projectile points in later Archaic and early ceramic-era assemblages was observed, something also suggested at Fort Polk (McGimsey 1996:143; see Chapter 6). Little reworking or resharpening of bifaces was noted, which may be related to the ready availability of raw material. A final trend suggested in the Lake Anacoco sample was a tendency for the flake to retouched flake ratio to increase in later periods, suggesting a greater production of nonutilized debitage. The sample sizes and changes in the ratios were small, however, leading the author to question the widespread applicability of this trend; instead, different functions or activities associated with the different sites and components might be producing the pattern (McGimsey 1996:143).

Multivariate Interassemblage Comparative Analyses

Assemblage variation over time was examined using data from the 1982 testing program of the University of Texas at San Antonio (Gunn 1984a:164–170; Gunn and Kerr 1984b), to which several thousand artifacts from the Eagle Hill site (16SA8) collected during the FPAS project were added (Kerr 1984:121). The Eagle Hill site was not examined during this 1982 testing program because it had been almost completely destroyed years before

(Servello and Bianchi 1983:390–403). A principal-components analysis was run over the 56-site sample using a series of environmental and assemblage variables (Gunn 1984a:155–160), and results indicated that sites characterized by small flakes, scarce (i.e., unusual or extralocal) raw materials, and relatively limited assemblages occur in lower-lying streamside locations, whereas larger and more diversified assemblages occur in the upland ridge-crest settings. The analysis also indicated that ceramic-period sites tended to have the largest assemblages with the broadest range of artifacts and hence activities and that some assemblages were characterized primarily by tool use and resharpening, suggesting fairly limited activity. A subsequent cluster analysis making use of data from 99 artifact-bearing levels in 14 sites, spread among streamside (n = 2), interface (n = 5), and ridge-top (n = 7) locations, produced 13 clusters, suggesting considerable variability in site use (Gunn 1984a:160–164) (Figure 3.9). Specific assemblage characteristics of each cluster were noted in general terms, and the primary data were provided, allowing future researchers the option of exploring and evaluating the patterns further (Kerr 1984:116, 118–119, 122–123, 125).

In brief, groups of clusters encompassing ceramic and preceramic occupations were observed over the 99-level/14-site sample, with the individual clusters representing groups of levels that appear to reflect common patterns of site use or activity. The results generally complement those from the principal-components analysis, although since relationships between individual proveniences rather than assemblage variables were what was being explored, greater variability within and greater differences between the ceramic and preceramic occupations were indicated. Paleoindian settlement was reported to have focused on ridge crests, this being a time when these areas were presumably moister and hence possessed more attractive vegetation/biomass. Assemblages were characterized by the presence of formal tools. Early Archaic occupations, in contrast, were spread over all three zones, with larger and more diversified occupations where tool manufacturing and use occurred being located on ridge crests and smaller assemblages with less diverse or intensive assemblages occurring in interface/ridge slope and streamside settings. These smaller assemblages may alternatively date to the mid-Holocene, when occupation closer to water may have been preferred, given the presumed drier conditions in the uplands at this time. Late Archaic assemblages were small, with a lower intensity of occupation, although use of a wide range of settings is indicated. Woodland assemblages occurred over all landforms and exhibited considerable variability in flake size, tool incidence, and intensity of occupation, suggesting a range of differing activities and comparatively more intensive use of the area were occurring.

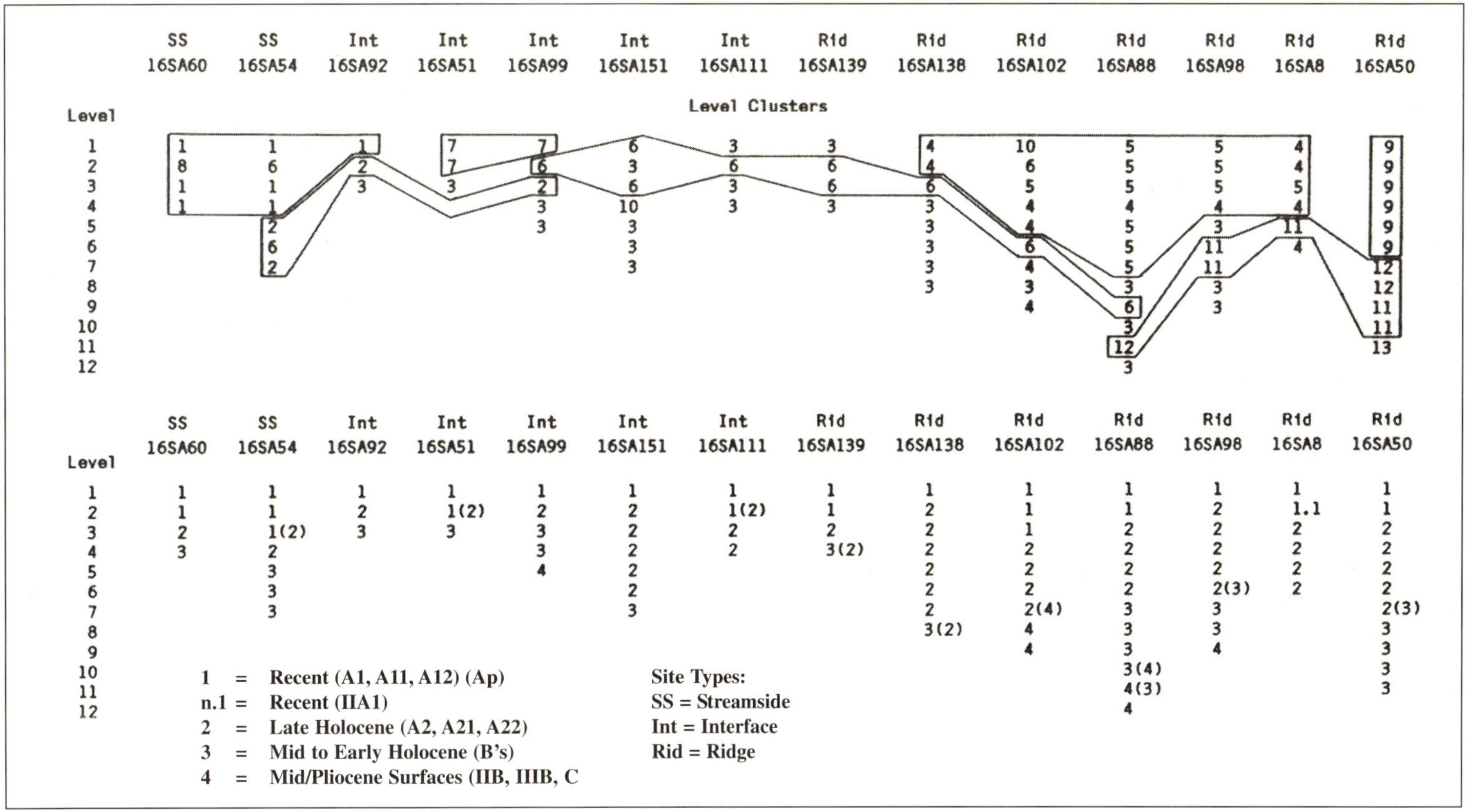

Level Clusters

	SS	SS	Int	Int	Int	Int	Int	Int	Rid	Rid	Rid	Rid	Rid	Rid
Level	16SA60	16SA54	16SA92	16SA51	16SA99	16SA151	16SA111	16SA139	16SA138	16SA102	16SA88	16SA98	16SA8	16SA50
1	1	1	1	7	7	6	3	3	4	10	5	5	4	9
2	8	6	2	7	6	3	6	6	4	6	5	5	4	9
3	1	1	3	3	2	6	3	3	6	5	4	5	5	9
4	1	2			3	10			3	4	4	4	11	9
5		6			3	3			3	6	5	3	4	9
6		2				3			3	3	5	11		12
7									3	3	5	11		12
8											6	3		11
9										4	3			11
10											12			13
11											3			
12											3			

	SS	SS	Int	Int	Int	Int	Int	Int	Rid	Rid	Rid	Rid	Rid	Rid
Level	16SA60	16SA54	16SA92	16SA51	16SA99	16SA151	16SA111	16SA139	16SA138	16SA102	16SA88	16SA98	16SA8	16SA50
1	1	1	1	1	1	1	1(2)	1	1	1	1	1	1	1
2	1	1	1	1	2	2	1(2)	1	2	1	1	2	1.1	1
3	2	1(2)	2	3	3	2	2	2	2	1	2	2	2	2
4	3	2	3		4	2	2	3(2)	2	2	2	2	2	2
5		3				2			2	2	2	2(3)	2	2
6		3				2			2	2(4)	2	3		2(3)
7		3				3			2	4	3	3		3
8									3(2)	4	3	3		3
9										4	3	4		3
10											3(4)			3
11											4(3)			3
12											4			

1 = Recent (A1, A11, A12) (Ap)
n.1 = Recent (IIA1)
2 = Late Holocene (A2, A21, A22)
3 = Mid to Early Holocene (B's)
4 = Mid/Pliocene Surfaces (IIB, IIIB, C

Site Types:
SS = Streamside
Int = Interface
Rid = Ridge

Figure 3.9 — Assemblage clusters by level and physiographic setting in the Eagle Hill locality (from Gunn 1984a:162).

A predominantly focal adaptation was inferred for Paleoindian times, giving way to a diffuse foraging strategy during the early Holocene (Gunn and Kerr 1984b:173). Following an apparent occupational hiatus or period of very low utilization, an increasingly complex use of the area occurred in the late Holocene during the terminal Archaic and ensuing Woodland/late prehistoric periods. It must be remembered, of course, that none of these assemblages have features or, save for Eagle Hill (16SA8), particularly dense and diversified assemblages indicative of extended use of specific locations. Accordingly, one must be careful to realize that the variability that has been recognized on Peason Ridge is almost all within what many archaeologists might consider to be small and unimpressive sites. The use of multivariate analytical procedures would appear to be an effective way to document relationships between a number of variables over numerous sites, although interpretation of the results must be done carefully and cautiously, and the results from such exploratory data analyses must above all make sense. The Eagle Hill and 1999 HPP multivariate analyses (see Chapter 5) both clearly indicate that even presumably small and uncomplicated sites, like those in many parts of Fort Polk, and especially on Peason Ridge, may actually exhibit appreciable variability and fall into a number of fairly discrete groups.

A comparative analysis of materials from 42 components from the installation found during the Prentice Thomas and Associates, Inc., testing program was conducted as part of a large-scale survey of Peason Ridge (Ezell and Ensor 1999:360–393; see also Ensor et al. 2001:26–27). The data examined included primary, secondary, and tertiary flakes, bifacial thinning flakes, chunks/shatter, cores/core decortication flakes, projectile points, other bifaces, unifaces, utilized flakes, and pecked stone/groundstone; assemblages were placed into one of four time periods including San Patrice, Middle to Late Archaic, Middle Woodland, and Caddoan, with each group of sites examined using correspondence analyses.

A number of general trends were noted over the sample: "Middle Woodland sites produced over twice as many artifacts as Archaic and Caddo sites and about three times that of San Patrice sites. . . . Caddo sites and bifacial thinning flakes are closely associated at the Main Fort. San Patrice sites are closely aligned with utilized flakes, unifaces, bifaces, cores, and chunks/shatter. Middle Woodland and Archaic assemblages are dominated by projectiles/point knives and primary, secondary, and tertiary flakes that may indicate bifacial reduction of pebbles" (Ezell and Ensor 1999:371). Initial reduction was evident at San Patrice components, which fell into two groups. One was characterized by extensive reduction debris and a wide range of tool forms, while the other was characterized by a low diversity of tool forms, predominantly bifaces, unifaces, and groundstone. Later Archaic components were found to be large and diversified on the Main Fort, with appreciable evidence for initial- to early-stage reduction manufacturing activity, while on Peason Ridge sites tended to be smaller and characterized by later-stage manufacturing or resharpening debris. Woodland sites tended to be uniform in content in both areas and were characterized by "a diverse range of tool/debris categories, reflecting a wide range of activities from lithic procurement to biface manufacture to camp maintenance activities" (Ezell and Ensor 1999:380; see also Ensor et al. 2001:443). Woodland sites on Peason Ridge tended to have smaller assemblages, suggesting somewhat shorter if still diversified occupations. Caddoan sites fell into two groups, one characterized by unifaces and extensive initial-stage reduction and manufacturing debris and the other by arrow points, unifaces, late-stage manufacturing/resharpening debris, other bifaces, and utilized flakes. These groups were interpreted to represent short-term lithic procurement and hunting/gathering activities, respectively.

The analyses suggested to the authors that longer-term occupations in the Fort Polk area likely occurred during Late Paleoindian San Patrice and Middle Woodland times (Ezell and Ensor 1999:387, 391). Middle and Late Archaic and Caddoan components, in contrast, appeared directed to shorter-term hunting and/or lithic-procurement activities (Ezell and Ensor 1999:391). An analysis of toolkit diversity was also conducted, with differences noted from period to period. Diversity was found to be highly correlated ($r = 0.86$) with the total number of tools present over the entire assemblage, although later prehistoric Middle Woodland and Caddoan assemblages had lower numbers of tool categories than expected (Ezell and Ensor 1999:391). These assemblages were thought to represent more specialized patterns of site use. Greater use of the Peason Ridge area by groups employing a somewhat more curated technology was suggested by the greater incidence of tools and late-stage lithic reduction/manufacturing debris. Differences between the Main Fort and Peason Ridge areas were also noted:

> Lithic procurement took place at both Peason Ridge and the Main Fort during San Patrice times. Caddoan sites at the Main Fort appear to reflect short term hunting/gathering camps. However, during the Middle to Late Archaic periods, the Main Fort became a focus for chert procurement, with very little evidence of this activity at Peason Ridge. Similarly, Middle Woodland occupation at the Main Fort resulted in a uniformity of site types in the present sample with lithic procurement, biface manufacture, and perhaps maintenance tasks occurring at the same locale. This suggests longer site occupation spans. Middle Woodland sites at Peason Ridge appear

to represent shorter-term occupations with little evidence of lithic procurement [Ezell and Ensor 1999:392–393].

These conclusions are based on a comparatively small sample of assemblages and hence must be viewed as hypotheses to be tested. The quantitatively based comparative analysis of information gathered by earlier investigators is fairly unusual, however, making this analysis particularly praiseworthy.

Nine artifact categories encompassing debitage size categories, stone tool types, and prehistoric ceramics from 21 sites with known Woodland or Caddoan components were compiled and used to conduct a multivariate correspondence or reciprocal averaging analysis (Ensor et al. 2001:443–448). Two groups of sites were identified: one, found on two of the sites, was characterized by larger flake sizes, cores, and tested cobbles and was apparently associated with lithic raw material procurement. At almost all of the other sites, smaller debitage categories, arrow and dart points, and sherds were found. Short-term camps were inferred because of the low tool variability. One site exhibited evidence for both lithic raw material procurement and domestic/campsite activity. Specialized lithic raw material procurement within a larger settlement strategy directed to routine subsistence activities was inferred, with at least three site types occurring: small and short-term limited-activity camps, specialized quarrying/procurement stations, and sites where both occurred. The incidence of each site type further suggests far more short-term camps (six times as many in this sample) are likely to be present in this general area than lithic raw material procurement loci.

Predictive Modeling on the Kisatchie National Forest

U.S. Forest Service archaeologists and their contractors have devoted considerable effort to predictive modeling activity over the past 15 years, with much of the effort directed to delimiting site density within broad, replicable environmental zones; this work has brought a great deal of rigor to this type of analysis locally (e.g., Hillman 1980; Johnson et al. 1986:90–120; Phillips and Willingham 1990:187–229; Willingham and Phillips 1987:172–220). The 1984 Kisatchie National Forest cultural resources overview noted that, to successfully accomplish cultural resource work on the Forest, "establishing a predictive model was seen as a primary goal" (Keller 1984:53). In that overview it was noted that sites in the upland areas of the Forest dominated by longleaf pine tend to be quite small, typically less than 10 m in diameter, and consisted almost exclusively of the remains of limited activities such as hunting or butchering. Although the absence of any reliable predictive model for the area outside of the longleaf uplands was noted, Keller also observed that "[i]t is apparent that areas adjacent to flowing streams contain the largest numbers of sites and that these contain the highest density of cultural material. Such streamside situations, including the territory within approximately 100 meters of the actual stream course, have the highest cultural resource potential on the Kisatchie National Forest. Stream size does not appear to be a deciding factor since several sites are located adjacent to springs and/or other spatially limited water sources" (Keller 1984:54). The predictive models of site location developed on Fort Polk, both in the 1988 HPP effort and in 1995, and the subsequent modeling analyses conducted on the Forest itself since 1984 have shown that proximity to water is one of the single most critical variables constraining settlement in this part of Louisiana.

The earliest example of predictive modeling–oriented research on the Kisatchie National Forest was by Hillman (1980) and was based on an analysis of environmental associations of 112 historic and prehistoric sites found during a survey of approximately 4,000 acres spread over a number of Ranger Districts. Hillman stratified the landscape into three major zones that, with only fairly minor revision, continue to be used to this date by U.S. Forest Service CRM personnel. These zones were (1) bottomland areas, (2) heavily dissected ridge lands, and (3) low rolling hills. Site density was described as high along the terraces in Zone 1 and throughout Zone 2, while it was described as low in Zone 3 (reported in Phillips and Willingham 1990:20). The use of extent of landscape dissection as a variable to define site probability areas, which has been common to all subsequent predictive modeling analyses by U.S. Forest Service personnel on the Kisatchie National Forest, appears to derive from this study.

A second predictive model was advanced by Johnson et al. (1986:90–120), which was based on an examination of the environmental associations of 146 historic and prehistoric sites located during an intensive survey of 5,016 acres of forest in the Winn Ranger District that had been damaged by tornado action. Once again three topographic zones were delimited, corresponding to (1) "low relief, gently sloping bottomland and immediately adjacent terraces," (2) "low relief and slightly dissected ridgeland," and (3) "highly dissected landscape" (Johnson et al. 1986:14–15). Site and isolated find incidence varied between zones, being 2.87, 1.76, and 4.98 sites and isolated finds per hundred acres in Zones 1 through 3, respectively (Johnson et al. 1986:90). The analysis also indicated both historic and prehistoric sites tended to occur near the boundaries of these zones; that is, in transition zones. A detailed analysis of site incidence by soil type was also conducted, documenting the utility of this variable as a predictor of site location as well

(Johnson et al. 1986:96–115). Recognizing the difficulty in replicating the analysis elsewhere, a call was made for the development of objective criteria for measuring degree of dissection (Johnson et al. 1986:116). This challenge was met, and answered, in the investigations reported a year later by Willingham and Phillips (1987).

The most comprehensive analysis of prehistoric settlement on the Kisatchie National Forest conducted to date was by Willingham and Phillips (1987) and was based on an analysis of 162 historic and prehistoric sites found during intensive surveys of 15,387 acres spread over all five Ranger Districts. Three major physiographic zones, corresponding to bottomlands and adjacent terrace areas, minimally dissected uplands, and heavily dissected uplands, had been previously identified within the general region, based on earlier predictive modeling efforts within the Forest (Hillman 1980; Johnson 1984a, 1984b). Significant differences in site type and density were observed over these zones, with the greatest site densities occurring in the bottomland and heavily dissected upland zones. In addition, large numbers of sites were observed in the transitional areas between these zones. Historic sites, in particular, were noted to occur at the minimally dissected/heavily dissected upland interface, while prehistoric sites tended to occur at the bottomland/minimally dissected upland interface.

Critical to predictive modeling efforts is the replicability of the analysis; that is, independent researchers, given the same site locational data, should be able to duplicate the environmental coding and hence the results. Difficulties with analytical replicability, as noted above, plagued early research along these lines at Fort Polk. This same weakness, Willingham and Phillips (1987:210) recognized, characterized some earlier Forest Service modeling efforts, notably Hillman's (1980) and Johnson et al.'s (1986) studies, and they accordingly directed considerable effort to overcoming this problem. Using USGS 7.5-minute quadrangle sheets to obtain a consistent measure of drainage characteristics, they distinguished three environmental zones using the following criteria:

> The boundary used to separate Zone I from Zone II and III was the first contour line at the base of the first slope component above the bottomland as indicated on USGS topographic maps. Zones II and III were differentiated by the quantity of dissection as determined by drain frequency. Using a modification of Strahler (1957), dissection was measured by the number of drains that occur within a given quarter section. A mean value of dissection was then computed for each zone. For the purposes of this study, Zone II is characterized by <15 drains per quarter section and Zone III is distin-

guished by ≥15 drains per quarter section [Willingham and Phillips 1987:210].

The three geographic zones defined on the basis of landform and drainage characteristics essentially correspond to bottomlands and adjacent terrace areas (Zone I, all areas within 10 feet or one contour line of a marked water-course); minimally dissected uplands (Zone II, <15 mapped drains per 7.5-minute USGS quarter section); and heavily dissected uplands (Zone III, >15 mapped drains per 7.5-minute USGS quarter section).

A series of finer-grained variables were also coded for each site, including soil type, slope percentage, elevation, distance to nearest permanent water source, elevation above the water source, and stream rank. Soils and slope data were derived from county soils maps, while elevation and drainage information were coded from USGS quadrangle sheets. In brief, Willingham and Phillips (1987:218) found that of their total sample of 162 sites, the majority (n = 89 sites, 55 percent), including the vast majority (n = 14, 74 percent) of sites potentially eligible for the National Register of Historic Places, occurred within 500 feet of a permanent water source. Almost all sites (n = 145, 89.5 percent) were located no more than 60 feet above permanent water, with the highest percentage (n = 61 sites, 37.6 percent) between 20 and 40 feet above water. A general observation of relevance to land management and to determining where major sites tend to be located was that "the level of site significance in terms of eligibility status tends to decrease on all Ranger Districts as the distance from Zone I increases" (Willingham and Phillips 1987:218).

Significant differences in site type and density were observed within and between the three major environmental zones advanced for the Forest area. Accordingly, predicted site probability areas were defined as follows:

High Probability:
Zone I   areas elevated above the floodplain.
Zone III   areas within 500 feet of the nearest permanent water source; areas within 500 feet of Zone I.

Moderate Probability:
Zone I   floodplain.
Zone II   areas within 500 feet of the nearest permanent water source; areas within 500 feet of Zone I.
Zone III   areas between 500 and 1000 feet of the nearest permanent water source; areas between 500 and 1000 feet of Zone I.

Low Probability:

Zone II   areas greater than 500 feet of the nearest permanent wa-
           ter source.
Zone III   areas greater than 1000 feet of the nearest permanent
           water source [Willingham and Phillips 1987:220].

These probability areas and the three environmental zones subsumed within
their definition saw successful use for a number of years by U.S. Forest
Service CRM personnel, and subsequent investigations demonstrated their
utility (e.g., Phillips and Willingham 1990:226–227). These strata were also
used to guide Forest Service archaeological survey work. High-probability
areas were examined using linear transects spaced 50 m apart with subsurface testing every 30 m, moderate-probability areas were examined using
transects spaced 100 m apart with subsurface tests opened every 50 m, and
in low-probability areas subsurface testing was judgmentally employed in
areas of less than five percent slope or on crests or elevations (Phillips and
Haikey 1992:13).

Willingham and Phillips's 1987 analyses, particularly their discussions
of the importance of distance to water and elevation above water, profoundly
influenced the 1988 Fort Polk HPP predictive modeling effort. The probability areas advanced by Willingham and Phillips, however, while of demonstrated utility and a considerable advance over previous efforts, contain
so many conditions for their definition that they have proven extremely difficult to use. Mapping the upland zones within typically irregular project
survey tracts that have greater or less than 15 drains per quarter section, for
example, and then using these data to define high-, moderate-, and low-
probability areas using the criteria listed above is a particularly arduous
enterprise. Even more challenging is finding these areas on the ground. This
is not an indictment—similar problems beset the operationalization of the
1988 Fort Polk HPP predictive model, particularly determining which parts
of survey tracts lay within 60 feet in vertical elevation of a mapped water
source, which is why the 1995 model used variables that could be easily
located on maps and on the ground (see Chapter 4). Phillips and Willingham
(1990:22–23), in fact, recognized these problems early on and eliminated
elevation above water as a criteria for identifying site probability areas, which
was a lesson that helped guide the 1995 predictive modeling effort on Fort
Polk. Because the probability areas proposed in both the 1988 Fort Polk and
the Kisatchie National Forest predictive models could only be determined
on a very approximate basis even using Geographic Information System
(GIS) technology, greatly simplified but actually more reliable criteria for
delimiting site probability zones were developed in the 1995 model.

Conclusions

As has been demonstrated by this review, an extensive body of research directed to modeling archaeological site occurrence and function has been conducted in the Fort Polk area. This work has incorporated large numbers of sites and isolated finds from large areas. While early modeling efforts, such as the 1976–1979 FPAS and the 1981 New World Research surveys, were based on the analysis of comparatively small, randomly selected tracts and low numbers of sites, with many environmental attributes calculated by hand, in recent years analyses have appeared that use much larger sample sizes and advanced GIS technologies. This research has led to increasingly greater accuracy in our site location models and has produced a number of ideas and observations about archaeological site location and past human settlement in west-central Louisiana.

Chapter 4

The 1988 and 1995
Fort Polk Predictive Models

T wo predictive models were developed for Fort Polk during the preparation of the historic preservation plans. While developing the 1988 Historic Preservation Plan (HPP), locational and environmental data about the installation and from 1,657 sites and isolated finds (excluding four recorded cemeteries) (Table 4.1) were used to generate three cultural resource probability zones. These were as follows: Zone 1, floodplain areas; Zone 2, locations beyond this floodplain category yet within either 300 m horizontal distance or 60 feet vertical distance of a water source mapped on the U.S. Geological Survey (USGS) 7.5-minute quadrangle sheets encompassing the fort; and Zone 3, all other areas (upland areas more than 60 feet above and 300 m distant from a mapped water source). Site probabilities were found to differ among these three zones, as described below. Zone 1, occupying floodplain areas, was listed as "Site Probability Indeterminate." Significant sites were thought to occur in this zone, but survey coverage had not been sufficient to settle the matter one way or the other. Zone 2, encompassing terrain intermediate between the floodplain zone and the uplands, was classified as a "High Probability" zone, on the basis of the numbers of all components and particularly the diagnostic components identified. Zone 3, occupying the upland areas of the base more than either 60 feet in vertical elevation or 300 m distance (whichever came second) from a mapped water source, was classified as a "Low Probability" zone.

During the preparation of the revised HPP in the 1990s, the entire cultural resources database recorded on Fort Polk as of July 1, 1995—a sample of 2,785 sites and isolated finds—was examined using the base Geographic Information System (GIS) to generate a revised predictive model of site location; this work occurred in July and August 1995 (Table 4.1). Every effort was made to render the cultural resource probability zones for the revised model as comparable as possible to those used in the earlier model, while at the same time making the delimitation and on-the-ground detection of these zones as easy as possible. The three zones that were defined were as follows: Zone 1, floodplain areas, defined as areas with floodplain soils;

Table 4.1 — The 1988 and 1995 Fort Polk predictive models site and isolated find analysis samples

	Sites	Isolated Finds	Totals
1988 Analysis Sample			
Historic	133	44	177
Prehistoric	832	581	1,413
Historic sites from maps	67	—	67
Cemeteries	4	—	4
Totals	1,036	625	1,661
1995 Analysis Sample			
Historic	199	56	255
Both historic and prehistoric	91	14	105
Prehistoric	1,350	1,075	2,425
Totals	1,640	1,145	2,785

Zone 2, locations within a 200-m buffer of Zone 1 or within a 200-m buffer of a mapped water source; and Zone 3, all other areas. These three zones were assigned site probabilities of Indeterminate, High, and Low, respectively. These three zones are much easier than the earlier zones to locate on maps and in the field, since the variable of vertical elevation above nearest water source has been removed, and the easily measured high-probability zone accounts for a higher percentage of all sites and all significant sites than the comparable zone in the 1988 HPP model, as documented below.

The 1988 predictive model guided all survey work at Fort Polk through 1995, while the 1995 model has guided all subsequent intensive survey work through April 2002, when the current volume was finalized. Because these models have proven fairly successful and because analyses associated with their development revealed a number of important observations about past human settlement in the west-central Louisiana area, how they were developed is explored in greater detail in this chapter. All of the primary data used in both of these analyses have been presented in the 1999 HPP Map and Inventory volumes and are available to researchers in hard copy and electronic format (Anderson et al. 1996a, 1999a).

The Development of the Fort Polk Predictive Models

The analytical procedures used to derive environmental and locational assemblage information for each site and isolated find examined on Fort Polk during the preparation of the 1988 and 1999 HPPs are discussed in detail in the HPP volumes (Anderson et al. 1988:205–232, 1999b:268–289, 339–377). A major aspect of the analysis during both the 1987–1988 and 1999 HPP projects was collecting basic inventory data about the sites and isolated finds recorded on the installation. At the time the original HPP was prepared, the site file records from Fort Polk were maintained at the offices of the Louisiana Division of Archaeology in Baton Rouge. From December 16–19, 1986, photocopies were made of all the state's site files and other records (i.e., maps and analysis notes) pertaining to Fort Polk, a major effort involving duplicating thousands of pages at a local copy shop. This information included complete copies of all records in the Division of Archaeology site files for Vernon, Natchitoches, and Sabine Parishes, as well as copies of USGS maps with plotted site locations. In addition, photocopies were also made of all reports of archaeological investigations and findings on the installation that were not available in original form. These data were reviewed to compile component and assemblage data from each site and isolated find and to prepare a map volume with all site and isolated find locations hand-plotted on USGS quadrangle sheets and 1:50,000 Army terrain analysis maps (Anderson and Macek 1987). A series of environmental measures (described below) were hand-coded from these maps and used to generate the 1988 predictive model, as well as conduct a range of other analyses. The data and results of these analyses were reported in the 1988 HPP Inventory and Technical Synthesis volumes (Anderson et al. 1987, 1988).

Beginning in late 1993, when planning for the 1999 HPP effort was initiated, the records collection process was repeated. This time, however, copies of all primary site files, reports, and other records were available from the Cultural Resource Manager's office on Fort Polk, where a permanent curation facility had been established in 1992. Duplicate copies of all site forms, together with the original copies of all field and analysis notes, photographs and slides, and other project records, including the camera-ready versions of all project reports, were maintained in the curation facility. Most importantly, the collections from all prior cultural resource investigations funded by the Army were also present, offering the opportunity to examine artifacts directly. As the HPP effort proceeded, all new reports, notes, or other materials that came into the curation facility were examined and incorporated into the 1999 HPP database.

From 1993 to 1996 several trips were also made to the U.S. Forest Service's Kisatchie National Forest offices in Pineville, Louisiana, where Alan Dorian, the Forest Archeologist, provided information on all of the work conducted by the Forest Service or its contractors on the Vernon and Kisatchie Ranger Districts near Fort Polk. This included photocopies of reports, site forms, and analysis notes. In addition, Dorian or his assistants routinely sent copies of reports of ongoing investigations in these districts to Anderson, together with site forms and other records. In 1995, the staff of the Cultural Resource Consulting Division of the South Carolina Institute of Archaeology and Anthropology (SCIAA), under the direction of Steven D. Smith and as part of a cooperative agreement with the National Park Service, conducted much of the coding of primary data from the installation compiled since 1988. Specific SCIAA staff who helped in the data compilation effort included Cindy Abrams, Mark Groover, Ramona Grunden, and Jill Quattlebaum, many of whom had worked extensively on Fort Polk (e.g., Abrams et al. 1995; Clement et al. 1998). This work entailed the entry of a wide range of information from site forms and reports into a series of standardized databases and encompassed all of the sites and isolated finds reported on the installation through July 1, 1995. While the HPP was in development all subsequent data were also entered, primarily by Anderson, so the data files in the inventory are complete through February 1999 (Anderson et al. 1999a).

The primary site file, report, and collections records were used to generate a comprehensive list of sites and isolated finds on Fort Polk, whose locations were plotted on USGS 7.5-minute quadrangle sheets when not already done (site locational data are recorded in the state site files, but isolated finds have not been uniformly reported or recorded over the years). Truthing (i.e., checking the accuracy of) these locations was accomplished by crosschecking among the state site forms and map records, the data in the various reports, and the original field records, when available. The maps were then sent to the U.S. Army's Construction Engineering Research Laboratory in Champaign, Illinois (USACERL) for incorporation into the GIS then under development for Fort Polk (Majerus and Rewerts 1994). Between 1993 and 1995 personnel from USACERL digitized all site locational data from quadrangle sheets and established links between this data and files with information about individual sites. This work was done by Larry Abbott, Cindy Balek, Craig Neidig, Jahsheed Deen, and Chris Rewerts, under the direction of Kim Majerus. All data were maintained under the site or isolated find number, which forms the unique identifier linking information for a property in the multiple files comprising the inventory and in the GIS.

Once the information was digitized, a second round of truthing was necessary to ensure the accuracy of the GIS output; this work was largely accomplished by Chris Rewerts, Cindy Balek, and Anderson, with technical assistance and managerial support provided by Kim Majerus. When all were satisfied that the database was clean, environmental associations for each site and isolated find (described below), as well as the maps comprising the HPP Map volume, were produced at Fort Polk by Rewerts and Anderson using the installation GIS. This GIS allows users to create, update, display, and print maps using a wide range of data layers that have been developed, including maps for cultural resources. A number of locational variables were recorded for the sites and isolated finds reported on Fort Polk, including Universal Transverse Mercator (UTM) zone, easting, and northing coordinates; USGS quadrangle name; and township, range, section, quarter section, and subsection. Township and range locational data were taken from the site forms in cases in which these were available and were obtained from the USGS quadrangle sheets in the case of isolated finds, for which site forms are not filled out in Louisiana. UTM data were calculated by hand in the 1988 HPP and generated using the digitized cultural resources GIS data layer in the 1995 analysis. Since the accuracy of UTM coordinates for sites and isolated finds is critical for the successful use of the installation GIS, for both resource management and for research, considerable effort was directed toward verifying their accuracy. Collecting accurate site locational data is one of the most important responsibilities of archaeologists engaged in fieldwork; it is the foundation on which much subsequent work is based.

ENVIRONMENTAL INFORMATION RECORDED IN THE 1988 PREDICTIVE MODELING EFFORT

The following measures were hand-coded in the 1988 Fort Polk HPP analysis for each site and isolated find, a sample of 1,657 properties: drainage basin, landform type, elevation, distance to nearest water, stream rank of nearest water, type of nearest water (i.e., intermittent or permanent), elevation above and distance to nearest permanent water source, stream rank of nearest permanent water source, distance to nearest confluence of two or more water sources, stream rank of water source immediately below nearest confluence, major soil association, soil series, specific soil type, slope of specific soil type, geological formation immediately underlying the site, and site aspect. Specific coding information for each of these variables, by site and over a comparative sample of 362 randomly selected locations, was presented in the 1988 inventory volume (Anderson et al. 1987, 1999a:appendixes 17 and 18). Specific attributes are described below.

Drainage Basin

Drainage-basin information was recorded by comparing the location of the site, as plotted on USGS 7.5-minute quadrangle sheets, with drainage-basin locations recorded on the installation Terrain Analysis Maps and by Cantley and Kern (1984:fig. 3) (Figures 4.1 and 4.2). While most of these assignments could be made directly from the smaller-scale maps, use of the USGS quadrangle data facilitated decision making when sites were near drainage

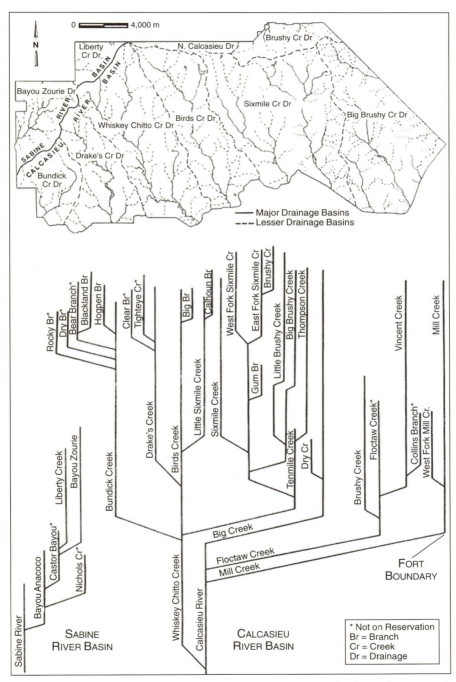

Figure 4.1 — Drainage patterns on the Main Fort at Fort Polk (from Thomas et al. 1982:50, 4–34).

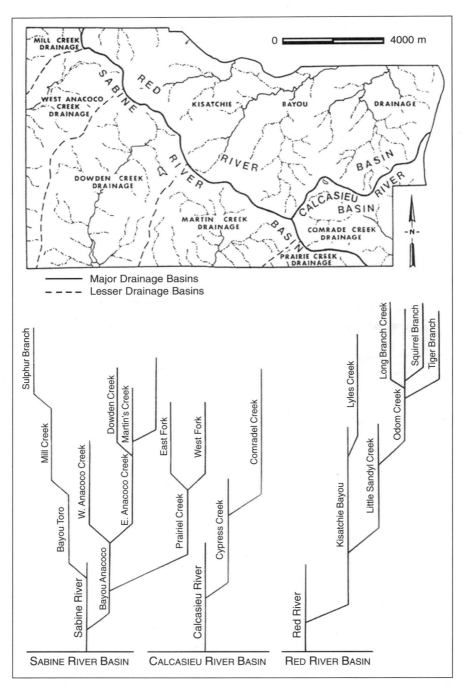

Figure 4.2 — Drainage patterns on Peason Ridge at Fort Polk (from Thomas et al. 1982:49, 4–35).

divides. Sites directly on drainage divides were assigned to the drainage with the nearest mapped watercourse.

Landform Type

Landform categories were assigned following Ruhe's (1975) criteria. All sites were initially classified into one of two major landform categories: either bottomland or ridge zone. These were in turn subdivided into a series of secondary (i.e., crest, terrace, slope, no assignment) and tertiary (crest, knoll, side, saddle, nose, terrace, no assignment) categories.

Elevation

Elevation values were recorded directly from the USGS 7.5-minute quadrangle sheets. Measures were taken to the nearest 10-foot contour interval. When sites spanned multiple contour lines, the highest and lowest values were recorded, as well as an average (midpoint) value.

Distance to Nearest Water

Distance was measured in meters to the nearest intermittent or permanent watercourse, as shown on the 7.5-minute quadrangle maps on which the sites were plotted. Use of USGS quadrangle data to determine water-related variables reflected a concern for analytical replicability. These maps provide a standardized, readily accessible coding framework, so observational problems that may arise when other criteria are used are avoided.

Stream Rank of Nearest Water, Nearest Permanent Water, and Water Source below the Nearest Confluence

Stream ranking was measured using Strahler's (1957) criteria.

Type of Nearest Water

Type of nearest water was measured directly from USGS 7.5-minute quadrangle sheets. Two categories were used: intermittent (dotted blue lines on the maps) and permanent (solid blue lines on the maps) water sources.

Elevation of the Site above Nearest Water

The elevation of the site above the nearest water was measured directly from the USGS 7.5-minute quadrangle sheets for the Fort Polk area. Measures were taken to the nearest 10-foot contour interval. When sites spanned multiple contour lines, an average (midpoint) value was recorded.

Distance to Nearest Permanent Water Source

This distance was measured in meters to the nearest permanent watercourse, as illustrated on the 7.5-minute quadrangle maps on which the sites were plotted.

Distance to Nearest Confluence of Two or More Water Sources
Distance was measured in meters to the nearest confluence of two water-courses, as shown on the 7.5-minute quadrangle maps on which the sites were plotted.

Major Soil Association
Soil association was plotted directly from the Fort Polk Terrain Analysis Engineering Soils Map (Fort Polk 1978). The major soil associations, recorded by type, were described as (1) sandy, moderately well-drained to well-drained soils on undulating to rolling hills; (2) sandy, well-drained soils on hilly to steep uplands; (3) clayey, moderately well-drained soils on gently to strongly sloping uplands; (4) silty or sandy, poorly drained floodplain soils; (5) silty, moderately well-drained soils on nearly level to undulating terraces; and (6) sandy, well-drained soils on dissected rolling to steeply sloping terraces.

Soil Series
Data on soil series were coded directly from Fort Polk Soil Survey aerial photographs. Fine-grained soil maps had been prepared for approximately three-quarters of the Main Fort at the time of the 1988 HPP, and the remainder were completed for the entire installation soon thereafter. These soils data, and the soil series and type categories employed, it should be noted, were subsequently entered into the installation GIS system as a separate data layer. This soils information was then used to generate a number of additional derivative data layers, such as slope and depth to C horizon, as described below. Major soil series present on Fort Polk were described in detail in the HPP (Anderson and Joseph 1988:188–190). They are reported here to give readers some understanding of the kinds of deposits within which sites are found on the installation.

Beauregard Series. The Beauregard series consists of deep, moderately well-drained, slowly permeable soils that formed in loamy Pleistocene-age and Tertiary-age uplands. These soils are on broad, nearly level and gently sloping coastal plains. They are saturated for short periods during winter and early spring. Water runs off the surface at a medium to slow rate. Slopes are predominantly 1 to 3 percent but range from 0 to 5 percent.

Betis Series. The Betis series consists of deep, somewhat excessively drained, rapidly permeable, sandy upland soils. They formed in thick sandy sediments of marine deposits. These soils are on broad, nearly level to sloping broad interstream divides. Slopes are dominantly 2 to 5 percent but range from 0 to 8 percent.

Briley Series. The Briley series consists of deep, sandy, well-drained, moderately permeable soils that formed in sandy and loamy Coastal Plain sediments. These soils are on gently sloping to moderately steep broad interstream divides. Slopes are dominantly 2 to 5 percent but range from 1 to 20 percent.

Caddo Series. The Caddo series consists of deep, poorly drained, slowly permeable soils that formed in thick beds of unconsolidated loamy sediments. These soils are on nearly level to very gently sloping terraces of middle to late Pleistocene age. Slopes range from 0 to 3 percent.

Cahaba Series. The Cahaba series consists of deep, well-drained, moderately permeable soils that formed in loamy and sandy alluvium. They are on nearly level to gently sloping stream terraces in the Coastal Plain. Slopes range from 0 to 6 percent.

Guyton Series. The Guyton series consists of deep, poorly and very poorly drained, slowly permeable soils that formed in thick loamy sediments. These soils are in Coastal Plain local stream floodplains and in depressions on late Pleistocene-age terraces. A water table is at a depth of 0.5 foot below the surface to 1 foot above the surface most of the time. Water runs off the surface at a very slow rate or is ponded. Slopes range from 0 to 1 percent.

Malbis Series. The Malbis series is a member of the fine, loamy, siliceous, thermic family of Plinthic Paleudults. These soils have dark grayish-brown, fine sandy loam A horizons, yellowish-brown loam upper Bt horizons, and mottled sandy clay loam lower Bt horizons that contain more than five percent plinthite. They are very low in calcium and become firm or very firm at depths greater than 50 inches.

Ruston Series. The Ruston series consists of deep, well-drained, moderately permeable soils that formed in loamy marine or stream deposits. These soils are on very gently sloping to sloping uplands of the southern Coastal Plain. Slopes range from 0 to 8 percent.

Sawyer Series. The Sawyer series is a member of the fine, silty, siliceous, thermic family of Aquic Paleudults. These very strongly acidic soils have dark grayish-brown silt loam surface layers; yellowish-brown silty clay loam upper subsoils; yellowish-brown mottled with gray silty clay loam middle subsoils; and mottled red, strong brown, and gray silty clay lower subsoils.

Susquehanna Series. The Susquehanna series is a member of the fine, montmorillonitic, thermic family of Vertic Paleudalfs. These soils have dark gray and yellowish-brown fine sandy loam A horizons and mottled red and gray, firm, plastic, clayey B horizons.

Vaiden Series. The Vaiden series consists of deep, somewhat poorly drained, very slowly permeable soils on level to sloping uplands and stream terraces. These soils formed in thick beds of acid clays, usually underlain by chalk or marl. Slopes are dominantly 0 to 8 percent but range to 17 percent.

Specific Soil Type

The specific soil type data were hand-coded directly from draft soil maps that had been prepared for approximately three-quarters of the Main Fort when the analysis was conducted in 1987; a fairly large sample was coded (n = 669 sites). Soils data are now available in a GIS data layer for the entire installation and were used to determine specific soil types for each site and isolated find in the 1999 HPP analysis.

Slope of Specific Soil Type

Slope data were included in the specific soil type descriptions. Considerable vertical relief may occur within individual soil patches, depending on their size and location within the landscape.

Engineering Geology

Engineering geology was plotted directly from the Fort Polk Terrain Analysis Engineering Geology Map (Fort Polk 1978). The major geological categories recorded, by type, were (1) layered mixtures of predominantly sand with silt and clay, (2) thick layers of clays and silts separated by thin layers of predominantly sand, (3) alluvium, and (4) Pleistocene terrace deposits of sand and silt with lenses of clay and gravel.

Site Aspect

This measure was recorded for all sites on sloping terrain. Aspect refers to the direction, or compass bearing, of the slope faces. This measure was coded by compass bearing of slope to nearest water using cardinal (N, E, S, W) and intermediate (NE, SE, SW, NW) readings. Cultural properties located on level terrain, specifically those on ridge crests and most sites in bottomlands (excluding those on bottomland knolls), by definition, have no aspect and were classified as level. Sites located on the crests of knolls, where site boundaries dropped off in all directions, were also classified as level.

ENVIRONMENTAL INFORMATION RECORDED IN THE 1995 PREDICTIVE MODELING EFFORT

Environmental information from Fort Polk used in the 1999 HPP was obtained from GIS data layers developed by the Legacy Resource Management Program and USACERL and maintained by the Environmental and

Natural Resources Management Division at Fort Polk. The Fort Polk GIS, or "PRISM Kajun Kaleidoscope," was installed in July 1994 and includes

> spatial map databases, a relational database management system (DBMS) and tabular databases, and computer menu and graphic user-interface (GUI) building tools to guide computer users through easy-to-use, "point-and-click" paths to accomplish tasks. PRISM allows decision support using computer data including maps and geographic data, remote sensing data, global positioning system (GPS) data, tabular data, computer files, and data accessed through a modem or computer network [Majerus and Rewerts 1994:1].

The GIS is designed to assist ongoing cultural resource management, forest management, endangered species programs, and watershed management and erosion control programs to further the installation's military mission in the most efficient and effective manner possible. The system can be easily used to produce summary maps, tables, and reports, examples of which are found in the remainder of this chapter and in colored format in the 1996 HPP Map volume (Anderson et al. 1996a).

In the development of the 1995 predictive model, 2,785 sites and isolated finds were used, representing all of the historic properties on Fort Polk for which final reports, site forms, and collections were available for inspection at the time the model was developed (Table 4.1). A random sample of 2,136 points was also generated using the GIS from within areas on the installation that had already been intensively surveyed, and this sample was used to help evaluate the 1995 model. Installation map data are maintained within a GRASS (Geographic Resource Analysis Support System, developed and supported by USACERL) GIS, linked to tabular data using an Informix relational database management system. An extensive data dictionary is part of the documentation for the Kajun Kaleidoscope GIS and details how data layers were developed and the accuracy and resolution of the information (Majerus and Rewerts 1994). Specific data layers and other environmental data calculated from these data layers that were used in the analyses reported in this volume are described below. The actual data values obtained for each site and isolated find, as well as for the random sample of nonsite locations, for each of the environmental variables described below, are documented in summary form in the analyses that follow. The primary data for individual sites and isolated find locations are presented in the 1999 HPP Cultural Resources Inventory Primary Data volume, which also includes all of the information presented in the 1988 inventory volume (Anderson et al. 1987, 1999a).

Soil Type

The soils information is derived from Natural Resources Conservation Service soil maps and is at 20-m resolution (Anderson et al. 1999a:appendixes 8–11). Soils data are not available from minor portions of the Main Fort. The data layer was created using the soil survey data for Fort Polk in the following manner:

> The soil polygon boundaries were traced onto a mylar overlay from photocopies of the original soil survey sheets. The map was georeferenced by matching prominent road intersections on the soil sheets with the UTM coordinates for the same loci on 7.5' USGS topo sheets. The boundaries of the soil polygons were digitized and edited, and the individual polygons labeled. A cell file was created and the appropriate category descriptions for the soil classes were added. Pixel resolution for the cell file is 20 meters. Minimum average RMS [root mean square] residual achieved for this map was 14.01 meters [on Peason Ridge; on the Main Fort it varied between 0.776 m and 3.25 m]. Because the original soil survey data was not ortho-photo rectified and inherent errors were introduced by photocopying and tracing, these soil polygons should not be inferred to represent actual ground truth conditions [Craig Neidig in Majerus and Rewerts 1994].

Potential Maximum Soil Depth of Archaeological Components

The data layer with information about the potential maximum soil depth of archaeological components was developed by Larry Abbott of USACERL. The data layer is described as providing information on

> the potential maximum soil depth of Late Pleistocene through Holocene cultural components at Fort Polk. This model is based on the assumption that the soil profile is not truncated, and that the upper Bt horizon is a time stratigraphic unit related to the Late Pleistocene. Thus, the potential archaeological record includes the A (or Ap) to the first subhorizon of the B horizon (e.g. Bt/E; Bt1; Btg; Bg; Bt2) for upland soils, and all the horizons (A to C) of the bottomland (alluvial) soils. Holocene-age cultural components would be expected in upland soils above this maximum soil depth, and at possibly great depths in the alluvial soils. This is a "model" that needs testing before it can be used as a guideline [Larry Abbott in Majerus and Rewerts 1994].

Five depth groups were prepared on the basis of a reclassification of the primary soils data from that GIS map layer. These groups are less than 50 cm, less than 100 cm, less than 150 cm, greater than 150 cm, and no data (Anderson et al. 1999a:appendix 14).

Soil Slope
Soil slope categories were derived from a direct reclassification of data on the soils map and are at 20-m resolution. The categories include no data, which indicates a lack of coverage, 0–5 percent slopes, 5–8 percent slopes, and slopes greater than 8 percent (Anderson et al. 1999a:appendix 15).

Elevation and Aspect
Elevation and aspect were derived from 100-m resolution digital terrain elevation data (DTED) and 30-m resolution digital elevation map (DEM) data for Fort Polk. DTED are derived from the Defense Mapping Agency and are available for the entire installation. The 30-m resolution DEM data are derived from USGS 7.5-minute quadrangle sheets and are available only for the eastern half of Peason Ridge on the Kisatchie, Kurthwood, and Simpson North quadrangles. Elevation and aspect data at 30-m resolution are not available for the remainder of Peason Ridge. Values of "no data" reflect this lack of coverage. Aspect values of "no aspect" mean the area is level or nearly level, precluding calculation of a meaningful aspect (Anderson et al. 1999a:appendixes 8–11).

Distance to Floodplain and Upland Soils
Distance to nearest floodplain and upland soils is derived from data obtained from Natural Resources Conservation Service soil maps at 20-m resolution. Soils data are not available for minor portions of the Main Fort. The soils data were reclassified into floodplain and upland soils; floodplain soils correspond to the Indeterminate Probability Zone in the revised HPP predictive modeling analysis. Distance values are Euclidean, or straight-line, measures calculated using the UTM coordinates for the analysis point (a random sample pixel, or a site or isolated find boundary pixel if the site area is larger than a single pixel), and the nearest pixel with the attribute in question—in these cases, upland or floodplain soils. An example of the 20-m pixel grid is shown in Figure 4.3, in this case showing how the 200-m buffer for the High Probability Zone in the 1995 analysis was obtained. Distance measures for each site and isolated find and for the random sample analysis points, as well as the UTM coordinates for these points, are in the HPP (Anderson et al. 1999a:appendixes 8–11).

Figure 4.3 — The 20-m pixel grid used to portray environmental data and calculate distances in the Fort Polk GIS. The example illustrates site probability zones from the 1995 analysis.

Distance to Nearest Water Body

The data file for distance to nearest water body contains information about the distance, elevation, and absolute elevation of the nearest intermittent and permanent stream from known sites and isolated finds and random sample points on Fort Polk. The elevation of the nearest water body is derived from 30-m resolution DEM data obtained from USGS 7.5-minute quadrangle sheets and from 100-m resolution DTED compiled by the Defense Mapping Agency. DEM data were not available for the three quadrangles comprising the extreme northern part of Fort Polk (LaCamp 1978 7.5-minute; Slagle 1954 7.5-minute; and Simpson South 1974 7.5-minute) when the analyses were conducted, hence elevation and aspect data at 30-m resolution were not available from this area. Distance measures are calculated the same way as for distance to upland and floodplain soils. The absolute elevation is the difference in vertical elevation between the sample point and the body of water where the distance measurement is taken. The resolution of the streams map used in the analysis, from which distance was calculated, is 20 m (Anderson et al. 1999a:appendixes 8–11).

Geological Formation

The source for the surficial geology GIS data layer used in the 1995 analysis is the "Geological Map for Vernon Parish, Louisiana" in Welch (1942). Categories include No Data, Recent Alluvium, Pleistocene Prairie Formation, Pleistocene Montgomery Formation, Pleistocene Bentley Formation, Pleistocene Williana Formation, Miocene Blounts Creek Member, and Miocene Castor Creek Member (Anderson et al. 1999a:appendix 16). The location of these formations on the Main Fort is presented in Figure 4.4. A new map and study of the geological formations in the vicinity of the installation has recently been produced (McCulloh and Heinrich 1999) and has since been incorporated in the installation GIS, allowing analyses to proceed with finer-grained geological data.

Site and Environmental Associations on Fort Polk: Results of the 1988 and 1995 Analyses

In the 1988 and 1995 analyses, somewhat different approaches to examining the environmental associations of prehistoric sites and isolated finds were taken. Environmental data were hand-coded in 1988 and derived from a GIS in the 1995 analysis. Sample sizes, additionally, were much larger in the 1995 analysis. During the 1988 analysis, considerable effort was directed to resolving environmental associations for each major period in prehistory in an effort to resolve settlement change over time. The 1988 HPP analysis sample consisted of 1,454 prehistoric sites and isolated finds, 368 with temporally diagnostic artifacts. A total of 1,693 components were identified, 532 of which could be identified to a specific era based on the presence of diagnostic projectile points or ceramics (Anderson et al. 1988:198–199) and 1,161 of which were unidentifiable to specific period. The greater total number of components than actual sites and isolated finds, of course, reflects reoccupation; some sites produced diagnostics from differing periods. The 1995 analysis, in contrast, focused on the entire site assemblage, encompassing both historic and prehistoric sites and isolated finds (although

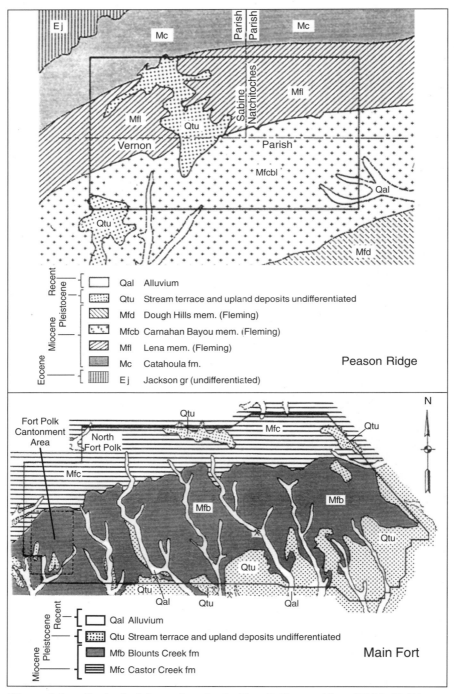

Figure 4.4 — Geological formations in the Fort Polk area (from Welch 1942).

only 105 of the 2,785 had just historic components) in an attempt to refine the predictive model developed during the 1988 study. While the 1988 analysis combined site data from across the installation, in the 1995 analysis data from the Main Fort and Peason Ridge were examined separately. This procedure appears to have had great utility, since considerable differences in land use are evident between the two areas. The results of each approach are presented and compared in the pages that follow.

To document whether observed discrete component distributions were a reflection of cultural factors or were merely due to chance, the natural distributions of the coded environmental attributes were examined. Summary environmental measures were used where available during both the 1988 and 1995 analyses. Data on stream rank and stream basin extent on Fort Polk had been previously calculated by Cantley and Kern (1984:112–114). Summary data on engineering soils and engineering geology, data categories examined in 1988, although not published, were calculated from the base Terrain Analysis Maps using a dot-grid acreage scale. Figures on the acreage of the soil series and types mapped on Fort Polk were provided by the base's environmental office in 1988 and generated using the GIS in the 1995 analysis. Using these summary measures, the site data from the installation could be compared against the total occurrence of these variables within the study universe, that is, on Fort Polk.

Where summary environmental data were not available, an attempt to generate such measures was made using random sample data to arrive at an unbiased representation of the physical environment (Kellogg 1987). In the 1988 HPP analysis, a stratified random sampling procedure was used, with two points being selected from within every section occurring on Fort Polk. In all, 362 points were selected, 112 from Peason Ridge and 250 from the Main Fort. The following environmental variables were coded for each random sample point in the same manner the site data were recorded: major, secondary, and tertiary landform type; absolute elevation; type of, stream rank of, distance from, and vertical elevation above nearest water; stream rank of and distance from nearest permanent water; type, stream rank, and distance of the stream below the nearest confluence; and aspect (Anderson et al. 1987, 1999a:appendixes 17, 18). In the 1995 analysis, a simple random sampling procedure was used to select pixels, or sample points, from nonsite locations within areas that had been intensively surveyed. A total of 667 sample points were drawn on Peason Ridge and 1,469 on the Main Fort. All of the environmental measures described above were calculated for these locations in the same manner as they were for the sites and isolated finds. These variables included soil type, minimum and maximum slope, elevation above nearest water, aspect, distance to upland and floodplain soils, and distance to intermittent and permanent water sources. The object of this sampling scheme was as much to see whether site locations were somewhat different from nonsite areas as it was to characterize the overall local environment. The use of random sample data as a baseline against which site environmental data may be compared has seen extensive successful archaeological application in recent years (Cabak et al. 1996; Goodyear et al. 1979; Hodder and Orton 1976; Kellogg 1987; Plog and Hill 1971).

Nearest Water Characteristics

In the 1988 examination of nearest water characteristics (Tables 4.2 to 4.4), the majority (75.34 percent) of prehistoric components on Fort Polk recorded at that time occurred near intermittent water sources (Table 4.2), a pattern reinforced by the 1995 analysis, as documented below. No great differences were observed when diagnostic as opposed to nondiagnostic components were examined. The analyses also noted that most prehistoric components on Fort Polk tended to occur closest to small Rank 1 drainages (Table 4.2). Only about one-third of all prehistoric components in the sample were located on Rank 2 or higher streams. Sites yielding diagnostic components tended to occur in somewhat higher than expected densities on higher-order Rank 3 streams, however, although they were underrepresented on Rank 2 streams. Prehistoric components were situated considerably closer to water, on the average, than points in the random sample (162.7 m vs. 199.8 m; see Table 4.2), and sites yielding diagnostic prehistoric components were themselves closer than those yielding nondiagnostic components (143.4 m vs. 172.1 m). Examining these distance to water measures period by period, later sites tended to be somewhat closer to water than earlier sites, although given the comparatively small sample sizes and large standard deviations for most periods, the validity of the observation was uncertain (Table 4.2).

Examining the distribution of prehistoric components by arbitrary 50-m intervals, the analysis indicated that the vast majority of sites and isolated finds in every period occurred within 300 m of water (Table 4.3). Interestingly, comparatively few prehistoric components were found within 50 m of water in the sample. The magnitude of this patterning is evident when the archaeological and random sample data are compared; a considerable difference is evident between the sample and component data (12.15 vs. 1.74 percent). This suggests that local prehistoric inhabitants may have avoided areas in immediate proximity to water, possibly to avoid low, wet ground conditions. Sites in floodplain areas, if covered with alluvium or in dense ground cover, are also likely to be less visible and hence harder to detect than those in upland settings. It now appears this patterning was at least partially an artifact of the archaeological surveying procedures used in earlier work on the installation, which did not routinely employ subsurface testing in lower-lying areas. Work conducted at Fort Polk since the mid-1980s has included extensive systematic shovel testing over large areas, including in the floodplain zone, with the result that comparatively more sites have now been found in or adjacent to this area, as discussed below.

The 1988 analysis also showed that elevation above nearest water source was a particularly sensitive measure of where prehistoric components were likely to occur on Fort Polk (Table 4.4). In every period most sites were situated within a comparatively narrow band approximately 10 to 40 feet above the nearest water source, and comparatively few sites were recorded above or below this range. There thus appears to have been an optimal intermediate zone that was utilized extensively and that was situated not too close to water yet not too far from it. Examining this distribution at a finer scale, by 10-foot intervals, the vast majority of all prehistoric components (90.75 percent), and an even higher incidence of the locations yielding diagnostic components (93.18 percent), were located within 60 vertical feet of water. These same measures indicate an underutilization of areas in close proximity to water (i.e., floodplains), the same patterning indicated by the distance to water analysis. Nondiagnostic components tended to be elevated somewhat higher above water than diagnostic components (30.2 vs. 26.0 feet), a finding in agreement with the observation noted previously that they tended to occur at a greater distance (Table 4.2). These figures suggest a pattern of decreased prehistoric use of higher elevations.

The results of the distance to water and elevation above water analyses conducted with the 1988 Fort Polk sample were in close agreement with results obtained by Willingham and Phillips (1987) using site data from the Vernon and Kisatchie Districts of the Kisatchie National Forest. In that analysis, base camps (sites likely to yield diagnostic components) were shown to occur closer to water, both horizontally and vertically, than temporary site types (where diagnostics might be less commonly expected). While some differences in the average distance and elevation values obtained by the two analyses are evident, these appear to be due to the markedly different sample sizes utilized. Willingham and Phillips (1987:217–220) concluded that distance to water and elevation above water were particularly significant predictors of site location in the general region and, as discussed below, these variables played a major role in the 1988 Fort Polk predictive model while distance to water remained critical in the 1995 model.

The 1988 analysis also examined distance to nearest permanent water and distance to the nearest confluence regardless of water type (i.e., a confluence of either intermittent or permanent water sources or of one with the other) (Table 4.5). Most prehistoric components tended to be farther

Table 4.2 — Prehistoric components on Fort Polk: occurrence by type of nearest water, stream rank of nearest water, and distance to nearest water, in meters (1988 HPP analysis sample)

	Nearest Water Type				Stream Rank				Distance Summary			
	Intermittent	Permanent	Total	No Data	R1	R2	R3	R4	Min	Max	Avg	SD
Early Paleoindian	1	—	1	—	1	—	—	—	200	200	200.0	0.0
MiddlePaleoindian	9	4	13	—	9	2	2	—	75	500	246.2	147.1
Late Paleoindian	17	7	24	—	15	2	6	1	50	450	199.2	135.7
Early Archaic	4	1	5	—	4	—	1	—	100	300	181.0	89.8
Middle/Late Archaic	25	11	36	—	22	4	9	1	0	425	130.7	93.3
Late Archaic	41	14	55	1	36	7	12	—	0	550	144.5	116.8
Late Archaic/Woodland	50	18	68	—	46	6	12	4	25	525	159.7	113.3
Early Woodland	—	1	1	—	—	—	1	—	50	50	50.0	0.0
Middle Woodland	13	4	17	—	11	3	3	—	15	200	92.1	48.4
Middle/Late Woodland	16	3	19	—	13	3	2	1	25	500	176.3	111.0
Unspecified Woodland	6	3	9	—	6	—	3	—	15	150	82.8	45.4
Late Woodland	28	2	30	—	25	4	1	—	0	550	139.2	111.7
Unspecified Formative	135	32	167	3	117	27	20	3	0	550	134.7	103.8
Early Caddoan	35	10	45	—	31	5	7	2	0	550	128.0	107.8
Caddo (Projectile Points)	11	3	14	—	11	1	1	1	50	275	121.8	69.1
Caddo (Ceramics)	6	6	12	1	5	3	2	2	25	250	143.8	74.0
Late Caddoan	8	3	11	—	7	—	4	—	50	325	129.5	78.1
Unknown Prehistoric	811	275	1,086	75	722	223	115	26	0	725	172.1	129.8
Total Prehistoric	1,216	397	1,613	80	1,081	290	201	41	0	725	162.7	121.3
(% of Total)	(75.34)	(24.61)	(100.00)	—	(67.02)	(17.98)	(12.46)	(2.54)				

Table 4.2 (cont.) — Prehistoric components on Fort Polk: occurrence by type of nearest water, stream rank of nearest water, and distance to nearest water, in meters (1988 HPP analysis sample)

	Nearest Water Type				Stream Rank					Distance Summary		
	Intermittent	Permanent	Total	No Data	R1	R2	R3	R4	Min	Max	Avg	SD
Total Diagnostic	405	122	527	5	359	67	86	15	0	550	143.4	103.8
(% of Total)	(76.85)	(23.15)	(100.00)		(68.12)	(12.71)	(16.32)	(2.85)				
Total Nondiagnostic	811	275	1,086	75	722	223	115	26	0	725	172.1	129.8
(% of Total)	(74.68)	(25.32)	(100.00)		(66.48)	(20.53)	(10.59)	(2.39)				
Occurrence in												
Random Sample	283	79	362		261	48	44	9	0	675	199.6	139.5
(% of Total)	(78.18)	(21.82)	(100.00)		(72.10)	(13.26)	(12.15)	(2.49)				
Main Fort	191	59	250		180	30	32	8	0	675	190.9	134.8
(% of Total)	(76.40)	(23.60)	(100.00)		(72.00)	(12.00)	(12.80)	(3.20)				
Peason Ridge	92	20	112		81	18	12	1	0	625	219.9	147.9
(% of Total)	(82.14)	(17.86)	(100.00)		(72.32)	(16.07)	(10.71)	(0.89)				
Stream Length (m)*			728,750		493,650	151,300	71,700	12,100				
(% of Total)			(100.00)		(67.74)	(20.76)	(9.84)	(1.66)				
Main Fort			537,850		364,250	114,550	48,350	10,700				
(% of Total)			(100.00)		(67.72)	(21.30)	(8.99)	(1.99)				
Peason Ridge			190,900		129,400	36,750	23,350	1,400				
(% of Total)			(100.00)		(67.78)	(19.25)	(12.23)	(0.73)				

From Cantley and Kern 1984:112–114.

Table 4.3 — Prehistoric components on Fort Polk: distance to nearest water, by 50-m intervals (1988 HPP analysis sample)

Distance Groups (m)	0–49	50–99	100–149	150–199	200–249	250–299	300–349	350–399	400–449	450–499	500–549	550–599	600–649	650–699	>700	Total
Early Paleoindian	—	—	—	—	1	—	—	—	—	—	—	—	—	—	—	1
Middle Paleoindian	—	—	3	1	2	3	—	—	2	—	2	—	—	—	—	13
Late Paleoindian	—	5	4	2	4	1	2	1	3	2	—	—	—	—	—	24
Early Archaic	—	—	2	1	—	1	1	—	—	—	—	—	—	—	—	5
Middle/Late Archaic	1	4	18	2	5	3	1	1	—	1	—	—	—	—	—	36
Late Archaic	1	11	16	10	8	1	4	—	2	—	—	2	—	—	—	55
Late Archaic/Woodland	—	14	14	12	15	3	3	1	2	3	—	1	—	—	—	68
Early Woodland	—	1	—	—	—	—	—	—	—	—	—	—	—	—	—	1
Middle Woodland	1	4	8	2	2	—	—	—	—	—	—	—	—	—	—	17
Middle/Late Woodland	—	1	5	4	4	3	—	1	—	—	1	—	—	—	—	19
Unspecified Woodland	1	2	4	2	—	—	—	—	—	—	—	—	—	—	—	9
Late Woodland	1	6	10	3	5	3	—	1	—	—	—	1	—	—	—	30
Unspecified Formative	4	30	59	30	18	6	6	9	—	1	3	1	—	—	—	167
Early Caddoan	1	10	17	6	5	2	—	2	—	1	—	1	—	—	—	45
Caddo (Projectile Points)	—	3	5	3	1	1	1	—	—	—	—	—	—	—	—	14
Caddo (Ceramics)	—	2	3	2	2	3	—	—	—	—	—	—	—	—	—	12
Late Caddoan	—	1	5	3	1	—	—	1	—	—	—	—	—	—	—	11
Unknown Prehistoric	18	168	287	171	130	63	85	48	50	25	18	14	3	3	3	1,086
Total Prehistoric	28	262	460	254	203	93	103	65	59	33	24	20	3	3	3	1,613
(% of Total)	(1.74)	(16.24)	(28.52)	(15.75)	(12.59)	(5.77)	(6.39)	(4.03)	(3.66)	(2.05)	(1.49)	(1.24)	(0.19)	(0.19)	(0.19)	(100.00)

Table 4.3 (cont.) — Prehistoric components on Fort Polk: distance to nearest water, by 50-m intervals (1988 HPP analysis sample)

Distance Groups (m)	0–49	50–99	100–149	150–199	200–249	250–299	300–349	350–399	400–449	450–499	500–549	550–599	600–649	650–699	>700	Total
Total Diagnostic	10	94	173	83	73	30	18	17	9	8	6	6	0	0	0	527
(% of Total)	(1.90)	(17.84)	(32.83)	(15.75)	(13.85)	(5.69)	(3.42)	(3.23)	(1.71)	(1.52)	(1.14)	(1.14)	(0.00)	(0.00)	(0.00)	(100.00)
Total Nondiagnostic	18	168	287	171	130	63	85	48	50	25	18	14	3	3	3	1,086
(% of Total)	(1.66)	(15.47)	(26.43)	(15.75)	(11.97)	(5.80)	(7.83)	(4.42)	(4.60)	(2.30)	(1.66)	(1.29)	(0.28)	(0.28)	(0.28)	(100.00)
Occurrence in Random Sample	44	46	55	45	45	33	31	23	19	8	7	3	2	1	0	362
(% of Total)	(12.15)	(12.71)	(15.19)	(12.43)	(12.43)	(9.12)	(8.56)	(6.35)	(5.25)	(2.21)	(1.93)	(0.83)	(0.55)	(0.28)	(0.00)	(100.00)
Main Fort	33	33	42	23	38	20	27	11	11	5	4	1	1	1	0	250
(% of Total)	(13.20)	(13.20)	(16.80)	(9.20)	(15.20)	(8.00)	(10.80)	(4.40)	(4.40)	(2.00)	(1.60)	(0.40)	(0.40)	(0.40)	(0.00)	(100.00)
Peason Ridge	11	13	13	22	7	13	4	12	8	3	3	2	1	0	0	112
(% of Total)	(9.82)	(11.61)	(11.61)	(19.64)	(6.25)	(11.61)	(3.57)	(10.71)	(7.14)	(2.68)	(2.68)	(1.79)	(0.89)	(0.00)	(0.00)	(100.00)

Table 4.4 — Prehistoric components on Fort Polk: elevation above nearest water, in 10-foot intervals (1988 HPP analysis sample)

Distance Groups (ft.)	0–9	10–19	20–29	30–39	40–49	50–59	60–69	70–79	80–89	90–99	100–109	110–119	120–129	Total	No Data	Min	Max	Avg	SD
Early Paleoindian	—	—	1	—	—	—	—	—	—	—	—	—	—	1	—	20	20	20.0	0.0
Middle Paleoindian	—	1	5	2	—	3	—	—	—	2	—	—	—	13	—	10	90	38.7	26.5
Late Paleoindian	—	7	5	2	5	3	—	—	—	2	—	—	—	24	—	10	90	31.7	23.0
Early Archaic	—	1	2	—	—	1	—	1	—	—	—	—	—	5	—	10	70	34.0	25.1
Middle/Late Archaic	1	13	12	4	2	1	1	—	1	1	—	—	—	36	—	0	90	23.6	19.6
Late Archaic	2	20	11	8	4	5	2	1	—	1	1	—	—	55	1	0	100	26.4	21.3
Late Archaic/Woodland	—	22	11	13	9	7	3	—	2	—	1	—	—	68	—	10	100	29.1	19.8
Early Woodland	—	1	—	—	—	—	—	—	—	—	—	—	—	1	—	10	10	10.0	0.0
Middle Woodland	1	7	6	3	—	—	—	—	—	—	—	—	—	17	—	0	30	16.5	8.6
Middle/Late Woodland	—	4	8	2	2	2	1	—	—	—	—	—	—	19	—	10	60	26.3	15.0
Unspecified Woodland	1	6	1	1	—	—	—	—	—	—	—	—	—	9	—	0	30	12.2	5.3
Late Woodland	1	8	12	3	1	4	1	—	1	—	—	—	—	30	—	0	60	23.7	15.2
Unspecified Formative	3	48	39	33	21	10	8	2	1	1	—	—	1	167	3	0	120	26.9	18.2
Early Caddoan	1	16	12	10	4	2	—	—	—	—	—	—	—	45	—	0	50	21.3	12.0
Caddo (Projectile Pts.)	—	5	2	3	3	1	—	—	—	—	—	—	—	14	—	10	50	25.0	14.0
Caddo (Ceramics)	—	4	3	3	2	—	—	—	—	—	—	—	—	12	1	10	40	22.5	11.4
Late Caddoan	—	4	3	1	1	—	2	—	—	—	—	—	—	11	—	10	60	26.4	19.1
Unknown Prehistoric	19	256	244	189	141	123	50	34	15	8	6	—	—	1,085	76	0	100	30.2	19.3
Total Prehistoric	29	423	377	277	195	162	68	38	19	15	8	—	1	1,612	81	0	120	28.8	18.8
(% of Total)	(1.8)	(26.2)	(23.4)	(17.2)	(12.1)	(10.0)	(4.2)	(2.4)	(1.2)	(0.9)	(0.5)	—	(0.1)	(100.0)	—				

Table 4.4 (cont.) — Prehistoric components on Fort Polk: elevation above nearest water, in 10-foot intervals (1988 HPP analysis sample)

Distance Groups (ft.)	0–9	10–19	20–29	30–39	40–49	50–59	60–69	70–79	80–89	90–99	100–109	110–119	120–129	No Data	Total	Summary Statistics			
																Min	Max	Avg	SD
Total Diagnostic	10	167	133	88	54	39	18	4	4	7	2	—	1	—	527	0	120	26.0	17.7
(% of Total)	(1.9)	(31.7)	(25.2)	(16.7)	(10.2)	(7.4)	(3.4)	(0.8)	(0.8)	(1.3)	(0.4)	—	(0.2)	—	(100.0)				
Total Nondiagnostic	19	256	244	189	141	123	50	34	15	8	6	—	—	—	1,085	0	100	30.2	19.3
(% of Total)	(1.8)	(23.6)	(22.5)	(17.4)	(13.0)	(11.3)	(4.6)	(3.1)	(1.4)	(0.7)	(0.6)	—	—	—	(100.0)				
Random Sample	13	114	73	61	57	24	15	1	4	—	—	—	—	—	362	0	80	25.4	16.4
(% of Total)	(3.6)	(31.5)	(20.2)	(16.9)	(15.7)	(6.6)	(4.1)	(0.3)	(1.1)	—	—	—	—	—	(100.0)				
Main Fort	10	80	53	42	39	14	8	1	3	—	—	—	—	—	250	0	80	27.1	17.0
Peason Ridge	3	34	20	19	18	10	7	—	1	—	—	—	—	—	112	0	80	24.7	16.2

Table 4.5 — Prehistoric components on Fort Polk: occurrence by type of nearest water and distance to nearest permanent water, in meters (1988 HPP analysis sample)

	Total Sites	No Data	Rank of Nearest Permanent Water				Distance Summary			
			R1	R2	R3	R4	Min	Max	Avg	SD
Early Paleoindian	1	—	1	—	—	—	1,475	1,475	1,475.0	0.0
Middle Paleoindian	13	—	4	7	2	—	100	1,910	879.6	535.4
Late Paleoindian	24	—	6	4	12	2	50	2,425	741.9	575.7
Early Archaic	5	—	1	1	3	—	105	1,600	1,201.0	622.3
Middle/Late Archaic	36	—	8	10	16	2	75	2,350	691.1	645.0
Late Archaic	55	1	9	12	31	3	50	2,350	839.4	630.7
Late Archaic/Woodland	68	—	9	17	35	7	50	2,350	866.2	663.5
Early Woodland	1	—	—	—	1	—	50	50	50.0	0.0
Middle Woodland	17	—	4	5	5	3	15	1,775	833.2	636.7
Middle/Late Woodland	19	—	3	10	5	1	200	2,000	1,093.4	583.7
Unspecified Woodland	9	—	—	2	6	1	15	2,350	930.0	894.6
Late Woodland	30	—	7	12	10	1	75	2,125	1,024.2	559.0
Unspecified Formative	167	3	31	60	66	10	15	2,375	881.3	594.2
Early Caddoan	45	—	9	9	23	4	50	2,350	928.3	611.7
Caddo (Projectile Points)	14	—	4	5	4	1	100	1,450	837.9	451.9
Caddo (Ceramics)	12	1	2	3	5	2	25	1,775	575.0	606.1
Late Caddoan	11	—	—	3	7	1	75	2,300	1,018.2	790.0
Unknown Prehistoric	1,086	75	86	425	477	98	0	2,675	751.3	586.5
Total Prehistoric	1,613	—	184	585	708	136	0	2,675	790.7	594.9
(% of Total)	(100.00)	—	(11.41)	(36.27)	(43.89)	(8.43)				

Table 4.5 (cont.) — Prehistoric components on Fort Polk: occurrence by type of nearest water and distance to nearest permanent water, in meters (1988 HPP analysis sample)

	Total Sites	No Data	Rank of Nearest Permanent Water				Distance Summary			
			R1	R2	R3	R4	Min	Max	Avg	SD
Total Diagnostic	527	—	98	160	231	38	15	2,425	872.0	612.3
(% of Total)	(100.00)	—	(18.60)	(30.36)	(43.83)	(7.21)				
Total Nondiagnostic	1,086	75	86	425	477	98	0	2,675	751.3	586.5
(% of Total)	(100.00)	—	(7.92)	(39.13)	(43.92)	(9.02)				
Occurrence in Random Sample	362	—	26	154	146	36	0	2,975	862.9	603.2
(% of Total)	(100.00)	—	(7.18)	(42.54)	(40.33)	(9.94)				
Main Fort	250	—	13	101	105	31	0	2,975	823.0	596.0
(% of Total)	(100.00)	—	(5.20)	(40.40)	(42.00)	(12.40)				
Peason Ridge	112	—	13	53	41	5	0	2,400	951.3	612.2
(% of Total)	(100.00)	—	(11.61)	(47.32)	(36.61)	(4.46)				

away from permanent water than from an intermittent source; only for the minority of sites was the nearest water source a permanent stream (Table 4.2). Permanent watercourses also tended to be Rank 2 or higher drainages. This was not altogether surprising, since few Rank 1 streams are mapped as permanent watercourses on local USGS quadrangle sheets, which were the source of the drainage information. The average distance of components from permanent water over most periods tended to fall between 750 and 1000 m, although given the large standard deviations these averages were considered to be of little predictive value. There was a slight tendency for components to occur between 100 and 300 m from permanent water, although in most of these cases permanent water represented the nearest water source (Anderson et al. 1988:215–217, 1999b:249). As noted in the distance to water analyses, sites of all periods tended to concentrate within roughly 300 m of watercourses, regardless of whether they were intermittent or permanent. While distance to water clearly shaped prehistoric settlement locally, this water source could be either intermittent or permanent; close proximity to a permanent water source does not appear to have been a critical concern (see also McGimsey 1996:145).

Prehistoric components at Fort Polk also tended to occur great distances from confluences, although this distance, on the average, was lower than the distance to permanent water (Table 4.6). A majority of these confluences were Rank 2, representing the joining of two Rank 1 streams. This reinforces the observation noted earlier that sites on Fort Polk tended to occur away from higher-order streams and at some distance from permanent water sources. This patterning, of course, is partially a reflection of the local physiography: the Fort Polk area is at the headwaters/interfluvial areas and away from the main channels of the major streams draining the region, and many of the local watercourses, as a result, are small. The analysis indicates that proximity to a confluence does not appear to have been a major factor shaping prehistoric land use in the Fort Polk area.

In the 1995 analysis these observations about site location in relation to distance to water, elevation above water, and drainage characteristics were strongly supported on the basis of data generated by the installation GIS and utilizing an appreciably larger sample size. As in the 1988 analysis, most sites and isolated finds on the installation occurred within 20 m vertical elevation of water. Likewise, sites occurred in close proximity to intermittent watercourses and at much greater distances from permanent watercourses (Figures 4.5 and 4.6).

LANDFORM CHARACTERISTICS

Until the 1988 HPP was released and distance to water and soils measures

were shown to be variables more easily replicated than landform characteristics, landform analyses received considerable attention in early attempts
to model prehistoric site location on Fort Polk. The Fort Polk Archaeological Survey team advanced a detailed landform classification scheme (Servello,
ed. 1983), although given its complexity and difficulty in application, subsequent investigators turned, to good effect, to greatly simplified landform
classification schemes. A particularly successful application of this kind of
analysis on Fort Polk was New World Research's tripartite classification of
installation physiography into summit, slope, and bottomland categories
(Thomas et al. 1982) (see Table 3.2). The 1988 HPP analysis made use of a
tripartite primary landform classification (bottomland terraces, upland ridge
slopes, and upland ridge crests) that was similar to that employed by New
World Research, with these categories in turn subdivided by the primary
Ruhe (1975) landform categories employed by the Fort Polk Archaeological
Survey team (saddle, knoll, nose, crests or level areas, and slopes). The occurrences of all prehistoric components found on the installation that fell
within these major and minor categories in the 1988 analysis sample are
given in Table 4.7. Random sample points were drawn and examined using
the same approach in an attempt to determine the incidence of these landforms in the natural environment, and this measure was useful for comparative purposes.

Comparatively few bottomland terrace components were noted (n = 185;
11.48 percent of classified components), at least in comparison with the
numbers of components observed in the uplands on ridge slopes (n = 1,197;
74.26 percent) and on ridge crests (n = 230; 14.27 percent) (Table 4.7).
Comparison with the random sample data indicates the degree to which prehistoric components are likely underrepresented in the bottomlands, reinforcing the observations noted in the distance to water analyses. Work on
Fort Polk since 1988 has shown that more sites were present in this zone
than was thought at the time or that were represented in the sample then
available for analysis. Of particular interest, a great majority of the prehistoric components were observed on ridge slopes, rather than in the bottoms
or on ridge crests, suggesting that selection for level ground was not a primary consideration shaping prehistoric land use. This observation, while
seemingly counterintuitive, was strongly supported by the analyses of aspect and slope data conducted during both the 1988 and 1995 analyses, as
reported in subsequent sections of this chapter. Much of this patterning appears due to characteristics of the local environment. As the random sample
data in Table 4.7 indicate, sloping terrain forms the majority of the landscape, a finding also reinforced by the 1995 slope and aspect analyses and
by the data in the installation GIS (see Table 4.8). Perfectly level terrain is

Table 4.6 — Prehistoric components on Fort Polk: occurrence by distance to nearest confluence, stream rank of drainage below nearest confluence, and type of water below confluence (1988 HPP analysis sample)

	Stream Type			No Data	Stream Rank				Distance Summary			
	Intermittent	Permanent	Total		R1	R2	R3	R4	Min	Max	Avg	SD
Early Paleoindian	—	1	1	—	—	1	—	—	1,625	1,625	1,625.0	0.0
Middle Paleoindian	—	13	13	—	—	11	2	—	250	1,910	996.9	495.8
Late Paleoindian	5	19	24	—	—	10	12	2	100	1,550	695.8	451.1
Early Archaic	2	3	5	—	—	2	3	—	125	1,675	920.0	714.2
Middle to Late Archaic	10	26	36	—	—	19	14	3	75	1,625	622.2	464.1
Late Archaic	18	37	55	1	—	26	24	5	125	1,625	718.2	432.2
Late Archaic to Woodland	23	45	68	—	—	36	25	7	50	2,175	696.7	459.8
Early Woodland	1	—	1	—	—	—	1	—	150	150	150.0	0.0
Middle Woodland	6	11	17	—	—	9	5	3	150	1,625	667.6	441.9
Middle to Late Woodland	8	11	19	—	—	13	5	1	175	1,625	877.6	467.0
Unspecified Woodland	3	6	9	—	—	4	4	1	125	1,425	711.1	519.8
Late Woodland	11	19	30	—	—	19	10	1	150	1,625	796.7	426.3
Unspecified Formative	68	99	167	3	—	105	49	13	25	1,625	697.8	409.3
Early Caddoan	17	28	45	—	—	25	16	4	125	1,625	668.9	429.5
Caddo (Projectile Points)	2	12	14	1	—	11	2	1	125	1,450	839.3	430.0
Caddo (Ceramics)	4	8	12	1	—	7	3	2	150	1,450	587.5	436.6
Late Caddoan	6	5	11	—	—	6	4	1	100	1,275	577.3	396.6
Unknown Prehistoric	359	727	1,086	75	—	620	358	108	0	2,275	665.1	400.8
Total Prehistoric	543	1,070	1,613	—	0	924	537	152	0	2,275	680.5	412.3
(% of Total)	(33.66)	(66.34)	(100.00)	—	(0.00)	(57.28)	(33.29)	(9.42)				

Table 4.6 (cont.) — Prehistoric components on Fort Polk: occurrence by distance to nearest confluence, stream rank of drainage below nearest confluence, and type of water below confluence (1988 HPP analysis sample)

	Stream Type			No Data	Stream Rank				Distance Summary			
	Intermittent	Permanent	Total		R1	R2	R3	R4	Min	Max	Avg	SD
Total Diagnostic	184	343	527	—	0	304	179	44	25	2,175	712.4	435.9
(% of Total)	(34.91)	(65.09)	(100.00)	—	(0.00)	(57.69)	(33.97)	(8.35)				
Total Nondiagnostic	359	727	1,086	—	0	620	358	108	0	2,275	665.1	400.8
(% of Total)	(33.06)	(66.94)	(100.00)	—	(0.00)	(57.09)	(32.97)	(9.94)				
Occurrence in Random Sample	155	207	362	—	0	219	107	36	25	1,825	688.9	362
(% of Total)	(42.82)	(57.18)	(100.00)	—	(0.00)	(60.50)	(29.56)	(9.94)				
Main Fort	99	151	250	—	0	139	80	31	25	1,825	692.8	361.8
(% of Total)	(39.60)	(60.40)	(100.00)	—	(0.00)	(55.60)	(32.00)	(12.40)				
Peason Ridge	56	56	112	—	0	80	27	5	75	1,500	680.1	364.2
(% of Total)	(50.00)	(50.00)	(100.00)	—	(0.00)	(71.43)	(24.11)	(4.46)				

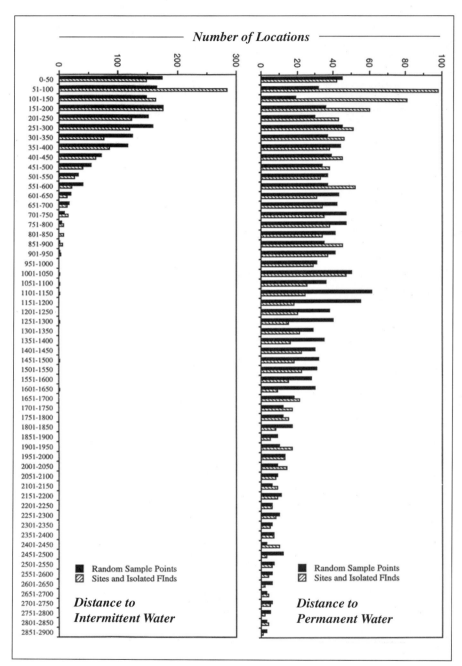

Figure 4.5 — Distance to permanent and intermittent water for sites and isolated finds, as well as for random sample locations, on the Main Fort, 1995 analysis sample.

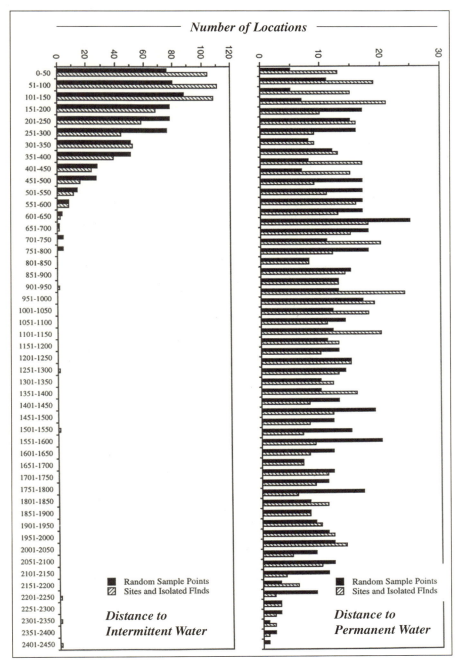

Figure 4.6 — Distance to permanent and intermittent water for sites and isolated finds, as well as for random sample locations, on Peason Ridge, 1995 analysis sample.

Table 4.7 — Prehistoric components on Fort Polk: occurrence by landform type (1988 HPP analysis sample)

Major Feature: Major Element: Minor Element:	Terrace Terrace Slope	 Level	 Subtot.	Ridge Crest Crest	 Knoll	 Nose	 Subtot.	 Saddle	 Knoll	Ridge Slope Nose	 Slope	 Subtot.	 Grand Total
Early Paleoindian	—	—	—	—	—	—	—	—	—	—	1	1	1
Middle Paleoindian	—	—	—	1	2	—	3	—	1	1	8	10	13
Late Paleoindian	—	3	3	2	4	—	6	—	2	1	12	15	24
Early Archaic	—	1	1	—	1	—	—	—	1	—	3	4	5
Middle/Late Archaic	—	8	8	1	1	—	2	—	—	9	17	26	36
Late Archaic	—	10	10	3	4	—	7	—	1	13	24	38	55
Late Archaic/Woodland	1	7	8	6	5	1	12	—	1	17	30	48	68
Early Woodland	—	—	—	—	—	—	—	—	—	1	—	1	1
Middle Woodland	1	2	3	—	1	—	—	—	—	6	8	14	17
Middle/Late Woodland	—	—	—	—	1	—	1	—	1	5	12	18	19
Unspecified Woodland	1	3	4	—	—	—	—	—	—	3	2	5	9
Late Woodland	—	4	4	—	3	—	3	—	—	7	16	23	30
Unspecified Formative	2	21	23	3	14	1	18	—	1	41	84	126	167
Early Caddoan	—	4	4	1	—	—	1	—	—	16	24	40	45
Caddo (Projectile Points)	—	1	1	1	3	—	4	—	—	3	6	9	14
Caddo (Ceramics)	—	—	—	1	—	—	1	—	—	4	7	11	12
Late Caddoan	—	—	—	—	1	1	2	—	—	4	5	9	11
Unknown Prehistoric	8	108	116	62	77	31	170	5	11	346	437	799	1,085
Total Prehistoric	13	172	185	81	115	34	230	5	19	477	696	1,197	1,612
(% of Total)	(0.81)	(10.67)	(11.48)	(5.02)	(7.13)	(2.11)	(14.27)	(0.31)	(1.18)	(29.59)	(43.18)	(74.26)	(100.00)

Table 4.7 (cont.) — Prehistoric components on Fort Polk: occurrence by landform type (1988 HPP analysis sample)

Major Feature: Major Element: Minor Element:	Terrace Terrace			Ridge Crest				Ridge Slope					Grand Total
	Slope	Level	Subtot.	Crest	Knoll	Nose	Subtot.	Saddle	Knoll	Nose	Slope	Subtot.	
Total Diagnostic	5	64	69	19	38	3	60	0	8	131	259	398	527
(% of Total)	(0.95)	(12.14)	(13.09)	(3.61)	(7.21)	(0.57)	(11.39)	(0.00)	(1.52)	(24.86)	(49.15)	(75.52)	(100.00)
Total Nondiagnostic	8	108	116	62	77	31	170	5	11	346	437	799	1,085
(% of Total)	(0.74)	(9.95)	(10.69)	(5.71)	(7.10)	(2.86)	(15.67)	(0.46)	(1.01)	(31.89)	(40.28)	(73.64)	(100.00)
Random Sample	0	62	62	13	7	19	56	7	11	152	91	254	362
(% of Total)	(0.00)	(17.13)	(17.13)	(3.59)	(1.93)	(5.25)	(15.47)	(1.93)	(3.04)	(41.99)	(25.14)	(70.17)	(100.00)
Main Fort	0	42	42	9	2	17	34	6	6	107	61	174	250
(% of Total)	(0.00)	(16.80)	(16.80)	(3.60)	(0.80)	(6.80)	(13.60)	(2.40)	(2.40)	(42.80)	(24.40)	(69.60)	(100.00)
Peason Ridge	0	20	20	4	5	2	12	1	5	45	30	80	112
(% of Total)	(0.00)	(17.86)	(17.86)	(3.57)	(4.46)	(1.79)	(10.71)	(0.89)	(4.46)	(40.18)	(26.79)	(71.43)	(100.00)

Table 4.8 — Slope categories for sites and isolated finds, and for random sample locations, on the Main Fort and Peason Ridge at Fort Polk (1995 analysis sample)

Landscape Slope Category	Main Fort			Peason Ridge		
	Acreage	Sites and Isolated Finds	Random Sample	Acreage	Sites and Isolated Finds	Random Sample
Flat to moderately sloping (0–5%)	30,331.52	568	726	16,447.67	405	329
(% of Total)	(28.62)	(29.46)	(49.42)	(48.64)	(53.86)	(49.33)
Moderately sloping (5–8%)	42,763.42	812	237	1,856.215	32	4
(% of Total)	(40.35)	(42.12)	(16.13)	(5.49)	(4.26)	(0.60)
Steeply sloping (>8%)	32,674.43	498	495	15,502.66	308	330
(% of Total)	(30.83)	(25.83)	(33.70)	(45.84)	(40.96)	(49.48)
No data	0	50	4	0	0	4
(% of Total)	(0.00)	(2.59)	(0.27)	(0.00)	(0.00)	(0.60)
Water bodies	204.10	0	7	10.181	7	0
(% of Total)	(0.19)	(0.00)	(0.48)	(0.03)	(0.93)	(0.00)
Total	105,973.48	1,928	1,469	33,816.77	752	667
(% of Total)	(100.00)	(100.00)	(100.00)	(100.00)	(100.00)	(100.00)

not all that common, particularly in close proximity to water, which appears to have been a critical factor. Slightly sloping terrain may also make a better camp location than flat terrain, since it might drain more readily, and it might also offer better vantages from which to look for game. Finally, while fairly large expanses of level terrain are noted in upland areas, they tend to occur at considerable distance from water and may have been avoided for this reason. These results tend to weaken the plausibility of models favoring prehistoric use of drainage divides, such as Guy and Gunn's (1983) Ridge Causeway hypothesis described in Chapter 3 (see also Meyer et al. 1996a:104).

A number of additional observations about prehistoric land use in the Fort Polk area can be derived from Table 4.7. Ridge side slopes, rather than ridge nose slopes, are more commonly represented in the sample, a finding at odds with interpretations emphasizing prehistoric use of ridge noses where game surveillance was presumably more favorable. The prehistoric occupants of Fort Polk apparently were at ease on both landform types. Components dating to later in the prehistoric sequence, after the Middle Archaic period, tended to be more commonly represented on terraces, an occurrence that may be a result of depositional conditions (i.e., more recent deposits may not be as deeply buried and hence may be more accessible) or actual greater use of this zone compared with the uplands during these periods. The results of subsequent research, notably the intensive site testing program undertaken in recent years and the excavations at 16VN791 and 16VN794, indicate that depositional factors are at least part of the reason for this patterning. Earlier components, particularly Late Paleoindian period San Patrice assemblages, have been found at depths of a meter or more on a number of sites on the installation, including in floodplain and terrace settings. Earlier components are thus likely underrepresented in survey assemblages in areas where deep deposits are likely, unless appropriate site-discovery procedures are employed. Landform analyses were not conducted during the 1995 predictive modeling effort, since they were not needed to yield useful probability zones, nor were the landforms readily delimited using the GIS.

SITE ASPECT CHARACTERISTICS

The 1988 analysis indicated that site aspect, the direction sites on sloping terrain face, was a comparatively minor factor shaping the location of prehistoric components (Table 4.9). Only approximately one-quarter of the prehistoric components in the 1988 sample were on level ground (n = 406; 25.19 percent). No pronounced preference for particular compass orientations was observed, although somewhat greater than average numbers of

Table 4.9 — Prehistoric components on Fort Polk: occurrence by landform aspect (1988 HPP analysis sample)

Landform Aspect	Level	NW	N	NE	E	SE	S	SW	W	Total	No Data
Early Paleoindian	—	1	—	—	—	—	—	—	—	1	—
Middle Paleoindian	3	3	—	—	—	—	1	3	3	13	—
Late Paleoindian	9	3	—	3	—	1	2	4	2	24	—
Early Archaic	1	—	—	1	—	1	1	1	—	5	—
Middle/Late Archaic	10	5	1	2	5	—	3	5	5	36	—
Late Archaic	17	7	3	3	3	3	7	11	1	55	—
Late Archaic/Woodland	19	12	1	7	4	7	4	12	2	68	1
Early Woodland	—	—	—	—	—	—	1	—	—	1	—
Middle Woodland	2	4	—	1	1	1	4	2	2	17	—
Middle/Late Woodland	1	3	—	1	1	3	1	6	3	19	—
Unspecified Woodland	3	—	1	2	—	1	—	1	1	9	—
Late Woodland	7	6	—	1	2	2	3	5	4	30	—
Unspecified Formative	39	23	6	15	14	18	14	23	15	167	3
Early Caddoan	5	4	3	3	4	5	7	12	2	45	—
Caddo (Projectile Points)	5	2	—	1	2	—	—	3	1	14	—
Caddo (Ceramics)	1	1	1	—	—	3	1	4	1	12	1
Late Caddoan	2	1	—	—	—	2	1	5	—	11	—
Unknown Prehistoric	282	96	65	116	81	119	83	161	82	1,085	76
Total Prehistoric	406	171	81	156	117	166	133	258	124	1,612	81
(% of Total)	(25.19)	(10.61)	(5.02)	(9.68)	(7.26)	(10.30)	(8.25)	(16.01)	(7.68)	(100.00)	—

Table 4.9 (cont.) — Prehistoric components on Fort Polk: occurrence by landform aspect (1988 HPP analysis sample)

Landform Aspect	Level	NW	N	NE	E	SE	S	SW	W	Total	No Data
Total Diagnostic	124	75	16	40	36	47	50	97	42	527	5
(% of Total)	(23.53)	(14.23)	(3.04)	(7.59)	(6.83)	(8.92)	(9.48)	(18.41)	(7.97)	(100.00)	—
Total Nondiagnostic	282	96	65	116	81	119	83	161	82	1,085	—
(% of Total)	(25.99)	(8.85)	(5.99)	(10.69)	(7.47)	(10.97)	(7.65)	(14.84)	(7.55)	(100.00)	—
Random Sample	107	37	19	36	14	61	17	64	7	362	—
(% of Total)	(29.56)	(10.22)	(5.25)	(9.94)	(3.87)	(16.85)	(4.70)	(17.68)	(1.93)	(100.00)	—
Main Fort	75	23	9	28	11	42	11	46	5	250	—
Peason Ridge	32	14	10	8	3	19	6	18	2	112	—

components had southwestern aspects and somewhat fewer than average had northern aspects. Given the general slope of the terrain in the region, which is to the south and the Gulf, this distribution may be an artifact of regional physiography; this inference is supported by the random sample data, which is characterized by a higher than average incidence of southeast and southwest aspects. East- to south-facing aspects have been shown to be preferred settings for extended settlement by prehistoric populations in regions characterized by moderate to pronounced daily or seasonal temperature fluctuations (Jochim 1976). The Fort Polk data, exhibiting no convincing concern for site aspect, may reflect the relatively mild local climate, a preponderance of short-term occupations, or both. No pronounced trends were observed within particular periods of occupation, suggesting that fairly consistent land use or site-selection practices may have been operating.

The 1995 analysis of slope generated using the installation GIS generally supported the findings of the 1988 analysis (Table 4.10; note that data were not available for all parts of the installation). No pronounced preferences for particular aspects were indicated, although a slightly bimodal distribution was evident for sites and isolated finds over both the Peason Ridge and Main Fort datasets, with peaks in northeast and southwest to western aspects. Likewise, northwest to northern aspects are somewhat less common than average. The southwestern trend is evident in the random sample data as well, however, suggesting that distribution is to some extent shaped as much by regional physiographic conditions as by cultural preference. As during the earlier analysis, a moderate number of sites had no aspect; that is, they were located on level ground.

SURFICIAL GEOLOGY

Examination of the geological associations of archaeological sites found on Fort Polk has received limited attention in past analyses, although Servello (1983) and his colleagues devoted considerable effort to identifying lithic raw materials and source areas on the installation, as have archaeologists working on the Kisatchie National Forest (see Chapters 2 and 3). In the 1988 HPP, prehistoric component distributions were examined over a series of engineering soils and geology categories obtained from installation Terrain Analysis Maps (Tables 4.11 and 4.12). These analyses indicated that many components were situated on sandy, well-drained soils located on gently to steeply sloping uplands and less commonly on poorly drained floodplain deposits. Sites and isolated finds also tended to occur most typically in areas where the prominent surficial geological features were unconsolidated sands, silts, or clays and less often in areas where either alluvium or gravel deposits were present.

Table 4.10 — Aspects for sites, isolated finds, and random sample locations on the Main Fort and Peason Ridge at Fort Polk (1995 analysis sample)

Aspect ° E of N	Main Fort				Peason Ridge			
	Sites and Isolated Finds		Random Sample Points		Sites and Isolated Finds		Random Sample Points	
	No.	(%)	No.	(%)	No.	(%)	No.	(%)
0	27	(1.85)	16	(1.09)	13	(1.99)	15	(2.25)
15	27	(1.85)	17	(1.16)	12	(1.84)	14	(2.10)
30	103	(7.04)	20	(1.36)	20	(3.06)	19	(2.85)
45	79	(5.40)	61	(4.15)	28	(4.29)	25	(3.75)
60	57	(3.90)	45	(3.06)	9	(1.38)	12	(1.80)
75	49	(3.35)	48	(3.27)	11	(1.68)	16	(2.40)
90	87	(5.95)	98	(6.67)	14	(2.14)	29	(4.35)
105	58	(3.96)	67	(4.56)	14	(2.14)	13	(1.95)
120	37	(2.53)	47	(3.20)	15	(2.30)	10	(1.50)
135	66	(4.51)	52	(3.54)	29	(4.44)	24	(3.60)
150	15	(1.03)	47	(3.20)	13	(1.99)	22	(3.30)
165	33	(2.26)	45	(3.06)	23	(3.52)	14	(2.10)
180	51	(3.49)	70	(4.77)	29	(4.44)	24	(3.60)
195	52	(3.55)	53	(3.61)	15	(2.30)	17	(2.55)
210	59	(4.03)	57	(3.88)	6	(0.92)	17	(2.55)
225	78	(5.33)	93	(6.33)	23	(3.52)	24	(3.60)
240	71	(4.85)	54	(3.68)	13	(1.99)	16	(2.40)
255	79	(5.40)	53	(3.61)	17	(2.60)	19	(2.85)
270	72	(4.92)	69	(4.70)	33	(5.05)	29	(4.35)
285	51	(3.49)	46	(3.13)	22	(3.37)	25	(3.75)
300	34	(2.32)	36	(2.45)	28	(4.29)	28	(4.20)
315	33	(2.26)	34	(2.31)	34	(5.21)	50	(7.50)
330	24	(1.64)	19	(2.31)	43	(6.58)	26	(3.90)
345	16	(1.09)	15	(1.02)	17	(2.60)	23	(3.45)
No aspect	276	(18.87)	307	(20.90)	192	(29.40)	156	(23.39)
Total	1,463	(100.00)	1,469	(100.00)	653	(100.00)	667	(100.00)
Mean	169.423		172.022		188.796		193.268	
Median	180		180		195		210	
Mode	90		90		305		315	
SD	93.488		87.691		102.867		105.658	

Table 4.11 — Prehistoric components on Fort Polk: occurrence by engineering soil association categories (1988 HPP analysis sample)

	ES1	*ES3*	*ES4*	*ES5*	*ES6*	*Total*	*ND*
Early Paleoindian	1	—	—	—	—	1	—
Middle Paleoindian	7	4	—	—	2	13	—
Late Paleoindian	14	3	4	1	2	24	—
Early Archaic	2	1	—	—	2	5	—
Middle/Late Archaic	16	6	9	1	4	36	—
Late Archaic	29	12	8	3	4	56	—
Late Archaic/Woodland	42	14	9	1	2	68	—
Early Woodland	—	—	1	—	—	1	—
Middle Woodland	7	5	5	—	—	17	—
Middle/Late Woodland	7	7	3	—	2	19	—
Unspecified Woodland	5	2	2	—	—	9	—
Late Woodland	18	7	2	1	2	30	—
Unspecified Formative	90	41	22	4	11	168	2
Early Caddoan	27	8	8	—	2	45	—
Caddo (Projectile Points)	9	4	1	—	—	14	—
Caddo (Ceramics)	5	2	4	1	1	13	—
Late Caddoan	8	1	1	—	1	11	—
Unknown Prehistoric	621	215	120	34	112	1,102	59
Total Prehistoric	908	332	199	46	147	1,632	61
(% of Total)	(55.64)	(20.34)	(12.19)	(2.82)	(9.01)	(100.00)	—
Total Diagnostic	287	117	79	12	35	530	2
(% of Total)	(54.15)	(22.08)	(14.91)	(2.26)	(6.60)	(100.00)	—
Total Nondiagnostic	621	215	120	34	112	1,102	59
(% of Total)	(56.35)	(19.51)	(10.89)	(3.09)	(10.16)	(100.00)	—
Acres Mapped	67,533	31,279	13,845	2,129	21,384	136,170	—
(% of Total)	(49.59)	(22.97)	(10.17)	(1.56)	(15.71)	(100.00)	—
Main Fort	49,995	26,206	11,722	2,129	15,520	105,572	—
Peason Ridge	17,538	5,073	2,123	0	5,864	30,598	—

ES1 = Sandy, moderately well-drained soils on undulating to rolling uplands
ES3 = Clayey, moderately well-drained soils on gently to strongly sloping uplands
ES4 = Silty or sandy, poorly drained floodplain soils
ES5 = Silty, moderately well-drained soils on nearly level to undulating terraces
ES6 = Sandy, well-drained soils on dissected rolling to steeply sloping terraces
ND   = No data

Table 4.12 — Prehistoric components on Fort Polk: occurrence by engineering geology categories (1988 HPP analysis sample)

	EG1	EG2	EG3	EG4	Total	ND
Early Paleoindian	1	—	—	—	1	—
Middle Paleoindian	7	4	—	2	13	—
Late Paleoindian	15	3	4	2	24	—
Early Archaic	2	1	—	2	5	—
Middle/Late Archaic	18	6	9	3	36	—
Late Archaic	32	11	8	5	56	—
Late Archaic/Woodland	45	12	9	2	68	—
Early Woodland	—	—	1	—	1	—
Middle Woodland	7	5	5	—	17	—
Middle/Late Woodland	9	7	3	—	19	—
Unspecified Woodland	5	2	2	—	9	—
Late Woodland	20	7	2	1	30	—
Unspecified Formative	101	39	22	6	168	2
Early Caddoan	30	6	8	1	45	—
Caddo (Projectile Points)	9	4	1	—	14	—
Caddo (Ceramics)	5	2	4	2	13	—
Late Caddoan	9	1	1	—	11	—
Unknown Prehistoric	679	204	120	99	1,102	59
Total Prehistoric	994	314	199	125	1,632	61
(% of Total)	(60.91)	(19.24)	(12.19)	(7.66)	(100.00)	—
Total Diagnostic	315	110	79	26	530	2
(% of Total)	(59.43)	(20.75)	(14.91)	(4.91)	(100.00)	—
Total Nondiagnostic	679	204	120	99	1,102	59
(% of Total)	(61.62)	(18.51)	(10.89)	(8.98)	(100.00)	—
Acres Mapped	69,316	30,832	14,959	21,934	137,041	—
(% of Total)	(50.58)	(22.50)	(10.92)	(16.00)	(100.00)	—
Main Fort	48,256	26,630	12,469	19,126	106,481	—
Peason Ridge	21,060	4,202	2,490	2,808	30,560	—

EG1 = *Layered mixtures of predominantly sand with silt and clay*
EG2 = *Thick layers of clays and silts separated by thin layers of predominantly sand*
EG3 = *Alluvium*
EG4 = *Pleistocene terrace deposits of sand and silt with lenses of clay and gravel*
ND = *No data*

Data on surficial geological formations for the Main Fort area, based on Welch's (1942) map of Vernon Parish, were available as a GIS data layer during the 1995 analysis. The distribution of sites and isolated finds on the Main Fort by major geological formation derived from this data layer is found in Table 4.13. While most sites tend to occur on the Miocene Blounts Creek Member and lesser numbers on the Miocene Castor Creek Member and the Pleistocene Williana Formation, these are the predominant forma-tions in the area (see Figure 4.4). Although the presence of gravel cherts has been noted in the Pleistocene Williana Formation (see Chapter 1), there do

Table 4.13 — Surficial geological formations for sites and isolated finds on the Main Fort at Fort Polk (1995 analysis sample)

Geological Formation	Eligible	Potentially Eligible	Not Eligible	Total Sites
Recent alluvium	9	22	127	158
(% of Total)	(15.52)	(15.07)	(7.37)	(8.20)
Pleistocene Prairie Formation*	1	5	22	28
(% of Total)	(1.72)	(3.42)	(1.28)	(1.45)
Pleistocene Montgomery Formation*	1	0	1	2
(% of Total)	(1.72)	(0.00)	(0.06)	(0.10)
Pleistocene Bentley Formation*	0	3	4	7
(% of Total)	(0.00)	(2.05)	(0.23)	(0.36)
Pleistocene Williana Formation	2	10	275	287
(% of Total)	(3.45)	(6.85)	(15.95)	(14.89)
Miocene Blounts Creek Member	30	86	968	1,084
(% of Total)	(51.72)	(58.90)	(56.15)	(56.22)
Miocene Castor Creek Member	15	20	325	360
(% of Total)	(25.86)	(13.70)	(18.85)	(18.67)
Miocene Williamson Creek Member*	0	0	0	0
(% of Total)	(0.00)	(0.00)	(0.00)	(0.00)
No data	0	0	2	2
(% of Total)	(0.00)	(0.00)	(0.12)	(0.10)
Totals	58	146	1,724	1,928
(% of Total)	(100.00)	(100.00)	(100.00)	(100.00)

* Minimally represented on Fort Polk

not appear to be an inordinate number of sites or sites eligible for the National Register of Historic Places (NRHP) associated with this formation.

SOIL CHARACTERISTICS

The distribution of prehistoric components by major soil series and specific soil types was also examined in 1988, using data from areas of the Main Fort where fine-grained soils mapping had been completed (Anderson and Joseph 1988:223–227; Anderson et al. 1999b:362–363) (Table 4.14). A preference for Briley, Ruston, and Susquehanna soil types and series was indicated, although these also appear to be the most common soil types in the Main Fort area, accounting for almost three-quarters of the mapped sample. The Briley, Ruston, and Susquehanna types are sandy, well-drained, gently sloping to sloping upland soils. The most pronounced pattern to emerge from the analysis was the occurrence of 15.87 percent of all prehistoric components and just over a quarter of all the diagnostic components on Guyton soils, a comparatively minor series that tends to occur in floodplains and on low terraces. The presence of large numbers of identifiable components on soils from this zone indicates that areas in and adjacent to the floodplain contain a disproportionate amount of unusual sites, reinforcing earlier findings noted in the distance to water analyses. The original soils analysis was supported by the 1995 reanalysis using GIS-derived data from across the entire installation (Anderson et al. 1999b:364) (Table 4.15). On the Main Fort, sites occurred in slightly higher than expected incidence on Guyton floodplain soils and on some Briley and Susquehanna types, although the incidence on Ruston types was slightly lower than expected in the reanalysis. The number of sites on Malbis soil types was also somewhat lower than expected given the natural occurrence of the series on the installation. On Peason Ridge, a slightly lower than expected incidence of sites was observed on Guyton soils. The Guyton soils distribution suggests that use of floodplain settings, which are small and quite localized on Peason Ridge, was not as important as on the Main Fort where floodplains are much larger and more extensive.

SLOPE CHARACTERISTICS

During the 1988 analysis, slope categories were determined using the 647-component sample from the Main Fort locations where fine-grained soils data were available (Table 4.16) (the same sample used in the soil type analyses). Interestingly, the vast majority of the prehistoric components occurred on sloping terrain of from 1 to 5 percent or on slopes greater than 5 percent (n = 540; 83.5 percent), a pattern in keeping with that observed over the landform and aspect distributions. Given the comparatively low incidence

Table 4.14 — Major soil series for prehistoric components on Fort Polk (1988 HPP analysis sample)

Soil Series	Beau	Betis	Briley	Cahaba	Guyton	Holly	Malbis	Osier	Ruston	Sawyer	Susq	Vaiden	Total	ND
Early Paleoindian	—	—	—	—	—	—	—	—	—	—	—	—	0	—
Middle Paleoindian	1	—	1	—	—	—	—	—	—	—	—	—	2	—
Late Paleoindian	—	—	1	—	2	—	—	—	1	—	3	—	7	—
Early Archaic	1	—	1	—	—	—	—	—	1	—	1	—	3	—
Middle/Late Archaic	1	—	3	—	4	—	—	—	2	—	4	—	14	—
Late Archaic	1	1	6	—	5	—	—	—	3	—	7	—	24	—
Late Archaic/Woodland	1	1	8	—	8	—	1	—	6	—	8	—	33	—
Early Woodland	—	—	—	—	1	—	—	—	—	—	—	—	1	—
Middle Woodland	—	—	1	—	3	—	—	—	2	—	—	—	6	—
Middle/Late Woodland	—	—	1	—	—	—	—	—	—	1	2	—	4	—
Unspecified Woodland	—	—	—	—	3	—	—	—	—	—	3	—	6	—
Late Woodland	—	—	1	—	1	—	—	—	1	—	4	—	7	—
Unspecified Formative	—	—	10	—	13	—	—	1	9	—	14	—	47	—
Early Caddoan	1	2	—	—	4	—	1	—	4	—	2	—	13	—
Caddo (Projectile Points)	—	—	2	—	1	—	—	—	—	1	1	—	4	—
Caddo (Ceramics)	—	—	—	—	2	—	1	—	—	—	1	—	4	—
Late Caddoan	1	—	1	—	1	—	—	—	1	—	—	—	4	—
Unknown Prehistoric	4	21	149	4	55	0	12	6	101	12	104	1	469	695
Total Prehistoric	10	25	185	4	103	0	16	7	131	13	154	1	649	695
(% of Total)	(1.54)	(3.85)	(28.51)	(0.62)	(15.87)	(0.00)	(2.47)	(1.08)	(20.18)	(2.00)	(23.73)	(0.15)	(100.00)	—

Table 4.14 (cont.) — Major soil series for prehistoric components on Fort Polk (1988 HPP analysis sample)

Soil Series	Beau	Betis	Briley	Cahaba	Guyton	Holly	Malbis	Osier	Ruston	Sawyer	Susq	Vaiden	Total	ND
Total Diagnostic	6	4	36	0	48	0	4	1	30	1	50	0	180	—
(% of Total)	(3.33)	(2.22)	(20.00)	(0.00)	(26.67)	(0.00)	(2.22)	(0.56)	(16.67)	(0.56)	(27.77)	(0.00)	(100.00)	—
Total Nondiagnostic	4	21	149	4	55	0	12	6	101	12	104	1	469	—
(% of Total)	(2.22)	(4.48)	(31.77)	(2.22)	(11.73)	(0.00)	(2.56)	(1.28)	(21.54)	(2.56)	(22.17)	(0.21)	(100.00)	—
Acreage of Series	239	5,424	14,485	201	4,699	2,043	3,634	424	16,681	376	17,920	581	66,800	(93)
(% of Mapped Area)	(0.36)	(8.12)	(21.68)	(0.30)	(7.03)	(3.06)	(5.44)	(0.63)	(24.97)	(0.56)	(26.82)	(0.87)	(100.00)	(0.14)

Beau = Beauregard   Susq = Susquehanna
Holly = Hollywood   ND   = No data

Table 4.15 — Soil types for sites, isolated finds, and random sample locations on the Main Fort and Peason Ridge at Fort Polk (1995 analysis sample)

Soil Type (Symbol) / Soil Description	Main Fort			Peason Ridge		
	Acres	Sites and Isolated Finds	Random Sample	Acres	Sites and Isolated Finds	Random Sample
Ba Beauregard fine sandy loam, 1–3% slopes	1,160.97	5	9	123.06	5	4
(% of Total)	(1.10)	(0.36)	(0.61)	(0.36)	(0.77)	(0.60)
Bd Betis loamy fine sand, 1–5% slopes	2,288.94	23	27	675.97	18	8
(% of Total)	(2.17)	(1.64)	(1.84)	(2.00)	(2.76)	(1.20)
Be Betis loamy fine sand, 5–20% slopes	4,461.24	50	56	320.04	7	2
(% of Total)	(4.23)	(3.57)	(3.81)	(0.95)	(1.07)	(0.30)
Br Briley loamy fine sand, 1–5% slopes	10,504.02	183	191	3,388.33	66	60
(% of Total)	(9.97)	(13.05)	(13.00)	(10.03)	(10.11)	(9.00)
Bs Briley loamy fine sand, 5–12% slopes	10,886.04	161	185	1,856.22	26	39
(% of Total)	(10.33)	(11.48)	(12.59)	(5.50)	(3.98)	(5.85)
Ch Cahaba fine sandy loam, 1–3% slopes	1,026.65	16	7	47.15	3	1
(% of Total)	(0.97)	(1.14)	(0.48)	(0.14)	(0.46)	(0.15)
Co Corrigan loam, 1–5% slopes	0.00	0	0	3,268.64	71	74
(% of Total)	(0.00)	(0.00)	(0.00)	(9.68)	(10.87)	(11.09)
GY Guyton soils, frequently flooded	10,347.26	174	118	2,341.22	32	29
(% of Total)	(9.82)	(12.41)	(8.03)	(6.93)	(4.90)	(4.35)
KH Kisatchie-Rayburn fine sandy loams, 5–30% slopes	22.63	0	0	14,890.25	254	279
(% of Total)	(0.02)	(0.00)	(0.00)	(44.09)	(38.90)	(41.83)

Table 4.15 (cont.) — Soil types for sites, isolated finds, and random sample locations on the Main Fort and Peason Ridge at Fort Polk (1995 analysis sample)

Soil Type (Symbol) / Soil Description	Main Fort			Peason Ridge		
	Acres	Sites and Isolated Finds	Random Sample	Acres	Sites and Isolated Finds	Random Sample
Hw Hollywood clay, 1–5% slopes	1,233.62	8	17	0.00	0	0
(% of Total)	(1.17)	(0.57)	(1.16)	(0.00)	(0.00)	(0.00)
Hy Hollywood clay, 5–12% slopes	766.5	6	11	0.00	0	0
(% of Total)	(0.73)	(0.43)	(0.75)	(0.00)	(0.00)	(0.00)
Ma Malbis fine sandy loam, 1–3% slopes	5,724.71	35	61	732.31	15	15
(% of Total)	(5.43)	(2.50)	(4.15)	(2.17)	(2.30)	(2.25)
Mb Malbis fine sandy loam, 3–5% slopes	5,712.26	40	41	189.97	3	4
(% of Total)	(5.42)	(2.85)	(2.79)	(0.56)	(0.46)	(0.60)
Mh Mayhew very fine sandy loam, 1–5% slopes	0.00	0	0	3,491.33	74	76
(% of Total)	(0.00)	(0.00)	(0.00)	(10.34)	(11.33)	(11.39)
Oc Osier loamy fine sand, 1–3% slopes	831.44	7	2	25.30	1	0
(% of Total)	(0.79)	(0.50)	(0.14)	(0.07)	(0.15)	(0.00)
Ra Rayburn fine sandy loam, 1–5% slopes	0.00	0	0	1,409.95	39	39
(% of Total)	(0.00)	(0.00)	(0.00)	(4.18)	(5.97)	(5.85)
Rs Ruston fine sandy loam, 1–3% slopes	10,587.44	132	169	10.58	1	0
(% of Total)	(10.05)	(9.42)	(11.50)	(0.03)	(0.15)	(0.00)
Rt Ruston fine sandy loam, 3–8% slopes	15,738.10	166	196	0.00	0	0
(% of Total)	(14.94)	(11.84)	(13.34)	(0.00)	(0.00)	(0.00)

Table 4.15 (cont.) — Soil types for sites, isolated finds, and random sample locations on the Main Fort and Peason Ridge at Fort Polk (1995 analysis sample)

Soil Type (Symbol) / Soil Description	Main Fort			Peason Ridge		
	Acres	Sites and Isolated Finds	Random Sample	Acres	Sites and Isolated Finds	Random Sample
Sf Sawyer very fine sandy loam, 1–5% slopes	964.68	17	31	48.63	1	2
(% of Total)	(0.92)	(1.21)	(2.11)	(0.14)	(0.15)	(0.30)
Ss Susquehanna fine sandy loam, 1–5% slopes	5,484.43	75	88	0.00	0	0
(% of Total)	(5.21)	(5.35)	(5.99)	(0.00)	(0.00)	(0.00)
Su Susquehanna fine sandy loam, 5–15% slopes	16,344.78	245	243	0.00	0	0
(% of Total)	(15.52)	(17.48)	(16.54)	(0.00)	(0.00)	(0.00)
Va Vaiden clay, 1–5% slopes	497.36	2	6	0.00	0	0
(% of Total)	(0.47)	(0.14)	(0.41)	(0.00)	(0.00)	(0.00)
Tp Trep loamy fine sand, 1–5% slopes	0.00	0	0	649.28	16	21
(% of Total)	(0.00)	(0.00)	(0.00)	(1.92)	(2.45)	(3.15)
Tr Trep loamy fine sand, 5–15% slopes	0.00	0	0	292.37	8	10
(% of Total)	(0.00)	(0.00)	(0.00)	(0.87)	(1.23)	(1.50)
Water	204.1	1	7	10.18	0	0
(% of Total)	(0.19)	(0.07)	(0.48)	(0.03)	(0.00)	(0.00)
No Data	558.45	56	4	0.00	13	4
(% of Total)	(0.53)	(3.99)	(0.27)	(0.00)	(1.99)	(0.60)
Total	105,345.62	1,402	1,469	33,770.76	653	667
(% of Total)	(100.00)	(100.00)	(100.00)	(100.00)	(100.00)	(100.00)

Table 4.16 — Prehistoric components on Fort Polk: occurrence by major soil slope categories (1988 HPP analysis sample)

Slope Categories	Level	1 to 5 %	>5 %	Total	ND
Early Paleoindian	—	—	—	0	—
Middle Paleoindian	—	2	—	2	—
Late Paleoindian	2	3	2	7	—
Early Archaic	—	2	1	3	—
Middle/Late Archaic	4	5	5	14	—
Late Archaic	5	11	8	24	—
Late Archaic/Woodland	8	15	10	33	—
Early Woodland	1	—	—	1	—
Middle Woodland	3	2	1	6	—
Middle/Late Woodland	—	2	2	4	—
Unspecified Woodland	3	—	3	6	—
Late Woodland	1	3	3	7	—
Unspecified Formative	13	18	16	47	—
Early Caddoan	4	6	4	14	—
Caddo (Projectile Points)	1	—	3	4	—
Caddo (Ceramics)	2	1	1	4	—
Late Caddoan	1	2	1	4	—
Unknown Prehistoric	59	250	158	467	695
Total Prehistoric	107	322	218	647	695
(% of Total)	(16.54)	(49.77)	(33.69)	(100.00)	—
Total Diagnostic	48	72	60	180	—
(% of Total)	(26.67)	(40.00)	(33.33)	(100.00)	—
Total Nondiagnostic	56	254	158	468	—
(% of Total)	(11.97)	(54.27)	(33.76)	(100.00)	—
Acreage Mapped	4,993	38,147	23,660	66,800	—
(% of Total Acreage)	(7.47)	(57.11)	(35.42)	(100.00)	—

ND = No data

of soils on the installation classified as level in the 1988 sample (7.47 percent; Table 4.16), the number of components recorded as occurring on level soils in this analysis (n = 107; 16.54 percent) is somewhat surprising. A considerably higher incidence of level ground was recorded in the landform and particularly the aspect analyses (see Tables 4.7 to 4.10), suggesting the soil slope classifications underrepresent level terrain.

In the 1995 analysis, soil slope values at 20-m resolution were available over the entire installation as a GIS data layer created from a direct reclassification of the soils data (Table 4.8). On the Main Fort, sites and isolated finds were distributed in roughly the same proportions as the slope categories themselves over the total sample. Slightly more sites than expected occurred on flat to moderately sloping terrain and on moderately sloping terrain, while somewhat fewer than expected sites occurred on more steeply sloping terrain. On Peason Ridge, similar patterns were indicated. Once again sites and isolated finds tended to occur slightly more often than expected on flat to moderately sloping terrain and less often than expected on steeply sloping terrain. The low incidence of moderately sloping terrain on Peason Ridge in the data layer, in comparison with the occurrence of this slope category on the Main Fort (5.49 percent vs. 40.35 percent), highlights the topographic differences between the two areas.

POTENTIAL MAXIMUM SOIL DEPTH OF ARCHAEOLOGICAL COMPONENTS

A final analysis conducted using the soils data available from the installation explored the potential depth of archaeological deposits using the 1995 site and isolated find sample (Table 4.17). As discussed previously, this GIS data layer is based on a straight reclassification of the primary soils data. The data layer, reproduced in large-scale color format in the 1999 HPP Map volume (Anderson et al. 1996a), provides researchers information on the potential depths at which archaeological deposits may occur over the installation. Over the sample, sites appear to be distributed in expected proportions over all depth categories, suggesting no areas are being overrepresented or underrepresented in the fieldwork at Fort Polk. Not surprisingly, however, NRHP-eligible or potentially eligible sites occur in appreciably greater than expected incidence in areas where the potential depth of archaeological deposits exceeds 150 cm and much less commonly than expected in areas of shallow deposits (i.e., less than 100 cm). Deep deposits offer a greater likelihood for the preservation and stratigraphic separation of cultural deposits, and sites with these characteristics have traditionally been considered to have much greater research potential.

Potential deposit depth information is valuable for management as well as research purposes, since it can be used to guide field investigations. The soils data indicate, for example, that the potential for deeply stratified deposits (i.e., more than 100 cm in depth) is likely only over a small fraction of the installation, on the order of 17 percent of the terrain on the Main Fort and just under 13 percent of the terrain on Peason Ridge (Table 4.17). While traditional shovel testing techniques are thus appropriate in most areas of the installation, alternative or additional procedures may be appropriate in

Table 4.17 — Potential depth of archaeological deposits for sites and isolated finds, by NRHP eligibility status, on the Main Fort and Peason Ridge at Fort Polk (1995 analysis sample)

	Acres	Eligible	Potentially Eligible	Not Eligible	No Data	Total
Main Fort						
<50 cm	24,670.27	11	39	299	3	352
	(23.28)	(18.97)	(26.71)	(17.41)	(42.86)	(18.26)
<100 cm	63,074.15	24	62	1,111	1	1,198
	(59.52)	(41.38)	(42.47)	(64.71)	(14.29)	(62.14)
<150 cm	6,790.80	4	3	89	0	96
	(6.41)	(6.90)	(2.05)	(5.18)	(0.00)	(4.98)
>150 cm	11,234.15	18	34	179	1	232
	(10.60)	(31.03)	(23.29)	(10.43)	(14.29)	(12.03)
Water bodies	204.10	1	8	39	2	50
	(0.19)	(1.72)	(5.48)	(2.27)	(28.57)	(2.59)
Total	105,973.47	58	146	1,717	7	1,928
	(100.00)	(100.00)	(100.00)	(100.00)	(100.00)	(100.00)
Peason Ridge						
<50 cm	19,460.51	14	50	357	0	421
	(58.47)	(46.67)	(61.73)	(55.69)	(0.00)	(55.91)
<100 cm	9,549.72	4	22	211	0	237
	(28.69)	(13.33)	(27.16)	(32.92)	(0.00)	(31.47)
<150 cm	1,910.78	6	3	41	0	50
	(5.74)	(20.00)	(3.70)	(6.40)	(0.00)	(6.64)
>150 cm	2,353.28	6	5	27	0	38
	(7.07)	(20.00)	(6.17)	(4.21)	(0.00)	(5.05)
Water bodies	8.20	0	1	5	1	7
	(0.20)	(0.00)	(1.23)	(0.78)	(100.00)	(0.93)
Total	33,282.49	30	81	641	1	753
	(100.00)	(100.00)	(100.00)	(100.00)	(100.00)	(100.00)

those areas where deeper deposits are possible. For this reason deep site-testing programs and geoarchaeological research in floodplain areas were recommended in the 1988 HPP and are now routinely carried out. During intensive site-testing work on the installation, in fact, excavation units are routinely taken to a meter or more in depth where conditions warrant such effort. Deep testing has even been incorporated into survey projects. During the 1995–1996 New South Associates, Inc., intensive survey on the Main Fort, for example, a program of deep site testing and geoarchaeological research was undertaken using a backhoe in the floodplain of Whiskey Chitto Creek to explore the possibility of much deeper deposits in that area (Cantley et al. 1997:796–806; see Chapter 2). Although the area examined was small, comprising three trenches 4 to 5 m long and 2 to 3 m deep, a great deal of data was recovered. The deeper floodplain soils were found to be ancient and hence stable, suggesting little channel movement in these locations. The stratigraphy in the trenches indicated cultural materials in this area could be expected to occur up to depths of ca. 1.25 m, in keeping with the expectations of the analysis and data layer.

The 1988 Fort Polk Predictive Model

In the development of the 1988 predictive model, the analyses described above showed that prehistoric sites on Fort Polk, including the vast majority of sites yielding diagnostic components, occurred between 50 and 300 m of a mapped water source and within 10 to 59 feet vertical elevation above this source. Comparatively few sites were documented at distances and elevations above these values, even though these upland areas offered excellent visibility as a result of deflation and erosion, were characterized by comparatively shallow deposits, and had been subject to extensive survey coverage. In areas below these distance and elevation values (i.e., within 50 m and 10 vertical feet of a mapped water source), which commonly encompassed floodplain areas, prehistoric components were likewise uncommon, although this appears to have been an artifact of the dataset available for analysis in 1988, since floodplain areas, particularly those characterized by Guyton soils, have since been shown to have moderate numbers of sites.

The locational and environmental analyses conducted during the preparation of the original (1988) Fort Polk HPP were used to create three site probability zones on Fort Polk. These three zones were as follows:

Zone 1   *Site Probability Indeterminate.* Floodplain areas, defined using the Terrain Analysis Engineering Geology category for alluvium (identical to the Engineering Soils silty or sandy, poorly drained floodplain soils category);

Zone 2   *High Probability.* Locations beyond this floodplain category, yet within either 300 m horizontal distance or 60 feet vertical distance of a mapped water source (all water sources mapped on the USGS 7.5-minute quadrangle sheets encompassing the Fort also occurred on the Terrain Analysis Maps, rendering these categories comparable); and

Zone 3   *Low Probability*. All other areas (upland areas more than 60 feet above and 300 m distant from a mapped water source).

Differing site probabilities were assigned to each zone. Zone 1, occupying floodplain areas, was listed as "Site Probability Indeterminate." Significant sites were thought to occur in this zone, but survey coverage as of 1988 was not sufficient to settle this matter one way or the other. Zone 2, encompassing the area intermediate between the floodplain zone and the uplands, was classified as a "High Probability" area, because of the large numbers of components identified in this area. Zone 3, occupying the upland areas of the base, more than either 60 feet in vertical elevation or 300 m distance (whichever came second) from a mapped water source, was classified as a "Low Probability" area. In the absence of an installation GIS, the probability zones were hand-drawn on a copy of the base Terrain Analysis Map that was included in the 1988 HPP Map volume (Anderson and Macek 1987). The three probability zones were entered into the installation GIS in 1993, however, and in the 1996 Map volume produced as part of the HPP revision these zones were depicted using a green, tan, and dark-brown Army jungle camouflage pattern, which has proven to be a big hit with Army personnel on Fort Polk and beyond (Figure 4.7). The 1988 HPP probability zones were believed to be considerably easier to replicate and locate on project maps and on the ground than probability zones developed during earlier predictive modeling exercises on the installation, all of which had made use of landform characteristics. The HPP zones were also similar to the site probability zones that had been developed by Willingham and Phillips (1987:219–220) and used with considerable success on the nearby Kisatchie National Forest.

The 1988 HPP predictive model guided all survey work at Fort Polk from the late 1980s through the end of 1995, when the 1995 model replaced it. Systematic shovel testing during this period, as per recommendations advanced in the 1988 HPP, occurred at roughly three times the intensity in High and Indeterminate Zones as in the Low Probability Zone. In terms of field procedures, shovel tests were placed at 30-m intervals along transects spaced 30 m apart in High and Indeterminate Probability Zones and at 50-m intervals along transects spaced 50 m apart in the Low Probability Zone. While both the Forest Service and the 1988 Fort Polk predictive models

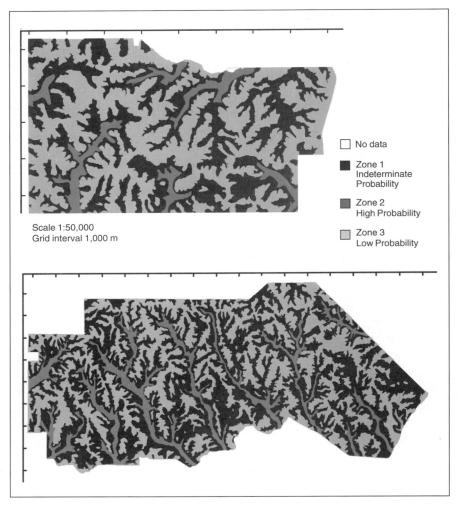

Figure 4.7 — The 1988 Fort Polk HPP predictive model.

were quite successful in documenting where the vast majority of archaeological sites were likely to occur, it soon became apparent that their constituent probability zones were difficult to delimit reliably on maps and to locate accurately on the ground. In particular, determining the parts of survey tracts that had 15 or more or fewer than 15 drains per quarter section, in the case of the U.S. Forest Service model, or that lay within 300 meters or 10 to 59 feet vertical elevation of a mapped water source, in the case of the 1988 Fort Polk model, could only be done on a very approximate basis. For this reason the model was revised and simplified in 1995.

Tests of the 1988 Predictive Model

The first test of the 1988 HPP predictive model on Fort Polk occurred during the Earth Search, Inc., 1993 survey of a 2,745-acre tract on the Main Fort, in which 16 of 20, or 80 percent, of the sites and 21 of 35, or 60 percent, of the isolated finds were found in the High Probability Zone (McMakin et al. 1994:227–228). The 1988 HPP predictive model was also evaluated by archaeologists from R. Christopher Goodwin and Associates, Inc., during the RCG-14 through RCG-18 survey projects reported in 1994 and 1995.

During the RCG-14 project, an examination of 985 acres on the Main Fort (Williams et al. 1994a:141–143), of 36 prehistoric sites encountered, 5 fell in the Indeterminate Probability Zone, 28 in the High Probability Zone, and 3 in the Low Probability Zone. The Indeterminate and High Probability Zones were surveyed the same way, that is, at 30-m transect intervals, yielding 33 sites, or 91.7 percent of the total found. Site density was approximately 6 sites per 100 acres in the High and Intermediate Probability Zones and less than one site (0.68) per 100 acres in the Low Probability Zone. The occurrence of three sites in the Low Probability Zone was attributed to a lower rate of mechanical disturbance in the upland areas and the existence of springheads and small drainage heads that do not appear on the USGS 7.5-minute quadrangle sheets, whose mapped watercourses were used to generate the 1988 model probability zones. Deeply buried deposits, with artifacts found at depths of more than a meter, were found at sites in all three probability zones but were particularly common on sites in the High Probability Zone.

The study thus indicated that upland areas cannot be automatically assumed to have shallow site deposits and that care must be taken to dig shovel tests deeply enough to locate potentially buried cultural horizons in all three probability zones. All of the sites were located within 100 m of water, with a mean distance of 30.6 m; that some of these water sources were unmapped explains why the sites did not all fall within the High Probability Zone as defined in the 1988 HPP analysis, which extended 300 m from mapped watercourses or floodplain soil margins. Relative elevation of the sites above the primary water source ranged from 0 to 6.1 m, which was again in close conformance with the 1988 predictive model. Mean site size was 2.4 acres, which was considered to be small and a reflection of the occurrence of numerous small camps and hunting stations. The possibility that large sites were palimpsests of numerous small scatters was advanced.

During the RCG-15 survey project, which encompassed 995 acres on the Main Fort along tributaries of Tenmile and Big Brushy Creeks (Williams et al. 1994b:142–143), all 36 sites located occurred in the Indeterminate (n = 12) and High (n = 24) Probability Zones, areas that received close transect interval survey coverage. All of the sites in the Indeterminate Probability Zone produced cultural materials at depths greater than 40 cm, while only a few sites in the High Probability Zone had artifacts at depths greater than 40 cm. The difference in artifact depth at sites in each zone between this project and RCG-14 was striking and indicates care must be taken before assuming appropriate shovel test depth when doing fieldwork. Once again sites were located close to water, in this case between 0 and 125 m horizontal distance, with an average distance of 35.7 m; elevation above the primary water source ranged from 0 to 7.6 m. Site size varied from 0.012 to 83.4 acres and averaged 3.5 acres. The median site size, 0.68 acres, indicated most were small scatters.

During the RCG-16 project, a 998-acre survey in the Fullerton Maneuver Area of the Main Fort (Williams et al. 1995a:155–157), once again the vast majority of prehistoric sites occurred in the Indeterminate and High Probability Zones (31 of 34; 91.2 percent). Site depth varied appreciably between the zones, with the deepest deposits found in the High Probability Zone and the shallowest in the Low Probability Zone. Site size varied from 0.02 to 2.9 acres, with an average of 0.43 acres; distance to water ranged from 10 to 170 m, with an average of 31 m; and elevation above water ranged from 0 to 9.1 m, with an average of 3.1 m. Likewise, during the RCG-17 survey project, 37 of 38 prehistoric sites were found in the Indeterminate and High Probability Zones; artifact deposit depth ranges were comparable to those observed during the RCG-16 project (Williams et al. 1995b:148–149). During the RCG-18 project, which was conducted over a 980-acre tract on Peason Ridge, 8 of the 10 sites located came from Indeterminate and High Probability Zones (Williams et al. 1994c:66). The general utility of the 1988 predictive model was supported by these projects.

The 1988 HPP predictive model was also examined with data from several survey projects conducted by Gulf South Research Corporation, Inc., specifically in the conclusions to the GSRI-2 and GSRI-4 through GSRI-7 reports (Jones et al. 1996a:164–165, 1996b:110, 1997:193, 197; Shuman et al. 1996a:107, 1996c:113–114). In the conclusions to the GSRI-2 report, the overall effectiveness of the model was challenged, at least in the Peason Ridge area, since a number of sites and isolated finds were found in the Low Probability Zone (Shuman et al. 1996a:107). The reevaluation of the 1988 HPP model with the far larger sets of site and isolated finds data available in 1995, in fact, indicated that both models are slightly less accurate on Peason Ridge than on the Main Fort. The High and Indeterminate Probability Zones in both models, however, do encompass the vast majority of all sites and isolated finds found on the installation (see Tables 4.18 and 4.19 and discussion below).

The 1988 predictive model was reexamined in the GSRI-4 report, a survey of 1,002 acres on the western end of the Main Fort. Again, a large number of sites, 8 of 15, plus 1 of 5 isolated finds, were found in the Low Probability Zone (Shuman et al. 1996c:113–114). While the authors argue that this generally supports the model, the site incidence in the Low Probability Zone is still much higher than expected from past work on the installation. Similar discrepancies were noted in the GSRI-5 through GSRI-7 analyses, in which 16 of 21, 7 of 8, and 23 of 29 prehistoric sites, respectively, and 4 of 7, 7 of 15, and 8 of 9 isolated finds, respectively, were found in High Probability Zones (Jones et al. 1996a:164–166, 1996b:110, 1997:193, 197). These differences appear to be due, at least in part, to the extensive shovel testing employed by Gulf South personnel in site-definition activity, at least in comparison with that in previous survey projects. Gulf South personnel routinely excavated at least twice as many, and in some cases several times as many, shovel tests around positive shovel tests than were opened by any previous contractor, particularly when evaluating isolated finds (see Figure 2.29). While providing excellent coverage at these locations, these procedures may well have inflated the number of small sites in upland areas. The care with which the survey teams documented their work, however, shows that more sites may be located in upland areas on Fort Polk than has been traditionally assumed. Most of the sites found in the Low Probability Zones during the Gulf South work appear to be quite small, and few have been deemed potentially eligible for inclusion on the NRHP.

The 1995 Fort Polk Predictive Model

The 1995 predictive model was developed using the installation GIS to conduct a site-probability analysis, in which a major goal was to replicate as closely as possible the 1988 zones, in terms of their location and mapped extent, but using criteria that were easier to determine both in the lab and on the ground. Using the GIS, potential probability zones were produced and then examined with the entire installation cultural resources assemblage. Selection of zone characteristics was guided by the results of the earlier 1988 HPP analysis and by an examination of site/isolated find–environmental associations using the GIS, as described in the preceding pages. These analyses had shown that distance to nearest water and distance to floodplain soils appeared to be particularly critical variables shaping site location on Fort Polk.

Accordingly, with the help of Chris Rewerts, the USACERL engineer who developed the Fort Polk GIS with Kim Majerus, the GIS was used to

Table 4.18 — Comparison of the 1988 and 1995 Fort Polk predictive models, using data from the Main Fort

	1988 Model					1995 Model				
	Sites	Isolated Finds	Possible Historic*	Total Properties	Acres	Sites	Isolated Finds	Possible Historic*	Total Properties	Acres
Zone 1 — Indeterminate	156	58	12	226	12,613.80	164	68	10	242	12,812.5
(% of Total)	(14.04)	(7.73)	(17.91)	(11.72)	(11.93)	(14.83)	(9.01)	(14.93)	(12.55)	(12.12)
Eligible	19	—	—	19	—	18	—	—	18	—
Potentially Eligible	27	—	—	27	—	36	—	—	36	—
Not Eligible	110	58	12	180	—	110	68	10	188	—
Zone 2 — High Probability	698	425	34	1,157	52,444.8	711	424	27	1,162	53,047.5
(% of Total)	(62.83)	(56.67)	(50.75)	(60.01)	(49.59)	(64.29)	(56.16)	(40.30)	(60.27)	(50.16)
Eligible	35	—	—	35	—	39	—	—	39	—
Potentially Eligible	98	—	—	98	—	89	—	—	89	—
Not Eligible	565	425	34	1024	—	583	424	27	1034	—
Zone 3 — Low Probability	250	266	21	537	40,550.1	197	254	22	473	39,893.7
(% of Total)	(22.50)	(35.47)	(31.34)	(27.85)	(38.34)	(17.81)	(33.64)	(32.84)	(24.53)	(37.72)
Eligible	4	—	—	4	—	—	—	—	0	—
Potentially Eligible	17	—	—	17	—	13	—	—	13	—
Not Eligible	229	266	21	516	—	184	254	22	460	—

Table 4.18 (cont.) — Comparison of the 1988 and 1995 Fort Polk predictive models, using data from the Main Fort

	1988 Model					1995 Model				
	Sites	Isolated Finds	Possible Historic*	Total Properties	Acres	Sites	Isolated Finds	Possible Historic*	Total Properties	Acres
No Data**	7	1	0	8	145	34	9	8	51	—
(% of Total)	(0.63)	(0.13)	(0.00)	(0.41)	(0.14)	(3.07)	(1.19)	(11.94)	(2.65)	—
Totals	1,111	750	67	1,928	105,753.7	1,106	755	67	1,928	105,753.7
(% of Total)	(100.00)	(100.00)	(100.00)	(100.00)	(100.00)	(100.00)	(100.00)	(100.00)	(100.00)	(100.00)

Grand Totals: 1,928 sites, isolated finds, and possible historic building complexes

* Possible historic sites delimited from aerial photographs, also MPRC and cemetery sites

** Eight locations examined by the 1988 analysis and 51 examined by the 1995 analysis had no associated probability zone data since small areas of the Main Fort were not encoded into the GIS data layer.

Summary:	Zone 1	Zone 2	Zone 3	Total*	Incidence in Zones 1 & 2
1988 Model	46	133	21	200	195
(% of Total)	(23.00)	(27.69)	(10.50)	(100.00)	(100.00)
1995 Model	54	128	17	179	182
(% of Total)	(27.69)	(65.64)	(6.67)	(89.50)	(93.33)

* Five eligible and potentially eligible sites in the 1988 model had no associated probability zone in the 1995 model.

Table 4.19 — Comparison of the 1988 and 1995 Fort Polk predictive models, using data from Peason Ridge

	1988 Model					1995 Model				
	Sites	Isolated Finds	Possible Historic*	Total Properties	Acres	Sites	Isolated Finds	Possible Historic*	Total Properties	Acres
Zone 1 — Indeterminate	30	19	0	49	2,466.4	28	19	0	47	2,965.3
(% of Total)	(7.35)	(5.54)	(0.00)	(6.51)	(7.38)	(6.88)	(5.52)	(0.00)	(6.24)	(8.87)
Eligible	8	—	—	8	—	6	—	—	6	—
Potentially Eligible	9	—	—	9	—	7	—	—	7	—
Not Eligible	13	19	—	32	—	15	19	—	34	—
Zone 2 — High Probability	228	160	1	389	15,295.4	259	173	1	433	16,868.6
(% of Total)	(55.88)	(46.65)	(50.00)	(51.66)	(45.75)	(63.64)	(50.29)	(50.00)	(57.50)	(50.45)
Eligible	18	—	—	18	—	20	—	—	20	—
Potentially Eligible	49	—	—	49	—	61	—	—	61	—
Not Eligible	161	160	1	322	—	178	173	1	352	—
Zone 3 — Low Probability	139	159	1	299	15,490.5	111	150	1	262	13,599.9
(% of Total)	(34.07)	(46.36)	(50.00)	(39.71)	(46.33)	(27.27)	(43.60)	(50.00)	(34.79)	(40.68)
Eligible	3	—	—	3	—	3	—	—	3	—
Potentially Eligible	20	—	—	20	—	10	—	—	10	—
Not Eligible	116	159	1	276	—	98	150	1	249	—

Table 4.19 (cont.) — Comparison of the 1988 and 1995 Fort Polk predictive models, using data from Peason Ridge

	1988 Model					1995 Model				
	Sites	Isolated Finds	Possible Historic*	Total Properties	Acres	Sites	Isolated Finds	Possible Historic*	Total Properties	Acres
No Data**	11	5	0	16	181.5	9	2	0	11	—
(% of Total)	(2.70)	(1.46)	(0.00)	(2.12)	(0.54)	(2.21)	(0.58)	(0.00)	(1.46)	—
Totals	408	343	2	753	33,433.8	407	344	2	753	33,433.8
(% of Total)	(100.00)	(100.00)	(100.00)	(100.00)	(100.00)	(100.00)	(100.00)	(100.00)	(100.00)	(100.00)

Grand Totals: 753 sites, isolated finds, and possible historic building complexes

* Possible historic sites delimited from aerial photographs, also MPRC and cemetery sites
** Five sites in the 1988 sample had no associated probability zone data in the 1995 analysis since these parts of Peason Ridge were not encoded into the GIS data layer.

Summary:	Zone 1	Zone 2	Zone 3	Total	Incidence in Zones 1 & 2
1988 Model	17	67	23	107	84
(% of Total)	(15.89)	(62.62)	(21.50)	(100.00)	(78.50)
1995 Model	13	81	13	107	94
(% of Total)	(12.15)	(75.70)	(12.15)	(100.00)	(87.85)

create a series of buffers of varying sizes about mapped watercourses and floodplain soils. The numbers of sites and isolated finds that occurred within these buffers were then calculated. In brief, the buffers were enlarged using 50-m intervals and the numbers of sites and isolated finds tallied until high predictive values were achieved for a relatively small proportion of the total acreage under examination. Beyond a certain point—in this case, beyond 200 m—increasing the size of the buffer did not appreciably increase the numbers of sites and isolated finds located within it, while it did increase the number of acres substantially. In this fashion we were able to improve upon the predictive accuracy of the 1988 model, while simultaneously greatly simplifying the delimitation of the site probability zones. Three site probability zones were again delimited and were portrayed in a yellow, tan, and dark-brown "Desert Storm" camouflage pattern, which was also a great hit with the military, which, after all, paid for the work (Figure 4.8). The 1995 model probability zones are as follows:

Zone 1   *Site Probability Indeterminate.* Floodplain areas, defined as locations where floodplain soils occurred as defined by the Natural Resources Conservation Service;

Zone 2   *High Probability.* Locations within a 200-m buffer of Zone 1 or within a 200-m buffer of a mapped water source; and

Zone 3   *Low Probability.* All other areas (i.e., uplands).

These three zones can be easily found on maps and in the field, particularly since the variable vertical elevation above nearest water source used in the earlier model has been eliminated. Because they are based on data in the installation GIS, furthermore, maps delimiting these zones can be readily produced to guide fieldwork; hard copies of such maps encompassing the installation are in the HPP Map volume (Anderson et al. 1996a).

Tables 4.18 and 4.19 document the effectiveness of the 1988 and 1995 predictive models on the Main Fort and Peason Ridge, and these data are summarized in Table 4.20, where they are also compared with data from a test of the U.S. Forest Service's predictive model for the Kisatchie National Forest (Phillips and Willingham 1990). A noticeable improvement in predictive ability is evident from the 1988 to the 1995 model, with a greater incidence of sites and isolated finds in the High and Indeterminate Zones and a lower incidence in the Low Probability Zone. Zones 1 and 2 in the 1995 predictive model account for a great majority of all sites (n = 1,884; 71.94 percent) and almost all the NRHP-eligible or potentially eligible sites

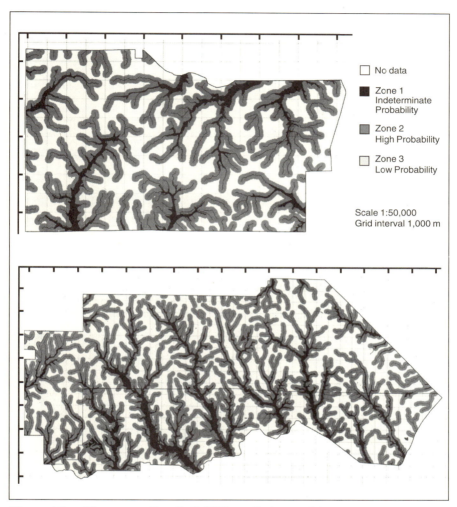

Figure 4.8 — The current Fort Polk HPP predictive model

(n = 276; 91.40 percent). As can also be seen, the acreage figures used to define the probability zones are almost identical in the 1988 and 1995 analyses, meeting one of the project concerns to ensure the zones were roughly equivalent in extent in order to avoid reducing the comparability of the overall installation survey effort and site database.

TESTS OF THE 1995 PREDICTIVE MODEL
The 1995 predictive model was used and tested on Fort Polk almost immediately following its development in the summer of 1995. A survey of 14,622

Table 4.20 — Comparison of the 1988 and 1995 Fort Polk and U.S. Forest Service predictive models

	1988 Fort Polk Model			1995 Fort Polk Model			USFS Model Evaluation**		
	All Sites and Isolated Finds	NRHP*	Acres	All Sites and Isolated Finds	NRHP*	Acres	All Sites and Isolated Finds	NRHP*	Acres
Zone 1 Indeterminate / Moderate Probability	275	63	15,080.20	289	67	15,777.8	33	2	2,097
	10.35%	20.52%	10.86%	11.03%	22.19%	11.34%	22.30%	6.25%	22.83%
Zone 2 High Probability / High Probability	1546	200	67,740.2	1,595	209	69,916.1	94	29	4,955
	58.19%	65.15%	48.78%	60.90%	69.21%	50.23%	63.51%	90.63%	53.95%
Zone 3 Low Probability / Low Probability	836	44	56,040.6	735	26	53,493.5	21	1	2,132
	31.46%	14.33%	40.36%	28.06%	8.61%	38.43%	14.19%	3.13%	23.21%
Totals	2657	307	138,861.00	2,619	302	139,187.4	148	32	9,184
	100.00%	100.00%	100.00%	100.00%	100.00%	100.00%	100.00%	100.00%	100.00%
Incidence in Zones 1 and 2 (High, Indeterminate Probability) / Incidence in High and Mod. Prob. Areas	1821	263	—	1,884	276	—	127	31	—
	68.54%	85.67%	—	71.94%	91.39%	—	85.81%	96.88%	—

* National Register of Historic Places eligible and potentially eligible sites

** From Phillips and Willingham 1990:227

acres of the Main Fort conducted by New South Associates, Inc., and initiated in late 1995–1996 made use of the revised model (Cantley et al. 1997).
In all, 9,172 acres of the High/Indeterminate Probability Zones and 5,450
acres of the Low Probability Zone were examined. The vast majority of the
sites (n = 319; 94.3 percent) and isolated finds (n = 357; 86.4 percent) were
found in the High/Indeterminate Probability Zones, a somewhat higher percentage than in the sample used to develop the model (Cantley et al.
1997:921–922).

Data from the 1996–1997 SCIAA survey of 12,538 acres on the Main
Fort were also used to evaluate the 1995 predictive model. Close agreement
was noted, with 81 percent of the sites and isolated finds being in the High/
Indeterminate Probability Zones (Clement and Peterson 1998:423–427). The
proportions of sites in each zone were observed to remain roughly the same
over all major time periods, including both historic and prehistoric components. The overall project analysis did indicate, however, that chert quarry
sites occurred widely over the landscape; two of the five quarries found
were in Low Probability Zones in the uplands (Clement and Peterson
1998:424). Several sites were also found in the Low Probability Zone that
were considered worthy of further investigation (Clement and Peterson
1998:424). The analysis highlighted the fact that low probability should not
be interpreted to mean "no probability" and that field crews working in these
zones must expend appropriate levels of effort in site discovery. Changes in
the locations of watercourses over time and the existence of water sources
that were not mapped on the USGS quadrangle sheets were also suggested
as reasons that significant sites might occur in the Low Probability Zone
(Clement and Peterson 1998:424; see also Campbell and Weed 1986:10-18
to 10-35).

The 1995 predictive model was evaluated for the first time on Peason
Ridge during a survey of 6,407 acres conducted in 1998 (Ensor et al., eds.
1999). In all, 79.1 percent of the sites and 85.55 percent of the isolated finds
were recorded in the High Probability Zone, a slightly higher incidence than
in the sample used to generate the 1995 predictive model. Of 14 sites considered potentially eligible for inclusion on the NRHP, 13 were in the High
Probability Zone, a finding in close agreement with the expectations of the
model (Ezell and Ensor 1999:340). Another major test of the 1995 model,
this time in lands to the south of Fort Polk, occurred during the 1999–2000
survey of 4,579 acres in the Rustville Training Area (Ensor et al. 2001:449).
Although the High Probability Zone encompassed only approximately 60
percent of the survey area, over 97 percent of all sites were found in this
zone. The authors noted that this was a much higher incidence than previously observed and suggested it was due to extensive disturbance that had

occurred in the upland areas, a very low incidence of historic settlement in the immediate area, and a selection for stream margins by the late prehistoric populations whose remains dominated in the collections.

Evaluations of the 1995 model continue and deviations from expectations are routinely examined, such as the recovery of appreciably higher or lower site densities in survey areas. During Panamerican Consultants, Inc.'s 6,535-acre survey on the northeastern part of the Main Fort in 1999–2000, for example, 24 of 27 sites and 11 of 19 isolated finds were found in the High Probability Zone (Buchner and Saatkamp 2000:195). The incidence of sites and isolated finds was far below expectations for the installation, however, prompting analyses directed to explaining why these densities occurred (Buchner and Saatkamp 2000:196–197; see Chapter 2). Another value of a predictive model of site location, thus, is that it can help to highlight unexpected findings. A second evaluation of site occurrence and density using the 1995 probability zones occurred during Panamerican Consultants, Inc.'s 4,212-acre survey on the Main Fort and limited-use area that occurred in 2000; all 39 sites and 20 of 22 isolated finds were found to occur in the High Probability Zone. Again, site density was much lower than expected, prompting further comparative analyses and explanations (Buchner and Saatkamp 2001:287–288; see Chapter 2). A third evaluation using this approach, during the 4,862-acre survey by Panamerican Consultants, Inc., along Whiskey Chitto Creek in the limited-use lands south of the Main Fort, found a site density by probability zone comparable to that recorded on the installation as a whole and only slightly lower than that recorded by the only other major survey project undertaken along Whiskey Chitto Creek to date (cf. Bundy 2002b:662–663; Cantley et al. 1997).

Care must be taken, however, to ensure that probability zones do not tend to become self-fulfilling prophecies guiding fieldwork, that is, assertions that influence whether and how many sites are likely to be found during given projects. Enough work has occurred to show that significant and unexpected cultural resources can occur in all three probability zones and that site incidence can vary greatly depending on the intensity of fieldwork and local environmental conditions. A classic example of this was observed when Lake Anacoco immediately west of Fort Polk was drawn down in 1995; the margins and bottom of the reservoir, long denuded of vegetation, produced a far higher site density than has been observed in comparable settings on Fort Polk (McGimsey 1996:144). Thus, while the nearly 5,000 sites and isolated finds recorded to date on Fort Polk constitute a remarkable and valuable assemblage, the number would unquestionably be far higher if the entire installation were cleared and eroded or in plowed fields rather than grown up in dense vegetation as at present.

Conclusions

The 1995 Fort Polk predictive model appears to have a comparable predictive accuracy to that of the model in use on the Kisatchie National Forest developed by Willingham and Phillips (1987). It also appears to be easier to use and places more acreage into the Low Probability Zone, translating into lower survey costs. The only published test of the Kisatchie model by U.S. Forest Service personnel that examined site incidence by probability areas, equivalent to Fort Polk's site probability zones, is highly instructive in this regard (all other published U.S. Forest Service analyses, it should be noted, give data on site incidence by topographic zones, which contain combinations of high, moderate, and low probability areas; see Chapter 3 for full definitions). This analysis is based on a sample of 148 sites found during an intensive survey of 9,184 acres (Phillips and Willingham 1990:227) (Table 4.20). The results indicate that the occurrence of sites in the U.S. Forest Service probability areas is not appreciably different from the incidence observed in the probability zones defined at Fort Polk. It must be cautioned, however, that the U.S. Forest Service model test case is based on a small and potentially nonrepresentative sample.

Both models have more than 90 percent of the significant sites in their high and moderate or indeterminate probability zones. The U.S. Forest Service model, in fact, appears to be a slightly better predictor, at least in this sample, accounting for 96.88 percent of all significant sites compared with 91.39 percent of the significant sites on Fort Polk (although the Fort Polk site and isolated find dataset, it must be noted, is 16 times larger). Interestingly, though, the Fort Polk High and Indeterminate Probability Zones occupy less acreage (ca. 61.6 percent vs. 77 percent of the total area) and the Low Probability Zone thus much more acreage (ca. 38.4 percent vs. 23 percent of the total area) than in the U.S. Forest Service model test case. These differences translate into much lower survey costs, since less land must be surveyed at a high level of intensity using the Fort Polk model.

The Fort Polk probability zones, additionally, are easier to define both in the lab and in the field, since they do not necessitate use of a dissection index (i.e., number of drains per quarter section) and since the probability zones are defined in terms of strict distances from easily observed phenomena, such as watercourses or floodplain margins. The U.S. Forest Service probability areas, in contrast, occur across each topographic zone. This does not mean that one model should replace the other, only that each has its own particular strengths and weaknesses that should be considered when doing fieldwork in west-central Louisiana. It is recommended that the Fort Polk probability zones be used to define survey intensity zones and procedures, but that in the field particular care should be taken on those portions of the landscape within these zones that correspond to the U.S. Forest Service high and moderate probability areas.

The analyses associated with the 1988 and 1995 predictive modeling on Fort Polk shed considerable light on past land use in this part of west-central Louisiana. Site locations are closely linked to distance to nearest water, elevation above water, landform type, soil type, and soil slope. Equally important, a number of measures, such as the rank and distance of the nearest permanent water or of the nearest confluence, appear to have little predictive utility.

Chapter 5

Prehistoric Assemblages in the Vicinity of Fort Polk

In this chapter diagnostic artifacts found on Fort Polk are described and a series of assemblages are examined to explore variability in settlement and land use on the installation. Because the dating of assemblages is fundamental to most forms of archaeological analysis and because the cultural sequence in this part of Louisiana has been somewhat ambiguous and in need of clarification, considerable effort was made to document all of the temporal diagnostics, specifically projectile points and ceramics, found on prehistoric sites and isolated finds on Fort Polk. Data about these artifact categories were obtained from an examination of reports, site files, and collections and encompass all work conducted on the installation through early 2002. Many of these artifacts were examined directly. Since it was not possible to reanalyze all of the collections, however, which would have required an immense effort, some items that went unreported initially may have been missed and some published artifact classifications may be in error. Information for nondiagnostic artifact categories such as debitage or stone tool forms other than projectile points was also compiled, and this was obtained almost exclusively from published reports or unpublished analysis notes. Due to varied analysis and reporting procedures, detailed analyses of these categories of artifacts were restricted to a subset of assemblages that had been collected and reported in a consistent fashion, specifically the data from the first 32 intensive testing projects conducted by Prentice Thomas and Associates, Inc., in the 1990s (see Chapter 2). Assemblage information for each site and isolated find, by site number and project since some sites were revisited a number of times, as well as the data from the 32 testing projects, has been presented in the 1999 Historic Preservation Plan (HPP) Cultural Resources Inventory Primary Data volume (Anderson et al. 1999a:appendixes 5–7). Updated electronic files, encompassing diagnostics found since that date, have been prepared and are on file at Fort Polk and are also available from the authors.

Wherever possible, the original published typological assignments were recorded, although in some cases alternative identifications were used, specifically when the original typological assignments were clearly in error or when the use of more appropriate categories was indicated. For ceramics, the original descriptive data about paste and surface finish were also recorded when available. In conjunction with the production of the 1988 HPP, an analysis of all the pottery and projectile points found on the installation through 1984 had been conducted. Charles E. Cantley examined the projectile point data, and David G. Anderson worked with the ceramics. This work was accomplished in conjunction with a contract between the Interagency Archeological Services Division of the National Park Service in Atlanta and Commonwealth Associates, Inc., to uniformly package and curate the artifact assemblages collected on Fort Polk through 1984. Although some materials from this earlier work were missing or still in the hands of the original investigators, the reanalysis covered many of the pre-1984 assemblages collected on the installation. In practice, the descriptions of materials found on the installation during projects conducted after the mid-1980s, beginning specifically with the Multipurpose Range Complex survey and testing project reports (Campbell and Weed 1986; Campbell et al. 1987), have been of such a high standard that only minimal inspection and reanalysis of the collections has been necessary to verify the nature of the diagnostics recovered. In most reports compiled since the mid-1980s, in fact, every projectile point and many of the unusual or decorated ceramics have been illustrated, and many reports additionally include detailed measurement/attribute data for these artifact categories. Detailed reporting standards mandating these efforts were put in place on the installation in the 1988 HPP and updated in the 1999 HPP, and this has ensured that the archaeological data generated by cultural resource management work on Fort Polk can be accessed and used to address a range of research questions, not the least of which concern the identification of and the variability within possible temporal diagnostics.

Projectile Points Found on Fort Polk

A total of 3,299 points and point fragments have been found on Fort Polk through April 2002, a sample several times the number (n = 564) reported in the 1988 HPP, which indicates the amount of work that has taken place on the installation over the past decade (Table 5.1; Anderson et al. 1999a:appendix 6). To facilitate future identification and analysis, brief descriptive information about each type is provided in the pages that follow, together with photographs of examples of these types that have been found on Fort Polk. The projectile point information is arranged alphabetically for

Table 5.1 — Fort Polk projectile points: total by type and period

Type	Period	Artifacts	Components
Agee	LP	1	1
Alba	LP	86	75
Angostura	EA	3	3
Arrow points, type unknown	LP	74	65
Bassett	LP	57	36
Bayougoula	LP	1	1
Big Sandy/Early Side-Notched	EA	5	5
Birds Creek Cluster	LA	44	25
Bonham	LP	12	12
Bulverde	MA	8	7
Calcasieu	W	25	21
Calf Creek	MA	1	1
Carrollton	MA	15	15
Castroville	W	3	3
Catahoula	LP	17	17
Cliffton	LP	29	28
Clovis	EPI	4	2
Colbert	LP	36	26
Cuney	LP	24	23
Cypress Creek II	MA	4	4
Darl	W	2	2
Dart Point Group 1 (NWR)	U	8	6
Dart Point Group 2 (NWR)	U	29	20
Delhi	LA	21	19
Dickson	W	1	1
Dooley Branch Cluster	W	98	61
Eccentrics	U	2	1
Edgewood	W	28	21
Elam	LA	1	1
Ellis	W	164	120
Ensor	LA	73	28
Epps	LA	21	19
Evans	MA	66	49
Fairland	W	1	1
Figueroa	W	3	1
Form X	LA	1	1
Fresno	LP	3	3
Friley	LP	198	144
Gary	W	208	153
Godley	W	47	37
Hardin	EA	1	1

Table 5.1 (cont.) — Fort Polk projectile points: total by type and period

Type	Period	Artifacts	Components
Hayes	LP	11	11
Kent	LA	112	96
Lange	W	18	16
Livermore	LP	1	1
Lone Oak	W	1	1
Lowe	W	5	5
Macon	LA	12	11
Marcos	W	80	32
Marshall	MA	22	21
Martindale	EA	3	3
Matamoros	LA	1	1
Maud	LP	2	2
Midland	LPI	6	6
Mississippian Triangular	LP	1	1
Morhiss	W	4	4
Morrill	MA	4	4
Motley	LA	68	54
Neches River	MA	3	3
Nolan	MA	2	2
Palmer/Kirk Corner-Notched	EA	22	19
Palmillas	W	78	61
Pelican	LPI	4	4
Perdiz	LP	36	33
Plainview/other Paleoindian point	LPI	6	5
Points or fragments, type unknown	U	780	331
Unidentified dart points	U	41	26
Unidentified dart fragments	U	138	62
Unidentified arrow fragments	LP	54	32
Unidentified arrow preforms	LP	22	19
Pontchartrain	LA	23	20
Reed	LP	2	2
Rio Grande	EA	1	1
San Patrice, *var. Coldwater*	LPI	1	1
San Patrice, *var. Dixon*	EA	8	8
San Patrice, *var. Hope*	LPI	19	16
San Patrice, *var. Keithville*	EA	21	18
San Patrice, *var. Leaf River*	EA	2	2
San Patrice, *var. St. Johns*	LPI	31	27
San Patrice, *var. unspecified*	LPI	34	33
Scallorn	LP	11	9
Scottsbluff	EA	8	8

Table 5.1 (cont.) — Fort Polk projectile points: total by type and period

Type	Period	Artifacts	Components
Shumla	W	6	4
Sinner	MA	23	17
Summerfield	LA	10	1
Trinity	LA	12	11
Wade-like	LA/W	1	1
Wells	EA	3	3
Williams	W	54	41
Woden	LA	8	8
Woodland Dart Points	W	3	3
Yarbrough	LA	56	36
Total		3,299	2,195

Total: 743 sites + 149 isolated finds = 892 assemblages with points

LP = Late Prehistoric	MA = Middle Archaic	LPI = Late Paleoindian
EA = Early Archaic	W = Woodland	U = Unknown Prehistoric
LA = Late Archaic	EPI = Early Paleoindian	

dart and arrow point types, respectively, to facilitate easy reference. Typological assignments and associated illustrations typically follow those employed by the original report authors, subject to occasional modification in later publications. It should be noted that very few original identifications were altered in the current projectile point analysis although, as noted below, some of the classifications were questioned.

Many projectile points found on Fort Polk and in western Louisiana in general occur widely in eastern Texas, where an extensive body of research exists on the classification and dating of these forms. Excellent overviews of Texas projectile types have appeared through the years (e.g., Prewitt 1995; Story 1990; Suhm and Jelks 1962; Suhm et al. 1954; Turner and Hester 1993), and the summaries that follow draw heavily on these works. A comparable study based on projectile points from across Louisiana remains to be produced, although Webb's (1981) *Stone Points and Tools of Northwestern Louisiana* is an excellent initial effort. Recent distributional analyses of projectile point forms in Louisiana undertaken by Saunders and Allen (1997:5, 7), like those recently completed for Texas by Prewitt (1995), represent important research that needs to be continued locally. The description of point types that follows, it should be noted, owes a great deal to the efforts of James Morehead, L. Janice Campbell, and other archaeologists from Prentice

Thomas and Associates, Inc., in reporting lithic materials from Fort Polk. Morehead's work in particular spans an exceptionally long period of involvement, from the original Big Brushy excavations in the late 1970s to analyses of most of the lithic artifacts recovered during the intensive testing projects conducted by Prentice Thomas and Associates, Inc., from the 1990s to 2002.

The discussion that follows encompasses the 82 types reported through early 2002 on Fort Polk. Nearly half of these types are fairly common on the installation, with 10 or more reported specimens. Almost a third (n = 27 types and varieties), however, are represented by no more than one to three specimens. In some cases when illustrations of artifacts were provided in the original reports or when the artifacts themselves could be reexamined, it was clear that some of the more unusual types had been misidentified, as noted below. Accordingly, to minimize the confusion associated with typing local points, readers are urged, wherever possible, to (1) refrain from using type names drawn from great distances, unless the point is known from previous research to occur with some incidence in Louisiana and (2) make use of locally documented types whenever possible (e.g., Campbell and Weed 1986:4-12). The typological principle to be employed is thus a variant of Occam's Razor: whenever two or more type names may apply to an artifact, the name that has been most commonly reported in the past and that represents a type known to occur with some incidence in the study area is the name that should be used. A corollary of this is to avoid naming new taxa of any kind, from pottery and projectile point types and varieties to archaeological phases, foci, or cultures, unless (1) there are compelling reasons to do so (i.e., the taxa must be useful) and (2) there are large samples of data from unambiguous contexts to support the new category.

Rare or unusual type names should be employed only if a more common type name cannot be justifiably substituted and only if the artifacts exactly or closely fit the type description. Rare types that are poorly defined or are used in distant areas with few or no reported examples in intervening areas should be avoided. At Fort Polk, a number of types have been recorded that occur well beyond their currently known geographic range, such as the Castroville, Figueroa, and Livermore types, which occur primarily in southwestern Texas. Rare or unusual projectile point types whose use should probably be avoided on Fort Polk, or at least used with caution, include the Agee, Bayougoula, Castroville, Darl, Dickson, Elam, Fairland, Figueroa, Form X, Fresno, Hardin, Livermore, Lone Oak, Matamoros, Maud, Morrill, Nolan, Reed, Rio Grande, San Patrice, *var. Coldwater*, Summerfield, Wade, and Wells types. This does not mean use of types originating at great distances should not be considered, only that their use should be justified. Some rare

forms may indeed be correctly identified and may represent unusual exten-
sions of the accepted range of these forms. Their presence may reflect large-
scale or long-distance interaction, perhaps as part of exchange or mating
networks. The fact that people apparently came from across large areas to
obtain knappable stone from the Fort Polk area, in fact, indicates that unusual artifacts will occasionally turn up that are well outside their normal
area of occurrence. Minimally, anyone using unusual type names should
provide some discussion as to why the category is appropriate. The use of
poorly defined and overly general catchall typological categories that encompass considerable morphological variability and probably a wide range
of time periods should also be avoided. Story (1990:220), noting a "lack of
comparability in the classification of some of the Archaic point styles" from
investigator to investigator in the east Texas area, has argued that "since
much information is carried on the shoulders of artifact typologies, archeolo-
gists should be more critical in their definition and recognition of cultural-
historical types (and varieties). Toward this end, more comparative type
collections should be set up (perhaps using casts) and uniform standards of
illustration should be instituted" (Story 1990:220). The Palmillas dart point
type is a classic example of such a category that, unfortunately, is widely
employed on Fort Polk and in western Louisiana in general (see discussion
below). More detailed documentation of local points, such as exemplified
by Baker and Webb's (1976) examination of the Catahoula type, is clearly
needed.

DART POINT AND UNUSUAL TOOL TYPES FOUND ON FORT POLK

Dart and arrow points and point fragments, as well as a few unusual chipped
stone tool types, are described in this section. The numbers in parentheses
following the type name refer to the number of these artifacts found on Fort
Polk and reported using that name and the number of sites and isolated finds
that they were found on, or components (assuming one component per location) (Table 5.1). The descriptions that follow are presented to help in the
identification of local artifacts and should be viewed as an introductory sorting
guide rather than a formal compendium of type descriptions. References
typically include the locations of the original type description and subsequent descriptions from common projectile point guides, plus reports from
the Fort Polk area where extended discussions of the type have been presented. Typed and illustrated specimens reported from Fort Polk, it should
be noted, do not always closely conform to classic type specimens.

Albany Scraper (n = 8/8 components). These tools are hafted unifacial scrapers characterized by side notching and a single straight to concave beveled

edge (Figure 5.1, *a–c*). Occasional specimens exhibit flaking over both faces. Albany scrapers were first defined by Clarence Webb (1946:9) based on specimens found in northwestern Louisiana and are a Late Paleoindian/Early Archaic tool form associated with San Patrice points in the Louisiana area. Similar tool forms occurring at the same time level from elsewhere in the Southeast include an unnamed notched uniface in Mississippi, Waller knives in the Florida area, and Edgefield scrapers in Georgia and the Carolinas (McGahey 1996:357, 360, 380, 384; Michie 1972). The tool also resembles the Cody knife and may be related to it (Story 1990:202). At Fort Polk, Albany scrapers have been found at several sites, typically with San Patrice points. These sites on Fort Polk include 16VN153, 16VN162, 16VN675, 16VN866, 16VN791, and 16VN1235 (Campbell et al. 1990:70; Largent et al. 1993c:49; Mathews et al. 1996:52; Meyer et al. 1995a:43; Morehead et al. 1994:46, 1997:65). *References*: Story 1990:202; Turner and Hester 1993:277; Webb 1946, 2000:4.

Angostura (n = 3/3 components)

This point is characterized by a leaf-shaped to nearly lanceolate biface with an oblique- to parallel-flaked blade. The haft area lacks shoulders and is slightly contracting, with a flat to slightly indented base. The haft area is basally and laterally ground. Angostura points occur throughout the Plains and into the western part of the Eastern Woodlands, including much of Texas and into Louisiana (Prewitt 1995:90). Turner and Hester (1993:73) have observed that "specimens attributed to the type in Texas vary widely in shape and flaking, causing problems in definition." The point was first described as the "Long point" at the Long site in the Angostura reservoir in South Dakota (Hughes 1949). The point form is considered to be early Holocene in age and has been dated to 8855 ± 75 rcbp at the Richard Beene site, 41BX831, in south Texas (Thoms 1992). Justice (1987:30–34) considers the Angostura to be a variety of Agate Basin within the larger Lanceolate Plano cluster. *References*: Hughes 1949; Justice 1987:33–34; Suhm and Jelks 1962:167–168; Suhm et al. 1954:402; Turner and Hester 1993:73–74; Webb 2000:2.

Big Sandy/Early Side-Notched (n = 5/5 components)

These points are characterized by pronounced side notches, often with squared basal ears, flat to slightly concave heavily ground bases, pronounced shoulder barbs, and (in all but the earliest stage forms) a resharpened, serrated and sometimes beveled blade (Figure 5.1, *d–f*). The forms appear to be part of an early side-notched horizon extending across the Southeast and into eastern Texas and the eastern Plains and dating ca. 10,200–9500 rcbp (Ander-

Figure 5.1 — Dart point forms from Fort Polk: a–c, Albany scraper; d–f, Big Sandy/ Early Side-Notched; g–p, Birds Creek.

son et al. 1996b:15; Justice 1987:60–71). Type names describing these points include Big Sandy, Bolen, Taylor, San Patrice, *vars. Dixon* and *St. Johns*, and Cache River Side-Notched (Bullen 1975:51; Cambron and Hulse 1975:14–17; Cloud 1969; Kneberg 1956:25; Michie 1966:123). Turner and Hester (1993:81) argue that use of the Big Sandy type designation in Texas should only be done with caution, and a similar admonition is warranted in Louisiana. Occasional specimens are reported in the literature from east Texas (Prewitt 1995:93), although the form is uncommon. *References*: Justice 1987:60–71; Perino 1985:36, 58, 374; Turner and Hester 1993:81.

Birds Creek Cluster/Birds Creek Point
(n = 44, excluding 29 16VN791 specimens/25 components)
This cluster is a grouping of morphologically similar terminal Middle Archaic and initial Late Archaic point types that co-occur on Fort Polk. The taxa was advanced by L. Janice Campbell and her colleagues (1990:64–73), based on stratigraphic excavations at 16VN791 on Fort Polk (Figure 5.1, *g–p*). The principal point types are Ensor and Epps. The cluster is described as including "two similar types, Ensor and Epps. These are medium-sized, side-notched points, characterized by bases that flare out widely, so much so that the bases are frequently almost in line with the edges of the blades. The orientation of the side-notches varies with some examples perpendicular to the long axis of the point to somewhat oblique; in the latter case, weak barbs may be present. Basal morphology is uniformly convex, but not strongly so, and never concave. The blades are usually narrow triangles with straight to slightly convex edges" (Campbell et al. 1990:64). At 16VN791, Birds Creek cluster points were stratigraphically below Dooley Branch cluster points (Campbell et al. 1990:69–73). A total of 29 specimens were placed in the Birds Creek cluster at 16VN791, the type site. Since these were also described by their respective type (i.e., Epps, Ensor), that is the way they were reported in the 1999 HPP Inventory and herein. A terminal Middle Archaic/initial Late Archaic date for the cluster, ca. 6300–3770 B.P./5500–3500 rcbp, is supported by the presence of a Birds Creek cluster point in the 90- to 110-cm level at 16VN791 in deposits radiocarbon dated to 5160 ± 170 rcbp (Beta-33068; Campbell et al. 1990:72). Use of point cluster terminology has seen increasing use in the Eastern Woodlands following the appearance of Justice's (1987) widely distributed projectile point handbook, which makes extensive use of the concept. Although the Birds Creek cluster taxa has been used extensively by archaeologists from Prentice Thomas and Associates, Inc., who have come to refer to it as a distinct point type (e.g., Morehead et al. 1995b:44), the Birds Creek cluster taxa has not been widely adopted by other researchers working on Fort Polk, who prefer instead to report points using the traditional types that make up the cluster. As it has come to be used, however, the taxa has appreciable utility. *Reference*: Campbell et al. 1990:64–73.

Bulverde *(n = 8/7 components)*
This point is characterized by a large straight-sided triangular blade, pronounced square to barbed shoulders, and a square stem with a straight base (Figure 5.2, *a*). The point form occurs in central and eastern Texas into western Louisiana; it is particularly common in central Texas (Prewitt 1995:94). The point was first named by J. Charles Kelley (1947a:124) from the Lehmann

Figure 5.2 — Dart point forms from Fort Polk: a, Bulverde; b, Calcasieu; c, Carrollton; d, Castroville?; e–g, Delhi; h–q, Dooley Branch.

Rock Shelter in the Edwards Plateau area of central Texas. A terminal Middle Archaic/initial Late Archaic age is inferred in central Texas, from roughly 5700 to 5100 B.P./5000 to 4500 rcbp (Turner and Hester 1993:82). A clear association with Evans points has been documented in southern Arkansas (Schambach 1970:389, 1998:114–117; Schambach and Early 1982:SW57).

Justice (1987:184) places Bulverde points into his Terminal Archaic Barbed cluster. The point type is considered to be associated with the Middle Archaic Sixmile phase on Fort Polk, as defined by Morehead et al. 1996a:170–171; see also Morehead et al. 2002:36–38 and Chapter 6 herein. A point resembling a Bulverde was found at the Conly site in northwestern Louisiana and was dated to between 7500 and 8000 B.P. (Girard 2000a:36–37). *References*: Johnson 1962; Kelley 1947a:124; Perino 1985:55; Schambach 1998:46–51; Suhm 1957; Suhm and Jelks 1962:169–170; Suhm et al. 1954:404; Turner and Hester 1993:141–142.

Calcasieu (n = 25/21 components)
This dart type is characterized by a triangular blade with straight to slightly excurvate lateral margins, pronounced barbed shoulders, deep corner notches, and an expanding stem with a straight to convex base (Figure 5.2, *b*). It is distinguished by an asymmetry in the angle the hafting notches form with the base on each side of the point; the two base-notch angles may differ by up to 30 degrees or more. The type, which was defined by James A. Green (1991) based on materials collected in the Calcasieu drainage, is apparently fairly common in west-central Louisiana. The validity of the type has been questioned, since examples of points with similar hafting characteristics have been infrequently observed over a wide range of point types ranging in age from late Middle Archaic to Middle Woodland (Morehead et al. 1994:44). In spite of this, the type has been reported at a number of sites in the Fort Polk area. *References*: Green 1991:96–97; Morehead et al. 1994:44; Thomas et al. 1993d:39.

Calf Creek (n = 1/1 component)
This dart point type is described by Perino (1985:62) as having "straight to convex sides, deep narrow basal notches and a long rectangular stem. Some stems may expand slightly. The basal edge may be straight to slightly convex and sometimes has a small notch. Barbs may be squared to rounded and in line with the base of the stem, when in new condition." The type was defined by Dickson (1968) on the basis of examples found at the Calf Creek site in Searcy County, Arkansas. The point type is found in low incidence in northeastern Texas (Prewitt 1995:94) and has been described as occurring in "southwestern Missouri, eastern Oklahoma, western Arkansas, northwestern Louisiana, and most of eastern and central Texas" (Perino 1968:62; see also Justice 1987:60). Related types include Andice and Bell in Texas, the latter of which is thought to date to between 8000 and 5500 B.P. (Turner and Hester 1993:71–72, 80). A Middle Archaic age is inferred for the type, which is believed to be associated with grassland bison-hunting groups (Mathews

et al. 1998a:56). A single specimen is reported from Fort Polk, at 16VN478, made on Edwards Plateau chert from central Texas (Mathews et al. 1998a:56, 87). *References*: Dickson 1968; Justice 1987:59–60; Perino 1985:62.

Carrollton (n = 15/15 components)
This point type is characterized by a crudely made short triangular blade, pronounced squared to slightly barbed shoulders, and a large square to slightly expanding or contracting stem with an expanded or straight base (Figure 5.2, *c*). The length of the haft element may approach 40 percent or more of the entire point length, giving the blade a stubby appearance. The stem and basal area are frequently smoothed. The type was first named by Crook and Harris (1952) in their overview of the Carrollton and Elam foci. It resembles the Bulverde, although the workmanship is reported as cruder, and Bulverde points lack the characteristic basal smoothing (Suhm and Jelks 1962:171). The Carrollton type occurs in northeastern Texas into western Louisiana (Prewitt 1995:96). A Middle Archaic age is inferred in Texas, where it was identified as a constituent of the Carrollton focus of the Trinity aspect of the Archaic culture. Justice (1987:184) places Carrollton points in his Terminal Archaic Barbed cluster. An age of 4500–4000 rcbp for the type is indicated in north-central Texas (Story 1990:217–218). *References*: Crook and Harris 1952; Perino 1985:67; Schambach 1998:61–62; Suhm and Jelks 1962:171–172; Suhm et al. 1954:406; Turner and Hester 1993:141–142; Webb 2000:10.

Castroville (n = 3/3 components)
This point is characterized by a large triangular blade with straight to excurvate margins, deep barbs formed by basal notching, and a squared to expanding stem with a convex or sometimes straight base (Figure 5.2, *d*). Barbs are commonly nearly as long as or in some cases even longer than the stem, due to the distinctive basal notching; barb width ranges from narrow and pointed to wide with squared ends. The type was defined by J. Charles Kelley (1947a:124) based on work at the Lehmann Rock Shelter in the Edwards Plateau area of central Texas. The point is common in central and southwestern Texas (Prewitt 1995:96) and rare in western Louisiana. Specimens reported on Fort Point may be misidentified (e.g., Cantley 1993:160, 163 illustrates a point that lacks the distinctive basal notching). Turner and Hester (1993:86) date the form to ca. 2900–2360 B.P./2800–2400 rcbp in Texas, while Story (1990:217–218) places it between ca. 2950 and 2750 B.P./2850 and 2600 rcbp. Suhm and Jelks (1962:173) state that it is closely related to the Williams type but has a wider and more angular stem and larger barbs. *References*: Kelley 1947a:124; Suhm and Jelks 1962:173–174; Suhm et al. 1954:408; Turner and Hester 1993:86–88.

Clovis (n = 4/2 components)
This is a lanceolate point with parallel-sided lateral margins, pronounced basal thinning or fluting, and basal and lateral grinding (Figure 2.10). The type, defined by Sellards (1952) based on specimens from the Blackwater Draw site near Clovis, New Mexico, as well as from elsewhere in the Southern Plains and Southwest, dates to the Early and Middle Paleoindian subperiods, from ca. 13,450 to 12,900 B.P./11,500 to 10,800 rcbp. Fluted Clovis-like points are found throughout unglaciated North America and into Central America. *References*: C. D. Howard 1990; E. Howard 1935; Justice 1987:17–24; Sellards 1952; Story 1990:178–188; Suhm and Jelks 1962:177–178; Suhm et al. 1954:412; Turner and Hester 1993:91–95; Webb 2000:2.

***Coastview/Other Paleoindian** (n = 6/5 components); see Plainview, below.*
The Coastview point type was developed at Fort Polk by Gunn (1984a:164, 1984b:145) as a local equivalent of Plainview (see also Campbell and Weed 1986:4-8 and 4-9; Thomas et al. 1993a:128–129). Only one specimen has ever been reported on Fort Polk (at 16SA50, Eagle Hill II); the other five specimens are unidentifiable Plano-like lanceolates. Given the widespread acceptance and utility of the Plainview type, the Coastview name should be retired. These points all properly belong to Justice's (1987:30–35) Lanceolate Plano cluster. *References*: Gunn 1984b:145; Mahula 1982; Wallace 1982.

Darl (n = 2/2 components)
This is a long, narrow point with weakly defined shoulders, a broad rectangular to expanding stem, and a typically concave base. The shoulders form an obtuse angle with the haft, while the blade margins are straight to convex, often finely chipped and serrated, and sometimes beveled. The type was defined by E. O. Miller and Edward B. Jelks (1952:175) based on examples from the Belton Reservoir near Fort Hood, Texas. The type is found in central and southern Texas and is rare in extreme eastern Texas and western Louisiana (Prewitt 1995:100). An age of about 1712 B.P./1800 rcbp has been assigned the type in Texas by Turner and Hester (1993:101). Story (1990:222) suggests that Kent and Woden points may be local variants of the Yarbrough and/or Darl types. The presence of beveling means care must be taken to avoid confusing the type with resharpened Late Paleoindian/Early Archaic forms locally. The type is reported as quite similar in appearance to both the Fairland and Yarbrough types, although Darl points are described as having (typically) a narrower blade and a concave base as well as more frequent beveling (Perino 1985:98; Suhm and Jelks 1962:179). *References*: Miller and Jelks 1952:175; Perino 1985:98; Prewitt 1981; Suhm and Jelks 1962:179–180; Suhm et al. 1954:414; Turner and Hester 1993:101.

Delhi (*n* = *21/19 components*)
This is a large point with a slender triangular blade, weakly defined to well-defined downward sloping barbs, and a squared parallel-sided stem with a straight to slightly convex base (Figure 5.2, *e–g*). It is similar to the Motley type, differing primarily in stem morphology. Identified at the Poverty Point site by Ford and Webb (1956:58), the type is named for the nearby town of Delhi. The type is closely associated with the Poverty Point culture and time period, and it occurs widely in western Mississippi and Louisiana and less frequently in adjoining areas. It is extremely rare in eastern Texas (Prewitt 1995:101). A span of ca. 3520 to 2215 B.P./3300 to 2200 rcbp has been assigned the form by Justice (1987:179–180), who places Delhi points in his Terminal Archaic Barbed cluster. Schambach (1998:54–55) considered Delhi points found during his research in southern Arkansas to be a variety of the Motley type. *References*: Bundy 2002a:86; Cantley 1993:168; Ford and Webb 1956:58; Justice 1987:179–180; Perino 1971, 1985:102; Schambach 1998:54–55; Turner and Hester 1993:103–104; Webb 2000:13.

Dickson (*n* = *1/1 component*)
This type is characterized by a large triangular blade with straight to slightly convex margins, pronounced squared shoulders, and a short square to contracting stem with a flat base (Figure 5.3, *d*). A single well-made example was found at 16VN396 (Cantley and Kern 1984:233, 238). The Dickson type was defined by Winters (1967) from the Dickson Mounds site in Illinois, where it is associated with Middle Woodland Hopewell culture. Because the Dickson type occurs in the Midwest, primarily in Illinois and immediately adjoining areas, it is possible that the point has been misidentified. The Fort Polk example may instead be an unusually large and well-made Bulverde point or possibly a Morhiss point. Dickson points have been attributed to Black Sand and Havana Hopewellian cultures dated ca. 2500–1650 B.P. Justice (1987:190–191) places Dickson Contracting Stemmed points into his Dickson cluster, dated ca. 2600–2080 B.P./2500–2100 rcbp. Unless found with unequivocal Hopewell or Marksville materials, the type name should probably be avoided in future work at Fort Polk (see also Campbell and Weed 1986:4-10). *References*: Cantley and Kern 1984:233, 238; Justice 1987:190–191; Perino 1968:18; Winters 1967.

Dooley Branch Cluster
(*n* = *98, excluding 45 16VN791 specimens/61 components*)
This grouping of terminal Late Archaic/initial Woodland era points was developed by L. Janice Campbell and her colleagues (1990:64–73) based on stratigraphic excavations at 16VN791 on Fort Polk (Figure 5.2, *h–q*). The

Figure 5.3 — Dart point forms from Fort Polk: a, b, Pelican; c, Plainview; d, Dickson?; e, Pontchartrain; f–l, preforms.

principal point types are Ellis, Edgewood, Marcos, Summerfield, and Yarbrough (Campbell et al. 1990:64–73). Critical diagnostic attributes include "(1) an expanding stem formed by corner-notches, and (2) virtually straight bases, although some are very slightly convex or concave. Due to the method of stem formation, most are barbed to a greater or lesser degree, although some (i.e., the Yarbroughs) are not" (Campbell et al. 1990:64). At 16VN791, Dooley Branch cluster points were stratigraphically above Birds Creek cluster points and below Williams cluster points (Campbell et al. 1990:73). They were reported by their respective type (i.e., Ellis, Edgewood, etc.), hence that is the way they are reported herein. A Marcos point from 16VN791 was radiocarbon dated to ca. 2866 B.P./2780 ± 140 rcbp (Beta-33070; Campbell et al. 1990:72–73), providing an initial Woodland date for the form. Use of cluster terminology has not been widely adopted on Fort Polk but should help reduce the ambiguity involved in separating highly similar point types. The Dooley Branch cluster terminology has come to be equated with a distinct type by some researchers on Fort Polk (e.g., Morehead et al. 1995b:44–45), creating some confusion in its application. Since the Dooley Branch points found at 16VN791 were also described by their respective types, they were tallied by those types in the 1999 HPP Inventory and herein. *References*: Campbell et al. 1990:64–73; Morehead et al. 1994:44–45.

Edgewood (n = 28/21 components)
This is a small dart point with a triangular blade, pronounced shoulders, and an expanding stem with a concave to straight base (Figure 5.4, *a*). The haft-shoulder angle varies from acute with pronounced barbs to obtuse and lacking barbs, giving the point a corner- or side-notched appearance, respectively. Blade margins are varied and may be straight to slightly incurvate or excurvate. The shoulders are sometimes asymmetrical, as are the blade margins, which appears to be due to resharpening. The type was defined by Dee Ann Suhm, Alex D. Krieger, and Edward B. Jelks (1954:418) based on examples from Texas. The point form is common in central and eastern to northeastern Texas (Prewitt 1995:102) and into western Louisiana and occurs less commonly in adjoining areas. A transitional Late Archaic/initial Woodland period date, around 3000 B.P., is inferred for the form. At Fort Polk the type has been included in the Dooley Branch point cluster by personnel from Prentice Thomas and Associates, Inc., and a range of ca. 3000 to 1500 B.P. has been inferred (Campbell et al. 1990:64–73). Some points with side or corner notching classified as Edgewood in the general region appear to date appreciably earlier, to the Early Archaic period. On the basis of materials from Fort Polk, for example, Thomas and his colleagues (1993a:35–36) have proposed renaming the taxa Edgewood, *var. Dixon* as San Patrice, *var. Dixon*. Suhm and Jelks (1962:183) note that Edgewood points are similar in some respects to the Fairland, Frio, and Martindale types, although they tend to be smaller and broader. A stratigraphic place-

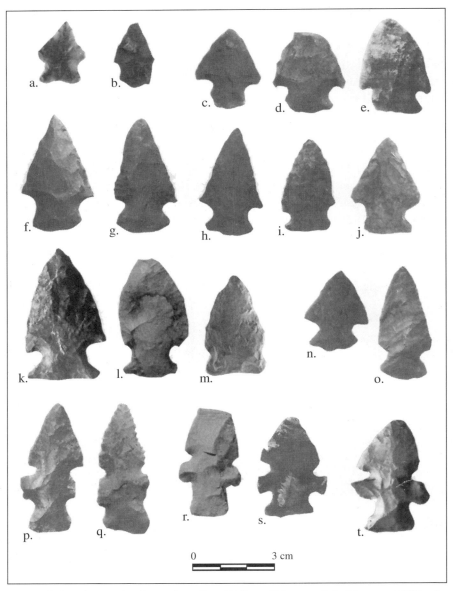

Figure 5.4 — Dart point forms from Fort Polk: a, Edgewood; b, Elam; c–j, Ellis; k–m, Ensor; n, o, Epps; p–t, Evans.

ment below the Williams type was indicated at Eagle Hill II (Gunn 1982a:230, 239). *References*: Cantley 1993:168; Duffield 1959; Perino 1985:120; Suhm and Jelks 1962:183–184; Suhm et al. 1954:418; Turner and Hester 1993:111.

Elam (n = 1/1 component)

This point is a small dart with a triangular blade, prominent shoulders that typically form an obtuse angle with the haft, and a long parallel-sided stem with a straight to convex base (Figure 5.4, *b*). Stem length may approach half the total length of the point. The Elam point was defined by Crook and Harris (1952, 1954:11), who called it the Elam Stemmed. The type is found in central and eastern Texas and is rare in western Louisiana (Prewitt 1995:102). Turner and Hester (1993:112) note that the form resembles the Ellis type but is smaller; some of their illustrated specimens appear to be resharpened, suggesting earlier-stage forms might be classified differently. Unless an unambiguous attribution can be made, the type name should probably be avoided in future studies on Fort Polk. A Late Archaic age for the type is advanced in Texas by Turner and Hester (1993:112). *References*: Crook and Harris 1952, 1954; Johnson 1962; Suhm and Jelks 1962:185–186; Suhm et al. 1954:420; Turner and Hester 1993:112; Webb 2000:9.

Ellis (n = 164/120 components)

These points are small, crudely flaked and thick, weakly barbed, and corner-notched, with a wide expanding stem and a straight to slightly convex base (Figure 5.4, *c–j*). Ellis points were originally defined at the George C. Davis site by Newell and Krieger (1949:166–167) and occur widely over Texas, being most common in the central and eastern parts of the state (Prewitt 1995:103) and in adjoining areas of western Arkansas and Louisiana. This is one of the most common dart point forms at Fort Polk, second only to Gary in incidence, and a co-occurrence of the two forms on Late Archaic and Early Woodland sites in the general region has been suggested (Servello, ed. 1983:907; see also Gray 2002:80). Because it is similar in morphology and manufacture to the Edgewood type, it is often difficult to distinguish the two forms. In part to help resolve this ambiguity, at Fort Polk the Ellis type was included in the Dooley Branch point cluster by archaeologists from Prentice Thomas and Associates, Inc., and a range of ca. 3000 to 1500 B.P. was inferred (Campbell et al. 1990:64–73; Thomas et al. 1993a:39). A date of 3355 B.P./3115 ± 615 rcbp on levels containing Ellis points was reported at 16VN18 at Fort Polk (Fredlund 1983:800). At 16VN794, Ellis points were found in strata inferred to date between 3800 and 2600 B.P./3500 and 2500 rcbp (Cantley 1993:211; Cantley et al. 1993b:256; Gray 2002:80). A broad range for the point form is inferred by some researchers working on Fort Polk, extending from the Late Archaic through the Middle Woodland; a peak in popularity during Tchefuncte and Marksville assemblages has been indicated, although the form is not a good diagnostic of these phases due to its seemingly long temporal occurrence (Morehead et al. 1996a:178–184,

2002:42; see also Bundy 2002a:86–87; Gray 2002:80). Turner and Hester (1993:113) suggest a range of ca. 4500 to 1260 B.P./4000 to 1300 rcbp in Texas for the form. *References*: Cantley 1993:169–170; Johnson 1962; Newell and Krieger 1949:166–167; Shafer 1973:181–187; Suhm and Jelks 1962:187–188; Suhm et al. 1954:420; Thomas et al. 1994a:51; Turner and Hester 1993:113; Webb 2000:9.

Ensor (n = 73/28 components)

This point is characterized by a wide variety of blade shapes, broad, expanding stems with shallow side or corner notches, and a straight base (Figure 5.4, *k–m*). Blade margins are frequently asymmetrical and range from straight to slightly incurvate or excurvate. The most distinctive attribute is the broad haft element, which in some specimens is the widest part of the point. The Ensor type was defined by E. O. Miller and Edward B. Jelks (1952:172) based on specimens found in central Texas. In Texas, otherwise similar specimens with pronounced basal notches or recurved basal edges are typed Frio or Ensor-Frio; resolution of the two types is considered difficult because of a gradation in basal morphology (Turner and Hester 1993:14). The two forms, Ensor and Frio, are widespread in central and southern Texas and somewhat less common in eastern Texas and into Louisiana (Prewitt 1995:103, 106). At Fort Polk the type has been included in the Birds Creek point cluster consisting of the Ensor and Epps types and dated to the terminal Middle Archaic/initial Late Archaic around 6300–3800 B.P./5500–3500 rcbp (Campbell et al. 1990:64–73). At 16VN791 a heat-damaged Ensor point was found immediately above a hearth-like feature dated to 5916 B.P./5160 ± 70 rcbp (Beta-33068; Campbell et al 1990:72). In Texas, where the type was defined and is widespread, it is dated much later: to the Woodland era ca. 2215–1300 B.P./2200–1400 rcbp or later (Turner and Hester 1993:114). These differences in age are appreciable and suggest that the dating or typological assignments attributed to the Birds Creek cluster may need to be rethought. Alternatively, this may well indicate, as Campbell and her colleagues have variously argued, that the Birds Creek cluster at Fort Polk is indeed something different. It is possible that Ensor-like points found in western Louisiana, for example, may be appreciably earlier than the classic forms from Texas or that different types are represented dating to appreciably different eras. *References*: Bundy 2002a:84; Cantley 1993:159–161; Gray and Buchner 2000:63; Miller and Jelks 1952:172; Perino 1985:125; Suhm and Jelks 1962:189–190; Suhm et al. 1954:422; Turner and Hester 1993:114.

Epps (n = 21/19 components)

This point type is characterized by a broad, expanding stem; large, well-defined and deep, curving notches; weakly defined to well-defined barbs; and an expanding stem with a straight to convex base (Figure 5.4, *n–o*). Blade margins are frequently asymmetrical and range from straight to slightly incurvate or excurvate. The haft element is sometimes the widest part of the point. A distinct medial ridge is present on some specimens. The type was defined by James A. Ford and Clarence Webb (1956) during their work at Poverty Point and was named for the nearby town of Epps, Louisiana. The type is common on Late Archaic sites in eastern Louisiana and is less common in western Louisiana. In eastern Texas it is only rarely observed (Prewitt 1995:104). While Justice (1987:199) has argued that Epps points may be reworked Motley points and contemporaneous in age, this does not appear likely since Epps points are thicker and cruder (see also Turner and Hester 1993:115). At Fort Polk the type has been included in the Birds Creek point cluster consisting of the Ensor and Epps types and dated to the terminal Middle Archaic/initial Late Archaic, perhaps from 6300 to 3800 B.P./5500 to 3500 rcbp (Campbell et al. 1990:64–73). An age for the form before classic Poverty Point age appears indicated. Justice (1987:198–201) places Epps points in his Late Archaic and Early Woodland period Motley cluster. *References*: Ford and Webb 1956; Justice 1987:198–201; Perino 1985:126; Thomas et al. 1994a:50; Turner and Hester 1993:115; Webb 2000:13.

Evans (n = 66/49 components)

This dart point form is one of the most distinctive in the entire cultural sequence in the Louisiana area and is readily identifiable by the presence of a second set of notches in the blade that are usually placed a short distance above the shoulder (Figure 5.4, *p–t*). The point itself exhibits ovate or convex blade margins and a straight to expanding stem with a straight to convex, lightly ground base. Shoulders are weakly defined to well-defined, are frequently asymmetrical, and vary appreciably in morphology, from acute to squared to obtuse in angle. The lateral blade margins are sometimes serrated. The Evans point was defined by James A. Ford and Clarence H. Webb (1956:64–65) during their work at the Poverty Point site, although the point is extremely uncommon at that site (Schambach 1998:52). A Middle Archaic to early Late Archaic age is inferred, from roughly 6300 to 3800 B.P./5500 to 3500 rcbp. The point form occurs in southern Arkansas and throughout Louisiana into east Texas (Prewitt 1995:104; Saunders 1996). In southeastern Arkansas Evans points are diagnostic markers of the Dorcheat phase of the Big Creek culture, based on work at the Big Creek and Cooper sites (Jeter and Williams 1989a:98; Schambach 1970:389, 1998:114–117; Schambach and Early 1982:SW57). Saunders and Allen (1997:6–8; Saunders et al. 1994:141–142, 151–152, 1997) have shown that the Evans point is restricted to Louisiana and southern Arkansas and immediately adjoining areas and, based on an occurrence in well-dated strata at Middle Archaic mound sites in northeastern Louisiana, that it occurs between 6000 and 5000 B.P. At Fort Polk, Evans points have been found in Middle and Late Archaic contexts at Big Brushy (Guderjan and Morehead 1983:904–907) and in deeper levels in a test pit opened at 16NA265/16NA274 (Thomas et al. 1993a:36). A Late Archaic/Early Woodland range of ca. 3800 to 2600 B.P./ 3500 to 2500 rcbp was attributed to the form at 16VN794 on the basis of its occurrence in the stratified deposits at that site (Cantley et al. 1993b:256; see also Bundy 2002a:83–84; Gray 2002:77–78). The point type is considered to be diagnostic of the Middle Archaic Sixmile phase on Fort Polk, as defined by Morehead et al. (1996a:170–171; see also Morehead et al. 2002:36–38; Chapter 6 herein). The Sinner type is a related form that is distinguished by multiple notches on the blade. *References*: Bell 1958; Ford and Webb 1956:64–65; Perino 1985:129; Schambach 1998:51–52; Turner and Hester 1993:81; Webb 2000:10.

Fairland (n = 1/1 component)
This is a large dart point with a triangular blade, narrow shoulders, and an expanding stem with an often finely chipped deeply concave to straight base. The haft-shoulder angle varies from acute to nearly squared with weak barbs to obtuse and lacking barbs, giving the point a corner- or side-notched appearance, respectively. The shoulders are sometimes asymmetrical, as are the blade margins, which appears to be due to resharpening. The Fairland type was named by J. Charles Kelley (1947a:124) based on excavations at the Lehmann Rock Shelter in the Edwards Plateau area of central Texas. Turner and Hester (1993:117) note that the form may be confused with the Edgewood and Ellis types, and it also closely resembles the Darl type. The single Fairland point found on Fort Polk, at 16VN34 in 1976, may be a manufacturing or idiosyncratic variant of one of these types. The Fairland type differs from Edgewood points in having much larger downward sweeping notches, and it differs from the Darl type in that the blade is much wider, the stem tips tend to flare outward widely and to be sharp, and the edges are rarely smoothed or beveled; Darl points are commonly beveled (Suhm and Jelks 1962:191; Turner and Hester 1993:101). The Fairland point type is common in central and southern Texas and extremely rare in eastern Texas and western Louisiana (Prewitt 1995:104). Use of other type names is recommended at Fort Polk. A transitional Late Archaic/initial Woodland period age around 3200 B.P. is inferred for the type. *References*: Kelley 1947a:124; Perino 1985:130; Suhm and Jelks 1962:191–192; Suhm et al. 1954:424; Turner and Hester 1993:117.

Figueroa *(n = 3/1 component)*

This small dart type is characterized by a short triangular blade, pronounced unbarbed shoulders, large side notches, and a broad expanding stem with a straight to convex base that is often as wide as the shoulders (Figure 5.5, *a*).

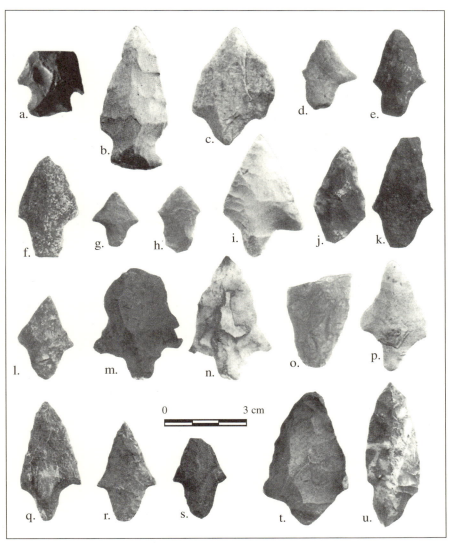

Figure 5.5 — Dart point forms from Fort Polk: a, Figeroa?; b, Form X?; c–u, Gary (c, var. Alsa; d, e, var. Colfax; f, var. Emory; g, var. Garyito; h, var. Hobson; i, var. Kaufman; j, k, var. Kemp; l, var. Kenedy; m, n, var. Maybon; o, var. Panna Maria; p–s, var. Range; t, u, var. unspecified).

The Figueroa type was first formally described by Leroy Johnson (1964:36–37) based on specimens from the trated examples (Turner and Hester 1993:118) include both side- and corner-notched forms, and the category appears to be something of a catchall, accommodating a number of resharpening and size variants. The type occurs in southwestern and south-central Texas, particularly along the lower Pecos, where a time range of 2215 to 1300 B.P./2200 to 1400 rcbp has been assigned (Prewitt 1995:105). The three specimens found on Fort Polk, while generally fitting the Figueroa description (Cantley 1993:162), occur well outside the geographic range of the type. Use of this category on Fort Polk should probably be avoided. *References*: Johnson 1964:36–37; Turner and Hester 1993:118.

Form X (n = 1/1 component)
This point is characterized by a triangular blade with straight to slightly excurvate margins, well-defined shoulders that form an obtuse angle with the haft, and an expanding stem with a straight to slightly convex base (Figure 5.5, *b*). This type was defined by Jelks (1965) based on material from the McGee Bend Reservoir project in eastern Texas. At McGee Bend, Woden and Form X points were attributed to the Late Archaic Brookeland focus. The single example found at Fort Polk, from 16VN928, was in a test unit that also yielded a Woden point in the immediately preceding 10-cm level. An Early Archaic age has been assigned to the related Woden type by Turner and Hester (1993:196), and if the Form X is related it would appear that some uncertainty exists about its age. *References*: Jelks 1965; Thomas et al. 1994a:50.

Gary (n = 208/153 components)
These points are characterized by triangular or ovate blades, weak to pronounced squared shoulders, a contracting stem, and a tapering rounded or convex base (Figure 5.5, *c–u;* Figure 5.6, *a–1*). Weak barbs are sometimes observed. Blade margins are varied and may be straight to slightly incurvate or excurvate. The shoulders are sometimes asymmetrical, as are the blade margins, which appears to be due to resharpening. Points may be well made to crude, and considerable variability is evident within forms typed as Gary. The Gary type was defined by Newell and Krieger (1949:164–165) at the George C. Davis site, where it was described as the Gary Contracting Stem type. Gary is more properly a supertype and a number of distinct varieties have been proposed based on subtle differences in shape and manufacturing treatment (e.g., Johnson 1962; Justice 1987:189–190; Schambach 1982:173–177, 1998:55–61). Gary points are common throughout the lower Mississippi Alluvial Valley and in adjoining areas of Mississippi, Tennessee, Arkansas,

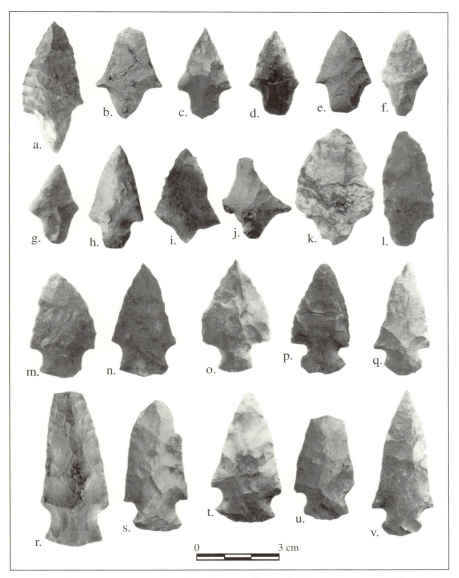

Figure 5.6 — Dart point forms from Fort Polk: a–1, Gary, var. unspecified; *m–v, Godley.*

and eastern Texas. While extremely common in eastern Texas, they do not extend much past the Trinity River (Prewitt 1995:107). The type has been found in numerous Late Archaic through Woodland contexts with a temporal range of ca. 4500 to 1200 B.P. It has been suggested that the point form may decrease in size over time, at least at the assemblage level (Ford and Webb 1956:52–54; Turner and Hester 1993:123). Justice (1987:189–190) places Gary points in his Dickson cluster, which dates from the Late Archaic through the Middle Woodland. An age of ca. 1950–1260 B.P./2000–1300 rcbp for the type is indicated in north-central Texas, while in eastern Texas it is commonly found with early pottery of the Mossy Grove culture, usually sand-tempered Goose Creek Plain (Story 1990:217–218, 222, 256). Gary is the most common projectile point type found on Fort Polk, and a number of variety designations have been used to describe these artifacts. Morehead and Mathews (in Prentice Thomas and Associates, Inc. 1992:20) have given reasons that variety names advanced by Johnson (1962) and used in Texas are preferred: "(1) names are easier to remember than numbers or letters; (2) the Johnson varieties seem more similar to Fort Polk Gary points than the Lower Valley varieties; and (3) the Johnson varieties have seen a fair amount of use in the region." Numerous named varieties have been identified at Fort Polk, including *vars. Kemp, Colfax, Emory* (Prentice Thomas and Associates, Inc. 1992:21), *Hobson, Maybon,* and *Panna Maria* (Gray 2002:78–79; Morehead et al. 1996a:186; Thomas et al. 1993a:27). The most common dart form on the installation, Gary points occur widely in both time and space locally, although there are suggestions that the point form is more common in some drainages on Fort Polk than in others, as indicated by the near absence of the form in the excavations at 16VN791 in the Birds Creek drainage (Campbell et al. 1990:97–98; see also Bundy 2002a:84–85; Gray 2002:78; Prentice Thomas and Associates, Inc. 1992:101). A "small Gary" was found at Eagle Hill II from a level that yielded a date of 1030 B.P./1130 ± 70 rcbp (Gunn 1984b:145). *References*: Cantley 1993:165–166; Ford and Webb 1956; Justice 1987:189–190; Newell and Krieger 1949:164–165; Perino 1985:144; Schambach 1982:173–177; Suhm and Jelks 1962:197–198; Suhm et al. 1954:430; Turner and Hester 1993:123–124; Webb 2000:7–8.

Godley (n = 47/37 components)
This point is characterized by a triangular blade with straight to slightly convex lateral margins, prominent unbarbed shoulders that typically form an obtuse angle with the haft, and a narrow expanding stem with a convex base (Figure 5.6, *m–v;* Figure 5.7, *a–f*). The Godley type was defined by Edward B. Jelks (1962) based on work at the Kyle site in Hill County, Texas. The point occurs in eastern Texas and western Louisiana and appears most common in east-central Texas (Prewitt 1995:107). Turner and Hester (1993:125) assign a Late Archaic to late prehistoric time range for the form in Texas. At Fort Polk Godley points are considered to be Woodland in age by some investigators (Bundy 2002a:89–90; Gray and Buchner 2000:64;

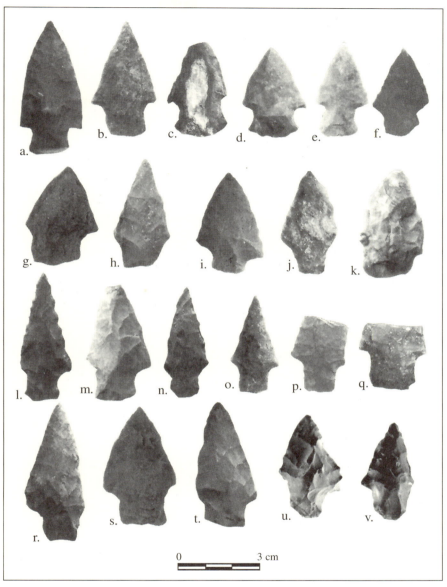

Figure 5.7 — Dart point forms from Fort Polk: a–f, Godley; g–v, Kent.

Thomas et al. 1994a:52). An age of ca. 2136–1538 B.P./2150–1650 rcbp for the type is indicated in north-central Texas (Story 1990:217–218). Separation of this type from Palmillas points is difficult. *References*: Jelks 1962; Perino 1985:152; Thomas et al. 1994a:52; Turner and Hester 1993:125.

Kent *(n = 112/96 components)*
This form exhibits considerable morphological variability but is typified by a large triangular blade (often exhibiting extensive reworking), a crude contracting to squared haft with a flat to convex base, and pronounced to weakly defined asymmetrical shoulders (Figure 5.7, *g–v*). The shoulders are sometimes squared or obtuse in angle, while the stem is typically one-third the length of the entire point. The point is crude in manufacture, with little or no fine retouch on the lateral margins; a prominent medial ridge is often present, giving the point a thick, squared cross section (Turner and Hester 1993:136). The Kent type was defined by Dee Ann Suhm, Alex D. Krieger, and Edward B. Jelks (1954:432) based on examples from Texas. Several varieties have been defined (Johnson 1962), although these have seen only infrequent and uneven use. On Fort Polk, where the form is common, when varieties of the Kent type are identified, they are typically called *var. Phalba* (e.g., Thomas et al. 1992:27–28; see also Bundy 2002a:85–86; Gray and Buchner 2000:64), which is characterized by a square to slightly contracting stem. Kent points occur widely across eastern and southeastern Texas (Prewitt 1995:112) and Louisiana and are dated ca. 2500–1366/4000–1500 rcbp, from the Late Archaic through the Middle Woodland period. Story (1990:222, 251) suggests that Kent and Woden points may be local variants of the Yarbrough and/or Darl types and notes that they are common on early ceramic Mossy Grove culture sites. Kent is thought to be related to the Pontchartrain type but is typically thicker and cruder, while Pontchartrain types are characterized by fine lateral retouch. The slightly contracting stem also suggests a relationship with Gary points. *References*: Campbell 1952; Johnson 1962; Perino 1985:201; Story et al. 1990; Suhm and Jelks 1962:199–200; Suhm et al. 1954:432; Turner and Hester 1993:136; Webb 2000:10–11.

Lange *(n = 18/16 components)*
These points have a large triangular blade with pronounced barbs and a slightly expanding, straight-sided stem (Figure 5.8, *b–f*). The shoulders range from acute with pronounced corner notches to squared, and they are asymmetrical on some specimens. The base is straight to slightly concave or convex. The Lange type was defined by Dee Ann Suhm, Alex D. Krieger, and Edward B. Jelks (1954:436) based on examples from Texas. The type is fairly common in central Texas and less common over the rest of the state (Prewitt 1995:114), extending into western Louisiana. It has been dated to ca. 2850–2600 B.P. at the Loma Sandia site in eastern Texas, where it is assumed to be Late Archaic in age (Taylor and Highley n.d.; Turner and Hester 1993:141). *References*: Perino 1985:219; Suhm and Jelks 1962:203–204; Suhm et al. 1954:436; Turner and Hester 1993:141–142.

Figure 5.8 — Dart point forms from Fort Polk: a, Kirk Corner-Notched; b–f, Lange; g, Lone Oak?; h, i, Macon; j–o, Marcos; p–r, Marshall.

Lone Oak *(n = 1/1 component)*

This is a crude dart form with a triangular blade, slight to well-defined barbs, and a large expanding stem with a convex to rounded base (Figure 5.8, *g*). The type was defined by Leroy Johnson (1962) based on specimens from northeast Texas. The form resembles the Palmillas type but is larger and cruder (Turner and Hester 1993:146); like the Palmillas type, the Lone Oak type appears to be poorly defined and too overly general to be a useful category. Lone Oak points are reported from northeastern Texas (Prewitt 1995:115), and a possible Early Archaic age has been assigned by Turner and Hester (1993:146). At Fort Polk the type has been considered part of the Woodland era Williams cluster (Morehead and Mathews 1992:22), a temporal assignment that may be more appropriate, particularly given its resemblance to Palmillas forms. Given the ambiguity surrounding its description and dating, use of the Lone Oak type name should be avoided in future studies on Fort Polk. *References*: Johnson 1962; Turner and Hester 1993:146.

Lowe (n = 5/5 components)
This point is characterized by an expanding stem with a straight base and sharp pointed ears. The blade is triangular with straight to slightly excurvate margins and straight to slightly barbed shoulders. The type Lowe Flared Base was defined by H. Winters (1963:90) from examples found in the Wabash Valley of Illinois, where it dates to the Early and Middle Woodland periods. A series of related forms occurs widely across much of the Midwest and Southeast during this time and includes the Bakers Creek, Swannanoa Stemmed, and Steuben Expanding Stemmed types. Justice (1987:208–213) places Lowe Flared Base points in his Lowe cluster and dates the form ca. 1712–1366 B.P./1800–1500 rcbp. The points resemble the Ellis and Ensor types, and Louisiana specimens may be more appropriately classified using one of these taxa. *References*: Cantley et al. 1997:825; Justice 1987:212–213; H. Winters 1963:90.

Macon (n = 12/11 components)
This point is a thick, square-stemmed dart point with straight to slightly excurvate blade margins, squared shoulders, and faint barbs (Figure 5.8, *h–i*). The type was defined by James A. Ford and Clarence H. Webb (1956) based on their work at the Poverty Point site in northeast Louisiana. The type is assumed to date to the Late Archaic and Early Woodland periods. *References*: Bundy 2002a:85; Campbell et al. 1990:62–63; Ford and Webb 1956; Meyer et al. 1996b:54; Webb 2000:13–14.

Marcos (n = 80/32 components)
This point is characterized by a large triangular blade, deep corner notches, pronounced barbs, and an expanding stem with a straight to slightly convex base (Figure 5.8, *j–o*). The type, defined by Dee Ann Suhm, Alex D. Krieger, and Edward B. Jelks (1954:442) based on examples from Texas, is common

in central and southeastern Texas into western Louisiana. Turner and Hester (1993:14) have noted that the type "is similar in form to Castroville, but the stem of Marcos expands more sharply and the notches are cut inward from the corners rather than upward from the base" and that more research is needed to differentiate it from similar forms. It is also similar to Ensor points but has a broader blade, longer barbs, and a narrower stem width (Suhm and Jelks 1962:209). At Fort Polk, where it is common, the type has been included in the Dooley Branch point cluster, consisting of the Ellis, Edgewood, Marcos, Summerfield, and Yarbrough types, and a range of ca. 3200 to 1366 B.P./3000 to 1500 rcbp has been inferred (Campbell et al. 1990:64–73; Thomas et al. 1993a:39). Turner and Hester (1993:147) suggest a range of 2750 to 1712 B.P./2600 to 1800 rcbp in Texas for the form. At 16VN791, a Marcos-like point was found at 80 cm below the surface in Test Pit 18, and charcoal from this area was radiocarbon dated to ca. 2866 B.P./2780 ± 140 rcbp (Beta-33070; Campbell et al. 1990:72–73, 91). At 16VN794, Marcos points were found in strata inferred to date between 3800 and 2600 B.P./3500 and 2500 rcbp, although the type was considered to be early Late Archaic in age (Cantley et al. 1994:211, 256; Gray 2002:79). A broad range for the point form is inferred by some researchers working on Fort Polk, extending from the Late Archaic through the Middle Woodland; associations with Tchefuncte and Marksville assemblages have been indicated, although the form is not a good diagnostic of these phases because of its seemingly long temporal occurrence (Morehead et al. 1996a:178–184, 2002:42; see also Bundy 2002a:87; Gray 2002:79). *References*: Perino 1985:240; Suhm and Jelks 1962:209–210; Suhm et al. 1954:442; Turner and Hester 1993:147–148; Webb 2000:11.

Marshall (n = 22/21 components)
This point is characterized by a large triangular blade with excurvate margins, pronounced shoulders with deep barbs, and a short squared to slightly expanding stem with an indented or concave base (Figure 5.8, *p–r*). The Marshall type was defined by Dee Ann Suhm, Alex D. Krieger, and Edward B. Jelks (1954:444; Suhm and Jelks 1962:211–212) based on examples from Texas. The point is commonly found in central Texas and is rare in western Louisiana. An Archaic age, 3200 B.P. or earlier, is suggested by Turner and Hester (1993:149). The point closely resembles the Castroville type. *References*: Perino 1985:241; Schambach 1998:40–42; Suhm and Jelks 1962:211–212; Suhm et al. 1954:444; Turner and Hester 1993:149–150; Webb 2000:11.

Martindale (n = 3/3 components)
This is a corner-notched form with well-defined shoulders and a pronounced basal depression, which gives the haft a fishtail or bifurcate-like appear-

ance. Considerable size and shape variation is evident within typed specimens, which is due in part to the fact that the type was extensively
resharpened. The type was defined by Dee Ann Suhm, Alex D. Krieger, and
Edward B. Jelks (1954:446) based on examples from Texas. Classic
Martindale forms appear primarily in central Texas, although similar forms
are identified in western Louisiana. The type appears to be a variant within
the Early Archaic corner-notched horizon dating to ca. 10,715–9850 B.P./
9500–8800 rcbp in the Southeast and may also be related to the slightly
later, terminal Early Archaic bifurcate horizon dating to ca. 10,050–8100
B.P./8900–7800 rcbp (Chapman 1985:146). The type appears closely related
to the Palmer and Kirk corner-notched types defined by Coe (1964), differing only in having more pronounced shoulders and an indented instead of
more flattened base. *References*: Prewitt 1981; Suhm and Jelks 1962:213–
214; Suhm et al. 1954:446; Turner and Hester 1993:151–152.

Matamoros (n = 1/1 component)
This is a triangular unstemmed point with straight to convex sides and a
straight to slightly concave or convex base. The blade is thick and typically
beveled, indicating use as a knife. The Matamoros type was named by R. S.
McNeish (Perino 1985:244) and defined by Suhm et al. (1954:448). The
type is common in central and southern Texas (Prewitt 1995:117) and extends into southern Tamaulipas in northeastern Mexico (Suhm and Jelks
1962:215). The type is rarely reported in Louisiana, although it should be
noted that triangular bifacial cutting tools are common locally and may be
confused with this type. A single specimen resembling the Matamoros type
was found at Fort Polk, at 16VN2523 on Peason Ridge, made of local
Citronelle gravel chert (Ezell and Ensor 1999:356). Given the use of local
materials and the distance from the major area of occurrence of the type, the
artifact in question may be a late-stage preform. A Late Archaic to late prehistoric range is inferred by Turner and Hester (1993:153). *References*: Perino
1985:244; Suhm and Jelks 1962:215–216; Suhm et al. 1954:448; Turner
and Hester 1993:153.

Midland (n = 6/6 components)
This is a small, thin, parallel to slightly expanding lanceolate point with a
flat to slightly indented base (Figure 5.9, *a*). Classic Midland points are well
made with fine, regular retouch along the margins and are similar to Folsom
points, lacking only the fluting. The type was defined by Fred Wendorf,
Alex D. Krieger, C. C. Albritton, and T. D. Stewart (1955) and Wendorf and
Krieger (1959:57) from examples found at the Scharbauer site near Midland, Texas. Turner and Hester (1993:155) have noted that classic Midland

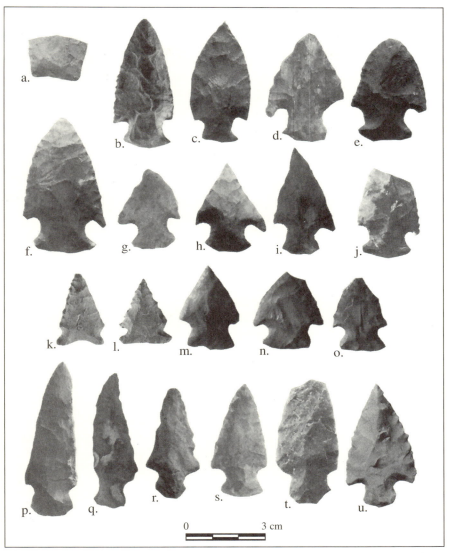

Figure 5.9 — Dart point forms from Fort Polk: a, Midland; b–j, Motley; k–o, Palmer Corner-Notched; p–u, Palmillas.

points occur in northern and central Texas, in and near the southern part of the Llano Estacado. Points with a similar morphology but that are thicker and less well executed occur in western Louisiana and have been called Midland. The relationship of the Louisiana specimens with classic Midland forms and with Folsom points is unknown. Midland points are assumed to be Paleoindian in age, perhaps contemporaneous with Folsom points (ca. 13,000–11,450 B.P./11,000–10,000 rcbp) (Frison 1978:25, 83). The Louisiana specimens resemble unfluted lanceolates commonly attributed to a Middle Paleoindian age in many parts of the Southeast. Justice (1987:35) places these points in his Lanceolate Plano cluster. *References*: Perino 1985:253; Turner and Hester 1993:155; Wendorf et al. 1955; Wendorf and Krieger 1959:57.

Morhiss (n = 4/4 components)
This point is characterized by a large triangular blade, small squared shoulders, and a long, broad rectangular stem with parallel to slightly contracting sides and a convex base. Stem length may approach 30 percent of the length of the entire point. The shoulders and blade margins are sometimes asymmetrical, which is the result of resharpening and use damage. The blade margins are typically excurvate but can vary, ranging from excurvate to straight to slightly incurvate. The Morhiss type was defined by Dee Ann Suhm, Alex D. Krieger, and Edward B. Jelks (1954:454) based on examples from Texas. The form occurs primarily in the southeastern Gulf Coastal Plain of Texas and is rare in western Louisiana (Prewitt 1995:121; Patterson 1995). Turner and Hester (1993:158) have assigned a terminal Late Archaic/ initial Woodland date to the form of about 2900 B.P./2800 rcbp. *References*: Perino 1985:258; Suhm and Jelks 1962:221–222; Suhm et al. 1954:454; Turner and Hester 1993:158–159.

Morrill (n = 4/4 components)
The Morrill point is characterized by a long, narrow triangular blade with straight to slightly convex lateral margins, small weakly squared to well-squared shoulders, and a long, broad rectangular stem with parallel to slightly expanding sides and a flat base. The point's shoulders vary from weakly barbed to squared to obtuse in angle with the haft, and they are sometimes asymmetrical, probably as a result of resharpening and use damage. The haft is nearly as wide as the blade in many specimens. The Morrill type was defined by H. Perry Newell and Alex D. Krieger (1949:167–168) based on specimens recovered from the George C. Davis site in eastern Texas. The type occurs primarily in east-central Texas and is uncommon in western Louisiana. Turner and Hester (1993:158) have assigned an Early to Middle Archaic date for the form in Texas. A close resemblance to the Wells type has been noted (Suhm et al. 1962:223). On the basis of work at the Cooper site in southern Arkansas, where these points were found in association with Bulverde points, which they also closely resemble, Schambach (1998:48– 49) designated them a separate variety of Bulverde, *var. Morrill. References*:

Johnson 1962; Newell and Krieger 1949:167–168; Perino 1985:259; Suhm and Jelks 1962:223–224; Suhm et al. 1954:456; Turner and Hester 1993:158–159.

Motley (n = 68/54 components)
This is a large point with a slender triangular blade, pronounced corner notches and well-defined barbs, and an expanding stem with a straight to convex base (Figure 5.9, *b–j*). Identified at the Jaketown, Motley Place, and Poverty Point sites and defined using materials from the Jaketown site in western Mississippi by James A. Ford, Philip Phillips, and William Haag (1955:129–131), the form is closely associated with the Poverty Point culture and time period. The type occurs widely in western Mississippi and Louisiana and less frequently in adjoining areas; only a few specimens have been observed in eastern Texas (Prewitt 1995:122). A span of ca. 3500 to 2500 B.P. is usually assumed for the form. Justice (1987:198–201) places the type within his Motley cluster, dated ca. 3650–2750 B.P./3400–2600 rcbp. *References*: Ford and Webb 1956; Ford et al. 1955:129–131; Justice 1987:198–201; Perino 1985:263; Schambach 1998:52–55; Thomas et al. 1994a:50; Turner and Hester 1993:162; Webb 2000:12.

Neches River (n = 3/3 components)
This is a triangular expanding to rectangular straight-stemmed point with straight to slightly convex lateral margins and a rounded base. The lower portions of the blade are typically serrated, indicating use as a knife. The Neches River type was defined by Jelks (1965). The type occurs primarily in extreme southeastern and eastern Texas (Prewitt 1995:117) and into western Louisiana. An occurrence coeval with the Sinner type and possibly with Birds Creek points is suggested at Fort Polk (Mathews et al. 1999:60, 131; Parrish et al. 1998:64; Thomas et al. 1999b:64). In Texas a Middle Archaic age is inferred by Turner and Hester (1993:163). *References*: Jelks 1965; Turner and Hester 1993:163.

Nolan (n = 2/2 components)
This is a large dart point with a square to slightly expanding stem, a straight alternately beveled base, weakly tapered shoulders that typically form an obtuse angle with the stem, and a large triangular blade with excurvate or convex margins. The steep, alternate beveling on the haft area is highly distinctive and reminiscent of beveling on Late Paleoindian through Early Archaic point and tool forms in the general region, such as Albany and Edgefield scrapers, Red River knives, and San Patrice, Palmer, and Dalton points. The Nolan type was defined by J. Charles Kelley (1947b:99) based on speci-

mens from central Texas, where it was described as the Nolan Beveled Stem type and noted as the key diagnostic of the Clear Fork focus (Suhm and Jelks 1962:225). A time range of roughly 6800 to 5100 B.P./6000 to 4500 rcbp is inferred in central Texas, where the point is most commonly observed (Prewitt 1995:123), although an earlier, Early Archaic, dating may be indicated by the beveling (Turner and Hester 1993:82). *References*: Kelley 1947b:99; Suhm 1959; Suhm and Jelks 1962:225–226; Suhm et al. 1954:458; Turner and Hester 1993:164.

Palmer/Kirk Corner-Notched (n = 22/19 components)

These points are small corner-notched forms with a straight to slightly concave, heavily ground base, barbed shoulders, and (in all but the earliest stage forms) a resharpened, serrated, and sometimes beveled blade (Figures 5.8, *a*, and 5.9, *k–o*). Larger forms are sometimes described using the Kirk corner-notched type. The Palmer and Kirk corner-notched types were named by Joffre L. Coe (1964:67–70) based on work at the Hardaway site in south-central North Carolina. Palmer and Kirk corner-notched points, or close morphological variants, occur widely across the Southeast and into Texas and the eastern Plains and are of Early Archaic age, occurring within a corner-notched horizon dating ca. 10,715–9850 B.P./9500–8800 rcbp. Whether the two types—which appear to reflect size variants rather than any temporal or behaviorally meaningful forms—even warrant taxonomic separation is a continuing source of discussion in the Southeast (Cable 1982; Chapman 1985; Justice 1987:71–82).

The Palmer type, as defined and used in Texas and Louisiana, appears closely related to the Martindale type, which is probably a contemporaneous variant. Palmer points have been identified by some investigators on Fort Polk (e.g., Abrams et al. 1995:157–160; Cantley 1993:168–170), although this has caused some consternation among other researchers (e.g., Morehead et al. 1995d:139), who argue that the local forms do not precisely match Coe's original type description (which states the points are made on prismatic flakes) and that use of local taxa, specifically San Patrice variants, is probably more appropriate. The Palmer and Kirk type designations, somewhat unfortunately, have been widely adopted across much of the East and no longer precisely correspond to Coe's original formulations. Use of these types in Louisiana, accordingly, would appear appropriate only if detailed descriptive and measurement data are provided and if relationships to local taxa are discussed. The San Patrice, *vars. Dixon* and *Keithville* taxa should be used on Fort Polk whenever possible. *References*: Coe 1964:67–70; Justice 1987:71–82; Perino 1968, 1985:207, 286; Story et al. 1990; Turner and Hester 1993:166.

Palmillas (*n = 78/61 components*)
The Palmillas point type has a triangular to leaf-shaped blade, slight to well-defined barbs, and an expanding stem (Figure 5.9, *p–u*). The type description indicates that the "chief characteristic is the small, bulbous stem, with expanded sides and convex base," although the description continues by stating that "occasionally specimens with straight bases should be included" (Suhm and Jelks 1962:229; see also Suhm et al. 1954:462). Blade margins are described as "straight to convex, occasionally concave or recurved" while considerable variability in shoulder morphology is also indicated (Suhm and Jelks 1962:229). The type is considered to be poorly defined and overly general, encompassing a range of forms and reflecting varying levels of skill in execution (Prentice Thomas and Associates, Inc. 1992:22; Schambach 1998:46; Turner and Hester 1993:167). Palmillas types are widely reported from southern Tamaulipas across eastern Texas and Louisiana (Prewitt 1995:124), although given the poor definition exactly what such a distribution means is unclear. The type is similar to the Williams type but tends to be smaller (Suhm and Jelks 1962:229). At Fort Polk the Palmillas type, along with the Calcasieu, Williams, and Lone Oak types, has been placed into a Williams cluster by archaeologists from Prentice Thomas and Associates, Inc. (Campbell et al. 1990:73; Prentice Thomas and Associates, Inc. 1992:22). The Williams cluster has been dated to the Woodland or Formative era, stratigraphically above the Dooley Branch cluster, and prior to and continuing through the introduction of arrow points (see also Bundy 2002a:88–89). Given its ambiguous description, the type name should probably be avoided in future studies at Fort Polk. *References*: Cantley 1993:167–168; Prentice Thomas and Associates, Inc. 1992:22; Schambach 1998:46; Suhm 1957; Suhm and Jelks 1962:229; Suhm et al. 1954:462; Turner and Hester 1993:167.

Pelican (*n = 4/4 components*)
This point is characterized by a lanceolate shape with weak shoulders that are typically the widest part of the point, although this may be due to resharpening (Figure 5.3, *a–b*). Hafts are squared and expand slightly toward the shoulders; lateral margins are ground, while bases are flat to slightly indented. Some specimens are basally thinned to the point of fluting. The Pelican type was defined by Sherwood M. Gagliano and Hiram F. Gregory, Jr. (1965:71) based on specimens from the Louisiana area. The type is found in Louisiana and Arkansas and in low incidence in east Texas (Prewitt 1995:126). In general shape, the Louisiana specimens resemble unfluted lanceolates attributed to a Middle to Late Paleoindian age in parts of the Southeast, suggesting an occurrence from ca. 12,900 to 11,450 B.P./10,800

to 10,000 rcbp. The Pelican type appears closely related to early varieties of San Patrice points, and an affiliation with Dalton points has also been suggested (Gillam 1996:406; Justice 1987:43). The Pelican type is very similar in shape to San Patrice, *var. Hope* (e.g., Webb 1981), and locally it has been tentatively associated with Anacoco I phase San Patrice assemblages (Morehead et al. 2002:25). *References*: Gagliano and Gregory 1965:71; Perino 1985:295; Turner and Hester 1993:174; Webb 2000:3–4.

Plainview (n = 6/5 components)
Plainview points are unfluted lanceolates with parallel lateral margins and straight to slightly indented, well-ground bases (Figure 5.3, *c*). Flaking is usually well executed and parallel or collateral in nature. Basal thinning is evident in some specimens. The type was originally defined by Alex Krieger (1947; also in Sellards et al. 1947) based on materials from the Plainview site in Texas. Unfluted lanceolates resembling Plainview points have been noted at a number of sites in western Louisiana, where they have been variously typed as Coastview (Gunn 1984b:145), Midland, and Angostura; the five specimens from Fort Polk were originally classified as Coastview/other Paleoindian. Plainview points in Texas have been dated to ca. 11,800–11,450/ 10,150–10,010 rcbp by Turner and Hester (1993:175). Justice (1987:30–35) places these points into his Lanceolate Plano cluster. *References*: Perino 1985:304; Sellards et al. 1947, Suhm and Jelks 1962:239–240; Suhm et al. 1954:472; Turner and Hester 1993:175–176; Webb 2000:3.

Pontchartrain (n = 23/20 components)
This is a long narrow point with straight to slightly convex lateral margins, small weakly squared to well-squared shoulders, and a short and narrow rectangular stem with a (typically) straight to convex or rounded base (Figure 5.3, *e*). The shoulders vary, from weakly barbed to squared to obtuse in angle with the haft; both the shoulders and the lateral margins are sometimes asymmetrical, probably as a result of resharpening and use damage. Broad, well-executed parallel flaking may be observed on the blade in some instances. The point type was named by James A. Ford and Clarence H. Webb (1956) based on their work at the Poverty Point site in eastern Louisiana. Pontchartrain points are common in eastern Louisiana and are much less frequently observed in the western part of the state and in eastern Texas (Prewitt 1995:127). The type is commonly found in Tchefuncte assemblages in eastern Louisiana and is thought to be related to the Flint Creek type of Alabama and Mississippi (Morehead et al. 1995b:47; Perino 1985:306). A range of ca. 3500 to 2000 B.P. is inferred in Louisiana, whereas Turner and Hester (1993:177) suggest a range of ca. 2500 to 1366 B.P./4000 to 1500

rcbp in Texas. *References*: Ford and Webb 1956; Perino 1985:306; Turner and Hester 1993:177; Webb 1982, 2000:9.

San Patrice (n = 116/105 components)

These points are typically characterized by a weakly to deeply indented concave base, weak shoulders, and extensive resharpening of the blade area (Figure 5.10, *a–s;* Figure 5.11, *a–k*). In all but the earliest-stage specimens, the shoulders are the widest part of the artifact. Basal and lateral margins are ground, and the base may exhibit thinning resembling fluting on some specimens. Points designated San Patrice are common in east Texas (Prewitt 1995:128), Louisiana, and contiguous portions of Arkansas and Mississippi. The type appears to be a local variant on a terminal Paleoindian/initial Early Archaic complex stretching from the Plains to the Atlantic coast and most commonly described using the Meserve and Dalton types, which are actually supertypes subsuming many local variants (including, in the Southeast, the Nucholls, Greenbrier, and Hardaway Dalton variants). The San Patrice type also appears related to the Pelican type, which differs largely in basal morphology.

A number of morphological variants within the San Patrice type itself have been named employing a type-variety system. Their occurrence on Fort Polk is presented in Table 5.1. A number of these points (n = 34), it should be noted, could not or were not classified to a particular variety and are reported as *var. unspecified.* Finally, San Patrice includes side- and corner-notched forms or varieties that encompass Early Archaic period types used elsewhere in the region, such as Kirk and Palmer. These varieties appear to reflect an evolution from lanceolate to side notching and then corner notching, a trend observed over much of the East during the Late Paleoindian/ initial Holocene era. Named San Patrice variants of Late Paleoindian age include *var. Hope* and *var. St. Johns* (Duffield 1963). San Patrice, *var. Hope* points are deeply indented lanceolates with weak shoulders and (in some cases) side notching; the type appears closely related to classic Dalton points from the central Mississippi Valley (Morse 1973; Morse and Morse 1983) (Figure 5.10, *e–j*). San Patrice, *var. St. Johns* points have a more varied, flat to indented, basal morphology and moderate to pronounced side- to corner-hafting notches; with extensive resharpening and basal attrition, these points increasingly resemble corner-notched forms (Figure 5.11, *a–e*). Basal thinning is common on both *var. Hope* and *var. St. Johns* points and in some cases may represent true fluting. Justice (1987:43–44) places the *St. Johns* and *Hope* varieties of San Patrice in his Dalton cluster and considers *var. St. Johns* to be a morphological correlate of the Hardaway Side-Notched type as defined by Coe (1964:67). On Fort Polk, Thomas and his colleagues

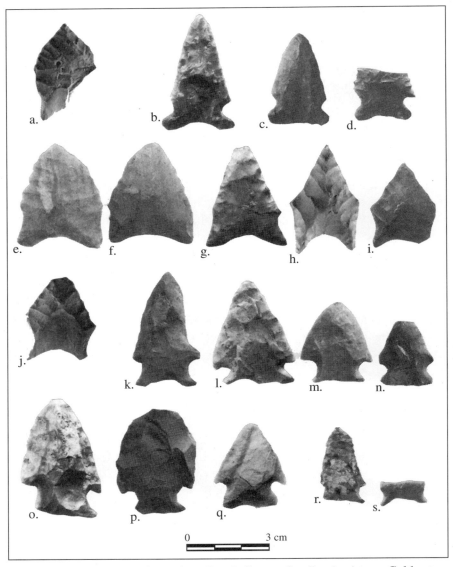

Figure 5.10 — Dart point forms from Fort Polk: a–s, San Patrice (a, var. Coldwater; b–d, var. Dixon; e–j, var. Hope; k–q, var. Keithville; r, s, var. Leaf River).

(1993a:35–36) have proposed an additional San Patrice variety, *var. Dixon,* characterized by pronounced side notches, replacing the type Edgewood, *var. Dixon* (Figure 5.10, *b–d*). Their argument for the creation of this variety is presented in Chapter 6 of this volume. Use of a San Patrice variety for

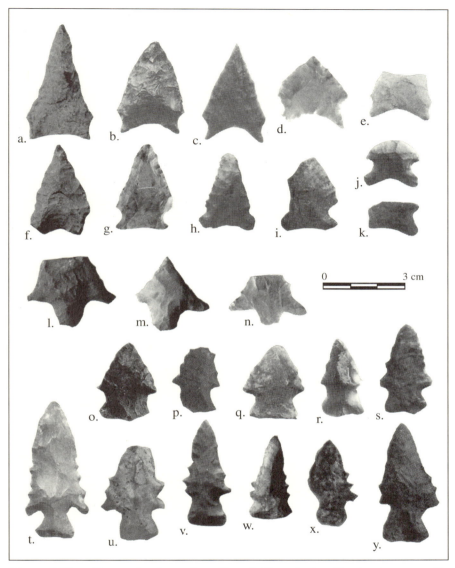

Figure 5.11 — Dart point forms from Fort Polk: a–k, San Patrice (a–e, var. St. Johns; f–k, var. unspecified); 1–n, Shumla; o–y, Sinner.

these points is appropriate until terminology is developed for the pan-south-eastern side-notched horizon that is now known to occur in Late Paleoindian/ initial Early Archaic contexts. A fourth San Patrice variety, *var. Coldwater*, was found at one site on Fort Polk (Abrams et al. 1995:414). Resembling the

Hope variant as well as the Coldwater point type from Mississippi (McGahey 1996), the point appears to date to the later Paleoindian era.

A fifth San Patrice variety identified on Fort Polk, *var. Keithville*, is characterized by a straight base and corner notching rather than side notching (Thomas et al. 1993b:46) (Figure 5.10, *k–q*). The *var. Keithville* form replaces the earlier Keithville type as defined by Duffield (1963; see also Turner and Hester 1993:134–135). Pronounced serrations and beveled blade edges are at times observed on specimens from Louisiana (Griffing 1994:110–111), although these attributes are uncommon on Fort Polk (Morehead et al. 2002:21). Neither the side-notched *var. Dixon* nor the corner-notched *var. Keithville* form exhibits evidence for pronounced basal thinning resembling fluting, which is something more commonly observed on the earlier *Hope* and *St. Johns* varieties. The sixth and final named variety found on Fort Polk, *var. Leaf River*, appears to be a late corner-notched form related to *var. Keithville* (Figure 5.10, *r–s*). San Patrice points are assumed to be contemporaneous with Dalton and initial Holocene side- and corner-notched horizons, with an estimated span of ca. 12,900 to 10,200 B.P./10,800 to 9000 rcbp. Within the San Patrice supertype, *var. Hope* is assumed to be earlier (probably pre–11,450 B.P./10,000 rcbp) and *vars. St. Johns, Dixon,* and *Keithville* later (post–11,850 B.P./10,200 rcbp), reflecting an evolution from lanceolate to first side-notched and then corner-notched forms. San Patrice points are common on Fort Polk, with many varieties observed (e.g., Bundy 2002a:82–83; Gray and Buchner 2000:60; Thomas et al. 1992:33–36). On Fort Polk, San Patrice, *vars. Hope* and *St. Johns* are considered diagnostic of the Late Paleoindian Anacoco I phase. San Patrice, *var. Dixon* is considered diagnostic of the Late Paleoindian/initial Early Archaic Anacoco II phase, and San Patrice, *var. Keithville* is considered diagnostic of the Early Archaic Anacoco III phase, as defined by Morehead et al. (2002:29–31; see Chapter 6). *References*: Duffield 1963; Suhm and Jelks 1962:243–244; Suhm et al. 1954:477; Webb 1946:13–17, 2000:3–4; Webb et al. 1971.

Scottsbluff (n = 8/8 components)

This point is characterized by a lanceolate shape with weak shoulders, a pronounced squared to slightly expanding stem, and fine parallel flaking of the blade. The haft area is basally and laterally ground. The type was named by E. H. Barbour and C. B. Schultz (1932) based on materials from the Scottsbluff bison kill site in Nebraska. Some examples have been resharpened and beveled to produce a scraping tool similar in shape to Albany or Edgefield scrapers (Michie 1972; Webb 1946); locally these bifacial tool forms are called Red River knives (Johnson 1989:38–39). Scottsbluff points have been described as follows:

[A] handsome point distinguished by: (1) small shoulders; (2) a well defined stem that is parallel-sided to slightly expanded with square corners and a generally straight base; and (3) more or less parallel-sided pressure flake scars that terminate smoothly at or near the midline of the point and that are the result of a carefully staged sequence of production. . . . Along with the closely related Eden points and a transversely bladed knife form (the Cody knife), it is considered to be diagnostic of the Cody Complex (Wormington 1957:136–137; Frison 1978:181–191) [Story 1990:205].

Scottsbluff points occur throughout the Plains and into the western part of the Eastern Woodlands and have been described as "widely scattered over much of Texas with the greatest concentration in east Texas and adjoining portions of Louisiana" (Turner and Hester 1993:183; see also Story 1990:205–210). Prewitt's (1995:129) distributional analysis shows them to be fairly common in southern and eastern Texas. Scottsbluff points are Early Archaic in age, and ranges of 10,238 to 9553 B.P./9120 to 8650 rcbp have been advanced for the type in Texas (Turner and Hester 1993:183); Story (1990:209) suggests a range of 11,250 to 10,235 B.P./9900 to 9100 rcbp. Justice (1987:46–51) places Scottsbluff points into his Scottsbluff cluster, which he dates to ca. 9850–9450 B.P./8800–8400 rcbp. *References*: Barbour and Schultz 1932; Perino 1985:348; Story 1990:205–210; Suhm and Jelks 1962:245–246; Suhm et al. 1954:478; Turner and Hester 1993:183–185; Webb 2000:6–7.

Shumla (n = 6/4 components)
This type is characterized by a triangular blade with weakly serrated lateral margins, pronounced barbs, and a squared stem with a flat base (Figure 5.11, *1–n*). The blade edges often exhibit fine retouch and are most commonly straight to slightly convex but sometimes include incurvate forms. The Shumla type was defined by Dee Ann Suhm, Alex D. Krieger, and Edward B. Jelks (1954:480) based on artifacts from Texas. Shumla points are common in southwestern Texas along the Pecos River and into northern Mexico, where a temporal range of ca. 3200–225 B.P./3000–2200 rcbp has been proposed (Turner and Hester 1993:186; Prewitt 1995:130). The point type is not reported from eastern Texas in Prewitt's distributional analysis, and it is thus likely to be extremely rare in western Louisiana as well. It is possible that the examples reported from Fort Polk are misidentified; three examples reported from 16VN794, for example, lack the distinctive basal notches and weak lateral serrations (Cantley 1993:166–167). Unless a clear match can be obtained, the type name should be avoided in future studies in western Louisiana. *References*: Bell 1960:86; Perino 1985:353; Schambach 1998:64;

Suhm and Jelks 1962:247–248; Suhm et al. 1954:480; Turner and Hester 1993:186.

Sinner *(n = 23/17 components)*

These darts are characterized by pronounced serrations or notches on the blade margins, squared to barbed shoulders, and a square to slightly expanding stem with a straight to irregular base (Figure 5.11, *o–y*). The serrations or notches appear to have served a cutting function rather than serving as hafting notches or spokeshaves; many examples are asymmetrical with damaged blades or haft areas indicative of resharpening and heavy use. The Sinner type was defined by Clarence H. Webb and his colleagues (1969) from the Resch site in Harrison County, Texas. Sinner points have been associated with the Avery (Gagliano 1967a:65; Thomas et al. 1994a:50) and Evans types in Louisiana. The multiple notches distinguish Sinner from the Evans point, which has a single large, deep notch in each blade margin. While a possible occurrence in the Woodland period was once suggested, Prentice Thomas and his colleagues (1997:19; see also Morehead et al. 2002:33–34) believe Sinner points may be an initial Middle Archaic form in the Fort Polk area, based on their general resemblance to Kirk Stemmed/Serrated points found farther to the east and dated to between ca. 8876 and 8600 B.P./8000 and 7800 rcbp (Chapman 1985:146). They also noted the resemblance of Sinner points to Neches River and Wesley points from eastern Texas and Avery and St. Helena points from southern and southeastern Louisiana (Jelks 1965:209; Gagliano 1967a:65; Gagliano et al. 1979; Perino 1991). The point type is considered to be diagnostic of the Middle Archaic Kisatchie phase on Fort Polk, as defined by Thomas et al. (1997:25; see also Morehead et al. 2002:32–34; see Chapter 6). Sinner points occur in low incidence in eastern Texas (Prewitt 1995:130) and appear to be more common in western Louisiana, where they are attributed to the Middle Archaic period. *References*: Turner and Hester 1993:187; Webb 2000:10; Webb et al. 1969:52–53.

Summerfield *(n = 10/1 component)*

This dart point is characterized by triangular blades with straight to excurvate, frequently asymmetrical lateral margins, pronounced straight shoulders forming a perpendicular to acute angle with the haft, and an expanding stem with a straight to slightly convex base (Figure 5.12, *a–c*). The type is reported from Oklahoma, where it has been assigned to a Fourche Maline and Late Archaic age at the Scott (34LF11) and Wynn (34LF27) sites (Galm and Flynn 1978). The specimens identified on Fort Polk are all from 16VN794 and should probably more properly be placed within the Ellis type or the

Figure 5.12. Dart point forms from Fort Polk: a–c, Summerfield; d, e, Trinity; f–j, Williams; k, Woden; 1, Yarbrough, var. Lindale; *m–o, Yarbrough,* var. unspecified.

Dooley Branch cluster. The points are "larger and generally exhibit more pronounced shoulder treatment and longer barbs than Ellis Points" (Cantley 1993:163), however, which is presumably why the Summerfield type was used. The appropriateness and effectiveness of the Summerfield type in western Louisiana remains to be evaluated. *Reference*: Galm and Flynn 1978:167–168, 229–230.

Trinity *(n = 12/11 components)*
This small dart point is characterized by a triangular blade, weakly defined shoulders, shallow ground side notches, and a straight base (Figure 5.12, *d–e*). The blade margins are typically straight to slightly convex. The Trinity type was named by Robert L. Stephenson (1949:56) based on survey data from the Trinity River area of east-central Texas. The point type is common in northeastern Texas along the Trinity and Red Rivers, and it is found extending into southwestern Arkansas (Prewitt 1995:133). A Middle to Late Archaic age is inferred by Turner and Hester (1993:190). *References*: Crook and Harris 1952; Perino 1985:382; Suhm and Jelks 1962:253–254; Suhm et al. 1954:484–486; Stephenson 1949:56; Turner and Hester 1993:190.

Wade-like *(n = 1/1 component)*
This is a triangular expanding stemmed dart point with pronounced corner notches and barbs. A single example has been reported from Fort Polk (Gray and Buchner 2000:64), where the authors infer a relationship with the Bulverde and Carrollton types in Justice's (1987:179–184) Terminal Archaic Barbed cluster. The Wade type was defined by Cambron and Hulse (1960:21) based on collections from sites near Wade Landing on the Tennessee River in northwestern Alabama. Wade points are common in northern Alabama and Georgia and occur in the Midsouth in the Tennessee and Kentucky area (Justice 1987:180, 183), but the type name is not typically used in the Louisiana area. *References*: Cambron and Hulse 1960:21, 1975:110; Justice 1987:180–183.

Wells *(n = 3/3 components)*
This form is characterized by a triangular blade, a long contracting stem with a flat to convex base, and pronounced to weakly defined shoulders. The shoulders are sometimes squared or obtuse in angle and asymmetrical, while the stem is typically one-third to two-thirds the length of the entire point. The blade margins are typically straight to slightly convex and are commonly serrated, while the stem is usually heavily ground. The Wells type was defined by Newell and Krieger (1949:167) based on work at the George C. Davis site in eastern Texas. The point type is common in east-central Texas (Prewitt 1995:135) and occurs rarely in western Louisiana. An Early Archaic age is inferred by Turner and Hester (1993:193). *References*: Newell and Krieger 1949:167; Shafer 1963; Suhm and Jelks 1962:257–258; Suhm et al. 1954:488; Turner and Hester 1993:193; Webb 2000:8.

Williams *(n = 54/41 components)*
These points have a large triangular blade with pronounced barbs and a

concave shoulder outline (giving a corner-notched appearance), an expanding stem, and a rounded, convex base (Figure 5.12, *f–j*). The Williams type was defined by Dee Ann Suhm, Alex D. Krieger, and Edward B. Jelks (1954:490; Suhm and Jelks 1962:259–260) based on materials from central Texas. The point form is common in central and east-central Texas (Kelly 1962; Prewitt 1995:135) and has also been reported in western Louisiana. A wide temporal range has been inferred for these point forms, extending from the Early Archaic to the Woodland period. In central Texas, the Williams type is assumed to be Middle to Late Archaic in age (Turner and Hester 1993:194), while on Fort Polk a range of ca. 3770 to 1366 B.P./3500 to 1500 rcbp has been inferred at 16VN794 (Cantley et al. 1993b:256) and it has a stratigraphic placement above the Edgewood type at Eagle Hill II (Gunn 1982a:230, 239).

Williams points are considered the principal type in what is called the Williams cluster, a grouping of terminal Late Archaic and Woodland era points developed by L. Janice Campbell and her colleagues (1990:64–73) based on stratigraphic excavations at 16VN791 on Fort Polk. Related forms appear to include the Calcasieu, Palmillas, and Lone Oak types. The cluster is described as "almost flatly equated with the Williams type, although it includes some specimens outside of Williams' range. These are medium-sized, corner-notched points with decidedly convex bases" (Campbell et al. 1990:64). At 16VN791, Williams cluster points were dated to the Woodland or Formative era since they were stratigraphically above Dooley Branch cluster forms and prior to and continuing through the introduction of arrow points (Campbell et al. 1990:64–73; see also Bundy 2002a:89). Use of point cluster terminology has not been widely adopted in Louisiana, but it should help reduce the ambiguity involved in separating highly similar point types. The temporal placement of the type, however, would appear to be in need of some refinement. *References*: Campbell et al. 1990:64–73; Schambach 1998:43–46; Suhm and Jelks 1962:259–260; Suhm et al. 1954:490; Turner and Hester 1993:194–195; Webb 2000:11–12.

Woden (*n = 8/8 components*)

This point is characterized by a triangular blade with straight to slightly excurvate margins, well-defined rounded or squared shoulders that typically form an obtuse angle with the haft, a rectangular stem that may be slightly expanding or more typically contracting, and a straight, often thick and unworked base (Figure 5.12, *k*). On some specimens the basal area has cortex from the parent material; the thick and minimally worked base is a distinctive characteristic of the type. The point is typically quite thick and crudely made and the blade margins are often asymmetrical. This type was defined by Jelks (1965) based on material from the McGee Bend Reservoir project in eastern Texas. At McGee Bend, Woden points were considered the principal diagnostic of the Brookeland focus, which was assigned to the Late Archaic period. The point occurs in southeastern and extreme eastern Texas and into western Louisiana (Prewitt 1995:136). An Early Archaic age has been assigned to the form by Turner and Hester (1993:196). Story (1990:222), however, suggests that Woden and Kent points may be local variants of the Yarbrough and/or Darl types. The Form X type is closely related, and one Woden and one Form X were found in a test unit at 16VN928, the former ca. 10 cm below the latter (Thomas et al. 1994a:50). It appears that some uncertainty exists about the age of the form in western Louisiana (Guderjan and Morehead 1983; Thomas et al. 1994a:50; see also Gray and Buchner 2000:63). *References*: Jelks 1965:142–144; Turner and Hester 1993:196.

Yarbrough *(n = 56/36 components)*

This point form is characterized by straight to convex blade margins, a square to slightly expanding stem, and a straight base. Shoulders lack barbs and are weak to pronounced, squared or obtuse in angle, and sometimes asymmetrical from resharpening (Figure 5.12, *l–o*). Bases and lateral haft margins are sometimes ground, making separation from Early Archaic forms difficult in surface specimens. Defined by H. Perry Newell and Alex D. Krieger (1949:168), the Yarbrough type was based on materials from east Texas. The point type is extremely common in eastern and northeastern Texas (Prewitt 1995:137), where it is assumed to date to the Middle and Late Archaic periods (Turner and Hester 1993:197) and possibly later, contemporaneous with Gary forms (Story 1990:220). Story (1990:222) suggests that Kent and Woden points may be local variants of the Yarbrough and/or Darl types. Three varieties, *vars. Lindale, Dike,* and *Mabank*, were defined by Johnson (1962) at the Yarbrough site, where the stratigraphic distributions indicated the former variety was earlier than the latter two. On Fort Polk, two examples of *var. Lindale* were found in the lower levels of the Big Brushy site, suggesting a date well back in the Archaic period (Guderjan and Morehead 1983). A range of ca. 6600 to 4500 B.P./5780 to 4000 rcbp for the form was inferred at 16VN794 (Cantley et al. 1993b:255–256), although it was also found in deposits extending appreciably later, well into the Woodland. At 16VN791 the form was inferred to date to the later part of the Late Archaic and was included in the Dooley Branch cluster, consisting of the Ellis, Edgewood, Marcos, Summerfield, and Yarbrough types (Campbell et al. 1990:64–73, 91; see also Bundy 2002a:87–88). During the FP-22 testing project, a Yarbrough-like point was found below a Birds Creek point at 16VN873 (Morehead et al. 1996b:118–119). Some ambiguity exists about the point form's temporal placement on Fort Polk (and beyond), which is probably due in part to the fact that expanding-stemmed points occur from the Early Archaic to the Woodland in the general region, rendering its diagnostic utility somewhat questionable. Yarbrough points resemble the Darl type, although the blade is not as slender or as commonly beveled, the shoulders are more pronounced, and the base is typically straight rather than concave (Suhm and Jelks 1962:261). *References*: Johnson 1962; Miller and Jelks 1952:172–175; Newell and Krieger 1949:168; Suhm and Jelks 1962:261–262; Suhm et al. 1954:492; Turner and Hester 1993:197.

ARROW POINT TYPES FOUND ON FORT POLK

Alba (n = 86/75 components)
This arrow form is characterized by a triangular blade with straight to slightly incurvate or excurvate lateral margins, pronounced squared to barbed shoulders, and a small square to slightly expanding stem with a straight base (Figure 5.13, *a–d*). The barbs are sometimes asymmetrical, reflecting breakage and reworking, and are often almost as long as the base. The blade margins are sometimes serrated. The point type was first described as Alba Barbed by Alex D. Krieger (1946:115) and was named after the town of Alba, Texas. The point type occurs widely throughout Louisiana and eastern Texas (Prewitt 1995:89) and into adjoining states, where it is found in Caddoan and Coles Creek assemblages dating ca. 1200–800 B.P. Justice (1987:235–237) places the Alba Barbed type and the related Agee, Bonham, Catahoula, and Hayes types in his Alba cluster, which he dates to between A.D. 900 and 1200. Story (1990:251) suggests that Alba might possibly be the earliest arrow point type (with Catahoula) found in eastern Texas. *References*: Justice 1987:235–237; Krieger 1946:115; Suhm and Jelks 1962:263–264; Suhm et al. 1954:494; Turner and Hester 1993:200; Webb 1959, 2000:14.

Bassett (n = 57/36 components)
This arrow form is characterized by a wide triangular blade with convex lateral margins, pronounced barbs that commonly extend to the base of the point or beyond, and a small contracting stem that terminates in a sharp to slightly rounded point (Figure 5.13, *e–q*). Considered diagnostic of the Belcher focus (Webb 1959:162), the type is thought to postdate 800 B.P. and may extend into historic times. Perino (1985:28) has suggested a range of ca. 500 to 300 B.P. The point is common in eastern and northeastern Texas (Prewitt 1995:92) and northwestern Louisiana, including the Fort Polk area (e.g., Bundy 2002a:90; Cantley 1993:158; Thomas et al. 1994a:53), and is less frequent in adjoining areas. Story (1990:251) observed that Bassett points

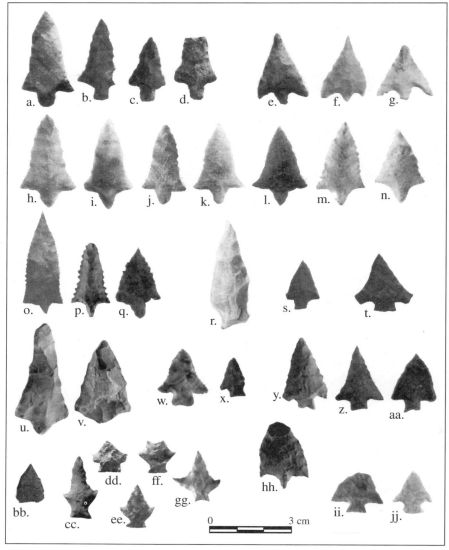

Figure 5.13 — Arrow point forms from Fort Polk: a–d, Alba; e–q, Bassett; r, Bayougoula; s, Bonham; t, Catahoula; u, v, Cliffton; w, x, Colbert; y–aa, Cuney; bb, Fresno; cc–gg, Friley; hh, unknown, possible Perdiz?; ii–jj, Scallorn.

are rarely found with Perdiz in eastern Texas and may have developed out of that type. At Fort Polk, the two types appear to be used interchangeably. *References*: Bell 1958; Perino 1985:28; Suhm and Jelks 1962:265–266; Suhm et al. 1954:494; Turner and Hester 1993:201; Webb 1948a:132, 1959, 2000:15.

Bayougoula Fishtailed (n = 1/1 component)
This arrow point form has a long triangular blade with straight to slightly convex margins, weak shoulders, an expanding fishtail- or hourglass-shaped stem, and a straight or concave base (Figure 5.13, *r*). The type was named by Stephen Williams and Jeffrey P. Brain (1983:222) after the Bayou Goula site in Louisiana, where the point form was described by Quimby (1957). The type occurs primarily in eastern Louisiana and is rare in the western part of the state. The type is associated with the Plaquemine culture, although Webb (1981) has demonstrated that it is also found on Caddoan sites. A range of ca. 800 to 500 B.P. is inferred for the type. *References*: Perino 1985:29; Quimby 1957:128; Thomas et al. 1994a:53; Webb 2000:17; Williams and Brain 1983.

Bonham (n = 12/12 components)
This arrow point is characterized by a triangular blade with straight to slightly convex lateral margins, pronounced squared shoulders with small barbs, and a small rectangular stem with a straight to slightly convex base (Figure 5.13, *s*). Individual specimens may be confused with the Alba type, although the latter has a wider blade and sharper barbs that form an acute angle with the stem, giving the point a deeply corner-notched appearance. The type Bonham Barbed was named by Krieger (1946:185) after the town of Bonham, Texas. The Bonham type occurs in northeastern Texas and western Louisiana and dates to the late prehistoric era from ca. 800 to 500 B.P. Justice (1987:237) places the Bonham Barbed type in his Alba cluster, which he dates to between A.D. 900 and 1200. *References*: Cantley 1993:157; Duffield 1961; Jelks 1962; Krieger 1946:185; Perino 1985:43; Suhm and Jelks 1962:267–268; Suhm et al. 1954:496; Turner and Hester 1993:202; Webb 2000:14.

Catahoula (n = 17/17 components)
This arrow form has a long, slender triangular blade with straight to slightly incurvate or excurvate margins, large rounded or squared outflaring barbs, and a small squared to slightly expanding stem with a straight to convex base (Figure 5.13, *t*). The barbs commonly extend to the base of the stem, giving the point the appearance of basal notching. The point type was named by Clarence H. Webb and Hiram F. Gregory in 1956 during work at the Sanson site on Catahoula Lake in central Louisiana (Baker and Webb 1976:226). The type was first formally described in Bell's (1960:16–17) projectile point guide. The point type occurs widely throughout Louisiana and eastern Texas, and a temporal range of ca. 1300 to 900 B.P. is indicated (Baker and Webb 1976; Patterson 1977; Prewitt 1995:96; Webb and McKinney 1975:96). Patterson (1987) described a variant, the Catahoula

Perforator, that appears to have been used as a hafted drill. Justice (1987:237) places the Catahoula type in his Alba cluster, which he dates to between A.D. 900 and 1200. The type is thought, possibly, to be the earliest arrow point type (with Alba) found in eastern Texas (Story 1990:251). *References*: Aten 1967, 1983; Baker and Webb 1976; Bell 1960; Patterson 1977, 1987; Perino 1985:70; Prentice Thomas and Associates, Inc. 1992:19; Turner and Hester 1993:206; Webb 2000:15.

Cliffton (n = 29/28 components)
This arrow form, actually a preform, is characterized by a triangular blade, pronounced squared shoulders, and a short contracting stem. Crudely made, the form typically has little or no fine retouch (Figure 5.13, *u–v*). The type was first described as Cliffton Contracting Stem by Alex D. Krieger (1946:115–116). Perino (1985:77) has suggested that the type is a preform for contracting-stemmed arrow point types such as Bassett and Perdiz. Turner and Hester (1993:208) argue that Cliffton forms are unfinished Perdiz points and that Cliffton has "little validity as a type." The form occurs widely across southern and eastern Texas (Prewitt 1995:97) and into Louisiana, and a late prehistoric age has been inferred from ca. 800 to 500 B.P. *References*: Krieger 1946:115–116; Suhm and Jelks 1962:269–270; Suhm et al. 1954:496; Turner and Hester 1993:208.

Colbert (n = 36/26 components)
This arrow form has a triangular blade with finely serrated incurvate or excurvate lateral margins, pronounced squared and barbed shoulders, and an expanding stem with a straight base (Figure 5.13, *w, x*). The shoulders are often quite wide, giving the blade a concave appearance. The type may be confused with the Alba, Homan, and Scallorn types. It occurs in eastern Texas and in adjoining parts of Louisiana and Arkansas, where a range of ca. 1150 to 400 B.P. has been inferred (Prewitt 1995:98; Turner and Hester 1993:209). *References*: Turner and Hester 1993:209; Webb 1963:180, 2000:16.

Cuney (n = 24/23 components)
This arrow form is characterized by a triangular blade with straight to slightly incurvate lateral margins, pronounced shoulders with well-defined barbs, and a small square to slightly expanding stem with a concave or notched base (Figure 5.13, *y–aa*). The barbs, which are usually pointed, commonly form an acute angle with the stem, giving the point a corner-notched appearance. The point was described by Dee Ann Suhm, Alex D. Krieger, and Edward B. Jelks (1954:498–499) based on materials from the Allen site in Cherokee County, Texas. The point type occurs widely in eastern Texas into

western Louisiana (Prewitt 1995:99), although it occurs infrequently in the Fort Polk area (Cantley 1993:157; Morehead et al. 1994:47–48). A range of ca. 800 to 300 B.P. is inferred for the type in the general region, although on Fort Polk a protohistoric age has been inferred for specimens found on some sites (Morehead et al. 1996a:194; see also Bundy 2002a:91–92; Gray 2002:81). *References*: Perino 1991:61; Suhm 1957; Suhm and Jelks 1962:271–272; Suhm et al. 1954:498–499; Turner and Hester 1993:211.

Fresno (n = 3/3 components)

This stemless arrow form is characterized by a triangular blade with straight to slightly convex or concave lateral margins and a straight to slightly convex or concave base (Figure 5.13, *bb*). Some specimens may be serrated, while those that are crudely made are probably preforms for this or other types. The point type was first described locally as the Fresno Triangular Blade by J. Charles Kelley (1947a:122) based on work at the Lehmann Rock Shelter in the Edwards Plateau area of central Texas. Stemless triangular points occur widely across the Southeast during the late prehistoric era, although they are comparatively uncommon in western Louisiana, at least in comparison with stemmed and notched forms. Turner and Hester (1993:213), however, note that the type occurs widely throughout eastern Texas, and Prewitt (1995:106) reports it from all across the state. A range of ca. 800 to 500 B.P. has been inferred for the type. *References*: Kelley 1947a:122; Perino 1985:138; Suhm and Jelks 1962:273–274; Suhm et al. 1954:498; Turner and Hester 1993:213.

Friley (n = 198/144 components)

This arrow form is characterized by a small triangular blade with pronounced outward- and commonly upward-flaring shoulders and a small expanding stem with a straight or convex base (Figure 5.13, *cc–gg*). The unusual shoulder morphology distinguishes this type, which is common in western Louisiana and eastern Texas (Prewitt 1995:106). The type was first described by Bell (1960:46) based on data provided by Clarence H. Webb and Hiram F. Gregory from the Friley site in Louisiana. A range of ca. 1300 to 900 B.P. has been inferred for the type. Friley points bear some resemblance to the Catahoula type, although the barbs are more recurved. The type is the most common arrow point found on Fort Polk and second only to Gary points in incidence. On Fort Polk they have an initial appearance during the Holly Springs phase of the Coles Creek culture and are most common in Caddoan assemblages (Bundy 2002a:90; Gray 2002:80–81; Morehead et al. 1996a:189–192, 2002:18, 51, 56). Justice (1987:227) places the Fresno in his Late Woodland/Mississippian Triangular cluster, which consists of a wide range of small triangular forms occurring across eastern North America and dating from ca. A.D. 800 to the historic period. *References*: Bell 1960:46; Perino 1985:139; Turner and Hester 1993:214; Webb 2000:16.

Hayes (n = 11/11 components)

This arrow form has a long, slender triangular blade, large squared shoulders, and a small diamond-shaped stem distinguished by a pointed to slightly rounded base. The tip is commonly sharply pointed, while the point body above the shoulders contracts markedly, giving the blade margin an incurvate, straight, and then incut appearance from the shoulder to the tip. The point is finely retouched and the blade margins are sometimes serrated. The type was described by H. Perry Newell and Alex D. Krieger (1949:162) based on materials from the George C. Davis site in eastern Texas. Hayes points occur widely throughout Louisiana and into northeastern Texas (Prewitt 1995:110), and a temporal range of ca. 1000 to 500 B.P. is indicated. The type is similar to both Alba and Bonham points, differing in stem shape and the presence of the incut tip. Justice (1987:237) places the Hayes type in his Alba cluster, which he dates to between A.D. 900 and 1200. *References*: Newell and Krieger 1949:162; Perino 1985:176; Suhm and Jelks 1962:277–278; Suhm et al. 1954:502; Turner and Hester 1993:218; Webb 2000:15.

Livermore (n = 1/1 component)

This arrow form is characterized by a long slender blade, pronounced squared to flaring shoulders, and a narrow stem with a convex base. The blade margins are steeply concave and sometimes serrated, while the stem ranges from expanding to contracting to squared. Many specimens are very crudely made. The type was defined by J. Charles Kelley, T. N. Campbell, and Donald Lehmer (1940:30) based on materials from the Big Bend area of Texas. The type occurs in western Texas, where it has been dated from 1020 to 595 B.P./1100 to 600 rcbp (Prewitt 1995:115; Turner and Hester 1993:220). The single specimen identified from Fort Polk, occurring well outside of the area where the Livermore type was defined, is almost certainly a crude variant of another form, quite possibly an Alba, Catahoula, or Hayes. Use of this type name should be avoided in western Louisiana. *References*: Kelley et al. 1940:30; Perino 1985:228; Suhm and Jelks 1962:279–280; Suhm et al. 1954:502; Turner and Hester 1993:220.

Maud (n = 2/2 components)

This stemless arrow form is characterized by a triangular blade with straight to slightly convex or concave lateral margins and a deeply indented concave to V-shaped base. The type was named by Dee Ann Suhm, Alex D. Krieger, and Edward B. Jelks (1954:504) after the town of Maud, Texas, near the Taylor site in Harrison County. The type occurs in extreme northeastern Texas and in adjoining parts of Louisiana and Arkansas, where a range of ca. 800 to 500 B.P. has been inferred (Prewitt 1995:118; Turner and Hester 1993:223). The type is rare in west-central Louisiana. The two examples found at Fort Polk may be unusual variants of a more common triangular type. *References*: Bell 1980; Perino 1985:246; Suhm and Jelks 1962:281–282; Suhm et al. 1954:504; Turner and Hester 1993:223; Webb 2000:15.

Perdiz (n = 36/23 components)

This arrow form has a triangular blade with straight lateral margins, pronounced barbed shoulders, and a long contracting stem that is usually pointed or less commonly rounded or even straight (Figure 5.13, *hh*). Considerable variability occurs within the type, which is distinguished by the long contracting stem. Barb size and shape vary appreciably; on some specimens the width at the barbs may exceed the overall point length. Most of the barbs form an acute angle with the stem, but some specimens are squared, with weak barbs. The point was named the Perdiz Pointed Stem by J. Charles Kelley (1947a) based on artifacts from central Texas. It occurs widely across Texas and Louisiana and in portions of adjoining states (Prewitt 1995:126). A range of ca. 800 to 500 B.P. has been inferred; the type spreads widely across Texas after ca. A.D. 1200 (Story 1990:251). It has been suggested by various authors that Cliffton points may be preforms for this type. On Fort Polk, the type may be confused with Bassett. *References*: Kelley 1947a; Perino 1985:297; Suhm and Jelks 1962:283–284; Suhm et al. 1954:504; Turner and Hester 1993:227–228; Webb 2000:15–16.

Scallorn (n = 11/9 components)

This arrow form has a triangular blade with finely serrated straight to slightly incurvate or excurvate lateral margins, pronounced barbed shoulders, corner notches, and a wide expanding stem with a straight to slightly convex or concave base (Figure 5.13, *ii–jj*). On some specimens the basal width approaches or equals that of the blade. The type was originally named Scallorn Stemmed by J. Charles Kelley (1947a:122), with a detailed description provided by Dee Ann Suhm, Alex D. Krieger, and Edward B. Jelks (1954:506). The point occurs widely across Texas and Louisiana and into adjoining states (Prewitt 1995:129). Jelks (1962:27) established three varieties: *var. Coryell*, characterized by an expanded stem; *var. Eddy*, characterized by a straight to slightly expanded stem; and *var. Sattler*, which has side notches. A range of ca. 1300 to 800 B.P. has been inferred for the Scallorn type (Story 1990:217; Turner and Hester 1993:230). Justice (1987:220–224) places Scallorn points in his Scallorn cluster, which he dates ca. A.D. 700–1100/1300–900 B.P. *References*: Jelks 1962:27; Justice 1987:220–224; Miller and Jelks 1952:176–177; Perino 1985:344; Suhm and Jelks 1962:285–286; Turner and Hester 1993:230; Webb 2000:16.

UNUSUAL HAFTED BIFACE FORMS

A few unusual bifaces were also found on the installation, including two eccentrics that are unusually chipped forms. Categories that were subsequently abandoned include the Dart Point Group 1 and Dart Point Group 2 clusters, tentatively advanced in the report on the Multipurpose Range Complex survey by Campbell and Weed (1986:7-33 to 7-35). Dart Point Group 1 (n = 8 points) subsumed bifaces that resembled the Bulverde, Castroville, Marcos, and Marshall types, while the Dart Point Group 2 (n = 29 points) category was defined as crosscutting the Ellis, Ensor, and Edgewood types (Campbell and Weed 1986:7-35). These groupings crosscut the subsequent Dooley Branch and Birds Creek clusters formally defined during the 16VN791 excavations and hence are not equivalent taxa. They represent an early attempt by the New World Research/Prentice Thomas and Associates research team to develop clusters of related points on the installation, a practice they have continued in subsequent investigations.

A large proportion of the projectile point assemblage consisted of dart (n = 179), arrow (n = 150), or point forms or fragments (n = 780) that were unidentifiable to type. That fully a third of the projectile points and point fragments (n = 1,109; 33.6 percent) recovered on the installation could not be classified to any specific type is not at all surprising. Such results are common in typological analyses in many areas. At Fort Polk these findings are probably due to factors such as (1) a conservative approach to classification by some investigators, (2) the existence of a wide range of variation in local point forms that is only beginning to be understood at present, and (3) the fact that many of the unidentified artifacts were fragmentary, with their bases damaged or missing and hence not amenable to sound typological analysis.

Because of the uncertainty inherent in temporal placement of many projectile point categories in the west-central Louisiana area, fairly broad temporal ranges were assigned for most of the types, reflecting an attempt to accommodate the evidence and opinions in the literature (cf. Bell 1958, 1960; Campbell and Weed 1986; Campbell et al. 1990; Ensor 1981; Justice 1987; Morehead et al. 1996a; Perino 1968, 1985; Prewitt 1981, 1995; Turner and Hester 1993; Webb 1981; Wyckoff 1984). Refinement of the morphological and chronological ranges for recognizably distinct point forms is an absolutely crucial area for future research. Examination of stratigraphic relationships between point forms, absolute dating, and attribute-based metric and functional analyses (i.e., to resolve or test for the existence of discrete point clusters/types) are all needed (Cantley et al. 1993b:258). Considerable uncertainty still characterizes the projectile point sequence in western Louisiana, but our knowledge of the variation at present is far better than it was two decades ago.

GENERAL TRENDS IN THE PROJECTILE POINT DATA

Projectile points have been found at 892 locations on Fort Polk to date, including 743 sites and 149 isolated finds. In all, 3,299 points have been recovered, of which 2,148 were identifiable to a particular type (Table 5.1). Of these, 528 (24.6 percent) were diagnostic arrow point types and the remainder (n = 1,620; 75.4 percent of all diagnostic points) were darts. That almost a quarter were arrow points, a tool form manufactured for only a few hundred years from approximately A.D. 800 to 1700, suggests fairly extensive late prehistoric and protohistoric use of the area, at least in comparison with earlier times.

A wide variety of point forms have been identified—some 82 types—with the most popular in order of incidence being the Gary, Friley, Ellis, San Patrice (all varieties combined), Kent, Dooley Branch, Alba, Marcos, and Palmillas types, which have 75 or more examples each. Forty-five types are represented by 10 or fewer specimens, and of these, 27 types are represented by three or fewer examples. While some of this variability appears to be due to the misidentification of some specimens or the use of inappropriate types, the general impression that one is left with is that a great many point forms occur in this part of western Louisiana. If this typological variability reflects cultural as well as the obvious temporal variability, then the area appears to have seen use by a wide range of peoples. That many of these visits were comparatively brief is suggested by the fact that most of the point types have almost as many components as individual artifacts. That is, with a few exceptions, typically where large-scale excavations occurred, few sites yielded more than one or two points of any particular type. To give an example, the 208 Gary points found on the installation came from 153 separate sites and isolated finds, while the 198 Friley points came from 144 locations. An average of 3.70 points per location were found over the 892 sites and isolated finds recorded to date that yielded points. This averages 1.50 points per component over the 2,195 separate components identified. These low numbers of points per location and component suggest fairly limited or abbreviated activities although, given extensive excavation at more sites, higher numbers would undoubtedly be recorded. As an aside, and illustrating this observation, the reason Ensor and Marcos points have a relatively low number of components compared to number of points is that these types were found in some quantity in the 16VN791 excavation block (Campbell et al. 1990:63). This example of a site yielding numerous points of a given type appears to be the unusual exception rather than the rule at Fort Polk, however.

Examining the occurrence of projectile points over time, both by total incidence and by number of observed components, a pattern of general increase is evident from Paleoindian times through the late prehistoric era (Figure 5.14, *top*). Minor declines in the overall incidence of points and components by period do occur at two times: once following the Late Paleoindian period and again after the Woodland period. For this reason, the incidence of points and components was also examined per 1,000 years (Figure 5.14, *bottom*). That is, the numbers were divided by the number of years assigned to each period, as follows: Early Paleoindian (1,000 years), Late Paleoindian (1,000 years), Early Archaic (2,000 years), Middle Archaic (3,000 years), Late Archaic (3,000 years), Woodland (2,000 years), and late prehistoric (1,000 years). Examining these distributions, the Woodland to late prehistoric decline is shown to be an artifact of the time periods involved. The only significant decline in the numbers of artifacts and components found in the Fort Polk area, accordingly, occurs following the Late Paleoindian period. A slight increase occurs from the Early Archaic to Middle Archaic, but the differences in the numbers are so slight as to be meaningless. The data suggest little change between these periods.

Extensive Late Paleoindian period use of the west-central Louisiana area is indicated by the large numbers of San Patrice components found on the installation. There appears to be little doubt that people 10,000 years ago found this area attractive. A number of classic Plains and southeastern Paleoindian and Early Archaic types have also been reported from the Fort Polk area, which is a pattern that has been observed elsewhere in Louisiana (Gagliano and Gregory 1965; Hillman 1985; Jeter and Williams 1989a; Johnson 1989). A considerable overlap of these major regional cultural traditions appears indicated. Whether the decline following the Late Paleoindian period is as severe as suggested by the graph, however, is debatable, and it may be more a reflection of our artifact typologies than any actual measure of population trends. A number of varieties of San Patrice points are known from the installation that span the Late Paleoindian and Early Archaic periods. Nearly a third of these San Patrice points (n = 34) could not be identified to a particular variety and hence could be either Late Paleoindian or Early Archaic in age. While they are here placed in the Late Paleoindian period, if some were placed in the Early Archaic period, the decline between these periods would be less pronounced. A decline would still likely occur,

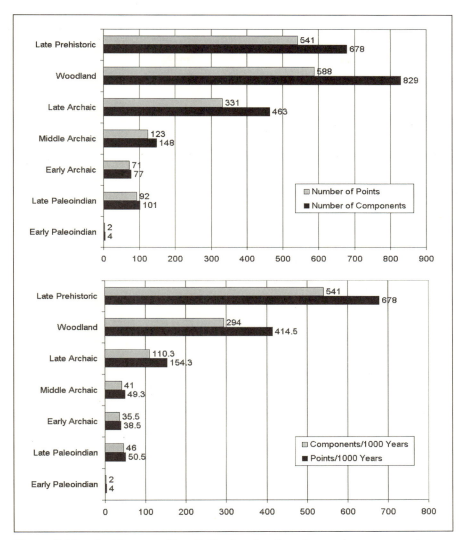

Figure 5.14 — Incidence on Fort Polk of projectile points and components by major period (top) and per 1,000 years (bottom).

however, as an examination of the incidence of artifacts and components per 1,000 years indicates (Figure 5.14, *bottom*). The data suggest use of the Fort Polk area declined appreciably after the end of the Late Paleoindian era and was fairly constant through the Early and Middle Archaic periods. With the onset of the Late Archaic period, use of the area increased steadily over time.

Middle Archaic diagnostics are beginning to be recognized in Louisiana, of which the most common forms occurring on Fort Polk are the Evans, Marshall, Sinner, Carrollton, and Bulverde types. While the archaeological visibility of the period is becoming more apparent, component incidence remains fairly low, which may reflect the hypothesized drought-induced abandonment or, at best, appreciably reduced use of the Coastal Plain uplands during the Hypsithermal interval (Campbell and Weed 1986; Gunn et al. 1982). As the Archaic period projectile point sequence becomes more precise, so too will our picture of settlement during this period.

Greater use of the Fort Polk area following the Middle Archaic period is indicated by the projectile point data. Fairly dramatic increases occur between both the Middle and Late Archaic periods and the Late Archaic and Woodland periods. The greatest number of points and components observed in any time period occurs during the Woodland period, although these figures are approached in the late prehistoric era by groups using arrow points. The decline in the number of points and components during the late prehistoric period (Figure 5.14, *top*), however, does not appear to reflect a decrease in land use since the numbers are actually greater than in earlier periods, as shown when time is controlled (Figure 5.14, *bottom*). While a pattern of pronounced increase is indicated, the relative number of points dating to the Late Archaic or Woodland period is somewhat uncertain. As noted in the review of the prehistoric cultural sequence and in the discussion of individual point forms (Chapter 6 and above), many dart point forms apparently had a long temporal occurrence, spanning portions of the Late Archaic through the Woodland period. Thus, while a dramatic upswing in use of the area is indicated following the Middle Archaic, the rate of increase after this time is uncertain.

Prehistoric Ceramic Artifacts Found on Fort Polk

A total of 4,843 prehistoric ceramic artifacts have been found at 565 sites and 45 isolated finds on Fort Polk as of late 1999; these are described by type, paste, and surface finish in Table 5.2 and by site in the 1999 HPP Inventory volume (Anderson et al. 1999a:appendix 6). This represents a considerable increase over the 1,321 ceramic artifacts from 204 sites reported in the 1988 HPP, and this, again, illustrates the amount of work that has occurred in recent years. Because many of the early investigators working on Fort Polk did not report paste or surface finish uniformly, a reanalysis of many of the early collections was conducted during the 1988 HPP production effort. As with the projectile points, typological assignments tend to

Table 5.2 — Prehistoric ceramics on Fort Polk: total by type, temper group, period, and surface finish

A. IDENTIFIED TYPES				
Type	*Period*	*Paste*	*Sherds*	*Sites*
Baked clay objects	LA/EW	No data	14	5
Baytown Plain, *var. Satartia*	MW/LW	Clay/organic	12	3
Belcher Ridged	C/Miss	Grog/clay	8	6
Beldeau Incised	LW	Grog	4	1
Bossier Brushed	C/Miss	Clay/no data	54	3
Canton Incised	C/Miss	Clay	2	1
Chevalier Stamped, *var. Chevalier*	LW	Grog	1	1
Churupa Punctate, *var. unspecified*	MW/LW	Clay	3	3
Churupa Punctate, *var. Boyd*	MW/LW	Sand	1	1
Coles Creek Incised, *var. Blakely*	LW	Clay	1	1
Coles Creek Incised, *var. Coles Creek*	LW	Grog	3	2
Coles Creek Incised, *var. Greenhouse*	LW	Bone	1	1
Coles Creek Incised, *var. Greenhouse*	LW	Clay/organic	6	2
Coles Creek Incised, *var. Hardy*	LW	Clay/grog, clay	12	7
Coles Creek Incised, *var. Mott*	LW	Grog	4	1
Coles Creek Incised, *var. Stoner*	LW	Clay/sand/organic	1	1
Coles Creek Incised, *var. Wade*	LW	Clay	1	1
Coles Creek Incised, *var. unspecified*	LW	Clay/sand/organic	2	2
Coles Creek Incised, *var. unspecified*	LW	Grog/sand	4	3
Coles Creek Incised, *var. unspecified*	LW	Grog	3	3
Coles Creek Incised, *var. unspecified*	LW	Clay	2	2
Crockett Curvilinear Incised	C/Miss	Clay/grog	4	4
Crockett Curvilinear Incised	C/Miss	Sand/clay	3	1
Davis Incised	C/Miss	Sand/clay	2	2
Dunkin Incised	C/Miss	Grog/sand	92	14
Dunkin Incised	C/Miss	Grog/bone	3	1
Dunkin/Mazique Incised	C/Miss	Clay	6	4
Dunkin/Mazique Incised	C/Miss	Clay/grog	4	3
Dunkin/Mazique Incised	C/Miss	Sand/clay	1	1
Dunkin/Sanson Incised	C/Miss	No data	9	1
Evansville Punctated	LW	Sand/clay	22	12
Evansville Punctated	LW	Grog	3	1
French Fork Incised, *var. French Fork*	LW	Clay	1	1
Harrison Bayou Incised	C/Miss	Clay/no data	4	4
Hickory Fine Engraved	C/Miss	No data	3	2
Indian Bay Stamped, *var. Shaw*	LW	Clay	2	2
Karnack Brushed-Incised	C/Miss	Sand	1	1
Kiam Incised	C/Miss	Sand/clay	1	1
Larto Red Filmed	MW/LW	Grog/sand	5	4

Table 5.2 (cont.) — Prehistoric ceramics on Fort Polk: total by type, temper group, period, and surface finish

A. IDENTIFIED TYPES (CONT.)				
Type	*Period*	*Paste*	*Sherds*	*Sites*
L'Eau Noire Incised, *var. Australia*	C/Miss	Sand/clay	1	1
Marksville Stamped, *var. unspecified*	EW/MW	Clay/grog	5	5
Marksville Stamped, *var. unspecified*	EW/MW	Grog/sand	17	11
Marksville Stamped, *var. unspecified*	EW/MW	Sand/clay	1	1
Marksville Stamped, *var. Yokena*	EW/MW	Clay	1	1
Marksville Incised	EW/MW	Grog/sand	27	17
Marksville Incised, *var. unspecified*	EW/MW	Sand	1	1
Marksville Incised, *var. unspecified*	EW/MW	Sand/clay	2	1
Marksville Incised, *var. unspecified*	EW/MW	Clay/bone	1	1
Marksville Incised, *var. Yokena*	EW/MW	Sand/clay	2	1
Marksville Incised, *var. Leist*	EW/MW	Grog	6	1
Mazique Incised, *var. unspecified*	MW/LW	Sand	1	1
Mazique Incised, *var. unspecified*	MW/LW	Grog/sand	57	7
Mazique Incised, *var. unspecified*	MW/LW	Clay/organic	1	1
Medora Incised	C/Miss	Grog/sand	2	2
Pease Brushed-Incised	C/Miss	Grog/sand	7	3
Pease Brushed-Incised	C/Miss	Clay	8	2
Pennington Punctate-Incised	C/Miss	Clay/grog	8	2
Pennington Punctate-Incised	C/Miss	Sand/clay	1	1
Pontchartrain Check Stamped	LW	Grog/sand	1	1
Salomon Brushed	MW/LW	Grog	6	2
Sanson Incised	C/Miss	Clay	1	1
Tchefuncte Plain	EW	Laminated	26	11
Tchefuncte Incised	EW	Clay/no data	4	3
Weches Fingernail	LW	Grog	2	2
Wilkinson Punctated	MW/LW	Clay	12	3
Williams Plain	C/Miss	No data	3	2
Total			509	194

LA = Late Archaic   *MW = Middle Woodland*   *C/Miss = Caddoan/Mississippian*
EW = Early Woodland   *LW = Late Woodland*

B. MAJOR PASTE GROUPING AT FORT POLK

Paste	*Count*	*Paste*	*Count*
Bone	75	Other	57
Clay/grog	2,747	Total	5,708
Sand	2,031	(Grog and bone)	(47)
No data	798	(Grog and sand)	(890)

Table 5.2 (cont.) — Prehistoric ceramics on Fort Polk: total by type, temper group, period, and surface finish

C. IDENTIFIED TEMPERS (SUMMARY)

Paste	Count
Bone	26
Bone/grog/sand	12
Clay	436
Clay/bone	2
Clay/grog	442
Clay/organic	49
Clay/sand	5
Clay/sand/organic	22
Clay/sand/bone	16
Grit/clay	8
Grog	983
Grog/sand	735
Grog/bone	19
Hematite	3
Laminated	26
No data	798
Organic	14
Sand	690
Sand/clay	433
Sand/grit	89
Sand/organic	21
Temperless	14
Total	4,843

D. IDENTIFIED FINISHES

Finish	Count
Baked clay objects	14
Brushed	71
Brushed-incised	43
Check stamped	1
Decorated, unid.	55
Engraved	12
Fingernail punctate	8
Fired clay	345
Incised	494
Pipe fragments	5
Plain	3,218
Punctate	66
Punctate/incised	20
Red filmed	8
Ridged	8
Stamped	28
Unidentified/other	436
Zoned-incised punctate	11
Total	4,843

follow those of the original report authors, save where the reanalysis indicated ambiguity or error in classification. Common ceramic taxa found on Fort Polk, as well as some of the more unusual specimens, are illustrated in Figures 5.15 through 5.21.

One thing is immediately evident, and that is that ceramics are decidedly uncommon on sites in this part of west-central Louisiana. There are, in fact, about the same number of sites and isolated finds reported from Fort Polk proper as individual sherds. While ceramics are the most common diagnostic prehistoric artifact in the collections, considering the vast amount of survey and excavation activity that has occurred on Fort Polk over the past 30 years, the total number of sherds recovered is extremely low. This suggests use of ceramics was not particularly important locally, which in

Figure 5.15 — Fort Polk ceramics: a–c, Baytown Plain; d–q, baked clay objects.

turn argues against extended settlement. The low number of prehistoric ceramics found in recent projects conducted in the limited-use lands south of
the Main Fort (e.g., Ensor et al. 2001:415), indicates that the low incidence
of these remains observed on Fort Polk proper likely characterizes conditions over much of this part of Louisiana.

Figure 5.16 — Fort Polk ceramics: a, Belcher Ridged; b–e, Bossier Brushed; f–h, Chevalier Stamped, var. Chevalier; *i–k, Churupa Punctate.*

Typological assignments are difficult to make for many of the specimens that have been found. Most of the ceramic artifacts recovered were sherds (n = 4,479), although small numbers of baked clay object fragments (n = 14), pipe fragments (n = 5), and pieces of fired clay (n = 345) were also found and are included in the total. The vast majority of the sherds are char-

Figure 5.17 — Fort Polk ceramics: a–l, Coles Creek Incised (a–c, var. Coles Creek; *d, e,* var. Greenhouse; *f, g,* var. Hardy; *h, i,* var. Mott; *j–l,* var. unspecified); *m, Davis Incised.*

acterized by a plain (n = 3,218) or unidentifiable (n = 436) surface finish, and pastes include either clay/grog (n = 2,747) or sand (n = 2,031) temper. Many sherds (n = 980) exhibited appreciable quantities of both sand and grog. A modest number (n = 825) of sherds had recognizable finishes other than plain or unidentifiable/eroded, and many of these (n = 454) could be

Figure 5.18 — Fort Polk ceramics: a–g, Dunkin Incised; h, j, Evansville Punctated; i, French Fork Incised, var. French Fork; *k, Harrison Bayou Incised; 1, m, Hickory Fine Engraved.*

identified to a specific type or variety (Table 5.2). Incised (n = 494), brushed (n = 71), and brushed-incised (n = 43) surface finishes are among the most common finishes reported and are typically described using taxa like Bossier Brushed, Coles Creek Incised, Dunkin Incised, Karnack Brushed-Incised, Marksville Incised, Mazique Incised, and Pease Brushed-Incised. Many of

Figure 5.19 — Fort Polk ceramics: a, Kiam Incised; b, L'Eau Noir Incised, var.
Australia; *c–g, Marksville Incised; h, i, Marksville Stamped; j–l, Mazique Incised;
m–p, Pennington Punctate-Incised.*

the remaining incised or brushed sherds found on the installation were not
identified to a type or variety by their discoverers, but they likely fall into
one of these taxa. Small numbers of stamped or punctated finishes have
been found, and these are most commonly attributed to the Evansville
Punctated or Marksville Stamped types.

Figure 5.20 — Fort Polk ceramics: a, Pitted plain; b–d, Sanson Incised; e–f, Tchefuncte Plain; g, unidentified brushed; h–k, unidentified incised; 1–n, unidentified incised-punctate.

The actual numbers of specimens identified to particular types are quite small. While 47 discrete types and varieties have been reported on the installation to date (including unspecified varieties of established types), 12 of these are represented by only a single sherd and another 14 are represented by no more than five sherds. Only eight taxa, in fact, had sample

Figure 5.21 — Fort Polk ceramics: a–c, Unidentified incised (Medora?); d–f, Pease Brushed-Incised; g, Wilkinson (Evansville) Fingernail Punctate.

sizes larger than 20 sherds (including all varieties): Bossier Brushed (n = 54), Coles Creek Incised (n = 40), Dunkin Incised (n = 95), Evansville Punctated (n = 25), Marksville Stamped (n = 24), Marksville Incised (n = 39), Mazique Incised (n = 59), and Tchefuncte Plain (n = 26). As with the projectile point assemblage, considerable variability occurs within the Fort Polk ceramic assemblage, suggesting these remains were left by a number of different groups. Also like the projectile point assemblage, most types are represented by only a few specimens, suggesting fairly limited or abbreviated activities using ceramics. An average of 7.94 ceramics per location were found over the 610 sites and isolated finds that yielded ceramics.

The difficulties of dealing with a ceramic assemblage characterized by small numbers of typically undecorated sherds exhibiting extensive variation in paste led Campbell et al. (1994b:155–157) to caution local researchers against assigning sand- or grog-tempered plain sherds to specific taxa such as Goose Creek or Baytown, respectively, in the absence of clearly associated diagnostic decorative types of these same series. Such a practice, they argued, creates a false sense of cultural affinity that may not be justified. They argued instead that use of readily replicable descriptive taxa should be employed until large enough samples in well-defined contexts could be obtained to permit the creation of valid taxa. In the absence of large sherd samples in secure contexts and given the admixture of paste categories observed, the appropriateness of some of the types that have been proposed by various researchers also needs to be reassessed. Otherwise similar sherds, for example, are sometimes assigned different type names by different investigators, and discussions with colleagues, including the reviewers of the published version of this manuscript, indicate appreciable ambiguity and uncertainty about many classifications. This is not altogether unexpected, given the widely varying backgrounds of the researchers working on Fort Polk over the past 30 years. The installation ceramic assemblage, fortunately, remains small enough so that a total reanalysis is a feasible undertaking for some future researcher; ideally this would be done with comparative analyses of type collections from the surrounding region.

The only plain finish that could be unambiguously sorted was Tchefuncte Plain (n = 26), with its characteristic laminated paste, although the Baytown Plain and Williams Plain types have been used to describe a few sherds of grog-tempered and grog-and-sand–tempered plainwares, respectively. Grog-tempered plainwares, some with appreciable sand present, are among the earliest ceramics in eastern Texas, where they are commonly classified as Williams Plain (Schambach 1970:271–299, 1998:24–26, 81–88; Story 1990:247). Attempting to sort small sherds of grog-tempered plain ceramics into types or varieties locally is, with rare exceptions (i.e., *var. Satartia;* see Chapter 6), as Campbell and her colleagues implied, likely to be an exercise in futility. Incising was the most common surface finish (n = 494), followed by brushed, punctated, and brushed-incised.

Fourteen baked clay object fragments, a hallmark of the Poverty Point and slightly earlier and later cultures in Louisiana, have been found on Fort Polk in recent years, including five at 16VN804 and six at 16VN839

(Morehead et al. 1996a:55–56, 1996b:59–61, 83–94; see also Chapter 6) (Figure 5.15, *d–q*). Two of the larger fragments from 16VN804 and one from 16VN839 are pyramidal in shape and may be from possible bipyramidal or octahedral shapes; most specimens are crude and amorphous in shape. They were made from a mixture of fired silt or loess and very fine sand and were described as virtually indistinguishable from similar materials found at the Poverty Point site. Both of these assemblages, however, were attributed to the initial Late Archaic Birds Creek phase, which is assumed to date prior to Poverty Point times. Classic Poverty Point shapes appear to be extremely rare locally (McGimsey 1996:144).

Paste information was available for 4,045 of the ceramic artifacts recovered to date from Fort Polk (see Table 5.2). Three major temper categories have been recognized in previous analyses: sand, clay/grog, and bone (e.g., Anderson 1984:245; Thomas et al. 1982). Of these, clay/grog tempering is the most common, occurring in just over two-thirds of the sample (n = 2,747; 68.1 percent—some of these sherds also had sand and other inclusions present). Sherds with sand tempering were also common, with sand present in just over half the sherds (n = 2,031; 50.4 percent—again some of these sherds had grog or other tempering elements present). Many sherds contained an admixture of pastes, of which clay/grog with sand or grit was the most common (n = 890; 22.1 percent). A small number of sherds also had small fragments of crushed bone present in the paste (n = 75; 1.86 percent). Bone tempering is observed in Early Woodland assemblages in eastern Texas, usually in low incidence and typically with sand and/or grog associated; Cooper Boneware, defined from the Cooper site in southern Arkansas, is the principal type (Schambach 1998:21–24; Story 1990:247). Bone temper is also sometimes found on later prehistoric Caddoan and Coles Creek sites in western Louisiana. Minor paste categories account for the remainder of the variation observed, of which Tchefuncte-like temperless and laminated pastes (n = 40) were the most prevalent.

While a near-bewildering array of descriptions has been offered for the pastes found on ceramics at Fort Polk, almost all of the assemblage can be described as sand tempered, grog tempered, or sand and grog tempered. Appreciable variability is evident within these larger classes (hence the widely varying paste descriptions in the literature), and lesser constituents such as bone, organic material, and hematite are also observed. The variability that has been observed suggests that people visiting the Fort Polk area came from a number of different places (if they brought their pottery with them) or made use of a number of subtly different manufacturing procedures (if they made it locally). The sherds present may, in part, be remains from groups of varied origin coming to exploit the chert resources, as is thought to have occurred throughout prehistory. Few large or single-component ceramic samples have been found on the installation to date, making comparative analyses with assemblages from other parts of the general region difficult.

The variation in ceramic surface finish and paste that has been observed may also be due to the location the area occupies, which is near the headwaters or minor tributaries of three major drainages, the Red, the Sabine, and the Calcasieu Rivers. Sherds with grog tempering can be generally assumed to have lower Mississippi–lower Red River Valley ties, while sherds with sand tempering can be generally attributed to the cultures of east Texas and the upper Red River Valley area. Few sand-tempered sherds, for example, have been found along the lower Red or Mississippi Rivers, while clay/grog tempering becomes progressively more uncommon farther to the south and west in Texas (Aten 1983; Aten and Bollich 1969; Perttula et al. 1995; Phillips 1970). An overlap of macroregional ceramic "temper zones" appears to be occurring in the Fort Polk area, and this pattern is reinforced by the diversity of possible types identified.

No obvious patterning in the occurrence of sand-tempered as opposed to grog-tempered ceramics has been noted on Fort Polk, suggesting the area is a true zone of mixing or cultural overlap. Importantly, however, an analysis of materials from a number of sites in the Lake Anacoco region just to the west of Fort Polk found that grog-tempered materials were uncommon (10.6 percent of the total sample) and that grog was almost always a secondary inclusion to sand (McGimsey 1996:135, 144). An affinity of the local wares with sand-tempered ceramics from eastern Texas, such as the Goose Creek series, was indicated. The data suggest that Fort Polk is at or near the distributional limits of predominantly grog-tempered assemblages and that the area was a "transitional zone between the grog and sand inclusion spheres" (McGimsey 1996:144).

An examination of the installation ceramic assemblage by period was conducted during the 1988 HPP, and findings suggested a general pattern of increasing ceramic utilization over the course of the Woodland period, followed by a decline in the Caddoan era (Anderson et al. 1988:200–202). Appreciably different results were obtained in the current analysis, which employed identified types and varieties (Figure 5.22). By far the greatest number of ceramics occurs during the late prehistoric Caddoan and Mississippian eras (n = 228 sherds; 63 components). The fact that comparatively large numbers of arrow points, a contemporaneous artifact type, were also found reinforces the idea that appreciable use of the area occurred during the late prehistoric era. This use was still of fairly limited duration and intensity, however, since we are talking about no more than a few hundred artifacts over almost 5,000 sites and isolated finds. The Fort Polk area may

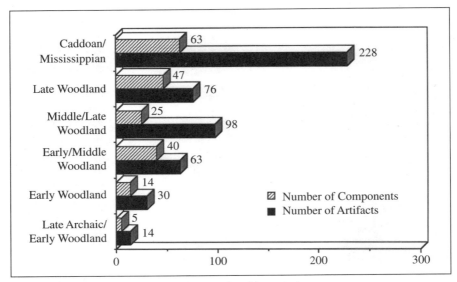

Figure 5.22 — Fort Polk ceramics: number by period.

have been something of a buffer zone between the complex Caddoan chiefdoms to the north and west and the equally complex chiefdoms of the lower Mississippi Valley. Alternatively, it may have been a Caddoan hunting territory that Mississippian populations rarely entered, as indicated by the low number of possible Plaquemine diagnostics found (Chapter 6).

Long-Term Land Use on Fort Polk: Univariate and Bivariate Analyses

The resolution of past land-use patterns, employing large numbers of assemblages from the Main Fort and Peason Ridge, was also a major focus for research. The objectives were to see whether different site types were present and, at a more general level, to see whether the two areas, with their differences in terrain and proximity to knappable stone, were used differently in the past (Table 5.3). Information on field procedures, numbers and size of units, and assemblage composition was compiled and used to explore these questions. All of the data used in the analyses that follow are presented in the 1999 HPP Inventory Primary Data volume (Anderson et al. 1999a).

Although both areas are characterized by hilly terrain, Peason Ridge is much more dissected than the Main Fort, as can be readily seen when slope data from the two subunits are compared (see Tables 4.8 and 4.16). Steeply sloping terrain accounts for just under one-third of the acreage on the Main Fort but for almost half of the acreage on Peason Ridge. Peason Ridge is at the headwaters of the region's major streams or closer to them than the Main Fort and has far less floodplain area or even level terrain. Another factor strongly influencing land use is the occurrence of knappable cryptocrystalline gravels in the southern part of the Main Fort area, where streams have cut into the underlying Miocene-age Williana Formation. Knappable stone is uncommon elsewhere in southern and eastern Louisiana, and how these gravels were used has been the subject of considerable research. Differences in lithic raw material procurement and use between Peason Ridge and the Main Fort have been examined by a number of previous investigators (see Chapters 2 and 3), prompting the comparative analyses advanced here.

The vast majority of sites discovered to date on Fort Polk have been examined using close-interval systematic shovel testing, providing well-controlled and standardized data on site size. Data on assemblage content and stratification at these sites have proven to be more ambiguous, however, as a result of the shallow depth of many of the shovel tests, which were rarely taken beyond 50 to 75 cm. Earlier comparative work on the installation, notably by Cantley and Schuldenrein (1984) and by Campbell and Weed (1986), in fact, showed that artifact density values derived from shovel test data were often markedly different from those obtained when larger, 0.5- or 1.0-m, units were excavated (see Chapter 3).

For this reason, data from the sites that have been intensively tested were considered particularly useful for an examination of assemblage variability on the installation. The five large-scale excavation assemblages collected to date, while a useful check, were not considered a large enough site sample to delimit settlement and land-use patterns. The analysis focused only on recently tested sites. While more than 600 sites have been intensively tested on Fort Polk, many were excavated between 15 and 20 years ago and were not reported in a consistent fashion and hence are not readily useful for comparative analyses (see Table 2.1 and discussions in Chapter 2). Fortunately, several hundred sites have been tested in a consistent manner by archaeologists from Prentice Thomas and Associates, Inc., in recent years as part of an ongoing effort to evaluate the significance of sites determined through survey work to be potentially eligible for inclusion on the National Register of Historic Places (NRHP) (as documented in Chapter 2). These sites have been excavated and reported in a standardized manner, with excellent detail provided on the number, placement, and volume of units and on the number and kinds of artifacts recovered. Data from the first 32 testing projects conducted by Prentice Thomas and Associates, Inc., were used. In all, 301 tested sites were examined, 196 from the Main Fort and 105

Table 5.3 — Intensive site-testing assemblages used in the comparative analyses between the Main Fort and Peason Ridge: summary data (n = 301 tested sites)

	Main Fort			Peason Ridge		
	Total Sample	Eligible	Not Eligible	Total Sample	Eligible	Not Eligible
Number of Sites	196	51	145	105	25	80
Average Site Size (m²)	13,874.70	21,094.61	11,335.34	4,321.77	9,191.00	2,800.14
Total Area Excavated (m²)	1,265.50	397.50	868.00	678.00	198.00	480.00
Average Area Excavated (m²)	6.46	7.79	5.99	6.46	7.92	6.00
Total Volume Excavated (m³)	935.88	326.94	608.94	427.47	131.61	295.86
Average Volume Excavated (m³)	4.77	6.41	4.20	4.07	5.26	3.70
Total Artifacts	217,497	96,256	121,241	13,808	8,378	5,430
Artifact Incidence (average/site)	1,109.68	1,887.37	836.14	131.50	335.12	67.88
Artifact Density (#/m²)	171.87	242.15	139.68	20.37	42.31	11.31
Artifact Density (#/m³)	232.4	294.41	199.10	32.30	63.66	18.35
Assemblage Diversity (average/site)	0.2903	0.4111	0.2478	0.0892	0.0861	0.0821
Debitage:Tools	26.67	23.42	29.94	18.87	21.95	15.45
Debitage:Cores	45.65	44.19	46.88	156.99	266.10	95.23
Curated:Expedient	0.92	1.00	0.85	1.71	1.45	2.08
Cortical:Noncortical	0.92	0.92	0.92	0.42	0.36	0.51
Debitage:All Bifaces	96.16	85.24	106.95	59.88	62.60	56.04
Debitage:Bifaces except Points	158.34	139.87	176.69	116.04	123.28	106.25

Table 5.3 (cont.) — Intensive site-testing assemblages used in the comparative analyses between the Main Fort and Peason Ridge: summary data (n = 301 tested sites)

	Main Fort			Peason Ridge		
	Total Sample	Eligible	Not Eligible	Total Sample	Eligible	Not Eligible
Unifaces:All Bifaces	2.51	2.52	2.50	1.94	1.70	2.26
Debitage	205,143	90,271	114,902	13,030	7,983	5,047
Cortical Debitage	83,182	38,413	44,769	2,918	1,636	1,282
Noncortical Debitage	90,373	41,867	48,506	7,016	4,493	2,523
Chunks	31,588	9,991	21,597	3,096	1,854	1,242
Cores	4,494	2,043	2,451	83	30	53
All Bifaces	2,180	1,083	1,097	219	128	91
Points	856	423	433	106	63	43
All Unifaces	5,479	2,732	2,747	424	218	206
Utilized Flakes	4,091	1,968	2,123	256	149	107
Ceramics	1,217	541	676	526	196	330

from Peason Ridge (Table 5.3). The total is 301 instead of 320 (the total originally examined in these 32 projects) because several sites were combined or were shown to no longer exist. Taken collectively, the area examined in the 301-site intensive-testing data sample was more than 1,900 m² and the volume of fill was more than 1,350 m³. This is roughly five times the total area (ca. 359 m²) and volume (ca. 300 m³) examined in the five major data-recovery excavations conducted to date on the installation.

It must be emphasized, of course, that sites that are intensively tested represent the more complex or unusual assemblages found during survey work and hence are not strictly representative of all of the variability found on the installation. In particular, isolated finds and most small, low-density lithic scatters found during survey projects are not typically considered potentially significant cultural resources and hence are not subject to intensive testing. Additionally, it must be stressed that the current analysis focuses on total site assemblages in an effort to resolve broad general patterns of land use. Many of the tested sites are multicomponent and while analyses have been conducted by several investigators working on Fort Polk to tease out individual components and to examine groups of sites by time period, this was not attempted here. Finally, it should be obvious that Fort Polk sites themselves are only small parts of much larger cultural systems and that we will need to conduct analyses like these with assemblages from over a much larger area. Given these caveats, the 301 sites still have much to tell us about life in western Louisiana.

The tested sites on the Main Fort are far larger, on the average (13,874.70 vs. 4,321.77 m²), than the sites on Peason Ridge. They also tend to have a far richer and more diversified artifact assemblage. Almost an order of magnitude difference, in fact, exists in average artifact density per unit area excavated (171.87 vs. 20.37 artifacts per square meter) and per unit volume excavated (232.4 vs. 32.3 artifacts per cubic meter) between the sites on the Main Fort and those on Peason Ridge. Average assemblage size was 1,109.68 artifacts on the Main Fort, compared with 131.5 on Peason Ridge. The highly desiccated terrain on Peason Ridge and the minimal local lithic resources do not appear to have made it as attractive a place to live or visit as the Main Fort area, which has larger drainages and knappable stone in great quantity.

When specific aspects of the assemblages from these two areas are examined, the differences are all the more evident (Table 5.3). Average assemblage diversity is far greater on the Main Fort than on Peason Ridge (0.2903 vs. 0.0892), as is the incidence of all major classes of artifacts, including debitage (205,143 vs. 13,030), bifaces (2,180 vs. 219), points (856 vs. 106), unifaces and utilized flakes (5,479 vs. 424), and ceramics (1,217 vs. 526). Interestingly, even though Main Fort sites have, on the average, 10 times the number of artifacts as sites on Peason Ridge, their average diversity (calculated by comparing the number of categories present by the total number potentially present) is only about three times as high. That is, sites on the Main Fort, on the average, exhibit only three times as many artifact categories as sites on Peason Ridge.

Appreciable initial lithic reduction and manufacturing activity took place in the Main Fort area, which is due to the proximity of the chert gravel sources. The total number of cores (4,494 vs. 83) is far greater on the Main Fort, and the ratio of debitage to cores is far lower (45.65 to 156.99). That greater initial reduction took place on the Main Fort than on Peason Ridge is also supported by the sheer number of cortical flakes (83,182 vs. 2,918 flakes) as well as the average ratio of cortical to noncortical flakes (0.92 vs. 0.42) and debitage to tools (26.67 vs. 18.87).

Of course, these figures are averages, and in reality appreciable diversity exists over the 301 assemblages and within each locality. When assemblage size is compared with volume of fill over the sample, for example, only weak correlations are evident over the total sample: $r = 0.41$ on Peason Ridge and $r = 0.15$ on the Main Fort (Figure 5.23). Similar results were obtained when assemblage size was compared with the area excavated. Correlations are almost nonexistent over the total sample: $r = 0.04$ on Peason Ridge and $r = 0.13$ on the Main Fort (Anderson et al. 1999b:382). When NRHP eligibility status is considered, the distributions indicate that large, dense sites tend to be considered eligible and small sites ineligible; eligible sites also tend to have far greater numbers of most categories of artifacts (Table 5.3). The occurrence of NRHP potentially eligible and ineligible sites has been examined using scatterplots of site size by number of artifacts recovered over assemblages found during two large-scale survey projects; this was done to demonstrate that a full range of site size and density classes was receiving further evaluation (Buchner and Saatkamp 2000:203–205, 2001:296–298). A third analysis by the same contractor used histograms to make the same point (Bundy 2002b:664–665). Such self-evaluation, through controlled analyses directed toward ensuring all site classes receive research and management consideration, should occur more often.

Assemblage diversity, measured on the basis of number of categories present (to ensure interval-level data were employed), was observed to be fairly closely tied to assemblage size (Figure 5.24). Correlations of $r = 0.37$ on Peason Ridge and $r = 0.67$ on the Main Fort were observed between assemblage size and diversity. The scatter of outliers away from the regression lines in all of these figures, parenthetically, indicates the extent of variability in the assemblages. The moderate to strong positive correlations suggest sample size must be controlled for when interpreting site function, which

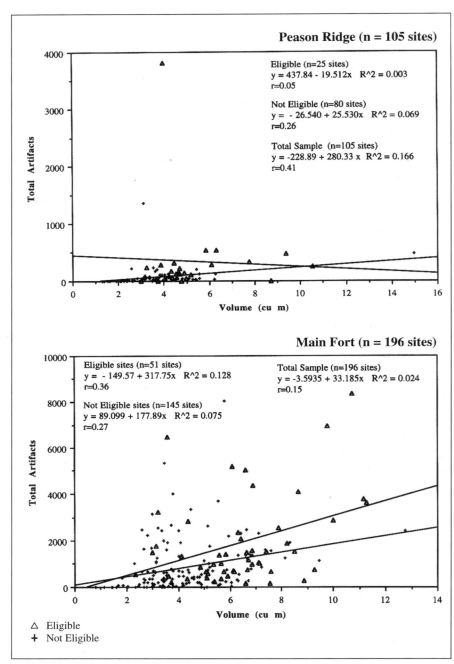

Figure 5.23 — Assemblage size by volume of fill excavated on the Main Fort and Peason Ridge in the intensive site-testing assemblages, with assemblages denoted by NRHP eligibility status (n = 301 tested sites).

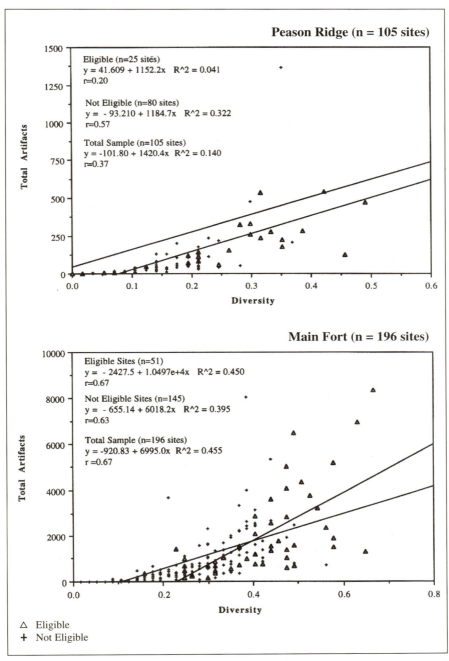

Figure 5.24 — Assemblage size and diversity relationships on the Main Fort and Peason Ridge in the intensive site-testing assemblages, with assemblages denoted by NRHP eligibility status (n = 301 tested sites).

was one reason cluster analyses were used in the current analysis (see be-low).

Looking at specific tool categories, in fact, it is clear that the site assem-blages taken collectively are quite different between the two areas (Table 5.3). Sites on Peason Ridge exhibit a lower average incidence of debitage to tools, a lower average incidence of unifaces relative to bifaces, and a higher curated-to-expedient tool ratio. Compared with the Main Fort area, assem-blages on Peason Ridge exhibit more curated tools, more bifaces than unifaces, and far less initial-reduction activity, as measured in the ratios of debitage to cores and cortical to noncortical flakes. The Peason Ridge as-semblages are what one might expect in a stone-poor area. The assemblages give every indication of being formed by groups that had to bring in their toolkit and raw materials rather than having the option of producing expedi-ent tools on the spot, at or near source areas.

These analyses show that the Fort Polk data are ideally suited to explor-ing questions of site assemblage composition as shaped by patterns of long-term land use, specifically, the effect of repeated visitation. If size alone is examined, most of the Peason Ridge assemblages fall quite comfortably at the lower end of the Main Fort range, as indicated in the various scatterplots, initially suggesting that incidence of reoccupation may be operating. Peason Ridge was more remote from the centers of most prehistoric settlement sys-tems, inferred to have been along or near the major streams of the region, and hence the area probably saw much less revisitation. The differences in assemblage composition between the two areas (i.e., ratios of bifaces to debitage, curated to expedient tools, etc.), however, strongly suggest that something other than intensity of reoccupation is operating to shape these differences (although this likely did play some role).

Use of the Peason Ridge area appears to have entailed somewhat differ-ent organizational strategies than use of the Main Fort throughout prehis-tory. Initial reduction activity, however, was likely similar in both areas, although less occurred on Peason Ridge. A moderate correlation ($r = 0.62$) was noted between the incidence of debitage and cores on Peason Ridge sites. This was only slightly lower than that noted on the Main Fort ($r = 0.69$) (Figure 5.25). Far less initial reduction, however, was occurring on Peason Ridge, as the assemblage totals for cores and cortical flakes indicate (Table 5.3). The difference in the amounts of material being reduced appears tied to the availability of knappable stone in the two areas, as well as to provision-ing strategies. Groups using Peason Ridge did not consistently bring chert cobbles with them to serve as stone sources; groups on the Main Fort had gravel sources close at hand. Greater use of curated tools and bifaces (per-haps as portable flake sources) is instead indicated on Peason Ridge.

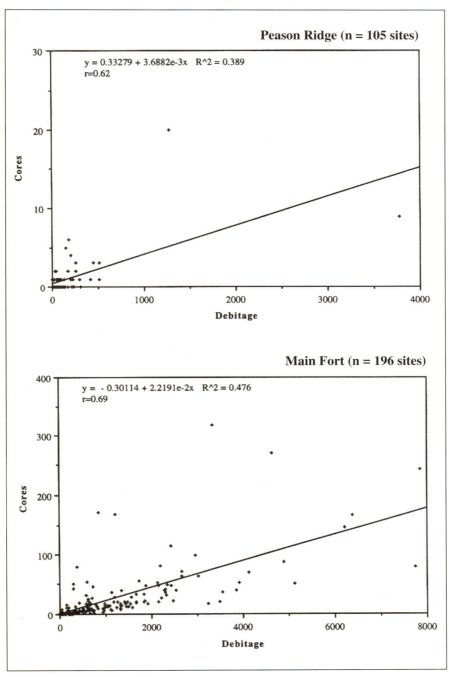

Figure 5.25 — Relationships between cores and debitage in the intensive site-testing assemblages on the Main Fort and Peason Ridge (n = 301 tested sites).

Extremely high correlations (r = 0.92, r = 0.93) were observed in the incidence of cortical to noncortical flakes in the assemblages from both areas (Figure 5.26). This appears to be due to the nature of the dominant local raw material itself—small chert gravels less than 8 to 10 cm in length. Use of this material appears to have produced consistent proportions of cortical and noncortical flakes. The distributions, quite simply, indicate that chert gravels were reduced following pretty much the same procedures in both areas. This is not surprising, as there are only a limited number of ways pebbles can be reduced practically (see Chapter 3). The incidence of curated to expedient tools was likewise found to be highly correlated (Figure 5.27), although the correlation on the Main Fort sample (r = 0.89) was somewhat higher than that on the Peason Ridge sample (r = 0.77). This difference may be related, in part, to sample size; the Main Fort assemblages are typically much larger than those on Peason Ridge. Where larger assemblages are more common, as they are on the Main Fort, an evening out of variability more readily apparent in small scatters may occur. That is, while individual episodes of site use may vary somewhat, over time and with more revisits, differences in assemblages, viewed in totality, tend to become smoothed out. The smaller, presumably single- or low-component assemblages, accordingly, probably give us a better picture of the variability in land use than can be resolved from large, dense, multicomponent sites.

Long-Term Land Use: Multivariate (Cluster) Analyses

To explore the assemblages collectively over all artifact categories, a series of hierarchical agglomerative cluster analyses were performed with a subsample of 173 assemblages, encompassing sites reported in the first 18 intensive testing projects conducted by Prentice Thomas and Associates, Inc. A total of 77 sites from Peason Ridge and 96 from the Main Fort were examined. These analyses were first conducted using 56 artifact categories and, when the output proved very difficult to interpret, they were done using 10 artifact categories, consisting of summary data for cores, cortical flakes, noncortical flakes, bifaces other than points or point fragments, formal unifaces, utilized flakes, ceramics, cobble tools, arrow points and arrow point fragments, and dart points and dart point fragments. An example of a 10-category solution for the 77 Peason Ridge assemblages examined is presented in Figure 5.28. The artifact data by category for each site used in these analyses, for both the 56- and 10-category analyses, are presented in the HPP Cultural Resources Inventory Primary Data volume (Anderson et al. 1999a:appendix 7).

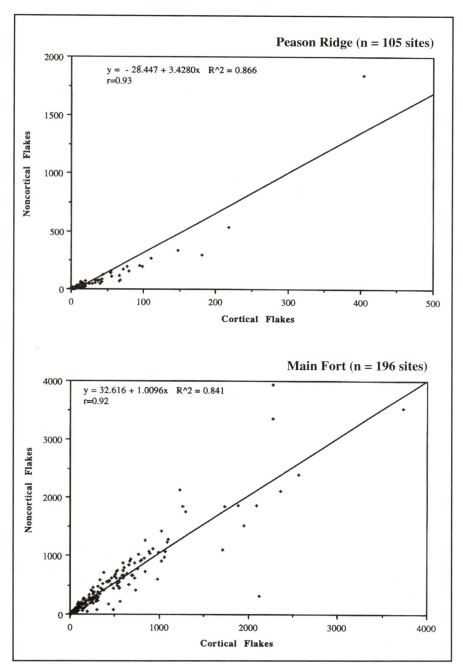

Figure 5.26 — Relationships between cortical and noncortical flakes in the intensive site-testing assemblages on the Main Fort and Peason Ridge (n = 301 tested sites).

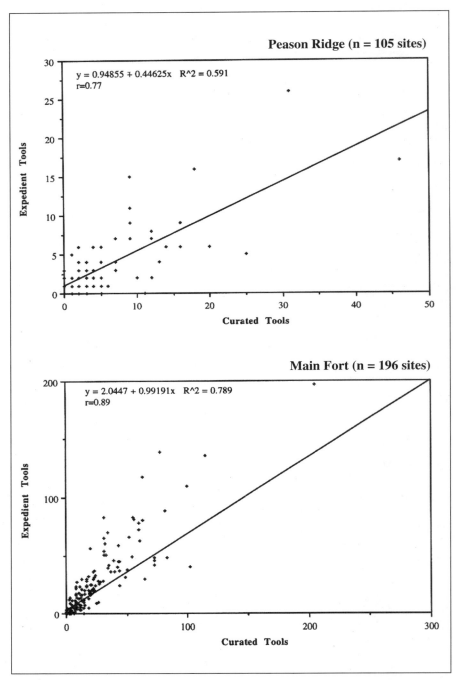

Figure 5.27 — Relationships between curated and expedient tools in the intensive site-testing assemblages on the Main Fort and Peason Ridge (n = 301 tested sites).

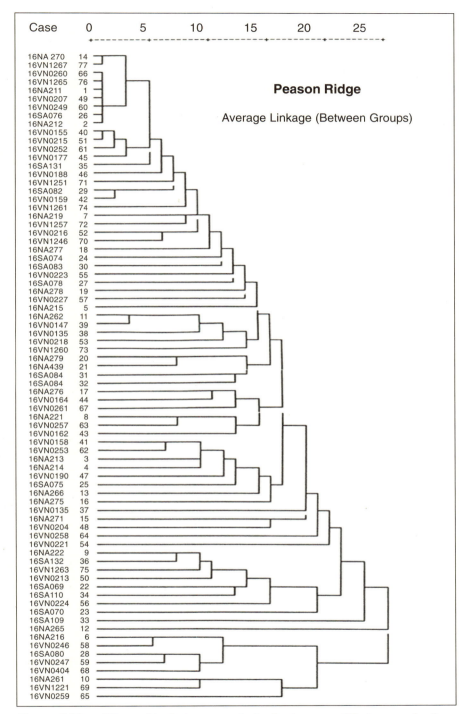

Figure 5.28 — Hierarchical cluster analysis dendrogram, 77-site sample, from Peason Ridge at Fort Polk, 10 assemblage variables, count data, chi-square distance measure solution.

The resulting dendrograms, produced using an average-linkage (between groups) procedure, made use of count data for each artifact category. Inspection of the primary data, handled by producing spreadsheets listing site assemblages in the order in which they appeared on the dendrograms, indicated that individual sites were joined to the dendrograms and groups of related sites were formed, in large measure, based on the total size of each site assemblage, the number of artifact categories present, and the number of artifacts present in each category. This resulted in some logical and informative clusters of sites, as well as some quite curious groupings.

In the Peason Ridge analysis, groups of sites were formed that corresponded to light scatters of debitage alone, light scatters of tools with little or no debitage, and a series of denser assemblages with appreciably more debitage, tools, or ceramics, with major clusters usually differing by no more than the presence or absence of a single artifact category. Considerable intergradation was evident between assemblages, with breaks between major site clusters typically due to appreciable differences in the numbers of artifacts in some categories. Some groupings were, however, simply curious, being artifacts of the clustering algorithm itself. These were typically discrete clusters of otherwise similar assemblages, with proportionally the same amounts of tools and debitage and differing from one another only in magnitude (i.e., having 10, 10, and 20 of a series of categories instead of 5, 5, and 10). These clusters may reflect reoccupation and/or the performance of similar tasks. The clusters did strongly indicate, however, that assemblage composition was quite varied on Peason Ridge, even within the typically small assemblages found there.

On the Main Fort, groupings of sites were formed, in a similar fashion to those on Peason Ridge, by assemblage size, number of categories, and number of artifacts in each category. Again, some groupings made perfect sense, while others were less obvious and appeared related more to assemblage size than to obvious functional differences from other such clusters that differed only in having larger or smaller numbers of artifacts otherwise distributed in the same proportion over the various categories. A few Main Fort sites that clustered together were different from most other sites and were probable quarrying areas, with large numbers of cores and debitage and few formal tools. Interestingly, however, quarrying and initial-reduction debris (i.e., large numbers of cores and debitage) appeared most commonly on sites where many other tool forms were present, suggesting that, for the most part, quarrying was embedded in a range of activities and not commonly done in isolation. Other clusters on the Main Fort consisted of groups of sites with large quantities of debitage but with few bifaces, few unifaces, or few utilized flakes. One of the largest single groupings consisted of sites with considerable debitage and utilized flakes but few other formal tools. These sites represent locations where extensive reduction and manufacturing and the use of expedient tools occurred, but where there was little use or at least discard of formal tools. These sites may reflect gearing-up areas, where formal tools were made for transport elsewhere.

The cluster analyses indicate that Fort Polk's seemingly uncomplicated prehistoric lithic scatters actually subsume considerable variability. They also indicate that many of the larger sites on the installation are actually the collective result of numerous smaller scatters from multiple periods of use. Small, single-component sites, as a result, are thus likely to be much easier to interpret and more likely to yield significant information than the larger, more complex sites. The analyses also indicate that evaluating large numbers of assemblages can give us a much better picture of local land use than analyses based on one or a few sites. Similar analyses, with assemblages that can be dated to specific time periods, should prove quite rewarding.

Chapter 6

The Prehistoric Cultural Sequence on Fort Polk

A tremendous amount of archaeological and historic research has occurred in west-central Louisiana in recent years and on Fort Polk in
particular, and our understanding of the nature of past human occupation
and use of this area has grown accordingly. In this chapter the prehistoric
cultural sequence in the Fort Polk area is presented using a period-by-period
format, together with a review of the kinds of research needed to help refine
this sequence. Basic understanding of cultural sequences and how they are
derived is crucial to effective research and resource management, since the
significance of many cultural properties is directly linked to the amount of
light they can shed on various periods in the past. Diagnostic artifacts remain the most effective tool archaeologists have to quickly and easily date
sites and assemblages. Their identification, description, dating, and associations are important research topics for future cultural resource investigations on the installation. The identification and dating of assemblages is, of
course, only one of many research topics to be addressed, as the discussion
that follows illustrates; some of the major research goals are described, as
well as questions for which we would like to know the answers for each
period of prehistory. Temporal diagnostics are tools by which assemblages
can be dated and then used to answer questions about what the people who
produced them were doing at that period in time. The cultural sequence
presented here is based on primary data collected on and near Fort Polk. The
temporal framework is based on research from across the surrounding region, however, since the archaeological assemblages, phases, and cultures
represented on Fort Polk have in many cases been documented elsewhere in
far greater detail. To interpret the Fort Polk archaeological record, general
syntheses of the prehistory of Louisiana, eastern Texas and the Texas Gulf
coast, and the lower Mississippi Valley, as well as more focused studies, are
referenced as appropriate in the pages that follow.

Calendar years before present (B.P.) as well as radiocarbon years (rcbp)
are used, taking advantage of the recent extended radiocarbon calibration
(Stuiver et al. 1998) (Table 6.1). Increasingly sound calibrations are being

developed linking the calendrical and radiocarbon time scales well back into the Late Pleistocene, to the limits of the radiocarbon dating technique (Hughen et al. 2000; Kitigawa and van der Plicht 1998; Stuiver et al. 1998). The development of this extended radiocarbon calibration and the increased use of dating procedures that provide calendar ages, such as optically stimulated luminescence (OSL) and thermoluminescence (TL) dating, permit researchers to use calendar dates with confidence. Given the great difference between uncalibrated radiocarbon and calendar ages in the Late Pleistocene and Early Holocene, and the fact that plateaus, jumps, and even reversals are evident in the radiocarbon record, using calendar time wherever possible is absolutely essential (e.g., Fiedel 1999; Sherratt 1997:271–272; Taylor et al. 1996:520). In general, the farther back in time we go, the greater the difference between these scales, with radiocarbon time being increasingly too young, or recent, by up to 2,000 and more years during the Paleoindian era, with profound consequences for our interpretation of the archaeological record. The 1,450-year offset between calendar and radiocarbon time at 10,000 rcbp (really 11,450 B.P.), increases to over 2,000 years at 12,000 rcbp (really ca. 14,065 B.P.) and to almost 3,500 years at 18,000 rcbp (really ca. 21,392 B.P.). Even in the later Holocene the differences may be important. The onset of the Early Woodland period, traditionally set at 3000 rcbp, is actually 3200 B.P. Using radiocarbon dates alone to discuss events in the past can give a highly misleading and erroneous picture of how much time is actually involved. Cultural historical sequences and, indeed, most archaeological writings will increasingly employ the more accurate calendar dates in the years to come. The timeline presented in this chapter makes use of this new approach to chronology by providing dates in both calendar and radiocarbon years (Table 6.1).

The Establishment of a Prehistoric Cultural Sequence in West-Central Louisiana

Most of the reports describing cultural resource investigations conducted on Fort Polk have included sections discussing, in greater or lesser detail, the presumed local cultural sequence. Until the mid-1980s, however, these summaries relied heavily on sequences generated in other areas and assumed that these were more or less congruent with developments on Fort Polk. Many interpretive analyses in these reports, in fact, consisted of extended discussions on the similarity or dissimilarity of assemblage data from Fort Polk to those found in other parts of the region. Typically, comparisons focused on materials in sequences developed in the lower Mississippi Alluvial

Table 6.1 — The Fort Polk cultural sequence in calendrical and radiocarbon time (calibrations from Stuiver et al. 1998)

Conventional (approx.)	rcbp	Period	Culture (phase)	Diagnostic Artifacts	Climactic Event
0 B.P./A.D. 1950	50	Modern U.S. National	Industrial Revolution	Glass, nails, forged metal, Herty cups	Pronounced warming
298 B.P./A.D. 1652	250				Little Ice Age ends
524 B.P./A.D. 1426	500	Caddoan/ Mississippian	European colonization (Belcher focus)	Belcher Ridged	Neo-Boreal
ca. 595 B.P./A.D. 1355	600				
672 B.P./A.D. 1278	750		Caddoan/Plaquemine (Bossier focus)	Bossier Brushed	Little Ice Age begins
694 B.P./A.D. 1256	800				
790 B.P./A.D. 1160	900		Coles Creek		Medieval Warm Period/ Neo-Atlantic
929 B.P./A.D. 1021	1000	Late Woodland	Early Caddo (Alto focus)	Davis Incised, Kiam Incised, Dunkin Incised, Crockett Curvilinear Incised Alba points	
953 B.P./A.D. 997	1050				
ca. 1020 B.P./A.D. 930	1100				
ca. 1130 B.P./820 A.D.	1200		Coles Creek (Holly Springs)	Coles Creek Incised, French Fork Incised	
1261 B.P./A.D. 689	1300		Troyville/Baytown		
1298 B.P./A.D. 652	1400			Arrow Points (<1300 B.P.)	Scandic/ Vandal Minimum
ca. 1366 B.P./A.D. 583	1500			Churupa Punctate? Baytown Plain, var. Satartia	
1520 B.P./A.D. 430	1600				
ca. 1590 B.P./A.D. 360	1700	Middle Woodland	Marksville (Whisky Chitto)	Marksville Incised, vars. Leist Yokena, Spanish Fort	Sub-Atlantic
ca. 1712 B.P./A.D. 238	1800				
ca. 1940 B.P./A.D. 10	2000			Marksville Incised Marksville Stamped	
ca. 2215 B.P./265 B.C.	2200				
ca. 2584 B.P./635 B.C.	2500	Early Woodland	Tchefuncte	Tchefuncte Plain	Sub-Boreal

Table 6.1 (cont.) — The Fort Polk cultural sequence in calendrical and radiocarbon time (calibrations from Stuiver et al. 1998)

Conventional (approx.)	rcbp	Period	Culture (phase)	Diagnostic Artifacts	Climactic Event
ca. 3185 B.P./1235 B.C.	3000	Late Archaic	Poverty Point	Motley, Epps points	Sub-Boreal
ca. 3770 B.P./1820 B.C.	3500		(Leander)		
ca. 4477 B.P./2528 B.C.	4000		(Birds Creek)	Birds Creek points	
ca. 5122 B.P./3172 B.C.	4500				
5728 B.P./3779 B.C.	5000	Middle Archaic	Watson Brake (Sixmile)	Evans points	Atlantic/Hypsithermal
6291 B.P./4342 B.C.	5500			Sinner points	
ca. 6809 B.P./4861 B.C.	6000		Big Creek Culture (Kisatchie)	Johnson/Bulverde points?	
ca. 7807 B.P./5857 B.C.	7000				
ca. 8876 B.P./6926 B.C.	8000	Early Archaic	?		Cold episode
10,189 B.P./8240 B.C.	9000		(Anacoco III) Corner-Notched horizon	San Patrice, *var. Keithville*	Boreal
ca. 10,715 B.P./8765 B.C.	9500		(Anacoco II) Early Side-Notched horizon		
ca. 11,250 B.P./9300 B.C.	9900				
ca. 11,450 B.P./9500 B.C.	10,000	Late Paleoindian	(Anacoco I)	San Patrice, *var. Dixon*	
ca. 11,850 B.P./9900 B.C.	10,200		San Patrice/Dalton	San Patrice, *var. St. Johns*	Younger Dryas ends
ca. 12,500 B.P./10,550 B.C.	10,500			San Patrice, *var. Hope*	Younger Dryas begins
12,900 B.P./10,950 B.C.	10,800				
13,000 B.P./11,050 B.C.	11,000	Middle Paleoindian	Clovis	Clovis points	Intra-Allerød cold period Allerød
13,450 B.P./11,500 B.C.	11,500				
14,065 B.P./12,115 B.C.	12,000?	Early Paleoindian	Pre-Clovis	?	Bølling-Allerød warm period Bølling
14,750 B.P./12,800 B.C.	12,500				

Valley (e.g., Belmont 1967; Phillips 1970; Phillips et al. 1951); along the middle course of the Red River in northwest Louisiana and southwest Arkansas (e.g., Gregory and Curry 1978; Schambach 1982; Schambach and Early 1982; Webb 1981); in the Sabine River/east Texas area (Aten 1983; Gibson 1978a; Story 1990); or in the lower Gulf Coast/Atchafalaya River area (Gibson 1978b).

Most prehistoric sequences employed in Louisiana make use of generalized Paleoindian–Archaic–Woodland–Mississippian (Griffin 1946, 1967) or Paleoindian–Mesoindian–Neoindian (Stoltman 1978; Willey 1966) stage terminology, with the term *Formative* substituted for the Late Archaic/Early Woodland or Neoindian stages in some formulations. These broad stages are then subdivided into finer subdivisions, some of which are characterized by one or more subregional or smaller-scale archaeological cultures, foci, or phases. These subdivisions are particularly numerous in the post-Archaic era because of the widespread occurrence of ceramics, which are artifacts that are temporally sensitive and that exhibit appreciable morphological variation, some of which has been assumed to reflect cultural variability. Many archaeological phases in Louisiana and beyond, in fact, are identified primarily by groupings of ceramic types or varieties, and that is certainly the case on Fort Polk. The prehistoric cultural historical framework that is perhaps the most influential in the Fort Polk area derives from Phillips's (1970) monumental overview of the human occupation in the lower Mississippi Valley, which built upon the earlier synthesis by Phillips, Ford, and Griffin (1951). Phillips formulated and reviewed in-depth evidence for sequential cultural phases in various portions of the lower Mississippi Valley and adjoining areas, beginning in Late Archaic times and carrying on through to the Mississippian period.

Following his broad outline, the terminal Archaic and later cultures across much of Louisiana are generally described by most researchers using Poverty Point, Tchefuncte, Marksville, Baytown, Coles Creek, and Caddoan/Mississippian culture or phase terminology (e.g., I. Brown 1984; Jeter and Williams 1989a, 1989b; Neuman 1984; Phillips 1970; Smith et al. 1983). In some research conducted in northwestern Louisiana, however, a somewhat different cultural sequence and approach to systematics is in play (e.g., Girard 2000b:8–9), with Woodland occupations sometimes described using subdivisions of the Fourche Maline culture (Schambach 1998, 2002) and local Caddoan developments typically described using foci (e.g., Perttula 1992; Perttula and Bruseth, eds. 1998); the use of foci terminology derives directly from long local use, particularly in Texas, of the Midwestern taxonomic system (McKern 1939). Some local phases and foci for earlier periods have also been developed, such as the Bellevue focus (Fulton and Webb

1953; Story 1990:291; Webb 1984) and a series of phases developed in the Natchitoches area (Gregory and Curry 1978), although they have seen little application in the Fort Polk area. Complicating the matter further, in eastern Texas, particularly along the Gulf coast, still different taxonomic designations exist for some of these cultures and periods (e.g., Aten 1983; Story [1990:256], for example, does not believe the term *Woodland* is appropriate for use in eastern Texas, preferring to refer to local developments as part of the Mossy Grove culture/tradition). In this volume, the Paleoindian–Archaic–Woodland–Caddoan/Mississippian stages and substages are used to refer to explicit time periods. Archaeological assemblages from Fort Polk are identified first by their temporal placement within one or more of these periods and then by reference to an appropriate archaeological phase, focus, or culture, if one has been developed.

"THE PROBLEM WITH FORT POLK ARCHAEOLOGY"

Until the mid-1980s most reports summarizing cultural resource investigations on Fort Polk included discussions of prehistoric occupations that were, for the most part, fairly general in scope and extensive in geographic scale, encompassing work from across the state and beyond. The goals of these discussions were to provide a general temporal and cultural framework from which archaeological remains found on Fort Polk might be interpreted. Only infrequently, however, did these early researchers attempt to use the results of their investigations to develop a local sequence. Some of the earliest efforts using local data were those by Frank Servello and his colleagues (e.g., Servello, ed. 1983:161–168), Gunn and Kerr (1984b), and Cantley (1984:256–262) (Figures 6.1 and 6.2). These efforts, although serving as a valuable guide for subsequent investigations, were typically based on small site or artifact samples or else were supported by comparatively few radiocarbon dates or stratigraphic columns. In the 1986 Multipurpose Range Complex (MPRC) report Campbell and Weed provided explicit reasons the development of a cultural sequence at Fort Polk has proved difficult, many of which remain true to this day:

> There are innumerable facts that have contributed to the perpetuation of temporal vagueness, but seven of the most critical were and are: (1) high frequencies of sites, most of which are marked by flake-dominated collections; (2) a low incidence of diagnostic lithics; (3) infrequent occurrence of ceramics, in general, and decorated sherds, in particular; (4) paste/temper/decortication inconsistencies between established sequences (e.g., Lower Mississippi Valley, Caddoan area) and Fort Polk ceramics; (5) wildly disproportionate ratio of sites

investigated only by survey and those that have been excavated (even through limited testing); (6) a paucity of sites with midden or stratified deposits; and (7) an overall dearth of absolute dates for comparative analysis [Campbell and Weed 1986:4-2].

During the 1986 MPRC testing work, these difficulties were characterized as "the problem with Fort Polk archaeology," which Campbell and her colleagues (1987:18) argued could only be overcome by working with the assemblages actually present on the installation and not by lamenting that the kind of sites archaeologists would like to find were rare or absent. Since the MPRC work, fortunately, large numbers of sites have been intensively tested on the installation, and two more large excavations have been undertaken. Evidence for stratification has been found at a number of these sites, and several radiocarbon dates have been obtained. Despite these advances, developing a cultural sequence has proven to be a major challenge in a locality like Fort Polk, where there are almost more sites and isolated finds than diagnostic points and sherds and where deeply stratified sites that offer a clear separation between datable assemblages, or even unambiguous single-component assemblages, are rare (see also Story 1990:217, who discusses similar problems in the resolution of the Archaic sequence in eastern Texas). A primary reason there have been so many innovative analyses of debitage, in fact, has been the desire to detect changes in assemblages over time to help date sites that yield few diagnostic points or ceramics (Fredlund 1983; Guderjan and

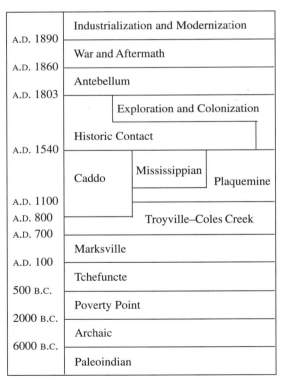

Figure 6.1 — The cultural sequence employed in the State of Louisiana's Comprehensive Archaeological Plan (from Smith et al. 1983:fig. 8).

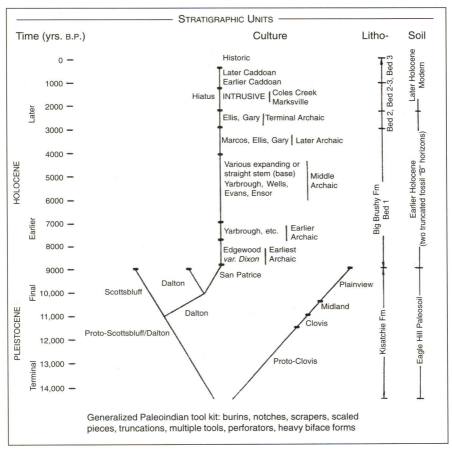

Figure 6.2 — The cultural sequence for Fort Polk from the FPAS project (from Servello, ed. 1983:168).

Morehead 1980:15–25, 1983:931–933; Gunn 1984a; Kerr 1984; see Chapters 2 and 3).

Indeed, in all of the excavations that have been undertaken on Fort Polk, cultural features remain exceedingly rare and consist primarily of groupings of stone or ceramic artifacts. Preservation of organic material like charcoal and bone is very poor in the typically acidic, sandy soils occurring over much of the area (see Chapter 1). Most features are like the paired sandstone manos and metates found at 16VN398 (Thomas et al. 1994a:67–73) and 16VN573 (Campbell et al. 1994a:62) (see Figures 3.5 and 3.6) or the moderately large cluster of sherds (n = 67) found at 16SA73 (Prentice Thomas and Associates, Inc. 1992). Features exhibiting organic or charcoal staining

are almost unheard of, although a few examples exist that have been interpreted as possible pits or hearths (e.g., 16VN1064, Thomas et al. 1993c:47–
49; 16VN839, Morehead et al. 1996a:130–146), post molds (e.g., 16VN513,
Thomas et al. 1994a:88), or midden staining (e.g., 16VN527, Morehead et
al. 1996a:83–106). One of the best prehistoric cultural features found to
date was a well-defined cluster of sandstone rocks found from 125 to 140
cm below the surface at site 16VN1064, which is located on a ridge overlooking two tributaries of the East Fork of Sixmile Creek (Thomas et al.
1993c:47) (see Figure 3.5). The feature contained three flakes, one of which
was fire damaged, and a burned piece of petrified wood. It was interpreted
as a rock-lined hearth, although unfortunately no charcoal was present. The
age of the feature could not be determined, but later prehistoric Woodland
or Caddoan remains were found in the overlying levels.

The low incidence of features on Fort Polk and the scarcity or absence
of charcoal when features are found mean that developing a secure absolute
chronology for the installation has proven difficult, since there are few opportunities for the radiocarbon dating of assemblages. In the absence of abundant preserved carbon, greater use of alternative absolute dating procedures
should be considered, such as OSL or TL dating. Indeed, a number of OSL,
Oxidized Carbon Ratio (Frink 1992, 1994), and TL dates have been run on
Fort Polk in recent years, supplementing the comparatively small number of
radiocarbon dates obtained through the years (Table 6.2). Beginning in the
mid-1980s and continuing to the present, however, our knowledge of the
local cultural sequence has been changing dramatically, as more and more
work has been done on Fort Polk. Our current view of the prehistoric cultural sequence is the result of almost two decades of continuous refinement,
primarily by archaeologists from New World Research, Inc., and Prentice
Thomas and Associates, Inc., under the overall leadership of L. Janice
Campbell and Prentice M. Thomas.

THE DEVELOPMENT OF A LOCAL CULTURAL SEQUENCE
The first detailed cultural sequence for the Fort Polk area based primarily on
evidence collected from the installation itself was published in 1986 and
1987 in the summary reports on survey and testing activity in the MPRC,
projects that generated a vast amount of new primary information (Campbell and Weed 1986:9-1 to 9-55; Campbell et al. 1987:22–33) (Figure 6.3).
Using a period-by-period format, factual and interpretative discussions of
the nature of the local archaeological record were provided, encompassing
the major periods of prehistory, including the Paleoindian, the Early and
Middle Archaic, the Late Archaic, the Formative/Woodland, and the Caddoan-
Mississippian eras.

Stage	Period	Culture	Regional Phase	Diagnostics
Lithic	Paleoindian	Clovis Folsom Undefined	Undefined Undefined Undefined	Clovis Points Folsom Points Pelican, Coastview
	Late Paleo.	San Patrice	Undefined	San Patrice Points *var. Hope, St. Johns* Albany Spokeshave
Archaic	Early/Middle Archaic	Undefined	Undefined	Edgewood Point *var. Dixon* Dart Point, Group 1 Dart Point, Group 2 (probably during Middle Archaic)
	Late Archaic	Undefined	Undefined	Dart Point, Groups 1 & 2 Motley, Gary, Pontchartrain "Pebble Line" tools Ground Stone Quartz Crystals (reported by locals)
Formative	Woodland	Tchefuncte	Undefined	Dart Point, Groups 1 & 2 Plain ceramics with laminated paste
		Marksville	Whiskey Chitto	Dart Point, Groups 1 & 2 (latter predominate) Dixon Points Reworked Garys Friley Points Marksville design elements
		Coles Creek	Holly Springs	Friley, Hayes, Livermore Points Stamped, Incised, Incised Sherds
	Caddo/Mississippian	Bossier	Calhoun Branch	Brushed, fingernail impressed, engraved ceramics Hayes, Alba, Bassett, Friley Points Knives

Figure 6.3 — The preliminary cultural sequence for the Fort Polk area, west-central Louisiana, 1987, based on the New World Research MPRC research program (from Campbell and Weed 1986:9-3, 9-4).

Table 6.2 — Radiocarbon, thermoluminescence, and OCR dates from Fort Polk sites

A. Radiocarbon Dates

Date rcbp	Calendar B.P. (2 sigma) max (cal ages) min	Lab No.	Site Name	Archaeological Culture	References
3115 ± 615	4868 (3355) 1823	UGa-1877	16VN18	Late Archaic/Early Woodland? Ellis points	Fredlund 1983:800; McGimsey and van der Koogh 2001:4–5
2780 ± 140	3322 (2866) 2513	Beta-33070	16VN791/Beechwood	Late Archaic/Early Woodland? Marcos point	Campbell et al. 1990:72–73
3675 ± 65	4226 (4057, 4052, 3983) 3784	UGa-2031	16VN24/Big Brushy	Late Archaic/Ellis, Evans, Gary, and Kent points	Guderjan and Morehead 1980:13, 1983:917, 935; McGimsey and van der Koogh 2001:8–9
1130 ± 70	1256 (1053, 1028, 1008) 927	UGa-3703??	16SA50/Eagle Hill II	Late Woodland/Coles Creek	Gunn 1984b:145; McGimsey and van der Koogh 2001:12–13
5160 ± 170	6288 (5916) 5593	Beta-33068	16VN791/Beechwood	Late Archaic? Ensor (?) point	Campbell et al. 1990:72: McGimsey and van der Koogh 2001:4–5
1015 ± 80	1064 (931) 739	UGa-3704??	16SA50/Eagle Hill II	Late Woodland/Coles Creek	Gunn 1984a:164; McGimsey and van der Koogh 2001:12–13
modern	n/a	UGa-2531	16SA50/Eagle Hill II	??	McGimsey and van der Koogh 2001:12–13
1520 ± 70	1545 (1408) 1291	Beta-48679	16VN794		Cantley et al., eds. 1993:119; McGimsey and van der Koogh 2001:4–5
1890 ± 110	2113 (1859, 1852, 1824) 1550	Beta-48677	16VN794		Cantley et al., eds. 1993:119; McGimsey and van der Koogh 2001:4–5

Table 6.2 (cont.) — Radiocarbon, thermoluminescence, and OCR dates from Fort Polk sites

A. RADIOCARBON DATES (CONT.)

Date rcbp	Calendar B.P. (2 sigma) max (cal ages) min	Lab No.	Site Name	Archaeological Culture	References
3920 ± 90	4776 (4409) 4090	Beta–48679	16VN794		Cantley et al., eds. 1993:119; McGimsey and van der Koogh 2001:4–5
4030 ± 110	4833 (4517, 4467, 4448) 4155	Beta–50531	16VN794		Cantley et al., eds. 1993:119; McGimsey and van der Koogh 2001:4–5
4170 ± 110	4968 (4812, 4757, 4726, 4722, 4708, 4654) 4416	Beta–48680	16VN794		Cantley et al., eds. 1993:119; McGimsey and van der Koogh 2001:4–5
5050 ± 90	5988 (5858, 5828, 5750) 5600	Beta–49294	16VN794		Cantley et al., eds. 1993:119; McGimsey and van der Koogh 2001:4–5
5770 ± 140	6890 (6616, 6612, 6595, 6593, 6565) 6290	Beta–49293	16VN794		Cantley et al., eds. 1993:119; McGimsey and van der Koogh 2001:4–5
1030 ± 50	1054 (946, 942, 933) 795	Beta–48675	16VN794		Cantley et al., eds. 1993:119; McGimsey and van der Koogh 2001:4–5
??	A.D. 635–885	??	16VN839	Feature 1, Birds Creek phase?	Morehead et al. 1996a:141
??	A.D. 350–650	??	16VN839	100–110 cm, baked clay objects	Morehead et al. 1996a:141
??	A.D. 635–885	??	16VN527	Marksville?	Morehead et al. 1996a:95

Table 6.2 (cont.) — Radiocarbon, thermoluminescence, and OCR dates from Fort Polk sites

B. Thermoluminescence Dates

Date rcbp	Calendar (2 sigma)	Lab No.	Site Name	Archaeological Culture	References
7500 ± 1252	n/a	UMC-2146	16SA50/Eagle Hill II	Archaic	Gunn et al. n.d.; McGimsey and van der Koogh 2001:37
7110 ± 575	n/a	UMC-1974	16SA50/Eagle Hill II	Archaic	Gunn et al. n.d.; McGimsey and van der Koogh 2001:37
8090 ± 410	n/a	UMC-1995B	16SA50/Eagle Hill II	Archaic	Gunn et al. n.d.; McGimsey and van der Koogh 2001:37
8910 ± 525	n/a	UMC-1995A	16SA50/Eagle Hill II	Archaic	Gunn et al. n.d.; McGimsey and van der Koogh 2001:37
12,800 ± 2100	n/a	UMC-2605A	16SA50/Eagle Hill II		Gunn et al. n.d.; McGimsey and van der Koogh 2001:37
10,250 ± 550	n/a	UMC-2605B	16SA50/Eagle Hill II		Gunn et al. n.d.; McGimsey and van der Koogh 2001:37
10,200 ± 500	n/a	UMC-2716	16SA50/Eagle Hill II	Paleoindian/Early Archaic	Gunn et al. n.d.; McGimsey and van der Koogh 2001:37
1290 ± 105	n/a	UMC-1172	16SA50/Eagle Hill II	Coles Creek	Gunn et al. n.d.; McGimsey and van der Koogh 2001:37
1250 ± 120	n/a	UMC-1707	16SA50/Eagle Hill II	Coles Creek	Gunn et al. n.d.; McGimsey and van der Koogh 2001:37
22,300	n/a	UMC-3292A	16SA50/Eagle Hill II		McGimsey and van der Koogh 2001:37
27,900	n/a	UMC-3292B	16SA50/Eagle Hill II		McGimsey and van der Koogh 2001:37

C. Oxidizable Carbon Ratio (OCR) Dates

Date B.P.	Calendar (2 sigma)	Lab No.	Site Name	Archaeological Culture	References
28786	n/a	ACT #2318	FP - Restricted Road Trench	strata C2	Cantley et al. 1997:803 (no. 5)
37726	n/a	ACT #2319	FP - Restricted Road Trench	strata 2BTB?	Cantley et al. 1997:803 (no. 6) Note: date in book reads "1938"
107	n/a	ACT #2321	FP - Lookout Road Trench	strata A1	Cantley et al. 1997:805 (no. 1)
3356	n/a	ACT #2322	FP - Lookout Road Trench	strata A2	Cantley et al. 1997:805 (no. 2)
6030	n/a	ACT #2323	FP - Lookout Road Trench	strata E	Cantley et al. 1997:805 (no. 3)
9627	n/a	ACT #2324	FP - Lookout Road Trench	strata Bw1	Cantley et al. 1997:805 (no. 4)
15449	n/a	ACT #2325	FP - Lookout Road Trench	strata Bw2	Cantley et al. 1997:805 (no. 5)

Table 6.2 (cont.) — Radiocarbon, thermoluminescence, and OCR dates from Fort Polk sites

C. Oxidizable Carbon Ratio (OCR) Dates (cont.)

Date B.P.	Calendar (2 sigma)	Lab No.	Site Name	Archaeological Culture	References
18058	n/a	ACT #2326	FP - Lookout Road Trench	strata 2Btb	Cantley et al. 1997:805 (no. 6)
25210	n/a	ACT #2327	FP - Lookout Road Trench	strata 2Btgb	Cantley et al. 1997:805 (no. 7)
639	n/a	ACT #2328	FP - Mill Creek Trench	strata A1	Cantley et al. 1997:799 (no. 1)
782	n/a	ACT #2329	FP - Mill Creek Trench	strata A2	Cantley et al. 1997:799 (no. 2)
2192	n/a	ACT #2330	FP - Mill Creek Trench	strata C1	Cantley et al. 1997:799 (no. 3)
3857	n/a	ACT #2331	FP - Mill Creek Trench	strata C2	Cantley et al. 1997:799 (no. 4)
4705	n/a	ACT #2332	FP - Mill Creek Trench	strata C3	Cantley et al. 1997:799 (no. 5)
7421	n/a	ACT #2333	FP - Mill Creek Trench	strata C4	Cantley et al. 1997:799 (no. 6)
9978	n/a	ACT #2334	FP - Mill Creek Trench	strata 2Bw1b?	Cantley et al. 1997:799 (no. 7)
12967	n/a	ACT #2335	FP - Mill Creek Trench	strata 2Bw2b?	Cantley et al. 1997:799 (no. 8)
19240	n/a	ACT #2336	FP - Mill Creek Trench	strata 3C5	Cantley et al. 1997:799 (no. 9)
23244	n/a	ACT #2337	FP - Mill Creek Trench	strata 4Bw1b	Cantley et al. 1997:799 (no. 10)
29356	n/a	ACT #2338	FP - Mill Creek Trench	strata 4Bw2b	Cantley et al. 1997:799 (no. 11)
31911	n/a	ACT #2339	FP - Mill Creek Trench	strata 4Bw3b	Cantley et al. 1997:799 (no. 12)
34439	n/a	ACT #2340	FP - Mill Creek Trench	strata 4Bw4b	Cantley et al. 1997:799 (no. 13)
					Note: date in book reads "31911"
1938	n/a	ACT #2314	FP - Restricted Road Trench	strata 2Btb?	Cantley et al. 1997:803 (no. 6)
3890	n/a	ACT #2315	FP - Restricted Road Trench	strata Bw	Cantley et al. 1997:803 (no. 2)
11804	n/a	ACT #2316	FP - Restricted Road Trench	strata Bc	Cantley et al. 1997:803 (no. 3)
20496	n/a	ACT #2317	FP - Restricted Road Trench	strata C1	Cantley et al. 1997:803 (no. 4)
1150 ± 34	A.D. 732–868		16VN2729 - Test Pit 1, 10 cm		Morehead et al. 2002:123
1361 ± 41	A.D. 507–589		16VN2729 - Test Pit 1, 20 cm		Morehead et al. 2002:123
1807 ± 54	A.D. 35–251		16VN2729 - Test Pit 1, 30 cm		Morehead et al. 2002:123
2208 ± 66	390–26 B.C.		16VN2729 - Test Pit 1, 40 cm		Morehead et al. 2002:123
9480 ± 284	8098–6962 B.C.		16VN2729 - Test Pit 1, 50 cm	San Patrice	Morehead et al. 2002:123

Table 6.2 (cont.) — Radiocarbon, thermoluminescence, and OCR dates from Fort Polk sites

C. OXIDIZABLE CARBON RATIO (OCR) DATES (CONT.)

Date B.P.	Calendar (2 sigma)	Lab No.	Site Name	Archaeological Culture	References
1711 ± 52	A.D. 135–343		16VN2730 - Test Pit 3, 13 cm		Morehead et al. 2002:123
2137 ± 65	317–57 B.C.		16VN2730 - Test Pit 3, 23 cm		Morehead et al. 2002:123
2831 ± 85	1051–711 B.C.		16VN2730 - Test Pit 3, 33 cm		Morehead et al. 2002:123
3507 ± 105	1767–1347 B.C.		16VN2730 - Test Pit 3, 43 cm		Morehead et al. 2002:123
5096 ± 153	3452–2840 B.C.		16VN2730 - Test Pit 3, 53 cm	San Patrice, *var. Keithville*	Morehead et al. 2002:123
6033 ± 181	4445–3721 B.C.		16VN2730 - Test Pit 3, 63 cm		Morehead et al. 2002:123
8021 ± 241	6553–5589 B.C.		16VN2730 - Test Pit 3, 73 cm	San Patrice, *var. Keithville*	Morehead et al. 2002:123
10,205 ± 307	8869–7641 B.C.		16VN2730 - Test Pit 3, 83 cm		Morehead et al. 2002:123
12,147 ± 365	10,927–9467 B.C.		16VN2730 - Test Pit 3, 93 cm		Morehead et al. 2002:124
14,632 ± 439	13,560–11,804 B.C.		16VN2730 - Test Pit 3, 103 cm		Morehead et al. 2002:124
788 ± 23	A.D. 1116–1208		16VN2730 - Test Pit 4, 10 cm		Morehead et al. 2002:124
1327 ± 39	A.D. 545–701		16VN2730 - Test Pit 4, 20 cm		Morehead et al. 2002:124
1655 ± 49	A.D. 197–393		16VN2730 - Test Pit 4, 30 cm		Morehead et al. 2002:124
3725 ± 111	1997–1553 B.C.		16VN2730 - Test Pit 4, 40 cm		Morehead et al. 2002:124
4148 ± 124	2446–1950 B.C.		16VN2730 - Test Pit 4, 50 cm		Morehead et al. 2002:124
4580 ± 137	2904–2356 B.C.		16VN2730 - Test Pit 4, 60 cm		Morehead et al. 2002:124
7425 ± 222	5919–5031 B.C.		16VN2730 - Test Pit 4, 70 cm		Morehead et al. 2002:124
9378 ± 281	7990–6866 B.C.		16VN2730 - Test Pit 4, 80 cm	San Patrice, *var. Keithville*	Morehead et al. 2002:124
9847 ± 295	8487–7307 B.C.		16VN2730 - Test Pit 4, 90 cm		Morehead et al. 2002:124
1002 ± 30	A.D. 888–1008		16VN2733 - Test Pit 4, 10 cm	Friley point	Morehead et al. 2002:124
1481 ± 44	A.D. 381–557		16VN2733 - Test Pit 4, 20 cm	Dunkin pottery	Morehead et al. 2002:124
3607 ± 108	1873–1441 B.C.		16VN2733 - Test Pit 4, 30 cm		Morehead et al. 2002:124
1054 ± 31	A.D. 834–958		16VN2734 - Test Pit 3, 10 cm	Bassett point	Morehead et al. 2002:124
1755 ± 52	A.D. 91–299		16VN2734 - Test Pit 3, 20 cm	Colbert, Kent points, Evansville Punctated	Morehead et al. 2002:124

Table 6.2 (cont.) — Radiocarbon, thermoluminescence, and OCR dates from Fort Polk sites

C. OXIDIZABLE CARBON RATIO (OCR) DATES (CONT.)

Date B.P.	Calendar (2 sigma)	Lab No.	Site Name	Archaeological Culture	References
2587 ± 77	791–483 B.C.		16VN2734 - Test Pit 3, 30 cm		Morehead et al. 2002:124
1194 ± 35	A.D. 686–826		16VN2736 - Test Pit 3, 10 cm		Morehead et al. 2002:124
1702 ± 51	A.D. 146–350		16VN2736 - Test Pit 3, 20 cm		Morehead et al. 2002:124
2667 ± 80	877–557 B.C.		16VN2736 - Test Pit 3, 30 cm	Gary	Morehead et al. 2002:124
494 ± 14	A.D. 1428–1484		16VN2764 - Test Pit 1, 10 cm		Morehead et al. 2002:124
1062 ± 31	A.D. 826–950		16VN2764 - Test Pit 1, 20 cm		Morehead et al. 2002:124
1851 ± 55	11 B.C. to A.D. 209		16VN2764 - Test Pit 1, 30 cm		Morehead et al. 2002:124
2085 ± 62	269–11 B.C.		16VN2764 - Test Pit 1, 40 cm		Morehead et al. 2002:124
2319 ± 69	507–231 B.C.		16VN2764 - Test Pit 1, 50 cm	Marksville pottery	Morehead et al. 2002:124
2525 ± 75	725–425 B.C.		16VN2764 - Test Pit 1, 60 cm		Morehead et al. 2002:124
2702 ± 81	914–590 B.C.		16VN2764 - Test Pit 1, 70 cm		Morehead et al. 2002:125
3799 ± 113	2075–1623 B.C.		16VN2764 - Test Pit 1, 80 cm		Morehead et al. 2002:125
4063 ± 121	2355–1871 B.C.		16VN2764 - Test Pit 1, 90 cm	Epps point	Morehead et al. 2002:125
4326 ± 129	2637–2118 B.C.		16VN2764 - Test Pit 1, 100 cm		Morehead et al. 2002:125

The 1987 sequence was subsequently modified by Campbell and her colleagues in 1990 using data collected from the large-scale stratigraphic excavations at 16VN791 (Campbell et al. 1990:96; see discussion of this work in Chapter 2). The work at 16VN791 has proven to be of great importance in efforts to develop a cultural sequence on the installation. The authors combined a number of what were formerly treated as separate dart point types into three point clusters and offered stratigraphic evidence supporting the hypothesis that these clusters are closely tied to particular time periods. From earliest to latest, these are the Birds Creek, Dooley Branch, and Williams dart point clusters; all arrow point forms combined to form a fourth and most recent group (see detailed descriptions of these taxa in Chapter 5). The Birds Creek cluster consists of Ensor- and Epps-like points with widely flaring bases and hafting often approaching side notching; the Dooley Branch cluster consists of Edgewood, Marcos, Summerfield, and Yarbrough-like points with expanding straight-based stems and corner notching; and the Williams cluster consists of Williams-like corner-notched points with convex bases. The distributions of specimens in the Williams dart point cluster and the arrow point cluster were found to be essentially identical, suggesting either a highly compressed upper stratigraphy or the co-occurrence of the two forms, possibly for different tasks.

In 1991, Prentice Thomas and Associates, Inc., was awarded a continuing services contract for intensive testing of sites considered potentially eligible for inclusion on the National Register of Historic Places, and since that time they have examined more than 500 sites, creating an archaeological dataset based on controlled excavations several times larger, in terms of both surface area examined and volume of fill excavated, than all the previous excavations undertaken on the installation combined (see Chapter 2). The site-testing data, coupled with the results of the five large-scale block unit excavations that have occurred on the installation and the results of other survey and testing work, have offered an unprecedented opportunity to refine the local cultural sequence. The Prentice Thomas and Associates, Inc., research team has done just that, refining the cultural sequence every few years since their initial efforts in the 1980s and early 1990s (e.g., Campbell et al. 1994a, 1994b; Morehead et al. 1995a, 1996a, 2002; Thomas et al. 1997). The most recent Fort Polk sequence, developed by Prentice Thomas and Associates, Inc., and released in early 2002, is depicted in Table 6.3.

The remainder of this chapter consists of a discussion of the prehistoric/ Native American cultural sequence for the Fort Polk area, using a period-by-period format. The sequence that is presented is essentially the one developed by archaeologists from Prentice Thomas and Associates, Inc., and closely follows the most recent update (Morehead et al. 2002:17–61). The

Table 6.3 — The cultural sequence for the Fort Polk area of western Louisiana as of 2002 (from Morehead et al. 2002:18–19; Thomas et al. 1997:13–14).

Period	Culture	Phase	Diagnostics and Secondary Traits
Proto-historic			European and aboriginal ceramics; Cuney points; possibly Bayougoula points and spikes(?). Secondarily, European gunflints and native flints, which resemble *pièces esquillées;* formal bifaces rare to absent.
Caddo Foci or Mississippian	Belcher		Belcher Ridged: Pease Brushed-Incised ceramics; Bassett and Cliffton (?) points. Secondarily, almost all formal tools are flake-based.
	Plaquemine		Coles Creek Incised *var. Hardy,* L'Eau Noire Incised ceramics; Bassett points. Formal bifaces extremely rare.
	Bossier	Calhoun Branch	Brushed, Finger Nail Impressed, Engraved, Ridged (Belcher?) ceramics; Bassett, Hayes, Alba and Friley points. Secondarily, about 80% of formal tools are unifaces.
	Alto		Pennington Punctated-Incised, Crockett Curvilinear Incised, Hickory Fine Engraved; Alba, Catahoula, Friley, Hayes and Scallorn points. Secondarily, about 80% of formal tools are unifaces; some blade technology.
Late Woodland	Coles Creek	Holly Springs	Mazique Incised, Coles Creek Incised *vars. Stoner, Greenhouse, Coles Creek, Blakely,* and *Hardy;* possibly French Fork Incised; Colbert, Alba and Gary points; possibly Friley and Catahouta points. Secondarily, formal bifaces outnumber formal unifaces.
	Baytown		Yokena Incised, Alligator Incised, chalky plainwares equivalent to Baytown Plain *var. Troyville;* Dooley Branch, Kent-like, Godley, Gary *var. Maybon,* Colbert, Alba-like and crude arrow points.
Middle Woodland	Marksville	Whiskey Chitto	Marksville Incised, Marksville Stamped. Churupa Punctated ceramics; Dooley Branch, Ellis, Godley, Kent, Gary, Palmillas-like and Dickson(?) points. Secondarily, ceramic wares are usually sandy; bifaces commonly amount to 60% or more of formal tools; blade technology present; ground stone common.
Early Woodland	Tchefuncte		Tchefuncte Plain, Tchefuncte Incised(?), notched rims; Birds Creek and Dooley Branch cluster points, also Godley and Gary points. Secondarily, bifaces and unifaces are about equal.

Table 6.3 (cont.) — The cultural sequence for the Fort Polk area of western Louisiana as of
2002 (from Morehead et al. 2002:18–19; Thomas et al. 1997:13–14).

Period	Culture	Phase	Diagnostics and Secondary Traits
Late Archaic	Calcasieu (II)	Leander	Motley, Epps, Delhi, Gary and Kent points; possibly Calcasieu. Secondarily, bifaces are more common as formal tools; points are the most common formal tools, some ground stone is present.
	Calcasieu (I)	Birds Creek	Birds Creek points; Texas types present as minority element points; Dooley Branch appears at the end of the phase. Secondarily, formal unifaces are dominant in base/seasonal camps; some ground stone; baked clay objects present. Birds Creek hearth at 16VN791 had uncorrected C-14 date of 3210 B.C.
Middle Archaic	Evans	Sixmile	Evans points and first appearance of Birds Creek. Secondary traits: biface-uniface ratios variable; many *pièces esquillées,* denticulated and serrated pieces rare: baked clay objects of bipyramidal or amorphous form. Possibly related to the Big Creek Culture of Arkansas and northeast Louisiana, but its exact form is unclear.
Early/ Middle Archaic	Kisatchie	Kisatchie	Sinner points, possibly Yarbrough *vars. Lindale* and *Dike* and similar forms. Secondary traits include the dominance of unifaces among formal tools (over 60%) many components with diverse but small to moderate-sized assemblages. Relationship with Early Archaic of East Texas, which has Kirk or Kirk-like points, unclear.
Late Paleoindian	San Patrice	Anacoco	San Patrice *var. Hope, St. Johns,* (early?), *Dixon, Keithville* (late?), *Leaf River;* possibly Pelican points; Albany tools. Secondarily, flake, blade and bifacial reduction; curated technology; majority of unifacial formal tools; multiple tools; *pièces esquillées,* burins, becs, notched pieces, denticulates: primary flakes common, biface trimming flakes rare; many large flakes; some ground stone: use of local raw materials; embedded procurement. San Patrice *var. Brazos* or Brazos Fishtail is found from Peason Ridge to Colorado River and Llano Estacado. Relationship with Dalton, Midland, Plainview and Scottsbluff unclear, but is at least contemporaneous.
Paleoindian			Clovis, Coastview(?) points; Folsom(?); Pelican late? Secondarily, core-flake and blade technology; curated tool kits; embedded procurement; exotic raw material; burins; end scrapers; multiple tools; *pièces esquillées;* ground stone rare.

discussion that follows also makes use of information presented in the 1988 and 1999 Historic Preservation Plans (HPPs) and data compiled since 1999, offers critical commentary on the efficacy of what has been proposed, and tries to place cultural developments on Fort Polk into a broader regional perspective. This sequence must, of course, be viewed as somewhat tentative and hypothetical in nature—as an evolving construct. Some of the proposed phases are based on evidence drawn from multicomponent and mixed site deposits and, less commonly, from single-component assemblages. Accordingly, revision and refinement will unquestionably occur, particularly over details like the temporal ranges and associations of particular ceramic, dart, or arrow point types, and probably even over more general matters like the existence of particular phases. Given the massive archaeological dataset developed on the installation, however, it is appropriate to put it to use in this fashion, developing a framework for examining local assemblages and comparing them with assemblages found elsewhere in the region.

The Fort Polk Prehistoric Cultural Sequence

THE PALEOINDIAN ERA (>11,450 B.P./10,000 RCBP)
Paleoindian sites and assemblages in Louisiana can be placed into three broad temporal and cultural groupings, the Early, Middle, and Late Paleoindian periods, corresponding to the pre-Clovis, Clovis, and post-Clovis Pleistocene occupation of the region. A number of syntheses exist summarizing our knowledge of this period in the Southeast and adjoining eastern Texas area, including the Louisiana area (e.g., in chronological order, Mason 1962; Williams and Stoltman 1965; Anderson 1990; Story 1990:168–210; Anderson and Sassaman 1996; Morse et al. 1996; Goodyear 1999; and Anderson 2001, n.d.a, n.d.b). On Fort Polk there is no evidence for Early Paleoindian assemblages and only limited evidence for Middle Paleoindian assemblages. Late Paleoindian assemblages, in contrast, are widespread and represent some of the most common materials found on the installation.

Late Pleistocene/Early Paleoindian Adaptations (before ca. 13,450 B.P./>11,500 rcbp)
The Late Pleistocene glacial maximum, or period of most intense cold and greatest ice sheet extent in the last glacial cycle, occurred at roughly 21,400 B.P./18,000 rcbp. So much water was tied up in ice on the land that sea levels were 100 m below where they are at present. Soon thereafter, by ca. 15,000 B.P., postglacial warming was underway and progressed rapidly for the next two thousand years, during the Bølling and Allerød, with only brief and

comparatively cold reversals, known as the Older Dryas (ca. 14,100–13,950 B.P./12,100–11,950 rcbp) and the Intra-Allerød Cold Period (ca. 13,400–13,100 B.P./11,400–11,100 rcbp) (e.g., Allaby and Allaby 1999; Björck et al. 1996; Yu and Eicher 1998). Sometime during this late glacial period the initial colonization of the New World probably occurred, since this is when human populations are first recognized across much of the hemisphere. Any earlier arrivals, predating the Bølling warming, apparently did not reproduce sufficiently to leave a widespread recognizable and hence incontrovertible and uncontroversial archaeological record.

The age of these earliest occupations is still a matter of considerable controversy in American archaeology, with estimates for the time of entry ranging from ca. 40,000 to 13,500 B.P. (e.g., Adovasio et al. 1999; Bonnichsen 1991; Bonnichsen and Turnmire 1999; Fiedel 2000; Meltzer 1997; Stanford 1983). While the human occupation of the Beringia region of Alaska and the Yukon territory may date as early as 15,000 B.P., at the present there is no unequivocally accepted evidence for human occupation south of the Canadian ice sheets prior to about 12,500 rcbp, with the Monte Verde site in Chile currently the earliest widely accepted site of this period. The first clear evidence for human occupation in the Southeast is attributed to Early Paleoindian groups, who apparently were present in the area by or shortly after 12,000 rcbp. No evidence for Early Paleoindian, pre-Clovis age occupation has been found to date in the work at Fort Polk, however, nor anywhere in Louisiana.

Late Pleistocene/Middle Paleoindian Adaptations (ca. 13,450–12,900 B.P./11,500–10,800 rcbp)

Middle Paleoindian occupations in Louisiana are recognized by the presence of lanceolate Clovis fluted projectile points, which are occasionally reported from various parts of the state (Gagliano and Gregory 1965; Hillman 1985; Marckese 1993). Clovis technology spread widely during and just after the Intra-Allerød Cold Period at ca. 13,400–13,100 B.P./11,400–11,100 rcbp and was replaced by a number of subregional cultural traditions by soon after the start of the Younger Dryas at ca. 12,900 B.P./10,800 rcbp (Anderson and Faught 1998, 2000:512; Fiedel 1999:105–106, 2000; Taylor et al. 1996). During this period human populations expanded rapidly over eastern North America and settled permanently in a number of areas. These people were highly mobile, ranged over large areas, and targeted a wide range of biota, including megafauna. Some parts of the region were highly favored, particularly the major rivers of the Midsouth and Midwest, including the Mississippi, Ohio, Cumberland, and Tennessee, and portions of Florida and the Atlantic Coastal Plain. These areas are assumed to have been rich in game, plant foods, and other resources of value to these early populations and to have been staging areas from which the settlement of the larger region occurred and from which subregional cultural traditions emerged (Anderson 1990:187–189, 1996a:34–39; Dincauze 1993:51–56). The Gault site in central Texas (Collins et al. 1992) and the McFaddin Beach locality on the northeast Texas Gulf coast (Stright 1999) are potential staging areas in closest proximity to western Louisiana, and these may be where local Clovis groups originated (see also Story 1990:178–188). Clovis settlement also appears to have been shaped, to some extent, by the occurrence of high-quality chert sources; these populations preferred these raw materials for their toolkits, which included some of the finest chipped stone artifacts ever made in prehistoric North America (Goodyear 1979).

Comparatively few Clovis points are known from the Louisiana area, at least in comparison with many other parts of the Southeast, but this appears to be largely because, unlike most states, no systematic fluted point survey has been put in place (Anderson and Faught 1998). Clovis points are assumed to occur from roughly 13,450 to 12,950 B.P./11,500 to 10,900 rcbp or slightly later, based on dates obtained at sites located farther to the west (Fiedel 1999; Haynes 1993). Four Clovis points have been found on Fort Polk to date, three from the vicinity of Eagle Hill on Peason Ridge and a fourth from site 16VN1505 on the terrace overlooking Big Brushy Creek on the Main Fort (Abrams et al. 1995:217). Late Pleistocene environmental conditions and their impact on human populations have been the subject of some research in Louisiana away from Fort Polk. Saucier (1994:134), for example, showed that Paleoindian settlement tended to occur along the edges of stream floodplains in the vicinity of Maçon Ridge, raising the possibility that a similar pattern might occur in the Fort Polk area, as indicated by the find at 16VN1505.

At 16VN1505, a Clovis base, a Plainview base, and two San Patrice points were found (Abrams et al. 1995:217; Meyer et al. 1996a:122–135). This large site was initially examined in 1992 during the South Carolina Institute of Archaeology and Anthropology's 8,027-acre survey (see below), during which 104 shovel tests were excavated, yielding 844 artifacts, including the Clovis base. The site was subsequently tested in the fall of 1994 by Prentice Thomas and Associates, Inc., personnel using seven 50-x-50-cm and five 1-x-1-m units from which over 4,000 artifacts were recovered at depths up to 90 cm, with the earliest materials, not surprisingly, typically in the lowest deposits. In Test Pit 4 a San Patrice, *var. Keithville* point, a Plainview base, and a San Patrice, *var. St. Johns* point were found at depths of 60 to 70 cm, 80 to 90 cm, and 90 to 100 cm, respectively (Meyer et al. 1996a:130, 228–229). The Paleoindian assemblage at the site was interpreted as the remains of one or more small camps and quarry workshops at which hunting and reduction of local cobbles occurred.

The three Clovis points found at the Eagle Hill II site (16SA50) were recovered during the Fort Polk Archaeological Survey testing program and included one extremely large and well-made example (see Figure 2.10) as well as two bases that appear to be from unfinished bifaces (Servello and Bianchi 1983:432). A number of well-made formal tools were present in apparent association with the Clovis point, and the assemblage was described as including

> a few other bifaces, numerous burins, notches and multiple tools, as well as endscrapers, sidescrapers, pièces esquillées, denticulates, and marginally modified (truncated and retouched) flakes (Servello and Bianchi 1983:428–431). Analysis of the debitage present indicated a heavy reliance on controlled core-flake reduction for the production of tool blanks and a low incidence of bifacial production and maintenance, qualified by the observation that the biface manufacture incorporated some unusual practices, notably scalar retouch produced by striking directly into the edge of a piece—perhaps on an anvil (Servello and Bianchi 1983:421–425) [Morehead et al. 2002:17].

The presence of Clovis points at Eagle Hill is thought to be due to the dramatic location on the landscape, which would have facilitated rendezvous and interaction between widely dispersed populations, and because the nearby source of high-quality Eagle Hill chert provided the kind of material these populations prized (Goodyear 1979).

No local phases for the Middle Paleoindian Clovis materials found on Fort Polk were proposed in the 2002 sequence suggested by archaeologists from Prentice Thomas and Associates, Inc. (Morehead et al. 2002:19). No evidence for exploitation of large now-extinct game animals, a hallmark of Clovis culture, was found, although there is evidence from elsewhere in Louisiana (Avery Island on the central coast) for such associations (Gagliano 1964, 1967a, 1970). Given the presence of well-preserved Miocene fossil deposits on the installation, the presence of Late Pleistocene–age fossils, while extremely unlikely, should not be dismissed completely.

Terminal Pleistocene/Late Paleoindian Adaptations
(ca. 12,900–11,450 B.P./10,800–10,000 rcbp)

The Late Paleoindian era was a time of tremendous cultural and climatic change. The Clovis culture came to an end about 12,900 B.P., and after this, regional and subregional cultural traditions became widely established, population levels grew dramatically, and technological organization changed to accommodate a new climate and new biota. The terminal Pleistocene extinctions were largely complete at the start of this period and human populations were likely quite low in many areas, while at the end of the period, people were present in large numbers across the region. The Younger Dryas occurred during this time, from ca. 12,900 to 11,650 B.P./10,800 to 10,100 rcbp, marked by a major return to cold conditions whose onset appears to have occurred quite quickly, within a few years or decades, and which probably had a major impact on local cultures (Alley et al. 1993; Björck et al. 1996:1159; Dansgaard et al. 1989, 1993; Hughen et al. 1998, 2000). The interval within the Late Paleoindian dated ca. 10,500–10,100 rcbp, furthermore, is a major radiocarbon plateau, encompassing almost 1,000 calendar years. Thus, the 800 radiocarbon "years" of the Late Paleoindian era are actually closer to 1,500 calendar years, which is a more realistic span to accommodate the dramatic changes that took place (Fiedel 1999:106–107). Late Paleoindian projectile point forms exhibit appreciable stylistic variability and in some cases fairly restricted spatial distributions, which is interpreted as evidence for increasing regionalization or isolation of groups as population levels rose and group mobility decreased.

Late Paleoindian occupations are common at Fort Polk and are identified by a range of unfluted projectile point types, including Midland (n = 6), Coastview/unknown lanceolate (n = 6), Pelican (n = 4), all varieties of San Patrice (n = 116), Angostura (n = 3), and Scottsbluff (n = 8). The latter two types are Plains Archaic forms that, together with one or more varieties of the San Patrice points, appear to correspond to an Early Archaic time level in the Southeast (see below). Late Paleoindian and Early Archaic assemblages on Fort Polk have been subdivided into three distinct phases in the most recent cultural sequence by archaeologists from Prentice Thomas and Associates, Inc.: the Anacoco I, II, and III phases (Table 6.1; Morehead et al. 2002:19–31). These phases are distinguished primarily by varieties of San Patrice points, which exhibit the evolutionary continuum observed elsewhere in the Southeast from lanceolate Dalton-like forms to side- and then corner-notched forms of the Big Sandy/Bolen and Palmer/Kirk clusters (Thomas et al. 1997:15). The replacement of fluted point forms by weakly fluted or nonfluted points, many exhibiting evidence for resharpening, is thought to reflect a change in hunting strategy from megafauna to smaller game, especially deer (Morse 1973:30). In addition to game animals, the gathering of wild plants was in all probability an important part of the Paleoindian diet, although the absence of subsistence evidence from most sites of this period makes evaluation of the role of plant foods difficult.

A derivation of San Patrice points from "Clovis or some other early fluted complex" has been inferred (Story 1990:197), much as Dalton points in the central Mississippi Valley are now believed to have evolved directly from Clovis points (Bradley 1997; Morse 1997). San Patrice, *var. Hope* is clearly a local Dalton equivalent (as apparently are some *var. St. Johns* points), while *vars. St. Johns*, *Dixon*, and *Keithville* represent later side- and corner-notched forms within the same cultural tradition. It has been argued by previous Fort Polk researchers that "San Patrice is a culture that developed in Paleoindian times and persisted in west-central and northwestern Louisiana into the time frame occupied by Early Archaic groups elsewhere" (Mathews et al. 1995:111; see also Servello, ed. 1983:26; Campbell and Weed 1986:9-1 to 9-20; Morehead et al. 2002:20–21; Thomas and Campbell 1978). The varieties of San Patrice thus represent a temporal as well as cultural continuum spanning the Late Paleoindian and Early Archaic periods.

Points classified as San Patrice are common in east Texas (Prewitt 1995:128; Story 1990:197–205), Louisiana, and contiguous portions of Arkansas and Mississippi. Late Paleoindian forms include San Patrice, *vars. Hope* and *St. Johns*, which were defined by Duffield (1963) based on work at the Wolfshead site in Texas. San Patrice, *var. Hope* points are lanceolates with deeply indented bases and weak shoulders and side notching and/or extensive resharpening of the blade area in later-stage specimens. In all but the earliest-stage specimens, the shoulders are the widest part of the artifact, reflecting this resharpening. Basal and lateral margins are ground, and the base may exhibit thinning resembling fluting on some specimens. San Patrice, *var. St. Johns* points have a more varied basal morphology and pronounced side to corner hafting notches, resembling both classic Dalton forms and later notched forms (Duffield 1963). With extensive resharpening and basal attrition, in fact, these points tend to change over their use life from lanceolate/side-notched to corner-notched forms, making classification difficult with some specimens.

The age of the various San Patrice forms is inferred through cross-dating with similar point forms in other parts of the region and from a limited number of radiocarbon dates. Late Paleoindian subperiod Dalton points are fairly tightly dated to between ca. 12,500 and 11,250 B.P./10,500 and 9,900 rcbp across the Southeast (Goodyear 1982; Jeter and Williams 1989a:75–81), and some San Patrice points, notably *vars. Hope* and *St. Johns*, appear to be a subregional expression of this type and closely related to classic Dalton points from the central Mississippi Valley (see also Ensor 1987; Morse and Morse 1983; Story 1990:190–205; Jeter and Williams 1989a:81–82). One notable difference, however, at least on Fort Polk, is a near absence of San Patrice points with pronounced serrations and beveling, which is attributed to bifacial rather than unifacial resharpening (Morehead et al. 2002:21). This may be a result of the widespread occurrence of knappable stone in local gravel deposits, which reduced the need for extensive resharpening or re-working (see McGimsey 1996:143). In eastern Texas, Story (1990:196, 202) has shown that the distributions of San Patrice and Dalton points only par-tially overlap, suggesting differing adaptations—to woodlands and to a wide range of environments, respectively. Dalton points were found in northeast-ern Texas, while San Patrice, *vars. Hope* and *St. Johns* were found more to the south into the Gulf Coastal Plain and into east-central Texas. A major concentration of San Patrice sites is located due west of Fort Polk across the Sabine River in eastern Texas, while virtually no Dalton sites are reported from the same area (cf. figs. 27 and 28 in Story 1990). Dalton and early San Patrice varieties do appear to be more or less contemporaneous, however. At the Big Eddy site in southwest Missouri, for example, a San Patrice, *var. Hope* point was associated with a date of 10,185 ± 75 rcbp (AA-26653; Ray 1998:167; see also Lopinot et al. 1998, 2000). San Patrice, *var. St. Johns* and classic Dalton points were also found in this stratum, which yielded dates from general level fill of 9450 ± 61, 10,400 ± 75, 10,340 ± 100, 10,430 ± 70, and 10,336 ± 110 rcbp (Hajic et al. 2000:31; Lopinot et al., eds. 1998, 2000). It is unlikely that Dalton or related San Patrice varieties continued much later than 11,450 B.P./10,000 rcbp, however, given the fairly appreciable numbers of radiocarbon dates that have accumulated for side- and corner-notched points beginning at ca. 10,200 rcbp/11,850 B.P. and particularly af-ter 10,000 rcbp/11,450 B.P.

Toward the end of the Late Paleoindian era in the Southeast, sometime around 11,850 B.P./10,200 rcbp, side-notched projectile points appear and then soon occur widely over the Southeast. These have been variously de-scribed, with named types including Bolen in the Florida area (Neill 1958, 1963:99), Early Side-Notched in the Tennessee River Valley of northern Alabama (Driskell 1996), Hardaway Side-Notched in North Carolina (Coe 1964:67), Kessel Side-Notched in the West Virginia area (Broyles 1966), San Patrice, *var. St. Johns* and *var. Dixon* in the Louisiana and southern Arkansas area (Duffield 1963; Thomas et al. 1993a:35–36), and Taylor in South Carolina (Michie 1966:123). A range of ca. 11,450–10,200 B.P./10,000–9000 rcbp is traditionally assigned these forms, although there are indica-tions that they may appear somewhat earlier, around ca. 11,850 B.P./10,200 rcbp, based on dates in this time range obtained at Page Ladson, Florida, and Dust Cave, Alabama (Chapman 1985:146–147; Driskell 1994:25–26, 1996; Dunbar et al. 1988). Side-notched points themselves appear to continue no later than ca. 10,700–10,200 B.P./9500–9000 rcbp, after which time corner-notched types, such as Palmer and Kirk, and Hardin Stemmed points occur.

Because the point form extends into the Early Archaic, individual side-notched points found in surface or mixed excavation contexts in western Louisiana cannot be unequivocally placed in a Paleoindian or Early Archaic time period.

San Patrice, *var. Dixon* is a side-notched form named at Fort Polk, where it was proposed as a replacement for Edgewood, *var. Dixon*. The variety was formally defined in the FP-3 testing report:

> San Patrice, *var. Dixon* is proposed as a type name to replace Edgewood *var. Dixon*. In order to introduce this type-variety, some introductory comments regarding its former nomenclature [are] needed. The Edgewood type was defined by Suhm, Krieger and Jelks (1954; see also Suhm and Jelks 1962) who suggested a Late Archaic date of circa A.D. 0. *Var. Dixon* and two others were described by Johnson (1962) based on analysis of the deeply stratified deposits at the Fred Yarbrough site where the former occurred in lower levels than other Edgewood varieties. Duffield (1963) noted a strong affinity between this Edgewood variety and San Patrice, *var. St. Johns*. The variety is also similar to points that Webb et al. (1971) referred to as side-notched points varieties A and B at the John Pearce site (16CD56). These were later named Keithville *var. A* and *var. B* by Webb (1981).
>
> Edgewood *var. Dixon*, as identified by Johnson (1962), is physically very similar to San Patrice, *var. St. Johns*. The principal differences are slight: 1) more pronounced basal ears; 2) thinned bases, not channel flakes, although the thinning flakes may be very long; 3) stem-forming notches are sometimes struck from the corner, and 4) greater thickness, on an average (Duffield 1963; Johnson 1962; Morehead 1983; Perino 1985; Webb et al. 1971). The second difference noted above is, perhaps, the most critical as the other three overlap.
>
> Edgewood *var. Dixon* points have been identified at Fort Polk previously (cf. Servello 1983). Two examples of points that could fit the definition, but which are now identified as San Patrice, *var. Dixon*, were recovered during the FP-3 project. . . .
>
> The evidence from previous Fort Polk projects suggests contemporaneity, as well as morphological similarity between San Patrice points and those that have been classified as Edgewood *var. Dixon*. For example, the Dixon variety of Edgewood has been reported from 16VN24, the Big Brushy site (Guderjan and Morehead 1980, 1983) where it was recovered from a level directly overlying

a deposit that yielded a San Patrice, *var. Hope* point; in association with San Patrice, *var. St. Johns*, and in the level above a San Patrice, *var. Hope* at 16VN77, the Comes Lupi site (means wolf's companion in Latin) (Morehead 1983); and at four sites on Peason Ridge (Brassieur 1983).

Associational data from the Yarbrough site (Johnson 1962) is ambiguous, but an early date is possible; additional data from the Wolfshead site (Duffield 1963) is likewise unclear. However, at the John Pearce site (Webb et al. 1971), as well as the Fort Polk sites documented above, the excavation data point to a chronological relationship between points previously classified as Edgewood *var. Dixon* and examples of San Patrice, *var. St. Johns*.

It is our opinion that the preponderance of stylistic and technological characteristics, in addition with the stratigraphic data from Fort Polk, favor a transitional or very early Early Archaic date for this type. Most likely, they are coeval with San Patrice, *var. St. Johns*, and may actually be a poorly executed example of that type-variety [Thomas et al. 1992:35–36].

Hafted unifacial tool forms that appear to be contemporaneous with these early side-notched forms include the Albany (Webb 1946) and Edgefield scrapers (Michie 1968a, 1972). The Albany scraper occurs in low incidence on Fort Polk (n = 8), indicating it was not a particularly common tool form in local assemblages.

- *San Patrice Culture on Fort Polk*

San Patrice points are among the most common diagnostic hafted bifaces found on Fort Polk, with a total of 116 specimens found on 105 sites to date (Anderson et al. 1999a:appendix 6). A number of dense, well-defined San Patrice components have been found at appreciable depths during intensive testing operations on Fort Polk, such as at 16NA266 and 16NA277 (Thomas et al. 1993a:75–85, 100–110), 16VN692 (Thomas et al. 1993b:120–145), 16VN772 and 16VN1421 (Mathews et al. 1997:86, 114–127), 16VN873 (Morehead et al. 1996b:112–126), and 16VN135 and 16VN162 (Morehead et al. 1994:67–71, 94–95). The number and exceptional condition of components prompted the archaeologists from Prentice Thomas and Associates, Inc., to advance an Anacoco phase designation for these materials (named after the town in Vernon Parish north of the Main Fort), which has since been subdivided into three subphases (Morehead et al. 1996a:160–166, 2002:24–28). Given the excellent stratigraphic separation of San Patrice assemblages on Fort Polk—they are almost invariably at the base of cultural deposits and are frequently isolated from overlying materials by sterile or nearly sterile levels—and the fact that the point forms used to define them are well dated in the general region, these phases are among the most secure of any advanced for the Fort Polk area to date. The Anacoco I and II phases, which date to the Late Paleoindian and Late Paleoindian/Early Archaic periods, respectively, are described here, while the Anacoco III phase is described in the Early Archaic discussion below.

The *Anacoco I phase*, as defined by Morehead et al. (2002:25–27), is identified by the presence of San Patrice, *var. Hope* and *var. St. Johns* points, with Pelican points tentatively assumed to be associated. San Patrice, *var. Brazos*, also known as the Brazos Fishtail (cf. Morehead et al. 2002:26; Story 1990:203–205), a form found in Texas, is also associated with this phase, based on the reclassification of one San Patrice point found on Peason Ridge (cf. Brassieur 1983:260; Morehead et al. 2002:26). Large sites with extensive and diverse assemblages have been identified, as well as much smaller sites characterized by a few tools and pieces of debitage. These have been interpreted as possible base camps and short-term camps or special-activity work stations, respectively. Formal tools, particularly unifaces, are common. Assemblages are dominated by local lithic raw materials, with no emphasis on high-quality or extralocal materials. The phase has been tentatively dated to between 12,500 and 10,700 B.P./10,500 and 9,500 rcbp (Morehead et al. 2002:27), although a somewhat earlier range from perhaps 12,900 to 11,250 B.P./10,800 to 9,900 rcbp may be more appropriate, if a direct evolution of *var. Hope* from Clovis forms occurred, and given the emergence of side-notched forms after ca. 11,850 B.P./10,200 rcbp.

The *Anacoco II phase*, as defined by Morehead et al. (2002:27–28), is identified by the presence of San Patrice, *var. Dixon* side-notched points. Albany scrapers are also present but appear to continue to occur later in time, with corner-notched Early Archaic *var. Keithville* points, and hence are not diagnostic. Other than the adoption of side-notched points, the assemblages are very similar to those of the Anacoco I phase, although with a somewhat lessened incidence of formal as opposed to expedient or more casually made tools. The reworking of points into end scrapers is also thought to be characteristic of the phase locally (Morehead et al. 2002:27). The Anacoco II phase has been tentatively dated to between ca. 10,950 and 10,235 B.P./9,600 and 9,100 rcbp (Morehead et al. 2002:28), although a range of ca. 11,850–10,700 B.P./10,200–9500 rcbp is suggested here, given the general replacement of side-notched by corner-notched forms elsewhere in the Southeast after this time (Chapman 1985:146).

The San Patrice culture on Fort Polk appears to be the first to make extensive use of local gravel cherts, as opposed to high-quality extralocal materials requiring different reduction strategies (e.g., Servello, ed. 1983:157–159; Mathews et al. 1995:111; Morehead et al. 2002:21). A well-defined San Patrice component exhibiting extensive evidence for quarrying and reduction of local gravel cherts was found at 16VN687 during the FP-24 project (Meyer et al. 1996b:79–91). The site is on a ridge nose east of and overlooking Whiskey Chitto Creek on the Main Fort. Dense chert gravel deposits on the steep side slopes on the northern and western margins of the site may have attracted early populations. A total of 6.6 m^3 of fill were opened at the site in 30 50-x-50-cm and 2 1-x-1-m units. Large quantities of stone tools and debitage were found in a number of the units at depths up to 140 cm. A fairly diversified San Patrice assemblage was found below 80 cm, including three points from 90 to 100 cm. A Yarbrough-like point occurred just above this in the 80 to 90 cm level. Besides several hundred pieces of debitage and a number of crude bifaces and utilized flakes, the assemblage also included two end scrapers, a pebble adze, a denticulate, a spokeshave or notch, and a pièces esquillée. A raw material procurement area and workshop was inferred. The upper 30 cm of the deposits appear to represent a Bossier focus Caddoan occupation (see below), while between 30 and 80 cm, dense but mixed deposits were found. The site illustrates a common stratigraphic pattern on Fort Polk, notably that of sites with isolated and well-defined lower components, overlain by extensively mixed deposits caused by repeated reoccupation and low rates of soil accumulation.

Campbell et al. (1987:46) have noted, however, that at least a few San Patrice points in the Fort Polk area are made of high-quality chert or novaculite, while raw materials used on later Archaic and Woodland period sites are highly variable. Following arguments developed by Goodyear (1979), the incidence of high-quality material used by these early populations is taken to imply a raw material conservation strategy by fairly mobile groups. Technological organization within local San Patrice groups appears to have been shaped by the occurrence of local raw materials. Multiple tools—retouched flakes with more than one working surface—only tend to occur on Peason Ridge, at some distance from the chert gravel sources on the Main Fort, suggesting a concern for raw material conservation (Morehead et al. 2002:23; Thomas et al. 1993b:154–155). A low incidence of cores was also noted in San Patrice assemblages on Peason Ridge, which also suggests conservation was practiced in the use of raw materials in this area. Finally, a low incidence of biface thinning flakes was observed on many San Patrice sites in the general region, suggesting a heavy reliance on unifacial flake tools (Thomas et al. 1993b:154–156).

One example of the kind of San Patrice sites that occur on the installation was a small, probably single-component assemblage found on a small ridge knoll approximately 100 m east of the Comrade Creek floodplain on Peason Ridge during the FP-19 project (Mathews et al. 1995:88–95). The site, 16VN259, was characterized by artifacts over an area about 25 m in diameter at a depth of about 40 cm. In the 2.82 m³ of fill and 6.75 m² of surface area examined, a total of 54 artifacts were found, including a San Patrice base (*var. unspecified*), two bifaces, two utilized flakes, and seven formal tools, including two end scrapers, one raclette, one dihedral burin, and three tools with multiple working edges. In addition, 39 pieces of debitage, one piece of ground sandstone, one unworked piece of petrified wood, and one piece of ferruginous sandstone were recovered. The ratio of tools to debitage is extremely high (1:3.25), and extrapolating over the entire site area (ca. 500 m²), it is possible that several hundred tools might be present. The authors interpreted the assemblage as "a special purpose work station with a few secondary activities" directed primarily to hide working, given the large number of unifacial tools (Mathews et al. 1995:93). Given the large number of tools, the site may have also been a residential base camp, following arguments raised over the interpretation of classic Dalton sites with numerous formal tools, like the Brand site in northeast Arkansas (cf. Goodyear 1974; Morse 1975a, 1977; Schiffer 1975).

What is particularly intriguing about the 16VN259 assemblage is the presence of two tools made of Edwards Plateau chert, which comes from central Texas in the general vicinity of the Colorado River (Banks 1990:58–61). The use of high-quality chert, frequently materials obtained from great distances, is characteristic of Paleoindian period assemblages across the continent. These selection practices appear closely linked to a technological organization oriented toward extensive range mobility and the use of highly formalized and curated tools (e.g., Goodyear 1979; Kelly and Todd 1988). The fact that the 16VN259 assemblage is small, fairly shallow in depth, largely undisturbed, and apparently reflects a single period of occupation means that it could tell us a great deal if it could be excavated in its entirety. Careful plotting of the recovered tools could provide valuable information about the kinds of activities that took place. Similar well-defined San Patrice components have been found at considerable depth at a number of sites during the testing program, such as 16VN873 (Morehead et al. 1996b:112–126), 16VN135 and 16VN162 (Morehead et al. 1994:67–71, 94–95), and 16VN1059 (Morehead et al. 1995b:80–88). These sites form a protected data bank that future generations of archaeologists should be able to draw upon to better understand these early occupations.

- *Late Paleoindian/Early Archaic Plains Lanceolates on Fort Polk*
In the western part of both the Southeast and the lower Midwest, including

Louisiana, low numbers of lanceolate projectile points occur that resemble classic Great Plains Paleoindian fluted and unfluted forms such as Folsom, Plainview, Scottsbluff, Midland, Agate Basin, and Angostura. Gagliano and Gregory (1965), for example, documented 64 Scottsbluff points from across Louisiana, and Midland, Plainview, Angostura, and other Plains types have also been fairly widely reported (e.g., Hillman 1985:206–207; Servello, ed. 1983:26). The Scottsbluff type is reported to be "especially common (for an early type) in the Little Missouri and Little River regions of southwestern Arkansas, the Sulphur River drainage of northeastern Texas, and the Sabine River drainage of northwestern Texas" (Story 1990:205). Story (1990:210) also notes that Scottsbluff points found in the forested Gulf Coastal Plain tend to be made of nonlocal raw stone, suggesting movement from the Plains to the Woodlands, while San Patrice points from the same area are typically made from local stone, usually chert or petrified wood. The distributions suggest that at least some overlap and possibly interaction between populations from the Plains and Eastern Woodlands cultural traditions was occurring, although the nature of this behavior is not well understood at present (Anderson 1995; L. Johnson 1989; Munson 1990; Story 1990; Wyckoff and Bartlett 1995). When Plains forms are found in the East they are assumed to have the same general cultural affiliation and age as those in the West. Until comparative typological analyses can be undertaken, however, the use of these taxa should proceed with caution and with an awareness that the forms may not date the same as on the Plains or represent a comparable culture and adaptation. Some of these artifacts, furthermore, are almost certainly misidentified given the variability in examples in the collections. Some are probably bifacial preforms, or later types like the Guilford Lanceolate or Brier Creek Lanceolate found further east (Coe 1964:43; Michie 1968b).

Midland, Plainview/Coastview, Pelican, Angostura, and Scottsbluff points, as noted previously, have all been found on Fort Polk in low incidence and only rarely in apparent single-component assemblages (Table 5.1). An isolated Pelican-like point was found at 16VN147 on Peason Ridge, located on a low ridge overlooking an unnamed tributary of Dowden Creek (Morehead et al. 1994:72–75). Only nine flakes were found with the point in a combined 5.75-m^2 test excavation, suggesting minimal site use. A second Pelican point, again part of a very light scatter of only 14 artifacts, was found at 16VN351 at a depth of 60 to 70 cm on a ridge nose overlooking Brushy Creek on the Main Fort (Campbell et al. 1994b:44, 85–86). The excavation and dating of such sites may help date the type and its relation to San Patrice or other complexes. Gunn (1984a:164), for example, has suggested that Middle to Late Paleoindian Coastview types, which occur in west-central Louisiana, appear to be a variant of Plainview.

The archaeological work on Fort Polk has produced important information regarding the dating of the Plains forms locally, through their associations with specific San Patrice varieties. A Scottsbluff point was found
stratigraphically above a San Patrice, *var. St. Johns* and a San Patrice, *var.*
Hope point at 16SA92 (Morehead et al. 2002:20, 27; Servello and Bianchi
1983:471). A Plainview base was found during intensive testing operations
at 16VN1505 on the Main Fort, stratigraphically between a San Patrice, *var.*
Keithville and an underlying San Patrice, *var. St. Johns* (Meyer et al. 1996a:50,
129–130, 228–229). At 16VN675, also on the Main Fort, a Midland point
base was found in Test Pit 2 (at a depth of 130 to 140 cm) stratigraphically
between a side-notched Albany scraper (at 150 to 160 cm) and a San Patrice,
var. Keithville point (Meyer et al. 1995a:42–43, 80–97), again arguing for a
contemporaneity of these forms and possibly an overlap of the ranges of the
peoples with these differing technological traditions in the Fort Polk area.
The site is located on a long low ridge to the east of and overlooking the
floodplain of a tributary of Birds Creek. The presence of the Midland point
between the San Patrice diagnostics was attributed to either the scavenging
of an earlier component or else the presence of a number of periods of site
use, some by peoples with San Patrice and others by peoples with Plains
affinities. The latter explanation was considered the most likely since the
deposits were so deep; additionally, the levels where the diagnostics were
found had such extensive quantities of tools and debitage (897 pieces of
debitage and 40 tools in the lower meter of deposits in a 1-x-2-m unit) that
attributing all the material to a single occupation was considered unlikely.
The authors suggested that the evidence points to a contemporaneity of San
Patrice and Midland points in the area.

Folsom points occur in small numbers in the Eastern Woodlands, including a few dozen specimens recorded east of the Mississippi River
(Munson 1990). They are usually described using that type name, although
some are reported using local names, such as the Sedgwick type in northeast
Arkansas (Gillam 1996:406; Morse and Morse 1983:63). In some places
where they are present, such as in western Illinois, their distribution appears
to parallel the occurrence of Late Pleistocene grasslands, suggesting they
represent an eastern extension of their inferred Plains adaptation (Munson
1990). No Folsom points have been reported to date on Fort Polk, or over
much of Louisiana for that matter, which is somewhat surprising, given the
occurrence of other western Paleoindian point forms. A few specimens are
noted from northwest Louisiana, however (Webb 2000:3).

▪ *Paleoindian Research Directions*
Paleoindian research in Louisiana, as well as general research themes, has

been discussed in some detail in the Comprehensive Archaeological Plan for the state (Smith et al. 1983:131–139). Much of our knowledge about the occurrence of Paleoindian sites has come from surface finds gathered by archaeologists and collectors, rather than from controlled excavations. Fluted points have been found in surface contexts in moderate quantities in Louisiana, although they are quite rare in comparison with the incidence of points of later periods (Gagliano 1964; Gagliano and Gregory 1965; Gregory and Curry 1978:22; Webb 1948b). Projects need to be initiated devoted to recording these artifacts, and indeed diagnostics from all periods, particularly those of amateur collections. Can measures of local population density be developed for this period, perhaps using numbers of diagnostic artifacts as a proxy measure for people? Were populations increasing rapidly, as might be suggested by the increasing numbers of diagnostics between the earlier and later portions of this period?

Regional population density is believed to have been relatively low during the Early and Middle Paleoindian periods, as indicated by the small numbers of sites that have been found. This low population density has been interpreted by some as reflecting a fairly low level of sociopolitical integration. In actuality, however, fairly sophisticated information exchange and mating networks would have had to have been in place for such low-density, mobile populations to remain reproductively viable (Wobst 1974, 1976), which suggests a greater complexity to these societies than is traditionally inferred. Were fairly sophisticated information exchange and mating networks in place? In this regard, did the Eagle Hill area serve as an aggregation loci during this or subsequent periods? Much more extensive occupation of the region is indicated in the Late Paleoindian period, indicating populations may have been growing rapidly and filling in the landscape. Because of the extreme rarity of Early and Middle Paleoindian components, land surfaces dating to the terminal Pleistocene era in the Fort Polk area must be carefully examined for possible evidence of early occupations.

The nature of Paleoindian settlement systems in western Louisiana is not well understood at present, although the Eagle Hill locality in the northern part of Peason Ridge appears to have been something of a focus for these early populations. A number of Paleoindian and Early Archaic components have been identified in the vicinity of Eagle Hill, partly because of the high-quality lithic raw materials outcropping nearby (i.e., Eagle Hill chert) but also because of the commanding position of the hill in the regional landscape, which would have facilitated population rendezvous throughout prehistory. At 463 feet, the summit of Eagle Hill is one of the highest points in the immediate region. Its singular nature is further enhanced by the fact that it lies at a divide between three major river systems, the Sabine, the Calcasieu, and the Red (Nials and Gunn 1982:127), and hence may have served as an aggregation loci for populations in any or all of these drainages. The occurrence of major sites and site clusters in such locations is particularly common during these earlier periods, when periodic rendezvous between groups for social as well as biological reasons (i.e., obtaining marriage partners) were critical (Anderson 1995; Anderson and Hanson 1988). The presence of large numbers of Paleoindian and Early Archaic sites in the Eagle Hill area should thus come as no surprise, even if the area appears to be a marginal environment in comparison with the major riverine zones.

Sites with undisturbed San Patrice deposits may offer the opportunity not only to inform us about late Paleoindian lifeways locally but also to potentially help resolve the ongoing debate over the nature of Dalton settlement in the general region. To date, Dalton settlement in the Southeast has really only been seriously explored in the central Mississippi Valley (e.g., Gillam 1995, 1996; Morse 1975a, 1977; Price and Krakker 1975; Schiffer 1975). Whether settlement models derived from that area are even applicable in the Louisiana area is, of course, open to question, but the observations that have been advanced are useful to consider. In brief, Morse (1975a, 1977) posits that during Dalton times portions of the central Mississippi Alluvial Valley were inhabited by bands living in permanent or semipermanent base camps exploiting territories oriented along major watersheds. Within each territory, the base camps tended to be centrally located in areas roughly 10 km in diameter, allowing for reoccupation of different locations. Outlying logistical stations, most of which are thought to be male hunting/butchering camps, were scattered throughout the remainder of the territory. The Brand site in northeast Arkansas, excavated by Morse and Goodyear (Goodyear 1974), has been interpreted as being this type of site. Other specialized sites included vegetable food processing and collecting loci, cemeteries, and quarry areas.

If Morse's model is correct and has widespread applicability, the scattering of San Patrice sites in the west-central Louisiana area may represent portions of a Dalton "territory." Larger sites, such as those in the Eagle Hill area or sites like John Pearce in northwest Louisiana (Webb et al. 1971:42), may have served as base camps, while smaller sites may be outlying hunting stations or other special-purpose camps. Schiffer (1975) and Price and Krakker (1975) have taken considerable exception to Morse's model. They have argued against the existence of linear, drainage-oriented territories, suggesting instead that Dalton groups "occupied territories which crosscut major physiographic and resource zones" (Schiffer 1975:111). The presence of year-round settlements has also been challenged; greater annual mobility, perhaps between seasonally occupied camps, has been suggested as an alternative settlement model. The Brand site, with its extensive formal tool assemblage, was interpreted as a seasonal base camp rather than a temporary hunting station (Schiffer 1975:110–111). The careful examination of lithic raw material sources may help indicate the extent of these Dalton settlement systems and the distances these groups may have traveled in resource procurement forays. Recent work by Gillam (1996) has shown that Dalton settlement in northeast Arkansas may well have been oriented along rivers but was even more strongly shaped by the occurrence of local raw material sources, which may also apply in Louisiana. Specific models of Paleoindian settlement in the Fort Polk area should be developed, employing site and locational data from the installation and beyond and informed by sound anthropological theory about hunter-gatherer behavior (e.g., Binford 1980, 1982, 2001; Kelly 1995). The research on Dalton settlement conducted in northeast Arkansas by researchers like Gillam, Morse, and Schiffer offers a good place to start.

THE ARCHAIC ERA (CA. 11,450–3200 B.P./10,000–3000 RCBP)

Initial Holocene/Early Archaic Adaptations (ca. 11,450–8900 B.P./10,000–8,000 rcbp)

The Early Archaic period roughly corresponds to the period from the end of the Younger Dryas to the onset of the Middle Holocene Hypsithermal warming episode (Anderson 2001; Anderson et al. 1996b:14–15; I. Brown 1994:48; Stoltman 1978:714; Story 1990:211–212). Early Archaic components across much of the Southeast are recognized by the occurrence of successive side- and corner-notched and bifurcate-based points (e.g., Anderson and Sassaman 1996; Bense 1994:65–67; Chapman 1985:146–148; Coe 1964; Ellis et al. 1998:161–162), together with forms reminiscent of Plains types such as Agate Basin, Scottsbluff, Cody, Eden, and Angostura in the western part of the region (Ellis et al. 1998:160; Jeter and Williams 1989a:84, 87–89; Johnson 1989:27–49; Lepper 1999:378–380; Spiess et al. 1998:235–238). Band-level groups are assumed to have been present, making use of resources over most if not all parts of the landscape (Anderson 1996a:160–163). Elaborately made scraping, cutting, and piercing chipped stone tool forms continued to be used, although this highly formal toolkit was gradually replaced by less well made and more expedient tool forms. Lower-quality raw materials were increasingly utilized in stone tool manufacture. The gradual abandonment of the highly curated toolkit that appeared in Middle Paleoindian times is believed to be directly related to an emergence and increasing importance of foraging, generalist strategies over the region during the later Paleoindian and Early Archaic periods (Cable 1982, 1996; Meltzer 1984,

1988; Meltzer and Smith 1986; Morse 1973, 1975b, 1997). Over time and as human populations grew, group ranges are thought to have become progressively smaller. Existing settlement models emphasize appreciable seasonal movement by small groups with periodic aggregation events by larger numbers of people for information exchange and mating network maintenance (Anderson 1996b; Daniel 1998). Wild plant and animal foods made up the entire diet, although local populations were undoubtedly becoming increasingly familiar with their natural environment, and some plant species that were later domesticated may have begun to be collected at this time.

In the Fort Polk area Early Archaic occupations are identified by the presence of San Patrice, *vars. Dixon, Keithville,* and *Leaf River* points. San Patrice, *var. Keithville,* a straight-based corner-notched form resembling the Kirk Corner-Notched type, was first recognized by Webb (2000:4–5; Perino 1991). San Patrice, *var. Leaf River* is a related form that is also characterized by corner notching (Perino 1991:192). A number of classic southeastern Early Archaic diagnostics also occur, such as the successive Big Sandy/ Early Side-Notched types (n = 5) and the Palmer and Kirk Corner-Notched types (n = 22). These latter designations were typically made by researchers from elsewhere in the Southeast, particularly from the eastern portion of the region, where these type names are commonly employed (e.g., Coe 1964; Driskell 1996). These points would have almost certainly been assigned San Patrice variety status by local researchers. Coeval with these are forms that occur at this time level on the Great Plains, such as Angostura and Scottsbluff, which are dated to between 11,450 and 8900 B.P./10,000 and 8000 rcbp (Frison 1978:83; Jeter and Williams 1989a:84–85; Stanford 1999:321). Other less common point forms that occur on Fort Polk and may date to this time level include Hardin (n = 1), Martindale (n = 3), and Wells (n = 3).

Early Archaic assemblages on Fort Polk are subsumed into the Anacoco II and III phases. The *Anacoco II phase*, described previously, is identified by the presence of Early Side-Notched points, typically classified locally as San Patrice, *var. Dixon.* This phase begins toward the end of the Late Paleoindian era and continues until side-notched point forms are replaced by corner-notched types sometime around or after 10,700 B.P./9500 rcbp. The *Anacoco III phase* (Morehead et al. 2002:29–31) is identified by the presence of San Patrice, *var. Keithville* corner-notched points, as well as other Early Archaic corner-notched taxa such as Palmer or Kirk. Albany scrapers are also present, continuing from the earlier Anacoco II phase, and hence these are not useful as a diagnostic. A pronounced decrease in the incidence of formal unifacial tools of all kinds occurs, coupled with an increase in the incidence of more generalized or expedient tools and of formal bifacial tools other than points. Groundstone abraders, manos, and metates appear. A major shift in settlement and technological organization appears to have occurred locally. Most identified Anacoco III phase components are located on the Main Fort in the Calcasieu drainage basin; little evidence for use of the Peason Ridge area is indicated (Morehead et al. 2002:30). A retrenchment of populations closer to larger drainages or the emergence of group ranges restricted to a specific drainage may be indicated, if the pattern is not merely due to sampling error. Reworking of points into end scrapers is uncommon, unlike during earlier phases; elsewhere in Louisiana, however, at the Baskin site along Maçon Ridge, 16 of 34 *var. Keithville* points recovered had been reworked into end scrapers (Griffing 1994:110). The Anacoco III phase has been tentatively dated to between 10,325 and 9500 B.P./9200 and 8500 rcbp (Morehead et al. 2002:31), although a range of ca. 10,715–9850 B.P./9500–8800 rcbp is suggested here, given the general duration of corner-notched forms elsewhere in the Southeast (Chapman 1985). A Hardin Stemmed point was also found on the installation but, while likely contemporaneous, cannot be unequivocally associated with this phase. No evidence for bifurcate forms, such as the MacCorkle, St. Albans, LeCroy, and Kanawha types that date ca. 10,050–8600 B.P./8900–7800 rcbp, was observed on the installation, although these types are common farther to the east in the South Appalachian area and the Midsouth (Chapman 1985). The Kisatchie phase, discussed below, may encompass terminal Early Archaic/initial Middle Archaic occupations in the Fort Polk area.

On Fort Polk, as noted previously, stratigraphic evidence was found at 16VN1505 to support the contention that *var. Keithville* is later than *var. St. Johns* (e.g., Meyer et al. 1996a:130). The occurrence of a San Patrice, *var. Keithville* point in a level 10 cm above a Hardin-like point at 16VN772 (Mathews et al. 1997:59, 60, 86) further supports the likelihood that *var. Keithville* is Early Archaic in age, given the dating of Hardin points (see Justice 1987:46–53). A single example of San Patrice, *var. Leaf River* was found at 16VN1308, which overlooks Little Brushy Creek on the Main Fort (Morehead et al. 1995a:43–44, 154–163). The variety, originally defined in Mississippi (Perino 1991:192), is not common on Fort Polk. The specimen from site 16VN1308 appears to be a heavily resharpened corner-notched point and resembles a reworked *var. Keithville* form or possibly an Early Archaic corner-notched form such as a Palmer or Kirk (after Coe 1964).

A number of groundstone tools were found in deeply buried and undisturbed San Patrice levels at 16VN1421 on the Main Fort (Mathews et al. 1997:120–121, 150–152). The artifacts, found with a San Patrice, *var. Keithville* point, included a mortar and pestle, two abraders, one possible small stone bowl fragment, and one unidentifiable ground fragment. One of the abraders and the bowl-like fragment are described as having a high hematite content, and their shape appears to be the result of the grinding of this material for pigment. The incidence of groundstone tools is unprecedented for a San Patrice assemblage and suggests that by late in this tradition, when *var. Keithville* assemblages were prevalent, increased plant processing may have been occurring, as well as the preparation and use of pigment. The assemblage from 16VN1421 also produced an unusual incidence of biface thinning flakes compared with San Patrice, *vars. Hope* and *St. Johns* assemblages, which may reflect a change in technology (i.e., greater resharpening?) or, alternatively, may simply be the result of sampling error. So few sites of this period have been examined that the range of variation within them is not well understood.

- *Early Archaic Research Directions*

Early Archaic research in Louisiana, along with general research themes, has been discussed in some detail in the Comprehensive Archaeological Plan for the state (Smith et al. 1983:141–149) and in a detailed overview by Jeter and Williams (1989a:81–88). The Fort Polk archaeological record indicates that a temporal and spatial overlap of southeastern Early Archaic side- and corner-notched point forms and central and southern Plains Paleoindian and Archaic lanceolate point forms occurs in the west-central Louisiana area, which lies near the boundary of these major cultural areas (Johnson 1989; Story 1990:209–210). The temporal range and physical characteristics of point types generally attributed to the Early Archaic period in the general Louisiana area, however, are currently not well documented. This problem actually applies to the entire Archaic sequence, as Story has recently noted in a summary from eastern Texas: "The lack of a robust chronological framework, either absolute or relative, is a major impediment to the study of Archaic remains in the Gulf Coastal Plain. It is not an exaggeration (or much of an exaggeration) to describe the Archaic chronologies in much of the study area as among the least well established in North America" (Story 1990:213). Measurement and description, as well as assiduous efforts at dating Archaic assemblages, should receive intensive research attention (Mahula 1982:221).

A generalized foraging adaptation by small, highly mobile groups is inferred at this time level, although studies of settlement patterns are in their infancy locally. A number of general settlement models for this time period have been proposed from various parts of the Southeast (e.g., Anderson and Sassaman 1996; Claggett and Cable 1982; Neusius and Wiant 1985). The large number of undisturbed San Patrice sites that have been found in recent years on Fort Polk should be of great help in addressing the nature of early settlement systems. Explicit settlement models for this period should, in fact, be proposed and tested using site locational and assemblage data from the installation and beyond (e.g., as attempted by Anderson and Hanson [1988] and O'Steen [1996] in other parts of the Southeast). Resolution of Archaic settlement patterns in the Fort Polk area, however, is complicated by later reuse of earlier projectile points (Campbell and Weed 1986:4-11) and by the difficulty of attributing cultural affiliations or temporal estimates to lithic scatters lacking diagnostic artifacts like ceramics or specific projectile point types. That is, although large numbers of nondiagnostic lithic assemblages have been found on Fort Polk, it is not possible, in the absence of unambiguous temporal diagnostics, to attribute these to preceramic occupations, much less specific periods in the Archaic or Paleoindian eras (see also Campbell et al. [1987:26] for a discussion of this problem). Attempts have been made to date Fort Polk lithic assemblages using tool and debitage characterics (e.g., Campbell and Weed 1986:7-47 to 7-61; Morehead et al. 1996a:159–194; Servello 1983; Thomas et al. 1997; see Chapters 2 and 3), with some success, but the results are frequently ambiguous. Continual refinement of the local Early Archaic sequence and settlement patterns, using ever larger and better dated or stratigraphically isolated assemblages, will occupy researchers for years to come.

Middle Holocene/Middle Archaic Adaptations in the East (ca. 8900–5700 B.P./8000–5000 rcbp)

The Middle Archaic is a time of dramatic cultural change in eastern North America. During this period ceremonial shell/earthen mound construction is initiated, long-distance exchange networks spanning much of the region appear, new tool forms, such as bannerstones and grooved axes, are adopted, and there is increased evidence for interpersonal violence or warfare (Sassaman and Anderson, eds. 1996; B. Smith 1986). While fairly simply organized foraging groups are still present, they increasingly come to be found in geographically marginal areas, which is one possible explanation for the relatively uncomplicated archaeological record from this time period found at Fort Polk. The Middle Archaic is widely viewed as the time of human adaptation to the climate interval known as the Hypsithermal, with temperatures warmer in the summer and winters colder than at present in the northern hemisphere (Ganopolski et al. 1998). Lakes were at low levels or dry over large areas, which would have made areas with permanent water more favorable for settlement (Webb et al. 1993:454). El Niño episodes may have been milder and less frequent (Hamilton 1999:350–351; Sandweiss et al. 1996). Across the lower Southeast, pine forests, replacing oak, began to re-expand dramatically from a low in the Initial Holocene, and cypress swamps began to develop along the slowing river systems (Jacobson et al. 1987; Watts et al. 1996:32–36; Webb et al. 1993:448–450). At the onset of the Middle Archaic, the Middle Holocene climate appears to have been hotter and dryer than at present, particularly in the lower Midwest and Midsouth, leading to a reduction in upland vegetation, increased surface erosion, and aggrading floodplains (Knox 1983:32–34; Schuldenrein 1996:9–10, 26–27; Wright 1992). These warming and drying trends may have rendered riverine areas more favorable and upland areas less favorable to human populations (Brown 1985:219–221; Brown and Vierra 1983:167–168; Sassaman 1995:182). As populations grew and mobility decreased, competition and interaction between groups appear to have increased, probably because people were forced closer and closer together on the landscape. These trends are manifest in a number of areas, such as in the use of personal status items as indicted by the growth in exchange networks; in the procurement of food or other natural resources as suggested by the increased evidence for warfare; and in collective ceremonial behavior, as reflected in the construction and use of elaborate mound centers in several areas. In some areas tribal societies are thought to have emerged, linking groups from across large areas (e.g., Anderson 2002; Bender 1985a, 1985b; Braun and Plog 1982; Saitta 1983).

Until quite recently the Middle Archaic period was very poorly known in west-central Louisiana, a situation duplicated over much of the state and surrounding region (e.g., Jeter and Williams 1989a; Neuman 1984; Story 1990). The examination of Middle Archaic mound groups in eastern Louisiana like Watson Brake and their association with Evans points, which are fairly common on Fort Polk, however, has led to much better recognition of and appreciation for sites of this period (e.g., Russo 1996; Saunders et al. 1997). A number of apparently single-component assemblages characterized by Sinner and Evans points have been found on Fort Polk in recent years, most during the intensive site-testing work by archaeologists from Prentice Thomas and Associates, Inc., prompting them to propose Kisatchie and Sixmile phases for assemblages yielding these point types, respectively.

The *Kisatchie phase*, encompassing Sinner assemblages on Fort Polk, was proposed as a terminal Early Archaic/initial Middle Archaic phase dating ca. 9500–8600 B.P./8500–7800 rcbp or possibly 8900–7800 B.P./8000–7000 rcbp, based on the presumed age of this point form (Thomas et al. 1997:25; see also Morehead et al. 2002:32–34). Thomas et al. (1997:19) suggest that Sinner points may be an initial Middle Archaic form in the Fort Polk area, based on their general resemblance to Kirk Stemmed and Kirk Serrated points found farther to the east that are dated to between ca. 8900 and 8600 B.P./8000 and 7800 rcbp (Chapman 1985:146; Coe 1964). A resemblance was proposed between Sinner points and Neches River (Jelks 1965:209) and Wesley (Johnson 1962; Perino 1991) points from eastern

Texas and Avery (Gagliano 1967a:65), St. Helena (Gagliano et al. 1979), and Kirk, *var. St. Tammany* (Gagliano 1963, 1967b) points from southern and southeastern Louisiana (as summarized in Morehead et al. 2002:31). The Kisatchie phase, named after the Kisatchie Wold physiographic region (see Chapter 1), was described as follows:

> The Sinner point . . . itself is the primary diagnostic, as are Neches River points with wide, short stems. Sinner is distinguished by the presence of two or more sets of notches above the shoulders (Webb 1981). These notches are shallow and better described as deep serrations on most of the specimens we have recovered. Otherwise, Sinner is almost indistinguishable from Evans, but as Webb (1981) noted, almost invariably occurs on local raw material. The area above the notched-serrated portion of the blade may exhibit shallow serration due to lamellar retouch applied bifacially and bilaterally. This retouch is distinct from the serrations which are wider and deeper. It is reminiscent of the retouch seen on San Patrice points.
>
> The formal tools are dominated by points, mostly Sinner. Also present in quantity are perforators and endscrapers. There are far fewer pièces esquillées, denticulated/serrated pieces, sidescrapers, burins, notches and multiple tools. . . . Ground stone is present, including one piece of site furniture—a pitted stone from 16VN734. Formal unifaces and formal bifaces are roughly equal. However, the most diverse assemblages are heavily dominated by formal unifaces. There are proportionally far fewer generalized flake tools in Kisatchie toolkits than in Anacoco III.
>
> The debitage has evidence of initial, core-flake and bifacial reduction. Site 16VN675, which appears to be a base camp when only the tools are examined, seems to have had a secondary function as a quarry workshop. Another quarry workshop component is 16VN1447, which appears to be a short-term hunting-related camp, in terms of tools. Because procurement does not appear to be associated with any specific kind of site in terms of tools and their implied activities, it is likely to have been embedded in the settlement and subsistence system. The advanced cores are almost equally divided between controlled reduction strategies and less structured approaches [Morehead et al. 2002:33; see also Thomas et al. 1997:20].

Sinner points are found in low incidence on Fort Polk (n = 23 points/17 sites or isolated finds; see Chapter 5), mostly on the Main Fort. Because of the low sample size employed in the formulation of this phase and the uncertain dating of the principal diagnostic used in its recognition, the Kisatchie phase should be considered a highly tentative formulation. One question in particular that needs to be addressed is the relationship of Sinner to Evans points and to Sixmile phase assemblages. Morehead et al. (2002:34) suggest that the Evans type may be derived from Sinner, while other authors suggest Sinner may be a local variant of Evans (e.g., Gregory 1995) or a contemporaneous type (Webb 1981).

A dense, possibly single-component Sinner assemblage was found at site 16VN675 along Birds Creek during the FP-16 testing project on the Main Fort (Meyer et al. 1995a:93–94). The assemblage was found in a 1-x-2-m test unit from 130 to 170 cm and was characterized by preforms, bifaces, end scrapers, gouges, pièces esquillées, perforators, notches, hammerstones, and a considerable quantity of cores and debitage from both initial and later-stage reduction. The assemblage was interpreted as the remains of a complex campsite that may have been seasonally reoccupied. A small apparently single-component Sinner assemblage was also found on Peason Ridge at 16VN134, located on a ridge line to the west of and overlooking the Dowden Creek floodplain (Morehead et al. 1994:60–66). The presence of a large number of formal tools suggests a range of activities may have been occurring. Sites with both Evans and Sinner points present are extremely rare on Fort Polk, however, suggesting the inferred temporal or cultural difference may indeed be valid. Of 49 sites or isolated finds with Evans points and 17 with Sinner points reported from the installation in the 1999 HPP sample, only one had both types present (Anderson et al. 1999a:appendix 6; see also Table 5.1).

The later Middle Archaic *Sixmile phase* was advanced by the Prentice Thomas and Associates, Inc., research team encompassing assemblages with Evans points on Fort Polk, a type readily identifiable by the presence of deep single notches on either side of the blade (Morehead et al. 1996a:170–171, 2002:36–38; Thomas et al. 1997:21). Saunders and Allen (1997:6–8; Saunders et al. 1994, 1997) have shown that the Evans point is restricted to Louisiana and southern Arkansas and immediately adjoining areas and, based on an occurrence in well-dated strata at Middle Archaic mound sites in northeastern Louisiana, that it occurs between roughly ca. 6000 and 5000 B.P. Evans points are fairly common at Fort Polk (n = 66). The Sixmile phase was described as follows:

> The Sixmile phase is named after Sixmile Creek, as one of the most important of these components, 16VN1068, overlooks the confluence of East Fork Sixmile Creek and an intermittent tributary. . . .

Most Sixmile components appear to be station camps or short-term, hunting related camps.

Only the component at 16VN1068 has a diverse, substantial assemblage, which is plausible for a base camp. Given this and the generally limited size of the Sixmile assemblages, we have inferred that the phase is no more than the fringe of an Evans-using culture whose core is distant from Fort Polk. The only candidate for the larger unit is the Big Creek culture of Arkansas and northern Louisiana (Schambach 1970; Jeter et al. 1989). The occasional appearance of a novaculite Evans point or novaculite debitage provides additional, nontypological support for some kind of link to the north. None of the components appear to be procurement-oriented, an unusual finding in itself for groups who used Fort Polk.

The Evans point . . . is the only recognized diagnostic. Schambach (1970) acknowledges the presence of Bulverde in many Dorcheat components, however, we have only encountered one point which is even remotely similar to Bulverde in Sixmile components. Bifaces and unifaces each comprise about half of the formal tools, but most of the generalized tools are retouched utilized flakes. One metate has been recovered. The debitage collections reinforce the impression of transitory occupations [Morehead et al. 2002:36–37; see also Thomas et al. 1997:21].

Other points recovered on Fort Polk that may date to the Middle Archaic period are the Bulverde and Yarbrough types (Morehead et al. 2002:34–36; Thomas et al. 1997:20; see Chapter 5). Bulverde points are dated to the late Middle Archaic/initial Late Archaic in central Texas, from roughly 5728 to 5100 B.P./5000 to 4500 rcbp (Turner and Hester 1993:82), and are found in undisputed association with Evans points in the Big Creek culture of southern Arkansas (Schambach 1970:389, 1998:114–117; Schambach and Early 1982:SW57). The type has a more western distribution than Evans points and, in fact, is absent from the Big Creek type site in central Arkansas where over 500 Evans points were collected (Schambach 1998:115), although the two forms are found together at other sites in that area. Of the seven sites and isolated finds yielding Bulverde points in the Fort Polk sample, one also yielded an Evans point; Evans points, as noted, were observed at 49 sites and isolated finds (Anderson et al. 1999a:appendix 6; see also Table 5.1). This distribution suggests a minor overlap or co-occurrence of the two forms locally.

The temporal placement of Yarbrough points on Fort Polk suggests a Middle Archaic age, although they were initially placed in the Late Archaic/

Woodland Dooley Branch point cluster (Campbell et al. 1990:64–73; see Chapter 5). Yarbrough varieties are common in eastern Texas, where they are assigned a Middle and Late Archaic age (Prewitt 1995:137; Turner and Hester 1993:197; see Chapter 5). A rough morphological similarity of Yarbrough to Bulverde points was noted by Morehead et al. (2002:36), although earlier or later points are likely present among the typed specimens, given a long occurrence for similar forms in the area (and explaining their inclusion initially in the Dooley Branch point cluster). At the Big Brushy site (16VN24; Guderjan and Morehead 1980, 1983; see Chapter 2), although the deposits were somewhat mixed, a succession was observed from Angostura-like and San Patrice types to Edgewood, Williams, and Yarbrough points and on through a range of later Archaic and Woodland forms (see Figure 2.9; see also Guderjan and Morehead 1983:902). At 16VN794 a range of ca. 5780–4000 rcbp was inferred on the basis of the age of deposits in which some specimens occurred (Cantley et al. 1993b:255), and at 16VN873 a Yarbrough-like point was found stratigraphically below a Late Archaic Birds Creek point (Morehead et al. 1996b:118–119, 2002:34). The data from Fort Polk, although limited, do support a Middle Archaic or early Late Archaic placement for the Yarbrough type, although whether it should be included with the Kisatchie or Sixmile phases remains an open question (Morehead et al. 2002:36).

▪ *Middle Archaic Research Directions*
A pressing research issue locally is identifying terminal Early Archaic/initial Middle Archaic components to fill the ca. 3,500-year gap between the end of the Anacoco III phase at ca. 9500 B.P./8500 rcbp, characterized by assemblages with corner-notched points, and the onset of the later Middle Archaic Sixmile phase at about 6000 B.P., characterized by assemblages dominated by Evans points. The Kisatchie phase characterized by Sinner points has been proposed to fall within this interval, but even if its estimated maximum age range of 8900–7800 B.P./8000–7000 rcbp is correct, a lot of unfilled time remains. A general abandonment of the area between ca. 7800 and 5750 B.P./7000 and 6000 rcbp has been suggested or, alternatively, that the Fort Polk area was occupied by people using an as-yet unrecognized assemblage, like that identified by Johnson points in Texas (Morehead et al. 1999b, 2002:24; Schambach 1998:35–36; see also Story 1990). Unless corner-notched points extend later in time and Sinner points earlier, there is also a troubling roughly 600-year gap at the early end of this interval as well, from ca. 9500 to 8900 B.P./8500 to 8000 rcbp, during the terminal Early Archaic period. Bifurcate horizon points fill this interval farther to the east in the region (e.g., Chapman 1985:146) but are nonexistent in the Fort Polk area.

Successfully identifying Middle Archaic assemblages locally will entail determining whether there are any currently overlooked forms, plus establishing the temporal range of points like the Bulverde, Evans, Sinner, and Yarbrough types, as well as Early Archaic corner-notched forms in general. At present, only the Evans point can be said to be fairly well-dated locally, because of its association with terminal Middle Archaic mound groups, and even its full temporal range is unknown.

The recent excavations at the Conly site in northwest Arkansas near the Red River between Natchitoches and Shreveport conclusively showed that there are indeed as-yet largely unrecognized Middle Archaic assemblages in the Louisiana area. At Conly, a dense midden with well-preserved charcoal and bone, including human burials and subsistence remains, was found, together with an extensive lithic assemblage that included both chipped and groundstone tools (Girard 2000a, 2001). Eight radiocarbon dates securely place the midden between ca. 7500 and 8000 B.P. (Girard 2000a:62). Some of the projectile points recovered do not readily fit established local types, although several Johnson points (Bartlett 1963:28–29; Schambach 1998:xiii, 35–36, 111–112) and points that resembled Carrollton, Delhi, Macon, and Bulverde types were present (Girard 2000a:35–38, 41–43); points and types similar to those illustrated by Girard have been found at Fort Polk. Johnson points are part of the Middle Archaic Tom's Brook phase defined by Schambach (1998:111–112), and the other forms would appear to date to this time level as well. Given the tight dating and unambiguous context of the remains in the midden at Conly, which is sealed under several meters of clay alluvium with no evidence for subsequent occupation, plus the excellent preservation and diversity of materials found, the site provides a baseline for examining initial Middle Archaic assemblages in the Louisiana area.

In northeast Louisiana, the Evans type has been found to be associated with Archaic mound sites, a cultural development that is just beginning to be understood (e.g., Russo 1994, 1996; Saunders et al. 1994). Particularly striking in the associated material culture is the occurrence of fired clay tablets, or "Watson Brake Objects," an artifact category common at a number of northeast Louisiana Archaic mound sites such as Watson Brake, Frenchman's Bend, Hedgepeth, and the Lower Jackson Mound (Saunders et al. 1998). Their function is uncertain, although they may have served as cooking stones, much as soapstone slabs were used at this time level in other parts of the Southeast (e.g., Sassaman 1993a). Fired clay slabs have not been found to date on Fort Polk. How local Middle Archaic assemblages relate to the more elaborate cultural developments associated with the mound-building cultures to the northeast and east are important research questions to be explored locally. Saunders and Allen's (1997:6–8) analysis of the occurrence of Evans points over the region, like Prewitt's (1995) analysis of projectile-point distributions in Texas, is the kind of work needed to place local assemblages into a larger perspective. Distributional analyses are needed for all diagnostic artifacts and assemblages, in fact, and should be linked with efforts in adjoining states.

While it is tempting to suggest that the Evans assemblages found at Fort Polk represent task groups or tribal segments from the mound-building societies in northeast Louisiana, the fact remains that mound building occurred over only a fairly small part of the Southeast during the terminal Middle Archaic. Assemblages from this time level in western Louisiana, where no such mounds are known, may represent the remains of relatively uncomplicated foraging groups who perhaps consciously opted out of the more complex sociopolitical lifestyles of the peoples in eastern Louisiana, a strategy of resistance noted in other parts of the region (Sassaman 1995, 2001). The Middle Archaic sites present in western Louisiana may thus represent the continuation of a highly mobile foraging adaptation similar to that noted in the South Appalachian area at this time (Anderson 1996a:171, 176; Sassaman 1991, 1995).

Differing opinions about the nature of Middle Archaic settlement in west-central Louisiana exist in the literature and must be resolved. One view, generally adopted by most of the researchers working in the Fort Polk area, is that the interriverine uplands were fairly minimally occupied as a local response to Middle Holocene desiccation and a decline in exploitable upland biomass (Gunn and Brown 1982:182). The few small Sinner and Evans components found to date are thought to be typical of occupations dating to this time level. Floodplain areas near larger drainages would have probably been favored occupation loci during this period, but whether substantial archaeological remains actually occur in such settings remains to be determined in the western Louisiana area. One of the few intensive studies of an exposed and eroded floodplain margin, that at Lake Anacoco a few miles west of Fort Polk, which was drawn down in late 1995, did not find evidence for Middle Archaic occupation in spite of a substantial program of survey and testing (McGimsey 1996:57). This led the author to conclude that a retrenchment of Middle Archaic populations to near permanent drainages "is not evident in western Louisiana, unless groups moved to the largest river valleys" (McGimsey 1996:146). An alternative explanation for the apparent low incidence of Middle Archaic components is that the Fort Polk area was more densely occupied than is currently thought but that the diagnostic markers are unrecognized, perhaps being represented by point forms currently assumed to date later in time. There is no question that some components are being missed, given the broad temporal ranges currently attributed to many dart points in the region, the fact that substantial gaps in occupation are indicated by the date ranges assigned to phases in the Fort Polk area at present, and the fact that recent excavations at the Conly site have documented a series of early Middle Archaic point forms currently unrecognized or assumed to date later in time on Fort Polk. Given the evidence that Evans and Bulverde points date to this period, and probably Sinner and Yarbrough points as well, however, the low number of observed components cannot be solely attributed to a lack of suitable diagnostics.

Initial Late Holocene/Late Archaic Adaptations (5700–3200 B.P./5000–3000 rcbp)

During the Late Archaic period, essentially modern characteristics of climate, sea level, and vegetation emerged. Mound construction, long-distance prestige-goods exchange, and warfare expanded, culminating in dramatic cultural expressions like Poverty Point, Stallings Island, Green River/Indian Knoll, and Old Copper. A major increase in regional population levels is indicated, with sites found in all parts of the landscape (Anderson 1996a:165–166; Griffin 1967:178–180; B. Smith 1986:28–35). An amelioration in climate that appears to have contributed to these developments occurred during the initial Late Holocene, with temperature, precipitation, and lake levels reaching conditions similar to those at present (Webb et al. 1993:454–457). Precipitation and flooding increased, as did channel migration in major river systems (Knox 1983:33, 39; Schuldenrein 1996:7–10).

Late Archaic period sites in west-central Louisiana are identified by a range of dart point types (noted for specific phases below), baked clay objects, and, in rare cases, evidence for bannerstones and lapidary items (Campbell and Weed 1986:9-20 to 9-23; Jackson 1984a:28; Morehead et al. 2002:38–44; Thomas et al. 1997:21–25; Webb 1981). Large numbers of sites of this period are found on Fort Polk, many occurring on terrace margins and ridges and knolls overlooking tributaries (Morehead et al. 2002:38). Sandstone manos and metates have been found at several sites, suggesting some plant-processing activity was occurring locally (e.g., Figures 3.5 and 3.6; Morehead et al. 1995a:123–127; Thomas et al. 1994a:67–73); these kinds of artifacts are not very common, however, suggesting plant-food procurement was not particularly extensive. No evidence for the use of domesticates of the Eastern Agricultural Complex have been found, although flotation processing and detailed paleosubsistence analyses that might identify such remains have rarely been conducted locally and then typically only in conjunction with large-scale excavations (e.g., Cummings 1993; Raymer 1993a).

Two Late Archaic phases have been proposed for the Fort Polk area, Birds Creek and Leander, based on assemblages found to co-occur during the large-scale excavations at 16VN791 and the subsequent intensive testing program (Campbell et al. 1990; Morehead et al. 1996a:171–179, 2002:38–44; Thomas et al. 1997:21–25). The Leander phase was originally named Dooley Branch, after the projectile point cluster originally thought diagnostic of the phase, but it was renamed when subsequent work showed these point forms continued to occur into the Woodland period. The *Birds Creek phase* (Morehead et al. 2002:39–41; Thomas et al. 1997:23–24), named after the drainage on the Main Fort that contains 16VN791, where the phase and point type/cluster of the same name were recognized, is dated to the earlier part of the Late Archaic period, ca. 6300–5100 B.P./5500–4500 rcbp. Components are recognized by the presence of Birds Creek cluster points, consisting of Ensor- and Epps-like points with widely flaring bases and hafting often approaching side notching. These point types are fairly common on Fort Polk; the Prentice Thomas and Associates, Inc., research team has started calling these forms Birds Creek points in recent reports (Table 5.1; see Anderson et al. 1999a:appendix 6 for a listing of all sites with these points). Two site types are recognized, those with extensive, diverse toolkits and those with smaller, less diverse assemblages, which are interpreted as base camps and short-term camps, respectively. Most components of the phase are found on the Main Fort in the Calcasieu drainage, which is a distribution similar to that observed with Anacoco III and Kisatchie phase assemblages. Little use of the Peason Ridge area, at least by peoples using Birds Creek points, is indicated. This may reflect a continuation of the Middle Holocene pattern of limited use of interriverine areas locally, which may support an early Late Archaic date for the phase. Given the number of sites found and the large size of the presumed base camps, populations resident in the immediate area are inferred to have been present year-round (Campbell et al. 1990, 1994a:46; Morehead et al. 2002:39).

Groundstone tools, baked clay objects, and Evans points are also occasionally noted in Birds Creek phase assemblages, and unifaces dominate chipped stone tool assemblages, with bifaces being less common. Direct procurement and use of local chert gravels is indicated at several sites, with pebbles more or less directly worked into tools, leaving a lot of debris and suggesting fairly minimal concern with raw material conservation. Archaic lithic raw material reduction appears to have been less frugal with raw material than reduction in later periods, as analyses at 16VN18 demonstrated (Fredlund 1983:854; see Chapter 2). Later occupations appear to have reduced cobble cherts far more effectively, obtaining much greater numbers of tools—albeit of a smaller size—from the same quantity of material. An overlap with the Sixmile phase is indicated by the proposed dating of the phase and the occasional presence of Evans points. A somewhat longer duration, perhaps to ca. 4475 B.P./4000 rcbp or later, is suggested here, given the dating of Poverty Point–like assemblages in the general region, which are considered to postdate components of the Birds Creek phase. The fact that baked clay objects have been recovered in some quantity in association with Birds Creek points suggests a later dating as well and perhaps an overlap with the subsequent Leander phase.

The *Leander phase* (Thomas et al. 1997:24–25; see also Morehead et al. 2002:41–44), dating to the later part of the Late Archaic from ca. 5100 to 3200 B.P./4500 to 3000 rcbp, has been considered a local Poverty Point–related complex that

> postdates Birds Creek and antedates Tchefuncte. . . . Given the character of these assemblages and that some of them are on Peason [Ridge], we would guess that the center of this phase is north and possibly east of the Main Post, hence the name Leander phase, after the locality of that name north of Fort Polk.
>
> Leander phase components are identified by the presence of point types such as Motley, Epps and Delhi which are strongly associated with the Poverty Point Culture as well as other types generally attributed to Late Archaic and Woodland. Some of the more substantial components have blade industry and Jaketown-like perforators. However, exotic stone is quite rare.
>
> . . . The typical site is a short-term hunting-oriented camp, although a few may be seasonal or base camps. A special purpose work station has been found at the terrace margin of site 16VN527 (Morehead et al. 1996a). Procurement may have been embedded. Thus far only one component has had site furniture identified [a mano and a metate at 16VN1136]. It generally looks as though the center of this phase is beyond the borders of the Military Reservation.
>
> The diagnostic artifacts are Motley and Epps points with strong necks or, more rarely, the classic weak necks of the type site, as well as Delhi and Pontchartrain-like points. Also present are Kent and Gary points, the latter being classifiable as Gary Typical (Ford and Webb 1956); however, like Dooley Branch, Gary seems to peak in popularity in Woodland times at Fort Polk. Jaketown-style perforators and blade technology are present but seldom in large numbers. Baked clay objects were found at 16VN804 on the FP-22 project (Morehead et al. 1996b).
>
> The most common tools after points are endscrapers, perforators and pièces esquillées. Celts, serrated and denticulated pieces

are present in lesser numbers, but burins have not yet been identified except as an expression on one multiple tool. Chipped stone technology includes core-flake, blade and bifacial components. Bifaces are slightly more common as formal tools than unifaces, and critical classes like endscrapers, piercers, pièces esquillées and celts have both bifacial and unifacial variants. The cores are about equally divided between controlled and ad hoc reduction strategies [Thomas et al. 1997:24–25].

Calcasieu points are also attributed to the Leander phase (Morehead et al. 1996a:175). The point types assigned to the Leander phase are fairly common on Fort Polk (Table 5.1), as are baked clay objects (see below). An overlap or continuity of some kind with Birds Creek phase populations is suggested by the presence of Epps points, and some Leander phase point types also occur during subsequent Woodland periods and phases.

- *Baked Clay Objects at Fort Polk*
Although baked clay ball forms are known to have persisted later in time in the general region—into the Woodland period (J. Johnson 1987:204; Phillips 1970:870)—they are commonly recovered in preceramic contexts in Louisiana and have been found on several Birds Creek and Leander phase sites on Fort Polk in recent years (Morehead et al. 1996a:55–56, 139–141, 1996b:59–61, 83–94) (see Figure 5.15, *d–q*). At site 16VN839, for example, located at the end of a ridge overlooking the confluence of a major tributary with Birds Creek on the Main Fort, deep, artifact-rich deposits dating to the Late Archaic period and after were found in 1995, including the first baked clay objects recovered on the installation (Morehead et al. 1996a:55–56, 130–146; see Figure 5.15, *o–q*). Six fragments were found: four small amorphous pieces and two larger fragments exhibiting crude pyramidal shapes that may have derived from possible bipyramidal or octahedral shapes. Made from fired silt or loess and very fine sand, the artifacts were described as virtually indistinguishable from similar materials found at the Poverty Point site. All but one of the baked clay object fragments were found in a single 1-x-1-m unit in levels yielding large numbers of stone tools and debitage, including two Birds Creek and one Evans point (Morehead et al. 1996a:139–141). Two radiocarbon dates were obtained from the unit, one on charcoal collected from the 100- to 110-cm level and the other on charcoal from a small oval charcoal stain located at 88 cm. Both dates were in the middle part of the first millennium A.D., which was considered much too late (Morehead et al. 1996a:141). Five apparent baked clay object fragments were also found at 16VN804, a site along the western margin of the Birds

Creek floodplain, in the same levels as Birds Creek cluster points (Morehead et al. 1996b:59–61, 83–94) (Figure 5.15, *e, i, j, 1, m*). One specimen was intact and crudely pyramidal in form, while the other four were small fragments. Although none have been dated at Fort Polk, a cluster of at least 12 baked clay balls was dated to 3136 ± 90 rcbp at 16VN1646 in nearby Lake Anacoco; the component yielding the baked clay balls also produced Birds Creek, Delhi, and Palmillas points (McGimsey 1996:90). No fiber-tempered sherds, the first pottery to appear in many other parts of the region, have ever been found on Fort Polk. Fiber-tempered pottery, presumably of the Wheeler series, however, has been found in some quantity elsewhere in Louisiana, for example, at Poverty Point and at a group of sites along Bayou Teche near Lafayette (Weinstein 1995:158–159).

- *Late Archaic Research Directions*
A discussion of the Late Archaic/Poverty Point period research themes in Louisiana is presented in the Comprehensive Archaeological Plan (Smith et al. 1983:151–161; see also Byrd 1991). Among the questions that can be explored locally are the procedures used to recognize Late Archaic components. The Birds Creek and Leander phases have been documented at a number of sites, but the assemblages assigned to them are typically from the middle parts of shallow, artifact-rich stratigraphic columns, where the possibility of mixing with earlier and later components, much less reoccupation within specific periods, cannot be ruled out. While these phases are thus somewhat tentative in nature, they represent an attempt to partition later Archaic assemblage variability in the area and appear to be quite useful in that regard. As with all typological constructs, however, they should be subject to continual testing and empirical validation through stratigraphic and comparative analyses. Much better dating of the projectile point categories used locally is essential, and the morphological variation present within local assemblages and within defined point categories needs to be better documented and understood.

Likewise, settlement patterns during the Late Archaic period are not well understood at present. In recent years, as more and more work has been accomplished on Fort Polk, the presence of large numbers of extensive, highly diverse assemblages dating to the Late Archaic period has been recognized. A similar pattern was observed immediately to the west when Lake Anacoco was drawn down; the vast majority of the assemblages documented dated to the Late Archaic and early ceramic periods (McGimsey 1996:57). As a result, it has been suggested that some of these assemblages are the remains of groups living in the immediate area whose annual range included Fort Polk (Campbell et al. 1990, 1994a:46; Morehead et al. 2002:39). The excavation of large areas at undisturbed Late Archaic components will be essential if questions about site size, composition, and season of occupation are to be considered. How Late Archaic use of the immediate Fort Polk area ties in to developments elsewhere in the region is a major and as of yet unresolved question. In particular, the nature of the relationships between populations in west-central Louisiana and those associated with the Poverty Point complex in northeast Louisiana deserves more attention. In the mid-1980s Campbell et al. (1987:34; see also Morehead et al. 2002:38) suggested that much of the Archaic period use of the Fort Polk area was for procurement of lithic raw materials that were then distributed through trading networks. During the Poverty Point era, they argued, the area may have been a source for lithics, salt, and Catahoula sandstone. It is difficult to accept that the resources of the Fort Polk region would have been completely ignored by Poverty Point peoples, particularly given their interest in—indeed obsession with—exotic lithic raw materials (e.g., Carr and Stewart n.d.; Gibson 1974, 1994, 1998; Webb 1968, 1982, 1991).

THE WOODLAND ERA (3200–1000 B.P./3000–1100 RCBP)

Early Woodland Adaptations (3200–2200 B.P./3000–2200 rcbp)
The first several centuries of the Woodland period, toward the end of the Sub-Boreal climatic episode, were a time of somewhat colder and fluctuating climatic conditions in eastern North America, within which were two fairly dramatic short-term cold events, one right at the start of the era and the other some two to three centuries later (Anderson 2001; Fiedel 2001; O'Brien et al. 1995; see Story [1990:244–246] for a summary of climatic evidence from eastern Texas during the Late Holocene). While it is unlikely that these climatic developments could have brought about the collapse of the fairly complex societies and exchange networks that occurred about this time in parts of the region, they may have played a role and made the Early Woodland a period of stress greater than these societies typically had to buffer against. During the Early Woodland period, pottery was adopted across much of the Eastern Woodlands (Griffin 1967:180), while in the Louisiana area the Poverty Point culture came to an end. The term *Tchefuncte* has been applied to Early Woodland components in the southern portion of the lower Mississippi Alluvial Valley that are characterized by ceramics of that series; the interval in which they occur is known as the Tchula period, dated ca. 2500–2000 B.P. (Ford and Quimby 1945; Jeter and Williams 1989b; Kidder 2002:69–72; Phillips et al. 1951:431–436; Weinstein 1986, 1995). Although this sequence uses the traditional starting date for the Woodland period of ca. 3000 rcbp (e.g., Anderson and Mainfort 2002), Tchefuncte culture itself

may have begun somewhat after that date, perhaps ca. 2800 rcbp, and appears to have extended into the subsequent Middle Woodland period to ca. 2000 B.P. (Hays and Weinstein 1996:82; Weinstein 1995:153).

Tchefuncte-like sherds, characterized by a temperless, laminated paste, are comparatively rare on Fort Polk, with only 30 identified (Table 5.2; see also Anderson et al. 1999a:appendix 5 for count data by site). Occasional sherds are found and used to infer the presence of components of this period (e.g., 16SA79, Prentice Thomas and Associates, Inc. 1992:61–76, 95–100; 16VN358, Campbell et al. 1994b:89–96; 16VN1059, Morehead et al. 1995b:80–88; 16VN1263, Thomas et al. 1994b:90–95). At 16VN358 a Trinity point came from the same level as Tchefuncte ceramics and was thought to be associated. The most extensive Tchefuncte ceramic assemblage found to date on the installation, at 16SA79 on Peason Ridge, consisted of only eight sherds, fortunately from largely undisturbed context (Prentice Thomas and Associates, Inc. 1992:71). The largest Tchefuncte assemblage from the Main Fort consisted of six sherds at 16VN1138, which were unfortunately from badly disturbed deposits (Morehead et al. 1995a:138–145). Tchefuncte components are sometimes difficult to recognize in the Fort Polk area. The characteristic paste lamination in the Tchefuncte sherds found at 16SA79, for example, was only recognized when the sherds were ground on a lapidary machine. The 16SA79 materials also lack the chalky paste common to Tchefuncte assemblages elsewhere, suggesting they are a distinct cultural or manufacturing variant. The authors suggested that at least some of the Tchefuncte materials observed on Fort Polk were late and likely overlapped with early Marksville materials (see also Morehead et al. 2002:46). No other diagnostic artifacts (i.e., projectile points, formal tools, or other ceramic types) are known to date exclusively to the Early Woodland period locally; most dart point types thought to occur at this time level, such as those in the Dooley Branch cluster, also occur in earlier and later periods as well. Because of the low incidence of readily identifiable components and the small numbers of diagnostics when such assemblages were found, no Early Woodland phases have been defined at Fort Polk (Morehead et al. 2002:45–46; Thomas et al. 1997:25–26). Gregory and Curry (1978:43; see also Girard 2000b:42) defined the Lena phase to encompass sites with Tchefuncte sherds found in southern Natchitoches Parish; these sites were characterized by Gary and Pontchartrain points and Lake Borgne Incised and Orleans Punctated ceramics.

- *Early Woodland Research Directions*
A discussion of the Tchefuncte culture in Louisiana and relevant Tchula period research themes is provided in the Comprehensive Archaeological

Plan (Smith et al. 1983:163–170; see also Girard 2000b:42–43; Hays and Weinstein 1996; Weinstein 1986, 1995). The Early Woodland period remains very poorly defined locally, meaning that the discovery and examination of undisturbed assemblages dating to this period would be extremely important. A major research challenge thus consists of defining the nature of Early Woodland occupations locally and relating them to more visible Tchefuncte manifestations in the lower Alluvial Valley and along the Gulf coast. Likewise, the relationship of materials found on Fort Polk to cultures identified in eastern Texas, such as Mossy Grove (Story 1990:256–292), must also be explored. No Tchefuncte ceramics were observed in the Lake Anacoco area west of Fort Polk, although appreciable sand-tempered remains thought to be of the Goose Creek series were found, suggesting some early ceramics locally may be of these east Texas types (McGimsey 1996:135, 144; see also Story 1990:246–247). Tchefuncte ceramics have been found at a number of locations in eastern Texas, such as at the Resch site in the Sabine River drainage northwest of Fort Polk (Story 1990:246). Sand-tempered Goose Creek Plain ceramics are frequently found associated, and at Resch a sherd of Alexander Pinched pottery was found, suggesting ties much farther to the east (Webb et al. 1969).

Middle Woodland Adaptations (2200–1600 B.P./2200–1700 rcbp)

The Middle Woodland period occurs during the Sub-Atlantic climatic amelioration, which occurred ca. 2450–1600 B.P. and is when the Hopewell culture and its variants appeared across eastern North America. Fluctuations in climate were not as common or extreme during this period, placing less stress on subsistence systems, which James B. Griffin (1960, 1961:712–713) noted may have helped facilitate the development and spread of Hopewellian iconography and exchange. The more moderate conditions may have allowed for the more regular generation of food surpluses, which could have helped fuel the monumental construction, ceremony, and exchange observed at this time. Early Middle Woodland period components in Louisiana are recognized by the presence of Marksville ceramics, named after the mound complex along the lower Red River (Toth 1974, 1979; see also Kidder 2002:72–79). The later Middle Woodland period, after roughly A.D. 300 and continuing into the subsequent Late Woodland period, is characterized by Baytown/Troyville culture materials, identified primarily by Baytown Plain and Mulberry Creek Cord Marked grog-tempered pottery and a few minor decorated types (Gibson 1982; Kidder 2002:72–79; Neuman 1984; Webb 1984). Several summaries exist detailing the evidence for Middle Woodland occupations in Louisiana (e.g., Gibson 1970; Neuman 1984:137–168; Toth 1974; Webb 1984). No major ceremonial centers are known from the immediate Fort Polk area, although Marksville ceramics were found during excavations at the Coral Snake Mound along the middle course of the Sabine just to the west (McClurkan et al. 1966, 1980; Story 1990:279–292), at the Fredericks site near Natchitoches (Girard 2000b:42–44), and at the Bellevue mound in extreme northwestern Louisiana (Webb 1984). Gregory and Curry (1978) have proposed Fredericks, Coral Snake, and Briar Bend phases for Marksville assemblages in Natchitoches and Sabine Parishes. Other archaeological cultures that likely influenced Middle Woodland developments in the western Louisiana area include Mossy Grove (Story 1990:256–292) from eastern Texas and Fourche Maline in northwest Louisiana and beyond (Schambach 2002).

Diagnostic early Middle Woodland Marksville ceramics are comparatively rare on Fort Polk, and most assemblages are characterized by only one or a few sherds, typically varieties of Marksville Stamped and Marksville Incised (Table 5.2). A provisional *Whiskey Chitto phase*, initially advanced by Campbell et al. (1987:30), has been proposed to encompass sites characterized by Hopewellian artifacts in the region. This phase, which the authors stress is a tentative construct, has been most recently described as follows:

> The diagnostics for Whiskey Chitto are Marksville pottery types, notably Marksville Stamped and Marksville Incised . . . specimens which exhibit motifs and rim forms like Marksville in the Lower Mississippi Valley. Fabric characteristics are predominantly grog-tempered (cf. Campbell and Weed 1986), but sandy pastes are also present and some specimens have flecks of bone. In the area of ceramic fabric, the sherds have more in common with the Lower Mississippi Valley than east Texas. This seems reasonable as it is less than 100 linear miles from Fort Polk to the Crooks site (16LA3) [Ford and Willey 1940] and less than 70 miles from Fort Polk to 16AV1—the Marksville type site. The scattered instances of bone temper may be indicative of some relationship to Fourche Maline cultures to the north and west where bone tempering has a long history.
>
> Dooley Branch, Ellis, Gary, Kent, the Williams cluster and similar dart points . . . are present but are not diagnostic because of their temporal span; thus we rely solely on the presence of identifiable Marksville sherds to establish a component. . . . An important secondary trait of Whiskey Chitto phase assemblages is that formal bifaces outnumber formal unifaces. In fact, in individual components other than base camps, formal bifaces often have a two to one majority over unifaces.

Points are the most common formal tool, followed by perforators, denticulated-serrated pieces and endscrapers. Less common are notches, celts, sidescrapers, serrated pieces, pièces esquillées; there has been only one burin. Interestingly, the multiple tools associated with Whiskey Chitto components each have perforator-class modifications as one element of their morphology. Except for points, the major tool classes have unifacial and bifacial variants.

Core-flake, blade and bifacial reduction are present. Although blades are not nearly as common as flakes, blades and at least one blade core have been recovered. . . . It may be that, like Leander and probably Tchefuncte, these peoples were not full time residents. Although some components seem consistent with . . . base camps, we believe they were probably seasonally, rather than permanently, inhabited. The camps may have been occupied during periods when people were engaged in activities focused on lithic procurement and hunting.

The dominance of bifaces among the formal tools is an interesting phenomenon. . . . To no small extent, bifacial technology climaxes in the Marksville Period rather than the Late Archaic at Fort Polk [Morehead et al. 2002:47–48].

Although Marksville ceramics occur in only very small quantity on Fort Polk, they do indicate that the area participated at some level in the interregional ceremonial/exchange network known as the Hopewell Interaction Sphere (Caldwell 1964; Struever and Houart 1972). Their presence locally may be related, at least in part, to lithic raw material procurement. While a majority of the components and all of the larger assemblages are found on the Main Fort, a number of small Marksville components are present on Peason Ridge (e.g., Brassieur 1983:314; Mathews et al. 1995:108–109). These sites may reflect an interest in the somewhat more unusual raw materials that occur in that area, such as petrified wood, Eagle Hill chert, and Fleming opal. The presence of Marksville components on the Main Fort, near the Citronelle gravel deposits, may likewise reflect exploitation of these sources.

The low number of Marksville sherds found on sites locally suggests fairly ephemeral contact from foraging or resource-procurement task groups based elsewhere. A possible exception to this pattern was observed at 16VN527, a large site on the lower slopes of the ridge line overlooking the Birds Creek floodplain (Morehead et al. 1996a:83–106). At this site a possible Marksville midden some 40 cm thick was found; this is one of the few unequivocal prehistoric features with organic staining detected on Fort Polk to date. Dense remains were found at depths up to 120 cm in a number of units, with the San Patrice, Evans, Birds Creek, Late Archaic/Poverty Point, Marksville, and Baytown or Coles Creek cultural complexes represented (Morehead et al. 1996a:104). Interestingly, four small fragments of steatite were also recovered from the site, although their age and associations are uncertain. The artifact-rich midden level was assigned to a Marksville occupation given the presence of two Marksville Incised sherds in the fill, although given the 1,395 pieces of debitage and cores and 47 chipped stone tools including Gary, Dooley Branch, and triangular types, plus one expanded stemmed point, such an assignment must be viewed as somewhat questionable. A bulk soil sample from the midden level was radiocarbon dated between A.D. 635 and 865, which is somewhat later than expected (Morehead et al. 1996a:95); dense occupation that included Marksville artifacts is clearly indicated, however. A bone-tempered Marksville Incised sherd was found at 16VN1508 (Meyer et al. 1996a:151, 156), and bone tempering has been observed on a little over one percent of the sherds from the installation (Table 5.2). Similar tempering has been observed at the Coral Snake Mound on the Sabine River to the west of Fort Polk (McClurkan et al. 1966) and in low incidence at a number of locations in eastern Texas (Story 1990:247), such as at the Resch site, where Cooper Boneware–like pottery was found and dated to between ca. 2350 and 1850 B.P./2400 and 1900 rcbp (Schambach 1982:161–162, 1998:21–24; Webb et al. 1969:24–28), suggesting possible ties with the peoples from this site or area. An early bone-tempered series thus exists in the general region and is the likely source or inspiration for some of the sherds found on Fort Polk.

The initial Middle Woodland Marksville culture occupations are succeeded in the Louisiana area by the later Middle Woodland Troyville and Baytown cultures, which are placed in the Baytown period from roughly A.D. 300 to 600 (Belmont 1982:78; I. Brown 1984; Gibson 1982). Over much of Louisiana, except for possibly in the extreme northeastern part of the state, assemblages of this period are placed in the Troyville culture; Baytown culture is typically used to refer to assemblages in eastern Arkansas and adjoining areas. Baytown period, Troyville culture components are difficult to recognize in the Fort Polk area, and no formal phases have been defined. Mulberry Creek Cord Marked ceramics, a key diagnostic of the period, have never been found on Fort Polk and indeed are rare throughout western Louisiana (Girard 2000b:45). Although a large number of plain sherds tempered with grog or grog and sand have been found on Fort Polk, they cannot be equated with the Baytown period, since grog-tempered plainwares have a long temporal occurrence, being found in Marksville and Coles Creek assemblages.

Grog-tempered plainwares with a chalky paste similar to Baytown Plain, *var. Troyville* are reported from Fort Polk and are thought to be diagnostic of the Baytown period (Morehead et al. 2002:50; they were not typed as such, however, in the original report), as are a few sherds of Baytown Plain, *var. Satartia*, a thin-walled, hard and compact ware (Girard 2000b:49; Phillips 1970:53) (Table 5.2). Other probable diagnostic markers of the Baytown period on Fort Polk include late varieties of Marksville Incised (*vars. Leist, Spanish Fort*, and *Yokena* and possibly *Steele Bayou*), Marksville Stamped, *var. Troyville*, Churupa Punctate, and possibly Alligator Incised, Indian Bay Stamped, and Larto Red. These types are associated with the Baytown period to the north of Fort Polk in the Natchitoches area along the Red River, where a major later Middle Woodland/initial Late Woodland assemblage has been documented at the Fredericks site (Girard 1998, 2000b:48–62, personal communication 1999). A range of dart points are thought to date to the period on Fort Polk, including Ellis, Kent, and Gary, *var. Maybon*, as well as other types associated with earlier and later Woodland occupations (Morehead et al. 2002:50; see also Thomas et al. 1997:27); arrow points, specifically the Colbert type, are also thought to appear at this time on Fort Polk. At the Fredericks site, Catahoula, Friley, and Scallorn are thought to be early arrow point types, dating to the Late Woodland Coles Creek period (Girard 2000b:74). Given the difficulties in identifying components dating to this time level on Fort Polk, whether arrow points came in during the Baytown period locally cannot be determined. A somewhat later inception, during the Late Woodland period (after A.D. 600), is suggested as more likely, given that this is the estimated age for their appearance over the larger region (Blitz 1988; Nassaney and Pyle 1999). While some researchers (e.g., Patterson 1982) have suggested that retouched flakes and microblades were used as arrow points appreciably earlier, possibly during the Archaic period locally, this idea has not been widely accepted. In eastern Texas, Story (1990:217, 246–251) places the appearance of arrow points about A.D. 700.

- *Middle Woodland Research Directions*

Discussions of current knowledge about the Marksville and subsequent Troyville–Coles Creek periods in Louisiana and relevant research themes have been detailed in the Comprehensive Archaeological Plan (Smith et al. 1983:171–193). Identifying local initial Middle Woodland assemblages in the absence of Marksville ceramics is a major challenge, as is identifying late Middle Woodland/initial Late Woodland Baytown period assemblages. While grog tempering is the predominant paste found on Fort Polk, a moderate incidence of ceramics characterized by a sand-tempered paste is also present (see Chapter 5). Some of these ceramics are equated with Woodland series described farther to the west in Texas, such as Goose Creek or Pease; decorated Goose Creek ceramics have also been found to the west of Fort Polk in the Lake Anacoco area (McGimsey 1996). What cultural relationships are implied by the occurrence and distributions of sand-tempered and sand/grog- and clay/grog-tempered wares is currently uncertain. Another major question relates to the presence of Middle Woodland Marksville components in the Fort Polk area. At what level did the occupants of the general west-central Louisiana region participate in the Hopewell Interaction Sphere? Finally, the relationship between Marksville and earlier Tchefuncte assemblages locally deserves attention; ceramics from late Tchula period assemblages often cannot be differentiated at the sherd level from Marksville (Kidder 2002:73), suggesting some late Early Woodland components may be misidentified.

Late Woodland Adaptations (ca. 1600–1000 B.P./1700–1100 rcbp)
The Late Woodland period is characterized by a mild decline in average global temperature from ca. A.D. 400 to 800—the Vandal Minimum—followed by the onset of a period of warmer climate thought favorable to agriculture in the East known as the Medieval Warm Period (Broecker 2001; Hughes and Diaz 1994; see also Anderson 2001; Griffin 1961:713). The early part of the Late Woodland period in the lower Mississippi Valley and along the Red River witnessed a continuation of the Troyville culture described previously, while the later part of the period, after ca. 1300 B.P., witnessed the emergence of the Coles Creek and early Caddoan cultures (Kidder 2002:79–90). By the end of the period, truncated pyramidal mounds fronting on plazas are observed at a number of Coles Creek sites in the general region, although none are known in the Fort Polk area. Along the Red River, late Fourche Maline/early Caddoan ceremonial centers have been identified at Mounds Plantation, Crenshaw, and Gahagan, although monumental construction at these sites is assumed to occur in subsequent periods after ca. A.D. 1000 (Schambach 1996:37–38; Webb and McKinney 1975:40). Most early Caddoan settlements are thought to be like those occurring later: small villages on tributary streams or lakes or dispersed villages in floodplains (Girard 1997; Story 1990:334–342). The first evidence for intensive maize agriculture occurs elsewhere in the Eastern Woodlands during this interval (e.g., Smith 1992), but no evidence for this has been found in Louisiana. Coles Creek occupations locally, in fact, appear to have made extensive use of wild plant and animal resources (Fritz and Kidder 1993; Kidder 1990, 1992, 2002). Over the general region, Coles Creek assemblages are dated to between ca. A.D. 700 and 1200 (Kidder 1992:147–148; Story 1990:170).

Late Woodland assemblages at Fort Polk are identified primarily by the presence of grog-tempered or grog-and-sand-tempered Chevalier Stamped, Coles Creek Incised, Evansville Punctated, French Fork Incised, Mazique Incised, and Pontchartrain Check Stamped ceramics. Most of these have Caddoan equivalents, such as Dunkin Incised/Mazique Incised, Davis and Kiam Incised/Coles Creek Incised, or Wilkinson Punctated/Evansville Punctated. Some of these types almost certainly extend later in time, particularly varieties of Coles Creek Incised like *var. Hardy* (e.g., Phillips 1970:74; Schambach and Waddell 1990:54). Many more clay/grog-and-sand-tempered incised ceramics actually occur on the installation than have been classified, with simple one- or two-line incising common, but most investigators have hesitated to assign these artifacts to a specific type or variety. A number of dart point types are found, most if not all continuing from earlier periods. Use of the bow and arrow becomes widespread at this time, and a number of arrow point types appear. The Alba, Catahoula, Hayes, Friley, Scallorn, and possibly the Colbert types are thought to date to this general period, although most of these forms also appear to continue into the early part of the subsequent Caddoan/Mississippian period.

A number of assemblages with presumed Late Woodland components have been found on Fort Polk, most characterized by small numbers of Coles Creek or contemporaneous sherds. Most are thought to be small, short-term camps apparently associated with lithic raw material procurement or travel through the area (Thomas et al. 1993e:110–111). Campbell et al. (1990:6) offered a provisional *Holly Springs phase* designation for sites with Coles Creek and related ceramics in the Fort Polk area characterized by

> stamped, incised and plain ceramics, in addition to Friley, Hayes, Livermore, Catahoula, Bassett and Alba points. While useful as an organizational framework, more data regarding Coles Creek assemblages and settlement patterns need to be obtained to better characterize these occupations at Fort Polk.
>
> Such data are beginning to accumulate; it now seems that Coles Creek components are more common than suspected earlier particularly in the southeast portion of the Main Post. Evidence of classic Coles Creek types was found at 16VN1053 (Campbell et al. 1994a) and at 16VN794 (Cantley et al., eds. 1993). As more of the classic types, such as Coles Creek Incised, are found and the body of evidence grows, we will be in a better position to characterize Coles Creek utilization of Fort Polk.
>
> The diagnostic artifacts recognized thus far include Coles Creek Incised, Mazique Incised and Evansville Punctated *var. Rhinehart.*

French Fork Incised has recently been identified and has been tentatively included as a diagnostic marker for this area. Points are not
diagnostic. The Colbert arrow type is carried over from Baytown,
and Alba makes its appearance, as does Friley. Ellis, Gary, Kent and
Godley dart points continue to be used [Campbell et al. 1990:6].

Coles Creek Incised, particularly *vars. Blakely, Coles Creek, Greenhouse*,
and *Mott*, were considered key diagnostics, as were *vars. Hardy* and *unspecified* if dart points were present, since *var. Hardy* and some Coles Creek
varieties continue into the ensuing Caddoan/Mississippian period (Morehead
et al. 2002:51; see also Kidder 1990:59; Phillips 1970:74). Other Coles Creek
types sometimes occur that are useful diagnostics. A classic sherd of French
Fork Incised pottery, for example, was found at 16VN873 (Morehead et al.
1996b:123). Bassett points are assumed to be appreciably later in time, while
Livermore points, a west Texas type, resemble Alba, Catahoula, or Hayes
points and are probably misclassified locally.

A few large diverse assemblages are attributed to the Late Woodland
period on Fort Polk that are thought to reflect seasonally utilized base camps,
and one assemblage, at 16VN1505, appears to have been a quarry/workshop
site (Meyer et al. 1996a); most remaining assemblages are small and appear
to be short-term hunting or special-activity stations (Morehead et al. 2002:51).
One unusual assemblage found on Peason Ridge on a low rise overlooking
Comrade Creek (site 16VN204) had 10 small blades or blade-like flakes
associated, six of which had been retouched (Morehead et al. 1996a:66–76).
The nature of the site is unknown although it is tempting to speculate that
the blades may have been used as scarifiers in some kind of religious activity. Unusual blade-like flakes of crystal quartz, for example, have been noted
at the roughly contemporaneous Toltec site in central Arkansas, where there
is extensive evidence for ceremony (Anderson 1985; Rolingson, ed. 1982).
Reuse of lithic materials from earlier occupations is indicated at some sites
(Morehead et al. 2002:51–52). The presence of comparatively large numbers of incised ceramics may reflect an increased use of the Fort Polk area
by populations centered farther to the east, in the Mississippi Alluvial Valley, or to the north and northwest in the Red River area.

- *Late Woodland Research Directions*
A discussion of the Middle to Late Woodland Troyville and Coles Creek
cultures in Louisiana and relevant research themes has been detailed in the
Comprehensive Archaeological Plan (Smith et al. 1983:181–191; see also
Kidder 2002:79–90). Use of the Fort Polk area by peoples making Coles
Creek and related types of pottery is clearly indicated, but what the geo-

graphic affiliations of these peoples were—that is, where on the landscape they originated, as well as what they were doing on Fort Polk—is largely unknown. The assemblages found at Fort Polk could represent the remains of activities by task groups from societies centered along the Red River or in the lower Mississippi Valley, where larger sites are known to have been present. Alternatively, local populations may be represented, who were perhaps affluent and fairly mobile foragers, much like the Coles Creek populations Schambach (ed. 1990) has described from southern Arkansas (see also Fritz and Kidder 1993). Finally, the impact of the bow and arrow on hunting and warfare locally and over the larger region should be considered. Did stone tool assemblages and particularly the exploitation of local lithic raw materials like cobble cherts change appreciably after the introduction of this technology? There is some suggestion for a change in reduction strategies, notably the production of smaller flakes (see Chapters 2 and 3).

THE LATE PREHISTORIC/EARLY HISTORIC ERA (1000–200 B.P./1100–350 RCBP)

The interval from ca. A.D. 800 to 1300 corresponds to the Medieval Warm Period (Broecker 2001; Hughes and Diaz 1994), a time thought favorable for agriculture, with peak warm temperatures in the northern hemisphere comparable to or only slightly lower than those at present (Crowley 2000; DeMenocal et al. 2000). During this period Mississippian and Caddoan cultures emerged and spread widely, including over much of Louisiana. The later part of the era, after the onset of the Little Ice Age around ca. A.D. 1300 (Grove 1988), was considered less favorable for agricultural populations, and there is some evidence for increased warfare and settlement nucleation and decreased long-distance exchange and monumental construction over the Eastern Woodlands (Griffin 1961:711–713; Milner 1999:125). By shortly after A.D. 900, Mississippian culture had emerged and was expanding in the central Mississippi Valley, reaching the Lower Valley one to two centuries later, where the local variant is called Plaquemine culture; this lasted into historic times. At the same time Coles Creek cultural systems were dominating the lower Mississippi, Arkansas, and Red River Valleys, Caddoan cultures were emerging, probably from a Coles Creek base, in northwest Louisiana along the middle course of the Red River and in the area from the Red to the Sabine and Trinity Rivers of eastern Texas (Skinner 1980:209–211; Story 1990:323–325).

Most late prehistoric/early historic assemblages found on Fort Polk appear to have Caddoan affiliations, although a few possible Plaquemine components have been identified by the Prentice Thomas and Associates, Inc., research team on the basis of the presence of Harrison Bayou Incised, L'Eau

Noire Incised, Mazique Incised, *var. Manchac*, and Coles Creek Incised, *var. Hardy*, if dart points are absent (Morehead et al. 2002:53–55; Thomas et al. 1997:28–29); Alba, Bassett, and Bayougoula Fishtailed points are also found with these assemblages. Because these points and pottery types also occur in Caddoan or Coles Creek contexts (Quimby 1951, 1957; Woodiel 1993:70–100), cultural differentiation can be challenging (e.g., Gibson 1991:79–80). Because most of these components are small, their identification as Plaquemine must be considered tentative. A minor Plaquemine component, for example, was inferred by the presence of a Coles Creek Incised, *var. Hardy* sherd and two Bassett points at 16VN1277 near Whiskey Chitto Creek on the Main Fort (Campbell et al. 1994b:130–140, 155). Minimally, the data collected to date from Fort Polk indicate that Plaquemine use of the area was fairly slight. Instead, greater use of the area, perhaps as a buffer zone or hunting territory, if not direct control, was by Caddoan groups (e.g., Smith et al. 1983:206).

Caddoan chronology and cultural developments have traditionally been classified using the Midwestern taxonomic system (McKern 1939), with two major aspects (Gibson and Fulton) subdivided into a number of foci (i.e., Alto or Alto-Gahagan, Haley, Bossier, Belcher, Glendora). A five-period sequence is in use in some areas, with Caddo I and II corresponding to the Gibson aspect, Caddo III and IV to the prehistoric Fulton aspect, and Caddo V to historic Caddoan (Davis 1970:40–54; see also Story 1990:325–334). An absolute chronological sequence has yet to be developed, however: "While difficulties can be expected in formulating proper local Caddoan sequences (ideally phases or subphases, with sociocultural associations), there should be no problem in defining useful area-wide chronological periods. . . . Yet such a straightforward temporal framework does not presently exist for Caddoan archaeology. The Caddo I through V sequences [come] the closest, except there is not agreement on the critical matter of how the periods should be delineated" (Story 1990:331). This is part of the reason the cultural sequence presented here employs periods with fixed temporal boundaries, with cultural developments discussed within or between each as warranted. Such an approach may be somewhat arbitrary, but at least calendrical dates do not have the baggage associated with stage designations like "Archaic" or "Woodland." Of course, until sound radiocarbon calibrations can be agreed upon, some confusion about the kind of time being used will still occur.

The earliest Caddoan developments in the northwest Louisiana area are described as the Alto-Gahagan focus, defined on the basis of work at sites such as George C. Davis in east Texas (Newell and Krieger 1949) and recognized at Mounds Plantation and Gahagan along the Red River (Webb and

Dodd 1939; Webb and McKinney 1975). Also known as the Alto focus, it has been dated to between ca. A.D. 800 and 1300 (Story 1990:169). A transition from Coles Creek to Alto-Gahagan focus Caddoan is evident at Mounds Plantation, where Webb and McKinney (1975:85, 120) have noted a continuation in mound building and in burial customs over these two cultures and a strong similarity in the local ceramics. As they conclude, "The findings at Mounds Plantation, Crenshaw and Gahagan, along with those on Red and Little Rivers above the Big Bend, contribute to our previous beliefs that the Red River Valley was the center of early Caddoan development, that early Caddoan origins were closely tied to the antecedent Coles Creek developments, and that Coles Creek–Alto transition occurred primarily along Red River" (Webb and McKinney 1975:124). Principal diagnostics of early Caddoan Alto focus assemblages on Fort Polk include Alba projectile points and Crockett Curvilinear Incised, Davis Incised, Dunkin Incised, Hickory Fine Engraved, Kiam Incised, and Pennington Punctated-Incised ceramics (Morehead et al. 2002:18, 56). Catahoula, Friley, Hayes, and Scallorn arrow points occur in Alto focus assemblages locally, as well as in earlier Late Woodland assemblages. At Fort Polk, Alto focus materials are the most common Caddoan remains found, occurring on more sites than later diagnostics (Morehead et al. 2002:56; see also Table 5.2).

By or soon after A.D. 1300, Bossier focus assemblages are found on Fort Polk, recognized by the presence of Bossier Brushed ceramics (Morehead et al. 2002:57). Other ceramic types that may be associated locally include Pease Brushed-Incised and Karnack Brushed-Incised, while arrow point types like Alba, Bonham, Fresno, Hayes, and Perdiz points may be associated as well, although most also occur earlier or later. Bassett points, "the resident type of Belcher Focus" (Webb and McKinney 1975:97), may be present but are clearly dominant later. While a moderate number of Bossier Brushed sherds have been found on Fort Polk (n = 51), most are from a single site, 16SA73, on the divide between the three major river systems in the area, the Sabine, the Calcasieu, and the Red (Prentice Thomas and Associates, Inc. 1992:47–57, 103). The Bossier focus is dated to between ca. A.D. 1300 and 1500 (Story 1990:169).

Late prehistoric/early historic Indian occupations on Fort Polk include assemblages characterized by artifacts of the Belcher focus (Webb 1959), dated ca. A.D. 1500–1700 (Story 1990:169). Belcher Ridged pottery sherds, the principal diagnostic, have been found on a handful of sites (Table 5.2), although Bassett points, thought to date primarily to this period, are more common, occurring on 36 sites. Cuney, Friley, and Perdiz points may also date to this period, and Cuney points are considered to be diagnostic of protohistoric assemblages locally by the Prentice Thomas and Associates,

Inc., research team (Morehead et al. 1996a:194, 2002:59–61). Use of the area for hunting by groups living elsewhere may be indicated by the comparatively large number of arrow points in comparison with the much lower occurrence of ceramics.

A possible early nineteenth-century Indian assemblage was found at 16VN928 during the FP-10 testing project (Thomas et al. 1994a:135–147). The site was located on a small knoll overlooking a number of intermittent tributaries of Bayou Zourie on the Main Fort. A total of 12 50-x-50-cm and 2 1-x-1-m units were opened, with just over 4 m^3 of fill removed. In all, 141 chipped stone tools, 1,304 pieces of debitage, and 4 pieces of groundstone were recovered from an area of about 1,375 m^2 in extent. Thirty-five points were found, including Bassett (n = 8), Bayougoula (n = 1), Gary and Gary-like (n = 8), Epps and Epps-like (n = 2), Godley (n = 1), Kent (n = 1), Sinner (n = 1), Woden (n = 1), Form X (n = 1), unidentified spikes (n = 3), and unidentified dart points (n = 8). Several sherds of what was identified as Pease Brushed-Incised pottery were also found together with a small number of early nineteenth-century historic artifacts, including seven sherds from "a minimum of two blue shell edged plates, a light blue transfer printed bowl, and possibly a cup" (Thomas et al. 1994a:141). Two olive hand-blown wine bottle fragments were also found and, most interestingly, a .54 caliber musket ball and two possible gun spalls, one of local gravel chert and the other of an unusual waxy brown and red chert. Two other objects were found made of local chert that were classified as pièces esquillées but that also may have been large gunflints. The .54 caliber size was described as a common diameter for trade guns of the eighteenth and early nineteenth centuries. The assemblage was interpreted as the remains of a historic Indian occupation whose peoples may have been reworking as well as possibly collecting earlier points and tools; some of the earlier prehistoric material may alternatively represent earlier use of the location. The site currently represents one of the few historic assemblages dating to the early nineteenth century on the installation.

Summaries of protohistoric occupations in and near west-central Louisiana, including possible settlements in the vicinity of Fort Polk (Morehead et al. 2002:60), have been presented by a number of authors (e.g., Gregory 1973; Kelley 1998; Kniffen et al. 1987; Perttula 1992; Story 1990:320–320, 346–355; Webb 1959; Williams 1961, 1964; Woodall 1980), in most cases incorporating archaeological site locational data. Initial European contact occurred in 1542, when surviving members of the de Soto entrada, searching for an overland route to Mexico, appear to have encountered Caddoan groups in the general northwest Louisiana area. The societies described by the de Soto chroniclers were reported to be extremely fierce and were accorded considerable respect by their neighbors (Garcilaso de la Vega in Varner and Varner 1951:466). The ferocity of these peoples and the fear they incited in their neighbors may have obviated the need for nucleated Caddoan centers during this later period.

A number of Indian groups were located in and near the northwest and west-central Louisiana area in ca. 1700, such as the Caddoan Adai, Doustini, Natchitoches, Ouachita, and Yatasi to the north; the Bidai to the west across the Sabine; the Opelousa and Avoyel to the east; and the Atakapa to the south by the coast (Kniffen et al. 1987:44–47, 49; Swanton 1911, 1946). Over the course of the next century and a half most of these groups declined markedly through disease, slave raiding, and warfare. Over this same interval settlements appeared and disappeared, brought about by the relocation and consolidation of some of these groups, the extinction of others, and the appearance of new peoples coming in from greater distances, in some cases encouraged to do so by the Spanish to serve as a buffer against Anglo-American encroachment (Kniffen et al. 1987:18–19, 73–98; Swanton 1911, 1942, 1946). Although no native groups are known to have resided directly on lands now controlled by Fort Polk, settlements are reported almost literally all around the installation, including immigrant groups like the Alabama, Apalachee, Biloxi, Chatot/Chatoh, Choctaw, and Koasati (Hunter 1994; Kniffen et al. 1987:73, 197). At present, populations of Native Americans are still present in the western Louisiana area, including the Apache, Choctaw, Choctaw-Apache, Tunica-Biloxi, and Koasati (Kniffen et al. 1987:299–311).

Louisiana Indians of the early historic era in the general vicinity of Fort Polk appear to have been actively engaged in the exchange and possibly procurement of lithic raw material (Campbell et al. 1987:127; Kniffen et al. 1987:49; Swanton 1911:272–274, 1946:543). Swanton (1946:543) observed that

> An early writer speaks of flint as abounding in the country of the Avoyel Indians, La. (Dyer 1917), and in fact there is flint near the Rapides [interpreted by Campbell et al. 1987:127 as near Alexandria, Louisiana] which may have been utilized by them. It is probable, however, that they derived their name, which seems to be the Natchez equivalent of Mobilian *Tasånåk okla*, "Flint People," very largely from the fact that they acted as middle men who obtained worked or unworked flint from the Arkansas Indians about the Hot Springs and passed it on to the Chitimacha and Atakapa on the coast, these last supplying the Karankawa further west (Dyer 1917, pp. 6, 7; Swanton 1911:24–26) [Swanton 1946:542].

> [T]he Avoyel tribe, just west of the Natchez, and their near rela-
> tives, were actively engaged in trading in flints—so actively that
> they were known as "Flint People" [Swanton 1946:543].

These references hint, at least indirectly, at the presence of raw materials
and the kinds of quarrying activities represented by the sites and assemblages on Fort Polk. Whether the Avoyel or other groups of Indians during
the early historic era in Louisiana procured lithic raw materials directly from
local sources or acted as middlemen in more long-distance exchange networks, or both, cannot be determined from these accounts. But they do suggest that lithic raw material acquisition and exchange preoccupied some of
the very last Indians to live in this part of Louisiana, just as these activities
appear to have done for thousands of years prior to this.

A probable later Caddoan camp and lithic reduction area, identified by
Perdiz and two Friley projectile points, was documented in Area B at 16VN18
(Fredlund 1983; see Chapter 2). Greater concern for maximizing the number of tools that could be produced from chert cobbles was observed during
this period than was seen during Archaic occupations at the same site. A
change in technological organization is also indicated by the fact that the
later assemblage at 16VN18 yielded much smaller tools than the earlier assemblage at the same site. Research at Fort Polk, as noted in Chapter 3, has
shown that changes in reduction and manufacturing practices did occur locally following the Archaic period and particularly with the adoption of
arrow points, which could be easily made from small flakes. An increase in
the incidence of bifacial thinning flakes observed in some later assemblages,
for example, may reflect the replacement of darts by arrow points (Clement
et al. 1998:422). Given the warlike nature of the Caddoans, raw material
procurement during the late prehistoric era, with groups potentially coming
from all over to exploit the local gravel cherts, may have been a more dangerous enterprise than during earlier periods, necessitating more efficient
procurement and use of local materials, perhaps to reduce the number of
return visits.

■ *Caddoan/Mississippian/Historic Indian Research Directions*
A discussion of late prehistoric Plaquemine, Mississippian, Caddoan, and
historic Indian cultures in Louisiana, including relevant research themes,
has been presented in the Comprehensive Archaeological Plan (Smith et al.
1983:193–233). As with every period, refinement of artifact taxonomies and
greater use of absolute dating procedures are needed to better understand
local developments, although it is unlikely the sample will ever approach
"the rather paltry 48 sites [with Caddoan components that] have been as-

sayed" from east Texas, with a total of 283 dates (Story 1990:325). Even given the large numbers of radiocarbon dates from that area, furthermore, gaps in geographic and temporal coverage remain; there will probably always be basic questions of chronology to address no matter how well we think we understand local sequences, particularly if our research questions require fine-grained temporal controls on data.

The Prentice Thomas and Associates, Inc., intensive site-testing project team characterized the Caddoan occupations on Fort Polk as follows:

> The large village and ceremonial settlement pattern characteristic of the Caddoan period to the north in the Red River region is not apparent at Fort Polk. Recent work, particularly testing projects, has demonstrated that most Caddoan sites are small; few appear to have been year-long (or otherwise long-term) habitations, and none have produced the large quantity of sherds generally found in the Caddo heartland of Louisiana to the north. Instead, the overall configuration and contents suggest that most Caddoan sites on Fort Polk functioned as camps. By camps, we are not referring to major base camps. Instead, the camps on Fort Polk appear to reflect habitations or activity stations used during periods of population dispersion from a central base camp [Thomas et al. 1997:30].

Jackson (1984a:39) has suggested that Caddoan populations may have been nucleated into villages only during part of the year. Group dispersal in the summer to locate agricultural fields in a wide variety of environmental settings or in the winter to ensure adequate overwinter hunting was considered possible. Some of the small Caddoan sites located on Fort Polk might reflect this kind of seasonal population relocation.

Whether Fort Polk served as a hunting territory or possibly a buffer or neutral zone between Caddoan and Mississippi Valley societies to the east is unknown but has been inferred (Campbell et al. 1987:127). Few Caddoan ceramics and no triangular arrow points were observed in the Lake Anacoco area immediately west of Fort Polk, suggesting late prehistoric occupation was rare in this area and supporting the idea of a buffer zone (McGimsey 1996:135). Fluctuations in intensity of use over time are also noted in other parts of the Caddoan culture area (Story 1990:327) that may reflect changes in the political or economic fortunes of individual groups. Settlement nucleation is increasingly evident throughout much of the lower Mississippi Alluvial Valley and in surrounding areas at this time. Fortified villages become common and farmsteads disappear in some areas, although not apparently among the Caddo. This has been linked to increasing regional population density and a concomitant expansion of warfare arising in part over political rivalries, ultimately based on the control of important resources such as trade routes, agricultural lands, or hunting territories. The minimal use, at least for extended occupation, of the Fort Polk area may well be related in some way to this pattern of regional competition. That is, the area may have been a buffer between major political entities, although this is admittedly speculative.

Franks (1990c:87) has argued that three major questions or topics need to be considered about the Caddoan occupation of the Fort Polk area. First, what was the size of the local resident population (if any)? Second, what kinds of sites are present and where are they located? Third, how can chronological resolution of these occupations be improved locally? Likewise, as Campbell and Weed (1986:12-12) have asked, are there differences between Woodland and late prehistoric Caddoan/Mississippian assemblages in the Fort Polk area and, if so, is this due to (1) differing land-use patterns between these two groups, (2) a shift in cultural ties from the cultures of the lower Mississippi Valley to those in the Caddoan area, or (3) an intrusion of Caddoan populations into the area, either replacing local populations or interacting with them? Was the area encompassing Fort Polk in use as a hunting territory or possibly a buffer or neutral zone between the Caddo and Mississippi Valley societies to the east (Campbell et al. 1987:127)? What are the relationships between Caddoan centers, such as those along the Red or Sabine, and outlying settlements or special activity loci such as the sites in the Fort Polk area appear to be? What is the nature of historic Indian use of the immediate Fort Polk area? Can additional documentary evidence of these occupations be found?

Chapter 7

Fort Polk's Historic Development

This chapter focuses on Fort Polk's historic period settlement as revealed by historic documents. It is a synthesis of a book-length county history (Smith 1999) that emerged as a result of the development of a historic context for Fort Polk (see Chapter 8). In the county history the reader was warned that the people of Vernon Parish, especially those settling within modern Fort Polk, left few written records of their lives. Further, like those of many rural southern counties, Vernon Parish courthouse records are decidedly incomplete and spotty. There are precious few sources about the Fort Polk region that professional historians would label primary. Thus that history and, by extension, this synthesis have been compiled using a mix of regional histories written by professionals, local histories written by avocational historians, oral histories and traditions gathered and copied down by native sons and daughters, newspaper clippings, and census records. As a further warning it is noted that the history herein is best seen as raw data for the historic context presented in the following chapter. It is history by an archaeologist, viewed through an archaeological eye (Eiseley 1971). That is, it is decidedly focused on the changing landscape and the details of that landscape, rather than broad social history.

Exploration and Settlement to 1821

The names of the first white explorers of Vernon Parish and the Fort Polk region will always remain lost to history. It is probable that the first European to set foot in what is now Vernon Parish was a French hunter-trader from Los Adaes, Natchitoches, or Post du Rapides, Louisiana. He probably ranged through the area between 1715 and 1725 on a hunting trip. Perhaps he was guided by an Indian or traveled alone along one of the numerous animal-Indian trails that traversed the region. The land would remain a hunting ground for a long time. Throughout approximately 200 years, regional settlement was delayed by the land's isolation from the major river transportation routes and the lack of fertile soils. Another major obstacle to settlement was the political maneuverings of European nations far from Vernon Parish.

With the discovery of the New World, Spain, France, and England began a long struggle for its control that would not end until the nineteenth century. During the sixteenth century, Spain explored and conquered the middle Americas. By the 1520s, they effectively controlled Mexico (Davis 1971:27). This gave Spain a foothold for expansion northward. Perhaps Spanish exploration of Louisiana began with Hernando de Soto's entrada during the early 1540s. The de Soto expedition landed in Tampa Bay, Florida, and embarked on a long exploration into the Southeast wilderness, eventually crossing the Mississippi River. Whether it entered the future state of Louisiana is a fiercely debated topic (Jeter et al. 1989:250). Some believe that the expedition led by Moscoso, de Soto's successor after his death, traversed northern Louisiana and passed into east Texas, reaching an area near modern Nacogdoches and Jefferson, Texas (Chipman 1992:40–41; Jeter et al. 1989:251); others (Hudson 1985) place the westward push by the de Soto expedition to the north of this route, bypassing Louisiana.

After considerable interest in exploring the North American continent in the early sixteenth century, there was a long pause before any European powers returned to the Louisiana region. Spain concentrated on the development of New Spain in Mexico. Its slow expansion north into Texas was led by "adventurers, prospectors, ranchers, friars, and soldiers" (Chipman 1992:43).

Meanwhile, the French settled in Canada. Their expansion into the interior was also led by the church but was driven just as passionately by the fur trade. In 1682, Robert de La Salle traveled down the Mississippi and found its mouth at the Gulf. He claimed the land for the French government, naming it Louisiana after his king, Louis XIV. La Salle returned two years later by ship and tried to find the Mississippi's mouth from the Gulf of Mexico. He missed it, however, and his expedition landed along the Texas coast. The Spanish naturally saw this French incursion into the Gulf as a threat, and they feared further intrusions. Their fears were well grounded since La Salle's goal was to establish a post at the Mississippi and split the Spanish settlements in Florida from those in Mexico (Jeter et al. 1989:251). This was accomplished in 1699 when Pierre Le Moyne, Sieur d'Iberville, found the mouth of the Mississippi and established Fort Maurepas (Davis 1959:30).

From this time until 1762, the French and Spanish maneuvered to determine the borderline between their possessions in the south-central part of America. Beginning in 1689 and continuing until around 1768, the Spanish launched a series of expeditions into Texas. The goals of later forays were to establish missions with the Tejas (Texas) Indians and also to maintain Spain's claim to Texas. These expeditions followed long-established Native American trade routes (Foster 1995). The main trail led all the way across Texas to a Natchitoches Indian settlement along the Red River (Figure 7.1). After serving the Spanish and Indians for hundreds of years as the Camino Real, or King's Highway, this trail would eventually serve as a gateway for the American westward expansion into Texas. During the latter part of the eighteenth century, it would also be a focus of the earliest settlements in northwest Louisiana.

In 1717, along the Camino Real—which today crosses Sabine and Natchitoches Parishes and generally follows Highway 6—the Spanish established the mission San Miguel de Los Adaes at an Adaes Indian village near modern-day Robeline, Louisiana (Chipman 1992:112). But the French had beaten them to the Red River. As early as 1690, French adventurer Henry de Tonti, searching for La Salle, had explored the Red River and found a Natchitoches Indian village near modern-day Natchitoches (Webb and Gregory 1986:19–20). This settlement was located at the river's head of navigation, just south of a great raft of debris and logs that clogged the river to the north. As the Spanish and French fought for control of the land, this site would become a strategic point in the struggle. Here, in 1714, Louis Juchereau de St. Denis founded Fort St. Jean Baptiste aux Natchitos, the first permanent settlement in northern Louisiana (Belisle 1912:39; Jeter et al. 1989:253; Webb and Gregory 1986:22).

The Spanish countered the French threat by founding San Miguel de Los Adaes and then, in 1721, Presidio Nuestra Señora del Pilar de Los Adaes. The latter was a military and government outpost and served the Spanish for most of the eighteenth century (Chipman 1992:123). Los Adaes was only 8 km from the French settlement. With its establishment, the line was drawn between the Spanish and French possessions in the New World. Halfway between the two European settlements was a small, rather unobtrusive stream called the Arroyo Hondo. It soon became an unofficial boundary and would figure prominently in the creation of a neutral zone between the two powers.

St. Denis's response to the Spanish presence was to form an alliance with the local Caddo, offering to buy all their surplus food. Each year, the chiefs of the Caddo were invited to Natchitoches to trade and receive gifts, thus helping to ensure the safety of the rapidly growing French population at the expense of the Spanish (Nardini 1961:32). Meanwhile, some 50 miles downstream of Natchitoches there was a great rapids that for ages had caused Native Americans to stop and portage their canoes. It was a favorite ambush spot and would obviously become another strategic point on the Red River as Europeans moved into northwest Louisiana. In 1723, the French established Post du Rapides at this location (Whittington 1935:30).

No sooner had the French built Post du Rapides than English and French traders arrived. Close behind came the earliest settlers to the land that would

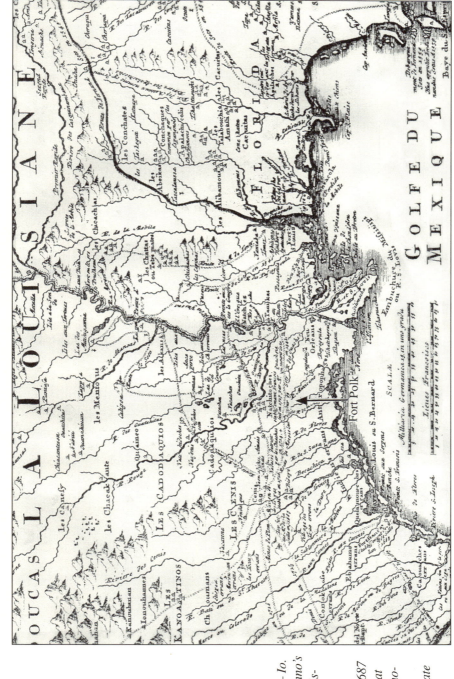

Figure 7.1 — Io. Bapt. Homanno's map of Mississippi and province of Louisiana, 1687 (map on file at the Hill Memorial Library, Louisiana State University).

eventually be divided into Natchitoches, Sabine, and Rapides Parishes (Vernon Parish was formed in 1871 from parts of these; see below). A 1722 census of Natchitoches indicated that 14 men, 10 women, 10 children, 20 Negro slaves, and 8 Indian slaves were already living there (Ditchy 1930:210). These people and the many who soon followed during the early eighteenth century probably ventured west to hunt and fish, and they eventually visited the Vernon Parish region.

Officially, through the first half of the eighteenth century, the Spanish at Los Adaes and the French in Natchitoches were enemies facing off along the Arroyo Hondo. Unofficially, both sides saw the need for mutual support and trade. For mutual survival, a tense truce was established between the two settlements. French and illicit traders supplied the Spanish with food (maize and beans), medicine, firearms, tobacco, liquor, and Indian trade items. The Spanish provided horses, cattle, and Indian slaves (Bolton 1962:39; Jeter et al. 1989:253; Webb and Gregory 1986:23).

Unlike the Spanish at Los Adaes, the French settling at Natchitoches profited from a shorter supply line that included a series of settlements established shortly after Louisiana was claimed. By 1714, when Natchitoches was founded, three small French settlements already existed at Fort St. Louis de la Mobile, Fort Maurepas, and Fort de la Boulaye. These settlements were inhabited by some two hundred people, and more were on their way. Between 1717 and 1731, new settlements were founded under the Company of the Indies, including New Orleans in 1721. Relatively speaking, French settlement was on firm, if not solid, footing, but French fortunes changed during the eighteenth century. It became evident that Louisiana was costing France far more than it was returning (Chipman 1992:172). The 1750s brought more conflict with the English. By 1760, it was clear the French would soon lose both their Canadian base and the Louisiana colony. Since they were about to lose Louisiana anyway, the French signed the secret Treaty of Fontainbleu in 1762, transferring the vast territory west of the Mississippi to Spain (Davis 1971:70).

The Louisiana acquisition was not necessarily a welcome development in Spain or in northwest Louisiana. Though the French were gone, Spain was left to contend with the English, who had gained all the French land east of the Mississippi. However, there was one bright spot. Since the Spanish were now in possession of the Gulf region, they no longer needed the economically draining posts in east Texas and Louisiana, including the presidio at Los Adaes (Faulk 1964:15). Spanish settlers in the area around the Adaes post were ordered to leave for San Antonio so as to consolidate and strengthen the Spanish position there. Many chose to flee to Natchitoches instead (Bolton 1962:114; Nardini 1961:76).

In northwest Louisiana throughout the latter part of the eighteenth century, English and colonial traders and settlers continued to arrive in the Natchitoches–Post du Rapides area thanks to the liberal policies of Spanish Governor Carondelet (Whittington 1935:34). In fact, as friction increased between the Spanish and the English and between the English and the colonists, the Spanish government in Louisiana looked more favorably toward the American immigrants. During the American Revolution, Louisiana's Spanish governor, Bernardo Galvez, called for support in attacking the English at Fort Butte, Baton Rouge, and Natchez. The population around Rapides was large enough to form a local militia that served under the Spanish in this campaign (Whittington 1935:31).

Overall, settlement within the modern boundaries of Natchitoches, Sabine, Rapides, and Vernon Parishes prior to the turn of the century was strung along the Red River and the Camino Real. Clusters of settlements could be found around the rapids on the Red River, at Natchitoches and nearby along Bayou Rio Hondo, and at Los Adaes. By 1799, the population of the district had increased to 3,000 whites and 2,000 slaves (Whittington 1935:37). The great increase reported in 1799 was due not only to Spain's liberal settlement policies but also to the monumental political changes that had occurred east of Louisiana. First, Americans had defeated the British in the Revolution, and the English influence in the west was gone. A steady migration began into America's heartland. Second, in 1795, Spain and the United States signed the Treaty of San Lorenzo. Spain's boundary with the new nation, except that of West Florida, was pushed west of the Mississippi (Haggard 1945a:1015). Third, Spain gave up her claim to the Mississippi River, opening the floodgate for Americans pushing west and opening the door for trade in New Orleans. The momentum of this migration carried into Louisiana, spilling additional settlers into the Red River area.

It was in this political and social setting that in 1797 Juan Baptiste D'Artigeau, the first recorded landowner in the Vernon Parish region, was deeded one square league on the Anacoco Prairie by Don Antonio Gilly Barbo, the Spanish commandant at Nacogdoches. He was joined by John Baptiste Lecomte that same year and Ambroise Lecomte in 1808. Although they were the first recorded occupants, it would seem likely that D'Artigeau had a few neighbors within 20 miles at this time, especially to the northeast. Still, documentary support for this supposition is scant. An 1805 census of Spanish claims indicated only 28 families living between the Sabine and the Arroyo Hondo (Haggard 1945a:1050–1051), an area north of Vernon Parish. Most likely none of these people lived in the Fort Polk region.

Many of the earliest arrivals to the Red River–northwest Louisiana region did not turn to the soil to make a living. Instead they were full-time traders, either dealing with the Native Americans or acting as middlemen between the French and Spanish. Though the Spanish either averted their eyes or only halfheartedly attempted to control American settlement and trade in Louisiana, they were more adamant that Protestant American settlers not infiltrate Catholic Texas. In the 1790s, Spanish authorities placed a permanent detachment of troops in Nacogdoches to keep out American immigrants and required all visitors to have valid passports (Chipman 1992:209–210). They also enlisted the aid of local landowners, including Ambroise Lecomte. Because the road from Alexandria to Nacogdoches cut through Lecomte's land, one stipulation of his land grant was that he arrest anyone passing through without a passport (Wise 1971:4).

THE NEUTRAL GROUND

At the turn of the nineteenth century, political events far from Vernon Parish continued to affect the local cultural landscape. In Europe, revolution had changed the fortunes of France and Spain, and they had gone to war between 1793 and 1795. As Napoleon rose in power, Spain was in no position to hold its North American possessions against the threats from both France and the United States. By 1800, Napoleon was positioned to expand his empire, and Spain was pressured into signing the second Treaty of San Ildefonso, giving Louisiana back to France (Chipman 1992:223; Davis 1971:128; Hofstadter et al. 1967:206). Napoleon originally saw Louisiana as a breadbasket for his possessions in the West Indies and as a part of his envisioned New World empire. However, faced with problems on the continent, Napoleon decided to forgo his overseas ambitions and concentrate on the conquest of Europe. Consequently, in 1803, France sold Louisiana to the United States for $15 million (Hofstadter et al. 1967:207; Morris 1965:132).

The money for Louisiana was well spent, but exactly what the United States had purchased was unclear. When Spain gave the land back to France, the wording of the treaty did not precisely delineate Louisiana's western borders. Not even the United States truly understood the extent of the new purchase. For this reason, President Jefferson planned and sponsored expeditions into the area, including those of Lewis and Clark (1804–1806), Dunbar and Hunter (1804), and Freeman and Custis (1806). The latter two expeditions planned to use the Red River as their route into the interior. However, Dunbar and Hunter never ventured out of Louisiana because of Spanish threats, and Freeman and Custis were forced to turn back when confronted by Spanish soldiers (Chipman 1992:224). By 1806, at both the international and local levels, tensions were running high between the Americans and the Spanish.

As the two nations bickered, intrepid Anglo settlers continued up the Red River, along the Camino Real, and into Texas. Spanish officials, both on the scene and in Mexico, could not agree on exactly what to do about these people. Some wanted to let the settlers enter Texas; others were adamant that they stay out. As the border problem was exacerbated by increasing encroachment, Don Nemesio Salcedo, Commandant General of the Interior Provinces, built up his forces along the Texas-Louisiana frontier to more than 1,200 soldiers (Faulk 1964:124; Haggard 1945a:1029). Salcedo ordered his men to patrol along the Camino Real and as far south as the Calcasieu River. These patrols probably reached into the Vernon Parish area. Alarmed, Major Moses Porter, the American commander at Natchitoches, sent a letter to the commandant of Nacogdoches, Captain Sebastian Rodriguez, requesting the withdrawal of all Spanish troops east of the Sabine. While the request was being forwarded to the Spanish governor, Rodriguez replied to Porter that his troops would stay put and continue to patrol as far east as the Arroyo Hondo. This response provoked the Americans, and, on February 5, 1806, American and Spanish troops faced off across the Camino Real at Juan Mora's Lagoon, about three miles east of Los Adaes. After the two sides exchanged insults, the Spanish officer in charge eventually began a slow retreat west to the Sabine, followed closely by the Americans (Haggard 1945a:1032).

Though excitement was high on the northwest Louisiana frontier, cooler heads prevailed. General Wilkinson, commander of the United States troops in Louisiana, offered to withdraw all soldiers east of the Arroyo Hondo if the Spanish would pull back west of the Sabine. The Spanish, realizing they would lose in any exchange of gunfire, quickly agreed, and a buffer zone or "Neutral Ground" between the two was established. This agreement, never actually formalized between the two countries, would hold for some 15 years and affect the course of settlement in the Vernon Parish region during the early antebellum period (Chipman 1992:224).

Where exactly was the Neutral Ground? Since it was never officially recognized by either country there is no exact answer. The Sabine was a clear and logical western border, and it was logical for the two sides to agree on the Arroyo Hondo as an eastern border because the land along it was well settled and well known. However, the Arroyo Hondo runs east into the Red River, not south to the Gulf. South of the Arroyo Hondo the land was practically unexplored and had no clear natural landmarks like the Sabine. Eventually, both the Spanish and the Americans accepted the Neutral Ground as "all the tract of country lying east of the Sabine and west of the Culeashue, Bayou Kisachey, the branch of the Red River, called Old river, from the Kisachey up to the mouth of Bayou Don Manuel, southwest of Bayou Don

Manuel, Lake Terre Noir, and Aroyo Hondo, and south of the Red River, to
the northwestern boundary of the State of Louisiana" (Crawford 1825:90).
The southern boundary was the Gulf of Mexico (Haggard 1945a:1045–1047).

This 40-mile-wide neutral strip, which included Fort Polk, was a land
apart. With no government, neither Spanish nor Americans could legally
settle there. Soon, into the Free State of the Sabine, as it was sometimes
called, "came the refuse of both Texas and Louisiana—criminals, robbers,
and smugglers—who raided and robbed in both provinces" (Faulk 1964:125).
Despite this "refuse," traders continued to cross the land and squatters quietly settled along streams and trails. Both continually demanded that their
governments do something to control the thieves. The traders were especially vocal as they were usually the targets of robbers. In addition to this
human mix, fugitive slaves hid in the region, and filibusters used the strip as
a base to launch expeditions into Texas.

During the period from 1806 until 1821, there were two kinds of settlers: those with legal claims to their lands, granted by the Spanish prior to
the establishment of the Neutral Ground, and squatters. The legal settlers
numbered around 251 and later reclaimed their land in American courts
(Crawford 1825; Haggard 1945a:1053). None settled in the Fort Polk area
as far as can be determined. Squatters were a curious breed. Some had been
thrown out of Texas after the failure of the filibuster expeditions or were
wanted as lawbreakers. Others were simply pioneers seeking free land. They
were universally poor and, it would appear, universally disliked by "respect-
able" persons. In 1806, for instance, the Bishop of New Leon described
them as follows: "Many Englishmen and Americans are living near the boundary line. They live without a ruler and without laws; they become frightened
like wild beasts when they see other human beings. They live in concubi-
nage and incestuous unions; they carry on illicit trade with the wild tribes. I
saw them with my own eyes. Many other horrible conditions exist, which I
prefer to leave unwritten" (quoted in Haggard 1945a:1051).

It is possible, but not likely, that a few squatter families settled in the
Fort Polk region at this time. If so, their habitations will probably never be
confirmed, for they were unlikely to leave any records and they would leave
few artifacts. To date no archaeological evidence of their presence exists.
The first census of the Territory of Orleans (Louisiana) in 1810, which included nearby Rapides County, counted 2,200 whites, of which "a few found
their way into the western part of the parish in the hammocks and along the
banks of the Calcasieu River" (Davis 1971:66; Whittington 1935:61). Still,
settlers might have been only a few miles away, for it was at this time that
the settlement of Hineston, just east of modern-day Fort Polk, is said to have
begun with the arrival of the Golemon family (Hardin 1939:429; Marler

1994:16). Within the borders of modern Vernon Parish, it is likely that squatters with hopes of farming settled along Bayou Anacoco and the Calcasieu River, where some fertile soils could be found, not the Fort Polk area.

Obviously, with at least 251 families and probably more living within the Neutral Ground, this border zone was hardly an effective barrier between the two nations. Furthermore, traders, both legal and illegal, traveled through the Neutral Ground along the Camino Real, Nolan's Trace, and other trails leading off the main thoroughfares.

One of the largest government-sanctioned trading enterprises was the House of Barr and Davenport. Organized in 1798 by Luther Smith, Edward Murphy (who started trading at Rapides), William Barr, and Peter Samuel Davenport, it was the main agency for Spanish trade across the Neutral Ground until 1812 (Haggard 1945b:66). Smith and Murphy operated from the Louisiana side, while Barr and Davenport operated from company headquarters at Nacogdoches (Faulk 1964:97). They mainly transported furs, pelts, livestock, and occasionally horses to Louisiana to exchange for various merchandise to ship back to Texas. One of the House of Barr's biggest competitors for Native American support was John Sibley, United States Indian Agent at Natchitoches. It was Sibley who, through Indian informants, discovered in 1806 that a detachment of Spanish troops had crossed the Sabine. He contacted the military at Natchitoches, initiating a crisis that led to the formation of the Neutral Ground (Nardini 1961:80). Sibley so successfully influenced the Indians toward the United States that the Spanish formally protested to the Spanish consul in New Orleans (Faulk 1964:68).

Settlers, traders, and Native Americans in the Neutral Ground were not alone. Fugitive slaves saw the Neutral Ground as a place of refuge and an opportunity to cross into Texas to gain freedom as Spanish citizens. Although slavery was practiced in Texas (Faulk 1964:96), a 1789 law guaranteed freedom to foreign slaves who entered the territory. When Louisiana was sold to the United States, the Spanish considered issuing a similar proclamation of freedom if the Americans made any hostile moves toward Texas (Haggard 1945a:1071). Slaves knew about this opportunity anyway, and many attempted to escape west. They would usually flee in groups and make their way across the Neutral Ground to Nacogdoches. There they would present themselves to Spanish authorities.

Traders, settlers, and both governments were harassed by the bandits and outlaws who moved into the Neutral Ground almost immediately after the two nations created the zone. Some of the bandits were organized into sizable gangs. For instance, one Jose Zepeda and his three hands were overcome by a larger party of bandits in 1811 (Haggard 1945a:1064). Don Apolinar Masmela and a detachment of 11 soldiers and 15 settlers were attacked in 1812. A year earlier, a party of 17 Spanish had been attacked on the Sabine by some 30 renegade Americans. In a separate incident, 30 or more brigands attacked traders along Bayou Pierre (Haggard 1945a:1064–1065). Outlaws became so numerous that, in 1810, American and Spanish forces cooperated in a joint operation, sweeping the Neutral Ground, burning homes, and moving out squatters (Haggard 1945a:1062–1063). Whether these forces went as far south as the Vernon Parish region is not known, but evidence indicates that they did pass down the Sabine to Bayou Toro (Haggard 1945a:1063, n. 63). Even after these efforts, Samuel Davenport of Barr and Davenport wrote, "The Neutral Ground is still infested by gangs of bandits" (in Haggard 1945b:78). It would continue to be so even after the land was granted to the United States.

The Neutral Ground also offered an excellent staging and recruiting area for private armies, collectively called filibusters, attempting to take Texas. Besides facing the exterior threat of the Americans, Spanish royalists had internal difficulties keeping revolutionary influences from creating discord. Don José Bernardo Gutiérrez de Lara, a revolutionary from northern Mexico, and others had staged unsuccessful revolts prior to the formation of the buffer zone. Gutiérrez met Irishman Augustus William Magee, and together they began recruiting an army made up largely of Neutral Ground desperadoes, who were offered $40 a month to join the expedition (Henderson 1951:44). The recruits, calling themselves the Republican Army of the North, gathered in camps in Natchitoches and Rapides and at a camp along the Sabine. They eventually formed a little army of about 130 men. In August 1812, they crossed the Sabine and attacked and captured Nacogdoches, Texas, where they recruited an additional 190 Mexicans, Indians, and other "disreputable characters from the Neutral Ground" (Faulk 1964:135). Gutiérrez's army marched deeper into Texas, winning battles at La Bahia and Salado Creek and capturing San Antonio. Meanwhile, the seeds of its own destruction were being sown within the band. Magee died mysteriously, and then Gutiérrez was replaced by José Alvarez de Toledo (Chipman 1992:236; Haggard 1945a:1055). Then, at Medina River in August 1813, the rebellion was crushed by the Spanish. Approximately 1,000 men in Toledo's mob were killed in the battle (Chipman 1992:237; Henderson 1951:59–61). Toledo retreated to Nacogdoches and, with some 300 men, women, and children, fled back into the Neutral Ground. Many of these survivors settled temporarily around Bayou Pierre (Haggard 1945a:1055).

The Gutiérrez-Magee Republican Army of the North was not the only filibuster group to use the Neutral Ground. Ex-French officer and adventurer Jean Joseph Amable Humbert soon recruited the vengeful survivors of the Gutiérrez-Magee expedition and crossed the Sabine for another attempt at Texas. Once there, however, the cause died for lack of funds, and the mob of discontents returned to the Neutral Ground. Five years later, yet another adventurer, John Long, arrived in Natchitoches, crossed the Neutral Ground again, and at Nacogdoches on June 23, 1819, declared Texas an independent republic. As his government was being formed, recruits poured across the Neutral Ground into Texas. But this mini-revolution also fell apart. Long drifted west to Mexico and was later killed by a soldier in Mexico City (Faulk 1964:139).

Although Long's motive for revolution was probably personal glory, he was spurred to action by the 1819 Transcontinental Treaty (Adams-Onis Treaty) between Spain and the United States. The treaty recognized Spain's claim to Texas (the United States acquired West Florida) and set the eastern Texas border at the Sabine and Red Rivers (Morris 1965:157). Two years later, when the treaty was finally ratified, Mexico declared its independence from Spain. Texas then became a Mexican problem.

Antebellum West-Central Louisiana

The ratification of the Adams-Onis Treaty in 1821 initiated legitimate Anglo-American settlement in the Fort Polk region. But the treaty did not initiate anything like what could be called a land rush and the population remained low throughout the early antebellum. Western Louisiana also remained isolated; roads were mere primitive trails. The Sabine River was an unreliable route for migration and commerce because of its logjams and shallowness during much of the year. There was a small population gain between 1826 and 1828 as a result of a combination of economic and natural crises along the Red River. That region was hit with floods, falling cotton prices, and a yellow fever epidemic in a matter of a few years (Whittington 1935:65–66). These misfortunes forced many foreclosures in Rapides Parish. Bankrupt farmers and plantation owners moved west into the pinelands or on to Texas, where they began new lives. But, while settlement along the Red River and its tributaries, like Bayou Rapides, Bayou Boeuf, and Bayou Robert, experienced "a veritable boom in immigration of farmers" during the early antebellum (Whittington 1935:65), sustained growth and settlement in the Vernon Parish area did not begin until the 1830s. Texas independence in 1836 helped significantly (Cantley and Kern 1984:42). Still, some 20 years later in 1860, the combined total population of Natchitoches, Sabine, and Rapides Parishes had reached only 47,885. Considering that population was concentrated along the Red River, the western pinelands were indeed sparsely settled. In fact, an estimate of between 2,500 and 3,000 is reasonable for the number of people living in the Vernon Parish region by the time of the Civil War (Smith 1999:47). Few of these lived within modern Fort Polk boundaries. While the exact number is impossible to know, certainly less than 700 were living there in 1860 (Smith 1999:47–48).

STOCKMAN-FARMERS, HUNTER-SQUATTERS

Subsistence farming was the principal occupation of the residents. These self-sufficient antebellum pioneers descended from a long-established line of stockman-farmers and hunter-squatters. The majority of those settling in the Vernon Parish region during the antebellum period were from the lower southern tier of states: eastern Louisiana, Alabama, Mississippi, Georgia, and South Carolina. In fact, most were from Louisiana. As early as 1850, 65.5 percent of the white population of Rapides Parish and 63.8 percent of the white population of Natchitoches Parish were native-born Louisianans (Hackett 1973:333). In Sabine Parish, 42 percent of the white population were born in Louisiana. Locally, in the Fort Polk region, Louisiana natives were an even higher percentage. By 1870, all 776 people living in the Rapides Parish western division (encompassing Fort Polk) were born in the United States, and 76 percent of them were born in Louisiana. White Anglo-Americans were the only ethnic group visible on this landscape. The 1870 population census indicates that only 13 African Americans were living in the western division of Rapides Parish.

The region's inhabitants were almost exclusively hunters, gatherers, and agriculturalists. Industrial development in the region was nonexistent, but one critical pioneer industry that was a necessity was the local mill. Mills were not only essential for grinding corn, but they also provided a meeting place to exchange news and stories. Mills became centers of community interaction. Early mills in Vernon Parish are difficult to locate and date exactly. One would think there would be one or two on every usable stream in the region. Census data, however, do not reflect this. According to the 1840 census, Natchitoches Parish had only 10 gristmills and 12 sawmills, while Rapides had no gristmills and only 9 sawmills. These numbers seem low, considering their importance. At any rate, the antebellum mills of Vernon Parish were likely small affairs in which an undershot wheel provided power to a set of belts that could turn either a grindstone or a saw, depending on need. Within or near Fort Polk, Clemmie Haymon built a mill on Birds Creek during the antebellum, as did Jim McMacallan on the Whiskey Chitto "a few miles north of Pitkin" (Foster 1976; Williams 1976:2). McMacallan's mill processed three products: corn, cotton, and wood. There might have also been a mill run by the Golemon family about this time on Little Six Mile about "7 miles NE of Fullerton" and still another called Weeks Mill "five miles SE of Walnut Hill" (Anonymous n.d.a). Finally, three miles south of the community of Providence on Bundick Creek, John Davis is said to have built a gristmill prior to the Civil War (Pool 1992:6).

Antebellum census data are also vague about other types of commercial development in west-central Louisiana. In 1840, Natchitoches Parish is noted as having only 49 retail stores and Rapides Parish only 25. Only 60 people were working in "commerce" in Natchitoches and 181 in manufacturing. In Rapides Parish at this same time, 22 people were employed in commerce and 193 in manufacturing. Census categories included bootmakers, brick makers, carpenters, wagon and carriage makers, saddle makers, coopers, blacksmiths, tanners, and other trades. It is important to note that most of these craftsmen would have had their establishments in the more populous Red River towns. In 1860, just prior to the Civil War, Sabine Parish had only five blacksmiths, one bootmaker, one leather shop, and one wagon establishment. Interestingly, at this time, Natchitoches had 34 people engaged in engineering and Rapides had 36. Overall, the census data point to a pioneer community in which individuals were heavily reliant on themselves and their immediate neighbors for most needs.

EARLY HAMLETS

As people began moving into the Vernon Parish region after the Neutral Ground issue was settled, most built small, subsistence-level farms consisting of a log house and perhaps a shed along some high ground near a creek, such as the Whiskey Chitto or the Anacoco. Eventually, some of these farmsteads grew into clusters of buildings housing several families, who were often related. Along the better and more-used trails, some of these homesteads soon expanded to include a store or mill, a ferry, or other small enterprises. These clusters of development within the pinelands eventually came to be identified with local prominent families or land features and were Vernon Parish's first hamlets and villages. Near Fort Polk, the most interesting of these little hamlets was Huddleston, probably Vernon Parish's first village. The site of Huddleston, originally called Petersburg, was just outside Fort Polk's main gate near modern St. Petersburg Church. It was first named for early settler Peter Eddleman, who may have settled there as early as the 1830s (Frazar 1933:20; O'Halloran 1951–1952:3/27/1952). A mail route was established from Lake Charles to Petersburg in 1841 (Wise 1971:48). However, Huddleston was not a post office until January 1847 (Post Office Department 1973), when Isaac Huddleston was appointed postmaster. Huddleston was the largest antebellum settlement in the Fort Polk region and Vernon Parish prior to the Civil War. By 1860 it had "several mercantile establishments, those of Hatch, Robinson & Co., J. P. Ettleman & Co. being among them" (Pritchard 1938:1159–1160). During the Civil War, Huddleston was a supply depot for Confederate troops passing through from Texas.

Another antebellum hamlet within or near Fort Polk was Liberty Creek. The exact location is not known, but it is assumed that it was near Liberty Creek, a small stream in the fort's northwest corner. It was once described as 65 miles from Alexandria, or 23 miles west of Hineston and 10 miles east of Huddleston (Pritchard 1938:1159–1160). This would place it near the present-day 8W-7W township line approximately along Liberty Creek. A post office was established there in October 1853 (Post Office Department 1973).

Serving the northern Fort Polk region was Walnut Hill, located just north of the Main Fort. The earliest settlers in the area were the Groves and Dail families, who one reference claims settled there as early as 1810 (Wise 1971:53). Walnut Hill had an inn and a store (Cupit 1963:29). A prominent landmark in the region, the inn became a polling place before 1840 (Whittington 1935:68). It was called Burton's Tavern or Stage Stand Hill (Wise 1971:53) and was owned by two men named Hawkins and Burton (Curry Ford in Hadnot n.d.b).

Although east of Fort Polk, Hineston, where the Golemon family were the prominent setters (Marler 1994:16), played an important role in the region's early development. Located just outside the Neutral Ground, Hineston was the last settlement before crossing the Calcasieu into no-man's land. By the 1820s, Hineston was the largest settlement on Rapides Parish's western frontier. It is depicted on most Civil War period maps. As it was at the junction of the Alexandria–to–Burr's Ferry road and the Opelousas-to-Natchitoches road, it also played a role as a Confederate campsite and depot.

From Hineston, the stage and post road followed the hills and dales to Walnut Creek, Huddleston, and then west to the Sabine River. At the Sabine was Burr's Ferry. Although far to the west of Fort Polk, it was nevertheless influential in Fort Polk's development. Burr's Ferry was the last stop before one entered Texas. Settlers arrived at Burr's Ferry, or Burr Ferry, as early as 1805, but Dr. Timothy Burr did not establish a ferry until around 1827 (Wise 1971:47). Burr built a plantation at Burr's Ferry, which included a gristmill, sawmill, and cotton gin. It is possible Burr built the ferry to transport his slaves back and forth from his plantation to his fields across the Sabine.

In the Peason Ridge region of modern Fort Polk, the hamlet of Kisatchie was situated immediately east of the installation. Of the hamlets mentioned herein, Kisatchie developed rather late. Scoggins (1961:4) claims the Dowdens settled there as early as 1818, but Kadlecek and Bullard (1994:175) place the first settlers as late as 1843. By 1848, Kisatchie had a school. A postal stop was established in the hamlet in 1854, discontinued in 1867, and reestablished in the 1870s.

FRONTIER SOCIETAL DEVELOPMENT

Within the context of communities and hamlets, churches and schools played an important role in community identity. Asked where they were from by an outsider, nineteenth- and early-twentieth-century rural people would most likely identify a nearby village or creek as their home. But within the local region, church affiliation was the primary means of community identification (Smith et al. 1982). On a frontier like Vernon Parish, churches were built and church communities established before there were hamlets and villages. A hamlet may have included a church or may have developed as a result of a church having been built first; but just as often a church would stand alone in the country, drawing the faithful from miles around. The first to spread the gospel in the region were circuit-riding ministers who were welcomed into the pioneer home as much for any news as for the "good news" they preached. As churches developed, these circuit riders would travel from congregation to congregation serving many needs within a large rural area. The most famous of such men in west-central Louisiana was the Baptist missionary Joseph Willis. He probably entered the area for the first time between 1813 and 1820 (Paxton 1888:143–144). Toward the end of his life, he settled along Ten Mile Creek. Willis, a mulatto, was active until his death in 1854. He was buried at Occupy Cemetery. Occupy Church No. 2 is today located four or five miles southeast of the Main Fort.

Census information provides insights into the religious mix on the Rapides and Sabine frontier during the antebellum period. In 1850, Rapides had two Baptist, two Christian, one Roman Catholic, and six Methodist churches. Sabine had four Baptist, one Roman Catholic, and eleven Methodist churches. Natchitoches had two Baptist, one Episcopal, one Free, four Methodist, and five Roman Catholic churches. Because Roman Catholicism was the predominant religion of the French and Spanish, the census indirectly supports Hackett's (1973) study, which indicated that Natchitoches still had a large French and Spanish ethnic mix during the early antebellum period, while both the Sabine and the Rapides Parish populations were largely Anglo-Americans.

However, by the Civil War, Anglo-Americans dominated the whole region. By the 1860s, the Rapides population supported one Baptist, one Christian, three Episcopal, eleven Methodist, and four Roman Catholic churches; Sabine's faithful attended nine Baptist, one Roman Catholic, and four Methodist churches; and Natchitoches believers attended six Baptist, one Episcopal, eight Methodist, and four Roman Catholic churches. The population statistics for Sabine Parish probably best represent the people living where Vernon Parish was to be established. Local historical sources indicate that these people were primarily Baptist and Methodist.

Schools were also established very early in the antebellum pinelands of Vernon Parish. Often a single building served as both church and school. Most children were educated at home during the early nineteenth century, but as soon as enough settlers arrived in an area, the community would gather together in a concerted effort to build a school and find a teacher. Funds to operate the earliest schools and pay teachers' salaries were derived from private tuition (Belisle 1912:166). With the formation of parishes, public schools were opened, although private schools continued to operate. Public schools were funded through the police juries.

Census figures indicate that in 1850, Rapides Parish operated 28 public schools, with as many teachers instructing 980 students. Sabine operated 33 schools with 33 teachers and 1,051 students. Natchitoches, interestingly, had only one school, one teacher, and 35 students. Information provided by parents to census takers indicated that 519, 783, and 705 children in Rapides, Sabine, and Natchitoches Parishes, respectively, were attending school. The difference between the two attendance figures may be attributed to children only attending public school part time.

Education was taken seriously—sometimes too seriously. One of the famous stories of disorder in the Fort Polk area describes the Rawhide Fight, traditionally dated to 1850 (Ford in Hadnot n.d.b). According to legend, the local community in and around Walnut Hill decided to build a schoolhouse. By the time a teacher was hired, the community was in high spirits over the new undertaking. Mysteriously, though, the school burned down before classes began. Two factions soon developed over who started the fire. A meeting was arranged—guns checked at the door—in an attempt to settle the issue. The meeting had the exact opposite effect of that desired.

Despite conflicting versions of the story, it is believed that the meeting was held either at the home of James Groves, a prominent Walnut Hill resident, or at Burton's Tavern (Cupit and Hadnot n.d.; Ford 1955; Wise 1971:54). Speeches on both sides apparently became more and more heated. Eventually a knife fight broke out and knives were soon replaced by clubs. The fight ended in the deaths of six men. The dead were laid out on dry rawhides, and from this the fight derived its name.

The Civil War and Reconstruction

Although no battles took place within modern Vernon Parish or Fort Polk, the Civil War brought upheaval and danger to the area, as it did all across the South. The Red River plantation owners risked losing their property and culture. In western Rapides and Sabine Parishes, few farmers owned slaves or had large landholdings to protect. These self-sufficient hunter-stockmen just wanted to be left alone. In the crucial 1860 election, more than 59 percent of voters in Sabine, Rapides, and Natchitoches Parishes supported the proslavery candidate Breckenridge (Cantley and Kern 1984:48). But in January 1861, three-fifths of Sabine Parish and more than half of Natchitoches Parish voters opposed secession. In Rapides Parish, where most of the large plantations were located, more than three-fifths of the population voted for secession (Cantley and Kern 1984:48).

Once the secession issue was decided, western Louisiana men answered the call to arms. Those who joined the Confederacy probably did so not because of the slavery issue, but so as "not to submit their destinies into the hands of a hostile Government," as was proclaimed in a series of resolutions at a public meeting in Alexandria on December 26, 1860 (Whittington 1935:139). Rapides Parish men eventually formed some 18 companies, most of which were absorbed into the Confederate army, and the men were sent to fight and die far from home (Bergeron 1989). Some of the most ardent secessionists in the parish's western frontier probably traveled to Alexandria or Cheneyville at first call and were marched to major muster grounds like Baton Rouge. Among those from the Fort Polk area who joined the Red River Rebels, for instance, were J. P. Groves, W. W. Goynes, J. M. Cavanaugh, and W. F. Roberts from Liberty Creek, and J. R. Miller, Z. R. Speights, J. Amons, Thomas Bonnette, J. W. Bush, and E. V. Cain from Huddleston (Hadnot n.d.a). Other volunteers in western Rapides and southwestern Sabine Parishes formed their own company called the Anacoco Rangers, which later became Company K of the Nineteenth Louisiana Infantry. Led by William W. Smart and later by John W. Jones, the company was shipped east to fight in campaigns in Tennessee, Alabama, and Georgia (Bergeron 1989:121–122).

Those from the Fort Polk area who had not joined at the war's start probably later joined the Calcasieu Rangers. This cavalry unit, under the command of Captain William Ivey, was organized in the fall of 1863. In 1864, it was officially mustered into Confederate service at Hineston and was used to patrol the local region for deserters and jayhawkers.

As young men joined the Confederacy's ranks, their farms were left to the older men, women, and children to manage. Women also volunteered to work in aid societies to make uniforms, cartridges, and food packages. If the region was like other Southern rural areas, many isolated farms were abandoned during this time, with the women and children moving to towns where they felt they would be safer. This left their farms to the mercy of the next band of raiders that came along. No doubt, many west Rapides Parish and Sabine Parish farms suffered this fate.

In Alexandria, those who did not join the ranks gathered supplies at a major depot and worked in a meat-packing plant that sent pickled beef to the front lines (Whittington 1935:148). The beef, which came from southwestern Louisiana and Texas, was transported along such trails as the Burr's Ferry–to–Alexandria road across the northern part of Fort Polk and the road that came north from Sugartown to Hineston (Marler 1994:21) east of Fort Polk.

As the war continued, food and other necessities became more scarce. This encouraged a brisk, illegal trade in cotton, which was supposed to be destroyed by Confederate authorities so as not to fall into Union hands. However, the authorities were easy to bribe, and some of this cotton went to Texas, probably along the route to Burr's Ferry through the Fort Polk area.

The Vernon Parish pinelands had little strategic value to either the North or the South, and the people who remained in the area saw no major action. Early in the war, it was relatively quiet around Vernon Parish. However, after the fall of Vicksburg and Port Hudson, Union strategists decided that control of Texas was critical. The best route into the Texas interior appeared to be up the Red River. Also, the presence of all that cotton around Alexandria probably motivated some Union generals to argue loudly for a campaign to capture Shreveport, the capital of Confederate Louisiana, which would, coincidentally, sweep through the cotton area (S. Smith 1986:2–4; J. Winters 1963:317–321). Thus, in the spring of 1864, the Union army, under the command of Major General Nathaniel P. Banks, began to move up the Red River, threatening destruction to Rapides Parish and Alexandria. This brought more military activity within the Fort Polk region, mostly confined to the road from Burr's Ferry to Hineston and the little hamlet of Huddleston.

THE RED RIVER CAMPAIGN

This Union move had long been anticipated by Confederate Major General Richard Taylor. He knew that his army of 6,000 troops, spread throughout north Louisiana and the Red River area from Bayou Teche to Alexandria, would need supplies and reinforcements if he was to stop Banks. He also knew that with regard to forage, the pinelands including the Fort Polk region were "utterly barren" (Taylor 1879:152). He was not alone in making this assessment—another general described the region between the Calcasieu and the Sabine as a "desert" (Walker 1864). Taylor's initial plans were to concentrate his forces around Alexandria, and he proceeded accordingly.

Beginning in late summer, 1863, gray-clad soldiers were seen along the western Rapides roads to Texas as the Confederate army prepared to defend the Red River. First, "works were ordered on the Sabine and the crossings of the upper Red River" (Smith 1864). One of these breastworks was built at

Burr's Ferry (Wise 1971:47). Second, along the roads leading to and from Texas, "depots were established, with small detachments to guard them" (Taylor 1879:152). Burr's Ferry, Huddleston, and Hineston became depots for storing forage, bread stuffs, salt, and corn in preparation for the Texas reinforcements en route to join Taylor's forces at Alexandria (Anderson 1864; Taylor 1864a).

The Union forces' thrust up the Red River was a joint operation of Banks's army and a gunboat flotilla under the command of Rear Admiral David D. Porter, combining some 30,000 troops, 13 gunboats, and 60 other vessels (S. Smith 1986:4). Porter began the campaign on March 12, 1864, entering the Red River at its mouth and capturing Fort De Russey, a Confederate stronghold near Marksville, Louisiana. Taylor abandoned Alexandria, moving his small army to the Carroll Jones plantation about 14 miles north of Hineston, close to the modern Vernon Parish–Rapides Parish line (J. Winters 1963:329). The roads to Alexandria, Burr's Ferry, Natchitoches, and Sabinetown all converged at this plantation. Here Taylor waited for Texas reinforcements commanded by Brigadier General Thomas Green. Porter's forces entered Alexandria around March 16, and Banks entered a few days later.

At Alexandria, Porter and Banks found that the water was too shallow at the rapids for the flotilla to continue northward. As they waited for the water to rise, they collected cotton and recruited more troops from among Union sympathizers and jayhawkers (J. Winters 1963:333).

But Taylor was also gaining strength as troops slowly arrived from Texas. Still, with Banks in Alexandria, Taylor's army was in a precarious position. He needed to keep it between Banks's troops and Shreveport and thus close to the Red River. At the same time, he had to protect the western routes, like the road from Burr's Ferry to Hineston, from which more Texas troops were expected to arrive. Taylor retreated even farther north, eventually to Mansfield. As he did so, Texas reinforcements were ordered to cross the Sabine farther and farther north of the Vernon Parish area. Eventually they crossed as far north as Sabinetown and Logansport (Bee 1864).

Banks moved north in early April, but at Natchitoches he made an error. Thinking the Confederates would not make a stand until he got to Shreveport, he took a well-traveled route toward the town—one that led away from the Red River and Porter's supporting navy and directly into Taylor's waiting army. On April 8 at Mansfield, the Confederates stood their ground and drove back the Union army, which was strung out for some 20 miles along the road (J. Winters 1963:347). Banks reorganized his troops the following day at Pleasant Hill, where both sides sustained heavy losses of around 1,500 men apiece (J. Winters 1963:355). Banks retreated the next day to Grand Ecore, his army diminished and demoralized.

While Taylor's army hounded Banks's retreat along the Red River, Taylor sent Colonel Vincent's Second Louisiana Cavalry on a wide swing south through the pinelands and Vernon Parish to try to "capture and destroy any small bands of the enemy found roving in that region" and to reach Opelousas, located south of Banks's army (Taylor 1864b). Felix Pierre Poche, a staff officer with the Twenty-Eighth Louisiana, got permission to follow them. Poche left a colorful description of the region, depicting the village of Many as "an ugly little town full of pine trees." He described the march down the road from Many, south through the heart of Vernon Parish and passing just west of Fort Polk, as the "most terrible journey that I have ever made in my life," for he was "always in the hideous and monotonous pine forests" (Poche 1972:112–113).

Meanwhile, at Alexandria, in a miraculous effort, the Federals built a dam and floated Porter's fleet over the rapids and continued their retreat back down the Red River (S. Smith 1986). Banks left the town on May 13. Someone—looters, troops, or both—started a series of fires that leveled a large section of the town. Taylor and Banks again met at Norwood's plantation near Yellow Bayou, but Taylor could not hold the retreating Federals (J. Winters 1963:376). This action effectively ended the Union's presence on the Red River and the presence of regular armies near the Vernon Parish region.

Irregulars continued to plague the area, however. In fact, the Union army's arrival along the Red River that spring brought deserters, draft-dodgers, and jayhawkers into the backcountry region and their raiding and plundering increased (Gallien 1968:355). General Taylor and other Confederate commanders made several attempts to route out these miscreants. As early as June 1863, Brigadier General Alfred A. Mouton issued secret orders to sweep the region that included Fort Polk:

> Information has been received that there are bands of outlaws, deserters, conscripts, and stragglers from a point above Hineston . . . in the parish of Rapides, down to the lower parishes extending into Calcasieu, through to the Bayou Teche, which are committing depredations, robberies and incendiarism, and who are openly violating the Confederate laws. . . . Such men can only be considered as outlaws, highwaymen, and traitors. In consequence: You will proceed . . . to scour the whole country . . . in search of these bands [who]. . . . must be exterminated, especially the leaders; and every man found with arms for the purpose of resisting Confederate laws, or against whom satisfactory evidence may be given, must be executed on the spot. No prisoners should be taken [Edmonds 1979:234].

While the results of this sweep are unknown, it is obvious that soon after, the region was once again filled with the same sort of desperadoes. In February 1864, Taylor reported that the same area was again inhabited by "large bodies of deserters and recusant conscripts whom it would require a large cavalry brigade to break up or force into service" (Taylor 1864c). This communication reveals much about the atmosphere in the region at this time. The woods and roads were dangerous for travel, especially for the Confederates. In small camps throughout the area, deserters and jayhawkers, probably mostly local Union sympathizers, were ambushing Confederate couriers and scouts. With Banks's retreat and north Louisiana in Confederate control, the jayhawkers probably went to ground. Colonel Dudley, who operated in western Rapides Parish, for instance, supposedly followed Banks and joined the Union army. The next major influx of Civil War soldiers into the Vernon Parish region would be the survivors returning home.

RECONSTRUCTION IN WEST-CENTRAL LOUISIANA

From 1862, when New Orleans fell, until as late as 1877, when President Hayes withdrew Federal forces, Louisiana was an occupied state (Davis 1971:266). Reconstruction—a word describing a historical period rather than an accomplishment—was a time of confusion, controversy, complexity, and political chaos. Census data show the war's impact on west-central Louisiana just prior to the formation of Vernon Parish. The Rapides plantation economy had been destroyed. Its 105,839 improved acres were reduced to 63,265, and their value dropped from $9 million to $1.5 million. In the pinelands, Sabine's 29,350 acres of improved lands in 1860 had fallen to 16,576 acres, with their value dropping from $414,746 to $223,805. The people, both black and white, were left to deal with a society and economy in total devastation.

Despite evidence from census data, west-central Louisiana was probably not as devastated as other parts of the South, in part because it was comparatively underdeveloped. The area was still full of desperados, and many farms had been destroyed or had fallen into disrepair, but there were still large tracts of virgin land. In many parts of the South and North, soldiers who until the war had never seen the land beyond their county found themselves restless and unable to settle back into home life. There was also a large population of African Americans with new-found freedom. Restlessness and freedom, combined with the passing of the Homestead Act in 1862 (Morrison 1972:2:454), prompted a large migration westward to cheap, available land, beginning during the war's ebb and continuing throughout Reconstruction. Texas was one of the more attractive goals for this migration. Its population increased by 35 percent between 1860 and 1870. To get to

Texas one had to pass through western Louisiana, and many Texas-bound migrants, like their antebellum predecessors, probably continued no farther than the Vernon Parish pinelands. Most of those who did settle in the region were Louisianans who simply moved across the state. As noted earlier, the 1870 Rapides population consisted primarily of Louisiana natives, as did the Natchitoches and Sabine populations. Of those Rapides Parish settlers born out of state, the largest contingent came from Mississippi or Alabama and made up seven percent of the population. Surprisingly, five percent came from Virginia or West Virginia.

The Late-Nineteenth-Century Landscape, 1871–1897

Martha R. Field, a correspondent for the *New Orleans Daily Picayune* under the pen name Catherine Cole, once described the late-nineteenth-century Vernon Parish landscape as the "most magnificent stretch of unbroken pine forest on the continent" (Cole 1892). Relishing the west-central Vernon pineland were its scattered residents, described as "happy and contented," "doing well," in "excellent health," "law abiding and hospitable," and leading "simple, moral, thrifty lives" (Cole 1892; Harris 1881:238–239; see also Poole 1889). Perhaps these sentiments were optimistic given Reconstruction's tumultuous times, the national financial panics of 1873 and 1893, and droughts. Nevertheless, life in Vernon Parish may have been better than life in the rest of the state in the late nineteenth century. Relatively isolated and remote, being on the outskirts of main settlement and development areas, the parish had not been as thoroughly devastated by the Civil War as the rest of the state. Perhaps the people were not as affected by the demoralizing corruption of Louisiana's Reconstruction. Without a substantial local African American population, race relations may not have been as raw and inflamed as they were in the cotton parishes along the Red and Mississippi Rivers. By the time of its formation, Vernon Parish was a forward-looking, optimistic, agrarian community in a relatively peaceful pineland, thriving amid abundant natural resources.

The most abundant of these resources was the pine forest, which was just beginning to be lumbered along the Sabine-Anacoco river system and along the Calcasieu River, Whiskey Chitto, and Bundick Creek drainages. During most of this period, lumbering was a lively cottage industry conducted by farmers and part-time lumbermen. Thus, the forest landscape in 1871 was much as it had been during the early part of the century: "The long-leaf pine forest is mostly open, so that a wagon can frequently traverse it with little more difficulty than the open prairie. The shade of the pine being very light, grasses and other plants requiring sunshine flourish underneath them, thus affording an excellent pasture, which fact has made stock-breeding the earliest industry of this [pine hill] region" (Hilgard 1884:128–129). Across mile after mile, travelers and settlers found postwar Vernon Parish covered with millions of pines reaching 100 to 150 feet in height, with trunks as large as 4 to 5 feet in diameter. The first limbs of these grand timbers were no less than 50 to 60 feet from the ground, creating a vast, canopied park (Maxwell and Baker 1983:5). "Here is a pine forest in all its splendor. It would seem that one could mow the trees down like grain if one just had a scythe big enough" (Cole 1892).

This seemingly unending pine forest running from the Red River uplands across the Sabine and deep into southeastern Texas was only rarely interrupted (Maxwell 1971:109). But one such break was the Anacoco Prairie, which had attracted the D'Artigeaus in the late eighteenth century. During the postwar years this "island of lovely prairie about three miles long by one mile wide" (Cole 1892) attracted even more settlers. The topsoils here were surprisingly fertile, black, and 2 feet deep, unlike the soils of the upland pine forest (Hilgard 1884:129). Other fertile soils were found along the Calcasieu's narrow bottomlands and in the Fort Polk area along the slopes and bottomlands of Whiskey Chitto and Bundick Creeks (Harris 1881:238–239; Hilgard 1884:128). But these small fertile areas were sharply confined to the bottomlands, for in the uplands above the streams around Fort Polk lay the unattractive hogwallow lands—a common epithet for any lands of "little account." Such lands consisted of infertile, sticky clay soils, lacking lime, excessively muddy and thus difficult to till in wet seasons, and easily deteriorated by drought (Hilgard 1884:130; Lockett 1969:47 [1874]). These soils were depleted after only a few years. Cotton grown there was susceptible to rust or blight, and the taproots suffered from the poorly drained subsoil (Hilgard 1884:130). Despite the poor soil, interspersed grassy areas in the pine-covered uplands made stock raising a profitable venture.

Despite the hogwallow lands that made up much of the Fort Polk area, late-nineteenth-century Vernon Parish was an attractive place to settle, especially for Southerners uprooted by the Civil War and restless (Sutherland 1980). And there was plenty of room for everyone. Even as late as 1881, private land was "almost without a price, there being so much vacant public land well adapted to farming upon which immigrants [could] settle without money or price, free from all fear of being disturbed" (Harris 1881:239).

THE FORMATION OF VERNON PARISH
Vernon Parish was formed out of parts of Rapides, Sabine, and Natchitoches Parishes on March 30, 1871. Its boundaries were designated as follows:

Commencing at the mouth of Bayou Toro, upon the Sabine River, thence up said Toro to the township line between three and four, (3 and 4) thence east on said township line to the road known as Bevils (now Hardins) and Natchitoches Road, thence along said road in a northward direction to the township line between four and five (4 and 5) north, thence east on said township line to the Devil Creek, thence down said creek to the range line between four and five (4 and 5) west, thence south on said range line to the parish line of Calcasieu, thence west on said parish line to the Sabine River, thence up the Sabine to the point beginning [Louisiana Historical Records Survey 1939:86–87].

Present-day Fort Polk's Main Fort lies entirely within Vernon Parish, while Peason Ridge straddles the tricorner where Vernon, Sabine, and Natchitoches Parishes meet.

Almost all we know about the formation of Vernon Parish comes from folk tradition. The few facts backed by documentation all revolve around the Smart family. It was John R. Smart who, while serving as a senator from Sabine Parish and on the Sabine Parish Police Jury, introduced the bill creating Vernon Parish (Wise 1971:78). Section 6 of the act creating the parish specified that the parish seat would be on or near Bayou Castor in Section 23, T2N R7W. This was land owned by Dr. Edmund Ellison Smart, son of John R., who had his office there and operated a store with I. O. Winfree (Wise 1971:3–4). The first Vernon Parish Police Jury, which included Dr. Smart as treasurer and Winfree as clerk of court, held its meetings in Smart's office; Smart soon after donated 80 acres of land for the parish seat and courthouse grounds. (The present-day courthouse stands on this same site.) He named the town Leesville. On August 14, 1871, the Police Jury opened sealed bids for the construction of Vernon Parish's first courthouse. John F. Smart—who apparently was not Edmund's brother but was surely related—was awarded the contract for $2,260 (Louisiana Historical Records Survey n.d.a). This two-story, 50-by-100-foot pine structure was used until 1897. Edmund Smart became a state senator in 1886 and president of the Vernon Parish Police Jury in 1899 (Louisiana Historical Records Survey n.d.a, n.d.b; Wise 1971:10). He was also Police Jury treasurer in 1891 (Louisiana Historical Records Survey 1941:1:66–68). John R. Smart would also serve as a senator for Vernon Parish. Another Smart, John F., would become the proprietor of the *Vernon News* in 1902 (Wise 1971:24). He may have been a son of or the same John F. who built the courthouse. In any case, all indications are that the Smart clan was instrumental in the creation and early growth of Vernon Parish.

LATE-NINETEENTH-CENTURY POPULATION AND SETTLEMENT

Perhaps three to four thousand people had settled by 1871 in the region that became Vernon Parish. From 1880 until 1890 the population grew only 14 percent, but the area experienced a 75 percent growth in the 10 years between 1890 and 1900, when the population stood at 10,327. Much of the growth in the 1890s was due to the building of the railroad in 1897, its promise of development, and the arrival of industrial timber giants, but earlier growth was the result of Vernon Parish rising out of Reconstruction ashes and beginning a transformation from a self-sufficient, isolated, frontier community to a general, diversified, farming community, actively participating in the greater regional economy.

The 1890 census provides the first solid data concerning the sporadic settlement in the Fort Polk region. In this census, the parish population is recorded by wards, numbered 1 through 6. While not a perfect fit, the Main Fort region is encompassed by Wards 4 and 5, with an insignificant fraction of the installation's old artillery range in Ward 6. In 1890, Ward 4 had the lowest population of the six wards; Ward 5 ranked fourth. The population of both wards combined was only 1,648, or 28 percent of the parish's total population.

The Fort Polk population remained sparse until the railroad came. The 1900 census, taken three years after the railroad's arrival, indicates that a significant shift and increase in population occurred in Wards 1, 2, and 4, where the railroad was built.

Despite this growth plenty of land was available. A sense of just how much can be perceived through the census records. In 1880 there were only 732 farms spread across the 870,400 acres of Vernon Parish. Ten years later there were still only 841 farms. Prime, fertile bottomland was still to be found, and the uplands must have been, for the most part, untouched.

According to the dates on the original government land surveys, most Fort Polk land was surveyed around 1881 to 1883, and the land in the Peason Ridge region was surveyed around 1879. Thus, it would appear that many of those who had settled in Vernon Parish during the antebellum period, and even in the 1870s and 1880s, simply took up residence as squatters, awaiting the opportunity to apply for legal title at a later date. Although settling on unsurveyed lands was not legal until after 1880 (Gates and Swenson 1968:394), this technicality was largely ignored. The Franklins, for example, came to the Anacoco region in 1828 and were still residing there when Thomas Franklin, the son of Jonathan, obtained a legal deed to their 120-acre farm in 1876 from the Government Land Office (O'Halloran 1951–1952:1/10/1952). Some waited even longer. Once surveyed, land was cheap and available from speculators. "There are thousands of acres of land ready for homestead entry, and thousands more to be had at a cost an acre of a little more than the price of one tree. While I was in Leesville, the pretty pine-girt parish seat, two gentlemen, agents from Alexandria, were going through the country listing lands—that is locating lands that can be bought. In the neighborhood of Leesville they had listed 7,000 acres of this mighty forest at a uniform price of $2.50 an acre" (Cole 1892). Though the government had passed a Homestead Act in 1862 and another in 1866 to assist blacks and "loyal whites" in obtaining land, few of either completed their land entries in Louisiana. These acts were mostly unsuccessful as a result of the backlog of unsurveyed lands, social and economic conditions of Reconstruction, and the closing of land offices (Oubre 1976). In fact, from 1871 to 1890, only 4,811 homestead entries were finalized in Louisiana (Gates and Swenson 1968:415).

Those who had settled in the area during the antebellum were predominantly white Anglo-Saxon, Protestant, rural agrarians. The new arrivals between 1871 and 1897 were no different. A look at the first census of Vernon Parish in 1880 reveals that of 874 male heads of household, 330 were born in Louisiana. The rest were primarily from other southern states: Mississippi, 172; Alabama, 108; Georgia, 76; South Carolina, 38; Florida, 36; Texas, 34; Tennessee, 17; North Carolina, 16; Arkansas, 12; Virginia, 7; Kentucky, 2; and Missouri, 2. The nativity of the wives in these households was of similar representation with 332 from Louisiana, 163 from Mississippi, and 89 from Alabama (McManus 1989). African Americans during this period only represented nine percent of the total population. This expanded to 12 percent after the railroad arrived and the lumber industry began attracting unemployed blacks from other areas of Louisiana. Other than African Americans there was a small group of nonwhites called the Redbones who lived in southeastern Vernon Parish. Davis's (1971:299) illustration of "cultural islands" in Louisiana indicates that the cultural hearth of the Redbones was centered around the intersection of the boundaries of Vernon, Rapides, and Allen Parishes. This area extended north to around Hineston, west and probably slightly into Fort Polk's eastern borders, and south to the Ten Mile region in modern Allen Parish. These people were a mixture of several European, African, and Native American cultures whose origins remain mysterious and a topic of controversy (Marler and McManus 1993).

AGRICULTURAL DEVELOPMENT
It was during the period between 1871 and 1897 that Vernon Parish's agrarian community began a gradual transition from predominately subsistence farming to a mix of subsistence and generalized or diversified farming. The latter is defined here as farming in which a cash crop is produced for sale at

a local or regional market. The number of general farms appears to have reached its peak during the late 1890s and early twentieth century, before logging became the prevalent occupation. Census data clearly support the notion that during the late nineteenth century, Vernon Parish was the home of the white, yeoman farmer, an owner-operator of independent mind and resources. Listed occupations in 1880, for instance, were overwhelmingly farming and housekeeping. Another large occupation category was laborer (as opposed to farm laborer), but one wonders how many of those declaring this occupation were actually also farm laborers. Interestingly, no one is listed as preacher, lawyer, inn or tavern keeper, or law enforcement officer. Obviously people fulfilled such functions, but more than likely they considered farming their primary occupation, which reveals the strong ties to agriculture at this time. The vast majority of women were housekeepers. Other occupations included 15 merchants/clerks, 10 millers or mill workers, four lumbermen, six schoolteachers, three physicians, four blacksmiths, five teamsters, a ferryman, a raftsman, three mail riders, three midwives, a nurse, and a seamstress (McManus 1989).

Farm size is another strong indicator of the region's subsistence and general farm mix. The average farm size in the state was 171 acres. The 732 farms spread across Vernon Parish's landscape during the 1880s averaged only 48 acres, the lowest average in the state. The census indicates there were no farms of 500 acres or larger, and 192 farms (26 percent) were smaller than 20 acres. Further supporting the independent owner-operator domination of the landscape are the census data regarding land tenure. In 1880, there were only 45 farmers on shares in Vernon Parish and one renter. Almost 94 percent of Vernon Parish farmers were owners; only 6 percent were on shares and only 1 percent were renters. Statewide, only 65 percent of Louisiana farmers were owners; 21 percent were on shares and 14 percent were renters. In 1890, there was a modest increase in tenancy across the state, with share tenancy rising by 6 percent. Some 56 percent of the state's farms were owned, 27 percent were sharecropped, and 17 percent were rented (Davis 1971:296). Vernon Parish's sharecropper population rose by 8 percent to 14 percent. Renters rose by 7 percent. Still, in Vernon Parish, 79 percent of the farms were owned.

The typical farmers in the Fort Polk region had much of their wealth tied up in cattle and hogs. In the pine uplands, the infertile soils made anything but subsistence-level farming difficult and chancy, but this was ideal grazing land: "[O]ne must not think these pine forests are bare of grass. To the contrary, the sweet succulent grass is almost knee deep on the Vernon hills; the cattle to be seen are rolling in fat" (Cole 1892). So, too, hogs were in "hog heaven" in the mast-filled pine forests. Both cattle and hogs roamed free, while crops were fenced in for protection from the animals. Traditional rural code of behavior dictated that animals could roam and graze on all open land regardless of ownership, as codified in Louisiana's free-range laws. The open-range tradition caused many problems when cutover and abandoned timber land was bought as public land.

Despite a slight increase in farm productivity and abundant signs of population growth and rural development, it would be wrong to paint a utopian landscape. The Vernon Parish countrymen were constantly challenged by the forces of nature. In 1896, the parish was threatened by smallpox. To oversee the threat, Dr. Smart was elected by the Police Jury to become the board of health's executive officer (Louisiana Historical Records Survey 1941:1:297–301). Statewide, yellow fever ravaged the countryside from 1878 to 1880 and again in 1883, 1897, and 1899 (Davis 1971:324). Severe frosts occurred in 1891, and a cold snap in 1892 ruined many crops (Daniel 1943:1071). Even as the railroad was bringing hope of economic prosperity, a catastrophic drought hit the northern parishes, including Vernon, in 1896–1897 (Hair 1969:272). With crops devastated, subsistence farmers were close to starvation. A Baton Rouge newspaper reported that thousands in Vernon and Sabine Parishes were without food and "almost naked" (Hair 1969:272). In January, M. N. Smart put forth a motion in a Police Jury meeting to appeal to the governor for aid to destitute parish farmers who had failed to make a crop. The motion was adopted (Louisiana Historical Records Survey 1941:1:389–391). Food was provided by the Louisiana State Relief Committee. In Sabine Parish, the railroad agreed to transport these provisions at no charge (Belisle 1912:121).

SMALL-SCALE TIMBER HARVESTING

Although Vernon Parish's halcyon days of industrial lumbering were a few years in the future, logging had begun in the parish's western portion during the antebellum period. It increased steadily during the 1880s. Timber near the Sabine and the Anacoco was cut out and rafted downriver to the mills along the Sabine's Texas bank near Orange (Maxwell and Baker 1983:53; Stokes 1959:87). In fact, logs were being floated down the Sabine from as far north as Hamilton, upstream of Vernon Parish (U.S. House of Representatives 1892:3). However, the lumber traffic floating down the lower Calcasieu surpassed the 1880s traffic on the Sabine River.

Around Lake Charles, a number of lumber mills were established at this time, processing a huge volume of Calcasieu logs. In 1876, the H. C. Drew Lumber Company began operating, and in 1884 the Calcasieu Lumber Company started up. Calcasieu Lumber soon became the Bradley-Ramsey Lumber Company and provided the city's largest payroll for more than 20 years

(Block 1996:42–43). Once, a Calcasieu company cut 148,000 board feet of lumber in 11 hours (Stokes 1959:86). Much of this timber came from the region below Vernon Parish, but Stokes (1959:86) indicates that the Whiskey Chitto and Bundick Creeks were among the Calcasieu tributaries used for rafting logs down to Lake Charles. These streams could only float logs during spring freshets. An 1881 government survey of the Calcasieu reported that above Phillips Bluff, the waters were "very rapid, shallow, [with] many timber obstructions . . . only suited for running saw-logs during short periods of flood" (U.S. House of Representatives 1881:2). Still, it is likely that in the 1880s, and even as early as the 1870s, Fort Polk timber was being cut and rafted to Lake Charles at a steady rate.

Along the Calcasieu, timber was cut all year and stored in the bayous until the spring floods. Then log rafts were constructed, like those on the Sabine (Kadlecek and Bullard 1994:77). Floater logs formed the cribs of these rafts; nonfloating logs were used as cross pieces. The cribs were tied together with rope. Farmers cut their own timber and hauled the logs to the creeks and rivers with oxen. Part-time loggers then floated the logs downstream to the mouth of the Calcasieu and sold them to timber buyers. Controlling the logs was difficult and dangerous work; some escaped to float freely out into the Gulf. On the Sabine, loggers made larger rafts, some with as many as 10 or 12 logs and measuring 30 or 40 feet long with a cook shack on top (Maxwell and Baker 1983:54).

It has been noted that there is little information about the mills operating during the antebellum period, and it is equally difficult to sort out the mills prior to the arrival of the big lumber operations. Kadlecek and Bullard (1994:77) write that a number of water-powered sawmills began to operate in the Kisatchie hills region in the 1890s. Perhaps some of the old gristmills were converted to sawmills. Some mills, including Stephens Mill on Mill Creek five miles southwest of Leesville, Langton and Hugh Mills on Sandy Creek, and the Koonce Brothers Mill on Big Sandy Creek, may actually have been started at this time rather than in the antebellum (Wise 1971:13). Within Fort Polk's Main Fort, several mills were operating (again, with the above chronological caveat), including Golemon Mill, Weeks Mill, and Haymons Mill, all on Little Six Mile Creek. Swain's Mill is shown on the 1880s Government Land Office survey maps along Six Mile Creek within Fort Polk. Few if any of these mills are reflected in the U.S. Census, however, which recorded only manufactories valued at $500 or more. In Vernon Parish, only three manufactories are listed in 1890; this category included mills and other kinds of manufactories.

Despite the early establishment of sawmills along the lower Sabine and Calcasieu Rivers, Vernon Parish's vast timber resources were, for all practical purposes, untouched. Until the railroads were built into the timberlands, only the best timber near rivers and streams could be cut and sold downstream for profit. The sawmills established up to this point served mostly local needs and were just beginning to have a national impact. As Charles Mohr reported, "The pine region west of the Red River valley . . . includes the whole parish of Vernon. The northern portion of this belt is one vast primeval forest. The small inroads made by the scattered settlers and the few small saw-mills which supply a small local demand are too insignificant to be taken into account" (Mohr in Sargent 1884:538–539). There were millions of *Pinus palustris* (longleaf pine) still awaiting the saw in western Louisiana. Sargent estimated that in 1880 as much as 3,741,000,000 board feet of merchantable pine was available for harvest in Vernon Parish alone (Sargent 1884:537).

THE TRANSPORTATION LANDSCAPE

As the population increased, it would be expected that road traffic also increased, but contemporary regional maps do little to expand our knowledge of the transportation system. Lockett's 1876 map, which was revised in 1891 (Lockett 1969), provides the most reliable information about the parish's major road network during the late nineteenth century. Figure 7.2 shows portions of the east-west route that ran from Alexandria through modern-day Fort Polk to Leesville, and on to Burr's Ferry. Within the fort, a branch road splits off from this road and runs south through Huddleston. This road disappears from maps around the turn of the century. The map also depicts the main trail running north-south from Many to Davis Mill and passing through Sibley's Mill and Huddleston. The railroad was to follow this route very closely.

Other important trails included a route running from the northeast corner of the parish through Walnut Hill to Huddleston and another little trail running from Huddleston south into Calcasieu Parish west of the Many–to–Davis Mill road. It is interesting to note how many of these nineteenth-century routes intersect at Huddleston. This road system is another indication that, before Leesville, Huddleston was the center of early west-central Louisiana traffic and, by extrapolation, probably its economic and political center as well. With the creation of Leesville, the political and economic center shifted.

With multiple deep wagon-wheel ruts and muddy puddles, there was no doubt that the thoroughfare between Leesville and Hineston was the main traveled road (Cole 1892), but its physical condition was an exception. Most of the other main roads were still little more than trails cut through the pine forest. Branching off at random intervals from these thoroughfares were

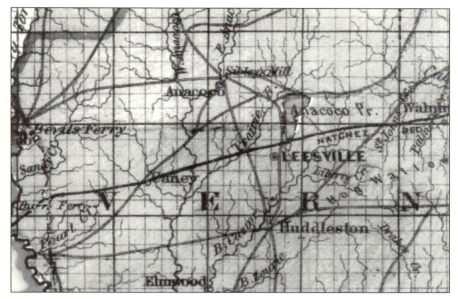

Figure 7.2 — Detail of Lockett's 1876 (revised 1891) map showing the Fort Polk area as a "Hog Wallow" land.

even smaller trails. These little trails, or "neighborhood" roads, appeared to be no different from the main thoroughfares, except that they would dead-end at little cabins and farms—utterly frustrating strangers. Field (writing as Cole) relates her experience with the Vernon Parish's transportation system in 1892:

> At the farmhouse I had been told to keep on the trail of the mail cart that passed down the day before. This was not easy to do on the carpet of dead pine needles, and Ned and I often left the buggy at the fork of a road to search ahead . . . for some sign of a trail; broken pine needles where a country's pony's unshod hoof had been—fresh signs of manure—these were signs enough to send us on our way.
>
> [Later] we pushed on, knowing now we were off course. . . . Nothing was left of the road, save where here and there a white gash on a tree showed the way had been blazed by somebody. We crashed on over roots and scrub oaks that, bending, lashed the ponies flanks [Cole 1892].

The travelers eventually "scuffed hopefully into the dust of a main traveled road" and found their way to Leesville. Government Land Office survey maps of various townships and ranges during the early 1880s indicate that these neighborhood trails were fairly numerous across the landscape, even in the Fort Polk region (Figure 7.3).

From Cole's description, it would appear that the road conditions in the 1890s had changed little since the time of the first pioneers, despite the road overseer system established when the region was tied to Rapides and Sabine Parishes. Under this system, police juries assigned residents sections of road for maintenance or new construction. A review of the Vernon Parish Police Jury minutes shows the jury spent considerable time assigning and reassigning road crews and voting on citizens' requests for new roads and changes in the current road system. A typical late-nineteenth-century entry for the Fort Polk region reads, "Mr. Davis presented a petition from the 4th Ward asking for a change in the road leading from Petersburg [Huddleston] to Whiscachitto Creek near the residence of Mr. [?]. A. Davis, which was laid over till next meeting and the following reviewers appointed to review said change" (Louisiana Historical Records Survey 1941:1:42). It is possible that at least a part of this road exists as Louisiana Avenue, which leads into Fort Polk today.

In 1912 road overseers were assigned to another little trail within Fort Polk as follows: "Leesville to Bull Branch—John Rus Smart; Bull Branch to A. James—Bill Cryer; A. James to Center Whiskey Chitto—J. T. Bates; Center Whiskey Chitto to Arnolds—S. A. Nolen; Arnolds to Parish line— Henry Davis" (punctuation revised; Louisiana Historical Records Survey 1941:1:700).

In 1897 the Police Jury passed a road law enacting various means by which roads would be built and maintained. The law stated that all males between 18 and 50 years of age, except ministers and a few others, were subject to work on the parish's public roads. A list was made and the men on the list were to be given 10 days' notice for road duty. This duty could not exceed 12 days per year. Fines were enacted for those who ignored the call. A standard road width of 18 feet was set, 14 of which were to be cleared of all obstructions. No stumps above six inches high were allowed within this 14-foot center. However, the overseer could ignore stumps and other obstructions if there was ample room to go around these obstacles. Bridges and crossways over sloughs or low areas could be as narrow as 12 feet. A $30 fine was enacted for obstructing roads (Louisiana Historical Records Survey 1941:1:4449–4453).

The Railroad Vote

A repetitive theme in west-central Louisiana history is the region's isolation. This was exacerbated by the poor road conditions and the Sabine River's unreliability, which combined to stymie Vernon Parish's industrial develop-

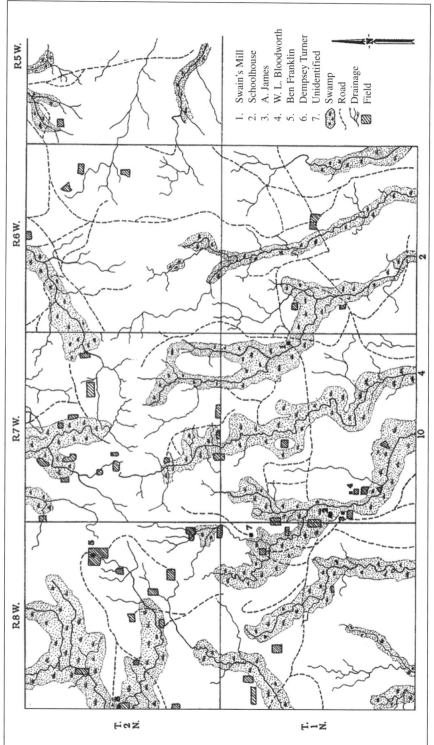

Figure 7.3 — Sketch compilation of Main Fort area plat maps, 1880–1883.

1. Swain's Mill
2. Schoolhouse
3. A. James
4. W. L. Bloodworth
5. Ben Franklin
6. Dempsey Turner
7. Unidentified

Swamp
Road
Drainage
Field

R5 W.
R6 W.
R7 W.
R8 W.

T. 2 N.
T. 1 N.

ment. All this changed with the completion of the Kansas City, Shreveport, and Gulf (KCS & G) Railway, which ran north and south through the parish's heartland. The Vernon Parish settlement pattern was radically altered. Its total cultural and natural landscape, and its history, would change with this railroad. Ironically, the decision to allow the railroad's entry passed by only four votes after at least one and perhaps two previous failures (Dalehite 1962:1; Louisiana Historical Records Survey 1941:1:303).

In fact, the railroad's construction may not have been as difficult as the struggle to get the west-central Louisiana population to agree to a property tax assessment to help pay for it. As early as 1890, Sabine Parish attempted to levy a five-mill property valuation for 10 years for the KCS & G Railway (Belisle 1912:118). Two years later, on January 3, 1893, the Vernon Parish Police Jury received a petition from some one-third of its residents to impose a five-mill tax to support the Natchez, Alexandria, and Texas Railroad Company's building of an east-west railroad through the parish. A special vote was to be held on February 9, 1893. The Sabine Parish initiative failed, and probably the Vernon Parish initiative also, because no further mention is made in the parish Police Jury records (Dalehite 1962:4; Louisiana Historical Records Survey 1941:1:150). The two parishes tried again in 1895; this time their respective elections were scheduled to coincide and include an election in DeSoto Parish (Belisle 1912:120). Vernon's referendum just barely passed 463 to 459, but Sabine's passed by a wide margin of 544 to 438. DeSoto's vote must have been positive, although the count is not known.

LATE-NINETEENTH-CENTURY VILLAGES, HAMLETS, AND POST STOPS

The parish's growth is best indicated in the list of small communities that appeared across the Vernon Parish landscape during this period. First and foremost among the new villages created during this period was Leesville, named for Robert E. Lee (Lawrence 1961; O'Halloran 1951–1952:12/27/1951). As stated earlier, the village was established with the legislation creating the parish, on land donated by Dr. Edmund Smart. Initially, only Smart's office and store were there. By 1880, seven families with 25 people lived at Leesville, including four Smart families (McManus 1989:164–165). In 1892, fewer than one hundred people were living in the town (Goodspeed Publishing Company 1975:206; Wise 1971:29). Cole (1892) described Vernon Parish's largest village: "Leesville, the parish seat, directly in the center of the parish, has a population of a couple hundred [compare Goodspeed reference above], several stores, a union church, two weekly newspapers and two hostelries for the convenience of the traveling public." With the founding of Leesville, Huddleston quickly disappeared. Illustrated on an 1870 map, Huddleston no longer appeared on maps after that date. Leesville would quickly become the main service town for those within Fort Polk and it remains so today.

Although Fort Polk's scattered population probably traveled to Leesville for major supplies, a number of smaller hamlets surrounded the modern borders of the fort at this time. Most were little more than post stops and general stores. Conrad, for instance, was a post office established around 1892 that lasted until 1898 (Post Office Department 1973). It is not illustrated on any contemporary maps and its exact location is a mystery. However, its mails were transferred to Slabtown when it closed, so it may have been in the parish's southeastern region in the Fort Polk area. Slabtown was the original name of the village that is today called Pitkin (Wise 1971:50). It was first settled in 1872 when a Mr. Millam constructed a water mill at the fork of Big Six Mile and Little Six Mile Creeks, just south of Fort Polk. Cora became a post office stop beginning in 1887 and grew throughout the postbellum period. It was located along the parish's eastern border, south of Hineston. The village was called Hueston; the post office Cora. Both were only a few miles east of the Fort Polk boundary. The hamlet Hicks, located along the old Alexandria–to–Burr's Ferry road between Hineston and Walnut Hill, remained a post stop throughout the postbellum period and probably served Fort Polk's population in the northeastern portion of the Main Fort. The population in the southwestern portion of the Main Fort might have also bought supplies at Rosepine, which was established in 1896, when Thomas Evans was granted 160 acres of land. He deeded 40 acres to Wyatt Herrington, who subdivided the town into 20 blocks one year later (Cupit 1963:40, 1983:105; Wise 1971:52). Rosepine was established with the railroad's arrival in mind. It would become a boom town only a few years later. Just north of the fort's main post, Walnut Hill continued to grow during the late 1800s. During the 1890s, this little village, with as many as 75 people, may have been second only to Leesville in population (Goodspeed Publishing Company 1975:206). Whiskachitto was a little post stop established in 1889 and discontinued in 1892. Whiskachitto was obviously on Whiskey Chitto Creek and may have been the only hamlet in Fort Polk prior to the railroad and lumber era. Six Mile is the only other possible hamlet, but there is no evidence that it was established during the antebellum period.

LATE-NINETEENTH-CENTURY SOCIETAL ORGANIZATION

Yet another indication of Vernon Parish's growth and transformation from an antebellum frontier backcountry to an established farming community was the fast growth of numerous social organizations after parish formation. As population increased, parish associations, branches, and chapters were organized. The Baptists formed the Vernon Association in 1871. In 1890, about 20 churches, some even outside the parish, were members of the association. Five miles northeast of Rosepine, Louisiana, and just south of the Kisatchie National Forest, the unincorporated community of Providence had its beginnings in the formation of Providence Baptist Church (Pool 1992:1). Meanwhile, the Kisatchie Baptist Church continued to grow; by 1887, it had some 57 members (Kadlecek and Bullard 1994:176). By 1890, the Southern Baptists had a total of 13 churches in the parish serving 585 members. There were also four Old-Two-Seed-In-The-Spirit Baptist churches—described in the 1890 census as very conservative and strongly Calvinistic—with 55 members. There were eight Methodist churches with 401 members. In all, there were 25 churches in the parish with 1,039 active members in 1890. This represents 18 percent of the parish population.

Freemason organization was yet another example of Vernon Parish's redevelopment after Reconstruction. At Walnut Hill, the N. H. Bray Lodge No. 208 was chartered on February 15, 1871, a month before the parish was formed (Dalehite 1963:1). The Anacoco Lodge No. 147 was restored on May 14, 1885, with members meeting at the Hardshell post office. On February 15, 1893, Freemasons in Leesville formed Lodge No. 240.

Public schools were very slowly being reestablished after the Civil War. In 1877, the state reorganized its board of education in an attempt to improve the condition of public education (Davis 1971:306). At that time, fewer than 20 percent of the state's educable white children were attending schools, and rural schools were described as "deplorable" and "dismal" (Davis 1971:306; Robertson 1952:1). Although some progress was made during this period, public education had a long way to go. In 1898, there were only 1,535 schools for whites and 741 for blacks statewide. Yearly, these were open, on average, 5.5 months (for whites) and 4.72 months (for blacks). Some 84,453 whites and 48,137 blacks attended that year (Fay 1898:108–109). The average school day lasted six hours.

Progress in Vernon Parish schools was as slow as in the rest of the state's schools. With parish formation, the Police Jury took responsibility for organizing the parish's schools, but initial interest may have been only cursory. On March 27, 1890, the Police Jury voted on a one-and-a-half-mill tax for parish public schools. Even though the motion was made and seconded, the entire jury voted against the tax. After citizens expressed further support, however, a tax was eventually assessed on July 11, 1891. The following year, $1,500 was raised (Wise 1971:5).

School names provide some of the first hard evidence of communities in the Fort Polk Main Fort area: Bundick Creek, Laurel Hill, Six Mile, Brushy Creek, Huddleston, and Whiskey Chitto. Attendance in the rural areas was poor and sporadic. Most of the teachers taught only from one to three months of the year. Although schools would improve slowly over the years, it was an uphill battle. Attendance improved also, and by 1899 there were as many as 72 schools for whites and seven for blacks in the parish (Wise 1971:11).

Politics were an important part of this rural community, and Vernon Parish's populace took their politics seriously. Traditionally, rural white farmers of the postbellum South were loyal Democrats. Through the 1880s, however, the rural white northern Louisiana parishes were submitting protest votes for Republican and Independent candidates as the Democratic party failed to support farm interests. For instance, Louisiana Democrats would not endorse the "subtreasury plan," which, if passed, would have provided low-cost federal farm loans allowing farmers to warehouse crops until prices rose—thus breaking the debt cycle of farmers caught in the lien system.

The people also thought their Democratic congressmen were doing nothing about Northern banker Jay Gould, who was buying up homestead land all through the northern parishes, including large tracts in Vernon and Natchitoches Parishes. Gould was, in fact, the largest landowner in Vernon Parish at the time and quite unpopular locally (Hair 1969:112). Eventually, Vernon Parish sent representatives to Natchitoches for the 1890 convention. Along with representatives from Sabine and Winn Parishes, they selected the Farmers-Union-Independent candidate Thomas J. Guice for the Fourth District congressional race (Hicks 1961:207). Though Guice did not win, the die was cast. In 1891, Vernon Parish Democrats renounced their party allegiance and joined the new People's party. During the governor's race in 1892, these Populists ran Robert L. Tannehill. Although Tannehill brought up the rear in the state election with only 9,804 votes, he won Catahoula, Grant, Winn, and Vernon Parishes (Daniel 1943:1082; Hair 1969:225).

The Populist movement continued to grow until 1896, when it began a gradual decline in popularity. Throughout this period, Vernon Parish was a Populist stronghold. The *People's Friend*, a Populist newspaper, was published in Leesville from 1888 until around 1897 (Wise 1971:24). In 1892, Vernon Parish sent People's party representative John Franklin to the state legislature (Hair 1969:226). In 1896, People's party candidate Lee McAlpin of Vernon Parish ran in the Fourth District but was defeated (Daniel 1943:1109). Later, some of these same people and their sons would become intensely involved with labor reform movements in the timber industry.

Timber, Trains, and a Landscape Transformed, 1898–1940

From the turn of the century until the late 1920s, Vernon Parish forests echoed with the sounds of chopping axes, shouting men, crashing trees, braying mules, and snorting steam engines. Out-of-state strangers—blacks, Mexicans, and Italians included—joined local farmers and their sons to work in the deep woods and at the new sawmills. Across the transforming Vernon Parish landscape, the people and culture of this isolated community were awakened to a wider world economy and, for some, unprecedented prosperity. During the peak lumber days, some of the larger mills employed an average of four hundred men and supported lumber towns and camps with populations often in the thousands. But just as suddenly as they came, the great lumber days ended. Less than 15 years after opening, the first lumber companies had cut all they could, closed their mills, abandoned their denuded forest land, and moved west. By 1933, 16 of the large mills built in Vernon and Beauregard Parishes stood abandoned (Cruikshank 1939:25; Stokes 1957:255). It was a time of "cut out and get out" for those who had purchased prime timberland a few years earlier.

The amount of lumber that was available and removed from Louisiana during this short period is beyond comprehension. In his 1880 study of Southern timber, Charles Mohr estimated that the state had some 5.9 million acres of longleaf forests (Burns 1979:198). The Bureau of Corporations (1913:132) reported in 1913 that Louisiana contained some 120 billion board feet of lumber. Foster (1912:20) reported that as much as 34.1 billion board feet of standing timber existed south of the Red River, an area of some 2.6 million acres that included Vernon Parish. How much was harvested? Winters estimated that 120 billion board feet of lumber were produced between 1880 and 1937 (Winters et al. 1943:1), a number that interestingly matches the Bureau of Corporations' 1913 estimate of available lumber.

Amazingly, even after this exploitation, some 41 billion board feet still remained. Not much of it was within Fort Polk, however. Fullerton Mill, one of the largest in the parish and state and located just south of the installation, had cut most of those trees, producing at its peak 120 million board feet of lumber per year (Burns 1979:202) and some 2.25 billion board feet over its lifetime (Fowler 1967:4). The effect of this harvest on the Vernon Parish and Fort Polk landscape was devastating. A 1943 Department of Agriculture publication noted that only three percent of Louisiana's longleaf pine forest supported uncut old growth forest, with an additional five percent partially cut (Winters et al. 1943:11). Surprisingly, most of this virgin forest was found in Vernon and Rapides Parishes. The rest of the pine forest was sawlog-size second growth (11 percent), undersized second growth (39 percent), or seriously damaged open lands (42 percent) (Winters et al. 1943:11).

Beyond the landscape, the effect on the economy and people was equally severe. With the lumber industry's rise, people prospered from employment and corporate taxation. But the economy's sharp rise was matched by an equally sharp fall when mills closed and companies left. The value of Vernon Parish land dropped from $40 million to $6 million after the timber was cut, and 70 percent of the land was cut over (Vernon Parish Planning Board 1949:8). From becoming one of the richest parishes in the state in the 1920s, Vernon became one of the poorest in the 1930s (Brown et al. 1935:1).

When the lumber barons and laborers migrated west at the beginning of the 1930s, the locals were left to return to their former agrarian lifestyle. The timing could not have been worse as the nation was entering a long economic depression. Much of the land had lost its only value—its timber. Looking to unburden themselves, the lumber companies sold their land to the federal government. Fort Polk's infertile, upland, hogwallow lands were among the now barren acres. In a national effort, partially to create jobs, the government began to restore the forests through the U.S. Forest Service and the Civilian Conservation Corps. The new employer, the U.S. Government, found new uses for these lands: forestry and, beginning in the 1940s, as a training ground for our national defense.

THE LUMBER BARONS

How had much of Vernon Parish and all of the Fort Polk landscape been so quickly and utterly transformed? The origins of the cut over began well before the first railroad spike was driven in Vernon Parish. As early as 1877, Henry J. Lutcher and G. Bedell Moore, founders of the great Lutcher and Moore Lumber Company, toured east Texas in search of timber. They never entered Louisiana during their tour, but they purchased thousands of acres on both sides of the Sabine, including 60,000 acres in southwest Vernon and northern Calcasieu (Beauregard) Parishes (Maxwell and Baker 1983:22–23). The lumber from these holdings was transported to Lutcher and Moore's mill in Orange, Texas. Lutcher and Moore were just the beginning.

More timber speculators came and by 1900 much of the government land in west-central Louisiana was held by relatively few speculators and lumber tycoons. The Wright-Blodgett Lumber Company of Illinois, for instance, came to Louisiana around 1890 and bought close to a quarter million acres in Vernon, Allen, Calcasieu, Rapides, and Sabine Parishes. At one time, it was the largest tract holder within present-day Fort Polk, owning some 180,000 acres between Six Mile and Whiskey Chitto Creeks. The name Wright-Blodgett never became synonymous with lumbering in Vernon Parish, as did Pickering Lumber and Gulf Lumber, because it sold its land to other establishments early on at a fabulous profit (Block 1996:143).

In fact, Wright-Blodgett had already sold most of its holdings by 1913 when the Department of Commerce and Labor issued its report (Bureau of Corporations 1913:134) on land purchases and speculation in the region.

The area studied in this report extended north-south from Natchitoches to Lake Charles and was bounded, generally, by the Red River (around Alexandria) on the east and the Sabine River on the west. All of Vernon Parish lay at the heart of this area, which spread some 65 to 85 miles east-west and 100 miles north-south.

The report found that 65 individuals and partnerships in the study area had purchased 1,000 acres or more from the government land office, totaling 1,021,000 acres at $1.25 per acre. Three of the 65 purchased more than 100,000 acres each: Nathan Bradley, 111,240 acres; Lutcher and Moore, 110,080 acres; and Franklin Head, 104,800 acres. Another 11 bought between 20,000 and 60,000 acres (Bureau of Corporations 1913:148). In this latter group were well-known northern industrialists, such as Jay Gould, who owned vast acreage in western Louisiana and, at one time, was the leading individual landowner in Vernon Parish with some 26,880 acres.

The study also plotted the landownership of 62 owners with more than 60 million board feet of timber each. Fourteen of the 62 companies owned 1.4 million acres, or two-thirds of the plotted land, producing 21.8 billion board feet of lumber (Bureau of Corporations 1913:139). Four of these companies—the lumber giants Long-Bell Lumber Company, Calcasieu Pine Company–Southland Lumber Company, Chicago Lumber and Coal Company Interests, and Lutcher and Moore Interests—owned half of the 1.4 million acres. Lutcher and Moore's land alone could supply 12.3 billion board feet of lumber. Curiously, Gulf Lumber, a major company in the area operated by S. H. Fullerton and the creator of Fort Polk's largest town of Fullerton, is not among the 14 landholders in the study. The answer to this mystery lies in the complex industrial conglomerates of the time, which rivaled those of today. Not only was much of the land in the ownership of a few companies, but also many of the 14 companies had close ties to each other. For example, S. H. Fullerton organized the Chicago Lumber and Coal Company, probably to hold the 54,960 acres of land reported in the 1913 study in trust while it was being cut over by his Gulf Lumber mills (Bureau of Corporations 1913:table 43). This acreage accounts for about half of the 106,000 acres owned by Gulf Lumber (Burns 1970:2; Fowler 1967:3). Another large landowner, Central Coal and Coke, is reported to have held 76,390 acres (plus the subsequent purchase of 24,200 acres from the Hackley and Hume Company). Chicago Lumber and Coal and Central Coal and Coke had a common director (Fullerton?) who was also a stockholder in Frost-Johnson Lumber Company. Two other directors of Chicago Lumber and Coal were stockholders in the Pacific giant Weyerhaeuser.

Present-day Fort Polk was dead center within these holdings. In reviewing study maps, it is obvious that much of Fort Polk was owned by one or more of these timber corporations. Cantley and Kern's (1984:59–62) study of landownership in 1910 indicates that S. H. Fullerton's Gulf Lumber Company and Nona Mills owned 80 percent of one township. It is known that Fullerton, who built a mill and mill town of unprecedented size just south of Fort Polk, purchased 106,000 acres of Vernon Parish pineland in 1906 from one or more speculators for around $6 million, or $60 an acre (Burns 1970:2; Fowler 1967:3). Fowler (1967:3) states that Fullerton bought a Wright-Blodgett tract in Vernon Parish. He may have paid $56.60 an acre (Block 1996:143). To put this in context, timber rights in Vernon Parish sold for $7 an acre in 1899 and $40 an acre by 1904. So, Wright-Blodgett and other early speculators made a fortune selling their holdings to the lumber companies. Other large Vernon Parish companies included the W. R. Pickering Company, with some 47,880 acres. Pickering had also bought sections of the Wright-Blodgett tract, paying around $35 an acre (Block 1996:5–12). Nona Mills owned 11,680 acres. And, still operating at the time of the government study, Lutcher and Moore Interests owned 120,800 acres in the parish along with Central Coal and Coke (Bureau of Corporations 1913:table 43). In summary, by the time the railroad was built, the power and wealth of Vernon Parish had been concentrated among a few interests. By 1915, these interests had become even fewer in number.

THE MILLS

Between 1890 and 1940 there were scores of large and small mills operating in and around Fort Polk. Early in this period, Leesville was at the center of those that cut and processed the timber within Fort Polk. One of Leesville's earliest mills was Nona Mills. Established around 1899, it had a tremendous impact on Leesville's growth (Hadnot in Wise 1971:13). With a daily capacity of 100,000 board feet, Nona Mills had a planing mill, machine shop, blacksmith shop, turpentine plant, and facilities for the workers. Nona contributed some $15,000 in monthly payroll to its 370 workers, which found its way into the local economy (Block 1996:180–184). The mill operated a general store—the largest in town in 1905—and a drugstore and hired a doctor. The company built a waterworks system to prevent widespread fires and an electric plant to keep the mills operating 24 hours a day—and all this was up and running by 1900 (Wise 1971:29). The company also contributed to a number of local projects for the community's benefit.

The W. R. Pickering Company built a mill at Pickering, six miles down the road from Leesville. Typical of most Vernon Parish lumber companies, the Pickering headquarters were out of state in Kansas City. (A connection to the Fullertons, big operators in Kansas City, is possible.) In Louisiana, Pickering purchased 130,847 acres in Sabine and Vernon Parishes, much of which was within the Fort Polk area and purchased from Wright-Blodgett (Block 1996:5). Pickering also owned more than 100,000 acres in Texas, as well as holdings in Missouri, Arkansas, and Oklahoma (Maxwell and Baker 1983:162, 199). The mill at Pickering, employing around 500 workers, was rated at 150,000 board feet daily, but around 1904 it was rated at as much as 200,000 board feet per day (Block 1996:6). It could cut boards as long as 36 feet. The Pickering Company had a reputation both in Texas and western Louisiana for its detrimental "cut out and get out" business practices. It closed on February 25, 1926 (Wise 1971:48).

Pickering also operated a mill at Cravens, about three miles south of Fort Polk, and yet another at a little stop at Barham, Louisiana, north of Leesville between Anacoco and Hornbeck (Wise 1971:13). The Cravens mill cut 200,000 board feet daily. Its two-story building housed two double-band saw heads and a separate lath mill with a daily capacity of 40,000 feet. Its annual output was about 50 million board feet (Block 1996:13). The smaller mill at Barham cut 65,000 feet of lumber and 20,000 feet of flooring (Block 1996:3, 11).

The Central Coal and Coke Company came to Vernon Parish just after the railroad arrived. In 1898, the company built both a mill and a town, located about three miles south of Pickering along U.S. Route 171. First called Taylor and then Keith (after a principal owner of the company, Charles S. Keith), the town was finally called Neame, apparently for financial backer Joe Neame (Wise 1971:49). Although Central Coal and Coke was known locally as the Delta Land and Timber Company, its brand, the 4 C Co., was stamped on wood products and nationally recognized (Wise 1971:49).

The Neame mill cut 200,000 board feet daily (Block 1996:107). It had two single-cutting band saws, a 52-inch gang saw, and an assortment of edgers, trimmers, cutoff saws, and slasher and drag saws, all of which kept 500 employees busy. The planing mill housed rip saws and a flooring machine (Block 1996:107). The Neame mill burned in 1925. Central Coal and Coke continued its operations down the road in Carson (McCain n.d.; Wise 1971:49). Although the Long-Bell Lumber Company built a piling operation at Neame in 1925, after the mill fire, the town waned. Neame's last mill was a small one built by C. N. Lockwood. As noted earlier, the Central Coal and Coke Company and Fullerton's operations were connected. Both had headquarters in Kansas City, Missouri. One of the larger operations in Texas with 120,000 acres (Maxwell and Baker 1983:157), Central Coal and Coke owned another 128,000 acres in Louisiana (Allen 1961:17), as well as holdings in Arkansas, Oklahoma, and Missouri.

The histories of the Fort Polk region and Fullerton Mill are closely intertwined. The story of Fullerton Mill and the town of Fullerton naturally begins with Samuel Holmes Fullerton. An immigrant from Ireland (or Scotland), Fullerton worked his way "up the ladder" from a laborer in Atchison, Kansas, to a multimillionaire (*American Lumberman* 1922; Burns 1970:2, 1979:200). Fullerton and his brother organized several lumberyards along the Santa Fe and Rock Island Railroads. Fullerton organized and owned several lumber and coal companies, railroads, and banks. At one time, early in his career, he "had a string of seventy retail yards in Oklahoma and Kansas" (Fowler 1967:3). His brother, Robert, president of the Chicago Lumber and Coal Company, was an influential lumberman in Mississippi (Hickman 1962:154, 204).

Samuel organized the Chicago Lumber Company, which soon became the Chicago Lumber and Coal Company. A subsidiary of this company, the Chicago Lumber and Coal Company of Texas, was formed by L. J. Boykin, who had previously worked for Nona Mills at Leesville (*American Lumberman* 1923:46). In 1920, Fullerton bought out the Texas subsidiary and reorganized it as the Boykin Lumber Company. L. J. Boykin served as general manager. Boykin Lumber Company handled the sale of lumber produced by the Fullerton mill (Burns 1970:2).

In 1906, Fullerton organized the Gulf Lumber Company, which became the largest company in the Fort Polk area (Miller 1997). The company's facility at Stables, just outside modern Leesville, was actually two mills. One cut 75,000 board feet a day; the other 60,000 feet. The complex had a four-room dry kiln and a planer (Block 1996:70–72). According to Fowler (1967:4), the mills at Stables operated until 1910. Block (1996:72), however, states that the "facility" burned in 1913 and again in 1916. The mill town of Stables was sold to the Newllano people in 1917 (see below).

Fullerton invested some $3.5 million in building a mill and mill town in southeast Vernon Parish, in the heart of the best, thickest pineland in Louisiana (Burns 1970:2). The mill at the new town of Fullerton began operations in 1907. By 1927, when it finally closed, it was the largest pine sawmill west of the Mississippi (Burns 1970:1). Stories that have become part of the area's oral history relate that Fullerton planned a "50-year run" but left after 20 as a result of stepped-up operations (Cantley and Kern 1984:269). Regardless of Fullerton's original plans, the mill's production record staggers the imagination. With an annual capacity of 120 million board feet (Burns 1979:199), it could produce as much as 350,000 board feet in a 10-hour shift. In a record one-day shipment, 35 cars with 789,000 board feet of lumber were sent down the tracks (Burns 1979:202). Fowler (1967:4–6) estimates that, in its lifetime, the mill cut 2.25 billion board feet, consuming 4.2 million trees.

Fullerton's mill payroll, nearly $1 million a year, was distributed to some 650 employees supporting 3,000 people. During World War I, the mill employed 2,000 people, with the town of Fullerton housing some 5,000 (Burns 1979:202). There were two sawmills at Fullerton, one of which could cut giant logs measuring 24 by 24 inches and up to 90 feet in length (Burns 1970:3). The mills had five double-cutting band saws and were fully electric, being run by the 500- and 1,000-kilowatt generators that powered the town. Fullerton had a lath mill and a planing mill. The laborers also collected turpentine for processing at a distillery in Rustville, just south of Fullerton. The lumber was processed in 12 dry kilns. A huge, overhead, "godevil" monorail lifted and transported the lumber around the yard.

Once ready for shipment, the lumber was loaded on railroad cars and moved out of Fullerton via the company's own Gulf and Sabine River Railroad. Although only 10 miles long, this railroad connected to the Santa Fe, Lake Charles, and Northern Lines, providing passengers two daily runs to Lake Charles (Burns 1970:3). The railroad company also operated Shay steam engines that hauled the logs along tramlines from the forests to the mills.

Fullerton, an experimenter, created an alcohol distillery five stories high to produce drinkable alcohol from sawdust and other lumber waste products. Prohibition severely handicapped this venture, as the alcohol had to be guarded and special arrangements made for shipping (Burns 1979:202). The alcohol plant closed early; Fullerton Mill stayed open until 1927.

As the southern Vernon Parish woods disappeared, the parish's northern part soon saw the arrival of lumbermen and mills. At Fort Polk's Peason Ridge Training Area, J. H. Kurth, Jr., built a mill and mill town around 1919, naming it Kurthwood (McDaniel 1983:4). Kurth was the son of German immigrant Joseph Kurth, who had built a lumber fortune in east Texas. His sons branched out as the Fullerton brothers had done. J. H. Kurth, Jr., first moved to Rapides Parish, where he operated the Pawnee Land and Lumber Company until 1919. On moving to Vernon Parish, he bought 3,000 acres of Jay Gould's estate near the Calcasieu (McDaniel 1983:4). Transporting part of the Pawnee Lumber Company's old mill town to this land, he built Kurthwood and opened the Vernon Parish Lumber Company.

The mill had two 14-inch single-cutting band saws and a "bull edger" (McDaniel 1983:5). It also had dry kilns and a planing mill. In the forests, Kurth used a Clyde four-line rehaul skidder and a 65-ton Shay steam engine. The Kurth Mill boasted a 300,000 board feet per day capacity. Like Fullerton, the town of Kurthwood was full of modern conveniences (see below). The Vernon Parish Lumber Company closed in 1929.

Obviously, the industrial giants just mentioned overshadowed all other Vernon Parish logging interests at the time. However, numerous smaller, locally owned and operated companies also thrived during this period or were formed shortly after the large companies had cut and run. Throughout western Louisiana, small lumber companies employed, and continue to employ, a significant number of people and the lumber industry maintained a strong presence in the region throughout the Depression. A map in a 1939 publication on forest resources shows nine mills operating in Vernon Parish: three in or near Leesville, two in north-central Vernon Parish near Kurthwood, three in the parish's northeast corner along State Route 107, and another in the southeast corner (Cruikshank 1939:27). Three of these mills (one a hardwood plant) were producing 40,000 board feet per 10-hour day; five were producing up to 10,000 board feet per 10-hour day. In addition, there was a cooperage plant and a turpentine still.

It is difficult to conceptualize the immense amount of lumber produced at Vernon Parish's ubiquitous mills, large and small, from 1897 until 1940 or to fully comprehend the impact this industry had on the parish. Indisputably, the Vernon Parish pinelands provided the nation with billions of board feet of pine during this period. While accurate statistics of production in Vernon Parish alone are unavailable, some additional (admittedly random) facts might shed light on the industry's tremendous impact on not only the parish but also the entire United States.

In looking at the parish's output, as previously noted, the Fullerton mill alone produced 2.25 billion board feet in its lifetime. In a 1912 publication, a map depicting the location of 82 Louisiana pine mills that produced more than 10 million board feet a year shows six mills in Vernon Parish (Foster 1912:12). This same publication states that Vernon Parish had the "best longleaf pine timber in the State" (Foster 1912:11). Census figures indicate that in 1909 an average of 46,072 people were employed each month in Louisiana's 702 lumber establishments—a 202.3 percent increase from 1899. Thirty-seven "Manufactories" operated in Vernon Parish in 1919 and 18 in 1929, many of which must have been lumber mills. Another source, the Vernon Parish Planning Board (1949:8), records 11 mills operating in Vernon Parish in 1920. Balance this information with the fact that Louisiana led the nation in the production of yellow pine from at least 1904 until 1919, and it becomes clear that Vernon Parish lumber found its way into a significant number of American houses in the early twentieth century. Despite the loss of mills at the end of the 1920s, Vernon Parish's contribution continued. A ca. 1945 Vernon Parish Chamber of Commerce publication claims that Vernon Parish led the state in timber production every year from 1930 to 1938, except for 1931 (Leesville–Vernon Parish Chamber of Commerce 1945:32).

TURPENTINE PRODUCTION
Lumber was (and is) far and away the primary resource extracted from the pinelands of Vernon Parish and west-central Louisiana. However, a small

naval stores industry also thrived in the parish. All over the Vernon Parish landscape but especially in the Fort Polk region, the remains of this industry are found in the form of broken clay Herty turpentine cups that are almost as ubiquitous as pine trees. Actually, the term *naval stores* refers to a number of related processes in which the gum (oleoresin) of primarily longleaf yellow pine (*Pinus palustris*) and some slash pine (*Pinus elliottii*) is extracted and processed into turpentine, rosin, tar, and pitch (Bond 1987; Brown 1919:167–187; Perry 1947; Robinson 1988; Sharrer 1981:241–270; Williams 1989:83–90). Early in colonial history, naval stores also referred to the timber used in building wooden ships, which was amply provided for by the North American forests (Williams 1989:83). In time, the term came to be associated more with liquid forms of extracted pine gum, especially turpentine and rosin.

Louisiana's peak turpentine days spanned from 1910 to 1925. In 1905, Louisiana, Texas, and Mississippi combined only accounted for 11 percent of the total U.S. production of naval stores. By 1918–1919, Texas and Louisiana produced 31 percent (Gamble 1921a:79). Louisiana's production alone was as follows: 1905, 0.8 percent; 1908, 4.6 percent; 1910, 2.8 percent; 1914, 8.3 percent; and 1918–1919, 15.5 percent (Gamble 1921a:81).

Initially, the lumber barons were not enthusiastic about the naval stores industry because turpentining kept the trees from being cut, and this did not mesh with their cut-and-run business practices. Generally, lumbermen everywhere looked upon naval stores largely as a nuisance (Speh 1921:111). The lumberman's attitude slowly changed with the invention of the cup method of turpentine extraction. Once convinced, the big companies like Lutcher and Moore, Great Southern, Industrial Lumber, and Gulf Lumber ran their own naval stores departments, with turpentine extraction running a few years ahead of cutting (Speh 1921:111). Many other timber owners sold turpentine rights to naval stores companies before selling or cutting the timber, especially in times of tight money (Foster 1912:31). In the west-central Louisiana region, the naval stores companies would usually come in one to three years before the cutting began (Hartman 1922:68).

It is doubtful that turpentine, tar, and pitch were extracted on an industrial level in Vernon Parish much before the turn of the twentieth century. One source states that the first naval stores company was Naval Stores of New Orleans, which moved into Vernon Parish around 1915 (Williams 1976:3), establishing camps at Hutton, Hornbeck, Slagle, and Old Groves Field. Fullerton's distillery was located at Rustville, just south of town. Fullerton employee Otis Richardson (1983:199) stated that where he worked, "The trees all showed the turpentine face." This explains why turpentine cups are found all around Fort Polk. The Fullerton operation at Rustville included "two 25 barrel kettles distilling 15 barrels of spirits a day, leaving 45 barrels of rosin. The idea is to keep three years ahead of the sawyer as it has been proven that it does not injure the pine for lumber to bleed the trees three years" (from a newspaper article in Block 1996:157). The Rustville operation employed as many as 225 men, most of whom were black. In fact, turpentining in western Louisiana was primarily done by black laborers living in temporary camps.

Turpentining was also conducted in the Kisatchie region after the railroad was built to Kurthwood (Kadlecek and Bullard 1994:81). Another still operated between Alco and Hutton around 1937 (Juneau 1937:1). In the Kisatchie region, sap was distilled in small camps and the turpentine was then shipped out by rail. One of only four stills operating in Louisiana in 1937 was at Leesville (Winters et al. 1943:27); it was most likely using stumpwood. Another still operating around 1938 and 1939 was in the northeast corner of Vernon Parish along State Route 107 (Cruikshank 1939:27). At that time, a forest survey study estimated that there were some 1.4 million acres of stumpwood available for the naval stores industry in the west-central Louisiana region spread out over an area of 5.7 million acres from Calcasieu Parish north to Sabine Parish and east to La Salle Parish (Cruikshank 1939:20).

At the turn of the twentieth century, an important innovation in sap extraction reduced the damage to trees, thus making it more palatable to the timber giants. It allowed the live trees to be exploited for gum more efficiently and then cut for lumber. The success of this new "cup-and-gutter" system brought turpentining to Vernon Parish on an industrial level.

While traveling in France, Dr. Charles Herty noticed that the French system of turpentine collecting consisted of cutting shallow chips into the tree and attaching metal gutters, which channeled the gum into clay cups. This eliminated the need to cut a deep cavity into the tree. Also, the gutter and cup could be moved up the tree's face, reducing the amount of inferior scrape. After experimenting with this system in the United States, Herty eventually convinced the industry of its merits, changing the way gum was collected (Veitch and Grotlisch 1921:135). Herty, in partnership with C. L. Krager, formed the Herty Turpentine Cup Company to manufacture the clay cups. The name Herty is now associated with the "flower pots" strewn over much of Florida, Georgia, and Louisiana (Smith and Rogers 1979:42).

The Herty cup was quickly adopted by the naval stores industry and by 1904 was in extensive use. By 1908, half the turpentine operations in Louisiana and Texas were using the cup-and-gutter system (Ostrum and Dorman 1945:3). Galvanized metal cups were invented around 1914, reducing the market for Herty cups, but the clay pots were manufactured and used as late as 1942, in which year the company dissolved (Forney 1985:277). One reason the Herty cups maintained their huge market share was that the metal cups would rust and stain, degrading the gum (Dunwody 1921:132). Herty cups did have one weakness though: they broke. Frost was one culprit. Another problem was that the clay flower pots hanging on the sides of trees became an irresistible temptation to deep-woods sharpshooting hunters (Ostrum and Dorman 1945:3). Anyone who has walked in the Fort Polk woods knows that Fullerton used both clay and metal cups (Richardson 1983:199).

The average distillery's layout included (1) a still house, consisting of an open shed containing the still and worm, (2) a shed for storing turpentine, (3) a cooperage for making rosin barrels, and (4) a rosin screen and rosin barrel platform (Brown 1919:179). Large plants, like those seen at Rustville, had housing for laborers, a blacksmith forge, and stables for the mules (Sharrer 1981:258). However, smaller field operations were probably more prevalent in Vernon Parish. Archaeological site 16VN1221, within Fort Polk, is a good example. This site was the processing point for turpentine collected in the surrounding woods for the Four L Company. Associated with the still and located some four miles to its west was a camp for the company's black workers. The stills and outbuildings for this camp, like many at this time, were portable, being brought to the site via a tramline (Thomas et al. 1993d:138). The site consisted of the remains of the distillery, a dam and pond, burned resin, tramlines, a barrel hoop concentration (cooperage), and domestic sites or camps. The investigators add that some long-term sites might include a church or store and a cemetery (Thomas et al. 1993:189). However, this seems unlikely within Fort Polk because the turpentine companies were in the area only a short time and the camps were portable.

Replanting the Forest

The speed with which the land was cut over between the late 1890s and 1929 was partially due to the fact that investors and industrialists were heavily bonded. To meet interest payments on their land and mills, they increased cutting and production despite current market rates. This created a lumber glut, which decreased profits, which led to the need to again increase production, thus completing a dangerous cycle (Foster 1912:24). A business depression in 1907 further complicated the situation. Then, World War I increased the demand for lumber. None of these events slowed production until the late 1920s, when Foster's prediction of disappearing forests was close to fulfillment.

While the lumber barons were rapidly depleting the forests and folks experienced a boom in material wealth, a few people worried about the future. As early as 1904, the Louisiana legislature passed an act creating a department of forestry for "the preservation of forests of this state, and the suppression and prevention of forest fires; to provide for the reforestation of denuded forest land, and for the proper instruction relative to forestry in the public schools" (Kerr 1958:3). Although this legislation had no immediate impact, it set the stage for future action.

In 1908, Louisiana passed another act creating a state conservation commission. The chairman, Henry E. Hardtner, became known as the Father of Forestry in the South (Kerr 1958:2). A successful industrialist who established the Urania Lumber Company in 1898 (Burns 1982:11; Kerr 1958:3), he was one of a few turn-of-the-century lumbermen who foresaw the pine landscape's bleak future. He became interested in the possibility that forests could be regenerated and experimented on his own lands. His fame in speaking on reforestation eventually led to an invitation to President Theodore Roosevelt's 1908 Conference of Governors on conservation. From that time forward, he worked for conservation in Louisiana.

The conservation commission's work resulted in another act in 1910, which provided for contracts between the state and landowners whereby denuded land could be reforested. Hardtner signed the first contract on 28,000 acres of his own land. The position of state forester was also established that year. Two years later, the commission was given full authority over all forestry matters, an arrangement that lasted until 1944 (Kerr 1958:6).

Eventually, a new but related wood industry helped stem the tide of the impending disaster overtaking the pinelands during the Depression. In 1923, State Forester V. H. Sonderegger traveled to New England to meet with paper companies. Louisiana pulpwood proved excellent for making paper. Slowly, paper mills replaced the lumber mills in Louisiana. Quick-growing pulpwood provided a fast economic return for tree farmers. As a result, paper mills became critical to the state's reforestation effort (Kerr 1958:13).

The creation of the Kisatchie National Forest, with some 84,825 acres now used by Fort Polk for training, was a long and complex process that began in the 1920s and continued through the 1930s. According to Burns (1982:18), the story begins with a local Kisatchie schoolteacher named Caroline Dormon. Her indefatigable efforts in protecting the pineland are legendary. First, she led the movement to keep the Kisatchie Wold virgin timber from being cut. She failed, but without pause continued her efforts to have it reforested. Recognition of her work led to a 1924 state act authorizing the state to cooperate with the federal government and allow it to purchase cut-over lands with the permission of local police juries (Burns 1982:20;

Kisatchie National Forest n.d.). In this same year, the U.S. Congress passed the Clarke-McNary Act allowing the purchase of cut-over lands for forests beyond the headwaters of navigable streams. With the state act passed, the state and federal governments worked together to create a national forest in west-central Louisiana.

Although Congress can pass acts, funding authorization is usually required for action to be taken, and this might not come for some time after an act's passage. Funding to purchase Kisatchie National Forest's first acres was not authorized until 1928 (Burns 1982:21). The land had to be found, legally titled, and purchased. This responsibility was left to Charles A. Plymale. Plymale came to Alexandria, Louisiana, on September 24, 1928, and immediately began the process of creating purchasing units. These units were "gross boundaries" within which the government could seek suitable land (Burns 1982:24). Not all the land within the boundaries was (nor is it today) owned by the government, but at least 50 percent has to be owned by the government for the area to be a National Forest. The Forest Service at first purchased, and now trades, lands within its boundaries with the goal of complete ownership. On average, the nation paid about $3 an acre for the purchase of the Kisatchie National Forest (Richardson 1960).

THE CIVILIAN CONSERVATION CORPS

The Depression hit the lumber industry as hard as many other industries throughout the country. Many lost their land to taxes or cut their trees to raise money. Lumber mill production dipped to 567 million board feet, the lowest it had been since 1889 (Kerr 1958:26). However, as a result of President Franklin Roosevelt's attempts to put the country to work, forestry and forests grew nationwide. In other words, while the Forest Service was able to acquire and create the National Forests, the goal of reforestation was accomplished through a combination of Forest Service leadership and the hard work of young men who joined the Civilian Conservation Corps (CCC).

The first action taken under Roosevelt's New Deal was the creation of the CCC in March 1933. This youth-oriented work program took thousands of men aged 18 to 25 off the streets and put them into the nation's forests where they constructed roads, bridges, and firebreaks; planted trees; and controlled mosquitoes, among other tasks. By 1941, when World War II suddenly created thousands of new jobs, the CCC had employed some 2.7 million men (Hofstadter et al. 1967:723).

Louisiana acted quickly to benefit from the CCC. State Forester Sonderegger was in Washington by April 1933, and by July the first camps were established in the state (Burns 1982:51; Kerr 1958:27). Over the course of the CCC's existence in Louisiana, as many as 53 camps were opened, and the youths constructed 3,000 bridges, 2,000 miles of telephone lines, 3,000 miles of truck trails, 3,000 miles of fire breaks, and 18 fire towers (Kerr 1958:27). They also improved highways, built recreational and picnic areas, created Valentine Lake, fought forest fires, and raised 220 miles of fencing, enclosing 80,000 acres of pinelands (Hardin 1939:415). Burns (1982:52, 61) adds that the CCC built levees, constructed state parks, surveyed the forest and state waterfowl, and helped construct air and army bases, including Camp Polk.

The Kisatchie National Forest had eight camps numbered F-1 through F-8. Camp F-4 was located 15 miles southeast of Leesville in the heart of the Vernon District, and F-2 was to its north near Provencal in Natchitoches Parish (Burns 1982:61). The Leesville camp was established in 1933 and remained open through the 1941–1942 enrollment period. In 1937, the CCC Official Annual indicates that camp F-4, making up the 5405th Company, was under the direction of First Lieutenant Henry H. West. The camp had a large recreation hall, first-aid building, and hot and cold water. According to the unit history, the unit originated in Georgia, and it spoke of the Georgia boys fitting well into the Leesville–De Ridder neighborhood (CCC 1937:107). Most of the original crew left the corps over the years though, and a glance at the roster indicates that by 1937, at least, the majority of enrollees were from Louisiana. Of these, most were from Leesville or De Ridder.

The history of the 5405th indicates that the company made a great contribution to the forest and the local community. By 1937, with the Winnfield camp's assistance, some nine million trees had been planted. Wise (1971:12) indicates that the CCC reforested 31,000 acres in Vernon Parish. Much of the work must have been done by the 5405th. The company built 150 miles of firebreaks, put up 65 miles of telephone lines, built 40 miles of "high service roads" including bridges, and fenced in 16,000 acres (CCC 1937:108). According to the Vernon Parish Planning Board (1949:20), the CCC's contribution in Vernon Parish included "three towers, 61 miles of telephone lines, 127 miles of firebreaks, 46 miles of roads, and 105 miles of plantation fences. A total of 42,080 acres were fenced, and 22,280 acres were planted." This tremendous accomplishment is even more notable when one recognizes that the 5405th's chief job—the one that took up most of their time to the point of morale problems—was fire suppression.

A Community Transformed, 1898–1940

Besides transforming the natural Vernon Parish landscape, the lumber industry radically altered the cultural landscape as well. The parish's preindustrial agrarian settlement pattern shifted from rivers to railroads and later to highways. Indeed the entire settlement system was made over. The population's ethnic mix and size shifted with the industry's fortunes. The political and social landscape changed also. There was little about Vernon Parish that was not affected in some way.

POPULATION AND SETTLEMENT SHIFT

Vernon Parish's population growth and decline between 1898 and 1940 was directly related to the rise and fall of the large lumber companies. The population increased by 75 percent between 1890 and 1900, with most of the growth occurring in the latter years after the Kansas City Southern (KCS) Railway and the timber giants established operations. This growth continued with a 98 percent increase between 1900 and 1920. In 1930, however, after the large mills had cut the timber and left, the census shows that the population was essentially the same as in 1920; it had decreased by 446 people. Although specific data are not available, one can reasonably assume that the population continued to rise during the early 1920s and fell during the latter half of that decade. This gradual downtrend continued through the thirties. The 1940 census recorded 905 fewer people in the parish than in 1930.

While many who came to the parish to work in the lumber industry in the early twentieth century stayed in the parish when the industry left, most of the African American population came and left with the large lumber companies. Blacks made up only a small minority of Vernon Parish's population prior to 1897. By 1900, the black population had more than doubled, and by 1910 it had nearly tripled. By 1920, African Americans in Vernon Parish numbered 5,103, representing 25 percent of the population compared with a 9 percent representation in 1890. However, the African American population declined to only 2,420 just before World War II. When the lumber and turpentine industries waned, African Americans migrated to northern urban regions.

Vernon Parish's nineteenth-century population was concentrated (if this word can be used) along the fertile Anacoco region in western Vernon Parish and along the Calcasieu in the northeastern section. The Fort Polk area was lightly settled. When the railroad was built, settlement concentrations shifted to the railroad line running through the center of the parish with Leesville as the center of population. With the lumber companies up and running full tilt in 1910, the greatest population concentration was in Leesville and in parish Ward 5—the region encompassing Fort Polk. In 1910, Leesville accounted for 12 percent and Fullerton for 7 percent of the parish population. Wards 1 and 5 together (including the two towns) contained 52 percent of the parish population. Ward 4, adjacent to both, accounted for another 19 percent. In other words, 71 percent of Vernon Parish's population lived in the three wards in which the lumber giants operated mills. In fact, Ward 5 quadrupled in population between 1900 and 1910. When Fullerton Mill closed, Ward 5 experienced a 49 percent drop in population. In 1930, population centers again shifted, this time to Ward 6, because the lumber activity in Vernon Parish had shifted to the Kisatchie region. But Leesville continued to have the greatest concentration of people, a trend that would continue to the present (Smith 1999:139–141).

Although Ward 5 had the largest ward population in 1910 (and probably 1920), settlement was concentrated heavily at Fullerton and along the railroad that ran from Fullerton to the KCS Railway's main line just south of modern Fort Polk. Within Fort Polk's boundaries, population remained scattered and sparse.

Cantley and Kern's (1984:54–64) examination of landownership within a small portion of Fort Polk provides valuable insights into the local settlement pattern. Cantley and Kern focused their attention on the settlement of one township, T1N R7W, which today is in the heart of Fort Polk. Specifically, they compared the township's 1910 tax assessor's plats of landownership to the 1910 census.

More than 80 percent of township land was under the ownership of the Gulf Lumber Company and Nona Mills, with an additional seven percent owned by other corporations. The corporations also owned the timber rights to 22 private parcels. Only 49 parcels were owned by private citizens, and these averaged only 55 acres. It is not known whether the parcels owned by the corporations had been previously owned by private citizens, but the 1913 Bureau of Corporations study strongly implies that, prior to the twentieth century, most land in this region had been purchased by timber speculators and lumber corporations as first-time purchases from the government.

Although there were 49 privately owned parcels in the township, private landownership does not correspond directly to actual population levels for several reasons: (1) some individuals owned multiple parcels, (2) some parcels were not settled by their owners, (3) some parcels were rented, and (4) some corporation parcels and many government parcels were occupied by squatters whose holdings do not appear on plat. But, recognizing some relationship between private ownership and actual occupation, how many people lived in the township? In trying to answer this question, Cantley and Kern examined tax plat maps and the U.S. Census for township T1N R7W. They found 72 possible households, of which only 20 could be confirmed as consisting of landowners. Twenty-two households were renters, although some of these may not have been renting in the township, but rather living

adjacent to it. Thirty landholding households were assumed to be in neigh-
boring townships since they were not in the tax assessment (Cantley and
Kern 1984:59). The 20 confirmed landowners provided a rough estimate of
the number of farms in the township, not counting squatters who may or
may not have been counted in the census. There is good reason to believe
that at least a few squatters were living within Fort Polk even as late as the
1930s. Juneau (1937) reports that, during the Depression, timber companies
in the Kurthwood area charged squatters $0.50 to $1 to settle on their cut-
over lands. The nominal rent prevented squatters from gaining landownership rights.

The general distribution and matrix of landownership did not change
dramatically in the examined township throughout the period from 1910 to
1940. In 1940, private citizens owned 12 percent of the land, down from 13
percent in 1910. Individual parcels numbered 67 compared with 49 in 1910.
Corporate landownership was reduced as a result of the U.S. Forest Service's
purchasing numerous acres of cut-over land from Gulf Lumber and other
lumber companies. The government owned 51 percent of the township in
1940, and corporate ownership was down to 36 percent (Cantley and Kern
1984:63).

Cantley and Kern only looked at one township in their study. The real-
estate tract register for Fort Polk (Office of the Chief Engineers 1975) provides a broader perspective of landownership distribution in the entire area
that became Camp Polk in the 1940s. The register is divided into several
sections including the Main Fort, the artillery range, and the Peason Ridge
acquisitions. It indicates that only 7,543.84 acres, or seven percent of the
Main Fort, was in private ownership, divided up into 160 separate small
tracts. At Peason Ridge, only three percent was in private ownership, divided into 30 separate tracts. It is not known how much of the property
purchased by the Forest Service was in private ownership, but one can assume that most of their property was purchased from lumber companies.
The small percentages of private ownership reflected in the register, combined with the data from the Cantley-Kern study, strongly support the assertion that very little of Fort Polk was ever in the ownership of private farming
citizens.

Although there is no one-to-one correlation between the number of parcels and the number of homesteads in any given region, in a rural area like
Fort Polk the number of parcels in private ownership gives an idea as to the
number of homesteads. In light of the data presented herein for the twentieth
century and given that the installation's hogwallow lands were sparsely settled
in the antebellum period and only slightly more populated before the land
speculators arrived, and also considering that the area was closed out by

land speculation around the late 1880s, it is not unreasonable to speculate that less than 15 percent of the land that became Fort Polk was ever settled or farmed. To put it more accurately, less than 15 percent of the land was ever purchased or otherwise legally claimed and used by private citizens. This 15 percent estimate is actually rather high and most assuredly incorporates any land that may have ever been settled by squatters.

In 1940, the U.S. Forest Service already owned 37 percent of the Main Fort and 29 percent of the Peason Ridge region, having purchased the land mostly from lumber companies. Still, lumber companies owned 36 percent of the Main Fort and 66 percent of Peason Ridge. All together, in 1940, the lumber companies and other commercial interests owned 59 percent of Fort Polk; the federal government, 34 percent; and private citizens, 6 percent.

AGRICULTURAL PERSISTENCE
While the southern and northern woods echoed with the sounds of falling trees, steam loaders, and steam engines, Vernon Parish farmers quietly pursued their husbandry. In those areas where lumber mills were busy, farmers and their sons became part-time lumbermen (Hadnot n.d.b). During down times at the mill, they returned to the fields. In fact, although the lumber mills brought the parish prosperity and employment, agriculture remained the main nontimber occupation throughout the twentieth century. Across the rural landscape, farming was still the primary occupation. This was especially true within the Fort Polk boundaries. Cantley and Kern's (1984:59) study, for instance, indicates that of 86 "occupations" listed in T1N R7W, 60 percent were in farming and 33 percent were lumber industry positions such as turpentine workers, tie cutters, and mill laborers. Perhaps only a few months before or after the census taker gathered his data, these percentages may have changed as a lumber mill hired or laid off people. In any case, many of these workers would go back to farming when the mills closed. In 1940, Vernon Parish had a working population of 4,689. Agriculture employed 43 percent of this population and the lumber industry 17 percent.

Farm census data for the twentieth century demonstrate the persistence of independent owner-operated, yeoman farms. At the turn of the century, most Vernon Parish farms (42 percent) were in the neighborhood of 100 to 174 acres, but from then on farms got smaller until in 1930, when half the farms were 20 to 49 acres (52 percent). Farms over 175 acres never represented more than 14 percent (in 1900) of the parish farms; by 1930 and 1940 this figure had dropped to around 2 percent. Within Fort Polk, the real-estate tract register of property purchased for the camp indicates that most farms there were very small: 38 percent of the tracts were between 20 and 49 acres and these probably were subsistence or self-sufficient farms.

Prior to the arrival of the railroads, 79 to 94 percent of the farms were farmer owned. This ownership trend continued even during the Depression, when the rest of the South was in high tenure. In 1900, 90 percent of farms were owned; in 1910, 82 percent; and in 1920, 85 percent. During the Depression, in 1930, 75 percent of farms were still wholly or partially owned, as were 72 percent in 1940. In contrast, Woofter's (1936:195) study of farm tenure in the South indicated that in 1910, 65.3 percent of all farms in 29 Louisiana parishes were tenant farms. Overall, in 1910, the state rate was 55 percent tenancy. The U.S. Census indicated that tenancy for all Louisiana farms in 1920, 1930, and 1940 was 57 percent, 66 percent, and 59.4 percent, respectively. Vernon Parish farmers for the most part retained their farms through the Depression. Even the majority of the black farm population in Vernon Parish owned their own farms until the 1940s.

Corn continued to be a farm mainstay and, except for around 1920, it increased over the years from its nineteenth-century production levels. Although sweet potato production declined drastically in 1940, the crop was still being produced on a relatively large scale. On the other hand, oats were abandoned in the 1930s. Perhaps farmers started to grow cotton on land previously used for oats. The cotton acreage in 1930 showed a radical increase after the decline seen between 1900 and 1920. Because raising cotton is time consuming, it is possible the decrease in cotton production during these earlier years was a reflection of farmers finding employment in the lumber industry. Once the mills closed, around the 1930s, farmers returned to their fields and to cotton.

Another reason for higher cotton production may relate to the use of fertilizers. By 1930, farmers were beginning to accept the advice of extension agents, who were promoting fertilizers to grow crops on infertile soils. Interestingly, cotton acreage in 1940 was half that of 1930, but yields were equivalent, probably as a result of improved agricultural practices. Wool production more than doubled between 1890 and 1900 and then dropped significantly in the 1920s, only to rise again in 1940.

Some subtle changes are seen in the parish's animal production during the twentieth century. It would appear that mechanization came late to the Vernon Parish farmer. The number of horses and mules combined grew gradually until 1940, when the number dropped radically. Cattle numbers fluctuated throughout the study period.

Like all farmers, Vernon Parish's agrarians were conservative in their trade, if not in their politics. The first agricultural agent, Horace A. Stewart, came to Leesville in 1909 (Curry Ford in Hadnot n.d.b). He had great difficulty getting the farmers to listen to his new ways. Once, he encouraged 12 young men to grow an acre of corn using fertilizer and new cultivation methods. The crops were successful, resulting in between 80 and 100 bushels of corn per acre; the average at that time was 15 bushels per acre. Although Stewart was the talk of Leesville, the farmers ignored him. His success came slowly by teaching schoolchildren and by forming 4-H and home demonstration programs (Curry Ford in Hadnot n.d.b).

Despite resistance, the work of the agricultural agents continued as they offered assistance in land terracing and hog and cattle vaccination. Agents also established demonstration programs, distributed fertilizers, and, beginning around 1926, promoted beef canning (Wise 1971:87). In the 1930s, a federal effort was initiated in the South to eradicate cow fevers, and all cattle were required to be dipped periodically to kill ticks. Western Louisiana farmers were adamantly against this program, at least partly because of the difficulty in rounding up the cattle in the summer and running them through concrete vats full of creosote. Apparently some federal agents were even killed while attempting to inspect regional farms. There are also stories of farmers dynamiting the vats (Armstrong 1958:165; Marler 1994:176).

THE CHANGING TRANSPORTATION LANDSCAPE

The twentieth-century transportation network emerged from the parish's nineteenth-century trails. Roads that served the pioneers were continually if slowly improved from 1897 to 1940. Generally, the main arteries today follow the main routes of the nineteenth century. Improvement and expansion of the system in the twentieth century was the result of several different economic and political developments: the most important was the rise of the lumber industry.

The lumber companies had to get into and out of the pinelands and transport their products to national markets. To accomplish this, lumber companies and railroads were intricately linked under the control of the industrial giants, who put up the capital to build the railroads and bought the land to cut the timber. On the one hand, the railroad enabled the lumber companies to move into the region. However, from a broader perspective, the railroad was planned and built in conjunction with speculators and industrialists purchasing timber resources back in the 1880s. In other words, most of the lumber barons were also railroad barons.

Once the lumber companies were up and running, new roads were built and more rails were quickly laid. In return, the companies brought prosperity to the parish. The parish government received increased revenues through taxation. These revenues, in turn, were used to construct new roads and maintain the old. Prosperity also allowed some to buy those new horseless carriages, and, as a result, the pressure to build new roads increased. Police jury records of the early twentieth century show that new roads continued to be a major concern. When the last of the great lumber companies left in the late 1920s, the road system received a boost from state and federal road programs, which led to the introduction of paved roads. During the Depression, the Civilian Conservation Corps (CCC) and Forest Service made additional improvements. The final boost to road development was in the early 1940s, when the U.S. Army moved into the parish. Bridges, culverts, and roads were improved or built to support the movement of military equipment and personnel.

In twentieth-century Vernon Parish, it would appear that "all roads led to Leesville." Those not leading to Leesville disappeared or became secondary roads, while those leading to the town became the parish's main arteries. Leesville, at the parish's geographical center, became not only the center of commerce, industry, and government but also the center of Vernon Parish's transportation web as well. This is evident when one looks at the 1930 parish highway map (Figure 7.4). With few exceptions, the majority of improved roads depicted on this map run through Leesville.

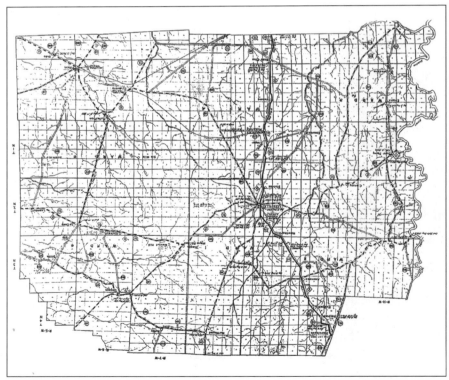

Figure 7.4 — Vernon Parish map, 1930 (Louisiana Highway Commission 1930).

There is a near complete absence of roads within the Fort Polk area during this time. A lone gravel road, State Highway 472, runs from LaCamp to Fullerton, and this became the Fullerton road within the installation today. Another gravel road, Route 118, runs from Cravens to Leesville, which is modern Route 10. There are two dirt roads, one running east and west from approximately the location of Coopers to Fullerton. It is possible that the modern Mill Creek and Holly Springs roads within the installation are remnants of this old road. The other is on the east border of Fort Polk. Most likely there were numerous unmarked trails in the fort region.

It is difficult to accurately project the Peason Ridge and Horse's Head Training Areas on road maps and, thus, difficult to determine the road system there. It would appear that there were few good roads within these areas. Figure 7.4 indicates that Highway 39, which is part of State Route 117 today, was probably an early-twentieth-century road connecting Kisatchie with Kurthwood and Leesville. Also, a secondary road, Route 172, ran southwest from the hamlet of Peason. Beyond this, there appears to have been no other roads except farm and logging trails. Most of these roads would have been constructed rather late.

Throughout the early twentieth century, Vernon Parish residents simply had to deal the best they could with bad roads, which became impassable when it rained. Agricultural Agent Stella Jones complained that the roads were so bad in the early 1930s that her monthly trip to Leander, a village located along State Route 21 on the parish's eastern edge, took two days (Jones in Wise 1971:86). During the Depression, relief efforts were hindered by the poor roads. Although there were improved roads in Vernon Parish, the relief fund in 1935 noted that "unfortunately, very few of our clients live on these [improved roads], and the rest of the road system, as a whole, is unimproved dirt roads that become impassable during the winter months" (Brown et al. 1935:6). Still, with unprecedented wealth from the lumber companies, Vernon Parish citizens took to the roads in automobiles early in the century. The first cars in the parish were ordered by Kyle Ferguson, a Mr. McFarland, and Arthur Franklin in 1907 (Werner and Rowzee n.d.). By 1919, as many as 306 automobiles, but no tractors, were registered in the parish (Louisiana Department of Agriculture and Immigration 1920:96).

Road improvements continued in the middle and late 1930s and the 1940s. As stated previously, the CCC, the Forest Service, and the army made major improvements. By 1945, Vernon Parish had four hard-surfaced roads (Leesville–Vernon Parish Chamber of Commerce 1945:27). By 1949, improvements resulted in 82 miles of hard-surfaced roads and 253 miles of graveled roads (Vernon Parish Planning Board 1949:60). At that time, there were 4,800 cars and 3,100 trucks registered in the parish. Three bus lines, five taxi companies, and the Kansas City Southern (KCS) lines provided public transportation, which was mostly used by Fort Polk soldiers. The KCS had two passenger trains leaving at 12:50 and 5:10 daily, squeezed between the heavy freight traffic. The bus lines ran five times daily.

Besides cars and buggies, railroads were the only other major form of transportation. Without doubt, the railroads opened Vernon Parish to the world and vice versa. Rails allowed the lumber companies to move into the parish, cut the timber, and send it to national and world markets. Rails created an opportunity and means for the farming community to move its crops to state and national markets. Rails brought thousands of men to Fort Polk and sent them away as soldiers, beginning in 1940. At the same time, rails brought the world's goods and services to Vernon Parish's rustic citizens.

Throughout the period from 1897 to 1940, the KCS line was the main freight and passenger route through the parish. The company's full name was the Kansas City, Shreveport, and Gulf Terminal Company, chartered for service in Louisiana on July 27, 1897. The KCS & G was under the control of the KCS, however, which remained the controlling company throughout the early twentieth century. A large Missouri-based corporation, the KCS owned or controlled many railway subsidiaries, such as the Texarkana and Fort Smith and the Arkansas Western (Poor's Manual 1915:761–765). The KCS still runs today along the line from Shreveport to Lake Charles. In Vernon Parish, it follows the same general line it always has, paralleling U.S. Route 171 from Hornbeck to Rosepine.

The KCS route through the parish drew population, development, and industry like a magnet. Many of Vernon Parish's lumber companies built their mills along its long north-south line. Even the Gulf Lumber Company built a mill and town just south of Leesville along this route (Miller 1997). But as the timber around this area was being depleted, the company reached deeper into the forests, building the town of Fullerton within the heart of the Fort Polk region. To get into and out of that area, branch lines were needed. Like the other great lumber barons, S. H. Fullerton solved the problem by building his own branch line, the Gulf and Sabine River Railroad (G & SR) chartered on September 1, 1906. He built one line from his mill at Stables southwest to Johnson, Louisiana—the line connected to the KCS at Stables— and another at Leesville that ran northwest. At Fullerton, he built a line running south to Nitram connecting with the east-west Jasper and Eastern Railway, the only other main line in the parish (Poor's Manual 1915:712). In 1915, the Stables–to–Johnson line was 11.75 miles long and the north branch stretched 15 miles. The Fullerton line, 17.81 miles long by 1915, was perhaps twice as long in 1921, as two branches ran northwest and northeast from Fullerton deep into the Fort Polk pinelands. R. W. Fullerton and

Robert Fullerton, Jr., were directors of the railroad along with S. H. Fullerton. J. T. Burlingame acted as the general manager at Fullerton (Poor's Manual 1915:713).

The G & SR was no mere logging train. Fullerton's railroad was a standard-gauge railroad that, through the Jasper and Eastern, connected to many points south of Vernon Parish and throughout southern Louisiana and Texas. During World War I, it made two daily passenger runs to Lake Charles (Burns 1970:3). Fullerton's railroad had nine locomotives, two passenger cars, 129 freight cars, and 14 service cars. Fullerton planned to expand the railroad to Merryville and Alexandria, but that may not have happened (Poor's Manual 1915:712). The G & SR was abandoned before 1935 (Poor's Manual 1935:64), probably when the mill closed. On the other hand, the 1930 highway map indicates a line running from Cravens to Pickering called the Louisiana Central Railroad. This line, running through the heart of Fort Polk, might have been part of Fullerton's old line.

At least three branch lines served the lumber companies in the Peason Ridge region. The Old River and Kisatchie (OR & K) ran from Old River to Jerguson, Louisiana, at least as early as 1906 (Poor's Manual 1906:321). At that time it had four locomotives, 36 logging cars, and four box cars. It was a true logging train with 3-foot-gauge rails running for 26 miles. The OR & K was owned by the Montrose Lumber Company in 1906, but by 1915 the Frost-Johnson Lumber Company owned the railroad, at which time three locomotives and 36 freight cars were running and the rail line had been reduced to 19 miles (Poor's Manual 1915:948). There was also a short branch line of 10.5 miles running from Sandel, Louisiana, in Sabine Parish to Peason. This railroad, the Christie and Eastern Railroad, is also shown on a 1930 Louisiana Highway Commission map. Not much is known about this branch, other than that it was a short private railroad abandoned by 1935 (Poor's Manual 1935:60).

Finally, the army built a railroad during the war to transport soldiers to and from Camp Claiborne and Fort Polk (O'Halloran 1951–1952:1/31/1952). This railroad was 47.66 miles long and used the old Hillger-Deutches-Edwards logging road (Gray 1955:32).

LUMBER TOWNS, HAMLETS, AND POST STOPS

The growth and decline of Vernon Parish's population in the twentieth century is clearly evident in the large number of little villages that sprang up across the landscape between 1897 and 1920 only to be abandoned in the late 1920s and the 1930s. Those villages and towns that depended solely on the mills for their survival had a short but intense life. Throughout the period from 1897 until World War II, Vernon Parish remained primarily a rural, country parish. Its largest towns were Leesville and Fullerton, both serving the Fort Polk region.

All that remains of Fullerton today is an extensive archaeological site within Fort Polk, but it stands as clear testimony to the wealth and prosperity experienced by its residents. In 1906, S. H. Fullerton arrived and literally carved a modern (essentially futuristic) town out of the forest. Named for its founder, Fullerton provided unprecedented material wealth for the common man. Other mill towns boasted similar success and a diversity of shops and facilities for its residents, but at its economic peak Fullerton was probably the largest mill town (except perhaps for Leesville) in Vernon Parish and it might have been the largest in all of western Louisiana.

Fullerton was a planned community (Burns 1979). The workers' houses were described as "comfortable" and, indeed, for the early twentieth century, they were very comfortable, with free electricity 24 hours a day, running water, iceboxes, indoor plumbing, and sewer connections (Burns 1970:1). There was little difference between the managers' and laborers' houses in terms of size or amenities, but each house style was a little different (Richardson 1983:198). The town had an elementary school and a high school with a checkout library and a concrete swimming pool. The pool was filled from the Whiskey Chitto through a drainpipe that occasionally discharged, besides cool water, a water moccasin into the throng of happy swimmers—lending extra excitement (Richardson 1983:199).

Two hotels were opened in Fullerton, the first of which burned. The original building was a two-story, U-shaped structure with a veranda and was heated by electricity (Richardson 1983:198). The second hotel was called the Hotel Des Pines and boasted individual rather than boarding-house dining, hot water, and baths in every room.

The town's business district contained a commissary, market, telephone office, bank, and drugstore with soda fountain, all in one large steel and concrete building. The commissary was supplied with fresh vegetables by local farmers. A post office, barber shop with three barbers, feed store, bakery, cafe, dairy, picture show, jail, blacksmith shop, refrigeration plant (icehouse), and train depot could also be found in town (Burns 1970:4, 8; Richardson 1983:199). Two dance pavilions (with separate facilities for whites and blacks), a ball park with a team that Red Smith once played on, a basketball court, and playgrounds provided the community with entertainment. A Masonic Lodge, two churches, and a hospital staffed by company doctors met the town's spiritual and health needs.

Of course, the Gulf Lumber Company owned the town and many (but not all) of its shops. Houses rented for around $20 a month for workers and $13 for foremen and were like modern condominiums in that rent included the cost of repairs and upkeep (Burns 1970:7–8). Employees with families paid $2.50 for medical service; single men paid $1.50. Burns (1979:203, 205) implies that, unlike many other lumber companies, Gulf Lumber did not issue scrip or tokens. Such a system of payment forced employees to spend their "money" in company stores, thus keeping them tied to the company. Instead, Gulf Lumber paid wages in cash.

White, black, and Mexican workers were segregated. The Mexican workers lived at Smokey Hill in houses built as part of Gulf Lumber Company's original camp number 1. (In fact, several camps were set up in the woods for workers. Richardson notes that there were seven in 1915.) Housing for blacks was less impressive than that for whites. Blacks were concentrated beyond the railroad spur in the Quarters, which were described by Richardson (1983:199) as "dreary, temporary settlements." Though segregated by their living areas and as laborers in the forests, workers were more integrated in the mills.

Fullerton's fortunes rose and fell with the mill. By 1927, most of the land had been cut over. The company pulled out and attempted to sell the town for about $50,000—a fraction of the corporation's $3.5 million investment (Burns 1970:5)—but there were no buyers. Operations died slowly. First the logging crews went; then the sawmill closed, as did the dry kilns. Then the people moved away. Fullerton made a celebration of the felling of the last tree, selecting one white and one black laborer to cut it down. Burns (1970:6) reports that the tree's rings dated it at around 800 years old. Later in the ceremony, the steam whistle was tied down, and its wail slowly and sadly changed pitch as it ran out of steam. Between 1933 and 1938, the U.S. Forest Service purchased 36,000 acres of Fullerton land at $1.40 per acre (Burns 1970:6).

Centrally located Leesville was Vernon Parish's seat of government and its predominant town in the late nineteenth century. It has never relinquished its prominence. Only Fullerton, in the 1920s, ever challenged Leesville. Wise (1971:29) states that Leesville was first incorporated in 1898, but Lawrence (1961) and Hernandez (1959) argue that the date was February 15, 1900. Leesville was incorporated as a town in 1915 (Vernon Parish Tourist and Recreation Commission n.d.).

Leesville, at the turn of the century, was the pride of Vernon Parish. This "enterprising little city of 1,300 inhabitants" was regarded as an example of modern, progressive Vernon Parish (*Vernon News* 1900). By 1897, Leesville had erected a jail "capable of accommodating twenty or thirty prisoners," and a new brick and stone courthouse was completed in 1899 (*Vernon News* 1900). Lining the streets were 10 general stores, four drugstores, three hotels, two restaurants, two barber shops, two blacksmith shops, two livery stables, boarding houses, a bakery, a butcher shop, two millinery stores, two ice cream parlors, a fruit and vegetable shop, and a photograph gallery. The *Vernon News* proudly noted that the town had three "club rooms and [a] billiard hall," but no saloons. There were enough residents to keep seven doctors, a dentist, seven attorneys, an undertaker, three tailors, and a shoe-maker in business. And, in 1928, the parish's first hospital was built in Leesville (Vernon Parish Planning Board 1949:40).

In 1904, two banks served the community: First National Bank of Leesville and the Bank of Leesville (Dalehite 1962:3). Later, by 1918, First State Bank and West Louisiana Bank had been established in town. Leesville was probably the site of most if not all of the banks in the parish during the early part of the twentieth century.

With plenty of empty land nearby to be occupied by new settlers, two real estate agents and a United States commissioner worked out of Leesville. In 1911, the town even had its own planned community to attract northern immigrants. Called McFarland Heights, this 76-acre tract was owned by the Leesville Real Estate and Improvement Company (*Earth News* 1911).

With the presence of Nona Mills, the town had a complete waterworks system. The water system was served by a 100-foot-high tower supporting a 35-foot-high, 30-foot-wide water reservoir that produced enough pressure to reach to the third story of the town's only three-story building (Wise 1971:29). An electric light plant was also constructed.

Leesville was also the center of west-central Louisiana news and infor-mation. At the turn of the twentieth century, the *Vernon News*, a weekly paper, was still in print. However, it was the *Leesville Leader*, established in 1898, that became the parish's main newspaper (Wise 1971:24). The *Leesville Leader* was the successor to the *Lightning* (or *Leesville Lightning*), which was first published sometime prior to 1898. The parish played an important role in social movements at this time. From these sprang the populist paper, *People's Friend*, in the late nineteenth century (Louisiana Department of Agriculture and Immigration 1928:187).

Leesville was home to many people, but some, however, were less than enamored with Leesville. Famed movie actress Joan Blondell was quoted in a 1931 newspaper article as saying that "on Saturday unless somebody stabbed somebody else, the day was unsuccessful for the town as well as our restaurant" (in Wise 1988). She may have had a point. For instance, on Sep-tember 25, 1930, an article in the *Leesville Leader* stated that "Saturday afternoon and night were rather disappointing. Only a few arrests were made, one man for being drunk, two for fighting and another for selling liquor. It is expected that there will be more doing around here next Saturday night" (in Wise 1988).

The town thrived in the 1920s. Its population grew to 2,518 in 1920 and 3,291 in 1930 (Hernandez 1959; Works Progress Administration 1936:1). Besides Nona Mills and Gulf Land and Lumber, there were other lumber companies in the county seat including Weber-King and Brown Lumber Companies (Louisiana Department of Agriculture and Immigration 1920:187). Like the rest of the parish, the town saw bad times after the mills left. However, smaller mills created some employment, and the town survived, unlike Fullerton. With the Depression, the population dropped to fewer than 3,000, and only one mill survived. A Works Progress Administration paper described Leesville in 1936 as having the "usual necessary community stores, most of which are located within a stretch of six blocks on Main Street" (Works Progress Administration 1936:2). The town also had two banks, a motion picture theater, two hotels (National House with 36 rooms and Hotel Leesville with 35), several restaurants and sandwich shops, and a bus station.

By 1940, despite the impact of the Depression, Leesville was doing well. It had maintained a population of 2,891 (Hernandez 1959; Laney 1940:205). Census data show that the town had 85 stores, including 21 food, two general, four merchandise, two clothing, two furniture, and four automotive stores. It also boasted 19 filling stations, three lumber and hardware stores, 25 restaurants, and two drugstores. If a Vernon Parish resident needed specialized drugs, merchandise, auto parts, hardware, or store-bought furniture and could not travel to Alexandria, he or she came to Leesville. There were 175 stores in Vernon Parish in 1940, 49 percent of them in Leesville.

The coming of Camp Polk in 1941, and then Fort Polk, was an economic boost as great as the railroad's arrival in 1897. Construction workers at the camp flooded the area looking for housing, food, and other services. By 1945, the population had increased to 18,000 (Hernandez 1959; Leesville–Vernon Parish Chamber of Commerce 1945:25). The town, with federal support, added 435 housing units for officers in an area that became known as Lee Hills. Two other World War II housing projects, Allendale and West End Heights, were built during the war, and more than 1,000 homes were constructed between 1941 and 1945 (Vernon Parish Planning Board 1949:36). A new sewage system and gas lines were installed. Most important, a new hospital was built around 1945 called the War Memorial Hospital.

As the seat of government, the town had built a two-story wood courthouse on land donated by Dr. Smart in 1871. This building lasted until around 1897. A brick and concrete courthouse, built by P. J. Duffy, replaced the original in 1899. Hadnot (1975) states that it cost $55,000 (probably confusing it with the third courthouse), but the Louisiana Historical Records Survey (n.d.b) records a cost of only $12,500. Extensive repairs had to be made to this building in 1902, when the foundation failed. Of course, there was a legal battle with the original contractor, but the records do not report the outcome (Hadnot 1975).

In 1917, in the midst of labor unrest and in keeping with its tradition of nineteenth-century Populism, Vernon Parish became the home of a socialist experimental colony called Newllano, just south of and connected to Leesville. The Newllano del Rio Co-operative Colony was the creation of Job Harriman. A true socialist who had failed continually in California politics, Harriman eventually decided that the future of socialism lay in demonstrating its economic viability through cooperative communities. The Newllano Colony began in Antelope Valley, California, in 1914. The location proved to be a poor choice. A planned reservoir turned out to be unfeasible because it would not capture enough water. Harriman was soon on the road seeking another location. The answer to his problem was found in Stables, Louisiana, a mile south of Leesville. Gulf Lumber had recently cut over the lands in that area and planned to abandon its mill and mill town with up to one hundred shacks, a hotel, an office, a school, warehouses, and drying sheds (Davison 1994:11). The colony purchased 20,000 acres of land surrounding Stables, much of it within present-day Fort Polk. In October 1917, 300 of the 1,000 California colonists began moving to Louisiana. Newllano was founded on a series of socialist principals including (1) collective ownership of "things used productively," (2) member labor to the community, (3) member profits to the community, and (4) general suppression of individual rights and privileges over the good of the whole (Davison 1994:5–6). Women had equal rights with men.

The colony's economic foundations were never stable. Membership in the colony cost $2,000, of which $1,000 was paid in cash on entering, plus $200 for additional adults in the family, $150 for children between 12 and 21, and $100 for children under 12. The remainder of the fee was worked off at a dollar a day. Despite continual unrest and financial problems, the colony survived with what appears to have been an ongoing turnover in membership. There was no rent for housing, no bills for water and electricity, and free meals at the hotel. Everyone was supposed to wear simple, unadorned clothing. Each member was to find suitable work and to labor at it eight hours a day for the colony.

The colonists immediately had trouble adjusting to local farming conditions. When the colony could not meet payments, the Gulf Lumber Company approved a new deal whereby property could be purchased 1,000 acres at a time at $6 an acre. However, by 1919, only 15 families remained at Newllano.

A new board member, George Pickett, was named and it was largely through his force of personality that the colony survived. He was fortunate in capturing the heart and money of socialist publisher Theodore Cuno, who gave the colony $6,000. The money met the second installment owed to Gulf Lumber. From this point on, Pickett's power and the colony grew. In 1924, Pickett consolidated his power in a special election and took over as the president.

Under Pickett's leadership, Newllano grew slowly, and by 1935 it had some 28 different cottage and larger industries besides farming and lumber. Enterprises included a laundry, print shop, gristmill, tailor shop, paint shop, machine shop, garage, hotel, power plant, butcher, bakery, service station, recreation center, candy shop, coffee shop, sheet metal shop, and tailor and sewing room. The colony's main industry, however, was lumber products. Newllano had a sawmill, planing mill, shingle mill, and crate factory. The farm economy was based on raising poultry, sheep, hogs, and a goat herd; running a dairy; cultivating truck gardens and a nursery; and growing the usual crops. Raising goats was one of Pickett's special experiments. To this day, the hill south of Newllano is known as Billy Goat Hill.

The reasons for the colony's ultimate failure were numerous and complex but intrinsically tied to the ideology on which it was founded. Each year it was on the brink of economic collapse, being saved often by outside donors or a fresh supply of new members. Anyone could join as long as new members signed a form agreeing to its first principles. Not surprisingly, many elderly people saw the colony as a means of late-life care and paid the initial $1,000 but could not contribute productive labor. Social outcasts and trouble-makers also filtered in, adulterating the colony's socialist principles.

Unrest and dissension were constant problems and led to one of the colony's largest upheavals, the May Day Revolt of 1935 (Davison 1994:70). The general assembly fell into cliques and was subject to power plays as personalities clashed. No authority existed to police the troublemakers. The colony had also made bad economic decisions, including oil speculation. These and other problems eventually forced Newllano to enter receivership in 1937. One of the colony's many rescuers, J. B. Pollard (who donated $5,000 in 1930), was appointed overseer (Wise 1971:42). Not until 1965 were final legal bills paid and settlements resolved. While the colony had closed down by 1938, the village survived and was incorporated in 1942. Today it is a Leesville suburb.

Within modern Fort Polk there were five little hamlets, besides the large village of Fullerton. Little is known about Whiskey Chitto, Bee, Front, Pringles, and Six Mile. William Davis was the postmaster at Whiskey Chitto from 1889 to 1892. Beside his name in the postal records is a notation saying "no papers." A later entry indicates that the Whiskachitto post office also operated between June 1908 and January 1909, with Davis again as postmaster (Post Office Department 1973). While the exact location of the Whiskachitto post office is not known, it would be safe to say it was on Whiskey Chitto Creek near the school. Another post stop was Pringles, located somewhere near the headwaters of the west branch of Six Mile Creek. Bee was possibly located along Bee Branch, a branch of the Whiskey Chitto. The tiny hamlet of Front was located in the very northwest corner of Fort Polk's main post and was the final stop on the Leesville East and West railroad. A little more is known about Six Mile. It is found along Six Mile Creek southeast of Leesville. While the 1882 Government Land Office map does not show Six Mile, it locates Swain's Mill on Six Mile Creek's. northeast bank (in the northeast corner of Section 13) just across from where the hamlet would later develop. The Government Land Office survey also shows a road meandering east in the direction of Six Mile's location and splitting up a mile or so before it gets to the hamlet. Cantley and Kern's (1984) study indicated that the land was owned by Nona Mills and Gulf Lumber in 1910, although the area around the mill was owned by C. R. Haymons. Several members of the Haymons family owned land in the township at that time. Another owner was E. M. Brack. The Six Mile post office operated from 1903 until 1908, at which time the mail was transferred to Leesville (Post Office Department 1973). In addition to these post offices were several small kin-based settlements that dotted the parish landscape. They perhaps never had a general store or post office but came to be named for the family who lived there and built a home or a cluster of homes as the family grew. Jetertown is a prime example of these little communities and will be discussed in the next chapter.

While Leesville and Fullerton served the Fort Polk settlers for most needs and the little hamlets of Whiskey Chitto, Front, Pringles, and Six Mile served their immediate needs, the people of Fort Polk were surrounded by numerous other villages and lumber towns. For instance, Cooper, a stop along the KCS south of Leesville, was home to the Lockwood and Bass Lumber Company, the Arbuthnot and McCain Lumber Company, and the Lockwood and Ross Company from 1903 to 1907 (Hadnot in Sandel 1982:96; Wise 1971:48). The nineteenth-century post office and hamlet called Cora, located east of Fort Polk, survived into the 1930s. Cravens was a moderately sized to large mill town and rail stop located south of Fullerton in Ward 5 along the Jasper and Eastern (or Gulf, Colorado, and Santa Fe) rail line. The Pickering Lumber Company owned the mill there (Wise 1971:50). The town had many amenities, including a hotel, commissary, schoolhouse, church, and blacksmith shop. An 1896 map of the town depicts a "Negro quarter" with 53 houses, a wood quarter with 26, and a white quarter with 100 (Block 1996:14). In 1909, Fortier (1909:322) noted that the village was "the trading center for a considerable district." LaCamp was a crossroads between Hineston and Leesville along modern State Route 121. A post office was stationed there from 1926 until 1929, when the mails transferred to Leander, just down the road to the east. LaCamp was another lumber town, although not on a main rail line. The mill at LaCamp was owned by the Louisiana Sawmill Company and operated around 1920 (Louisiana Department of Agriculture and Immigration 1920:187). Leander was the first hamlet one encountered when entering Vernon Parish along State Route 121 from Hineston to Leesville. Mayo was located along State Route 21 just north of the Main Fort. It had a solid population from the very beginning that reached 50 by 1900 (Fortier 1909:142).

Neame was another lumber town located along the railroad about 12 miles south of Leesville. Built by Central Coal and Coke in 1898, it was originally called Taylor, then Keith, and finally Neame after financier Joe Neame (Wise 1971:49). Central Coal and Coke provided a commissary and a market and also paid a doctor to treat company employees. Two churches and two schools were built, one each for whites and blacks. During World War I, the company also operated a cannery. At its height, Neame had an ice cream parlor, barber shop, pool hall, railroad round house, swimming pool, pressing shop, lodge for Woodmen of the World, boarding house, and open-air movie theater. It also had a band and its own baseball team (Block 1996:110). Klondike, a section on the north side of town, housed white and Mexican families (McCain n.d.:3). South of town, a suburb called Doggie provided saloons, gambling parlors, and bawdyhouses for the mill workers. The population was two hundred in 1900. Eventually the mill employed as many as nine hundred men (Fortier 1909:215; Wise 1971:49). One mill worker was Gene Austin, who became a famous recording star (McCain n.d.). After the mill burned in 1925, the town was quickly abandoned. The Kansas City Railway attempted to raise strawberries in the area and, just before World War II, the area was mined for gravel.

Pickering, a lumber town south of Leesville, was built by the W. R. Pickering Lumber Company in 1898. According to Fortier (1909), some 4,000 lumber cars were loaded and shipped out of Pickering annually. By 1900, with a population of 1,000, the thriving town challenged Fullerton in size (Fortier 1909:307). Most of the 800 people who lived there in 1908 worked in the mills or the woods. Pickering had a large department store, a hotel, a school, and its own physician. The town also had its own "notorious" section called the "bottom" (Wise 1971:48). Pickering's development suffered greatly after 1926 when the mill experienced its second fire (Wise 1971:48). Nevertheless, the town faded away slowly; however, in 1936, 300 people were still living there.

With the construction of the Gulf, Colorado, and Sante Fe Railroad, the nineteenth-century settlement called Slabtown became the hamlet of Pitkin, an important mill, rail stop, and road junction. Its population of 54 in 1900 probably rose much higher during the peak lumber days (Fortier 1909:450).

Rosepine, another lumber town along the KCS Railway, was on the scale of Stables, Pickering, Neame, and Pinewood. Although a settlement prior to the railroad, Rosepine began its real growth when the railroad arrived. Rosepine flourished and died with the rise and fall of the lumber industry, as did Pickering, Neame, and Pinewood. In 1900, Rosepine's population was 75 (Fortier 1909:396), but the town grew much larger. Wise (1971:52) and Cupit (1963:40) reported that it had at least 1,000 people by 1906. During its heyday, it supported a bank (Rosepine Banking Company), two hotels, five dry-goods stores, three groceries, a drugstore, a barber shop, three restaurants, two churches, a school, and seven saloons (Dalehite 1962:3; Wise 1971:52). The local mill, Rosepine Lumber Company, left around 1908, and by 1912 the town had died (Cupit 1963:44–45).

Rustville, named for Paul D. Rust, Gulf Lumber's secretary (Block 1996:157), was a stop on Fullerton's rail line. Most of the town's residents were African Americans who worked at the turpentine still that Fullerton operated there. At its peak, Rustville had 129 cottages, a commissary, a meat market, a church, and its own school (Block 1996:158–160).

Slagle still exists today along State Route 8, formerly Route 21. It was one of the rare mill and lumber towns not located along a major rail line. However, at its peak, Slagle was probably quite large and in the size range of Cravens, Pitkin, or Pinewood. The mill was operated by the White Gandlin Lumber Company (Louisiana Department of Agriculture and Immigration 1928:187). Wise (1971:53) quoted a 1931 article reporting that E. P. Ferguson of Glenmora purchased the entire town, including the store, mill, dry sheds, sawmill, and some 100 houses for white families and another 150 houses for black families. The first Slagle post office opened in 1919 and operated until around 1930. Slagle, Mayo, and Walnut Hill were so close together that they were probably essentially all part of one large community.

Stables, near Leesville, was the other town owned by Gulf Lumber. Although often overshadowed by Fullerton, it was a fully functioning town in its own right. Two mills operated there, and the town's structures included 215 cottages, a commissary, and a boarding house (Block 1996:71). Many of the laborers from Stables helped build Fullerton. The town peaked in 1908, having reached a population of around seven hundred (Block 1996:72). Stables was sold to the Newllano colony in 1917, after Gulf Lumber cut all the trees in the area and began concentrating on its operations at Fullerton. The Stables post office was established in 1905 or 1906, implying that Gulf

Lumber began its operations in the area around that time (Block 1996:71; Post Office Department 1973).

The early-nineteenth-century settlement of Walnut Hill survived into the twentieth century within the complex of the crossroad communities of Mayo, Slagle, and Walnut Hill. Its post office operated until 1925, at which time the mail was moved through Slagle (Post Office Department 1973). Walnut Hill had a population of 75 in 1900 (Fortier 1909:583).

North of Leesville, the Peason and Horse's Head areas of Fort Polk also saw the rise and fall of many lumber towns and villages. The old nineteenth-century Natchitoches Parish settlement of Kisatchie remained a small post office stop through the twentieth century, serving Fort Polk's Peason Ridge region. It still exists today as a small hamlet. Kisatchie, as with many rural communities, was the name given both to the place where post office, school, store, church, and cemetery were established and to the greater community, whereby people from the surrounding area referred to themselves as living at Kisatchie. The latter usually covered a wider area, and only rarely are historians able to reconstruct such a community. However, in this case, the Kisatchie community was "approximately nine miles long and two miles wide" (Kadlecek and Bullard 1994:175).

Kurthwood, a lumber town of some prominence in the 1920s, was on the caliber of Pickering, Stables, and Fullerton. Kurthwood was built by Joseph H. Kurth, Jr., the son of lumber baron Joseph Kurth (McDaniel 1983:4). After working in east Texas, Kurth Jr. moved to Rapides Parish and built the small Pawnee Land and Lumber Company, which operated until 1919. Then he moved to north Vernon Parish, where he bought thousands of acres in and around the present-day Peason Ridge Training Area and established the Vernon Parish Lumber Company. Kurthwood town equaled Fullerton in all respects, except perhaps in total size. It had all the amenities of Fullerton, including an ice plant, three hotels (one for blacks), a feed store, school, commissary, church, ball park, movie house, doctor's office, barber shop, and pool. Homes for the mill workers had electricity, telephones, and running water (McDaniel 1983:5). The town even had a plant for making and bottling Chero-Cola and an automobile agency (McDaniel 1983:8, 12). Kurth Jr. was Kurthwood. He constructed his own home in Kurthwood, from which he operated the town and mill he built. He was intimately involved in the lives of the people who worked there and was even the town's first postmaster (Post Office Department 1973). He bought one of the first radios in the parish and set it up for all to listen to important news and sports events.

The Vernon Parish Lumber Company closed in 1929. The last tree was cut with much ceremony and sadness, as it had been at Fullerton. On the closing of the company, many were left without jobs. Some moved, taking their homes with them to be rebuilt in Leesville and other nearby towns. Those who stayed no longer paid rent for housing. Unlike Fullerton, however, Kurthwood remains today. In 1930, the Anderson-Post Hardwood Company bought part of the Kurth property.

Finally, Peason, in Sabine Parish, was a lumber town and rail terminus for the Christie and Eastern Railroad. The size of Kurthwood, this village thrived from around 1916 to 1935. Peason's peak population ranged between 1,500 and 2,000 inhabitants. The mill at Peason employed some 450 people. Mill houses, typically with pyramid-shaped roofs, were built for the employees. The houses also had electricity and water (Jones 1979:5a). Today only the railroad bed exists.

TWENTIETH-CENTURY SOCIETY AND POLITICS

Although the lumber business brought an influx of new people, including ethnic minorities, to Vernon Parish, its cultural milieu did not change at all. At the turn of the century and continuing until the onset of World War II, the people of Vernon Parish remained a decidedly rural, white Southern community. Independence, self-sufficiency, and Protestantism were at the heart of the culture.

The churches in Vernon Parish were an obvious reflection of its Protestantism. From 1897 to 1940, most of the religious population was Southern Baptist. The Southern Baptists never represented less than 45 percent of membership in all denominations in Vernon Parish throughout the period between 1900 and 1940. Methodists were the next in representation. Non-Protestants were never more than 14 percent of the total church population.

The population explosion that occurred in Vernon Parish at the turn of the twentieth century coincided with a statewide movement to improve education (Smith 1938). Although educational progress continued slowly, Vernon Parish schools did improve. At the state level, the new constitution of 1898 provided for public schools and began the process of standardization by setting age limits for children (6 to 18 years old). It authorized kindergartens, provided for state funds apportioned on a per educable basis, and directed the state general assembly to develop a plan for its schools (Robertson 1952:3). Constitutional reform was quickly followed by the establishment of standards for teacher examination and certification. Vernon Parish rural folk at the turn of the century were still reluctant to support schools through taxation. A 1900 parish superintendent's report noted that although a tax as high as six mill was authorized under the state constitution, "all the aid we received last year from the parish was a two-mill tax" (Cain in Robertson 1952:19). The superintendent pointed out that the parish had numerous schools but a lack of funding, and careless parents and teachers made the needed conversion to larger centralized schools unlikely at that time (Robertson 1952:19). He was right: the scattered population had 72 public schools for whites and seven for blacks in 1899. A total of 2,883 white and 213 black students attended, taught by 73 teachers for the white and seven for the black students (Wise 1971:11). Also, 250 students attended five private schools. In 1907 and 1908, Vernon Parish's numerous schools were organized into equally numerous school districts. For instance, within Fort Polk, Six Mile and Whiskachitto school districts served the scattered, scant population (Wise 1971:18). The parish's school buildings at this time were fairly typical of those found across the rural upland South. Most were small, one- or two-room buildings of rough-hewn logs.

With the increase in wealth from the lumber industry, Vernon Parish became more amenable to providing local support. Through the first three decades of the twentieth century, major progress was made. In 1910, the parish voted a four-mill tax for schools (Wise 1971:34) and, around 1909, even set up a Teachers Institute (Wise 1971:21). By 1934, the people's attitudes toward education had changed dramatically. A study of the parish school system reported at that time that the people of Vernon "vote school taxes freely" (Arnold 1934:5).

By the 1930s the Whiskachitto, Six Mile, and Cypress (and perhaps Flactor) schools served the community within the area that is now Fort Polk. Whiskachitto had as many as four teachers and 63 students in daily attendance. A 1933 State Department of Education bulletin provides more details about these schools. In 1932–1933, Whiskachitto had two teachers and 58 students—all in elementary school—and was open 88 days a year (Foote and Sisemore 1933). The school cost $3,000 to build in 1928. Flactor had two teachers and 43 elementary students, while Cypress also had two teachers and 41 students (Foote and Sisemore 1933). Fifty-five Whiskachitto students were transported to the school over 25 miles of dirt roads.

During the early part of the century, schools, like churches, still represented communities and towns, and the people identified with these institutions. School consolidation, however, continued during the first half of the century, and as this took place, schools lost their community identity. By 1949, the number of parish schools had dropped to eight high schools and four elementary schools for whites and one high school and four elementary schools for blacks (Vernon Parish Planning Board 1949:43). Nonetheless, schools were still often the center of social activities, especially football. Leesville's first football team was started in 1910 (Wise 1971:39). By 1929, the team was playing an eight-game schedule with schools such as Oakdale, Vernon, De Ridder, Natchitoches, Merryville, and other out-of-parish high schools (Wise 1971:34).

Labor Unrest

Lumbering brought unprecedented prosperity to many in Vernon Parish. For the first time, some residents had an income well beyond subsistence levels. Local merchants and farmers profited from the increase in customers. Such benefits were largely responsible for the warm welcome local residents gave the lumber industry without regard for future conservation. Not all, however, were satisfied. The dangerous working conditions, poor wages for unskilled labor, long hours, and abrupt cutbacks in production and personnel contributed to an undercurrent of discontent. The noisy, frenzied pace of industrial production was a shock to the slower-paced agrarian lifestyle of west-central Louisiana (Cook and Watson 1985:126). Nationally, indeed globally, labor movements were fueling the fires of unrest at the turn of the century; it was not long until the South was also inflamed. Only a few years before, Vernon Parish farmers were making their voices heard and votes count in a populist revolt. At the turn of the century, unhappy lumber workers began to make the parish, once again, a center of discontent.

Unrest in the mills and fields had a precedent back in the 1870s when workers at Orange, Texas, struck over long hours and poor pay (Allen 1961:166). But real dissension, to the point of violence, was yet to come. In 1907, the unrest spread to west-central Louisiana. Laborers walked out of Long-Bell's mills protesting a plan to increase hours and cut wages because of a business depression. This strike included the De Ridder mill just south of Vernon Parish. The dispute was quickly settled, but both management and labor were alerted to the probability of future strife.

The De Ridder walkout brought the region to the attention of the national union movement. At the same time, alarmed mill owners organized the Southern Lumber Operators' Association to defend themselves against the union threat. The union movement in the western Louisiana region was led by Arthur L. Emerson and Jay Smith. Emerson was an experienced woodsman from Tennessee who drifted from job to job. John Kirby, president of the Southern Lumber Operators' Association, said that Emerson had been fired from Gulf Lumber for stealing blankets at a boarding house in Fullerton (Fickle 1975:62). Whether or not this is true, it seems that Emerson did indeed work "undercover" at Fullerton "testing and polling [mill laborers] about their willingness to support a union" (Fickle 1975:64). Emerson and Smith organized the first local at Carson, Louisiana, south of Fullerton, on December 3, 1910. Emerson was elected president of the Brotherhood of Timber Workers at Alexandria in 1911. That year the organization's membership reached 25,000. Locally, in Fullerton and Leesville, Emerson evidently encountered a large measure of sympathy. In 1908, Pat O'Neil established *The Toiler*, a weekly socialist newspaper published in Leesville (Cook and Watson 1985:129). The paper was a recruiting organ for the Industrial Workers of the World.

Through 1911, mill operators, led by John Kirby of the Southern Lumber Operators' Association, challenged the union's organizing efforts by requiring their employees to swear they would not join the union. As tensions grew, mill operators threatened and executed lockouts and hired detectives to trace union members. An 11-mill lockout in the De Ridder area put 3,000 laborers temporarily out of work (Cook and Watson 1985:132). Meanwhile, both sides appealed to African American laborers. The unions claimed their goal was to improve the living and working conditions of blacks and whites alike. The operators countered that once the unions were formed, white laborers would use the unions to take all the jobs (Fickle 1975:68).

Violence finally broke out in 1912 at Graybow (or Grabow) just southwest of De Ridder in Beauregard Parish. Graybow was the site of the Galloway Lumber Company. The owner swore he would not give in to union demands. Tempers rose for a few days prior to July 7, as union men toured towns like De Ridder, Bon Ami, and Carson, rallying support and giving speeches. On July 7, Emerson was beginning to speak at Graybow. Among the crowd were both well-armed lumbermen and the operators' hired gunmen. Alcohol was free-flowing, and it was only a matter of time before the first shots were fired. When they were, four or five men died, and 40 more were injured (Allen 1961:174; Fickle 1975:78). Both sides claimed the other fired first. Interestingly, it was Emerson who asked that the governor call in troops, which he did. The troops, together with local authorities, rounded up 64 union members and six company men.

The bloodshed temporarily sobered both sides as the Graybow incident was sorted out by legal authorities. Mill operators began bickering among themselves, some admitting that conditions were indeed bad at some mills. But at the same time, they rallied to step up efforts to defeat the union. Meanwhile, union members became closer as they rallied around their jailed comrades. Mass meetings were held in Leesville during the rest of the year, and socialists won seats in local elections (Fickle 1975:81–82). The long trial ended in the fall when all 64 union men were acquitted. However, the union had won only a small battle. In the end, the Graybow riot worked against the union movement in western Louisiana. The operators blacklisted Graybow participants, locked out others, and hired nonunion labor. Reforms, such as small pay increases and fewer hours, were instituted by some mill operators. Meanwhile, the trial practically bankrupted the union. After an unsuccessful strike at Merryville, Louisiana, the "Louisiana-Texas Lumber War" ended with the operators victorious (Fickle 1975:83). Although the union did not die out completely, unionism never gained a strong foothold in west-central Louisiana after that and in 1944, Louisiana had only six union-organized lumber establishments (Allen 1961:185).

According to Allen (1961:187), many factors caused the unions to fail during this period. In the South, more lumbermen were married and had children than in the North, where unions were more successful. Also, large southern industrial operators at this time could relatively easily afford temporary strikes. Most of a mill's operating cost was labor. A closed mill brought no profit, but it also brought cost savings. Owners had other mills operating elsewhere in the country, so a temporary lockout or strike in western Louisiana was not considered critical to their overall bottom line.

Unionism and socialist colonies like Newllano were in keeping with the populist trend in the parish's political history. Likewise, during the Depression years, Vernon Parish was enamored with the controversial Governor Huey Long. As Wise (1977:1) quips, "His supporters, in fact usually kept only two pictures on the home fireplace mantel—one of Jesus Christ and one of Huey P. Long." Vernon Parish voted for Long by a three-to-one margin over any of Long's opponents. During Long's impeachment proceedings, the Police Jury even formally endorsed the embattled governor. Long, knowing he was strongly supported in the region, visited Leesville during the Fourth of July celebrations in 1929. A crowd of 20,000 was estimated to have attended (Wise 1977:11).

The Depression and the Army

Exactly how the Great Depression affected the people of Vernon Parish is difficult to measure. On the one hand, many people who had been employed in the lumber industry were out of jobs by the 1930s. On the other hand, except for one year during the 1930s, Vernon Parish led the state in lumber production, and it is assumed that the mills were thus hiring. The effect on farms and farmers is equally problematic. Census data indicate that tenancy did not rise as sharply as in other parishes, so many Vernon Parish farmers retained their land, but many had to get loans to keep going. Stella Jones recalled that in 1932, the courthouse was filled with farmers waiting their turns to apply for loans (Jones in Wise 1971:86). One source of temporary employment for local youth was the CCC. Another was through the 1933 Federal Emergency Relief Act, which provided grants to state relief projects (Morris 1965:343). However, in 1934, the unemployables in Vernon Parish were dropped from the rolls and referred to local agencies. The Police Jury responded by passing a one-cent gasoline tax to care for unemployables and mothers aid cases (Brown et al. 1935:1).

A 1935 Vernon Parish Relief Fund report provides an insight into the extent of local distress. The fund assisted mothers without resources, the blind, the aged, the infirm, and families without support. When the fund began, applications flooded in and the organization had to hire additional personnel to process the forms. Eventually 599 applications were received, of which 314 were accepted (Brown et al. 1935:5). The report indicates that many of these people were helped with clothing for their children. Fund personnel made 956 home visits in 1935 and arranged for local doctors to examine the high school children. The doctors found many children suffering from hookworms and anemia. They also recommended tonsillectomies for 98 percent of the children and arranged for a school bus to transport them to Shreveport for their operations. Of the $17,627 expended through the fund, $14,000 came from a gas tax. All told, in 1935, the fund directly assisted 190 adults and 205 children, not counting those examined in school.

Certainly the wealth in the parish decreased during the Depression years compared with that of the lumber years. One measure of this can be seen in the material culture. In 1930, the parish had 2,148 car registrations; the total dropped to 1,344 in 1935 and 1,107 in 1937 (Anonymous n.d.b). In 1937, 791 trucks were registered and only 168 residences and 132 businesses had phones. One exception was an increase in homes with radios from 226 in 1930 to 1,600 by 1937.

The Depression ultimately ended as a result of world events far removed from western Louisiana. As the United States prepared for global war in 1940, the U.S. Army sought land to practice maneuvering large numbers of men and materials. Despite the hard work of the Forest Service and the CCC, large tracts in Vernon Parish were still composed of relatively open, rolling, "submarginal," cut-over land with little occupation (Burns 1982:73)—precisely what the army required. The army chose a location seven miles southeast of Leesville and called it Camp Polk after General Leonidas Polk, the "fighting bishop" of the Confederacy (Wise 1971:26). These lands, some 27,615 acres in all, were mostly owned by the Forest Service (Burns 1982:74).

THE ARRIVAL OF THE U.S. ARMY

Through the spring and summer of 1940, military vehicles and green-clad soldiers were seen more and more frequently marching and convoying up and down western Louisiana's formerly quiet, dusty roads. No part of the parish was spared the army's invasion as the entire parish was within its planned maneuver area. Most activity, however, was concentrated in and around modern-day Fort Polk where the army engineers arrived to prepare for battle. Camp Polk not only billeted the troops and served as a depot but also was the monitoring umpires' headquarters (Casey 1971:27).

Just prior to the famous Louisiana Maneuvers, Vernon Parish experienced a major road improvement project—the first benefit of the army's presence. In order to make western Louisiana's bridges and culverts safe for tanks, the engineers were loaded "aboard trucks filled with lumber and tools. Every shaky bridge and culvert [was] strengthened, steep ditches [were] regraded, poor roads [were] improved" (Perret 1991:41).

The first of the Louisiana Maneuvers began in April and May 1940, pitting tanks against tanks in a mock battle (Perret 1991:40–41; Pollacia 1994). Leesville and the area east toward Leander (or the northern part of the modern Main Fort) became the battleground. At one point, Leesville was actually the scene of a tank battle. As citizens watched from rooftops, tanks raced through town firing blanks at each other in mock combat (Pollacia 1994:84).

The big "battle" occurred between September 15 and 28, 1941, when 19 divisions were locked in mock combat from Lake Charles to Shreveport (Miller 1987:324). General Mark Clark drew up the plans for the second maneuvers using a Standard Oil Company map of Louisiana and Texas. Drawing a circle around Shreveport and a line of departure south of that, he ordered Lt. General Ben Lear to move south with his 130,000-man Red army and attack Lt. General Walter Kruger's 270,000-man Blue army across the Red River. Kruger was to move north from Lake Charles through the Vernon Parish region and stop Lear's advance. In Lear's command was George Patton and in Kruger's, Dwight Eisenhower. Kruger and Eisenhower bottled up Lear and Patton's armor against the Red River, winning round one (Perret 1991:43–44). In the second round, Lear was ordered to defend Shreveport. This time Kruger had Patton on his team. It was during this battle that Patton made his famous 300-mile flanking movement through Texas and attacked Shreveport unexpectedly from the north.

Unfortunately many Americans' first glimpse of Vernon Parish in the early 1940s was the stumped, open, brushy landscape left behind by the lumber mills. Few knew that its former wooded beauty had been transformed into the lumber in many of their own homes. As a result, maneuver veterans rarely reminisce glowingly about west-central Louisiana. A friend of Eisenhower described Camp Polk as an area "where I don't think any human beings have been for fifty years. We found snakes all over the place, rattlers. We killed fifteen, twenty rattlers a day, and we were just torn apart by the ticks. A lot of men had poison oak. . . . It was a hundred degrees in the day time and forty or thirty at night" (in Miller 1987:323). Powell Casey, a Louisiana native, thought he was ready for the mosquitoes, but "they seemed to have grown since we left" (Casey 1971:27). Chiggers were also a big problem, for which storekeepers prescribed coal oil as a remedy (Casey 1971:27).

The men ran into more trouble once they hit the roads outside of the camp. The ground had a firm but thin crust, which trapped trucks and tanks. Once wet, the dirt roads became impassable. Rain greeted the soldiers on opening day of the first Louisiana Maneuvers, turning roads into quagmires for the remainder of the exercises; the second maneuvers opened with a hurricane (Miller 1987:327). Despite attempts to protect reforested areas, damage occurred. Soldiers cut some trees for camouflage, and, in open areas, trucks and tanks rutted the ground that had only recently recovered from rutting by log skidders.

With people out of work, the army was, like the lumber mills decades before, an economic godsend. Estimates that the army was going to spend some $28 million locally on the maneuvers and construction of the fort were actually conservative. By the end of World War II, the costs had risen to more than $44 million (Pollacia 1994:148; Wise 1971:26). During the mock battles, some 11 million pounds of bread, 8.5 million pounds of meat, and 9 million potatoes were consumed in 18 million meals (Miller 1987:323). Some of these supplies were purchased locally.

THE CONSTRUCTION OF FORT POLK AND WORLD WAR II

On January 11, 1941, the War Department of the United States government entered into a contract with W. Horace Williams Company of New Orleans for the construction of a military base to be known as Camp Polk. Benham Engineering Company of Oklahoma City, Oklahoma, served as architect and engineer for the construction. Employing 9,000 carloads of freight; 7,500 truckloads of sand, gravel, and lumber; 35,000,000 kegs of nails; 220,000 barrels of cement; 4,300,000 square feet of wall board; 3,924,00 square feet of roofing paper; and 3,000 pieces of machinery, the construction crew at Camp Polk reached a peak of 14,000 with an average weekly salary of $500,000. The laborers were organized into three eight-hour shifts of some 2,000 men each (Alexandria *Daily Town Talk* 1983:102). As the land was taken over by the military and the fort shot up faster than a slash pine, farmers and the military attempted to coexist. But cattle grazed on the parade grounds and hogs found shade under the barracks and eventually farmers were told to remove their stock (Cantley and Kern 1984:64). The originally scheduled construction was completed by August 1941, while additional expansion and construction was finalized by December 10, 1942, at a total cost of nearly $22 million (Completion Report I 1941:1–10, 56; Completion Report II 1942).

A memorandum between Captain Frisby of the 4th Engineers and Benham Engineering Company dated January 11, 1941, outlined 56 directives for the construction of the base. These included a number of specifications regarding the overall arrangement of the site. Buildings were to be constructed in blocks, with at least 50 feet between structures and at least 100 yards between tank parks and barracks. No structure was to be constructed with a footing greater than 8 feet in height. Service structures, including kitchens and storerooms, were to be built with their widest opening facing the service road. Officers' quarters were to be built near their group areas, and the base post office, telephone and telegraph building, utility shop, firehouse, theater, guest house, and service club were all to be built near the center of the base. Between each regimental group sufficient space was to be provided for athletic fields and drill grounds, and parking areas were to be left for private vehicles at each regiment. Water plants were to be built on high ground, and sewage plants at the lowest available point. All guardhouses were to be constructed as a single unit including a kitchen and mess hall, orderly room, tool room, and storehouse, and this unit was to be established behind wire fencing. Sentry boxes were to be placed where traffic would require direction in all types of weather. Finally, Benham engineers were instructed to number all structures consecutively, to plan names or numbers for all streets, and to recommend a name for the base (Completion Report I 1941:25–30). Street names in the southern portion of the base were named for states, with Louisiana Avenue taking precedence as the main artery of the base. Streets in the north fort area were numbered. The designs of most of the buildings were presented as accepted plans in use at other installations, although several experimental barracks were advanced at Camp Polk. In all, a total of 1,728 structures were built during the 1941–1942 phase of construction at the base (Completion Report I 1941:62–63).

With construction occurring at an unprecedented pace, Leesville, for the moment, was stunned. Between January 16, 1941, and February 15, 1941, the population jumped from 3,500 to 15,000, and it eventually reached 18,000 during the war. Streets were jammed with cars and people. But the town soon recovered. Businesses boomed and money poured in as new businesses were created. Rents went through the roof. One local resident remembered that "there were people staying in chicken houses, sleeping in barns, or we'd shed them" (Oaks in Cantley and Kern 1984:64). Banks stayed open until nine in the evening. Vernon Parish's state trooper allotment rose from 15 to 127 to control the roads (Alexandria *Daily Town Talk* 1983:102). Meanwhile, the army also bought land in the Peason Ridge area to establish a firing range. Although eight families were forced to leave, most people in the Kisatchie area were happy for the new job opportunities brought by the army (Scoggins 1961:23).

Camp Polk's construction and the war not only affected Leesville but also the surrounding communities. Simpson, for instance, became a "rushing little city. . . . It was very common to see a continuous line of motor vehicles traveling the main and side roads both day and night. The construction of the camps and conversion of people to the military gave everybody in Simpson a job, and there was more money in Simpson than ever before in its history" (Lewis 1956:18).

The war again transformed the rural parish landscape and its people, as had the timber industry. This time the transformation was not through the removal of timber, but through furious activity. The remaining woods and broad open spans of cut-over land were suddenly overrun with masses of men and equipment. Farms were invaded by thirsty, hungry soldiers, and the quiet countryside erupted with intermittent gunfire. Occasionally, short and long artillery rounds passing overhead would scare the wits out of those living next to firing ranges (Scoggins 1961:24). During the war, some eight million men passed through the gates of Camp Polk, maneuvered around Vernon Parish and western Louisiana, and spent time seeking entertainment in Leesville before going overseas to battle.

FROM CAMP TO FORT

Camp Polk not only supported the Louisiana Maneuvers of World War II but also served as the training base for the 3rd, 7th, 8th, 9th, and 11th Armored Divisions, the 95th Infantry, and the 11th Airborne Division. After the war the Camp was placed on standby and only open on a partial basis as a training facility for the National Guard during 1948 and 1949. Camp Polk was reactivated for the Korean War and served the 45th Infantry Division, Oklahoma National Guard, from 1950 to 1954. Closed at the end of the war, the camp again reopened in 1955, this time as headquarters for Exercise Sagebrush, in which 85,000 troops participated. The 1st Armored Division was also stationed at Camp Polk beginning in that year. The post again was placed on the inactive list in 1959 and was used only as a summer training base for the next two years (Fort Polk Museum n.d.; Servello, ed. 1983:66).

In 1961 the base was reopened as a result of the Berlin Crisis, and in June 1962, Camp Polk was designated an Infantry Training Center. Advanced training for the Vietnam conflict was conducted at Camp Polk following 1965, much of which was carried out in a "little Vietnam" established on Peason Ridge, and in October 1968, the base was established as a permanent installation. In July 1973, Fort Polk became the primary training center for basic infantry soldiers. Training activities at the base included Brave Shield IX, a joint training exercise featuring the 256th Infantry Brigade of the Louisiana National Guard against the 101st Airborne Division from Fort Campbell, Kentucky. Brave Shield IX marked the first time the National Guard had committed a brigade-sized force to a joint training exercise. By May 1976, when the Infantry Training Center struck its colors, over 1,000,000 men had received their training at Fort Polk (Fort Polk Museum n.d.).

The establishment of Fort Polk as a permanent installation marked a major turning point in the history of the base. Following the conclusion of the Vietnam conflict, Fort Polk served as home to the 5th Infantry Division (Mechanized), which included the 1st Brigade, 2nd Brigade, 5th Aviation Brigade, Division Artillery (DIVARTY), Division Support Command (DISCOM), Division Troops, and the 256th Infantry Brigade of the Louisiana National Guard. The 5th Division also provided support to the 2-152 Armor Battalion of Alabama, the 135th Artillery Brigade of Missouri, the 31st Armor Brigade from Alabama, the 32nd Infantry Brigade from Wisconsin, the 157th Infantry Brigade from Pennsylvania, and the 47th Infantry Division from Minnesota. The transition from temporary to permanent facility also entailed a dramatic increase in the funding allocated for construction on the base. Permanent construction at Fort Polk has been carried out at a cost of $461 million since 1975, with contracts for an additional $54 million currently in progress. In 1987 the base had 4,119 structures, of which nearly three-quarters were modern. Since 1984 Fort Polk has served as the Forces Command (FORSCOM) representative for the Office of the Secretary of Defense Model Installation Program (MIP). As of January 1, 1987, the population of the fort consisted of 15,214 active military personnel; 24,874 military dependents; 3,241 Department of the Army civilians; 1,419 contract employees; and 28,812 retirees (Fort Polk Museum n.d.).

From October 21, 1974, until 1992, the installation was the home of the 5th Infantry Division (Mechanized). With the stationing of the 5th Infantry Division (Mechanized), Fort Polk's new and primary mission responsibility was to support the Division and its mission. Additionally, Fort Polk was responsible for providing support for the 256th Infantry Brigade of the Louisiana National Guard. This National Guard unit is designated as the "roundout," that is, the third brigade of the Division.

In 1991, as a result of the Base Realignment and Closure Act, Fort Polk underwent a major mission change. The 5th Infantry Division (Mechanized) moved to Fort Hood, Texas, as the 2nd Armored Division. In 1993 Fort Polk became the new home of the Joint Readiness Training Center, which moved from Fort Chaffee, Arkansas. The XIII Airborne Corps came on board, which included the 42nd Field Artillery, the 108th Air Defense Artillery, and the 2nd Armored Cavalry Regiment. Fort Polk still maintained its mission as a training and validating center for mobilized National Guard and Reserve soldiers.

At present, Fort Polk continues to serve as the home of the Joint Readiness Training Center, one of the three combat training centers in the U.S.

Army. It is home to the XVIII Airborne Corps, which includes the 42nd Field Artillery Brigade, the 108th Air Defense Artillery Brigade, and the 2nd Armored Cavalry Regiment. Also, Fort Polk still supports mobile National Guard and Reserve training. Further, Fort Polk has become a vehicle-processing center for troops returning from European assignments. These new support missions have led to a major increase in the level of activity at ranges and training areas, increased construction in the cantonment area, modification of ranges, and creation of drop zones, landing strips, and other facilities.

Chapter 8

A Historic Period Context for Fort Polk

This chapter examines the historic archaeological sites on Fort Polk. Much less attention has been paid to these resources than to prehistoric sites, partially because there are so few and partially because at the survey and testing level it is difficult to approach the kinds of research questions that might shed light on the historic occupation of the installation. Still, there have been valuable and valiant attempts to understand the historic occupation of Fort Polk and these are discussed herein. The chapter is organized into a summary of previous research efforts and their results followed by a detailed discussion of a historic context first included in the 1999 Historic Preservation Plan (HPP) but proposed here as a method of organizing future research. The historic context argues that what has been missing in previous research is an overall framework that will allow for a systematic approach in understanding historic sites at the installation. This framework attempts to integrate the history developed by Smith (1999) with the archaeological resources discovered and analyzed during survey and testing projects. The purpose of such a context is to allow Fort Polk a programmatic method for evaluating a diverse set of historic sites for National Register eligibility and, as such, it also serves as a research design for future efforts.

Previous Investigations at Historic Sites on Fort Polk

A detailed review of previous archaeological research conducted on Fort Polk was presented in Chapter 2. A number of historic sites found during this fieldwork were examined in some detail, and this research will be discussed in the pages that follow. Hundreds of historic sites have been found on the installation, of course, but none have been the subject of large-scale excavation, and only a comparative few were found with sufficient integrity to warrant intensive testing. The sites below represent the largest and most unusual assemblages examined to date.

INVESTIGATIONS AT JETERTOWN (16VN1070)
A detailed program of archival research, mapping, controlled surface col-

lection, oral history, and artifact analysis was conducted during the fourth and sixth survey projects by Earth Search, Inc., ES-4 and ES-6, at the Henry Jeter Homestead site, or Jetertown, a cluster of four households variously built and occupied from the mid–nineteenth century until the establishment of Fort Polk (16VN1070; Franks 1990d:84–106; Franks and Yakubik 1990a:47–95). Oral historical evidence, obtained from a 90-year-old former resident, proved invaluable to resolving the location, character, occupation history, and use of many of the buildings in the site area, which had been destroyed 50 years earlier and were otherwise largely known only through archaeological research and abbreviated tax, census, and other legal records. The extent of the information that was recovered, in fact, clearly demonstrates the importance of oral historical research with former residents of the installation area. Given the advanced age of many of these people, there is considerable urgency to this need.

The artifact analyses included the documentation of the relative age of and functional and economic differences between the structures, as well as the use of space around them. Mean ceramic dating was employed, although it was found to have limited utility in resolving the actual age of the occupations and relative order in which they were established; the dates were tightly clustered and too early by 20 or more years (Franks and Yakubik 1990a:74–77). An innovative alternative dating analysis, involving the incidence of amethyst to clear window glass, yielded ratios that were progressively higher for the earlier structures, whose order of occupation had been previously determined from the oral history (Franks and Yakubik 1990a:74, 79). Another innovative analysis was directed to examining the incidence of various types of ironstone pottery in the vicinity of each former structure, and again results supported the use of this procedure as a relative dating tool locally (Franks and Yakubik 1990a:74–79). An analysis of the incidence of plain, embossed, decal decorated, and porcelain tableware was also undertaken in a largely successful attempt to rank the economic position of the occupants of each structure; ceramic prices were derived from period Sears, Roebuck and Co. catalogs (Franks and Yakubik 1990a:80, 82). Different structure assemblages were also compared using a series of functional groupings of artifacts: ceramic tableware, utilitarian ceramics, glass tableware, glass jars and lid liners, other (bottle) glass, turpentine cups, architecture, and personal items. Again, the analysis provided insight about the lives of the families occupying the structures (Franks and Yakubik 1990a:80–85). A comparison of the artifact assemblages recovered from the site surfaces and in shovel tests was undertaken, with no significant differences observed.

An intensive systematic surface collection was made around one of the four structures, the Henry Jeter house, using 10-m squares (Figure 8.1). Ar-

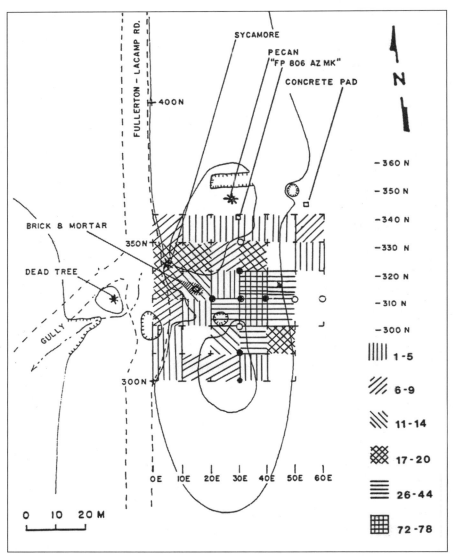

Figure 8.1 — Surface artifact scatter at the Henry Jeter house site, 16VN1070 (adapted from Franks and Yakubik 1990a:88).

chitectural debris was found to be strongly clustered in the immediate vicinity of the former house site, whose location was determined by the brick rubble from the chimney fall. Little postabandonment scattering of this material was indicated. Heavy concentrations of nonarchitectural materials were found north and west of the house and around the well depression, distributions that were inferred to reflect the intentional sweeping of those portions of the yard immediately adjacent to the house (Yakubik and Franks 1990:51–52). A low incidence of glass jar fragments in the immediate house area, coupled with a higher incidence at some distance away, south and east of the well, led to the suggestion that preserved foods may have been stored in an exterior building such as a smokehouse, a pattern confirmed locally by oral history (Franks and Yakubik 1990a:90). Turpentine cups were found in and around the house area, where informants indicate they were used as flower-pots and utensil holders.

A low incidence of nails and a high incidence of windowpane glass were also observed on the site. This was attributed to the demolition and re-moval of buildings with the establishment of Fort Polk, rather than their destruction or deterioration in place. In the 1988 HPP it was suggested that nails would be an important artifact category on historic sites (Anderson et al. 1988:253), an assumption that would appear unwarranted on at least some later historic sites on Fort Polk. Instead, Franks (1990d:105) suggested that windowpane glass would likely be a more telling indicator of a late-nineteenth- or early-twentieth-century house site. Franks (1990d:195) also challenged the assumption that ceramics would be more common than glass-ware on house sites and that this relationship would be reversed on tem-porary camps (Anderson et al. 1988:251; Campbell and Weed 1986:5-4). Instead, evidence from the Henry Jeter Homestead site indicated glass was far more common than ceramics (see also Yakubik and Franks 1990:72 for additional discussion and analyses). A call was made for greater effort in locating wells and privies, which are assumed to be ubiquitous on historic house sites (Franks 1990d:104). The oral history also noted that privies were not dug on the Jetertown site prior to the 1930s, nor were storm or root cellars built. Wells, in contrast, were a common feature, and informants stated that they were used as trash dumps (Yakubik and Franks 1990:51).

INVESTIGATIONS AT WILLIAM BRIDGES HOMESTEAD (16VN1076)

Despite historical evidence that there was little settlement in the Fort Polk area, some farmsteads dating to the mid–nineteenth century, pre–Civil War era, together with complementary archival data, have been found, most no-tably 16VN1076, examined by Earth Search, Inc., during the ES-5 and ES-7 projects (Franks 1990e:47; Yakubik and Franks 1990). The William Bridges Homestead site was named after a later occupant of the location, who filed a claim on it in 1911. Courthouse and tax assessor's records indicated that tracts of land in the general area of 16VN1076 had been claimed as early as the immediate pre–Civil War era, but no claim prior to Bridges's existed for the land where the site was located. The artifact assemblage, however, indicated occupation from the early part of the nineteenth century, making the site possibly one of the earliest historic occupations on the military reservation. Yakubik and Franks (1990:28, 30) argued that the early occupation on the site and in the area was because a major east-west road ran through the area, connecting Alexandria to Hickman's Ferry on the Sabine. The Self family had been in the area since at least 1860, when a claim for nearby land had been filed, and there were indications that the family had actually arrived as much as a decade before that. Occupation of 16VN1076 by a Self family member, or else someone who never registered a claim, was inferred. The site's presence indicates that, for at least some pre-twentieth-century occupation on Fort Polk, a few records may be available.

Despite the early ceramics, the early occupation was masked by later occupations. A surface debris scatter, two groups of three posts each from possible structures, and two depressions thought to represent wells were found during the fieldwork. A controlled surface collection was made over the site area, which was subdivided into a series of collection loci. Three posts covered with sheet metal were found together and were thought to reflect the remains of a corncrib, since this was a procedure used to keep rats and other pests out of the elevated storage area. The second group of posts was found near a depression thought to be a well and may have been part of an associated structure. A local informant told the crew that wells were located near houses, and a nearby scatter of nails, window glass, and other debris seemed to confirm this. A mean ceramic date of 1873.4 was obtained on ceramics from the site. Artifacts were divided into a number of functional groups and used to document intrasite variation. A concentration of architectural debris—nails, window glass, and metal debris—was found near the well, indicating a structure had once been in this area. Areas where outbuildings were inferred had more glass than ceramic artifacts, particularly jar or lid liners, suggesting some storage took place in these areas. A paucity of artifacts away from the presumed building sites was inferred to reflect sweeping of the yard, an activity documented by local informants.

Storm cellars and wells are the two principal subsurface features reported to have been present on Fort Polk–area historic sites, although no evidence for the former has yet to be found (Thomas et al. 1982:116; Yakubik and Franks 1990:51). Yakubik and Franks's (1990:51) interviews with local informants indicated, again, that privy pits were not common until the 1930s and that chimneys were more often of mud than of brick, making archaeological detection somewhat difficult. They also noted that the ubiquity of dogs and hogs meant that organic remains useful to documenting subsistence practices would be extremely unlikely. A detailed discussion of how the archaeological record of farmstead sites formed was presented:

[Y]ards were swept and domestic refuse was either fed to the animals or thrown into abandoned wells. In some cases, non-organic refuse was temporarily deposited in a central location until "clean up day," when it was then used as well fill (Mr. Lafate Franks, personal communication 1990). Consequently, few artifacts will be found horizontally distributed across most sites. Artifacts that are found in this context will fall into one of three categories. The first of these is lost items. These will generally be small articles such as buttons, coins, marbles, or toy parts. The second category is abandoned items that were left when occupation was terminated. These would include items such as the metal cans and washtubs found at 16VN1076. It might also include artifacts such as the plate and the bottle that were found in the vicinity of the house. The relatively large amounts of these artifacts that were found suggest they were whole (or at least nearly so) at the time of deposition. The third category includes small fragments of ceramics, glass, etc. that could have been easily overlooked during clean-up or covered over during sweeping the yard. This last category, while it certainly represents secondary refuse, may provide clues to the activity areas of the site. For example, tableware might be expected to be more prevalent in the area of the residence, as was the case at 16VN1076.

Two minor concentrations of debris might be expected at farmsteads. The first of these may indicate a central collecting area for refuse prior to clean up. It does not seem likely that this was located immediately adjacent to the residence, since such care was taken to keep this area clean. The second possible minor concentration of debris would occur on the perimeter of the yard and result from sweeping the yard.

The majority of the artifacts, however, would be deposited in abandoned wells according to informant accounts. If this is the case, the paucity of material recovered from these farmstead sites is not indicative of material poverty, but a reflection of the inhabitants' tidy, organized lifestyle. No wells have yet been excavated at Fort Polk, but the hypothesis that they contain the majority of the material culture of the settlers is supported by negative evidence.

In terms of the spatial organization of the farmsteads, major activity areas were closely arranged according to informants. Wells were immediately adjacent to the houses in order to facilitate water-carrying. Clothes washing and drying areas would also be nearby. It is generally agreed by informants that the chicken yard and smokehouse would be close enough to the house to protect them from animals and from theft. The barn would be slightly more distant, and adjacent to cattle and hog pens (Mr. Lafate Franks, Mrs. Naomi P. Copeland, personal communication 1990). Consequently, surviving features such as well depressions, fence posts, and structural supports might provide clues to former activity areas, as was the case at 16VN1076 [Yakubik and Franks 1990:51–52].

These observations can help guide and also be tested during subsequent historic sites research in the Fort Polk area.

The data from the site, where window glass was comparatively common and nails made up a relatively low proportion of the overall assemblage, again (as noted in the work at the Jetertown site) led the authors to conclude that earlier inferences about the archaeological signatures of early farmsteads were in need of rethinking and, more important, testing with as much data as possible (Yakubik and Franks 1990:70–72). In particular, in the 1988 HPP, it was suggested that window glass may not have been present at some early house sites and that a high incidence of nails, or at least a high incidence compared with ceramics and glass, might be one way to find the locations of former structures (Anderson et al. 1988:250–251). Neither of these expectations was realized at 16VN1076, where nails made up only about eight percent of the overall assemblage. Reuse of materials from earlier structures was common in the area, and structures were typically dismantled or scavenged rather than allowed to deteriorate in place, which were practices that would affect the occurrence of architectural debris.

FORT POLK CEMETERY NUMBER 2 (16VN1099)

During the Earth Search, Inc., ES-7 survey project, a small historic cemetery with 18 marked graves was located on the Main Fort. This was mapped, the inscriptions on each headstone were recorded, and photographs and a brief description of each grave were prepared (Yakubik and Franks 1990:56–69). The level of documentation was superb for a survey project, setting a standard that has rarely been equaled by subsequent investigators. The authors noted a number of patterns, notably that specific rows of graves represented family groupings; that unmarried children were buried near their parents, while married adults were buried by their spouses; that burials where inscribed headstones were lacking appeared to be those of children (due to the small size of some of these graves and their placement near adults); that children's headstones, when inscribed, more commonly bore epitaphs than did those of adults; and that decorative elements on headstones were about evenly distributed between adults and children. Most of the graves had footstones as well as headstones, making them easy to delimit. Materials used for headstones and footstones included marble and sandstone, while one grave had a wooden footstone. Eight of the graves were decorated with silk and plastic flowers, indicating the cemetery is still visited, even though the most recent marked interment dated to 1929. The oldest marked grave dated to 1849, consistent with the age of the occupation suggested by the artifactual and archival evidence collected at the William Bridges Homestead site (16VN1076), which is nearby. The headstones were classified by shape and method of manufacture, although the sample size was considered too small to permit much in the way of interpretation. Yakubik and Franks (1990:68) calculated a mean burial date for the cemetery by averaging the death dates on the inscriptions, arriving at 1894.3. While some old families were present in the cemetery, other families known to have been present in the area were not. The investigators concluded by suggesting that similar information could be collected from other cemeteries on Fort Polk and the resulting database used to explore the early settlement of the area.

INVESTIGATIONS AT HONOR CRYER HOMESTEAD (16VN1092)

Earth Search personnel continued their examination of historic settlement patterns at Fort Polk during the Earth Search, Inc., ES-8 survey project, during which limited investigations were undertaken at 16VN1092, the Honor Cryer Homestead site (Franks and Yakubik 1990b:52–68, 77–83). Cryer claimed the land in 1898 and was apparently living there at that time or soon thereafter. A light scatter of brick and other historic artifacts from a possible residence was found around two depressions that were interpreted as filled-in wells. Auger testing to a depth of 2 m below ground surface in these depressions failed to locate artifact-bearing deposits, although the procedure appears to be quite useful for the initial exploration of features of this kind. The occurrence of multiple wells is not surprising, since local informants indicated that additional wells were sometimes opened when the original wells went dry. About 100 m to the south a hand-hewn wooden spring box was found near a tributary of Whiskey Chitto Creek. These features were used for "keeping foods cool and as a source of water during periods of drought," according to a local informant (Franks and Yakubik 1990b:61). A similar spring box was found at 16VN1265 on Peason Ridge during a later survey (Largent et al. 1994a:112, 115–116) and was subsequently tested by Prentice Thomas and Associates, Inc., as described below (Thomas et al. 1994b:60–66). Finally, a group of fence posts from a possible animal pen was found about 200 m north of the presumed house area.

The 16VN1092 site assemblage, together with the results of past work on Fort Polk, was used as the basis for evaluating historic sites research to date on the installation (Franks and Yakubik 1990b:77–83). They noted that enough archaeological research had been conducted to demonstrate that existing archival and legal records presented an incomplete picture of early historic settlement, which was appreciably greater than had been inferred by previous researchers working primarily with documents (e.g., Anderson et al. 1988:280–281). In particular, a number of nineteenth-century residential sites had been examined for which no documentation existed. The initial claims in the area, dating from the 1840s through 1860s, were considered a particularly valuable source of information and their study crucial to the development of an accurate historic settlement model. In those portions of Fort Polk where land claim records had previously been examined, filing dates were either prior to the Civil War or after ca. 1880. While one claim is known that dated to 1845, many others postdated 1855, which was inferred to reflect filing under the Graduation Act of 1854:

> This act permitted the purchase of public lands at less than the minimum price of $1.25 per acre, depending on how long the lands had been available for sale. Lands that had been unsold for 10 to 15 years were priced at $1.00 per acre, lands that had been unsold for 15 to 20 years were priced at $.75 per acre, and so on to a price of $.125 per acre for lands unsold for 30 years or more. The act also permitted the preemption of land on which a settler was established at these prices (Gates 1968:186). This may suggest that the mid-to-late-1850s land claims may have been made by previously established settlers who saw the opportunity to gain title to their lands at a reduced price [Franks and Yakubik 1990b:78–79].

Postbellum land claims were all in the 1880s or later, which was inferred to reflect a belated desire by longtime residents to obtain legal title to their land in the wake of the expansion of the railroad and timber industries. Franks and Yakubik (1990b:79–83) also conducted an analysis of where land claims were filed in the antebellum and postbellum eras in the Whiskey Chitto and Drakes Creek areas of the Main Fort. The initial settlement was located near water sources and floodplains, while later settlement was more dispersed and was characterized by some speculation, a pattern noted by Joyce (1981) in the War Eagle Creek area of Arkansas.

THE 16VN424 CEMETERY AND 16VN1126 CONNERS HOUSE SITES

During the Earth Search, Inc., ES-11 project, a small cemetery, 16VN424, was recorded on Peason Ridge. Four graves were present. Measurements were made of the cemetery area and each grave, and detailed descriptions were given for each grave, including the inscriptions, headstones, and footstones (Franks and Jones 1991:24–25). Two of the interments were of Robert and Elizabeth Conners, husband and wife owners of a late-nineteenth- and early-twentieth-century farmstead identified as site 16VN1126 during the same project (Franks and Jones 1991:26–32). The report described the artifacts that were found and the results of an archival search. The tract containing the house site had been claimed in 1898, while in 1901 the timber on a 161.86-acre portion of it was sold for $600. The provisions of the timber sale included permitting tram construction and a right-of-way to facilitate removal of the longleaf pine that was being cut. The Conners couple died in the mid-1920s and, although the site itself is heavily disturbed, the assemblage recovered provides a good collection from an early-twentieth-century farmstead occupation.

A NAVAL STORES COMMUNITY: THE FOUR L STILL SITE (16VN1221)

A major timber industry turpentine-processing complex, 16VN1221, was initially documented by R. Christopher Goodwin and Associates during the RCG-6 intensive survey project and was then tested by Prentice Thomas and Associates, Inc., during the FP-6 project (Largent et al. 1993a:90–93; Thomas et al. 1993d:134–17). The site extends over a roughly 340-x-260-m area on a ridge overlooking an unnamed tributary of Dowden Creek (Figure 8.2). In all, besides the mapping of numerous surface features, 75 30-x-30-cm shovel tests were opened during the initial survey and 45 50-x-50-cm and 2 1-x-1-m units were opened during the testing program. The intensive testing subsurface investigations encompassed 13.25 m² in area and 8.725 m³ of fill. Archival investigations indicated the complex was operated by the Louisiana Long Leaf Lumber Company, from which the site name is derived. Two local informants, Mr. Odell Behan and Mr. Lois Brown, provided extensive detail about the operation on the complex:

> According to Mr. Odell Behan, whose father worked for the Four L company, 16VN1221 was the terminus of activities related to the procurement and final processing of turpentine. More specifically, this site was the location of one or more stills which were used to extract pure turpentine from the pine sap collected from stands surrounding the site. The majority of wage workers were African-Americans who lived in another company camp and who walked to and from work each day. This second camp was located four miles west of 16VN1221, just west of the north-south perimeter road that denotes the western boundary of Fort Polk, Peason Ridge.
>
> Mr. Behan also stated that a company store, measuring about 20 feet long and eight feet wide was located at the still site. The

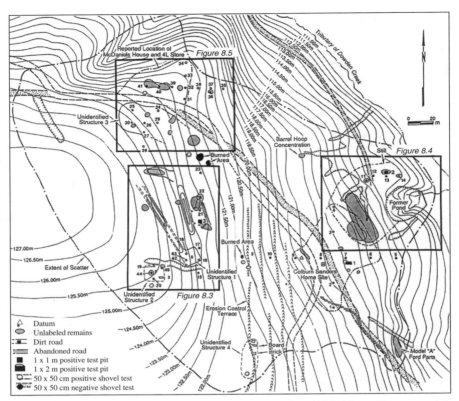

Figure 8.2 — Base map of the Four L Still site, 16VN1221 (from Thomas et al. 1993d:140).

majority of buildings were constructed in such a manner that they could be moved by rail when the turpentine collection ended and the whole complex was moved elsewhere. This movement was facilitated by the construction of tram railroad lines which served several purposes. After the turpentine potential was exhausted, the trees were cut and the trams were used to haul the logs to different sawmills. The trams were also used to move buildings from one site to the next in addition to transporting food and supplies to these camps. Tram railines [sic] can be distinguished from standard railines [sic] by the difference in the way the ties were made. Tram ties were usually squared on only two sides, while standard line ties were squared on all four sides.

According to Mr. Lois Brown, the pine stands surrounding 16VN1221 were separated into drifts which were numerically designated. These drifts were "hoed" once a year during the winter. Hoeing involved a gang of men and/or boys moving through the drifts with hoes and removing all the understory from each pine tree for a distance of 30 inches away from the tree. Hoes were purchased from the company for $1.00, but the handle had to be provided by the individual workers who, in this case, were usually Euro-American. The tree was then capped, creating a clean, bark free face down which the pine sap ran into aprons and finally into turpentine cups. Once a week each tree was "chipped" when the turpentine was collected by African-American workers. These workers collected the turpentine in small barrels which were later transferred to larger barrels and conveyed by wagon to the turpentine stills for processing. According to both men interviewed, the Four L turpentine camp at 16VN1221 ceased operations between 1932–1933.

After turpentine processing ceased, the majority of the area containing 16VN1221 was purchased from the Four L company in 1932 by two brothers, E. F. and M. C. Sanders. Each man bought 20 acre adjoining tracts for $40.00 per tract. . . . The brothers farmed cotton on the higher slopes . . . until the time of Government acquisition of the property.

Mr. Behan stated that the improvements included two houses, one of which was located in the southeastern portion of the site and occupied by M. C. Sanders. The second house was apparently the domicile of Mrs. Tishie McDaniels, the daughter of James Owers (16VN138). There are no records documenting a legal transfer of land to Mrs. McDaniels so the details of her occupation at the site are unclear. However, Mr. Behan identified the area of her home as being on the northern periphery in the former location of the Four L company store [Thomas et al. 1993d:137–138].

There were thus two major periods of site use, one associated with the naval stores industry in the 1920s up to roughly 1932 and the second with homesites occupied after that time until the area was incorporated into Fort Polk.

The site area was first examined on foot using transects spaced at 10-m intervals, with all features and artifact concentrations marked with flagging. In areas between concentrations artifacts were flagged individually. The site was divided into a number of subareas and each was reported separately. A turpentine still, inferred by the presence of a mass of burned resin, a small dam and pond, and two large sheet middens were located in the northeast part of the site (Figure 8.3). One of the sheet middens included the remains

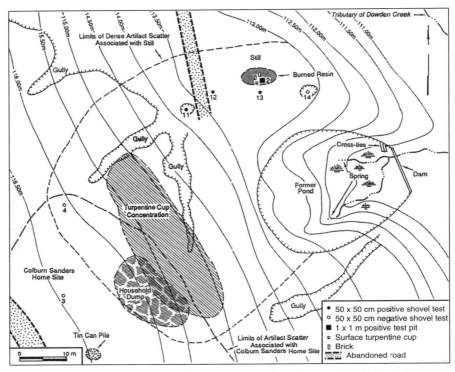

Figure 8.3 — Detail of the area of the turpentine still at the Four L Still site, 16VN1221 (from Thomas et al. 1993d:143).

of hundreds of metal turpentine cups, while the other was a scatter of glass, ceramics, and metal domestic debris associated with the Colburn Sanders house site located ca. 30 m to the south. The dam, which was of poured concrete and varied from 4 to 12 inches thick, was designed to collect water from a spring for the turpentine still boilers.

A cooperage shed, where barrels were apparently made, was found 100 m west of the turpentine still locality (Figure 8.4). A number of large pine posts were found with a 10-x-15-m leveled area that had brick and mortar concentrations probably from chimney falls at either end. The surrounding area yielded large numbers of metal barrel hoops, an earthen berm, resin piles, and a gully with turpentine aprons along its length. Just to the south were the remains of two unidentified structures, one with an elongated earthen berm stretching from it to the north. Sixty-five meters to the northwest was another concentration of features and debris, including sandstone slabs and old pine boards from an unidentified structure (Figure 8.5). In this same area were what the informants said were the remains of the Tishie McDaniels

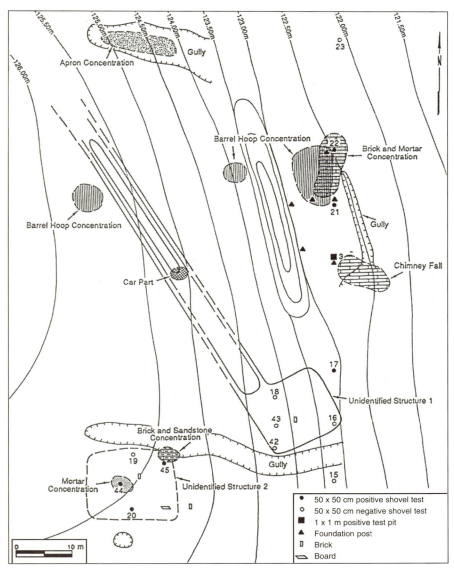

Figure 8.4 — Detail of the area of the cooperage shed at the Four L Still site, 16VN1221 (from Thomas et al. 1993d:149).

house site, built on the same location as the Four L company commissary, and a dense concentration of metal turpentine cups. In the southeast corner of the site another unidentified structure was located, together with debris from what the informants stated was the remains of the Colburn Sanders

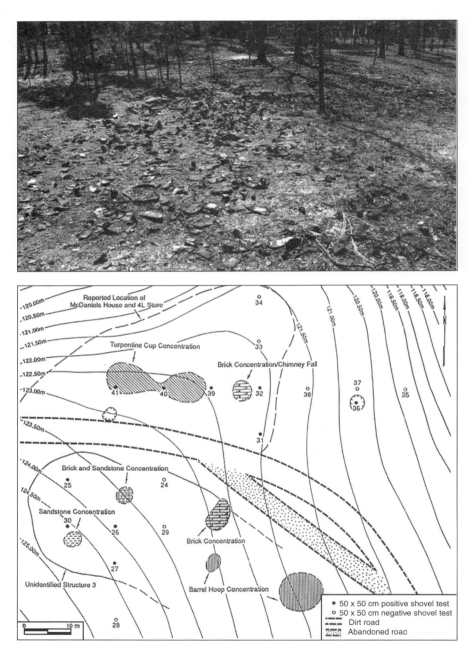

Figure 8.5 — Detail of the area of the company store (bottom) and the turpentine cup sheet midden (top) at the Four L Still site, 16VN1221 (from Thomas et al. 1993d:154, 160).

Figure 8.6 — Historic artifacts from the Four L Still site, 16VN1221: a, b, Raleigh's medicine bottles; c, f, wood stove door lids; d, e, turpentine cups (from Thomas et al. 1993d:170, 176).

house site. A well lined with mortar was located a few meters east of the presumed house, while another 20 m east was a deep depression that, upon excavation of a 1-x-2-m unit to a depth of a meter, appeared to be the remains of a privy.

Several hundred artifacts were found, whose character generally corresponded to the nature of the structures they were associated with (Figure 8.6). Structures associated with the turpentine-processing operation typically contained, besides architectural debris, metal turpentine cups, barrel hoops, and bottle glass fragments. A wider range of debris, including architectural and domestic items, was found at the house sites. The investigators provided a general summary of how a turpentine still operated:

> Turpentine stills were set up to process pine resin into turpentine and rosen. These are industrial sites with a variety of associated activities that required structures, often including, in addition to the still, a cooperage shed, a blacksmith shop and company store. Also, since the naval stores industry was labor intensive and since the activities took place in isolated areas of the forest, living arrangements for workers and supervisory personnel also had to be provided. As a result, the still operation was essentially an industrial complex.
>
> The primary industrial structures found at most stills include the still and a dammed pond or sluice-way from a nearby stream, in addition to the above referenced associated structures. . . . The cooper's shed was a very important part of the operation as it produced the wooden barrels necessary for the transport of the raw turpentine resin or gum from the forest and receptacles for the turpentine spirits and rosin. Several sheds were generally built to protect the open barrels of raw pine gum prior to distillation and store various equipment such as turpentine cups.
>
> Usually present at more substantial and permanent stills were the manager's quarters, the operator's quarters, and the turpentine workers' quarters. . . . The supervisory personnel generally occupied residences near the industrial complex, whereas the workers' quarters were established on the fringes of the operation. Large turpentine villages may have had populations in the hundreds, with additional company facilities such as a company store. Some companies even paid their workers with their own coinage which, of course, could only be redeemed at the company store [Thomas et al. 1993d:163–165].

Considerable quantities of artifacts remain at the site, particularly turpentine cups and cup fragments, of which thousands were observed.

THE JAMES OWERS HOMESITE (16VN138)

An early-twentieth-century house site located on a ridge overlooking the floodplain of a tributary of Dowden Creek on Peason Ridge was examined by Prentice Thomas and Associates, Inc., during the FP-6 project (Thomas et al. 1993d:77–92). The area is adjacent to an old road that runs to Hornbeck, a small community to the north. The Coleman and Annie Owers house site is located about 600 m to the north, while 16VN1221, the Four L Still site, is located 400 m to the southeast. In all, 31 50-x-50-cm and 2 1-x-1-m units were opened at the site, covering a total area of 9.75 m^2 and 4.825 m^3 of fill. During the late nineteenth and early twentieth centuries the land in the area was owned by various railroad and timber interests. In 1926 James and Louella Owers purchased 40 acres of property from the Louisiana Long Leaf Lumber Company, on which they lived until the land was acquired for incorporation into Fort Polk in 1943. A local informant described the homestead, which included a pine board and batten house with one or more mud cat chimneys, a well, and a barn. The county tax assessor's records for 1930 indicate that at that time 30 acres were in timber and 10 acres were under cultivation and that Mr. Owers had "one mule valued at $40.00, four head of cattle worth $35, and 25 goats worth $1.00 apiece" (Tax Assessors Records, Leesville Public Library, cited in Thomas et al. 1993d:80). Twelve shovel tests were placed in and around the house, eight were placed in the vicinity of the barn, and the remainder were dispersed over the site area. The 1-x-1-m units were placed into the presumed well depression and the house chimney fall.

Three concentrations of sandstone slabs, two with bricks, were found; one of these appeared to represent a chimney fall from the main house while the other two appeared to be foundation stones of outbuildings. Three depressions were also located, one a few meters north of the chimney that was assumed to be a well, one 30 m to the northwest that appeared to be a refuse dump on the basis of a surface scatter of artifacts, and a third, of unknown function, that was located 20 m to the southwest of the house depression. A scatter of historic material was found about 100 m to the southeast of the house, which may also represent a trash disposal area or possibly an outbuilding. In all, 301 historic artifacts were recovered. Glass, metal, and brick were found in the vicinity of the barn, while a much larger sample with a wider range of artifacts, including domestic ceramics, windowpane, and lamp glass, was found in the vicinity of the house. A test pit opened into the well depression was taken to 50 cm and intersected the edge of a dark circular stain that may be the well pit itself, although the function could not be determined. A second test pit uncovered a number of rocks and bricks from a probable chimney fall.

An analysis of artifacts by location within the site and by functional group was undertaken (Thomas et al. 1993d:89–91). The house area was dominated by architectural remains such as nails, window glass, and other building materials. The inferred refuse pit was dominated by kitchen items, suggesting it was filled with debris from the house, while the area of the barn had only a small number of domestic, architectural, and barn and stable items.

THE FOUR L HOME SITE (16VN1575) AND THE
TIN FIREPLACES SITE (16VN1795)

A dense surface scatter of historic artifacts that was designated the Four L Home site (16VN1575) was found by archaeologists from Gulf South Research Corporation during the GSRI-2 project (Shuman et al. 1996a:59–64). The site name derives from its early-twentieth-century owner, the Louisiana Long Leaf Lumber Company, which owned it from 1918 until 1942. The site assemblage was dominated by whiteware and bottle glass, with lesser amounts of nails, brick, and window glass. The presence of a structure was indicated, although no foundations were noted. The material cultural assemblage was similar to that noted on other timber industry sites in the region, suggesting that the site may have functioned as a workers' camp. A 1923 chauffeur's medallion that could have been used by a truck driver was also found, which is also consistent with logging activities. The Four L Still site (16VN1221), a major logging compound, is located about 915 m to the southeast and 16VN1575 was thought to be related, possibly being a workers' residence (Shuman et al. 1996a:63). A second historic scatter found during the same survey, 16VN1795, was characterized by brick and glass fragments, utilitarian ceramics, barrel hoops, and the remains of molded tin fireplaces, from which the site obtained its name (Shuman et al. 1996a:65). Located immediately northeast of the Four L Still site across a small draw, the Tin Fireplaces site was interpreted as a side camp or temporary quarters for at least some of those working at the larger site.

THE COLEMAN AND ANNIE OWERS HOMESITE (16VN139)

A historic house site, 16VN139, was initially documented during the RCG-6 intensive survey project and then was tested by Prentice Thomas and Associates, Inc., during the FP-6 project (Largent et al. 1993a:54–58; Thomas et al. 1993d:93–106). The site is located on a ridge overlooking an unnamed tributary of Dowden Creek. During the late nineteenth and early twentieth centuries the land in the area, which also includes sites 16VN138 and 16VN1221, was owned by various railroad and timber interests. In all, 25 50-x-50-cm and 3 1-x-1-m units were opened at the site during the testing phase, for a total area of 9.75 m² and 3.4 m³ of fill. In 1926 Coleman and Annie Owers purchased 40 acres of property from the Louisiana Long Leaf Lumber Company, on which they lived until the land was acquired for incorporation into Fort Polk in 1943. The county tax assessor's records for

1930 indicate that at that time Mr. Owers had 10 acres in cut-over pine and 10 acres under cultivation, a horse, two head of cattle, and an automobile (Tax Assessors Records, Leesville Public Library, cited in Thomas et al. 1993d:80).

A local informant who visited the site area with the Prentice Thomas and Associates team in 1993 described the property as follows:

> [T]he house was made of pine lumber using the board and batten construction technique. The house had at least one mud cat chimney and was located in the southern portion of the site near two large trees. A pole barn was located north of the house, while a smokehouse and an outhouse were located west and downslope of the house. A well was probably located north and east of the house near the small north-south oriented dirt road which passed the homesite. An agricultural field was located north of the barn and had mature corn in it when Mr. Behan and his father helped the Owers move after they sold their land to the U.S. Government [Thomas et al. 1993d:96].

During the fieldwork a small concentration of sandstone slabs was observed, which was thought to represent the foundations of a structure; six depressions were also noted. A feature originally thought to be a drip line was reinterpreted as a fire break. Artifacts were found over an area measuring 70 x 65 m. The three 1-x-1-m units were placed near a sandstone slab concentration believed to be the location of a structure and at the edges of two depressions. A board and more sandstone slabs, interpreted as part of the house foundation, were found in Test Unit 1. In Test Unit 2 a squared post mold was found at the depression margin that appears to be part of a structure associated with the depression, whose function was not resolved. In Test Unit 3, a circular stain was found with historic debris inside, and this may represent a filled-in well or a refuse pit.

A total of 395 historic artifacts were found, which all appeared to derive from the Owers occupation. The vast majority were the remains of household items, specifically ceramic and glass fragments, dating from the 1920 to 1940 period. Architectural items were a distinct minority, suggesting the house may have been dismantled and removed/scavenged rather than burned or allowed to deteriorate in place.

THE WILLIAM PERKINS HOUSE SITE (16VN65)

An early-twentieth-century house site, 16VN65, was examined on the Main Fort by Prentice Thomas and Associates, Inc., during the FP-9 testing project in 1993 (Campbell et al. 1994b:57–71). Archival records indicated the land belonged to Mr. and Mrs. William Perkins from 1909 to 1930 and that their home was part of a dispersed community that included a number of farmsteads, a mill, a schoolhouse, a church, and at least two cemeteries located within a few sections. Thirteen 50-x-50-cm and two 1-x-1-m test units were opened at the site, which was mapped, surface collected, and systematically examined with a metal detector. Eleven metal concentrations were recorded, and one of the 1-x-1-m units was opened within one of these while the other was placed in a depression that appeared to have been a filled-in well. A sheet midden of early-twentieth-century debris was observed in the southeastern part of the site. The unit in the probable well depression was opened to 90 cm and produced a large proportion of all the historic material found on the site (n = 142 of 227 total artifacts). A wide range of glass, ceramics, and metal artifacts were recovered from the site and were described in the report (Figure 8.7). Given the value of the ceramics, which appeared to derive from a plain white ironstone dinnerware set that was the least expensive in the 1909 Sears, Roebuck and Co. catalog, the occupation was interpreted to be the remains of a lower-class or lower-middle-class residence. Ceramic turpentine cup fragments were collected, suggesting Mr. Perkins may have worked in the lumbering industry, although the Earth Search informant interviews indicated these items were also used as flowerpots and utensil holders by local residents (Franks and Yakubik 1990a:84, 91).

THE BOXED SPRING HISTORIC SITE, 16VN1265

The Boxed Spring site was originally discovered during intensive survey work conducted by Goodwin and Associates, Inc., on Peason Ridge (Largent et al. 1994a:112, 115–116). It was tested by archaeologists from Prentice Thomas and Associates, Inc., during the FP-11 project. The site is located on a ridge slope near a minor tributary of Martin's Creek and is named for a spring box found by the creek edge (Figure 8.8). In all, 16 50-x-50-cm tests were dispersed over the site area, the spring box was excavated, a 1-x-2-m unit was opened into a small depression, and an irregular stone and brick pile was mapped (Thomas et al. 1994b:96–110). The spring box was made of rough-cut lumber and appears to have been placed as the well was excavated (Figure 8.9). Two rows of four large bolts each were observed protruding out of the ground in a small depression near the stone pile. The bolts were attached to massive timbers laid in a crisscross fashion, and this was thought to represent the foundation of one or more structures, possibly a sawmill. A crescent-shaped stone and brick concentration extending over a roughly 10-x-15-m area was also plotted, which may represent the remains of a chimney or some other structural component. Near this was a shallow

Figure 8.7 — Historic artifacts from the William Perkins house site, 16VN65: a, b, door hinges; c, porcelain vessel fragment; d, ironstone; e, stenciled porcelain; f, can lid; g, pewter decanter neck; h, i, shoe leather; j, bottle top (from Campbell et al. 1994b:66–67).

depression of unknown function about 4 x 7 x 0.5 m in extent. Large cow bones with butchering marks, bolts, a crank handle, and an unidentified machine part were also found. A general scarcity of domestic artifacts suggests use of the area for industrial purposes of some kind, possibly related to

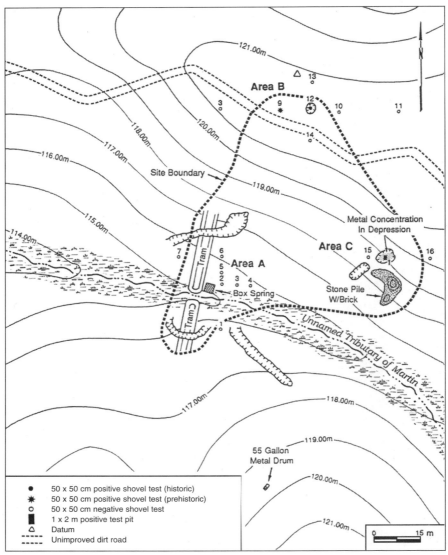

Figure 8.8 — Map of the Boxed Spring site, 16VN1265 (from Thomas et al. 1994b:98).

timbering. An archival search documented the existence of a number of owners from 1905 through its purchase for incorporation into Fort Polk in 1943, although there was no indication that structures were ever present on it. Briefly owned by the W. F. Diehl Lumber Company in the first decade of the twentieth century, the site may reflect a work camp site of some kind.

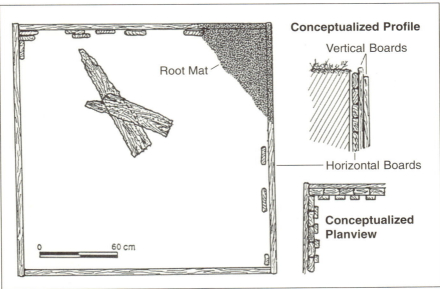

Figure 8.9 — Plan drawing and photograph of the spring box at 16VN1265 (from Thomas et al. 1994b:100, 101).

THE 1999 HPP SETTLEMENT ANALYSIS

The 1988 HPP provided a detailed and thorough critique of historic archaeological research at Fort Polk by J. W. Joseph, with a special emphasis on previous settlement analyses and development of historic site typology. Joseph updated his critique in 1999 (Anderson et al. 1999b:391–421), and this section is a condensed version of that update. Prior to the 1988 HPP, little systematic effort had been directed to the resolution of historic settlement patterning. The most comprehensive analyses of historic assemblages were those conducted by New World Research personnel (Campbell and Weed 1986; Thomas et al. 1982). Their assessment, derived from attempts to produce historic models for Fort Polk, was that such effort had relatively little chance of success as a result of the low density of sites of this period, coupled with their "general random distribution" (Thomas et al. 1982:138). These studies did produce an excellent historic site typology, however, as well as a good overview of the kinds of historic sites likely to be found on the installation.

The 1988 HPP historic settlement analysis explored the difficulties entailed in historic sites modeling in general, and at Fort Polk in particular, and reevaluated Thomas et al.'s (1982) contention that historic sites settlement patterning was not feasible for Fort Polk. The results of this analysis, while in general agreement with this conclusion, did provide a good general picture about historic settlement in the Fort Polk area, even if the results were not useful for predicting specific site locations.

For that reason, the 1999 revision looked first at models from other areas of the South to see what applicability there might be for Fort Polk. That evaluation suggested that modeling is feasible for historic sites, but that the variables that determine historic settlement patterning are both environmental and cultural in nature and that the cultural variables are of a type that are rarely recorded during archaeological surveys. It was also argued that the archaeological definition of "settlement" was overly dependent on physical remains and failed to address the perceived environment and its resultant settlement pattern at the time of historic occupation. Historic settlement patterns, according to the 1999 revision, must be based on the location of improved and unimproved land, roads, stores, churches, schools, and neighbors, in addition to the remains of former farms and houses. The majority of this information is not recovered during typical archaeological survey.

The 1999 HPP looked at a number of historic settlement pattern studies throughout the South. However, most were either in coastal areas or designed to look at lowcountry plantations. Still, they supported the argument that environmental variables alone cannot explain historic settlement (Goodwin et al. 1984; Hartley 1987; Joseph 1986; Singleton 1980; South and Hartley 1980; Wheaton et al. 1983). More applicable to Fort Polk was Orser and Nekola's (1985) examination of piedmont tenant farms in South Carolina. Orser and Nekola attempted to address the settlement patterning of tenant structures from Millwood Plantation, South Carolina, utilizing statistical correlations with environmental data. The environmental variables employed in their study included soil association; agricultural, pasturage, and woodland potential of the land; current vegetation; elevation; direction and aspect of slope; distance to the Savannah River; distance and direction to the nearest stream; rank order and type of nearest stream; and proximity to the confluence of the nearest stream. They also included cultural variables-distance to the nearest road, railroad, neighbor, and town—in calculating the settlement correlations (Orser and Nekola 1985:79). Their analysis, again, revealed that there was no strong association between environmental factors and site location. The strongest correlation was between site location and nearest road or railroad, although Orser and Nekola suggested that this association might be an artificial creation of the presence of two sets of roads and railroads in the project area, each set paralleling the other, so that all sites were in proximity to a transportation source. Thus, they concluded that tenant settlement patterning was "random," although they recognized that "it remains possible that the locations are not at all random in terms of social, familial, economic, and political factors which were not measured by the variables chosen for analysis" (Orser and Nekola 1985:83).

The 1999 HPP found the most useful historic settlement analysis for the Fort Polk area was Joyce's (1981) settlement study of the War Eagle Creek vicinity in northwest Arkansas. Joyce (1981:49–69) used original land grants from the period of 1836 to 1869 to determine the relative importance of both environmental and cultural variables in determining historic settlement. By employing land grants she was able to determine the universe of decisions made by settlers in selecting one tract over another. As she noted, one problem with settlement models based on archaeological data is that they invariably address settlement patterning as a product of the visible remains of occupations: foundation ruins, wells, privies, artifact scatters, and so on. However, settlers selected land in terms of agricultural or commercial potential, and construction loci were determined only after the initial plot of land had been secured. Thus, historic settlement patterning exists at two levels: property ownership patterns and individual structure locations. As Joyce wrote: "With property ownership the universe is the total purchasable region; whereas with the individual structure the universe is the purchased or claimed property. The confusion arises because settlement is usually viewed as a structure or activity center which generates physical remains, rather than a physical space which includes fields, woods, and improvements, as well as structures and refuse areas. The latter view probably more closely approximates the emic view of 'settlement' " (Joyce 1981:14). Joyce considered both environmental and cultural variables in constructing her model of the War Eagle settlement. Environmental factors included distance and rank of nearest water, topography, soils, and vegetation, while cultural variables included political factors, social factors, and economic factors. Joyce calculated political factors as those government decisions affecting the availability of land, primarily various land grant acts. Social factors considered by her study were limited to kinship, while economic factors included the proximity of the nearest road, community, and special activity sites (i.e., mills, tanneries, and distilleries) (Joyce 1981:15–48).

The War Eagle settlement model was characterized by two phases. During the initial phase of settlement, when nearly the entire universe of settlement locations was available, settlers chose tracts that met their needs and/ or wants. Having water within the boundaries of a purchased property was preferred over no water, and higher ranked drainages were preferred over lower ranks. Swamps and arid prairies were rejected as homestead sites. Soils with high to medium agricultural potential were preferred. Floodplain settings were favored, followed by sloping uplands and flat uplands. Mountainous settings were rejected. Wooded settings were the preferred habitats. Among the cultural variables, the various land grant acts each stimulated additional settlement in the area. Proximity to special activity sites was not an important consideration; however, proximity to a community was. The role played by transportation networks in establishing settlement could not be determined in the absence of comprehensive historic maps of the area. Finally, kinship was determined to be the most important variable regulating settlement. Settlers were willing to accept less desirable land if it was located within 1.25 miles of members of their kin. For example, a settler would chose a sloping uplands site over a floodplain site or a Rank 3 drainage over a Rank 4 drainage if the choice meant closer proximity to kin (Joyce 1981:92).

Once the prime lands of the War Eagle Creek area had been secured, a second phase of settlement occurred. During this phase the less desirable lands were selected. However, it is difficult to determine whether these acquisitions were for settlement purposes or intended simply as speculation. Land grant acts of this period greatly reduced the cost of land in the War Eagle Creek vicinity, and much of the activity reflected in land acquisition may not represent settlement (Joyce 1981:93–96).

The model produced by Joyce suggested that earliest settlement focused on the floodplains of major drainages, with War Eagle Creek being the preferred drainage. These settlements appear to have been kin based, and as land along War Eagle Creek was acquired, the preferred settlement locus shifted to upland slopes adjacent to the larger streams and creeks of the area and, in particular, locations marked by the confluence of drainages. Next in preference were upland flatlands crossed by water. Joyce's analysis suggested that many of the settlers arriving in the War Eagle Creek area came as extended families and that their land-selection practices reflected a desire to maintain these kinship connections. Thus, if only isolated tracts were available on War Eagle Creek but larger contiguous plots were available on the upland slopes, these contiguous plots would be selected in preference to the superior, but isolated, War Eagle Creek tracts. While Joyce was not able to determine the significance of roads to settlement patterning, she did note that this was something of a chicken-or-egg dilemma—in the absence of detailed maps it was impossible to determine whether roads or settlement came first (Joyce 1981:45). It seems likely that both instances were in existence and that some roads were adapted from existing trails, while others were created to provide access to favorable settlement loci.

While she did not consider them as social variables in her study, Joyce mentioned that ethnicity, religion, and national or regional ties might also influence settlement decisions. For example, Joyce noted that in the area of War Eagle Creek there is a community named Old Alabam composed of former citizens of Alabama (Joyce 1981:94). Given the importance that kinship plays in settlement patterning, these social variables should also be considered as affecting settlement patterning.

The 1999 HPP came to several important conclusions in looking at efforts in other areas. For instance, settlement loci seemed to be selected not only for particular environmental qualities but also to fulfill cultural needs, such as to be in proximity to kin and other support groups, communities, and transportation routes linking these cultural resources. Thus, historic settlement patterning cannot be projected from archaeological data alone. Second, the types of information produced from archaeological research are also inappropriate to the historic, emic, perception of settlement. While archaeological studies focus on structural remains, historic settlers appear to have been preoccupied with the agricultural potential of their lands, and the positioning of homesteads was not a critical concern. Finally, much of what appears random in historic settlement is patterned, but this patterning is the product of cultural decisions not recoverable in the archaeological record. Historic settlement pattern models thus must incorporate greater historical data if they are to produce meaningful settlement models. These conclusions led to the historic context discussed in detail later in this chapter.

Historic Site Typology for Fort Polk
The 1999 HPP also looked at previous attempts in the development of a historic site typology, a necessary part of any settlement analysis. The 1999 HPP began by noting that the recognition of Fort Polk's historic ancestry

has progressively widened over the course of archaeological investigations at the base. Early research by Servello (1983), for example, virtually ignored the nonindustrial components at the fort, as Servello wrote that the historic cultural environment of the base "has its roots in the logging era" (Servello, ed. 1983:67). The lumber industry clearly provided the greatest historic impact to the area, but it is an overstatement that this occupation provided the "roots" of historic settlement. A broader perspective of historic occupation was provided by Thomas et al. (1982), who defined five site types: (1) artifact scatters, (2) features with artifacts, (3) features without artifacts, (4) tramways, and (5) cemeteries. Thomas and his colleagues recognized the presence of farms (which they referred to as "homesteads") in the project area prior to the arrival of the lumber industry but, like Servello, discredited the notion of any significant historic settlement prior to the 1880s (Servello, ed. 1983:67; Thomas et al. 1982:137). As Thomas and his colleagues viewed the situation, historic settlement of the Fort Polk area was tied to the arrival of the Kansas City Southern Railroad, and "permanent settlement of the Fort Polk area prior to the late 1800s was sparse or nonexistent." As they pointed out, the success of the lumber industry was dependent on the arrival of the railroad (Thomas et al. 1982:137). However, the absence of rail transportation would not have precluded farming occupations and as later research discovered, there was moderate settlement prior to the arrival of the railroad.

Campbell and Weed (1986:5-4) expanded on the typology presented by Thomas et al. (1982) and divided Fort Polk historic sites into six types: (1) homesteads, (2) temporary work stations, (3) commercial/industrial sites, (4) trams, (5) cemeteries, and (6) historic scatters. Campbell and Weed also presented criteria through which each of these site types could be distinguished. As they noted, this typology exhibited some overlap, in that trams (and technically temporary work stations) are also commercial/industrial sites (Campbell and Weed 1986:5-2, 5-4). This typology also did not account for community occupations, schools, churches, and agricultural sites larger than homesteads. However, the criteria outlined by Campbell and Weed provided for a reasonably accurate typological assignment of historic sites based on archaeological survey data alone and were of considerable value to the development of Fort Polk historic archaeology. Their typology, as modified in the 1988 HPP, was, in fact, used extensively by subsequent researchers to describe site types found on survey projects. This historic sites typology has also been subject to evaluation and refinement in recent years, and one new site type was proposed, the industrial turpentine-still complex, on the basis of the extensive work conducted at the Four L Still site (Thomas et al. 1993d:185; see above).

Campbell and Weed were the first to attempt to define an archaeological signature for the various site types. Homesteads in the Campbell and Weed historic site typology were characterized by the presence of "distinctive homestead artifacts," which they defined as stove parts and window glass; an equal or greater percentage of ceramics to glass; the presence of wells, privies, and old road beds; and the presence of ornamental plants, which proved to be one of the securest indicators of homestead occupations (Campbell and Weed 1986:5-4, 11-2). Temporary work stations associated with turpentine were characterized by the appearance of glass in greater quantities than ceramics; the contribution of turpentine cup fragments as at least one-third of the entire assemblage; and the appearance of privies, structural remains, or old roads. Temporary stations associated with lumbering exhibited similar traits, although turpentine cups were expected to be absent or to contribute less than one-third of the total assemblage. Campbell and Weed (1986:5-4) classified commercial/industrial sites as those sites "restricted to all one artifact type," with associated concrete or earthen structures, while tramways were defined as earthen structures with no or only a single artifact type associated. Cemeteries were identified by grave markers, while historic scatters were characterized by few artifacts and the absence of homestead artifacts (Campbell and Weed 1986:5-4).

The 1999 HPP noted that the separation of temporary work stations from homestead sites was a critical distinction necessary to Fort Polk archaeology. It agreed that homesteads, as relatively permanent occupations, should possess significant quantities of architectural remains. However, Joseph (in (Anderson et al. 1999b:397) suggested that while Campbell and Weed chose to focus on window glass as a homestead diagnostic, poorer rural occupations of the middle to late nineteenth century might not have had glazed windows and instead might have made do with shutters. A more reliable index, he suggested, was the presence of nails and the percentage of nails to ceramics and glass. The assumption here was that temporary work stations probably employed tents and other types of impermanent architecture that would not leave substantial traces and that this architecture would be intended for reuse, also limiting the residue of these occupations. The presence of significant architectural evidence thus immediately suggests a nontemporary occupation.

Likewise, the 1999 HPP noted that Campbell and Weed's (1986) emphasis on the ratio of ceramics to glass reflected long-term versus short-term behavior. Ceramics are normally associated with the serving of food, whereas glass artifacts are more likely to be storage containers. Short-term occupations should not require elaborate food service, and hence one or two plates would most likely suffice for each individual. Short-term occupations would need significant quantities of storage vessels, as all foods were brought into the site (as opposed to being produced at the site), and hence a high percentage of glass artifacts should be anticipated for short-term occupations. Long-term occupations are more likely to produce their own foodstuffs and to have acquired and employed more elaborate service items, and hence the inverse relation was anticipated by the 1999 HPP for long-term occupations.

Indeed, Franks (1990d:195) had also previously challenged the assumption that ceramics should be more common than glassware at house sites and that this relationship would be reversed on temporary camps (Anderson et al. 1988:251; Campbell and Weed 1986:5-4). Instead, evidence from the Henry Jeter Homestead site indicated that glass was far more common than ceramics (see also Yakubik and Franks 1990:72).

The 1999 HPP Revised Historic Site Typology

Another site attribute observed by Campbell and Weed was that short-term lumbering and turpentine encampments were noted for their residents' considerable consumption of "recreational" beverages, and hence the high glass ratio of these sites may be a reflection of this aspect of human behavior. While Campbell and Weed (1986) provided a functional typology for distinguishing homesteads from encampments, the 1999 HPP researchers believed that their classificatory scheme was inconsistent. As noted, commercial/industrial sites did not include temporary encampments, and the logic for their characterization of these sites as "restricted to all one artifact type" was unclear. Thus, in order to provide consistency to the historic site typology for Fort Polk, the 1999 HPP suggested a revised typology (Table 8.1).

The 1999 typology divided Fort Polk historic sites into three classes: agricultural, commercial/industrial, and communal. Agricultural site types included farmsteads (Campbell and Weed's "homesteads") and plantations. Although plantations were expected to be a limited site type occurrence in the project area, at least one, 16VN15, was listed by Servello (Servello, ed. 1983:xxxv) and hence this designation was included in the typology. Commercial/industrial sites in this typology included those evidences of the lumber industry at Fort Polk such as temporary work stations and trams, as well as other commercial/industrial site types such as cattle dipping vats, stores, and other site types. Communal sites included cemeteries, towns, schools, and other site types. Finally, historic artifact scatters were listed as an independent class/type since these represent undefined historic archaeological sites. This typology did not address chronological variation among historic sites at Fort Polk. As noted above, Servello (1983), Thomas et al. (1982), and Campbell and Weed (1986) all attributed the bulk of Fort Polk's historic

Table 8.1 — Historic site typology for Fort Polk: class, type, and criteria

Site Class—Type—Criteria

A. Agricultural
1. Farmstead
a. presence of window glass
b. nails contribute 30 percent or more of total artifacts
c. number of ceramics equal to or greater than glass
d. wells
e. privies
f. ornamental plants
g. adjacent to old road

2. Plantation (not expected in the immediate Fort Polk area)
a. presence of window glass
b. nails contribute 30 percent or more of total artifacts
c. number of ceramics equal to or greater than glass
d. wells
e. privies
f. ornamental plants
g. adjacent to old road
h. appearance of multiple structure locations

B. Commercial/Industrial
1. Lumbering Temporary Work Station
a. glass artifacts more numerous than ceramics
b. limited or no architectural artifacts
c. turpentine cups less than 33 percent of assemblage
d. privies

2. Turpentine Temporary Work Station
a. glass artifacts more numerous than ceramics
b. limited or no architectural artifacts
c. turpentine cups greater than 33 percent of assemblage
d. privies

3. Turpentine Industrial Still Complex*
a. still
(1) proximity to water
(2) pond and dam or other water sources such as would be present at a mill
(3) concentrations of turpentine cups
(4) burned resin
(5) building materials
(6) turpentine-related artifacts should predominate

Table 8.1 (cont.) — Historic site typology for Fort Polk: class, type, and criteria

Site Class—Type—Criteria

    b. cooperage shed
       (1) evidence for a ramp for loading and unloading
       (2) barrel hoops
       (3) aprons
       (4) building materials
    c. associated structures (overseer's house, cooper's house, workers' quarters)
    d. store (possibly)
    e. place of worship (possibly)
    f. cemetery (possibly)

  4. Tram
    a. raised or excavated linear earthen features

  5. Cattle Dipping Vat

  6. Store

  7. Other

C. Communal
  1. Cemetery
    a. presence of marked or unmarked graves
    b. presence of grave shaft depressions
    c. presence of fence or wall enclosing cemetery

  2. Town
    a. presence of numerous domestic structures in proximity
    b. linear arrangement of structures

  3. School

  4. Other

D. Historic Artifact Scatter (absence of features/low artifact density)

Source: Adapted from Campbell and Weed 1986:5-4.

* *The Turpentine Industrial Still Complex site type was proposed for the commercial/industrial group of sites by archaeologists from Prentice Thomas and Associates, Inc., based on the work at the Four L Still site, 16VN1221 (taken from Thomas et al. 1993d:189).*

settlement to the late nineteenth century, with Servello emphasizing the impact of the lumber industry in the region, and Thomas and colleagues and Campbell and Weed recognizing the previous existence of small farmsteads. Obviously, this attribution is generally correct, as Fort Polk historic settlement was sparse prior to the arrival of the lumber companies, and hence late-nineteenth- and twentieth-century sites should be the most numerous occurrences. However, some farmsteads dating to the mid–nineteenth century, pre–Civil War era, together with complementary archival data, have been found on Fort Polk, including 16VN1076, examined during the ES-5 and ES-7 projects (Franks 1990e:47; Yakubik and Franks 1990).

The possibility of antebellum sites was suggested by Campbell and Weed's (1986:11-8, 11-10) attempt to chronologically segregate historic sites identified during the Multipurpose Range Complex (MPRC) survey through the application of *terminus post quem* (TPQ) dating, that is, by establishing the earliest artifact date for each site and thus the "date after which" each site was occupied. Using the end of the Civil War, 1865, as the barrier between antebellum and postbellum occupations, a surprisingly high number of sites dated to the antebellum period: 23 of the 43 TPQ-dated occupations. Campbell and Weed (1986:11-9) also provided date ranges for each of these sites, and only two of these same 43 sites were given a date range that began in the antebellum period. While the average TPQ date for the 43 sites was 1858, the average earliest date for the occupation ranges presented was 1904.45. Unfortunately, the authors did not specify how their date ranges were produced, except to note that "artifact date ranges were based on periods of widest distribution" (Campbell and Weed 1986:11-8, 11-10).

Presumably the "widest distribution" they referred to was the most frequent distribution by chronological period, yet this does not explain the earlier TPQ dates. In reviewing the date ranges of these sites, Campbell and Weed argued that "the few sites which yielded artifactual materials dating to the Antebellum period had collections which also included items used through the latter half of the nineteenth century and the early twentieth century. For this reason, the attempt to distinguish changes in settlement strategies was not made" (Campbell and Weed 1986:11-10). Campbell and Weed simply accepted the perceived wisdom of the time that Fort Polk historic sites dated to the late nineteenth century without fully evaluating this contention in light of their own material. As has been noted, subsequent research has shown that some antebellum settlement did occur on the installation.

Campbell and Weed did make a very important observation that sites occupied during the antebellum were also occupied in the postbellum period; the antebellum occupants undoubtedly selected superior land that would also have been desirable during the postbellum. Excavations at historic sites

16VN1092 and 16VN1076, for instance, noted that earlier occupations had been masked by later settlement.

Other modifications to the 1988 HPP historic site typology that were suggested included the subdividing of farmsteads into their individual components, such as domestic structures and outbuildings (Thomas et al. 1993d:185). The proportions of various artifact categories at a number of sites had also been examined, particularly by the Earth Search, Inc., survey team. While a high incidence of nails was predicted to occur at domestic sites in the 1988 HPP (>30 percent), this figure was rarely reached on any site and instead incidences were more typically about 10 percent. Likewise, the suggestion that ceramics would be more common than glass (excluding window glass) does not appear to be universally true. The Earth Search survey program also suggested that glass artifacts were even more common in outbuildings than in domestic structures. Finally, the presence of scatters of brick, mortar, and sandstone slabs used in chimneys and foundations was considered another characteristic of farmsteads.

Historic Site Patterning from
Historic Documentary/Cartographic Sources

The 1999 HPP detailed an analysis of 1880s plat maps for the Fort Polk region in an attempt to gain another perspective of historic settlement. Between 1880 and 1883 a series of plats were produced by the Surveyor General's Department of Louisiana, the Government Land Office (GLO). These plats, drawn by township and range, present physical features of the historic landscape pertinent to this study: the locations of drainages, agricultural fields, roads, and structures. As these maps were compiled at different times and by different surveyors, their details are not always consistent. Further, it is not known whether squatters are represented, and it is not known whether the fields represent active fields or cleared but abandoned lands from previous decades. Given these unknowns the maps still appear to provide a relatively good picture of settlement at the time the surveyors were in the area. These individual plats were produced as compilations for the Main Fort and Peason Ridge areas. The originals are on file at the U.S. Forest Service office in Pineville.

The maps indicate that settlement becomes less dense as one travels from north to south, and our consideration of the historic settlement begins with the area that encompasses Peason Ridge (Figure 8.10). The northernmost township and range considered is T6N R9W. Although outside Peason Ridge, this township and range offers important information regarding historic settlement in the area. Settlement density in T6N R9W is relatively high, with a total of 11 structures identified. The majority of these (n = 7)

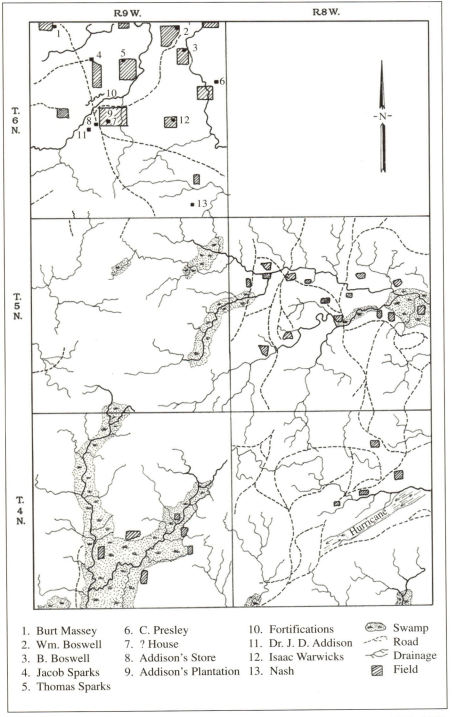

R9 W.   R8 W.

T. 6 N.

T. 5 N.

T. 4 N.

-N-

Hurricane

1. Burt Massey   6. C. Presley   10. Fortifications   Swamp
2. Wm. Boswell   7. ? House   11. Dr. J. D. Addison   Road
3. B. Boswell   8. Addison's Store   12. Isaac Warwicks   Drainage
4. Jacob Sparks   9. Addison's Plantation 13. Nash   Field
5. Thomas Sparks

Figure 8.10 — Sketch compilation of Peason Ridge area plat maps, 1880–1883 (from Anderson et al. 1988:258).

are focused on the two major drainages of the area: Middle Creek and Kisatchie Creek. With the exceptions of one small field in Section 25/26 and a second one in Section 6, the agricultural tracts are also focused on these drainages. The acreage of the agricultural fields is fairly extensive, ranging from a high of approximately 128 acres at the Addison Plantation to an average of 40 to 60 acres for the other fields along Middle and Kisatchie Creeks. The isolated field located in Section 25/26, in contrast, is only approximately 25 acres in size.

The settlement in this township and range is tightly clustered. Addison's store and the Addison Plantation appear to form the focus of this community, which is situated on Middle Creek and located at the juncture of the four main roads that serve the area. The presumed importance of this location is supported by the appearance of "fortifications" crossing the road just north of Addison's store. These are assumed to date to the Civil War era and, if so, provide some sense of the antiquity of this location (this also supports the contention that these maps represent not only contemporary features but also the remains of past activity). Kinship also appears to play an important role in community formation. For example, there are at least two apparent kin connections represented in the area: Wm. Boswell (Structure 2) and B. Boswell (Structure 3) and Jacob Sparks (Structure 4) and Thomas Sparks (Structure 5). An additional kinship connection may exist between the owner of the structure on the Addison Plantation (Structure 7; the name of the owner is illegible) and Dr. J. D. Addison (Structure 11).

Dwellings and fields are closely associated in this area. Of the occupations appearing in the northern part of T6N R9W, all are directly associated with agricultural fields. Furthermore, there are only three fields in this area not associated with houses. The common pattern appears to be for houses to be built in a corner of the agricultural fields, usually the corner farthest distant from the drainage. Perhaps this is related to periodic flooding and an effort to avoid flood impact on the domestic structures. Roads appear to serve houses and fields, with all of the structures except 6, 12, and 13 located in proximity to the five roads that traverse this township and range.

As one travels south in the Peason Ridge area the terrain becomes steeper, the drainages more numerous, and transit more difficult. There are no structures in the remaining four township and range sections that form Peason Ridge (T5N R9W, T5N R8W, T4N R9W, and T4N R8W). There are, however, numerous agricultural fields, which follow the pattern noted to the north and are distributed along the major drainages, Dowden Creek and Sandy Creek. The size of the fields decreases significantly, ranging from approximately five to 20 acres, with the majority consisting of no more than five acres. The numerous smaller tributaries of the major drainages attest to the heavily dissected nature of this section of Peason Ridge. Much of Dowden Creek is subsumed by swamplands, with agricultural fields located either within the swamps or on their immediate periphery. The road system has become chaotic, with far more miles of roadway than T6N R9W. These roads clearly serve as access routes to agricultural fields, and many terminate at agricultural plots. In general the road pattern is attributable to two types: those crossing drainages and those paralleling drainages. The latter presumably follow the ridge tops of the area and hence avoid the wetlands, while the crossing routes access fields adjacent to the streams and creeks and connect the ridge-top lanes. Within this pattern there are no distinct primary routes.

This distribution is evident and amplified in the townships and ranges forming the Main Fort (Figure 7.3). The number of drainages there is greater than that in the Peason Ridge area, and most fields continue to occur along the larger drainages: Whiskey Chitto Creek, Birds Creek, Bayou Zourie, and the West and East Forks of Six Mile Creek. Whiskey Chitto Creek appears to be the most heavily utilized. There are 10 fields on this creek, in addition to three houses and a school. The appearance of the school (Structure 2) and the dwellings of A. James (Structure 3) and W. L. Bloodworth (Structure 4) formed the closest analogy to a community in the area in 1880. Interestingly, the sole service occupation in the area, Swain's Mill (Structure 1) is somewhat isolated from other structures and does not appear to serve as a settlement focus. This is similar to observations made by Joyce (1981) in the War Eagle Creek area that service structures like mills and distilleries are not settlement hubs. While settlement of the area is light, there is some settlement clustering. With the exception of Swain's Mill, all structures appear on either Whiskey Chitto Creek or Bayou Zourie.

Agricultural fields remain fairly small, with an average size range of five to 15 acres. Fields away from the swamps are less common, although larger, with the field at Ben Franklin's (Structure 5) comprising approximately 60 acres. This is the largest field in the area. Franklin and Dempsey Turner (Structure 6) are the only farmers to build their homes on their fields, and they also appear to be the largest landholders. The James and Bloodworth dwellings, as well as an unidentified dwelling (Structure 7), are all built in proximity to several small plots, which presumably they owned.

As in the area to the north, the transportation networks exhibit no clear hierarchy. Again, roads appear to either cross streams or parallel them. One evident purpose of the roads is to access fields. Consider, for example, Ben Franklin's location (Structure 5). In addition to the large field where his dwelling is constructed, Franklin also appears to have owned an approximately 25-acre field south of Bayou Zourie that is linked to the larger field by a road that skirts the bayou. A second road connects Franklin with Dempsey Turner, while a branch of this road crosses another field and passes near a third. Finally, four small fields in the headwaters of Bayou Zourie may also have been Franklin's possessions. Thus, by road Franklin is linked to approximately 105 acres of improved land and to the smaller tracts on Bayou Zourie of approximately 60 additional acres.

Franklin is clearly one of the larger, if not the largest, landholders in the area. Considering the average amount of improved land recorded for Vernon Parish farms in 1880, 24.2 acres, it is evident that there are few fields depicted in the project area that possess this amount of land. As noted, the majority of fields appear to range from five to 15 acres. It would thus require two to five of these small fields to accumulate this average improved acreage. This suggests that individual farmers probably cultivated several small plots. Because of the heavily dissected, drained, and eroded nature of the area, larger fields were probably not feasible. In order to maximize the agricultural potential of their lands, farmers were forced to establish smaller fields in the best-suited, but spatially limited, portions of their property. The positioning of dwellings, barns, and other support structures was dependent on this patchwork of agricultural fields. The ideal locations for homesteads would be those that provided the best access to all of an owner's agricultural fields.

The location of Structure 7 may serve as an example of this settlement model. This structure is located at a fork in a tributary of Whiskey Chitto Creek in a moderately sloping upland environment. While this particular location offers no environmental advantages for settlement, its selection may be predicated on the basis of the distribution of agricultural fields. It is not possible to identify field ownership from the information presented on the plats; however, a hypothetical relationship between fields and structures can be developed on the basis of location. Structure 7 is well suited to serve four fields: two located to the south and situated near the confluence of Whiskey Chitto Creek and a major tributary and two others situated farther north on the tributary on which Structure 7 is located. Combined, these fields total approximately 40 acres. Similar relations between structures and the locations of agricultural fields may exist for W. L. Bloodworth (Structure 4), who is located immediately north of four small fields totaling approximately 20 acres, and A. James (Structure 3), who is located north of one field and south of a larger field in the Whiskey Chitto Creek swamp and who is connected by road to a third field in the area of Structure 7. These fields comprise approximately 35 acres. Such a distribution of fields is described historically by Hadnot (n.d.a), who wrote: "It is common on most farms for the various fields to contain from 5 to 20 acres, then have a high hill or swamp intervene before there is sufficient flatland to have another field." The historic settlement of Fort Polk is undoubtedly dictated by the necessity to be centrally located to numerous agricultural fields.

The number of fields shown in the 1880s plats does not correspond with the limited number of structures identified on these maps, which is an indication that the fields were not in use at the time the map was produced or that some may represent abandoned fields from an earlier period. In order to have 20 to 30 acres in active crop production, a farmer may have needed eight to 10 fields, allowing some to lie fallow and rejuvenate. Joseph (Anderson et al. 1999b:406) felt that this explanation still did not explain the density and distribution of fields depicted in Figure 7.3. Since most of these fields are situated on major tributaries, it is interesting to note that the network of roads follows these tributaries and connects these fields with areas to the north and south of the study area. Joseph suggested that the owners of these farms may have been located outside the study area and thus may have traveled to and from their individual plots along a longer route than their colleagues in the area of Fort Polk.

Joseph (Anderson et al. 1999b:406) came to several important conclusions about Fort Polk settlement based on this map analysis. Historic settlement density in the area of the Main Fort and Peason Ridge was expected to be light, as these areas are too severely dissected to provide an ideal setting for agricultural occupations. Settlement patterning suggests that the preferred agricultural pattern of developing large fields and settling in proximity to kin and community (the pattern witnessed in T6N R9W) was not feasible for most of Fort Polk. Instead, a number of smaller fields were created in the isolated areas suited to agricultural production, and settlement was dispersed in order to access these smaller tracts. The pattern of roads thus became more complicated, with many serving only to connect individual structures and fields. No primary transportation routes were noted in the area of the Main Fort in the early 1880s. The routes that did appear served either as transportation arteries between the major drainages or as connecting trunks crossing drainages. This pattern of a limited number of structures and a prevalence of fields in the area of the Main Fort suggests that many farmers who possessed land within the boundaries of the current fort preferred to live outside this area. Although the precise reasoning for this settlement preference is unknown, the dispersed settlement pattern necessitated by the terrain of the base and the disconnected nature of the transportation routes suggest that many of those who lived outside the area of the Main Fort preferred to live in communities established in more easily accessed locations and were willing to accept a longer daily commute as a consequence of this settlement strategy.

This analysis also suggested that settlement pattern models for Fort Polk will be difficult to produce from archaeological data alone. There does not appear to be any one combination of environmental factors that predicated historic settlement location and selection. Instead, settlement appears to be a factor of different sets of environmental data, specifically the locations of dispersed agricultural fields in a dissected terrain. Farmstead locations are thus selected from those settings providing the best access to these various fields. Because the exact locations of historic fields cannot be recovered archaeologically, it is impossible to precisely predict farmstead locations through archaeological data. However, it is possible to identify environmental zones that appear to be preferred habitats for these sites. Since the majority of fields appear along the major drainages of the area, farmsteads are also expected to focus on these drainages, although most likely in an upland setting that provides access to both the drainage and its tributaries. The distance from water therefore may be a useful measure of farmstead settlement patterning.

■ *Archaeological and Historical Data: The MPRC Survey and the 1880s*
As a means of comparing archaeological data with the historic distribution discussed above, the information presented by Campbell and Weed (1986) from the MPRC survey was combed to determine the locations of historic sites from approximately the 1880s in portions of T1N R7W. Sites were assigned an approximately 1880s date on the basis of either TPQ dates or Campbell and Weed's (1986:table 11-4) occupation date range. The locations of these sites are shown on Figure 8.11. The Birds Creek and Whiskey Chitto Creek drainages were traced from the Birds Creek topographic map, with the locations of swamps interpolated from their position on the 1880s plats for comparative purposes. Homesteads are denoted by triangles, while the symbol for artifact scatters is a circle. Darkened symbols indicate that the 1880s assignment is based on TPQ dating, while open symbols indicate Campbell and Weed's occupation range was used as the basis for this temporal assessment. Because Campbell and Weed base their occupation range on the frequency distribution of artifacts, their chronology yielded two separate datasets for the purposes of this analysis. For example, site 16VN657 has a TPQ of 1880 based on the presence of amethyst glass but is assigned an occupation range of 1920–1940 by Campbell and Weed, while site 16VN578, with an occupation range of 1870–1940, has a TPQ of 1810 based on the presence of pearlware. It is difficult to say which dataset is more accurate, and it is likely that both sets contain validly and invalidly dated sites, as evidenced by the location of several farmsteads where none are shown on the 1880s plats.

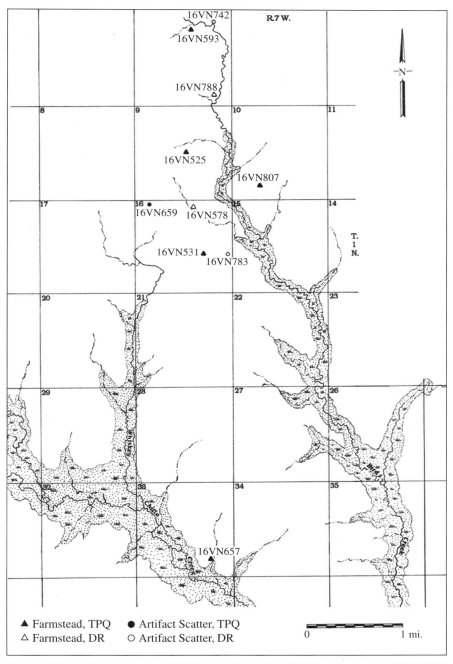

Farmstead, TPQ ● Artifact Scatter, TPQ
△ Farmstead, DR ○ Artifact Scatter, DR

0   1 mi.

Figure 8.11 — Distribution of 1880s sites from the MPRC survey, area T1N R7W.
TPQ, Terminus post quem; DR, date range (see text for discussion of these terms)
(from Anderson et al. 1988:261).

Only one site can be correlated with a location shown on the 1880s plats: 16VN742 is located in approximately the same position as a field shown on the 1880s plats. As this site is identified as an artifact scatter, it is possible that these artifacts are associated with the historic field. The positions of the remaining sites do not correspond with locations shown on the 1880s plats.

However, several of these sites are in positions that would fit the requisites of the settlement model proposed above. For example, 16VN788 is located at the confluence of Birds Creek and an intermittent drainage. This position would have provided access to the upper reaches of Birds Creek as well as this particular drainage. Site 16VN525 is situated on a dirt road above an intermittent drainage of Birds Creek. This road could have served both Birds Creek and this drainage. Site 16VN578 occupies a similar position to the south. Site 16VN807 is located in the *U* formed by the confluence of Birds Creek and two tributaries and represents an excellent settlement location. This site is accessed by a dirt road. Site 16VN657 is located on the terrace above Whiskey Chitto Creek at its confluence with an intermittent drainage, which also provides an excellent settlement locale. This site is also accessed by a dirt road. Site 16VN596 occupies a similar position in the northern portion of T1N R7W. These sites, all identified as homesteads by Campbell and Weed, thus fit the proposed settlement model, although they do not match the location of sites shown on the 1880s plats.

These sites may either predate or postdate the 1880s, which would explain their absence from the plats. Their distribution, however, supports the settlement model. It is also worth noting that these sites support the depiction of the area as shown on the 1880s plats. No fields are shown in the lower portions of Birds Creek, and no sites were identified in this region. At this time it is difficult to explain this absence, although it is potentially related to soil quality and/or erosion.

- *The 1999 HPP Conclusions*

The 1999 HPP concluded that historic settlement at Fort Polk appeared to be predicated on several factors. Most important among these was the nature of agricultural practices in the area. Because fertile cropland was limited in availability and extent, primarily because of the dissected nature of the locality, most farmers appear to have relied on three or more dispersed small (ca. five acre) fields. House settings thus would have been established in environments that provided access to these dispersed fields. Fields appear to have been located on the major and minor drainages of the fort, but house settings themselves were somewhat distant from these watercourses. Ridge noses and slopes overlooking one or several drainages were probably preferred habitats. Community and kinship, factors that Joyce (1981) demonstrated as integral to historic settlement in Arkansas, were not as critical in the immediate limits of Fort Polk, but may have played important roles beyond the base's boundaries. Based on data from historic maps, settlement density within the area of the fort was sparse, yet the number of agricultural fields presented on the maps far outnumbered those that would have been serviced by the limited number of structures shown. This information, plus the routes of early roads, suggests that many of those who farmed in Fort Polk lived outside the immediate area. Communal settings may not have been easily established in this dissected and isolated country; perhaps kinship and community were of such value that farmers were willing to travel greater distances to their fields in order to maintain familial bonds. The pattern presently depicted of Fort Polk's agricultural settlement is one that is dispersed, dissected, and dependent on the locations of several separate fields. Such settlement cannot be predicted with a high degree of reliability from environmental criteria. Settlement patterns for Fort Polk's other categories of historic sites are less easily produced. There is no distinctive pattern for lumber and turpentine work stations, trams, artifact scatters, or other commercial and communal sites. The physical extent of the lumber industry may have been so great that these resources were scattered across the range of the base, while the other sites types were either too limited in number (the commercial and communal sites) or too unknown in nature (the artifact scatters) for modeling to be effective. At this point their distribution can only be considered as random.

An Upland South Historic Context:
Cultural Geography, Archaeology, and History

The critique of previous research by Joseph (Anderson et al. 1999b) in the 1999 HPP came to the conclusion that historic sites cannot be properly studied and evaluated through archaeological analysis alone. In attempting to understand the past, historic archaeologists must deal with two subjective, often contradictory, and always elusive types of data—the written record and the archaeological record. Rarely do they overlap with ease, as was demonstrated by the combining of plat maps with the archaeological record to date. And yet, while some may believe that it is easier to mix oil and water, attempts at integration provide a perspective that enlightens the past. It is the method of integration that is the key. In that regard, one method of integration is to seek a common or unifying explanatory framework toward which both the historical and archaeological evidence commonly point. This framework is called a historic context. Historic contexts seek the integration of history, culture, and archaeology of a region. This not only allows for ordered research, but it also has a management advantage in that installations like Fort Polk can systematically evaluate large numbers of historic sites and determine their eligibility for listing in the National Register of Historic Places in a consistent manner. Multicultural and multiethnic regions may need more than one historic context, however, as has been demonstrated in Chapter 7. Fort Polk was settled almost entirely by white Protestant Anglo-Americans. Therefore a single unifying theme is possible for Fort Polk's historic resources. This does not cover up what diversity exists, however; in fact, it helps to highlight it. Sites like the Four L Still site (16VN1221), a turpentine community settled by African American laborers, stand out more vividly as sites worth preserving under this framework because they are obviously uncommon.

The first step in creating any historic context is the development of a thorough history of the region. This was first provided by Smith (1999) and has been summarized in Chapter 7 of this volume. The second step is to define, through this history, a unifying theme. Clearly Fort Polk folk represent a microcosm of a type of people who rapidly settled the Southeast beginning in the eighteenth century and continuing through the nineteenth century. Cultural geographers and folklorists first labeled these people and their culture as *Upland South*, and while the term is no longer in vogue in those disciplines, it does still fit well with the kinds of historic site resources seen at Fort Polk and indeed across Vernon Parish. For although the French D'Artigeau and Lecomte families were the first to settle in or at least claim land in Vernon Parish, it was the Franklins, Smarts, Brays, and numerous other Anglo-American families who established a permanent presence and shaped the cultural landscape that we see today. Arriving separately or in a train of wagons, Vernon Parish's first homesteaders, and those who followed, shared a common history, identity, and set of values. They were a people united by a singular culture. They were people of the Upland South. The following discussion looks at Fort Polk's historic sites and the previous archaeological work on these sites that exemplify the settlement patterns and the social, political, and archaeological traits typically associated with the Upland South.

DEFINING THE UPLAND SOUTH

The single most encompassing and unifying theme defining the people, culture, ideology, and landscape of the Fort Polk and Vernon Parish area is the cultural tradition of the Upland South. It is argued herein that this particular region is, practically speaking, a type site for Upland South culture. By *type site* it is meant that the region contains a vast majority of the characteristics and attributes of a culture previously defined as Upland South and, indeed, can be pointed to as a pure example or archetype of this culture. Although a few aspects of the Fort Polk area may have slight variance with what has been defined as traditional Upland South culture (see below), the people, their settlement and economic patterns, their ethnic mix, their worldview, and their woodland environment and way of life all fall deeply into the very core of Upland South culture as defined by folklorists, cultural geographers, and archaeologists. In essence, the people and culture of Fort Polk and Vernon Parish define Upland South culture as much as Upland South culture defines them. This is demonstrated in the following discussion.

Scholarly interest in the Upland South as a distinct region and culture began with an article by Kniffen (1965) and it has since been discussed, elaborated, and expanded on by numerous cultural geographers (Clendenen 1973; Glassie 1968; Jordan 1981; Jordan and Kaups 1989; Meyer 1975; Newton 1971, 1974; Otto 1985; Otto and Anderson 1982). Archaeologists also have found this tradition to be a useful explanatory framework for research on small southern yeoman farmsteads in regions along the Tombigbee River (Adams et al. 1981; Futato 1989; Smith et al. 1982) and in northeast Texas (Jurney and Moir 1987; Jurney et al. 1988), Arkansas (Sabo 1990; Stewart-Abernathy 1986), Missouri (Smith 1993), North Carolina (Clement et al. 1997; Stine 1989), and South Carolina (Joseph et al. 1991; Resnick 1988). Even urban sites in the larger region have fit within this research framework (Faulkner 1998). The Upland South defines both the cultural tradition of the white, yeoman, farmer-hunter-stockman plain folk and their geographical area of settlement in the upland South and southern portions of the northern states. Even prior to the cultural geographers' interest in an Upland South tradition, historians identified this ethnic group as a distinctive culture, using terms like *plain folk* (Owsley 1949). Frederick Jackson Turner (1920) also used the term *Upland South,* "though he often seems to attach a physiographic connotation to the term" without the cultural connotations (Newton 1971:72). Other regional variations on the term include *upcountry South, upper South,* and the *backcountry,* especially along the Appalachian chain (Crass et al. 1998; Fischer 1989; Ford 1986; Jordan and Kaups 1989; Otto and Anderson 1982:89). Anthropologists have even recognized the distinctive traits of the Scots-Irish southern farmer, preferring to label the region the "hill south" (Arensberg 1955).

The Upland South defines a tradition and ideology that originated among the Celtic and Welsh peoples who migrated to America as early as the 1670s and initially settled in western Virginia (Newton 1971) or, according to Jordan (1981:155), in the Delaware Valley. Blending with Chesapeake Tidewater, German, and English traditions of southern Pennsylvania, this multicultural amalgamation resulted in "an independent small farm owner/operator who relied on traditional solutions to everyday problems which affected their economic, social, and settlement systems" (Smith et al. 1982:9). These highly individualistic, often lowland Scot and Scotch-Irish peoples rapidly migrated down the Appalachian chain beginning as early as the 1720s. (While the term *Scots-Irish* is more technically correct, common usage of *Scotch-Irish* has become acceptable; see Jordan and Kaups 1989.) With the arrival of another influx of Scots highlanders, who were being forced from their lands between the 1760s and 1815 (some 52,000 Scots left for North America during this time [Johnson 1991:220]), they began to rapidly spread north through the woodlands of southern Ohio, Indiana, and Illinois; west through Kentucky and Tennessee; and south through upper Alabama, Mississippi, Arkansas, Louisiana, Texas, and the Missouri Ozarks (Glassie 1968:235; Kniffen 1965; Meyer 1975; Newton 1974), mixing freely with people of English and German ancestry. With localized exceptions, the land they settled was remarkably similar: mountainous or rolling, forested, and often rugged, with plentiful game and marginal agricultural soils. A seemingly unstoppable wave, the Upland South cultural tradition finally ran its course at the point where the Eastern Woodlands ended and the midwestern open prairies began. Within the Vernon Parish area, the initial migration of Upland South people was checked briefly by the problems associated with Spanish Texas. But even then, they surreptitiously penetrated the east-Texas Big Thickett, using the western Louisiana Neutral Ground as a refuge in times of danger.

It is difficult to say whether these people freely chose the backcountry lands of the Appalachians for their migration and settlement or whether they followed that route because the lowlands were controlled largely by the plantation class. However, cultural geographer Milton Newton (1974) goes so far as to state that these people were "preadapted" for the topography and climate found in the upper heartland of eastern America. Newton (1974:152) defines preadaptation as "a set of traits possessed by a particular human society or part of that society giving that group competitive advantage in occupying a new environment." Newton lists several settlement, economic, and social patterns that define the Upland South. These patterns will be detailed below. Otto and Anderson (1982:91) support this view and argue that "this woodlands-adapted agriculture of the plain folk permitted them to occupy the vast Southern forests in only two to three generations in the period between 1790 and 1840" (Otto and Anderson 1982:91). Though Upland South people lacked the capital and labor resources of the planter, the abundant woodlands offered easily obtained building materials, hunting subsistence, and grazing land for hogs and cattle. The rapidity of the migration, according to Otto and Anderson (1982:96), was due to the need for a "steady supply of fresh woodlands" that kept them migrating westward generation after generation, pushing the Native Americans ahead of them.

The concept of the pan–Upland South as a distinct cultural tradition and as defined here has some weaknesses primarily associated with the fact that social, economic, and settlement patterns that define it cover a wide geographical area of the eastern United States. Otto and Anderson (1982:90), for instance, draw the geographical limits of this culture (ca. 1835) as encompassing an area from Lancaster, Pennsylvania, to mid-Texas and from southern Iowa to northern Florida. Jordan and Kaups (1989:8–9) define a primary domain that spans the region from Delaware down the Appalachian chain, through upper Georgia and Mississippi, north to upper Ohio, and west to central Texas. Then they define an even broader area that encompasses practically the entire eastern United States, only excluding the lower Coastal Plain and the very upper part of Michigan and Wisconsin. We prefer a middle ground, with the southern and eastern extent ending at the interface of the piedmont and the Coastal Plain but then stretching through upper Georgia to east Texas. The northern border would appear to be along the Pittsburgh–Columbus–Indianapolis line (Interstate 70) reaching all the way to the Missouri-Kansas border. Regardless of its geographical extent, a pan–Upland South viewpoint encompasses an area and patterns that may not all be linked to white northern Europeans and their migration but, rather, are typical of historic period low-income rural people, black, white, and Native American. The answer to this question will require further historical and archaeological research.

A more serious challenge is a recent study that has questioned the ethnic origins of those traits attributed to the Celts by early cultural geographers. Jordan and Kaups (1989) contend that many traits normally ascribed to the Scotch-Irish were in fact originally northern European, primarily Finnish, and Native American. They wrote: "Our main thesis, to be defended in ecological, diffusionary terms . . . is that American backwoods culture had significant northern European roots" (Jordan and Kaups 1989:35). Further, they go on, "in our view, the role of the Celts in frontier America has traditionally been greatly overstated, the Indian influence consistently underestimated, and the Finnish contribution almost wholly ignored or, without adequate scholarly evidence, dismissed" (Jordan and Kaups 1989:37). Their argument is not that northern Europeans settled the Upland South geographical region themselves, but that the Celts were the cultural carriers of such traits as building traditions borrowed from early Swedish-Finnish settlement along the Delaware River in the late 1600s. Importantly, they do not dispute that the carriers of these traits were the poor white Protestant yeoman who served as the "economic foot soldiers" in a surge of migration of Europeans to the Southeast (Johnson 1991:220) and that these yeomen were primarily Scotch-Irish: "The Scotch-Irish subsequently supplied the largest single genetic input to the backwoods population, setting the colonization machine in rapid westward motion" (Jordan and Kaups 1989:247). What they do argue is that the traits (especially folk architecture) ascribed to the Scotch-Irish actually represent an amalgam of Scotch-Irish, Finnish, and Native American culture. They point to the evidence of this settlement and the log construction traditions of the Delaware River and the lack of a log construction tradition in Scotland or Ireland (Jordan and Kaups 1989:38–92).

Another problem is that there may be real cultural differences between successful white yeoman farmers on one end of a spectrum and those persons historians classify as "poor whites" on the other (Bolton 1994; Flynt 1979). In the purest, earliest form of Upland South culture, cultural geographers defined an independent, self-sufficient pioneer. He was a hunter-herdsman who moved frequently and swiftly west, searching for better game, fewer neighbors, and graze for his free-ranging hogs and cattle. Many of these people settled eventually and became successful yeoman farmers and even specialized farmers. Others lost their land in the Civil War and became poor, landless tenants competing with newly freed blacks. There was, of course, a spectrum of all combinations in between these two extremes of economic status. The problem is that many of their settlement patterns, economic patterns, and social patterns are similar, but their archaeological sites may not be distinctive. Further discussion of this problem will be addressed later, but suffice it to note at this point that these problems make the archaeological remains at Fort Polk increasingly valuable because the majority of the people who settled there were self-sufficient yeoman farmers archetypical of the Upland South. Their archaeological manifestations provide a type site for the study of these people and their culture.

Regardless of the above problems, it is the contention here that a distinct cultural tradition defined as the Upland South did and still does exist across the South and in Vernon Parish. There may be some problems with refining the traditions ascribed to Upland South people, but the people who settled Fort Polk were first and foremost Protestant, white, agrarian peoples of Celtic and English descent. Across the South there are regional variations or, better stated, local adaptations of Upland South culture. Thus, the use of "backcountry" in South Carolina, for instance, is correct, because it defines the people of the initial Scotch-Irish migration down the Appalachian chain in the eighteenth century. Elsewhere, people of direct Scottish descent on the piedmont of North Carolina adapted to a similar pineland (Clement et al.

1997). In still another region, the people of the northern Ozarks of Missouri (Smith 1993) adapted Upland South culture to the local environment of a rolling prairie between two sharply defined woodlands. Within the Fort Polk area, however, Upland South culture appears as an "unaltered" strain in the pineland of western Louisiana. The following discussion details the various historical and cultural patterns in Vernon Parish and Fort Polk that are characteristic of the Upland South tradition.

POPULATION

Ethnicity

First and foremost, the Upland South cultural tradition is wholly associated with white Anglo or northern European Americans. While this population was not totally Scots and Scotch-Irish, these groups represent a large percentage, mixed with English and Germanic peoples. This attribute of the Vernon Parish population has been documented in detail elsewhere (Smith 1999) and in Chapter 7. Population statistics note that throughout the history of Fort Polk and Vernon Parish, the population was overwhelmingly Anglo-American Protestant yeoman farmers. Admittedly, as far as is known the very first settlers to the region may have been a few Spanish rancheros and French who settled along the Calcasieu and Anacoco, but most of these people settled north of Vernon Parish near the Camino Real. Regardless of the possibility of a few French and Spanish settling in Vernon Parish, they soon became anomalous, for they had hardly arrived before the English and Anglo-Americans slipped into the region, hunting and herding, building homesteads, and cautiously avoiding all governmental authorities. This Anglo-American majority remained throughout the history of Fort Polk and Vernon Parish. The first reliable census data for the region (1880) indicate that the overwhelming majority of the people in Vernon Parish and Fort Polk were indeed white Anglo-Americans who had migrated into the region from other parts of Louisiana (probably the northern half). The rest were from the southern tier of Gulf states, primarily Mississippi, followed by Alabama and Georgia.

African Americans came to Vernon Parish in some large measure with the lumber companies at the turn of the twentieth century. By the 1920s they had reached as much as 25 percent of the population; however, they left with the lumber companies, and as a result probably did not influence the parish's cultural patterns to any large degree up to 1940, especially within Fort Polk. Other minorities, including Italians and Hispanics who also arrived during the lumber years, were even more transitory and their influence is difficult to measure. More than likely they blended into the dominant culture, but this remains a hypothesis to be tested. To some extent it is possible that the Redbones had some influence on the cultural patterns within Fort Polk, but as Redbone defining characteristics are vague and undocumented, it is impossible to determine their influence at this point. Discovering whether these minorities had a distinguishing impact on the cultural and archaeological patterns within Fort Polk is a worthy future goal.

Density

Concerning population density, previous research (recounted in Chapter 7) has demonstrated repeatedly that population density was low. Settlement was sparse and scattered (dispersed) in Vernon Parish throughout its history and apparently even more so within Fort Polk. The parish's settlement history did have periods of augmentation. For instance, when the land was declared no longer a Neutral Ground, settlement received an immediate boost. However, west-central Louisiana in the antebellum was more of a temporary stop for settlers heading into Texas, a staging ground during the filibustering campaigns, and a refuge for Texas settlers during the Mexican War. Those who were attracted to the area at this time were the hunter-stockman squatters who were in the van of the Upland South migration west and who would continue to move west when neighbors came too near or the game became too scarce. In other words, many of these early settlers probably moved on. When real settlement did occur, beginning in the late antebellum, the first of the Upland South yeoman farmers claimed the rich, fertile lands along the Anacoco Prairie and to a lesser extent those along the Calcasieu and Sabine, where subsistence farming could be accomplished with some hope of success. Meanwhile, the hogwallow lands were usually avoided. It is likely that fewer than 700 persons had settled in the Fort Polk region by the 1860s, and this included all of modern Ward 5 (Smith 1999:48). It is a generous figure. The first glimpse of the true parish population in 1880 indicates only 5,160 people for the entire parish, concentrated along the fertile land near rivers. By 1890, there were still only 1,648 people in Wards 4 and 5 combined, an area encompassing all of the main installation. By that time the speculators were buying up the rich pine uplands beyond the creek beds.

Purchase of the Fort Polk hogwallow lands by the lumber speculators and lumber barons in the 1880s and 1890s occurred at a critical juncture. The rich farmable lands in the parish were about filled to a capacity that was comfortable to the Upland South dispersed lifestyle. The vast majority of the settlers within the Fort Polk area were still hunter-stockman squatters living along the Whiskey Chitto, Birds, and Six Mile Creeks. Perhaps settlement would have begun to fill out along these creeks and then spread into the upland areas at this time. But, just as the land was surveyed and parceled, the speculators began purchasing large unclaimed tracts away from the creeks. Some of the original settlers who had the means made an effort to legally obtain their lands from the government to keep it from being gobbled up by timber speculators. Others without funds continued to live on the timber land as squatters, but further legal settlement (beyond squatting) was thwarted by the lumber barons and speculators. The landscape remained in the hands of the lumber companies through the 1920s. It was then purchased by the government. Evidence from the northern part of Vernon Parish indicates that squatters continued to settle and live on timber lands without interference from the lumber companies even during the 1930s. This most assuredly occurred to some degree within the Fort Polk area also but may have been restricted by the Forest Service's purchases.

In the Peason Ridge area, the land-use history was quite similar to that seen within the Main Fort. For instance, the land-use history at Peason Ridge of archaeological site 16VN138, the James Owers farmstead, is probably typical. The land was originally purchased as part of a large railroad land grant given to the Texas and Pacific Railroad Company, which transferred the lands to another railroad company, the New Orleans Pacific Railway Company, in 1884 (Thomas et al. 1993d:79). This railroad company for financial reasons sold the land to Jay Gould, a noted land speculator, who purchased 55,300.71 acres of west-central Louisiana for its timber assets (see Smith 1999) at a cost of $152,076.92, or $2.75 per acre. Within this vast land was Section 5 of T4N R9W, where the Owers family would settle. Gould's heirs sold the land to the Forest Lumber Company of Kansas City, Missouri, which in turn sold it to the Louisiana Long Leaf Company in 1918 (Thomas et al. 1993d:80). Owers eventually purchased 40 acres in the southeast quarter of Section 5 in 1926. Owers attempted to farm 10 acres, and the remaining 30 remained in timber. Thus, actual farming and homesteading did not occur on this property until the late 1920s. When the war started, Owers refused to sell his land to the federal government and he was taken to court. Owers lost, and in 1943, he received $1,150 for his farm.

Perhaps no more than three to six persons per square mile were living within the Fort Polk area at any one time. Within a township examined by Cantley and Kern (1984) only 20 households were confirmed as residents in 1910, and a projection of between 600 to 1,200 people was made for the total population of the region that encompassed the Fort Polk area at that time in its history (Smith 1999). With the Forest Service purchase of the cutover lands, this certainly remained the pattern until the arrival of the army in 1940. Additional support comes from the real-estate tract register, which indicated only some seven percent of the land was in private ownership at the time the army purchased the tracts at the Main Fort—and even less (three percent) at Peason Ridge. Additional support comes from the lack of historic archaeological sites recorded.

While there were 4,743 historic properties recorded on Fort Polk as of 2002 (i.e., isolated finds, historic sites, prehistoric sites, and multicomponent sites) (Table 2.1), only 290 historic archaeological sites and 70 isolated finds were present in the 1999 HPP analysis sample (Table 4.1), which includes not only homesteads but also cemeteries and industrial sites. In addition, there are 67 historic homesteads that were given site numbers as a result of identification by historic aerial photography but have not been confirmed on the ground. The work since 1999 has continued to report low numbers of historic sites in the area. Admittedly, the low numbers of historic sites are partially the result of early surveys not recording historic archaeological sites. However, some of these areas were resurveyed. Essentially, the low number is an accurate reflection of historic population density. As an educated guess, only around 15 percent of the fort was ever settled or farmed during its history, even if it is assumed that squatters lived on the land up until the Forest Service arrived.[1] Furthermore, this settlement was concentrated along the Whiskey Chitto, Birds, and Six Mile Creeks during most of the period of private settlement. Joseph's 1880s plat analysis provides additional support (Anderson et al. 1999b:400–407).

SETTLEMENT PATTERNS

Intersite Settlement
The Upland South intersite settlement patterns are distinctive: (1) adaptation to woodland areas with plentiful game and marginal agricultural lands that usually must be cleared (Otto and Anderson 1982); (2) dispersed, kin-structured settlement and hamlets; (3) in keeping with dispersed settlement, a low density of population (Jordan and Kaups 1989:66; Newton 1974) or, as Futato (1989:82) wrote, "The emphasis is . . . on dispersion of a substantial portion of the population"; (4) dispersed, low-order, central-place or community service sites (general stores, grist mills, churches, schools) (Newton 1974:151); (5) courthouse-town and county system that gives focus to civil order and concentrates the skill of the elite over the "peasantry" (Newton 1974:152; Zelinsky 1951:173), and thus the county system becomes the maximum unit of settlement (Futato 1989:82; Sabo 1990:143) and allows a minimum of people to represent both the elite and subordinate members of

[1] *That is, only a maximum of 15 percent of the land was in the ownership of or occupied by farm families and operated as farms. It does not mean that 15 percent was tilled for crops, a figure that would be much less.*

society (Newton 1974:151); and (6) domestic sites located on high ground, next to water early and later next to roads (Newton 1974:151; Sabo 1990:140–146; Smith et al. 1982:239).

Clearly previous historic research indicates a dispersed, low-density settlement pattern, and the scant number of historic archaeological sites supports this, as do the GLO maps discussed in the 1999 HPP. However, the archaeological data do not overlap as smoothly as desired, with both supporting and detracting observations. As noted, using the survey information conducted by Campbell and Weed (1986), the locations of archaeological sites were compared with historic locations on the GLO plats, but only one site corresponded directly to a cultural feature on the maps (16VN788), and that was an agricultural field with no structure illustrated near it. Several other archaeological sites did fit the settlement model proposed; that is, the farmsteads were located near major drainages, but they did not overlap with known historic sites on the GLO maps. Finally, the 1988 HPP looked at the archaeological data alone. To do this, farm sites, industrial sites, tram sites, and "communal" sites, meaning central places like schools and cemeteries, were plotted on distribution maps (Anderson et al. 1988:270–274). Although these data were not updated in the 1999 HPP, with 1988 data this analysis did find that most farmsteads were located on ridge slopes, noses, or crests (71 percent) with an additional 14 percent on bottom terraces. Some 43 percent were found on a slight (5 percent) slope and, of greatest interest, 52 percent of them were found 601 or more meters from permanent water (Anderson et al. 1988:276–278). Other conclusions drawn by Anderson et al. (1988) were discussed above; notably, that farmers utilized multiple fields because of the dissected nature of the environment, that house locations were positioned between these fields and usually away from major watercourses, and that because fields in the Fort Polk area far outnumber house locations, many farmers may have lived outside the area.

Where there is agreement between history and the archaeology, the history provides an explanation for the archaeological findings. Both agree that farms were dispersed, with fields consisting of numerous small plots. One reason for this, noted by the archaeologists, was that fertile land was limited to the lowland areas near streams. The upland pine landscape was barren for crop production. However, the HPPs do not recognize that the reason plots were small was that one man only could handle around "two acres of tobacco, perhaps eight acres of cotton, or 25 to 30 acres of corn" in any one year (Otto and Anderson 1982:92). Also, fertilization was not used by Upland South farmers so even the fertile land was unproductive after a while and new fields had to be opened while old fields were abandoned or lay fallow—the latter point was raised by the 1999 HPP. Furthermore, with hogs and cattle roaming free, the fields had to be fenced. A large field would be difficult to fence and maintain.

House sites indeed were located on high ground near water, but within the Fort Polk area many of the water sources contain wide, swampy boundaries. Likely, the farmsteads were located as close to water as possible without endangering the farm as a result of flooding or unhealthful standing water. Also, the archaeological data do not take into account whether a spring was located near these farm sites. Most likely the early settlers depended on springs rather than streams for water, and thus the farmstead was located at the junction of the upland and lowland, above the possibility of flooding but close to springs and the lowland fields. Wells were later phenomena (probably 1920s to 1930s), of course, and at that time, wells allowed settlement to shift from water sources to transportation sources (i.e., roads).

One area of disagreement herein is the conclusion by the HPPs that many who farmed in the study township lived outside of the region. This conclusion was made on the basis of the lack of farm structures illustrated on the GLO maps in the Main Fort region, but the historical data above explain why there are fields without structures. Multiple fields were worked by one farm. Some farmers may have settled in the uplands but commuted a short distance to fields in the lowlands where the land was fertile. Commuting for any distance would have been impossible, however. The roads were too poorly maintained for much commuting, and rain would have made them impassable. A long commute from another township would not have been practical for the farmer until maybe the 1920s. Further, it is likely that the GLO surveys did not depict all the structures (i.e., farmsteads) that actually existed at the time. Most likely they only depicted the larger farmsteads, and the homes of squatters and subsistence farmers may not have been labeled. This is implied archaeologically in that the only archaeological site matching a cultural feature on the GLO maps in the Campbell and Weed (1986) study matched an agricultural field. It is possible that there was a structure at that location after all that was just not labeled on the maps or that had been abandoned at the time. Still further, it must be remembered that a characteristic of the early Upland South hunter-stockman was to settle for a few years and move on. In this example from east Texas, the same settlement pattern is explained in the words of a resident:

> Very few of the descendants of the old settlers own any land. For the last forty years they have been in the habit of settling upon any land fit for cultivation. After finding a good, rich land (hammock) the pine woods settler will commence felling and cutting trees and underbrush away from where he expects to have his field. . . . After

working some one else's land for two or three years, he sells the improvements and his squatter's claim to one of his neighbors, and then hunts up another piece of land to improve and sell in a like manner. The consequence of this way of living is that they are always moving, and their children grow up without knowing the pleasures and comforts of a home that could be made comfortable and beautiful if the land was their own. . . . The people have been in the habit of using every man's land as their own for so many years that they believe the land has no owners. Most of the timbered lands in East Texas are owned in large tracts by non-residents and their agents who pay their taxes seldom know where the land is situated; hence the squatter has it all his own way [Caplen in Wright 1942:158–259].

Within the installation the land was, overall, poor farmland. Upland South subsistence farmers cleared the low hardwood areas because they knew that pinelands were very poor for farming (Otto and Anderson 1982:91–93). In fact, this is the reason most of the fields depicted on the GLO maps are located in low areas near water: this is where the hardwoods were, and Upland South people used the hardwoods as indicators of soil fertility (Otto and Anderson 1982:92). Upland South farmers would use the fields for a few years and then turn them into pasture land and open up new fields. Again, fertilizer was an unheard-of concept to these farmers until convinced of its value by twentieth-century agricultural agents, and even in 1923 only 668.75 tons of fertilizer were shipped to Vernon Parish, the 27th lowest amount in the state (Louisiana Department of Agriculture and Immigration 1924:122). The farmers had no manure to use because the pigs and cattle roamed. Thus, the GLO maps are probably depicting both contemporary and abandoned fields over the course of some 10 to 20 years. All these traits go a long way toward explaining why there was not a structure for every field. There is no documentary support for the conclusion that the fields were farmed by commuting farmers.

As noted, some archaeological studies have argued for a greater concentration of settlement in the Fort Polk region. Franks and Yakubik (1990b), for instance, argued that antebellum land claims support a conclusion that settlement was not as sparse as previously claimed. In their study of land claims within Townships T2N R8W and T1N R8W, Franks and Yakubik found a greater number of claims than expected in the antebellum period (Franks and Yakubik 1990b:77–83; Yakubik and Franks 1990:29). Some of the claims were surprisingly early (1845, for example). Their parcel maps indicate that 1,520 acres out of a total of 9,600 possible acres (n = 38 40-

acre claims in 15 sections, 640 acres per section) were claimed or, interestingly, about 16 percent of the land. Franks and Yakubik also dismiss Anderson et al.'s (1988:281) "commuting farmers" hypothesis for this reason.

The antebellum claims were indeed higher than one might expect. The weakness of Franks and Yakubik's argument, though, is that they did not know the ratio of actual settlers to private land speculators. It is quite possible that the larger 160-acre plats were purchased by speculators rather than people actually settling on the land: note the east-Texas example above. This was a common pattern across the South. Census data would also support the hypothesis that some or many of these were speculative. Further, even if the claims all represented settlers, this does not necessarily represent a dense population or settlement pattern, although it does represent a higher than expected number of land claims. It is also interesting to note that the claims for this particular township represent 16 percent of the land claimed by private citizens, a number close to the assertion herein that about 15 percent of the land was ever in private hands (Smith 1999). Overall, Franks and Yakubik's hypothesis deserves further attention. A special study of all antebellum land claims within the Fort Polk area would assist greatly.

Overall, census records and the GLO maps support the dispersed settlement pattern. Landownership tax maps are confusing, indicating a possible higher settlement density than supposed for the antebellum, but still one that is sparse and dispersed. Absentee land use is an interesting hypothesis but does not fit the practical aspects of the transportation system. There are many other more likely explanations for the lack of structures on the GLO maps. As Thomas et al. (1993d:192) point out, despite 20 years of survey on Fort Polk, evidence of antebellum settlement remains scarce.

Having argued against Franks and Yakubik's hypothesis of a greater population density based on land claims, it must be admitted that land claims do correspond, to some unknown degree, to actual settlement. In this regard, the historic data all suggest that private landownership was concentrated along the creeks and streams of Fort Polk. Archaeological data support this general pattern, although sites are located farther from streams on the Main Fort. This is to be expected, given the terrain. Maps do indicate that there was some settlement in the uplands. However, generally, pine-rich uplands were left to the speculators and the Upland South stockman's hogs and cattle. It is hypothesized here that further research will find a more clear pattern in which nineteenth-century settlement in the Fort Polk area (and in Vernon Parish, for that matter) was concentrated at the interface of the uplands near streams and creeks (no matter the distance to water) and that upland settlement was only widespread after the timber had been cut (beginning around 1920), when the people were using fertilization and rough but reliable roads were available for transport of goods to market. At that point, the pattern of historic settlement changed to occurrence primarily along the roads (e.g., Thomas et al. 1993d:181). This change probably began around 1920 but was more evident around 1930. The transportation needs of the lumber industry probably facilitated this change.

A dispersed settlement pattern of central-place locales (trading centers, hamlets, churches, schools, post stops) also accurately describes Vernon Parish and the Fort Polk region. Churches, schools, and hamlets were widely dispersed across the landscape from the initial settlement of the parish up to the arrival of the army and even today. Characteristically, as soon as a handful of people had settled in reasonable proximity, they would establish a church, a school, or a public building serving both functions. This area became a community that might later include a general store and mill. Once post offices were established, a place name was established, which was often the last name of the postmaster. Post offices/general stores might become hamlets consisting of no more than the store and the postmaster's house. Mills, on the other hand, could become community locales, but being tied to streams they often were isolated locales, although close enough to a community to serve the farmers there. Occasionally, mills would become hamlets also. As Newton (1974:151) explains: "At strategic points, such as bluffs overlooking streams, or where several ridge or valley roads converged at a likely millsite . . . a number of buildings might form the nucleus of a cross-roads hamlet; around the crossroad might be a mill, store, post office, church, or cemetery and several houses, although these were seldom located very close together."

Yet another indication of the sparse nature of settlement in the Fort Polk area is the relatively small number of community centers or hamlets that are known in this region. Within the Main Fort, the historical record documents Whiskachitto (school and post office), Six Mile (school, post office, and Swain's Mill), Front (probably a rail terminal), and Pringles (?), the latter two being only known on maps. Certainly there were churches also, as well as cemeteries (there are 13 cemeteries in the Main Fort and two within the Peason Ridge and Horse's Head Training Areas). The archaeological record adds Jetertown (see below) and an unnamed dispersed community identified by Campbell et al. (1994b:57–71). This last community, discovered during the test excavations at the William Perkins house site (16VN65) and the surrounding area, included farmsteads, a mill, a schoolhouse, a church, and two cemeteries within a few miles. In addition, there was, of course, the large village of Fullerton, and it is worth noting that while much smaller, both Front and Pringles also owed their existence to the arrival of the lumber industry. The Peason Ridge area was no exception to this pattern; the only known hamlet there was Peason, another mill town. Archaeology adds the Four L Still site (16VN1221), a turpentine-processing complex. The camp for the African American workers at this industrial complex was located four miles west of Fort Polk property.

Joyce's (1981:92) War Eagle Creek study found that kinship was a determinate to historic settlement. Smith et al. (1982:215) at Bay Springs, Mississippi, also found kinship to be a determining element in settlement decision making in the Upland South. While oral historical research has not been conducted extensively, a historic document search of those few historic sites studied at Fort Polk indicates this to be true there. Within Fort Polk an excellent example is seen at the site called Jetertown. Jetertown (16VN1070) consisted of four structures concentrated within approximately 500 m that housed the Henry, Charles, and John Jeter families and an earlier occupation by Henry, the father of the other two. The initial occupation of the area by Henry occurred around the late 1880s, and occupation continued through the early twentieth century. Note that Henry Jeter, in keeping with the settlement pattern proposed herein, arrived as a squatter and attempted to claim the land beginning around 1904 (Franks and Yakubik 1990a:47–50). Landownership became embroiled in continual filings and cross-filings not only because of earlier claims by lumber companies but also as a result of a family dispute when the mother died. Locally, the area became known as Jetertown, although it never appeared on maps (one important reason being that it never became a post stop).

Besides Franks and Yakubik's (1990a:47–50) study, Thomas et al. (1993d) found evidence of kin-based settlement at sites 16VN138 and 16VN139, two historic farms in close proximity that were purchased at the same time by Owers family members. Morehead et al. (1994:24) go as far as to state that "kinship may have played a very strong role in historic settlement decisions. In fact, in some cases, kinship may have been the primary reason for selecting one plot of land over another." They are no doubt quite correct, although more data are needed to confirm this statement.

The importance of transportation networks has been discussed previously both by Thomas et al. (1993d:181) and in the 1999 HPP. Note how closely Newton's description of Upland South transportation patterns follows those previously discussed at Fort Polk:

> Roads, their importance determined by their directness to the courthouse, conformed to the land—in the valleys in mountainous areas, on ridges in plain or hilly regions. Under the open-range custom and law of the Upland South, roads developed freely as the demands of users and the terrain indicated.

> The old roads, before the automobile, were the marshaling yards of the peasantry. Time and time again, older farmsteads were bisected by roads. . . . The newer faster roads bypassed many old farmsteads, often by-passing much of the country as well. But wherever later roads were built, Upland people built new houses on high ground next to the road, if land was available [Newton 1974:151].

Within Fort Polk, the 1988 HPP described the transportation routes around the 1880s as chaotic, "exhibit[ing] no clear hierarchy. Again, roads appear to either cross streams or parallel them. One purpose of the roads is to access fields" (Anderson et al. 1988:260). What Anderson and his colleagues were seeing was a snapshot of Newton's description of the effects of the open-range system. The roads were simply trails cut across the landscape as directly as possible to whatever central-place hamlet, agricultural field, or farmstead was a common enough objective for the road to be reused. Roads within Fort Polk probably never developed fully enough to establish more than one or two major routes that crossed the region, leading to Leesville and, for a short while, Fullerton or Pitkin.

Smith has added to knowledge of Upland South transportation patterns through study of another Upland South region (Smith 1993:77). At Fort Leonard Wood, Missouri, Upland South transportation routes were first indirectly influenced by the quality of soils and later directly by water transportation. As has been related, Vernon Parish was avoided by most people who bypassed the region by traveling up the Red River to Natchitoches and then west along the Camino Real. Poor soils were avoided by the planter class, but not by Upland South subsistence hunter-stockmen, who first arrived in the Vernon Parish region in the late 1820s. Interestingly, once these migrants were within Vernon Parish, the routes were primarily east-west, in keeping with their westward flow. Water became insignificant as a transportation method, because most of the major streams flowed north-south. Sometime around the 1860s, routes appear to trend toward Huddleston, the largest hamlet in the parish at that time. All major routes led to Huddleston. But this changed dramatically with the establishment of the parish. Quickly, all major routes shifted slightly to converge on the centrally located parish seat of Leesville, a trait noted by Newton.

Another interesting aspect of the macrotransportation system within the parish is the railroads. Again, previous research (Smith 1994) has shown that railroads had a major impact on Upland South transportation and settlement patterns, changing the course of settlement merely by their placement on the landscape. At Fort Leonard Wood and at Fort Bragg, North Carolina, preinstallation Upland South settlement was impacted not by the arrival of the railroad, but by its bypassing both areas. At Fort Leonard Wood, for instance, the railroad planned near the region before the Civil War was never built, and after the war it was shifted north. As in Vernon Parish, this shifted settlement to the railroad, isolating the Fort Leonard Wood region. At Fort Bragg, the development of Fayetteville was severely thwarted by the railroad's bypassing the town and the adjacent Upland South community (Clement et al. 1997).

Intrasite Settlement

Upland South intrasite settlement patterns include (1) hilltop farmsteads as a seemingly disordered cluster of buildings with barns and outbuildings arranged around the house in an "order determined by the owner's changing conceptions of convenience" (Newton 1974:151); (2) separate house and outbuildings (smokehouse, barns, cribs, pens, food-storage buildings) (Weaver and Doster 1982:63) serving multiple functions (Jurney and Moir 1987:230; Smith et al. 1982:10–11); (3) "house fac[ing] the probable path of human approach" (Weaver and Doster 1982:64); (4) dwellings shaded by trees (Weaver and Doster 1982:64); and (5) fields and pastures irregularly arranged, often following topographic features (Hart 1977).

Actually, cultural geographers and archaeologists have noted that buildings on the Upland South farmstead, while appearing disordered, do have a clear and patterned arrangement (Glassie 1975; Jurney and Moir 1987; Newton 1974; Pillsbury 1983; Smith et al. 1982; Smith 1993; Weaver and Doster 1982). Outbuildings are arranged around the main dwelling with the well, privy, storage shed, chicken house, and smokehouse close to the dwelling and the large animal pens, barns, and equipment sheds beyond the central core (Weaver and Doster 1982:63–64). Smith et al. (1982:241) have noted that this arrangement is often clearly defined by a road or alley between the inner and outer ring of buildings. Newton (1974:151) adds that early Upland South farmsteads bisected roads with buildings on either side and the road simply widened to form a "stomp." Later, the farmstead was set beside a road, with the house facing the road or probable direction of approach.

Glassie (1975) was the first of many to remark that the arrangement of outbuildings was associated with traditional sexual divisions of labor. Women's activities generally included household chores and care of the chickens, all performed within the inner circle of the farmstead. Men attended to duties associated with the outer ring of buildings like the planting and maintenance of crops and care of the large animals (Glassie 1975:144). Smith et al. (1982:240) and Adams (1990) have countered that this division was not necessarily hard and fast: women occasionally worked in the fields, and men often repaired equipment in the yards. Further, both Stine (1989) and

Joseph et al. (1991:160–165) support Smith and colleagues in noting that the male/female roles were not absolute at North and South Carolina Upland farms. Children tended the chickens. Smith et al. (1982:240–241) proposed that the division could also be explained along the general lines of farm economics: "the outer circle of outbuildings at Bay Springs [Mississippi] was oriented toward the production and storage of income related activities like cash crops and animal husbandry . . . with lesser amounts going to the households. The inner circle of outbuildings was oriented mainly around the production and storage of subsistence products . . . for household consumption." Both explanations have relevance and weaknesses. Glassie's male/female spheres generally hold if one recognizes that under special circumstances the lines were easily crossed. For instance, at harvest time everybody worked in the fields. Likewise, Smith and colleagues and Adams are generally correct in saying that the animals and crops of the outer circle were sold for cash or traded in barter, but so were eggs from the chicken coops in the inner circle and hams from the smokehouse. Regardless of the explanatory thesis, the arrangement of Upland South farmsteads is clearly patterned.

Smith et al. (1982:240–243) proposed a model of Upland South intrasite farmsteads in which the main house was centrally located on the highest ground, with a well in close proximity. Beyond the house a ring of outbuildings was found including smokehouse, chicken coop, privy, and storm cellar. Also found in this area was a place where odds and ends were stored outside (Smith et al. 1982:226). A road or trash accumulation from sweeping often helped define this area from the outer ring of buildings, which consisted of animal pens, barns, and sheds. In the fields, occasional sheds also could be found. One reason for the above arrangement, only briefly mentioned by Smith et al. (1982:241), was the sanitary drainage. Clearly the outer buildings, containing large farm animals, needed to be on a different drainage system from that of the dwelling. At Bay Springs, Mississippi, this was accomplished by having the house on the highest ground or, at the least, on a separate drainage from the barns. With some differences based on the prairie landscape, Jurney and Moir (1987:234–236) found similar patterns in Texas. A regional influence on the general location of barns may have been the prevailing winds. Also, there are data indicating that wells and privies were later additions to the Upland South farmstead. Generally, prior to the twentieth century, the nearby woodlot or other private place served as a privy, and springs were water sources. Based on previous archaeological research at other Upland South farmsteads (Carlson 1990; Joseph et al. 1991; Jurney and Moir 1987; Jurney et al. 1988; Smith et al. 1982; Stine 1989), the archaeological expression of a farmstead is often a broad, shallow artifact sheet midden, with small areas of intense past activity where features such as storm cellars, smokehouses, chicken coops, fireplace fireboxes, wells, and cisterns have intruded more deeply into the ground. Dumping of trash is often off-site, although occasionally a ring of trash separating the outer circle from the inner circle of the farmstead builds through time. Another aspect of rural life is considerable recycling of materials for multiple uses and therefore trash accumulations often are small.

Archaeological investigations at Fort Polk clearly fall in line with those described above. An excellent example is the William Bridges Homestead site (16VN1076). The archaeological expression of this site, detailed earlier in this chapter, included evidence of yard sweeping, surface trash accumulations, wells, a chicken coop, and a smokehouse in the Upland South pattern. Other historic house sites, 16VN65, 16VN138, 16VN139, and 16VN1221, also exhibited these site attributes (Largent et al. 1993a:54–58; Thomas et al. 1993d:93–106). Architectural items were a distinct minority, suggesting the house may have been dismantled and removed/scavenged rather than burned or allowed to deteriorate in place. This site thus exhibits the typical archaeological expression of an Upland South farm site, including evidence of recycling.

One final area concerning intersite/intrasite settlement is the location of agricultural fields. In the Upland South farm model the fields are arranged around the local topography. In the rolling uplands, agricultural fields can be expected to follow the natural wood line and ridge line and the road system. In the river valleys, fields should conform to the riverbeds and hill slopes. Illustrations of GLO township maps in Anderson et al. (1988:258, 261) provide what appear to be archetypical examples of Upland South fields. In the illustration of open, rolling T6N R9W, farms are arranged along roads, but in the more dissected topography of T5N R8W, fields are smaller and dispersed and, although the topographic features are not clearly illustrated, appear to be conforming to the valleys and drainages. This is also true on the Main Fort.

Architectural Features

Cultural geographers (Meyer 1975; Newton 1974) discuss Upland South architecture within the framework of settlement patterns. Upland South folk architectural patterns include (1) wide use of horizontal log construction (Kniffen and Glassie 1966:48); (2) universal modular (pen and crib) construction (Newton 1974:152) including single-pen, double-pen, dogtrot, and saddlebag housing (Wilson 1974); (3) the I-house as an indicator of economic attainment (Kniffen 1965:557); and (4) transverse crib barns (Meyer 1975:61). Historians such as Hadnot (n.d.a) and Wise (1971) both indicate that dogtrots were commonplace in Vernon Parish. Sandel (1982) offers a detailed description of the building of log and board and batten homes in the west-central Louisiana area from pioneer times to the 1940s:

> The first thing to do was to clear a place to build the log cabin that would be home. . . . The logs were notched to lock in place on the corners. Wood blocks were used as foundations, and logs were split and the flat side turned up to form the door. The roof was made of split boards or rived as it was called, they're about thirty inches long and each course covered the cracks in the course below. The fireplace and chimney was the last to be added. . . . The chimney was made of mud and straw on a wooden frame. They would place four poles about three or four inches in diameter upright to form the chimney. At about twelve feet the poles would be cut off and from thereon up the chimney would be made smaller to form the hips to make it draw better.
>
> In later years when lumber was available, the settlers built houses they called boxed houses. That simply meant the boards were nailed upright to form the walls. The boards would be twelve or fourteen feet long and would be nailed to the sills at the bottom and the plates at the top, very little framing was used in this kind of house. A narrow board would be nailed over the cracks between the wide ones and these were called bats. Usually there would be a wide hall between the two or four large rooms with a wide porch across the front of the house [dogtrot] [Sandel 1982:17–18].

There are no standing architectural remains of historic farms on Fort Polk, only small remnants of ruins or foundations. As noted, at sites like the Coleman and Annie Owers Homesite (16VN139), sandstone foundation stones and oral history both support Upland South architectural patterns. Modular pen construction can be seen in contemporary photographs, which indicate clearly the presence of Upland South architecture (Figure 8.12). Oral history also indicates the presence of log dogtrot housing (Franks 1990d). Stone and brick also served as the base for fireplaces. As Goodspeed Publishing Company (1974:108) notes at Fort Leonard Wood, Missouri, and as is most applicable at Fort Polk, "The hills furnished the stone fire-place . . . chimney sticks and mud for the poorer, and stone for the more able."

ECONOMIC PATTERNS

Newton lists three common economic patterns characteristic of the Upland South. These patterns are (1) adaptive food and feed complex including a

Figure 8.12 — Charlie and Martha Swain house located on Six Mile Creek (courtesy Museum of West Louisiana).

wide variety of crops like peas, squash, collards, pumpkins, potatoes, cabbage, cucumbers, okra, and turnips, but with the most important being corn, hogs, and cattle (Newton 1974:147); (2) stockman-farmers with hunting as primarily part of the farm economy (Kniffen 1965); and (3) an adaptable cash crop (Newton 1974:147). These patterns include both the subsistence farmer and the special or general farmer, except for the emphasis on hunting, which is a pattern associated with the earliest subsistence farmers. However, there are a whole range of patterns that can be included under the theme of Upland South economic adaptation, which may be defined as agriculturally based.

Usually a new family settled near a water source already cleared of pines by the Native Americans (called an "opening") and planted crops while building a cabin at the clearing's edge (Sitton 1995:49). Occasionally, settlers came upon areas where tornadoes had ripped up trees, providing them with ready-made agricultural fields (O'Halloran 1951–1952:4/27/1952). Upland South farmland often was initially cleared using slash-and-burn practices to open small plots (Otto 1985; Otto and Anderson 1982:92; Otto and Burns

1981:173). Trees were girded with an ax and left to die. Eventually, they would be cut down. Furrows were plowed around the stumps. Corn was the primary crop, with beans, squash, and gourds grown in and around the corn-fields (Sitton 1995:62). Field crops were supplemented with sweet potatoes, okra, and turnips grown in home gardens. Cane sugar, used to make syrup, was an important caloric source for the pinelands subsistence farmer. Cotton, on the other hand, was rarely grown in great quantities; the early settlers had no market for it, and even later, cotton was too labor intensive and risky. A ruined corn crop could be replanted or the hogs turned loose on it and fattened for market. A ruined cotton crop was "a total loss" and a disaster for the subsistence farmer (Sitton 1995:69). Enough cotton was grown to make clothing and to sell a few bales, if there was a place to take it for ginning. Big cotton fields were found only along the Red River.

Fencing was placed around the fields to keep out animals, for the open-range system of allowing the cattle and pigs to roam free was a strongly held tradition across the South, as it was in the Vernon Parish and Fort Polk region. In the early days, after a field was no longer productive, more land was cleared and the old field was abandoned, as is probably evidenced in the study by Anderson et al. (1988) of GLO maps in the region. Burning the woodlands was common practice and typical of Upland South agricultural practices. Farm activities were synchronized in an "annual round" to plant crops at different times, conduct repairs to housing and equipment, and harvest products (Newton 1971). The first Anglo-American settlers often found wild horses and cattle in the woods, which were lost by the Spanish or other settlers pushing west. These were fair game for the pioneer and part of the forest's bounty. Deer, rabbit, squirrel, and fish were plentiful, providing additional protein for the homesteader's table.

Raw materials grown or gathered from the forests were processed in the home. These cottage industries provided clothing and farming equipment that could not be easily obtained otherwise. Self-sufficiency was necessary for survival. Fort Polk pioneers were confined in the pinelands because of poor roads and often impassable streams. The closest source of supplies was Alexandria, Louisiana. The round trip to Alexandria took three weeks from east Texas, and Fort Polk residents saved perhaps a week. Regardless, the pinelanders made the trek only twice a year (Sitton 1995:63; Wright 1942:2). In Alexandria, settlers could purchase sugar, flour, salt, coffee, whiskey, ammunition, and perhaps a plow or some other farming implement, but not much more. Everything else was made, traded, or grown locally. An 1890s visitor to the parish wrote of the setters: "They raise all they consume; know nothing of luxuries beyond gorgeous cooking stoves; have dim ideas about life or property insurance outside of the towns; save their money in a stocking foot; go to camp meeting once a year; have a deer drive and a fishing bout whenever they can, and are happy and contented where you and I are sad and sour" (Cole 1892). Once determined to settle down, Upland South subsistence farmers eventually turned to generalized farming with less reliance on hunting, gathering, and fishing as part of their economy. They still were very flexible with the types of crops grown, although corn remained the main and most important crop. However, one characteristic of the Fort Polk area that has been stressed repeatedly is that squatting, and therefore subsistence-based agricultural practices, survived far into the twentieth century.

Fort Polk Agricultural Continuum

To understand the variety of agrarian development within Fort Polk, an "agricultural continuum" that describes the development of the agricultural economy is proposed (Figure 8.13). A similar continuum has been described in Missouri and North Carolina (Clement et al. 1997; Smith 1993) and, with minor modification, this one can be adapted to the Fort Polk region also. Within this continuum are found differing types or, perhaps, economic levels, of farming, defined by the degree to which farmers (1) depended on hunting versus farming, (2) participated in the market economy, (3) devoted land to crops versus woodlands, (4) devoted time and land to a particular crop or animal, and (5) owned property and material goods. Chronologically, the agriculturists in Vernon Parish and within Fort Polk can be loosely typed as (1) hunter-squatters, (2) subsistence-squatters, (3) pioneer farmers, (4) general (diversified) farmers, (5) specialized farmers, and (6) tenants, with degrees of tenancy from full sharecroppers to full renters.

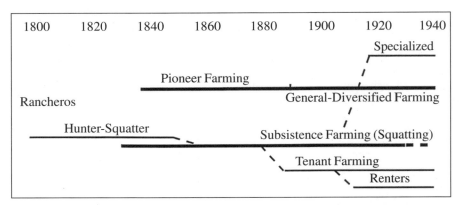

Figure 8.13 — Agricultural continuum, Vernon Parish (from Anderson et al. 1999b:438).

It is important to stress that the agricultural practices described are observable "types" or markers within an agricultural continuum. By definition these are generalized. A particular farm may be placed along this continuum only through a comparison of all the criteria in relation to another farm. There was a great deal of mobility within the agricultural economy and individuals could move along the continuum with good or bad fortune. In other words, these types do not represent a class system in any form, although they do represent different levels of economic and material wealth that, it is hoped, may be observed in the archaeological record. Also note that the chronology in Figure 8.13 is very generalized. Exactly when these types were first on the landscape is based on the historic research to date. Perhaps the dates can be refined with further archaeological and historical research.

There was one other farm type on the Vernon Parish landscape that existed very early; perhaps it was the first, but it had no real influence on the development of agriculture. The very first farmers may have been members of a Spanish or French family who were there before the first American hunter-squatter. These farms are labeled *rancheros*, to recognize that they would have been settled under Spanish authority, but they should not be confused with rancheros typical of west Texas. More likely they were small farms with houses constructed of logs like those soon to come. There is very little likelihood that such a farm would have existed within the boundaries of the Main Fort, but there is a very slight possibility of this type of farm in the Peason Ridge and Horse's Head areas.

Notwithstanding the ranchero, the development of the agricultural economy in this area essentially began with the hunter-squatter, defined by Price and Price (1978:7) as a person who was "highly mobile and [whose] subsistence was based on hunting, trapping, fishing, and trading with little emphasis, if any, on agriculture." Some raised cattle and pigs and these people are sometimes referred to as stockman-farmers (Sitton 1995). Essentially, this vanguard of the Upland South migration into the region devoted the vast majority of their family economic effort to hunting and gathering and left when the game became scarce or neighbors got too near. They raised some crops such as corn, but did not participate in a market economy and bartered for needs they could not get from the land. In the Vernon Parish region these are the people who migrated in and out of the region during the Neutral Ground period. The lifestyle may have persisted up to around the turn of the twentieth century, but more than likely the majority of such people were gone by the time of the Civil War.

Those hunter-squatters who did not move out of the area became subsistence farmers. Subsistence farmers, as defined here, were less mobile than hunter-squatters, devoting more time to raising crops. They participated only marginally in the developing market economy and were in the main self-sufficient and highly independent. Subsistence farmers were extremely flexible in their farm economy. They hunted, trapped, fished, bartered, grew a little cotton for clothing, let the pigs run in the woods, and grew corn for feeding both the family and their animals. Subsistence farmers were among the first lumbermen. They would cut timber seasonally and sell it to a mill downstream during the late nineteenth century—or, more likely, they would be hired by more wealthy farmers (see below) to do this work. During the twentieth century many would seek temporary employment in the woods with the lumber companies. Some subsistence farmers became pioneer or general farmers and eventually purchased their land free and clear. The land cleared for farming would remain small, and when it wore out more land would be cleared nearby. Other subsistence farmers were squatters who lived their entire lives on unclaimed land, government land, or timber land. Like the hunter-squatter, they would move, but usually within a short distance, to squat elsewhere when the old land was exhausted. As we have seen from the history within the Fort Polk area, the squatter lifestyle continued almost until the arrival of the U.S. Army. Within Fort Polk the majority of the farmers were subsistence farmers or squatters, with a sprinkling of others. Again, the distinction between the hunter-squatter and the subsistence farmer (squatter) is subtle, but it is largely dependent on time frame. The hunter-squatter was the early subsistence farmer who relied much more on the forest for subsistence. As game grew scarce from exploitation, the early hunter-squatter could and did move farther west. As the land became settled, the subsistence farmer had to become more flexible in obtaining subsistence.

First arriving around the 1840s and most prevalent in the 1870s and 1880s was the pioneer farmer. As defined here, the pioneer farmer arrived with the full intention of farming as a full-time occupation, of raising a cash crop, and of creating and participating in a market economy. These are the people who settled along the Anacoco and Calcasieu and were likely to become or even strove to become community leaders. This is not to say that they were absent in the Fort Polk area, but in the antebellum period they were more likely to seek good farmland to raise a cash crop. Some arrived as squatters but were able to successfully increase their landholdings and change their lifestyle. When able, they sought title to their lands from the government. More likely these pioneers came with some wealth in hand and perhaps they participated in some land speculation also. They purchased sections and quarter sections. They were entrepreneurs and, if possible, would find additional means of increasing their wealth, as opposed to simply farming. So they built the mills, provided the impetus for the formation of local government, and often ran for local office when the parish was formed. They hired the squatter to help cut timber to sell downstream. Before the Civil War, they brought a few slaves into the region, but they are in no way to be confused with plantation owners east of the parish. Pioneer farmers evolved into general farmers in the 1890s, the difference being that the pioneer farmer established the market economy, whereas the general farmer made it thrive. Pioneer farmers were those middle- to upper-class farmers of the mid–nineteenth century who created a local market, developed the sociopolitical community, and established a parish government in the 1870s.

General farming is defined as full participation in the local agricultural economy by raising a cash crop or a number of cash crops on at least 60 acres of land but usually much more. These farmers are essentially the same as pioneer farmers but of a later period, when the railroad came into the parish and opened the parish to the world. Along with crops, pigs and cattle were raised for market. Like all farmers in Vernon Parish, general farmers were very flexible, adapting their effort to the market and the environment. Crop diversity was their watchword. Corn remained the staple, but other grains were grown, along with fruits. General farmers owned their land and were full participants in a growing community, taking over from the pioneer farmers the social-leadership roles in establishing churches, fraternal organizations, and schools. It was the general farmer who was best represented by the statistics listed in the Census of Agriculture, reflecting the county's progress. General farmers did not participate much in the lumber boom, although some sons may have sought jobs in the woods, and they would sell their timber to a local mill. There were probably few of these people within the Fort Polk area because of the poor farmland.

The general farmer, like every farmer described above, was an opportunist. Starting around 1920 and definitely by the 1930s some began to specialize in cattle and sheep raising. Specialized farming is distinguished from general farming only in the degree to which farm labor and space were devoted to a single cash crop or commodity. Even specialized farmers were generalists to a degree; however, the majority of their effort went toward developing a single marketable commodity. Besides cattle and sheep farming, Vernon Parish farmers attempted to focus on cotton farming in the 1930s. Also, after the mills had cut and run there were attempts at fruit farms (satsuma oranges, for example) and truck farming. There is not much information about the success of these farms and they were not found within Fort Polk. Specialized farmers owned land and fully participated in community development and in the marketplace.

As a result of a variety of complex reasons, tenancy increased dramatically across the South after the Civil War. The term *tenant* represents a separate complex continuum of landless people (Orser and Holland 1984). Briefly, the term *tenancy* includes a range of economic levels from full sharecroppers (who owned almost nothing in the way of farm equipment and had only their labor to offer) to full renters (who owned everything they needed to farm except land). In this model, tenancy in Vernon Parish is thought to have developed primarily from subsistence farming although one must remember that by definition some tenants were general farmers who owned their own farm and rented another farm's land to grow additional crops. Also, during the 1930s some of those people who squatted on abandoned timber lands may have been counted by census takers as tenants, for some paid a nominal $1.00 a year rent. As can be seen, tenancy is a complex issue and thankfully one that can be practically ignored as a research topic within the area because parish-wide there were few "tenant farmers" in the classic southern sense of a landless black or white cotton sharecropper.

Finally, there was a type of tenant or squatter that Smith (1993:121–124) has called the "rural resident" in similar studies. These people were probably present in the parish in the late 1920s and 1930s through the Depression. They lived in the county but hired out, doing part-time work when they could find it. They did not farm as an occupation or at the subsistence level although they may have had a garden. They were the victims of the agricultural hard times of the 1920s and later the Depression. Some found jobs in the smaller lumber companies that formed in the parish after the large companies cut out. Others worked in town when the roads were finally able to make a daily commute possible. Obviously not all of the citizens of Vernon Parish were farmers, although the vast majority of those who did not work in the mills were. There were teachers, preachers, elected officials, blacksmiths, businessmen, and professionals (lawyers, for example). In the twentieth century there were gas-station attendants and mechanics and a long list of people who worked in local businesses. Some of these people also lived on farms and often did some farming. These professional classes add to the complexity of the economic patterns in the area, especially for the archaeologist studying this area.

Timber and Naval Stores Industry
Cultural geographers like Newton (1974) have not recognized any industry-related traits associated with Upland South culture, a culture that is predominately agriculturally based. However, geographically, the Upland South was covered with timber, the culture thrived on it, and thus, when the colonial naval stores industry developed and the timber industry of the late nineteenth and early twentieth centuries cut the great southern forests, the people of the forest adapted the industry to their economic strategy. For Upland South peoples, naval stores and timber represented a cottage industry and

another method of making additional income within their flexible agricul-
tural-hunting forest-dwelling lifestyle.

Upland South people participated in the timber industry in several forms.
First, and the most common method, was to cut timber and float it down-
stream at seasonal flood times to be sold to a mill. This was common in
Vernon Parish beginning sometime after the Civil War. In some areas of the
Upland South tie-hacking of hardwoods for railroad ties was a common
method of gaining cash from the earliest days of the railroads until the 1940s
(Smith 1993). This was not prevalent in Vernon Parish but it was done (see
Wright 1942). Finally, Upland South people turned to the industrial mills
for temporary employment. Upland South people were also familiar with
the naval stores industry, and in other areas of the Upland South like North
Carolina, turpentine, tar, and pitch production was a common method of
supplementing income (Clement et al. 1997). Within Vernon Parish, the naval stores industry came too late for it to become a cottage industry, but
naval stores were important to the local economy nevertheless. Site
16VN1221 provides an example of a turpentine operation in the Peason
Ridge Training Area occupied by African American laborers.

SOCIAL AND POLITICAL PATTERNS

Political, religious, and educational patterns, along with traditional folkways, are joined herein under social and political patterns. This is an expansion of Newton (1974:152), who confines Upland South social patterns to
(1) evangelical, atomistic Protestantism, coupled with anti-federalism; (2)
an open class system; (3) kin-structured settlement (previously discussed);
and (4) a county-courthouse political system (and remember, all important
roads led to the courthouse).

The patterns listed by Newton are clearly evident throughout the history
of settlement in the west-central Louisiana area. Without doubt, the settlers
in Vernon Parish and the Fort Polk area ordered their lives as Newton described. Their religious orientation included evangelical Protestant denominations dominated by Baptists, with a moderate Methodist presence, practically to the exclusion of other religious groups. Fundamentalist religious
beliefs dominated their doctrine. Anti-federalism in Newton's sense of the
word meant a distrust of centralized government, especially in the form of
the federal government's authority over local affairs. If one stretches this to
include an antiauthoritarian attitude, then surely Vernon Parish fits this description. Beginning around the 1880s, the parish was a hotbed of agrarian
populism, labor unrest, and antiestablishment political movements. In Vernon
Parish, socialist experimenters like the Newllano movement found sympa-
thetic support. Further, Vernon Parish was a strong supporter of Huey Long,

seen as the champion of the common man. Clearly, the people of Vernon Parish fit the Upland South model of fundamentalists and anti-federalists quite well.

Smith et al. (1982:213) found at Bay Springs, Mississippi, that although the settlement was kin based, a person's community often was defined by church affiliation. People within geographic proximity, who were not kin, would not necessarily identify themselves as being in the same community. The church they attended was more important. This was unlike the situation in the more mountainous regions of the South, where valleys and rivers restricted travel and helped to define the community. While Joyce (1981:94) did not address church affiliation in detail, she recognized that it might play a role in historic settlement patterning. At Bay Springs, topographic restraints were nonexistent. Creeks and hills were easily traversed. Given similar rolling topography at Fort Polk, albeit with poorer roads, it is hypothesized that church affiliation may have been important in defining communities here also. Schools also would be important community identifiers.

Exactly how this church affiliation as a community identifier corresponded to kin-structured settlement, another community link, is not clearly understood. Surely, "[t]he traditionalist places strong emphasis on knowing family genealogy" (Rafferty 1980:240), and who you were related to was as important as who you were. Within the Fort Polk area, settlement was indeed kin structured. Certainly people in kin-based communities like the Jeters attended the same church. Further, they may have interacted in a community sense with people not physically close to Jetertown but who attended that same church. When it came time for a log-rolling, picnic, raising of a school building, or other community activity, they may have turned to kin and church members for assistance rather than a nearby neighbor. This is a question for further study through oral history.

Discussion of the region's courthouse system seems unnecessary as this system was evident throughout the country. However, it should be noted that there is clear evidence of the importance of the courthouse and parish (county) seat in the development of the parish. Clearly Leesville's central location was conscientiously considered in the formation of the parish. Further, the development of the transportation system indicates that, as noted by Newton (1974), most if not all important state-maintained roads in the parish led to Leesville and were improved as major parish arteries.

Upland South Site Typology for Fort Polk

Utilization of an Upland South context for historic archaeological sites allows for another typology to be developed that might assist future researchers in developing a consistent and holistic evaluation of these properties from both the top (context) down and the bottom (archaeological manifestations) up. This typology begins, like the previous typology, with the recognition that overall, the archaeological manifestations at Fort Polk are farms, homesteads, community service centers (schools, general stores, mills, churches, cemeteries), industrial processing sites (turpentine stations and camps), and associated activity areas like trash dumps. In the vast majority of cases, the sites discovered have been farmstead sites from the early twentieth century. This is to be expected for two reasons (even though during much of this period the majority of the land was in the ownership of the timber industry). First, despite the timber industry, the peak population period for the installation was during this time. Second, beginning in the late nineteenth century and continuing through the present, inexpensive, durable materials were available to all people regardless of socioeconomic status in the form of dinnerware, packaging, and construction materials. Inexpensive glass, ceramics, and, to a lesser degree, metal packaging materials deteriorate slowly and were manufactured in mass quantities. This change makes twentieth-century sites easier to archaeologically "see" (see below) than earlier nineteenth-century occupations.

In this typology (Table 8.2) archaeological sites at Fort Polk are sorted into functional classes and types. Four classes of sites have been identified in the historic overview, are part of the agricultural continuum discussed previously, and should show up in the archaeological record: (1) agricultural sites, (2) community service centers, (3) industrial/special activity sites, and (4) transportation-related sites. This typology is based on previous work in another Upland South region (Smith 1993) and modified by local cultural attributes and previous archaeological research. For instance, the typology incorporates a typology first proposed by Campbell and Weed (1986:5-4). However, this typology takes a broader perspective, attempting to integrate the historical record with the archaeological record. Plantations have been eliminated again in this typology. In the classic definition, plantations as large landholding enterprises operated with slave labor to produce a cash crop, and these were rare or nonexistent in Vernon Parish, although there is evidence that a few landowners, such as the Smart family, called their landholdings plantations. Within Fort Polk, the land was hardly conducive to such enterprises. Additional evidence that Servello's (1983) site 16VN15 is indeed a plantation is needed before this type is added.

Within this typology site types within each class should have several distinct archaeological components. However, as these individual components make up an entire site, they are subsumed under their appropriate type for the purposes of discussion and context. It is recognized that for the purposes of site inventory, distinct archaeologic sites will remain independent.

Table 8.2 — Classes and types of archaeological sites in Vernon Parish and on Fort Polk (V. = Very; Med. = Medium)

Site Class/Type	Date Range	Visibility	Type Signature	Sensitivity
Agricultural				
Rancheros (1780–1810)	(none)	V. Low	V. Low	High
Hunter-squatter (1800–1860)	1820–1870	V. Low	V. Low	High
Subsistence (squatters)	1830–1940	Low-Med.	V. Low	High
Pioneer	1840–1890	Low	Med.	High
General	1890–1940	Med.	Med.	Med.
Specialized (1920–1940)	(present?)	High	Med.-High	Med.
Share-tenant	1870–1940	High	Low	Low
Renter	1870–1940	High	Low	Low
Rural resident	1920–1940	Med.	Low	Low
Community Service Centers				
Grain mills (1830–1940)	1850–1900	Med.	Med.-High	High
Sawmills (1880–1940)	1900–1930	Med.	Med.-High	Med.
General store/post office (1830–1940)	1850–1940	Low-Med.	Low-Med.	Med.
Schools	1830–1940	Med.-High	Med.-High	Med.
Churches	1830–1940	Med.-High	Med.-High	Med.
Cemeteries	1830–1940	Med.-High	High	Med.
Hamlets, Villages (1830–1940)	1870–1940	Low-High	Med.-High	High
Industrial Special Activity				
CCC camps	1930–1940	Med.	Med.-High	High
Civil War (1860–1865)	(none)	V. Low	Low	High
Portable sawmills	1910–1940	Low	Med.	High
Turpentine stills	1910–1930	High	High	Med.
Lumber camps	1900–1930	High	High	Med.
Historic scatters	1820–1940	Low-High	High	Low
Cattle dipping vats	1930s	High	High	Low
Stills	1830–1940	Low	Med.	High
Transportation				
Bridges (1850–1940)	1870–1940	High	High	Low
Ferries, fords	1820–1940	Med.	Low	Low
Roads	1820–1940	Low	Med.	Med.
Railroads (trams)	1900–1930	High	High	Low

For instance, under the agricultural sites class, the various components of a farmstead archaeological site (barns, dwelling, and outbuildings) are all subsumed under each site type such as a hunter-squatter or general farm. It is important to recognize, where possible, the fields and outbuildings removed from the farmstead that are part of the farm "site" also. Obviously, this will not always be possible, but it is important to make every attempt to do so. Note that trash dumps and cattle dipping vats are listed separately. This is in recognition of the practical problem of associating many of the trash dumps, inventoried as individual archaeological sites found in fields or hollows, with one particular farm or another. Such dumps may be far removed from their primary use area or the location of initial discard. Still, when dumps can be recognized as part of a particular farmstead, they should be incorporated into the research framework. Likewise, cattle dipping vats were shared among farmers. It also should be noted that this typology is not specific to Fort Polk but may be applicable to historic sites outside the artificial borders of the installation. It has been proposed as a regional, Vernon Parish, or west-central Louisiana typology.

Table 8.2, column two, provides an estimate of the general chronological range in which the various site types occurred within Vernon Parish and on Fort Polk. Some types listed have a slightly different date range in column one. The date range in the first column is for sites of that type beyond Fort Polk when the date range is believed to be different from that of the Fort Polk region. If only one range is provided, it addresses both the installation and the greater west-central Louisiana region. These are obviously generalized ranges for refinement in future research.

Column three of Table 8.2, labeled "Visibility," provides a hypothesized measurement of an archaeologist's ability to locate these sites on the ground during a typical cultural resource survey. The measurement is subjective and ranges from a very low to a high likelihood of finding such sites. This measurement is based on a number of site type attributes including (1) expected number and types of artifacts and features found at these sites; (2) degree of permanence of artifacts and features associated with these sites; (3) expected number of sites; (4) existence of other areas of research (e.g., archival) that would assist in locating such sites; and (5) intensity and length of site occupation (Adams and Smith 1985:326). It is important to point out that this column only measures the degree to which a site might be found and recognized as an archaeological site. It does not measure the archaeologist's ability to identify that particular site type, which is measured in the next column, "Type Signature."

An example of how sites have high or low visibility would be the hunter-squatter sites. Hunter-squatters came into the area with very little material culture, lived off the land, and moved on. Their contribution was significant because they set the stage for the unique character and culture of the area. Yet, because the people had little in the way of permanent material culture and built few outbuildings on their homesteads, the likelihood of finding such a site on a typical archaeological survey is expected to be very low. On the other hand, subsistence farmers of the twentieth century, while generally comparable in socioeconomic status to hunter-squatters, will have very large material culture assemblages, not because of their wealth but simply as a result of the permanent, inexpensive nature of their twentieth-century material culture like canning jars, ceramics, nails, and plastics (see Adams 1980).

The "Type Signature" column provides a subjective measure of the possibility of recognizing a discovered site as a particular site type. The site attributes discussed above are considered along with the expected artifact assemblage in determining the high, medium, or low possibility of recognizing the site type. Essentially, this column measures the archaeologist's ability, using any and all lines of possible evidence, to identity a particular site as an identified site type. For example, not only are early subsistence sites likely to be hard to find, but also, once one is discovered as a site, it will be difficult to recognize the site as a subsistence agriculture site as distinguished from a pioneer site of the same period. This also will be true of late-nineteenth and early-twentieth-century farm sites. The low cost of the artifacts usually found at such sites (nails, glass, ceramics) made them easily available to the general farmer, subsistence farmer, and rural resident. It is hypothesized that the material culture assemblages will look very similar and perhaps may not be distinguishable at all (Santeford et al. 1985:193; Stine 1989:366–367). Still, the occupants of these sites had different lifestyles and the frequency of their sites on the landscape will differ as well. Also the farmstead pattern may be different for these sites: a general and specialized farmer, for instance, should have a greater quantity of outbuildings and material culture than a subsistence farmer and should be working a larger number of acres. Therefore it will be important to attempt to distinguish these different cultural sites in order to determine how many of each should be preserved. Perhaps deed and other archival research may be able to assist in the effort to distinguish these sites.

The "Sensitivity" column of Table 8.2 measures the degree to which each site type can withstand modern cultural disturbance (in this case military training) and, if some are disturbed, the degree of loss to the culture history of the area.[2] Essentially, this column is a broad measure of the re-

---

[2]   *Of course, most of the pre-1930 sites had already been impacted by the timber industry during the removal of the pines.*

search value of a particular site in relation to the number of expected sites of that type. For example, as a site type, there are expected to be very few hunter-squatter sites (there were few of them in the past), and because there are expected to be few cultural remains associated with these sites, they are probably highly sensitive to postoccupation human impacts. If a hunter-squatter site were found and identified, it would be considered a rare and important research site, because so little is known about this time period, the people, and what their sites might look like archaeologically.[3] On the other hand, it is expected that the most common sites found during typical archaeological surveys will be twentieth-century farmsteads, and of those, the various types of subsistence sites will be the most common. Since there is expected to be a moderate number of these present, excavation of a few of these sites may be enough to define the type's particular archaeological signature.

Archaeological Manifestations of Upland South Sites

As noted, archaeologists studying historic sites at Fort Polk primarily have been concerned with artifact assemblages, attempting to define artifact patterns associated with different site types. This research is important because so many of the sites found at the installation are no more than artifact scatters without the other distinguishing characteristics discussed above. The 1988 and 1999 HPPs discussed these attempts in detail including their strengths and weaknesses. Within the framework of an Upland South context, additional observations may be made.

On the basis of previous research at other Upland South farm sites (Carlson 1990; Jurney and Moir 1987; Smith et al. 1982), it is evident that the archaeological expression of a farmstead is often a broad, shallow sheet midden, with small areas of intense past activity where features such as a smokehouse firebox, wells, and cisterns have intruded more deeply into the ground. A number of test excavations at historic farmsteads within Fort Polk support the intrasite patterns discussed herein, although impacts from the lumber industry have severely disturbed most of these sites, leaving an indistinct picture. Still, this research has indicated that Fort Polk domestic sites have surface expressions such as artifact scatters, depressions, wells, ornamental trees, occasionally fence lines, brick, and sandstone or other medium-sized stone used as ground supports for log structures (Campbell and Weed 1986; Campbell et al. 1987; Franks 1990d; Franks and Yakubik 1990a, 1990b; Largent et al. 1993a, 1993b; Morehead et al. 1994; Thomas

---

3   *In fact, one might have been found. An unusual early-nineteenth-century site, 16VN928 (Thomas et al. 1994a), is a good candidate for a hunter-squatter site and might be worth further research consideration.*

et al. 1993d, 1994b; Yakubik and Franks 1990). Characteristically, the archaeological matrix of Fort Polk sites, as with sites seen in other Upland South contexts, consists of sheet middens and clustered concentrations of artifacts assumed to be associated with activity areas.[4] Campbell and Weed (1986:5-4) also note that domestic sites contain distinctive "homestead artifacts like stove parts" and, critically, ornamental plants. Late sites (twentieth century) may have privies. Oral historical research connected to the archaeological testing indicates that wells were "generally close to the house," that yard sweeping was a tradition in the Fort Polk region, and that the farmstead was laid out in the Upland South pattern noted above (Franks and Yakubik 1990a:86–91).

As discussed previously there also have been attempts made to identify site types based on percentages of various categories of artifacts and their percentages in the assemblage. Campbell and Weed (1986:5-4) proposed such criteria as (1) the presence of window glass, (2) nails 30 percent or more of the total artifacts, and (3) ceramics equal to or greater than glass as part of a pattern distinguishing a domestic assemblage. Later Thomas et al. (1993d:184–186) revised these criteria noting that window glass was present at two historic sites in much lower percentages than originally thought (16VN138, 16VN139). Unfortunately, these criteria may not be of much help. Research at other Upland South farmsteads (Smith et al. 1982) warns that the date of the site's occupation, the method of excavation, and the location of test units all play a part in the percentages of architectural artifacts recovered.

Fine-tune dating of Fort Polk's archaeological sites using the artifact assemblages has proven extremely frustrating. Artifacts like ceramics and glass were durable items. Ceramics were reused and curated. Thus, Campbell and Weed's (1986:11-8, 11-10) experience in attempting to chronologically separate historic sites by *terminus post quem* dating seemed to offer conflicting conclusions. Meanwhile, glass and nails were recycled. In the Upland South, even farmhouses were often moved and reused (Smith et al. 1982). Most critically, and perhaps most devastating for any attempt to date sites by artifact assemblages alone, many Upland South homesites were occupied over several generations, and the earliest occupations may be masked by later occupations. At Fort Polk the evidence is clear that earlier sites do mask later sites.

---

[4] *Much of the work here was conducted at the survey and testing level using shovel tests, controlled surface collections, and test units so the data are not directly comparable with those of other Upland South sites. However, the distribution of artifacts appears to conform to this model.*

Anderson et al. (1988) also addressed the site chronology problem, noting that early log houses probably did not have window glass. Test excavations at an antebellum site (16VN1076) by Franks (1990e), for instance, produced no window glass. Franks and Yakubik's (1990a) testing of a long-term occupation site (Jetertown) found few windowpane glass artifacts and no nails. They assumed the structures there were dogtrot log houses or pen constructions. But the percentage of window glass and nails alone may not be a reliable marker for site dating either. Historic research herein indicates that at Fort Polk long pen construction extended into the 1940s. It is true that nails became inexpensive to make and were mass produced only after the 1880s and are more likely to be found in greater quantities at twentieth-century sites when balloon frame construction became common (see Adams 1980). If balloon framing was rare at Fort Polk, however, and it probably was, nails cannot be expected to make up a significant percentage of the artifact assemblage at any site. Likewise, Franks and Yakubik (1990a:105) found that glass artifacts were far more common than ceramics at twentieth-century farmsteads. Again, this is because glass became an inexpensive and versatile sanitary container and was in widespread use after automatic bottle-making machines came into common use (1904). Ceramics, on the other hand, were becoming more limited in use, primarily as tablewares. Middle-to late-twentieth-century sites, regardless of socioeconomic status, will contain abundant glass artifacts (see Adams 1980; Smith et al. 1982).

Despite these frustrations, Yakubik and Franks (1990) offer some hope that early sites may not all be invisible. For instance, site 16VN1076 was known from courthouse records to have been occupied in 1911 by William Bridges. Yet, an artifact assemblage dates to the early nineteenth century, making it one of the earliest in the Fort Polk region (Franks 1990e:47; Yakubik and Franks 1990).

Given the above problems with chronology and site identification, the ability to distinguish the site types proposed in the agricultural continuum seems dubious. In previous historic archaeological studies like this (Clement et al. 1997; Smith 1993) it has been proposed that the identified types of farms and farmers described in the agricultural continuum should have a distinguishing archaeological signature that allows archaeologists to distinguish a subsistence occupation from a general occupation. Indeed, this was why the continuum was originally proposed, in the hope of being able to see these different farm types within the archaeological record. However, in those regions previously studied (North Carolina and Missouri, respectively) the development of rural agriculture followed a pattern that generally ran from early hunter-squatters and pioneers (antebellum), to subsistence farmers and tenant farming (middle to late nineteenth century), to the introduction of general farming (late nineteenth century), to a combination of general, specialized, and tenant farming in the twentieth century. While this development is probably visible at sites in the western and northeastern portions of Vernon Parish, within Fort Polk, the extremely marginal agricultural lands, combined with the purchase of large tracts of land by the timber companies and their later sale to the U.S. government, may have stunted this development. Thus, the question for historical archaeologists working within Fort Polk is, can these different levels of agricultural development be observed in the archaeological record? Obviously, the archaeological signature of a specialized farmer in the 1930s should be quite different from that of the hunter-squatter of the antebellum—one reason being that the artifacts would be different. But what about the differences between a specialized farmer and a subsistence farmer: both were present in the parish in the 1920s and 1930s, a time when America's material culture was durable and cheap (ceramics, glass, metal). Previous work (Franks and Yakubik 1990a, 1990b) indicates that the differences between such farm types will be difficult to see archaeologically and clearly will not be evident at the survey and testing level. Stated again, it will be very difficult to find the early farmsteads and, once found, they will be difficult to assess because the archaeological expression is spread thinly across the landscape. Shovel testing may discover such sites, but it may not be a good way of assessing the sites.

The possibility of identifying these sites remains open since almost all or all archaeological work at historic sites has been at the survey and testing level, not at the excavation level. It will take a more intensive effort at a high-potential site to see whether the kinds of settlement and cultural patterns discussed in this chapter can be delineated. Testing or the mitigation of adverse impact at these sites may require intense, systematic shovel testing on a tight 2-m grid, or with a checkerboard pattern of 1-x-1-m units, or other means to determine the settlement and cultural patterns seen above. In other words, as the Fort Polk inventory is completed it would be useful to evaluate the agricultural continuum and Table 8.2 in light of the survey record. Much of what is proposed in this table may not be evident at the survey level but can be tested in site-testing strategies.

Beyond farmsteads there are very few examples of other types of sites. Community service centers are those low-order central places where local farmers and other members of the community would have had raw materials processed and products marketed, exchanged, traded, or purchased and where the community would have gathered for social-political-religious activities. The type sites include sawmills and grist mills, general stores, gas stations, post offices (often combined with general stores), schools and public assembly areas (often combined), and churches (and associated cemeteries).

Within the Fort Polk area these sites would include hamlets (Six Mile, Front, Pringles, Whiskey Chitto), schools (Whiskachitto, Six Mile), cemeteries (Zion Hill, Mill Creek, Holly Springs, Smith, Watson, and various numbered cemeteries), churches (Gravel Hill, Oak Grove, Johnsonville), and mills (Swain's Mill near Six Mile).

None of the social, political, communal, or central-place sites within Fort Polk have been investigated beyond the survey level, except cemeteries (Franks and Jones 1991), so their archaeological signatures are unknown. While mill sites may be more easily recognized than the others by such attributes as location and unique artifacts (millstones and dams), it is expected that general stores/post offices, churches, and schools will not be as easily recognized. At Bay Springs, Mississippi, for instance, Adams et al. (1981:215–252) found no distinguishing archaeological features or artifacts that would indicate that two sites excavated were a general store and a Masonic lodge, although they knew them to be. They could just as easily have been domestic sites. This is expected to be the case at Fort Polk. General stores, post offices, schools, churches, and even the hamlets may have little archaeological visibility at Fort Polk because the artifacts that remain behind are those found on domestic sites.

The industrial/special activity class of sites is defined as including sites that had a unique activity or process that was not community oriented. At Fort Polk, the most critical of these are associated with the lumber and turpentine industries, including lumber camps, small portable mills, turpentine camps and mills, tramways, and, of course, Fullerton (which is not within the fort proper but nearby and under the U.S. Forest Service's management). At Fort Polk, at least one site (16VN1221) has been identified as a distillery (Thomas et al. 1993d; see above). It is also possible that some evidence of Civilian Conservation Corps (CCC) activity is likely to be found on the installation.

Abundant evidence of the process of extracting turpentine has been found at Fort Polk; however, the vast majority of this is in the form of abandoned and broken turpentine cups. The process of boxing and transporting pine gum to the distillery did not create archaeological properties other than the possibility of an occasional lost or abandoned artifact like a tool and the ubiquitous turpentine cup. Of greater visibility would be distilleries and camps for laborers. According to Brown (1919:178) distilleries were generally located near water and/or a source of transportation like a railroad. Olmstead (1968:344) noted that forest distilleries were placed in ravines or valleys. Olmstead was describing still sites in the 1850s; however, water was always a necessity and it is likely that the sites would be found near a water source in the twentieth century also.

The average distillery layout consisted of (1) a still house, an open shed containing the still and worm; (2) a storage shed for storing turpentine; (3) a cooperage for making rosin barrels; and (4) a rosin screen and rosin barrel platform (Brown 1919:179). Large plants might also have contained housing for laborers, a blacksmith forge, and stables for mules (Sharrer 1981:258). These buildings and outbuildings and the resultant waste areas would leave a large archaeological signature, and indeed archaeological testing of such a site confirmed this (Largent et al. 1993a, 1993b; Thomas et al. 1993d). Site 16VN1221 was the processing point for turpentine collected in the surrounding woods for the Four L Company, and associated with the still was a camp for its black workers located some four miles west of the still. The stills and outbuildings for this camp, like many at this time, were portable and were brought to the site via a tramline (Thomas et al. 1993d:138). The archaeological site consisted of remains of the distillery, dam and pond, burned resin, tramlines, barrel-hoop concentration (cooperage), and domestic sites or camps. Of course, turpentine cups in concentration were another distinct feature (Thomas et al. 1993d:189). These identifying characteristics are very similar to those proposed by Brown (1919). Thomas et al. (1993d:189) add that some long-term sites might include a church or store and a cemetery. However, within Fort Polk this would seem less likely as the time the turpentine companies were in the area was short and the camps were portable.

Tar kilns are also a vague possibility at Fort Polk although there is no direct evidence for them. The lack of kilns is probably related to the fact that when pitch was in greatest demand (colonial and antebellum periods) the Vernon Parish region was far from any market. For the record, small kilns, one-time operations, were usually located on a slope or a hillock with the channel running downhill (Olmstead 1968:347). Kilns could be operated easily by farmers with little land and they required little expertise, thus they were "dispersed throughout the forests" (Williams 1989:88) or "far out in the country" (Gamble 1921b:42). Later, the industry changed to more large-scale operations, and there is a remote possibility that tar kilns might be found as part of still sites since the distilleries served as central points of processing and distribution.

Transportation-related sites are those physical manifestations on the landscape that assisted transportation, such as roads and ferries. Within Fort Polk, bridges and tramways are the most prevalent. Tramways for the lumber industry are ubiquitous across the landscape and other than their presence and location it is unlikely that they will yield much more information. Historic roads within the installation will be most difficult to find. Aerial photography combined with map research would provide a greater return than field survey.

Research Directions

This section provides a series of research questions that can be used to guide the direction of future research at Fort Polk and in west-central Louisiana. It is proposed that future research should take place in a multidisciplinary framework, sometimes called ethnoarchaeology, which essentially means the incorporation of the techniques and theories of archaeology, oral history, and history into a holistic approach to discovery of the past (Adams 1977; S. Smith 1991; Smith et al. 1982; Stewart-Abernathy 1986). All of these disciplines together can offer a more complete look at the history and culture of the area, which today is represented mostly by the archaeological resources.

Much of the previous archaeological work on historic sites has been guided by a few general themes first proposed in Louisiana's Comprehensive Archaeological Plan (Smith et al. 1983) and by a summary of research directions proposed in the Technical Synthesis portion of the 1988 HPP (Anderson et al. 1988:310–311). Both sets of research themes are still useful in guiding research concerning historic sites within the installation, as most questions have yet to be fully answered. The following sets of research questions are similar to those posed previously but are refined on the basis of knowledge gained from a recent historic overview prepared for the installation (Smith 1999) and within the framework of the Upland South historic context. The section also provides a brief digest of what has been learned to date regarding these questions.

Table 8.3 presents a list of the identified historic themes appropriate to the context and the Fort Polk region. Also presented in the table are the suggested areas, methods, or disciplines to be used in answering the research questions posed. Naturally, these are not the only questions that could be addressed; however, they are offered as a method for guiding future researchers in fruitful directions.

Finally, the questions and discussion are organized by the broad topics posed at the beginning of this chapter. There is considerable overlap in this arrangement, in that it is impossible to address one area without affecting another. Also, addressing one question will provide information that will assist in answering another. The following discussion addresses both Vernon Parish and the installation.

UPLAND SOUTH THEME

Generally, the study of all aspects of Upland South culture is the research direction prescribed for historic resources at Fort Polk, with several areas of inquiry. The Comprehensive Archaeological Plan has identified this topic as "Upland South Subsistence and Settlement Patterns"; however, research

Table 8.3 — Historic themes for the Upland South

Theme	Research Methods
Population and settlement patterns	Oral history, archaeology, government records, GIS mapping
Economics (agriculture)	Archaeology, oral history, cultural geography, history
Political/social life	Oral history, history, genealogy
Archaeological signature/visibility	Archaeology, GIS mapping
Material culture	Archaeology, oral history
Transportation patterns	Archaeology, cultural geography
Antebellum History in Vernon Parish	History, archaeology
Civil War and Postbellum in Vernon Parish	History, archaeology
Development of the Lumber Industry in Vernon Parish	Oral history, cultural geography
Forestry and Depression in Vernon Parish	History, oral history

should be broadened to include traditional folkways, political and social patterns, and industrial patterns—all within the Upland South framework. Oral history will be especially useful in defining folkways, political and social life, and traditional practices, while archaeology will provide the most useful method of determining settlement patterns.

Anderson et al. (1988:310) stated in 1988 that "perhaps the single most important . . . question facing researchers is resolving the nature of historic period settlement patterning on Fort Polk." Both their study and the Comprehensive Archaeological Plan call for research about the nature of historic settlement; the environmental, social, and economic factors influencing settlement; and how and why early settlers decided where to settle. These questions are still in the forefront of future research at the installation, but this historical study has provided some answers. To begin with, historic research indicates that regional settlement patterns in Vernon Parish were first determined by transportation routes and the quality of agricultural lands. Initially the region was bypassed because of its isolation: the flow of migration was to the north along the Red River and west across the Camino Real. During this period, settlement also was thwarted by political restrictions. The region was first settled by hunter-squatters who moved on and were followed, when the area was opened to settlement by the government, by subsistence farmers and pioneer farmers. Both generally preferred the rich lands surrounding Fort Polk. Those who chose the Fort Polk region in the antebellum era were subsistence, Upland South agriculturists. They probably made their own roads off the main trails, probably following animal paths along the lines of least resistance. This pattern continued until the arrival of the railroads; hence the randomness of the road system. However, with the formation of the parish, the more-traveled trails were those to Leesville, the seat of government and commerce. With the railroads, these roads, running to Leesville and other rail stops, became even more important.

At first (antebellum), on the local level, settlement decisions were tied to environmental factors like sources of water (springs and streams). However, as settlement developed (postbellum), community and kin played a more important role. Communities were organized along with churches and schools. Settlement decisions were affected not only by water sources but also by the presence of the community services available. At this same time kin became increasingly more important. Families grew and matured, requiring the large land tracts to be split into smaller ones. Married sons settled nearby, for instance. At the microlocal level, farmstead siting was chosen with winds, aspect, view, and drainage in mind. After the arrival of the railroad, and as Vernon Parish began to thrive with the lumber industry, settlement decisions were made based on the developing transportation system. A good road tied to the market was important to any farmer.

Of course, within the Fort Polk area these patterns were stumped in many ways by the lack of good soils in the antebellum period and later by the land purchases of the lumber industry. Still, some subsistence-level people settled there, and all the above rules of settlement pertained. However, community development was seriously affected in that almost no central-place hamlets, villages, or towns developed within the Fort Polk region. The settlement capacity never reached a level for local organization. Community services remained scattered, including mills, churches, and schools.

Importantly, archaeological survey and testing has been and is likely to be affected by this lack of development. Archaeologists have seen and are going to see a biased settlement pattern. The pattern will be biased by the nature of the artifact assemblages. Sites dating to the 1920s and 1930s will predominate not only because they were indeed more prevalent but also because the durability and quantity of material culture of this period masks earlier settlement, especially at the survey level.

With this summary in mind the following population and settlement pattern research questions for the future include the following:

1. The people, culture, and history of Vernon Parish and the Fort Polk region seem to constitute an archetypical example of Upland South life.

What aspects of the population and settlement seen there add to our definition of Upland South culture?

2. Can intersite and intrasite settlement patterns be distinguished at the historic archaeological sites within the installation or have impacts from lumbering and military training obscured them?

3. Can resident population estimates be better refined through time for the Fort Polk region?

4. Were farms (or acreage) actually worked by nonresidents commuting into the region, or are there other explanations for the seeming discrepancy between the different population estimates offered by deed and tax record research on the one hand and archaeological site surveys on the other (see above discussion regarding twentieth-century site artifact assemblages)?

5. Are there distinguishing characteristics between Redbone material culture assemblages and the material culture assemblages of white Upland South peoples?

6. To what extent was settlement kin based?

7. How were central-place sites dispersed across the Fort Polk landscape?

8. Are there distinctive intrasite settlement patterns—and can they be seen—for each of the agricultural sites described in the continuum discussed above?

9. Who were the first residents of Vernon Parish and the installation?

10. How accurate is the proposed summary of settlement development?

11. Recent research suggests a greater number of antebellum land claims than population and settlement data support. Is this true across the installation? Are the explanations herein for this phenomenon correct?

Economic questions include these:

1. Are the agricultural sites archaeologically distinguishable?

2. Can hunter-squatter sites be found?

3. Were there pioneer farmers in the Fort Polk region, as measured by large landholdings and large acres of cropland, prior to the Civil War?

4. Was general or specialized farming carried on later within Fort Polk; for instance, were there sheep herders there after the land was cleared?

5. What was the ratio of squatters to landowning farmers within the Fort Polk region?

6. Are there visible differences in material culture between farmers in the rich Anacoco region versus those in areas like Fort Polk?

Social and political life questions include these:

1. What were the traditional gender roles in the Upland South, and are they identifiable in the oral history and archaeology of this region?

2. What was the structure of kin relationships in the region?

3. How was the community within the installation defined—by residence, church, geographic proximity, topography, or kin? Was it the same for the rest of the parish?

4. What role did Leesville play in the development of the Fort Polk region and of the parish? Was it the center of political, social, and cultural development? Did its influence thwart the development of other central places within the installation?

5. Was Huddleston the center of sociopolitical life before Leesville?

6. Was the church the center of rural social interaction? To what level did the location of schools affect community identity?

7. Can central-place nodes like Six Mile, Pringles, and Front be identified on Fort Polk? Do they have a distinctive archaeological signature?

Archaeological visibility and signature questions include these:

1. Can we identify through archaeology the full range of possible sites known to exist at Fort Polk?

2. What do each of these type sites look like archaeologically? Are they distinguishable?

3. Are intrasite patterns at a Fort Polk, Vernon Parish, farmstead different or the same as those seen in other areas of the Upland South? Are there differences between the Anacoco region and the Fort Polk region?

4. Can trash dumps or historic artifact scatters be attributed to a particular farmstead occupation?

5. Can the archaeological record tell us more about the lives of the people who lived at the various types of farms in the Fort Polk region?

Material culture questions include these:

1. Are there any differences between the material culture assemblage of a Vernon Parish–Fort Polk farm site and that of another such site elsewhere in the Upland South?

2. What are the similarities and differences in the material culture assemblages between the various agricultural types?

3. What are the similarities and differences in the material culture assemblages found on yeoman farmsteads at Fort Polk versus the assemblages found on black tenant and white yeoman farmsteads in other regions of the South?

4. Are there regional differences between Anacoco and Fort Polk farmers?

Transportation system questions include these:

1. Did the proximity of Leesville affect the transportation system in the Fort Polk area as described above?

2. Did the creation of Leesville change the transportation network within the parish, as it would seem from historic maps?

3. What were the effects of the railroad on transportation and settlement patterns? Was the effect of the building of the railroad as pronounced as it seems?

4. Did road improvement efforts concentrate on roads leading to Leesville?

5. To what extent was the road system within the Fort Polk area tied to Huddleston prior to the creation of Leesville?

ANTEBELLUM HISTORY IN VERNON PARISH THEME

The theme of antebellum history in Vernon Parish is provided simply to recognize the necessity of continuing research into the early history of the area. Information concerning Vernon Parish may be available within Texas archives. Additional historical research should concentrate on primary sources. The next step is to dig deeper into the settlement history using the land records available to determine the earliest farmsteads and settlements. With this information, archaeological surveys should attempt to locate these specific sites. This will require a considerable effort to result in productive findings. Pioneer questions include the following:

1. Can we identify the earliest settled areas and sites (including those of possible Spanish and French settlers)?

2. When was the Fort Polk area first settled?

3. Were the first farmsteads all located in the valleys?

4. Where are the earliest roads? Do remnants exist?

5. What was the settlement concentration along the Sabine?

6. What are the similarities and differences between Vernon Parish pine settlers and the people in east Texas?

CIVIL WAR AND POSTBELLUM THEME

Vernon Parish seems to have been bypassed by the Civil War, yet there are tantalizing glimpses in the record to indicate that the region was plagued by deserters, guerrillas, and desperadoes during this time. As with many other areas of Vernon Parish history, there just does not seem to be much recorded about the war in the region or the effects suffered afterward. A fruitful area of research might be to dig deeper into this subject by tracing regimental histories and other archival sources. At least with Civil War records, there are plenty of them, and the extra effort taken to dig through them is more likely to be rewarded than research in other periods of American history. Civil War questions include:

1. Is there any archaeological evidence of military activity within the installation?

2. What was the local population distribution between those who fought for the South and those who fought for the North?

3. Were there any skirmishes or encounters between the military and guerrilla bands within the parish?

4. Was there a widespread migration out of the parish after the war as in other areas of the South, or was Vernon Parish an attractive place where many displaced southerners settled after the war?

THE DEVELOPMENT OF THE LUMBER INDUSTRY THEME

No other event had a greater impact on the parish than the arrival of the lumber companies once the railroad was built. Lumbering not only changed the landscape, but it also changed the lives of almost every resident: it brought in a dramatic increase in new residents, it brought prosperity to some, and it brought economic development for most of the parish. This research theme is, other than Upland South culture, the most important central theme for the history of the parish and Fort Polk. Areas of research abound, and it is one of the few themes listed here for which large amounts of additional documentation probably exist for historical research. Archival records in Kansas City, in Beaumont, Texas, in New Orleans, in Louisiana, in Chicago, and at the National Archives are bound to contain primary sources covering the various lumber companies within the parish. Archaeologically speaking, research potential is also fruitful, for lumber industry sites should be highly visible in the archaeological record and much work needs to be done. Just a few of the lumber industry research questions include the following:

1. Are there more records in existence for the W. R. Pickering Company, Fullerton Lumber Company (Miller 1997), and other Fort Polk–area companies that will shed light on the region?

2. What about other companies in other areas of Vernon Parish, including the naval stores industry?

3. What are the names of the speculators who bought land within the Fort Polk area? What is the land history of these parcels?

4. Are there archaeological remains of distilleries and labor camps (lumber and turpentine) other than those recorded?

5. What is the archaeological signature of these camps? What can the archaeology tell us about the lives of the people living in these camps?

6. The lives of these camps were short. How could excavation of these camps in light of the short-term occupations assist our understanding of the development of material culture and identification of artifact patterns in the early twentieth century?

Forestry and Depression in Vernon Parish Theme

Research at other installations (Smith 1993) found abundant data concerning the lives of people during the Depression. These records were the result of federal work programs. A search for such records for Fort Polk and Vernon Parish did not locate any. Additional archival work may bring these to light. Also, U.S. Forest Service records and CCC records at the National Archives may exist and assist in shedding light on the lives of people in the region during the Depression. Further, U.S. Army records probably exist at the National Archives concerning the development of the installation. Also, it is possible that when the army arrived, it made a careful survey of the lands, properties, and people of the area, and these records may still exist. For instance, detailed records of the properties purchased at the Savannah River nuclear site in South Carolina were made when that area was acquired. This work was done by the Army Corps of Engineers for property assessment, and the records include size of all structures, photographs of all structures, values, inventories, and a wealth of other data (Richard Brooks, personal communication, October 1, 1992). Finally, aerial photography may exist since the area was right in the middle of the Louisiana Maneuvers. Finding and analyzing these records would be time consuming but worth the effort for settlement pattern studies and could be used in a variety of ways, including assisting in GIS mapping. All of this could provide a microscopic level of detail and create a unique opportunity to reconstruct the Fort Polk landscape during the first part of the twentieth century. Forestry and Depression questions include the following:

1. Can the Depression landscape be fully recreated using the documents noted above?

2. How can these documents be used to detail the settlement patterns?

3. Does the U.S. Forestry Service have archival material related to land use in the area?

4. How were the lives of Vernon Parish residents affected by the Depression?

5. How was the lumber industry impacted? Did the lumber companies provide a level of employment sufficient to buffer some of the effects of the Depression?

6. How did Vernon Parish react to the arrival of the U.S. Army?

7. What was the nature of CCC activity in Fort Polk and Vernon Parish?

8. The CCC is known to have occupied a main camp and a side camp in Vernon Parish. How did they relate to one another and what activities were shared/dissimilar?

9. What lasting effects did the CCC have on the landscape?

These are just a few of the areas of inquiry that might be pursued in the course of research and management of the cultural resources at Fort Polk. The themes provided came directly out of the history. The questions serve as examples of the more promising areas of research to investigate and toward which future research can be directed. They are especially important in that the Fort Polk region seems, not only from the archaeological work but also through this history, a representative region of the Upland South. Study of this region and its sites can go a long way toward our understanding of this distinctive culture.

Conclusions

A s we have seen in the preceding chapters, the information collected by Fort Polk's cultural resource management program has contributed a great deal to our understanding of past life in western Louisiana. Fort Polk has an aggressive and proactive program, furthermore, that will continue to generate information and preserve and protect archaeological and historical properties on the installation in the years to come. The production of technical syntheses is a part of this process, giving resource managers and researchers an opportunity to assess their programs. Only by knowing what has been done and what has been learned can we determine what more is needed and how that work can be best accomplished.

The historic preservation plans produced at Fort Polk, first in 1988 and then again in 1999, prepared through lengthy consultation among the Army, the Louisiana State Historic Preservation Office, and the Advisory Council on Historic Preservation, provided detailed standards, procedures, and goals for the cultural resource program on the installation, which were adopted with the acceptance and implementation of these documents. These encompassed areas such as specific requirements for field investigation by project type (i.e., procedures to be used during intensive survey, site testing, and data-recovery/large-scale excavations), reporting standards by project type, curation standards, National Register of Historic Places evaluation standards and eligibility criteria to be used on Fort Polk, and treatment standards for historic properties (i.e., monitoring, stabilization, protection). Short- and long-term goals included such things as completing the National Register of Historic Places evaluation of all cultural resources found on the installation, expanding public outreach programs, ensuring the protection of cultural resources on the installation, and improving records management to facilitate greater access to and use of existing collections and reports. Preservation planning works when organizational/agency commitment is there, as it has been at Fort Polk. All of the standards and procedures advanced in the 1988 and 1999 Historic Preservation Plans were implemented and have been used to guide all subsequent cultural resource work on the installation, and all of the specific goals put forth in 1988 and most of those advanced in 1999 have been achieved, with the rest under active implementation.

Lessons Learned

When archaeological and historical data exist from large numbers of sites, as they do at Fort Polk (and from many other installations and, indeed, from each state), they need to be compiled and then carefully examined. Analyses of large numbers of assemblages, it is clear, can help us understand what was occurring at individual sites and help put the sites in a larger perspective as part of geographically extensive settlement systems and long-lasting cultural traditions or patterns of land use. Well-controlled test excavations at large numbers of sites, furthermore, can be as useful in building a cultural sequence as the extensive excavation of a few large, dense sites. Compiling primary data about nearly 5,000 sites and isolated finds spread over dozens of reports and in thousands of pages of records, however, requires immense effort. The payoff comes when these data are put to use, as we have tried to do here. Much more can and should be done with the primary electronic/ Geographic Information System data files available from Fort Polk, however, and we hope that researchers coming after us will make use of these data to go further than we have been able to and to learn new things about past life in this part of Louisiana.

We have also learned that while predictive models are valuable for guiding research and for telling us where on the landscape sites are likely to be located, we must avoid taking these models too seriously, that is, letting them become self-fulfilling prophecies about what is actually out there. The Low Probability Zone at Fort Polk, for example, contains significant sites, just not as many as the High Probability Zone. It still must be carefully examined. We must also continually evaluate the accuracy and effectiveness of our predictive models. Current research on Fort Polk, for example, has shown that sites may be present in floodplain as well as upland settings, deeply buried by colluvial or alluvial processes. Our knowledge of these areas remains limited; yet they too must be carefully examined. Sites of all periods are frequently found on elevated settings bordering major stream channels on Fort Polk. Occupation appears to have favored these areas because they were only infrequently flooded. Understanding former drainage patterns is thus also critical to locating archaeological and historical resources.

Most of the large, artifact-rich assemblages found on Fort Polk appear to be the remains of numerous small, short-duration visits rather than of one or a few periods of extended activity or settlement. We are just beginning to understand how to examine such sites through distributional and computer-mapping analyses directed to resolving individual components within the larger scatters (e.g., see Cantley et al. 1997:879–921). Gridded shovel test data have been collected from hundreds of sites on Fort Polk in recent years and constitute a vast database that can be used to conduct analyses of this kind. Close-interval shovel testing, we have learned, is an excellent means of resolving internal site structure, a necessary first step in most testing and large-scale excavation programs. Density maps can be used to locate and interpret individual concentrations and components and to guide the placement of larger test units in subsequent intensive testing programs, should these prove necessary.

We have also learned that, given the sandy soils and mixed artifact deposits that occur widely over Fort Polk, only limited information about chronology and culture history and the nature of individual occupations can be obtained through the hand excavation of large block units in sites with dense but somewhat mixed artifact assemblages. At least as much can be learned from numerous small stratigraphic columns, as the intensive testing program has demonstrated. Large block units like those used in the five data-recovery excavations undertaken to date at Fort Polk, while useful in establishing the broad outline of the local cultural sequence, were far too small to fully expose activity areas or the remains of possible camp structures. However, in settings where feature preservation is poor, as at Fort Polk, the locations of prehistoric camp huts, tents, or other structures can still be identified by the presence of distributional voids or low-density areas (e.g., Sassaman 1993b; Sassaman and Green 1993). Such places are missed if the block units cover comparatively small areas or are opened in the densest parts of sites. People only rarely live where they dump most of their trash, but those are the areas on which archaeologists tend to focus.

A number of alternative approaches to site excavation on Fort Polk have been advanced that should result in an improvement in information return (Cantley et al. 1993b:260–262). First, more geoarchaeological research is needed at the start of excavations to determine whether particular occupations are tied to particular strata or surfaces. Second, thinner (i.e., 5 cm) levels should be employed to increase stratigraphic resolution. Third, if the goal of the research is cultural historical, that is, the resolution of cultural sequences and chronology, smaller blocks (i.e., probably no more than 2 x 2 m or 4 x 4 m in extent) should be used, with careful vertical controls adopted, specifically the use of thin (i.e., 5 cm) arbitrary levels following natural stratigraphy wherever possible. Fourth, excavation of larger block units should proceed only if clear stratigraphic breaks are evident between components and there is minimal evidence for mixing. Finally, when discrete single-component occupation surfaces are recognized, heavy equipment can be used to remove overburden to just above the target horizon over a larger area, followed by the excavation of blocks encompassing a minimum of several hundred square meters. The procedure can be repeated for each successive occupation surface if these are separated by sufficient sterile deposits. Greater attention to single-component assemblages rather than excavations into mixed deposits, as well as the excavation of large areas, are clearly called for in future work on Fort Polk.

In other words, small, single-component sites are much easier to interpret and learn information about the past from than larger, more complex multicomponent sites. This point has been forcefully expressed by the Prentice Thomas and Associates, Inc., intensive site-testing team, who noted:

> It seems clear, after 20 years of professional work at Fort Polk, that single component sites or areas within sites are our best hope for coming to terms with the prehistoric occupations which are obviously present at Fort Polk. The only problem with an exclusively single component approach is that such places may have been relatively unattractive and, therefore, little utilized.
>
> Although multiple component sites are certainly useful for the initial establishment of a regional chronology, the separation of components at the typical Fort Polk multiple component site, where the components are vertically stacked at the same spot, has ranged in difficulty from analytically trying to nightmarish. Single component sites or multiple component sites in which the separations are horizontal are far less problematic [Morehead et al. 1995a:136].

Much greater consideration should be given, we believe, to sites with intact or minimally disturbed single-component assemblages, as well as to stratigraphically or horizontally isolated components within large, multicomponent sites.

The importance of intrasite distributional analysis cannot be overstated. An inexpensive procedure, it permits great savings in resources, helps guide unit placement during subsequent fieldwork, and allows for more accurate interpretation of site assemblages. Density/distribution maps can be produced quickly and easily and can reveal the existence of concentrations indicative of discrete components or else areas within landforms that were more intensively utilized in the past, perhaps because of microtopographic conditions (i.e., slightly better drainage, proximity to water). With such maps it becomes possible to place test units in or near all of the major concentrations on a site. Important areas are thus much less likely to be missed. More accurate unit placement will also lead to more accurate identification of what is being explored. Having such distribution maps may actually preclude the need for as many units as might be excavated at some sites, because concentrations can be precisely targeted.

The size of the concentrations revealed by such mapping, furthermore, can provide clues about the nature of the activities that formed them. Thus, small, discrete concentrations of artifacts may represent a number of separate camp or special-activity sites, each perhaps formed by a few people (see Figure 3.3). Where more extensive concentrations are observed, they may represent the activities of larger groups. Rings of debris, for example, might indicate a number of families were present, perhaps with the placement of a number of structures around an open area (Cantley et al. 1997:879–900). This is a more satisfying approach to site interpretation than simply and uncritically attributing components with large quantities of debris to the remains of extended settlement and calling components with comparatively few artifacts temporary work stations or special-activity areas, an approach that, unfortunately, has dominated much of the survey and testing work undertaken to date in the Southeast. Adding spatial information about the size and density of individual concentrations thus gives us a much better picture of what was occurring on these landforms in the past and a better basis for making decisions about how to evaluate and manage these resources.

Final Thoughts

Fort Polk bears traces of some of the first peoples to enter the New World upward of 13,500 years ago and has particularly dense occupations at the very end of the Pleistocene era some 11,000 to 12,500 years ago. Over the next 10,000 years, Indian groups from around the region came to the area to obtain stone for their tools, staying for longer or shorter periods. How these occupations are recognized and the kinds of activities people did when they were in the Fort Polk area have been the focus for much of the research that has taken place on the installation, as summarized here. Much has been learned about these first peoples, but much more can and should be done.

Historic settlement of the Fort Polk region, we have also seen, was influenced by the clash of European nations struggling for control of the New World, which created a lawless neutral zone in western Louisiana. Once that struggle was over, Fort Polk was bypassed by most westward-streaming pioneers for more fertile soils along the Calcasieu and Anacoco—or farther on in east Texas. Hardly the best of agricultural lands, the "hogwallow lands" of Fort Polk were avoided. Still, a few farmers and intrepid hunter-stockmen ventured into the area, settling close by the creeks and streams where narrow bands of fertile soils might allow a stand of corn. Undeveloped, it was largely without strategic value during the Civil War. Texas farmers-turned-soldiers only wanted to get through west-central Louisiana rather than occupy it, and the Union armies saw no cotton worth going after. Therefore, as in the Appalachian and Ozark regions, west-central Louisiana men marched off to war, leaving the area to outlaws and guerillas. Since no major armies passed through the region, many of the farms probably escaped the destruction that left the rest of the South a wasteland.

After the war, west-central Louisiana began to fill with people seeking a new beginning. Eventually, a few found the hogwallow lands a good place to live. But just as postbellum settlement was gaining momentum, the farmers were beaten to the land by speculators who saw the land's greatest resource, its trees, as a prime investment. This checked intensive settlement until the arrival of the railroad at the turn of the century transformed both the landscape and the culture of Vernon Parish. With the railroad came the means to remove the trees, and the quiet piney woods filled with the sounds of falling trees and steam engines. Mill towns sprang out of nowhere, their iron tentacles reaching deep into the woods and extracting the trees. Within a period not exceeding 25 years, some 10,000 years of natural pine forest development was obliterated. Meanwhile, over this same brief blink in time, the normally scattered population drew into dense clusters, first in southern Vernon Parish and the main part of Fort Polk, then in the northern part around Peason Ridge. When the trees were gone, these clusters of human occupation disappeared along with the trees. Left behind were stumps, tramlines, Herty cups, and ghost towns. The few people who stayed behind scattered again. They were mostly the same people or kin of the people who had been there before the mills opened. They simply put down their axes and picked up their plows.

In the 1930s, the Fort Polk landscape consisted of vast empty stump lands surrounding small tracts of cultivation. Acres upon acres of lands never farmed were never to be farmed, for the timber companies sold the land to the Forest Service, which promptly started replanting. One hundred and forty years earlier, European nations had dictated the course of land use and settlement at Fort Polk; now they did so again. War in Europe brought the U.S. Army to west-central Louisiana and the creation of Fort Polk. Today, the land is managed as a pine forest and military training center. Pine trees once again dominate the landscape.

If one were asked what best represents 10,000 years of human occupation in west-central Louisiana, one might be tempted to point to the three most ubiquitous, and least attractive, artifacts found scattered across its landscape: chert flakes, fired clay Herty cups, and hot sauce bottles. While this might seem a flippant response, it is not meant so. Geoarchaeological evidence points to a stable piney woods landscape. For most of those 10,000 years, Native Americans exploited the region's abundant woodland resources through seasonal hunting and gathering. Highly mobile, these Native Americans moved constantly and rarely settled for long periods of time or in densely populated clusters. Through the years Native American culture varied, but no matter their style of pottery or pattern of settlement they all camped at night and sharpened stone tools and spear and arrow points, leaving behind small chips. Historic settlement of the region was equally dispersed. However, for one fleeting moment in this long era, the entire landscape was radically, even catastrophically changed. While Herty cups do not represent timbering directly, turpentining is a related industry, and broken cups are so plentiful they can be considered part of the landscape, especially as they are typically not collected during archaeological survey. What better artifact to represent this fleeting moment of furious human activity. Today, the army maneuvers across Fort Polk's recovering pine forests. Soldiers carry with them meal kits, and in Louisiana these kits are often spiced with small, individual-serving hot sauce bottles. Army policy is for soldiers to carry out what they carry in, but these little glass bottles can often be found at the abandoned "hunting" camps of the modern army. Chert, baked clay, and glass—durable testimony to 10,000 and more years of human occupation.

References Cited

Abrams, Cynthia L., Steven D. Smith, Mark D. Groover, Ramona M. Grunden, Jill S. Quattlebaum, and Christopher Ohm Clement (editors)
1995   *Exploring Fort Polk: Results of an 8,027-Acre Survey in the Main Fort and Peason Ridge Portions of the Fort Polk Military Reservation, Vernon and Natchitoches Parishes, Louisiana.* South Carolina Institute of Archaeology and Anthropology, Cultural Resources Div., University of South Carolina, Columbia.

Adams, William H.
1977   *Silcott, Washington: Ethnoarchaeology of a Rural American Community.* Report of Investigations 54, Laboratory of Anthropology, Washington State University, Pullman.
1990   Landscape Archaeology, Landscape History, and the American Farmstead. In *Historical Archaeology on Southern Plantations and Farms,* edited by Charles E. Orser, Jr. *Historical Archaeology* 24(4):92–101.

Adams, William H. (editor)
1980   *Waverly Plantation: Ethnoarchaeology of a Tenant Farming Community.* National Technical Information Service, Washington, D.C.

Adams, William H., and Steven D. Smith
1985   Historical Perspectives on Black Tenant Farmer Material Culture: The Henry C. Long General Store Ledger at Waverly Plantation, Mississippi. In *The Archaeology of Slavery and Plantation Life,* edited by Theresa Singleton, pp. 309–334. Academic Press, New York.

Adams, William H., Steven D. Smith, David F. Barton, Timothy B. Riordan, and Stephen Poyser
1981   *Bay Springs Mill: Historical Archaeology of a Rural Mississippi Cotton Milling Community.* National Technical Information Service, Washington, D.C.

Adovasio, James M., D. Pedler, J. Donahue, and R. Stuckenrath
1999   No Vestiges of a Beginning nor Prospect for an End: Two Decades of Debate on Meadowcroft Rockshelter. In *Ice Age Peoples of North America: Environments, Origins, and Adaptations of the First Americans,* edited by Robson Bonnichsen and Karen L. Turnmire, pp. 416–431. Center for the Study of the First Americans, Oregon State University, Corvallis.

Advisory Council on Historic Preservation
1986   *Section 106 Step-by-Step.* Washington, D.C.
1989   *The Section 110 Guidelines: Annotated Guidelines for Federal Agency Responsibilities under Section 110 of the National Historic Preservation Act.* Washington, D.C.

Alexandria *Daily Town Talk*
1983   *Alexandria Daily Town Talk Centennial Album.* McCormick & Co., Allen, Louisiana.

Allaby, Alisa, and Michael Allaby (editors)
1999   *A Dictionary of Earth Sciences.* Oxford University Press, Oxford, England.

Allen, Ruth A.
1961   *East Texas Lumber Workers: An Economic and Social Picture, 1870–1950.* University of Texas Press, Austin.

Alley, R. B., D. A. Meese, C. A. Shuman, A. J. Gow, K. C. Taylor, P. M. Grootes, J. W. C. White, M. Ram, E. D. Waddington, P. A. Mayewski, and G. A. Zielinski
  1993   Abrupt Increase in Greenland Snow Accumulation at the End of the Younger Dryas Event. *Nature* 362:527–529.
American Lumberman
  1922   To Handle Chicago Sales. *American Lumberman* Chicago Whole Number 2463, July 29:73.
  1923   A Successful Lumber Organization Built by Good Management and Efficient Service. *American Lumberman* Chicago Whole Number 2496, March 17:46–47.
Anderson, David G.
  1984   The Ceramic Analysis. In *Cultural Resources Evaluations, Fort Polk, Louisiana*, edited by Charles E. Cantley and John R. Kern, pp. 243–252. Report R-2639, Gilbert/Commonwealth, Jackson, Michigan.
  1985   The Robert Chowning and Frank E. Chowning Collection: Lithic Artifacts from the Surface of the Toltec Mounds Site. Ms. submitted to the Arkansas Archeological Survey, Fayetteville. Copies available on request from the author.
  1989   Archaeology and History in West-Central Louisiana: Research Results of the Fort Polk Cultural Resources Program. In *Historic Preservation Planning on Military Bases: An Example from Fort Polk, Louisiana*, by David G. Anderson, L. Janice Campbell, James E. Cobb, John E. Ehrenhard, and Prentice M. Thomas, Jr., pp. 30–74. Interaction Special Publication No. 3, Interagency Archeological Services Div., NPS, Atlanta.
  1990   The Paleoindian Colonization of Eastern North America: A View from the Southeastern United States. In *Early Paleoindian Economies of Eastern North America*, edited by Kenneth B. Tankersley and Barry L. Isaac, pp. 163–216. Research in Economic Anthropology, Supplement 5. JAI Press, Greenwich, Connecticut.
  1995   Paleoindian Interaction Networks in the Eastern Woodlands. In *Native American Interactions, Multiscalar Analyses and Interpretations in the Eastern Woodlands*, edited by Michael S. Nassaney and Kenneth E. Sassaman, pp. 3–26. University of Tennessee Press, Knoxville.
  1996a   Modeling Regional Settlement in the Archaic Period Southeast. In *The Archaeology of the Mid-Holocene Southeast*, edited by Kenneth E. Sassaman and David G. Anderson, pp. 157–176. University Presses of Florida, Gainesville.
  1996b   Models of Paleoindian and Early Archaic Settlement in the Southeastern United States. In *The Paleoindian and Early Archaic Southeast*, edited by David G. Anderson and Kenneth E. Sassaman, pp. 29–57. University of Alabama Press, Tuscaloosa.
  1999   *JRTC and Fort Polk Historic Preservation Plan Cultural Resources Inventory Primary Data: Management Summary (Site Master List and National Register of Historic Places Determinations)*. Southeast Archeological Center, NPS, Tallahassee.
  2001   Climate and Culture Change in Prehistoric and Early Historic Eastern North America. *Archaeology of Eastern North America* 29:143–186.
  2002   The Evolution of Tribal Social Organization in the Southeast. In *The Archaeology of Tribal Societies*, edited by William A. Parkinson. International Monographs in Prehistory, Ann Arbor, Michigan, in press.
  n.d. a   Paleoindian Occupations in the Southeastern United States. In *New Directions in First American Studies: Extended Abstracts from the 1999 Clovis and Beyond Conference, Sante Fe, New Mexico*, edited by Bradley T. Lepper. Center for the Study of the First Americans, Texas A&M University, College Station, in press. Ms. on file, Southeast Archeological Center, NPS, Tallahassee.

n.d. b   The Pleistocene Human Occupation of the Southeastern United States: Research
          Directions for the Early Twenty-first Century. In *Beyond Clovis,* edited by Robsen
          Bonnichsen. Center for the Study of the First Americans, Texas A&M University,
          College Station, in press. Ms. on file, Southeast Archeological Center, NPS, Tal-
          lahassee.

Anderson, David G., and Michael K. Faught
   1998   The Distribution of Fluted Paleoindian Projectile Points: Update 1998. *Archaeol-
          ogy of Eastern North America* 26:163–187.
   2000   Paleoindian Artefact Distributions: Evidence and Implications. *Antiquity* 74:507–
          513.

Anderson, David G., and Glen T. Hanson
   1988   Early Archaic Settlement in the Southeastern United States: A Case Study from
          the Savannah River Basin. *American Antiquity* 53:262–286.

Anderson, David G., and Vince Macek
   1987   *Fort Polk Historic Preservation Plan Inventory Map Volume: Site Location Maps,
          Cultural Resource Probability Zones, and Areas Surveyed to Date on Fort Polk.*
          Garrow and Assoc., Atlanta.

Anderson, David G., and Robert C. Mainfort, Jr.
   2002   An Introduction to Woodland Archaeology in the Southeast. In *The Woodland
          Southeast,* edited by David G. Anderson and Robert C. Mainfort, Jr., pp. 1–19.
          University of Alabama Press, Tuscaloosa.

Anderson, David G., and Kenneth E. Sassaman (editors)
   1996   *The Paleoindian and Early Archaic Southeast.* University of Alabama Press,
          Tuscaloosa.

Anderson, David G., and Harry G. Scheele
   1993   *Proposed Revision and Updating: Fort Polk, Louisiana Historic Preservation
          Plan.* Interagency Archeological Services, NPS, Atlanta.

Anderson, David G., and Steven D. Smith
   1999   *Fort Polk Historic Preservation Plan Cultural Resources Action Plan/Planning
          Manual.* Southeast Archeological Center, NPS, Tallahassee.

Anderson, David G., and James R. Wilson (assemblers)
   1988   *Fort Polk Historic Preservation Plan.* Vol. 1, *Technical Synthesis of Cultural Re-
          source Investigations, Fort Polk, Louisiana* (David G. Anderson, J.W. Joseph, and
          Mary Beth Reed); Vol. 2, *Cultural Resources Planning Manual* (James R. Wil-
          son, David G. Anderson, and J. W. Joseph); Vol. 3, *Comprehensive Cultural Re-
          sources Inventory* (David G. Anderson); Vol. 4, *Inventory Map Volume* (David G.
          Anderson and Vince Macek). Contract CX5000-7-0007 final report prepared by
          Garrow and Assoc., for Interagency Archeological Services Div., NPS, Atlanta.

Anderson, David G., Dennis Finch, J. W. Joseph, Jenalee Muse, Marion Roberts, and Thomas
R. Wheaton
   1987   *Fort Polk Historic Preservation Plan Comprehensive Cultural Resources Inven-
          tory.* Garrow and Assoc., Atlanta.

Anderson, David G., J. W. Joseph, and Mary Beth Reed
   1988   *Fort Polk Historic Preservation Plan Technical Synthesis of Cultural Resource
          Investigations, Fort Polk, Louisiana.* Garrow and Assoc., Atlanta.

Anderson, David G., L. Janice Campbell, James E. Cobb, John E. Ehrenhard, and Prentice
M. Thomas, Jr.
   1989   *Historic Preservation Planning on Military Bases: An Example from Fort Polk,
          Louisiana.* Interaction Special Publication No. 3, Interagency Archeological Ser-
          vices Div., NPS, Atlanta.

Anderson, David G., Chris Rewerts, and Kim Majerus
  1996a   *JRTC and Fort Polk Historic Preservation Plan Inventory Map Volume: Site Lo-
          cations, Areas Surveyed, and Cultural Resource Probability Zones, Fort Polk,
          Louisiana.* Southeast Archeological Center, NPS, Tallahassee.
Anderson, David G., Lisa D. O'Steen, and Kenneth E. Sassaman
  1996b   Environmental and Chronological Considerations. In *The Paleoindian and Early
          Archaic Southeast,* edited by David G. Anderson and Kenneth E. Sassaman, pp.
          3–15. University of Alabama Press, Tuscaloosa.
Anderson, David G., Tiffanie Bourassa, Cindy Abrams, Mark Groover, J. W. Joseph, Kim
Majerus, Jenalee Muse, and Chris Rewerts
  1999a   *JRTC and Fort Polk Historic Preservation Plan Cultural Resources Inventory
          Primary Data.* Southeast Archeological Center, NPS, Tallahassee.
Anderson, David G., J. W. Joseph, Mary Beth Reed, and Steven D. Smith
  1999b   *JRTC and Fort Polk Historic Preservation Plan. Prehistory and History in West-
          ern Louisiana: A Technical Synthesis of Cultural Resource Investigations.* South-
          east Archeological Center, NPS, Tallahassee.
Anderson, Harold V.
  1960   *Geology of Sabine Parish.* Dept. of Conservation, Louisiana Geological Survey,
          Bulletin 24, Baton Rouge.
Anderson, S. S. (Adjutant General)
  1864   Letter to Maj. General Magruder, March 5. In *War of the Rebellion: The Official
          Record of the Union and Confederate Armies in the War of the Rebellion,* series 1,
          part 2, vol. 34:1027. GPO, Washington, D.C.
Anonymous
  n.d. a Lumber Industry. Paper in Vertical files, Vernon Parish Library, Leesville.
  n.d. b Fact Sheet. Vertical files, Vernon Parish. Hill Memorial Library, Louisiana State
          University, Baton Rouge.
Arensberg, Conrad M.
  1955   American Communities. *American Anthropologist* 57(6):1143–1162.
Armstrong, Amos Lee
  1958   *Sabine Parish Story: Land of Green Gold.* Jones and Stringfellow Printing Com-
          pany, Shreveport, Louisiana.
Arnold, Steven Gordon
  1934   *The Operation of the Unit County System of School Control in Vernon Parish,
          Louisiana.* Master's thesis, University of Oklahoma, Norman.
Aten, Lawrence E.
  1967   *Excavations at the Jamison Site (41LB2), Liberty County, Texas.* Report No. 1,
          Houston Archeological Society.
  1983   *Indians of the Upper Texas Coast.* Academic Press, New York.
Aten, Lawrence E., and Charles N. Bollich
  1969   A Preliminary Report on the Development of a Ceramic Chronology for the Sabine
          Lake Area of Texas and Louisiana. *Bulletin of the Texas Archeological Society*
          40:241–258.
Baker, William S., and Clarence H. Webb
  1976   Catahoula Type Projectile Points. *Louisiana Archaeology* (Lafayette) 3:225–251.
Banks, Larry D.
  1990   *From Mountain Peaks to Alligator Stomachs: A Review of Lithic Sources in the
          Trans-Mississippi South, the Southern Plains, and Adjacent Southwest.* Oklahoma
          Anthropological Society Memoir 4, Tulsa.

Barbour, E. H., and C. B. Schultz
  1932   The Scottsbluff Bison Quarry and Its Artifacts. *Nebraska State Museum Bulletin* 34(1).
Bartlett, Charles S., Jr.
  1963   The Tom's Brook Site, 3JO1: A Preliminary Report. In *Arkansas Archeology 1962,* edited by Charles R. McGimsey III, pp. 18–65. Arkansas Archeological Society, Fayetteville.
Bee, H. P. (Brigadier General)
  1864   Letter to Brigadier General J. E. Slaughter, April 1. In *War of the Rebellion: The Official Record of the Union and Confederate Armies in the War of the Rebellion,* series 1, part 3, vol. 34:722. GPO, Washington, D.C.
Belisle, John G.
  1912   *History of Sabine Parish, Louisiana.* Sabine Banner Press, Many, Louisiana.
Bell, Robert E.
  1958   *Guide to the Identification of Certain American Indian Projectile Points.* Special Bulletin No. 1, Oklahoma Anthropological Society, Norman.
  1960   *Guide to the Identification of Certain American Indian Projectile Points.* Special Bulletin No. 2, Oklahoma Anthropological Society, Norman.
  1980   Fourche Maline: An Archaeological Manifestation in Eastern Oklahoma. *Louisiana Archaeology* 6:83–125.
Belmont, John S.
  1967   The Culture Sequence at the Greenhouse Site, Louisiana. *Southeastern Archaeological Conference Bulletin* 6:27–34.
  1982   The Troyville Concept and the Gold Mine Site. *Louisiana Archaeology* 9:63–98.
Bender, Barbara
  1985a   Emergent Tribal Formations in the American Midcontinent. *American Antiquity* 50(1):52–62.
  1985b   Prehistoric Developments in the American Midcontinent and in Brittany, Northwest France. In *Prehistoric Hunter-Gatherers: The Emergence of Cultural Complexity,* edited by T. D. Price and J. A. Brown, pp. 21–57. Academic Press, Orlando.
Bennett, W. J., Jr.
  1982   *Cultural Resources Survey on the Vernon Ranger District, Kisatchie National Forest, Vernon Parish, Louisiana.* Archaeological Assessments Report 13, Pineville, Louisiana.
Bense, Judith A.
  1994   *Archaeology of the Southeastern United States: Paleoindian to World War I.* Academic Press, San Diego.
Bergeron, Arthur W.
  1989   *Guide to Louisiana Confederate Military Units 1861–1865.* Louisiana State University Press, Baton Rouge.
Bernstein, Nancy
  1984   The Oral History Project at Fort Polk. In *Cultural Resources Evaluations, Fort Polk, Louisiana,* edited by Charles E. Cantley and John R. Kern, pp. 263–279. Report R-2639, Gilbert/Commonwealth, Jackson, Michigan.
Bianchi, T. H.
  1983   Geomorphic Setting in the Fort Polk Region: An Abstract. In *U.S.L. Fort Polk Archaeological Survey and Cultural Resources Management Program,* 2 vols., edited by A. Frank Servello, pp. 71–76. University of Southwestern Louisiana, Lafayette.

Binford, Lewis R.
  1979   Organization and Formation Processes: Looking at Curated Technologies. *Journal of Anthropological Research* 35:255–273.
  1980   Willow Smoke and Dogs' Tails: Hunter-Gatherer Settlement Systems and Archaeological Site Formation. *American Antiquity* 45:4–20.
  1982   The Archaeology of Place. *Journal of Anthropological Archaeology* 1:5–31.
  2001   *Constructing Frames of Reference: An Analytical Method for Archaeological Theory Building Using Hunter-Gatherer and Environmental Data Sets.* University of California Press, Berkeley.
Björck, S., B. Kromer, S. Johnson, O. Bennike, D. Hammarlund, G. Lemdahl, G. Possnert, T. L. Rasmuson, B. Wohlfarth, C. U. Hammer, and M. Spurk
  1996   Synchronized Terrestrial-Atmospheric Deglacial Records around the North Atlantic. *Science* 274:1155–1160.
Blitz, John H.
  1988   Adoption of the Bow in Prehistoric North America. *North American Archaeologist* 9(2):123–145.
Block, William T.
  1996   *Early Sawmill Towns of the Louisiana-Texas Borderlands.* Dogwood Press, Woodville, Texas.
Bolton, Charles C.
  1994   *Poor Whites of the Antebellum South: Tenants and Laborers in Central North Carolina and Northeast Mississippi.* Duke University Press, Durham, North Carolina.
Bolton, Herbert Eugene
  1962   *Texas in the Middle Eighteenth Century.* Reprinted. University of California Publications in History, vol. 3. University of California Press, Berkeley. Originally published 1915, Russell and Russell, New York.
Bond, Stanley C., Jr.
  1987   The Development of the Naval Stores Industry in St. John's County, Florida. *Florida Anthropologist* 40(3):187–202.
Bonnichsen, Robson
  1991   Clovis Origins. In *Clovis Origins and Adaptations,* edited by Robson Bonnichsen and Karen L. Turnmire, pp. 309–329. Center for the Study of the First Americans, Oregon State University, Corvallis.
Bonnichsen, Robson, and Karen L. Turnmire
  1999   An Introduction to the Peopling of the Americas. In *Ice Age Peoples of North America: Environments, Origins, and Adaptations of the First Americans,* edited by Robson Bonnichsen and Karen L. Turnmire, pp. 1–26. Center for the Study of the First Americans, Oregon State University, Corvallis.
Bourgeois, Philip D., Jr., Paul LaHaye, James R. Morehead, James H. Mathews, Prentice M. Thomas, Jr., and L. Janice Campbell
  1999   *Fort Polk 43: The Results of a Forty-Third Program of Site Testing at Ten Sites, Fort Polk Military Reservation, Vernon Parish, Louisiana.* Prentice Thomas and Assoc., Report of Investigations No. 431, Fort Walton Beach, Florida.
Bradley, Bruce A.
  1997   Sloan Site Biface and Projectile Point Technology. In *Sloan: A Paleoindian Dalton Cemetery in Arkansas,* edited by Dan F. Morse, pp. 53–57. Smithsonian Institution Press, Washington, D.C.
Brassieur, Charles R.
  1983   Analysis of Cultural Materials Recovered by Peason Ridge Surveys. In *U.S.L.*

Fort Polk Archaeological Survey and Cultural Resources Management Program, 2 vols., edited by A. Frank Servello, pp. 237–328. University of Southwestern Louisiana, Lafayette.

Braun, David P., and Stephen Plog

1982 Evolution of "Tribal" Social Networks: Theory and Prehistoric North American Evidence. *American Antiquity* 47:504–525.

Broecker, Wallace S.

2001 Was the Medieval Warm Period Global? *Science* 291:1497–1499.

Brown, C. B.

1945 *Louisiana Trees and Shrubs.* Louisiana Commission of Forestry, Baton Rouge.

Brown, David O.

1982a Ceramic Analysis. In *Eagle Hill: A Late Quaternary Upland Site in Western Louisiana,* edited by Joel D. Gunn and David O. Brown, pp. 260–277. Special Report 12, Center for Archaeological Research, University of Texas at San Antonio.

1982b Chemical Analysis of Ceramics and Lithics from the Eagle Hill II Site. In *Eagle Hill: A Late Quaternary Upland Site in Western Louisiana,* edited by Joel D. Gunn and David O. Brown, pp. 163–180. Special Report 12, Center for Archaeological Research, San Antonio.

1984 Geomorphology of the Eagle Hill–Peason Ridge Area. In *Occupation and Settlement in the Uplands of Western Louisiana,* edited by Joel D. Gunn and Anne C. Kerr, pp. 15–31. Special Report 17, Center for Archaeological Research, University of Texas at San Antonio.

Brown, Ian W.

1984 Late Prehistory in Coastal Louisiana: The Coles Creek Period. In *Perspectives on Gulf Coast Prehistory,* edited by Dave D. Davis, pp. 94–124. University of Florida Press, Gainesville.

1994 Recent Trends in the Archaeology of the Southeastern United States. *Journal of Archaeological Research* 2:45–111.

Brown, James A.

1985 Long Term Trends to Sedentism and the Emergence of Complexity in the American Midwest. In *Prehistoric Hunter-Gatherers, The Emergence of Cultural Complexity,* edited by T. Douglas Price and James A. Brown, pp. 201–231. Academic Press, Orlando.

Brown, James A., and Robert K. Vierra

1983 What Happened in the Middle Archaic? Introduction to an Ecological Approach to Koster Site Archaeology. In *Archaic Hunters and Gatherers in the American Midwest,* edited by James Phillips and James A. Brown, pp. 165–195. Academic Press, New York.

Brown, Nelson C.

1919 *Forest Products: Their Manufacture and Use.* John Wiley & Sons, New York.

Brown, Robert F., P. G. Pye, and G. R. Carver

1935 Annual Report of Vernon Relief Fund, Report for Fiscal Year January through December 1935. Leesville. On file, Hill Memorial Library, Louisiana State University, Baton Rouge.

Broyles, Bettye J.

1966 Preliminary Report: The St. Albans Site (46KA27), Kanawha County, West Virginia. *West Virginia Archaeologist* 19:1–43.

Buchner, C. Andrew

2000 Literature and Records Search Results. In *An Intensive Phase I Cultural Resources Survey of 6,535 Acres within Portions of Training Areas Sixmile Creek 1, 2, & 3, and Slagle 7, 8, 9, 10 & 11 on Fort Polk Military Reservation, Vernon Parish, Louisiana,* edited by Andrew Saatkamp, C. Andrew Buchner, and Jay Gray, pp. 47–54. Panamerican Consultants, Memphis.

2001 Literature and Records Search Results. In *A Cultural Resources Survey of 4,212 Acres on Fort Polk Military Reservation and the Limited Use Area, Vernon Parish, Louisiana,* by Andrew Saatkamp, C. Andrew Buchner, and Jay Gray, pp. 51–70. Panamerican Consultants, Memphis.

2002 Literature and Records Search Results. In *A Cultural Resources Survey of 4,862 Acres in the Limited Use Area/Kisatchie National Forest, Vernon Parish, Louisiana,* edited by Paul D. Bundy and C. Andrew Buchner, pp. 61–73. Panamerican Consultants, Memphis.

Buchner, C. Andrew, and Andrew Saatkamp

2000 Summary and Discussion. In *An Intensive Phase I Cultural Resources Survey of 6,535 Acres within Portions of Training Areas Sixmile Creek 1, 2, & 3, and Slagle 7, 8, 9, 10 & 11 on Fort Polk Military Reservation, Vernon Parish, Louisiana,* edited by Andrew Saatkamp, C. Andrew Buchner, and Jay Gray, pp. 195–205. Panamerican Consultants, Memphis.

2001 Summary and Discussion. In *A Cultural Resources Survey of 4,212 Acres on Fort Polk Military Reservation and the Limited Use Area, Vernon Parish, Louisiana,* by Andrew Saatkamp, C. Andrew Buchner, and Jay Gray, pp. 287–298. Panamerican Consultants, Memphis.

Bullen, Ripley P.

1975 *A Guide to the Identification of Florida Projectile Points.* Kendall Books, Gainesville, Florida.

Bundy, Paul D.

2002a Laboratory Analysis. In *A Cultural Resources Survey of 4,862 Acres in the Limited Use Area/Kisatchie National Forest, Vernon Parish, Louisiana,* edited by Paul D. Bundy and C. Andrew Buchner, pp. 75–129. Panamerican Consultants, Memphis.

2002b Summary and Discussion. In *A Cultural Resources Survey of 4,862 Acres in the Limited Use Area/Kisatchie National Forest, Vernon Parish, Louisiana,* edited by Paul D. Bundy and C. Andrew Buchner, pp. 649–665. Panamerican Consultants, Memphis.

Bundy, Paul D., and C. Andrew Buchner (editors)

2002 *A Cultural Resources Survey of 4,862 Acres in the Limited Use Area/Kisatchie National Forest, Vernon Parish, Louisiana.* Panamerican Consultants, Memphis.

Bureau of Corporations

1913 *The Lumber Industry,* parts 1–3. Dept. of Commerce and Labor, GPO, Washington.

Burns, Anna C.

1970 *Fullerton, the Mill, the Town, the People, 1907–1927.* Alexandria, Louisiana.

1979 The Gulf Lumber Company, Fullerton: A View of Lumbering during Louisiana's Golden Era. *Louisiana History* 20(2):197–207.

1982 *The Kisatchie Story: A History of Louisiana's Only National Forest.* Ph.D. dissertation, University of Southwestern Louisiana, Lafayette.

Burns, Anna C., and Ronald W. Couch

1994 A History of the Kisatchie National Forest. Kisatchie National Forest, Pineville, Louisiana.

Butler, William B.

1987 Significance and Other Frustrations in the CRM Process. *American Antiquity* 52:820–829.

Byrd, Kathleen M.
1991   *The Poverty Point Culture: Local Manifestations, Subsistence Practices, and Trade Networks.* Geoscience and Man 29. Louisiana State University, Baton Rouge.

Cabak, Melanie A., Kenneth E. Sassaman, and J. Christopher Gillam
1996   *Distributional Archaeology in the Aiken Plateau, Intensive Survey of E Area, Savannah River Site, Aiken County, South Carolina.* Savannah River Archaeological Research Papers 8, Savannah River Archaeological Research Program, South Carolina Institute of Archaeology and Anthropology, University of South Carolina, Columbia.

Cable, John S.
1982a   Differences in Lithic Assemblages of Forager and Collector Strategies. In *Archeological Survey and Reconnaissance within the Ten-Year Floodpool Harry S. Truman Dam and Reservoir,* by Richard L. Taylor, John S. Cable, Andrea L. Novick, and James M. O'Hara, pp. 148–150. Commonwealth Associates, Report R-2324, Jackson, Michigan.
1982b   Organizational Variability in Piedmont Hunter-Gatherer Lithic Assemblages. In *The Haw River Sites: Archaeological Investigation at Two Stratified Sites in the North Carolina Piedmont,* assembled by Stephen R. Claggett and John S. Cable, pp. 637–688. Commonwealth Associates, Report No. 2386, prepared for U.S. Army Corps of Engineers, Wilmington District, Jackson, Michigan.
1996   Haw River Revisited: Implications for Modeling Late Glacial and Early Holocene Hunter-Gatherer Settlement Systems in the Southeast. In *The Paleoindian and Early Archaic Southeast,* edited by David G. Anderson and Kenneth E. Sassaman, pp. 107–148. University of Alabama Press, Tuscaloosa.

Cable, John S., Kenneth F. Styer, and Charles E. Cantley
1998   *Data Recovery Excavations at the Maple Swamp (38HR309) and Big Jones (38HR315) Sites on the Conway Bypass, Horry County, South Carolina: Prehistoric Sequence and Settlement in the North Coastal Plain of South Carolina.* New South Associates, Technical Report 385, Stone Mountain, Georgia.

Caldwell, Joseph R.
1964   Interaction Spheres in Prehistory. In *Hopewellian Studies,* edited by Joseph R. Caldwell and Robert L. Hall, pp. 133–143. Scientific Papers No. 12, Illinois State Museum, Springfield.

Cambron, J. W., and David C. Hulse
1960   The Transitional Paleoindian in North Alabama and South Tennessee. *Journal of Alabama Archaeology* 6:7–33.
1975   *Handbook of Alabama Archaeology.* Part 1, *Point Types,* edited by D. L. DeJarnette. Archeological Research Association of Alabama, Inc.

Campbell, L. Janice, and Prentice M. Thomas, Jr.
1989   Large Scale Survey and Testing Projects at Fort Polk: An Example of Preservation Planning in Action. In *Historic Preservation Planning on Military Bases: An Example from Fort Polk, Louisiana,* by David G. Anderson, L. Janice Campbell, James E. Cobb, John E. Ehrenhard, and Prentice M. Thomas, Jr., pp. 9–29. Interaction Special Publication No. 3, Interagency Archeological Services Div., NPS, Atlanta.

Campbell, L. Janice, and Carol S. Weed
1986   *Cultural Resources Investigations in the Proposed Multipurpose Range Complex Area, Fort Polk, Vernon Parish, Louisiana.* New World Research, Report of Investigations 85-6, Pollock, Louisiana. Contract No. CX5000-5-0015 to Archeological Services Branch, National Park Service, Southeast Regional Office, Atlanta.

Campbell, L. Janice, M. T. Swanson, John L. Lenzer, and Prentice M. Thomas, Jr.
  1980   *A Cultural Resources Survey of the Kisatchie Ranger District, Kisatchie National Forest, Louisiana.* New World Research, Report of Investigations 34, Pollock, Louisiana.
Campbell, L. Janice, Carol S. Weed, J. E. Keller, and J. A. Homburg
  1985   *An Examination of Prehistoric Site Distribution in the Whiskey Chitto Drainage: Results of Judgmental Survey in Portions of Vernon, Beauregard, and Allen Parishes, Louisiana.* New World Research, Report of Investigations 84-20, Pollock, Louisiana.
Campbell, L. Janice, C. Hays, Prentice M. Thomas, Jr., and James H. Mathews
  1987   *Archaeological Testing in the Birds Creek Drainage, Fort Polk Military Reservation, Vernon Parish, Louisiana.* New World Research, Report of Investigations 154, Fort Walton Beach, Florida.
Campbell, L. Janice, James R. Morehead, and A. Frank Servello
  1990   *Data Recovery at 16VN791: A Multi-Component Prehistoric Site in the Birds Creek Drainage, Fort Polk Military Reservation, Fort Polk, Louisiana.* New World Research, Report of Investigations 188, Fort Walton Beach, Florida.
Campbell, L. Janice, James R. Morehead, Prentice M. Thomas, Jr., James H. Mathews, and Joseph Meyer
  1994a *Fort Polk 7: The Results of a Seventh Program of Site Testing at Ten Sites, Fort Polk Military Reservation, Vernon Parish, Louisiana.* Prentice Thomas and Assoc., Report of Investigations No. 234, Fort Walton Beach, Florida.
Campbell, L. Janice, Prentice M. Thomas, Jr., James R. Morehead, James H. Mathews, and Joseph Meyer
  1994b *Fort Polk 9: The Results of a Ninth Program of Site Testing at Ten Sites, Fort Polk Military Reservation, Vernon Parish, Louisiana.* Prentice Thomas and Assoc., Report of Investigations No. 243, Fort Walton Beach, Florida.
Campbell, L. Janice, Joseph Meyer, James R. Morehead, Prentice M. Thomas, Jr., and James H. Mathews
  1997   *Fort Polk 26: The Results of a Twenty-Sixth Program of Site Testing at Ten Sites, Fort Polk Military Reservation, Vernon Parish, Louisiana.* Prentice Thomas and Assoc., Report of Investigations No. 335, Fort Walton Beach, Florida.
Campbell, L. Janice, James R. Morehead, James H. Mathews, Philip D. Bourgeois, Jr., Paul LaHaye, and Prentice M. Thomas, Jr.
  2000   *Fort Polk 48: The Results of a Forty-Eighth Program of Site Testing at Ten Sites, Fort Polk Military Reservation, Vernon Parish, Louisiana.* Prentice Thomas and Assoc., Report of Investigations No. 556, Fort Walton Beach, Florida.
Campbell, L. Janice, James R. Morehead, James H. Mathews, Philip D. Bourgeois, Jr., and Prentice M. Thomas, Jr.
  2001   *Fort Polk 49: The Results of a Forty-Ninth Program of Site Testing at Ten Sites, Fort Polk Military Reservation, Vernon Parish, Louisiana.* Prentice Thomas and Assoc., Report of Investigations No. 626, Fort Walton Beach, Florida.
Campbell, T. N.
  1952   The Kent-Crane Site: A Shell Midden on the Texas Coast. *Bulletin of the Texas Archeological Society* 23:39–77.
Cantley, Charles E.
  1984   Conclusions. In *Cultural Resources Evaluations, Fort Polk, Louisiana,* edited by Charles E. Cantley and John R. Kern, pp. 256–262. Report R-2639, Gilbert/Commonwealth, Jackson, Michigan.
  1993   Lithic Analysis. In *Data Recovery at Site 16VN794: Investigations into Site For-*

mation Processes and the Cultural Sequence of West Central Louisiana, edited by Charles E. Cantley, Leslie E. Raymer, John S. Foss, C. Stiles, Linda Scott Cummings, J. W. Joseph, and J. Raymer, pp. 155–215. New South Associates, Technical Report 119, Stone Mountain, Georgia.

Cantley, Charles E., and H. Edwin Jackson
   1984   Research Design. In *Cultural Resources Evaluations, Fort Polk, Louisiana,* edited by Charles E. Cantley and John R. Kern, pp. 79–95. Report R-2639, Gilbert/ Commonwealth, Jackson, Michigan.

Cantley, Charles E., and John R. Kern (editors)
   1984   *Cultural Resources Evaluations, Fort Polk, Louisiana.* Report R-2639, Gilbert/ Commonwealth, Jackson, Michigan.

Cantley, Charles E., and Leslie E. Raymer
   1993   Data Recovery Design and Methods. In *Data Recovery at Site 16VN794: Investigations into Site Formation Processes and the Cultural Sequence of West Central Louisiana,* edited by Charles E. Cantley, Leslie E. Raymer, John S. Foss, C. Stiles, Linda Scott Cummings, J. W. Joseph, and J. Raymer, pp. 53–94. New South Associates, Technical Report 119, Stone Mountain, Georgia.

Cantley, Charles E., and Joseph Schuldenrein
   1984   Survey Results. In *Cultural Resources Evaluations, Fort Polk, Louisiana,* edited by Charles E. Cantley and John R. Kern, pp. 109–122. Report R-2639, Gilbert/ Commonwealth, Jackson, Michigan.

Cantley, Charles E., and Joseph James Towler
   1984   Site Descriptions. In *Cultural Resources Evaluations, Fort Polk, Louisiana,* edited by Charles E. Cantley and John R. Kern, pp. 123–216. Report R-2639, Gilbert/Commonwealth, Jackson, Michigan.

Cantley, Charles E., Leslie E. Raymer, J. Raymer, and J. W. Joseph
   1993a   Environmental and Cultural Background. In *Data Recovery at Site 16VN794: Investigations into Site Formation Processes and the Cultural Sequence of West Central Louisiana,* edited by Charles E. Cantley, Leslie E. Raymer, John S. Foss, C. Stiles, Linda Scott Cummings, J. W. Joseph, and J. Raymer, pp. 3–52. New South Associates, Technical Report 119, Stone Mountain, Georgia.

Cantley, Charles E., J. W. Joseph, and Leslie E. Raymer
   1993b   Conclusions and Recommendations. In *Data Recovery at Site 16VN794: Investigations into Site Formation Processes and the Cultural Sequence of West Central Louisiana,* edited by Charles E. Cantley, Leslie E. Raymer, John S. Foss, C. Stiles, Linda Scott Cummings, J. W. Joseph, and J. Raymer, pp. 251–262. New South Associates, Technical Report 119, Stone Mountain, Georgia.

Cantley, Charles E., Leslie E. Raymer, John S. Foss, C. Stiles, Linda Scott Cummings, J. W. Joseph, and J. Raymer (editors)
   1993   *Data Recovery at Site 16VN794: Investigations into Site Formation Processes and the Cultural Sequence of West Central Louisiana.* New South Associates, Technical Report 119, Stone Mountain, Georgia.

Cantley, Charles E., L. Danielsson-Murphy, T. Murphy, U. McEnvoy, Leslie E. Raymer, John Cable, R. Yallop, Cindy Rhodes, Mary Beth Reed, and L. A. Abbott
   1997   *Fort Polk, Louisiana: A Phase I Archaeological Survey of 14,622 Acres in Vernon Parish.* New South Associates, Technical Report 427, Stone Mountain, Georgia.

Carlson, Shawn Bonath
   1990   The Persistence of Traditional Lifeways in Central Texas. In *Historical Archaeology on Southern Plantations and Farms,* edited by Charles E. Orser, Jr. *Historical Archaeology* 24(4):50–59.

Carr, Philip J., and Lee Stewart
n.d.   Poverty Point Chipped Stone Raw Materials: Inferring Social and Economic Strategies. In *Big Mounds, Big Power,* edited by Jon L. Gibson and Philip J. Carr. University of Alabama Press, Tuscaloosa, in press.

Casey, Powell A.
1971   *Try Us. The Story of the Washington Artillery in World War II: Louisiana Casualty Lists WWII.* Claitor's Publishing, Reading, Massachusetts.

Chapman, Jefferson
1985   Archaeology and the Archaic Period in the Southern Ridge-and-Valley Province. In *Structure and Process in Southeastern Archaeology,* edited by Roy S. Dickens and H. Trawick Ward, pp. 137–153. Tuscaloosa: University of Alabama Press.

Chipman, Donald E.
1992   *Spanish Texas, 1519–1821.* University of Texas Press, Austin.

Civilian Conservation Corps (CCC)
1937   Official Annual of District E, Fourth Corps Area, Civilian Conservation Corps. On file, Hill Memorial Library, Louisiana State University, Baton Rouge.

Claggett, Stephen R., and John S. Cable (assemblers)
1982   *The Haw River Sites: Archaeological Investigations at Two Stratified Sites in the North Carolina Piedmont.* Commonwealth Associates, Report No. 2386, prepared for U.S. Army Corps of Engineers, Wilmington District.

Clement, Christopher Ohm, and John K. Peterson
1998   Summary and Management Recommendations. In *Archaeological Survey of 12,538 Acres Fort Polk, Vernon Parish, Louisiana,* edited by Christopher Ohm Clement, Ramona M. Grunden, John K. Peterson, Jill S. Quattlebaum, and Steven D. Smith, pp. 411–431. South Carolina Institute of Archaeology and Anthropology, University of South Carolina, Columbia.

Clement, Christopher Ohm, Ramona M. Grunden, and Steven D. Smith
1995   Interpretations. In *Exploring Fort Polk: Results of an 8,027-Acre Survey in the Main Fort and Peason Ridge Portions of the Fort Polk Military Reservation, Vernon and Natchitoches Parishes, Louisiana,* edited by Cynthia L. Abrams, Steven D. Smith, Mark D. Groover, Ramona M. Grunden, Jill S. Quattlebaum, and Christopher Ohm Clement, pp. 405–444. South Carolina Institute of Archaeology and Anthropology, Cultural Resources Div., University of South Carolina, Columbia.

Clement, Christopher Ohm, Steven D. Smith, Ramona M. Grunden, and Jill S. Quattlebaum (editors)
1997   *Archaeological Survey of 4,000 Acres on the Lower Little River, Cumberland, Hoke and Moore Counties, Fort Bragg, North Carolina.* South Carolina Institute of Archaeology and Anthropology, University of South Carolina, Columbia.

Clement, Christopher Ohm, Ramona M. Grunden, John K. Peterson, Jill S. Quattlebaum, and Steven D. Smith (editors)
1998   *Archaeological Survey of 12,538 Acres Fort Polk, Vernon Parish, Louisiana.* South Carolina Institute of Archaeology and Anthropology, University of South Carolina, Columbia.

Clendenen, H. L.
1973   *Settlement Morphology of the Southern Courtois Hills, Missouri, 1820–1860.* Ph.D. dissertation, Louisiana State University, Baton Rouge.

Cloud, Ron
1969   Cache River Side-Notched Points. *Central States Archaeological Journal* 16(3):118–119.

Cobb, James E.
1989   Historic Preservation Planning at Fort Polk. In *Historic Preservation Planning on Military Bases: An Example from Fort Polk, Louisiana,* by David G. Anderson, L. Janice Campbell, James E. Cobb, John E. Ehrenhard, and Prentice M. Thomas, Jr., pp. 1–8. Interaction Special Publication No. 3, Interagency Archeological Services Div., NPS, Atlanta.

Coe, Joffre L.
1964   *The Formative Cultures of the Carolina Piedmont.* Transactions of the American Philosophical Society, n.s., 54, pt. 5. Philadelphia.

Cole, Catherine
1892   Newswoman Details Travels through Vernon Parish during 1880s, 1890s. *New Orleans Daily Picayune.* Republished in *The Leesville Leader,* September 27, 1992. On file, Vernon Parish Library, Leesville, Louisiana.

Coleman, Lisa E.
1992   *Cultural Resources Management Summary 92-12.* Kisatchie National Forest, Pineville, Louisiana.
1993a   *Heritage Resources Management Summary 93-25.* Kisatchie National Forest, Pineville, Louisiana.
1993b   *Heritage Resources Management Summary 93-27.* Kisatchie National Forest, Pineville, Louisiana.
1993c   *Heritage Resources Management Summary 93-31.* Kisatchie National Forest, Pineville, Louisiana.

Collins, Michael B., T. R. Hester, and P. J. Headrick
1992   Engraved Cobbles from the Gault Site, Central Texas. *Current Research in the Pleistocene* 9:3–4.

Completion Report I
1941   Benham Engineering Company. War Department, Office of the Constructing Quartermaster, Leesville, Louisiana. Ms. on file, Real Property Div., Fort Polk.

Completion Report II
1942   U.S. Engineer's Office, Galveston, Texas. On file, Real Property Div., Fort Polk.

Cook, Bernard A., and James R. Watson
1985   *Louisiana Labor: From Slavery to "Right to Work."* University Press of America, New York.

Crass, David Colin, Steven D. Smith, Martha A. Zierden, and Richard D. Brooks (editors)
1998   *The Southern Colonial Backcountry: Interdisciplinary Perspectives on Frontier Communities.* University of Tennessee Press, Knoxville.

Crawford, William H.
1825   Claims to Land between the Rio Hondo and Sabine Rivers in Louisiana. *American State Papers* 445.

Crook, W. W., and R. King Harris
1952   The Trinity Aspect of the Archaic Horizon: The Carrollton and Elam Foci. *Bulletin of the Texas Archeological Society* (Lubbock) 23:7–38.
1954   Traits of the Trinity Aspect Archaic: Carrollton and Elam Foci. *The Record* 12(1):2–16.

Crowley, Thomas J.
2000   Causes of Climate Change over the Past 1000 Years. *Science* 289:270–277.

Cruikshank, J. W.
1939   *Forest Resources of Southwest Louisiana.* U.S. Southern Forest Experiment Station, New Orleans.

Cummings, L. Scott
1993 Pollen and Phytolith Analysis. In *Data Recovery at Site 16VN794: Investigations into Site Formation Processes and the Cultural Sequence of West Central Louisiana,* edited by Charles E. Cantley, Leslie E. Raymer, John S. Foss, C. Stiles, Linda Scott Cummings, J. W. Joseph, and J. Raymer, pp. 131–138. New South Associates, Technical Report 119, Stone Mountain, Georgia.

Cupit, John T.
1963 *A Brief History of Vernon Parish, Louisiana.* Privately published, Rosepine, Louisiana.
1983 Rosepine. In *History of Beauregard Parish, Louisiana.* Curtis Media and Beauregard Parish Historical Society, De Ridder, Louisiana.

Cupit, John T., and Andrew Jackson (Jack) Hadnot, Jr.
n.d. *Family History of Some of the First Families in Vernon Parish.* Hadnot Collection, Vernon Parish Library, Leesville.

Dalehite, Bob
1962 *The Vernon Free-Stater.* Bulletin of the Vernon Parish Library. Existing issues include April and August. Vertical files, Vernon Parish Library, Leesville, Louisiana.
1963 *The Vernon Free-Stater.* Bulletin of the Vernon Parish Library. April. Vertical files, Vernon Parish Library, Leesville, Louisiana.

Daniel, I. Randolph
1998 *Hardaway Revisited: Early Archaic Settlement in the Southeast.* University of Alabama Press, Tuscaloosa.

Daniel, Lucia Elizabeth
1943 The Louisiana Peoples Party. *Louisiana Historical Quarterly* 26(4):1055–1149.

Dansgaard, W., J. W. C. White, and S. J. Johnsen
1989 The Abrupt Termination of the Younger Dryas Climate Event. *Nature* 339:532–533.

Dansgaard, W., S. J. Johnsen, H. B. Clausen, D. Dahl-Jensen, N. S. Gunderstrup, C. U. Hammer, C. S. Hvidberg, J. P. Steffensen, A. E. Sveinbjornsdottir, J. Jouzel, and G. Bond
1993 Evidence for General Instability of Past Climate from a 250 kyr Ice Core. *Nature* 364:218–219.

Davis, Edwin Adams
1959 *Louisiana: The Pelican State.* Louisiana State University Press, Baton Rouge.
1971 *Louisiana: A Narrative History.* 3rd ed. Claitor's Publishing Div., Baton Rouge.

Davis, Hester A. (editor)
1970 *Archaeological and Historical Resources of the Red River Basin.* Research Series No. 1, Arkansas Archeological Survey, Fayetteville.

Davison, James N.
1994 *Newllano: History of the Llano Movement.* Dogwood Press, Woodville, Texas.

Delcourt, Paul A., and Hazel R. Delcourt
1983 Late-Quaternary Vegetational Dynamics and Community Stability Reconsidered. *Quaternary Research* 19:265–271.
1985 Quaternary Palynology and Vegetational History of the Southeastern United States. In *Pollen Records of Late-Quaternary North American Sediments,* edited by V. M. Bryant and R. G. Holloway, pp. 1–37. American Association of Stratigraphic Palynologists Foundation, Dallas.

DeMenocal, Peter, Joseph Ortiz, Tom Guilderson, and Michael Sarnthein
2000 Coherent High- and Low-Latitude Climate Variability during the Holocene Warm Period. *Science* 288:2198–2202.

Dickson, Don
   1968   Two Provisional Projectile Point Types. *Arkansas Amateur* 7(6):5–7.
Dincauze, Dena F.
   1993   Pioneering in the Pleistocene Large Paleoindian Sites in the Northwest. In *Ar-
            chaeology of Eastern North America: Papers in Honor of Stephen Williams,* ed-
            ited by James B. Stoltman, pp. 43–60. Archaeological Report No. 25, Mississippi
            Dept. of Archives and History, Jackson.
Ditchy, Jay K.
   1930   Early Census Tables of Louisiana. *Louisiana Historical Quarterly* 13(2):208–213.
Dorian, Alan W.
   1988a   *Cultural Resources Inventory on the Kisatchie National Forest, Louisiana.* In-
            terim Report. On file with the Div. of Archeology, Baton Rouge.
   1988b   *Cultural Resources Management Summary and Evaluation Report of 16WN140:
            Kisatchie National Forest, Winn Ranger District, Winn Parish, Louisiana.* On
            file with the Div. of Archeology, Baton Rouge.
Dorian, Alan W., and Lisa E. Coleman
   1992   *Cultural Resources Management Summary 92-16, Kisatchie National Forest,
            Vernon Range District, Vernon Parish, Township 1 North, Range 6 West.* Man-
            agement summary letter on file at U.S. Forest Service, Pineville, Louisiana.
Driskell, Boyce N.
   1994   Stratigraphy and Chronology at Dust Cave. *Journal of Alabama Archaeology*
            40:18–33.
   1996   Stratified Late Pleistocene and Early Holocene Deposits at Dust Cave, North-
            western Alabama. In *The Paleoindian and Early Archaic Southeast,* edited by
            David G. Anderson and Kenneth E. Sassaman, pp. 315–330. University of Ala-
            bama Press, Tuscaloosa.
Duffield, Lathel F.
   1959   Archaeological Reconnaissance at Cooper Reservoir, Delta and Hopkins Coun-
            ties, Texas, February 1959. Mimeographed report submitted to the National Park
            Service by the Texas Archaeological Laboratory, University of Texas, Austin.
   1961   The Limerick Site at Iron Bridge Reservoir, Rains County, Texas. *Bulletin of the
            Texas Archeological Society* 30:51–116.
   1963   The Wolfshead Site: An Archaic–Neo-American Site in San Augustine County,
            Texas. *Bulletin of the Texas Archeological Society* 34:83–141.
Dunbar, James S., S. David Webb, and Michael K. Faught
   1988   Page-Ladson (8JE591): An Underwater Paleo-Indian Site in Northwestern Florida.
            Florida Anthropologist 41:442–452.
Dunwody, Robson
   1921   Proper Methods of Distillation and Handling in the Production of Turpentine and
            Rosin. In *Naval Stores, History, Production, Distribution, and Consumption,* com-
            piled by Thomas Gamble, pp. 127–133. Weekly Naval Stores Review, Review
            Publishing and Printing Company, Savannah.
Dyer, J. O.
   1917   *The Lake Charles Atakapas (Cannibals), Period of 1817–1820.* Galveston, Texas.
Dyson-Hudson, Rada, and Eric A. Smith
   1978   Human Territoriality: An Ecological Reassessment. *American Anthropologist*
            80:21–41.
Earth News
   1911   Advertisement for McFarland Heights. February, vol. 33. On file, Northwestern
            State University Library, Natchitoches, Louisiana.

Edmonds, David C.
   1979   *Yankee Autumn in Acadiana: A Narrative of the Great Texas Overland Expedition through Southwest Louisiana, October-December 1863.* Acadiana Press, Lafayette, Louisiana.
Eiseley, Loren
   1971   *The Night Country.* Charles Scribner's Sons, New York.
Ellis, Christopher, Albert C. Goodyear, Dan F. Morse, and Kenneth B. Tankersley
   1998   Archaeology of the Pleistocene-Holocene Transition in Eastern North America. *Quaternary International* 49/50:151–166.
Ensor, H. Blaine
   1981   *Gainesville Lake Area Lithics: Chronology, Technology, and Use.* Report of Investigations 13, Office of Archaeological Research, University of Alabama, University.
   1987   San Patrice and Dalton Affinities on the Central and Western Gulf Coastal Plain. *Bulletin of the Texas Archeological Society* 57:69–81.
Ensor, H. Blaine, Robert Patton, Raymond Ezell, Jeffrey L. Holland, and Lynn Marie Piatak (editors)
   1999   *Archaeological Survey of 6,407 Acres at Peason Ridge, Fort Polk, Vernon, Sabine, and Natchitoches Parishes, Louisiana.* TRC Garrow Associates, Atlanta.
Ensor, H. Blaine, Carmen Dickerson, T. Clay Schultz, and Mary Evelyn Starr
   2001   *An Archaeological Survey of 4,579 Acres in the Rustville Training Area, Fort Polk, Vernon Parish, Louisiana 1999–2000.* Office of Contract Archaeological Services, Dept. of Anthropology, University of Memphis, and Weaver and Assoc., Memphis.
Ezell, Raymond, and H. Blaine Ensor
   1999   Prehistoric Synthesis. In *Archaeological Survey of 6,407 Acres at Peason Ridge, Fort Polk, Vernon, Sabine, and Natchitoches Parishes, Louisiana,* edited by H. Blaine Ensor, Robert Patton, Raymond Ezell, Jeffrey L. Holland, and Lynn Marie Piatak, pp. 330–393. TRC Garrow Associates, Atlanta.
Faulk, Obie B.
   1964   *The Last Years of Spanish Texas.* Studies in American History IV. Mouton, London.
Faulkner, Charles H.
   1998   Here Are Frame Houses and Brick Chimneys. In *The Southern Colonial Backcountry: Interdisciplinary Perspectives on Frontier Communities,* edited by David Colin Crass, Steven D. Smith, Martha A. Zierden, and Richard D. Brooks, pp. 137–161. University of Tennessee Press, Knoxville.
Fay, Edwin W.
   1898   *History of Education in Louisiana.* Circular of Information No. 1, Contributions to American Educational History, edited by Herbert B. Adams. U.S. Bureau of Education, GPO, Washington, D.C.
Fickle, James E.
   1975   The Louisiana-Texas Lumber War of 1911–1912. *Louisiana History* 16(1):59–85.
Fiedel, Stuart J.
   1999   Older than We Thought: Implications of Corrected Radiocarbon Dates for Paleo-Indians. *American Antiquity* 64:95–115.
   2000   The Peopling of the New World: Present Evidence, New Theories, and Future Directions. *Journal of Archaeological Science* 8:39–103.
   2001   What Happened in the Early Woodland? *Archaeology of Eastern North America* 29:101–142.

Fischer, David Hackett
   1989   *Albion's Seed: Four British Folkways in America.* Oxford University Press, Ox-
            ford.
Flynt, J. Wayne
   1979   *Dixie's Forgotten People.* Indiana University Press, Bloomington.
Foote, J. M., and W. A. Sisemore
   1933   *An Administrative and Financial Study of the Vernon Parish School System.* State
            Dept. of Education, Bulletin No. 261. On file, Hill Memorial Library, Louisiana
            State University, Baton Rouge.
Ford, Curry
   1955   The Rawhide Fight. *Leesville Leader* January 20.
Ford, James A., and G. I. Quimby
   1945   *The Tchefuncte Culture, an Early Occupation of the Lower Mississippi Valley.*
            Memoirs of the Society for American Archaeology No. 2, Menasha, Wisconsin.
Ford, James A., and Clarence H. Webb
   1956   *Poverty Point, a Late Archaic Site in Louisiana.* American Museum of Natural
            History Anthropological Papers 46(1). New York.
Ford, James A., and Gordon Willey
   1940   *Crooks Site, a Marksville Period Burial Ground in LaSalle Parish, Louisiana.*
            Dept. of Conservation, Louisiana Geological Survey Anthropological Study 3,
            Baton Rouge.
Ford, James A., Phillip Phillips, and William G. Haag
   1955   *The Jaketown Site in West-Central Mississippi.* American Museum of Natural
            History Anthropological Papers 45. New York.
Ford, Lacy K.
   1986   Yeoman Farmers in the South Carolina Upcountry: Changing Production Pat-
            terns in the Late Antebellum Era. *Agricultural History* 60(4):17-37.
Forney, Sandra Jo
   1985   The Importance of Sites Related to the Naval Stores Industry in Florida. *Florida
            Anthropologist* 38(4):275–280.
Fort Polk
   1978   *Fort Polk Terrain Analysis Maps.* U.S. Army Engineer Waterways Experiment
            Station, Vicksburg.
Fort Polk Museum
   n.d.   One-page history of Fort Polk. On file, Fort Polk Museum, Fort Polk, Louisiana.
Fortier, Alcee
   1909   *Louisiana.* 2 vols. Southern Historical Association, Atlanta.
Foss, J., C. Cantley, R. Lewis, and C. Stiles
   1993   Pedological Investigations. In *Data Recovery at Site 16VN794: Investigations
            into Site Formation Processes and the Cultural Sequence of West Central Louisi-
            ana,* edited by Charles E. Cantley, Leslie E. Raymer, John S. Foss, C. Stiles,
            Linda Scott Cummings, J. W. Joseph, and J. Raymer, pp. 95–130. New South
            Associates, Technical Report 119, Stone Mountain, Georgia.
Foster, Emma Louise
   1976   Early History of Parish Is Traced by Homemaker. *Leesville Leader* July 15.
Foster, J. H.
   1912   *Forest Conditions in Louisiana.* U.S. Dept. of Agriculture, U.S. Forest Service,
            Bulletin 114. Washington, D.C.
Foster, William C.
   1995   *Spanish Expeditions into Texas, 1689–1768.* University of Texas Press, Austin.

Fowler, Barbara
    1967   History of Fullerton, Louisiana. Paper submitted to Dr. Yvonne Phillips, Social
            Studies 303, Northwestern State University of Louisiana, Natchitoches.
Franks, Herschel A.
    1990a   *Archaeological Survey of 414 Acres within the Comrade Creek Drainage Area,*
            Peason Ridge, Fort Polk, Vernon Parish, Louisiana. Earth Search, Fort Polk Re-
            port ES-1, New Orleans.
    1990b   *Archaeological Survey of 202 Acres within the Calcasieu River Drainage System,*
            Main Fort, Fort Polk, Vernon Parish, Louisiana. Earth Search, Fort Polk Report
            ES-2, New Orleans.
    1990c   *Archaeological Survey of 194 Acres in the Eastern Portion of the Main Fort (Ful-*
            lerton Lake Quadrangle), Fort Polk, Vernon Parish, Louisiana. Earth Search,
            Fort Polk Report ES-3, New Orleans.
    1990d   *Archaeological Survey of 243 Acres in the Eastern Portion of the Main Fort (Ful-*
            lerton Lake Quadrangle), Fort Polk, Vernon Parish, Louisiana. Earth Search,
            Fort Polk Report ES-4, New Orleans.
    1990e   *Archaeological Survey of 247 Acres on the Main Fort and Peason Ridge, Fort*
            Polk, Vernon Parish, Louisiana. Earth Search, Fort Polk Report ES-5, New Or-
            leans.
    1991a   *Archaeological Survey of 565 Acres on the Main Fort (Vernon Parish), Fort Polk,*
            Louisiana (1991). Earth Search, Fort Polk Report ES-10, New Orleans.
    1991b   *Archaeological Survey of 371 Acres on the Main Fort, Fort Polk, Louisiana (1991).*
            Earth Search, Fort Polk Report ES-13, New Orleans.
    1992a   *Archaeological Survey of 432 Acres on the Main Fort, Fort Polk (Vernon Parish),*
            Louisiana. Earth Search, Fort Polk Report ES-15, New Orleans.
    1992b   *Archaeological Survey of 274 Acres on the Main Fort (Fullerton Lake Quad-*
            rangle), Fort Polk, Louisiana. Earth Search, Fort Polk Report ES-16, New Or-
            leans.
    1992c   *Archaeological Survey of 417 Acres in the Eastern Portion of the Main Fort (Ful-*
            lerton Lake Quadrangle, Vernon Parish), Fort Polk, Louisiana (1992). Earth
            Search, Fort Polk Report ES-17, New Orleans.
Franks, Herschel A., and Kenneth R. Jones
    1991   *Archaeological Survey of 96 Acres on the Main Fort and Peason Ridge (Vernon*
            Parish), Fort Polk, Louisiana (1991). Earth Search, Fort Polk Report ES-11, New
            Orleans.
Franks, Herschel A., and Mark Rees
    1991   *Archaeological Survey of 392 Acres in Compartment 39 of Peason Ridge (Sabine*
            Parish), Fort Polk, Louisiana. Earth Search, Fort Polk Report ES-14, New Or-
            leans.
Franks, Herschel A., and Jill-Karen Yakubik
    1990a   *Archaeological Survey of 240 Acres in the Eastern Portion of the Main Fort (Ful-*
            lerton Lake Quadrangle), Fort Polk, Vernon Parish, Louisiana. Earth Search,
            Fort Polk Report ES-6, New Orleans.
    1990b   *Archaeological Survey of 316 Acres on the Main Fort (Vernon Parish) and Peason*
            Ridge (Natchitoches Parish), Fort Polk, Louisiana. Earth Search, Fort Polk Re-
            port ES-8, New Orleans.
Franks, Herschel A., Rhonda L. Smith, and Kenneth R. Jones
    1991   *Archaeological Survey of 202 Acres on the Main Fort (Vernon Parish) and Peason*
            Ridge (Sabine Parish), Fort Polk, Louisiana (1991). Earth Search, Fort Polk Re-
            port ES-9, New Orleans.

Frazar, Lether Edward
1933   *Early Annals of Beauregard Parish.* Monograph. De Ridder, Louisiana.
Fredlund, Glen G.
1983   Occupational Variability at 16VN18: A Multiple Component Site in the Bayou
        Zourie Area. In *U.S.L. Fort Polk Archaeological Survey and Cultural Resources
        Management Program,* 2 vols., edited by A. Frank Servello, pp. 771–858. Uni-
        versity of Southwestern Louisiana, Lafayette.
Frink, Douglas S.
1992   The Chemical Variability of Carbonized Organic Matter through Time. *Archaeol-
        ogy of Eastern North America* 20:67–79.
1994   The Oxidizable Carbon Ratio (OCR): A Proposed Solution to Some of the Problems
        Encountered with Radiocarbon Data. *North American Archaeologist* 15:17–29.
Frison, George
1978   *Prehistoric Hunters of the High Plains.* Academic Press, New York.
Fritz, Gayle J., and Tristram R. Kidder
1993   Recent Investigations into Prehistoric Agriculture in the Lower Mississippi Val-
        ley. *Southeastern Archaeology* 12:1–14.
Fulton, R. L., and Clarence H. Webb
1953   The Bellevue Mound: A Pre-Caddoan Site in Bossier Parish, Louisiana. *Bulletin
        of the Texas Archeological Society* 24:18–24.
Futato, Eugene M.
1989   *An Archaeological Overview of the Tombigbee River Basin, Alabama and Missis-
        sippi.* Report of Investigations 59. Div. of Archaeology, Alabama State Museum
        of Natural History, University of Alabama, Tuscaloosa.
Gagliano, Sherwood M.
1963   A Survey of Preceramic Occupations in Portions of South Louisiana and South
        Mississippi. *Florida Anthropologist* 16(4):105–132.
1964   *An Archaeological Survey of Avery Island.* Avery Island, Inc., Avery Island, Loui-
        siana.
1967a   *Occupational Sequence at Avery Island.* Coastal Studies No. 22, Louisiana State
        University Press, Baton Rouge.
1967b   Kirk Serrated: An Early Archaic Index Point in Louisiana. *Florida Anthropolo-
        gist* 20:3–9.
1970   Archaeological and Geological Studies at Avery Island 1968–1970. Progress re-
        port submitted to the International Salt Company, Avery Island, Louisiana.
Gagliano, Sherwood M., and H. F. Gregory
1965   A Preliminary Survey of Paleo-Indian Points from Louisiana. *Louisiana Studies*
        4(1):63–77.
Gagliano, Sherwood M., Susan Fulgham, and Bert Rader
1979   *Cultural Resources Studies of the Pearl River Mouth Area, Louisiana-Missis-
        sippi: Surveys and Assessments of Five Areas in Conjunction with Proposed Con-
        struction of Lake Pontchartrain Hurricane Protection Barrier.* New Orleans Dis-
        trict, U.S. Army Corps of Engineers, Contract DACW 29-77-0272 Final Report.
        Coastal Environments, New Orleans.
Gallien, Jeanie M.
1968   James Calvert Wise: Soldier and Politician. *Louisiana Studies* 6(4):348–377.
Galm, Jerry R., and P. Flynn
1978   *The Cultural Sequences at the Scott (34FL11) and Wann Sites (34FL27) and
        Prehistory of the Wister Valley.* Research Series No. 3, Archaeological Research
        and Management Center, University of Oklahoma, Norman.

Gamble, Thomas

    1921a   The Production of Naval Stores in the United States. In *Naval Stores, History, Production, Distribution, and Consumption,* compiled by Thomas Gamble, pp. 77–88. Weekly Naval Stores Review, Review Publishing and Printing Company, Savannah.

    1921b   "Tar Heeler" Making Pine Tar. In *Naval Stores, History, Production, Distribution, and Consumption,* compiled by Thomas Gamble, pp. 41–42. Weekly Naval Stores Review, Review Publishing and Printing Company, Savannah.

Ganopolski, Andrey, Claudia Kubatzki, Martin Claussen, Victor Brovkin, and Vladimir Petoukhov

    1998   The Influence of Vegetation-Atmosphere-Ocean Interaction on Climate during the Mid-Holocene. *Science* 280(5371):1916–1919.

Garner, Edward

    1982   Geology and Geomorphology of the Eagle Hill Locale in the Uplands of West Central Louisiana. In *Eagle Hill: A Late Quaternary Upland Site in Western Louisiana,* edited by Joel D. Gunn and David O. Brown, pp. 120–126. Special Report 12, Center for Archaeological Research, University of Texas at San Antonio.

Gates, Paul W., and Robert W. Swenson

    1968   *History of Public Land Law Development.* Public Land Law Review Commission, Washington, D.C.

Gibson, Jon L.

    1970   The Hopewellian Phenomenon in the Lower Mississippi Valley. *Louisiana Studies* 9(3):176–192.

    1974   The Rise and Decline of Poverty Point. *Louisiana Archaeology* 1:8–36.

    1978a   *An Archaeological Reconnaissance of the Lower Sabine River Valley, Toledo Bend Dam to Gulf Intercoastal Waterway, Louisiana and Texas.* Report No. 4, Center for Archaeological Studies, University of Southwestern Louisiana, Lafayette.

    1978b   *Archaeological Survey of the Lower Atchafalaya Region, South Central Louisiana.* Report No. 5, Center for Archaeological Studies, University of Southwestern Louisiana, Lafayette.

    1982   The Troyville-Baytown Issue. *Louisiana Archaeology* 9:29–64.

    1991   Islands in the Past: Archaeological Excavations at the Francis Thompson Site, Madison Parish, Louisiana. *Louisiana Archaeology* 14.

    1994   Empirical Characterization of Exchange Systems in Lower Mississippi Valley Prehistory. In *Prehistoric Exchange Systems in North America,* edited by T. G. Baugh and J. E. Ericson, pp. 127–176. Plenum Press, New York.

    1998   Elements and Organization of Poverty Point Political Economy: High-Water Fish, Exotic Rocks, and Sacred Earth. *Research in Economic Anthropology* 19:291–340.

Gillam, Chris

    1995   *Paleoindian Settlement in the Mississippi Valley of Arkansas.* Master's thesis, Dept. of Anthropology, University of Arkansas, Fayetteville.

    1996   Early and Middle Paleoindian Sites in the Northeastern Arkansas Region. In *The Paleoindian and Early Archaic Southeast,* edited by David G. Anderson and Kenneth E. Sassaman, pp. 404–412. University of Alabama Press, Tuscaloosa.

Girard, Jeffrey S.

    1997   Caddoan Settlement in the Red River Floodplain: Perspectives from the Willow Chute Bayou Area, Bossier Parish, Louisiana. *Louisiana Archaeology* 22:143–162.

    1998   *Excavations at the Fredericks Site (16NA2), Regional Archaeology Program, Management Unit 1, Ninth Annual Report.* Louisiana Div. of Archaeology, Dept. of Culture, Recreation, and Tourism, Baton Rouge.

2000a   *Regional Archaeology Program, Management Unit 1, Eleventh Annual Report.* Louisiana Div. of Archaeology, Dept. of Culture, Recreation, and Tourism, Baton Rouge.

2000b   Excavations at the Fredericks Site (16NA2), Natchitoches Parish, Louisiana. *Louisiana Archaeology* 24:1–91.

2001   *Regional Archaeology Program, Management Unit 1, Twelfth Annual Report.* Louisiana Div. of Archaeology, Dept. of Culture, Recreation, and Tourism, Baton Rouge.

Glassie, Henry

1968   *Pattern in the Material Folk Culture of the Eastern United States.* Monograph No. 1 in Folklore and Life, University of Pennsylvania, Philadelphia.

1975   *Folk Housing in Middle Virginia: Structural Analysis of Historic Artifacts.* University of Tennessee Press, Knoxville.

Goodspeed Publishing Company

1974   *History of Laclede, Camden, Dallas, Webster, Wright, Texas, Pulaski, Phelps, and Dent Counties, Missouri.* Reprinted. BNL Library Service, Independence, Missouri. Originally published 1889, Goodspeed Publishing, Chicago.

1975   *Biographical and Historical Memoirs of Louisiana.* Reprinted. Louisiana Classic Series, Claitor's Publishing, Baton Rouge. Originally published 1892, Goodspeed Publishing, Chicago.

Goodwin, R. Christopher, Jill-Karen Yakubik, and Cyd Heymann Goodwin

1984   *Elmwood: The Historic Archeology of a Southeastern Louisiana Plantation.* Jefferson Parish Historical Commission, Metairie, Louisiana.

Goodyear, Albert C. III

1974   *The Brand Site: A Techno-Functional Study of a Dalton Site in Northeast Arkansas.* Research Series No. 7, Arkansas Archeological Survey, Fayetteville.

1979   *A Hypothesis for the Use of Cryptocrystalline Raw Materials among Paleo-Indian Groups of North America.* Research Manuscript Series 156, South Carolina Institute of Archaeology and Anthropology, University of South Carolina, Columbia.

1982   The Chronological Position of the Dalton Horizon in the Southeastern United States. *American Antiquity* 47:382–395.

1999   The Early Holocene Occupation of the Southeastern United States: A Geoarchaeological Summary. In *Ice Age Peoples of North America: Environments, Origins, and Adaptations of the First Americans,* edited by Robson Bonnichsen and Karen L. Turnmire, pp. 432–481. Center for the Study of the First Americans, Oregon State University, Corvallis.

Goodyear, Albert C., John H. House, and Neal W. Ackerly

1979   *Laurens-Anderson: An Archaeological Study of the Inter-Riverine Piedmont.* Anthropological Studies 4, South Carolina Institute of Archaeology and Anthropology, University of South Carolina, Columbia.

Gray, Carl R., Jr.

1955   *Railroading in Eighteen Countries.* Charles Scribner's Sons, New York.

Gray, Jay

2001   Laboratory Analysis. In *A Cultural Resources Survey of 4,212 Acres on Fort Polk Military Reservation and the Limited Use Area, Vernon Parish, Louisiana,* by Andrew Saatkamp, C. Andrew Buchner, and Jay Gray, pp. 71–101. Panamerican Consultants, Memphis.

2002   Laboratory Analysis. In *A Cultural Resources Survey of 4,862 Acres in the Limited Use Area/Kisatchie National Forest, Vernon Parish, Louisiana,* edited by

Paul D. Bundy and C. Andrew Buchner, pp. 75–129. Panamerican Consultants, Memphis.

Gray, Jay, and C. Andrew Buchner
2000   Laboratory Analysis. In *An Intensive Phase I Cultural Resources Survey of 6,535 Acres within Portions of Training Areas Sixmile Creek 1, 2, & 3, and Slagle 7, 8, 9, 10 & 11 on Fort Polk Military Reservation, Vernon Parish, Louisiana,* edited by Andrew Saatkamp, C. Andrew Buchner, and Jay Gray, pp. 55–79. Panamerican Consultants, Memphis.

Green, James A., Jr.
1991   Calcasieu Point: A Formal Description. In *Central States Archaeological Journal* 38:96–97. Central States Archaeological Society, Kirkwood, Missouri.

Gregory, Hiram F.
1973   *Eighteenth Century Caddoan Archaeology: A Study in Models and Interpretations.* Ph.D. dissertation, Southern Methodist University, Dallas. University Microfilms, Ann Arbor.
1995   Regional Variation in Evans Points. Paper presented at the Annual Meeting of the Louisiana Archaeological Society, Natchitoches.

Gregory, Hiram F., and H. K. Curry
1972   An Archaeological Survey of the Diamond Ore Test Area, Peason Ridge, Vernon Parish, Louisiana. Ms. on file, Fort Polk Military Museum, Fort Polk, Louisiana.
1978   *Natchitoches Parish Cultural and Historical Resources, Prehistory.* Natchitoches Planning Commission, Natchitoches, Louisiana.

Griffin, James B.
1946   Cultural Change and Continuity in Eastern United States Archaeology. In *Man in Northeastern North America,* edited by Frederick Johnson, pp. 37–95. Papers of the Robert S. Peabody Foundation for Archaeology 3, Andover, Massachusetts.
1960   Climatic Change: A Contributory Cause of the Growth and Decline of Northern Hopewellian Culture. *Wisconsin Archaeologist* 41(1):21–33.
1961   Some Correlations of Climatic and Cultural Change in Eastern North American Prehistory. *Annals of the New York Academy of Sciences* 95:710–717.
1967   Eastern North American Archaeology: A Summary. *Science* 156:175–191.

Griffing, David L.
1994   The Baskin Site: An Early Archaic Site in Franklin Parish. *Louisiana Archaeology* 21:103–125.

Grove, J. M.
1988   *The Little Ice Age.* Methuen, London.

Grunden, Ramona M., and Christopher Ohm Clement
1998   Results: Fullerton 1, 2, and 4, Six Mile Creek 3, and Slagle 11. In *Archaeological Survey of 12,538 Acres Fort Polk, Vernon Parish, Louisiana,* edited by Christopher Ohm Clement, Ramona M. Grunden, John K. Peterson, Jill S. Quattlebaum, and Steven D. Smith, pp. 47–87. South Carolina Institute of Archaeology and Anthropology, University of South Carolina, Columbia.

Guderjan, Thomas H., and James R. Morehead
1980   Big Brushy: A Stratified Multiple Component Site at Fort Polk, Louisiana. *Louisiana Archaeology* 7:1–30.
1983   16VN24: A Stratified Multiple Component Site on Big Brushy Creek. In *U.S.L. Fort Polk Archaeological Survey and Cultural Resources Management Program,* 2 vols., edited by A. Frank Servello, pp. 859–935. University of Southwestern Louisiana, Lafayette.

Gunn, Joel D.
  1982a Eagle Hill Environment, Lithics, and Dynamic Utilization Analysis. In *Eagle Hill: A Late Quaternary Upland Site in Western Louisiana,* edited by Joel D. Gunn and David O. Brown, pp. 181–261. Special Report 12, Center for Archaeological Research, University of Texas at San Antonio.
  1982b Foreword: Overview of the Project and Conclusions. In *Eagle Hill: A Late Quaternary Upland Site in Western Louisiana,* edited by Joel D. Gunn and David O. Brown, pp. 1–6. Special Report 12, Center for Archaeological Research, University of Texas at San Antonio.
  1982c Excavation Activities and Techniques at Eagle Hill. In *Eagle Hill: A Late Quaternary Upland Site in Western Louisiana,* edited by Joel D. Gunn and David O. Brown, pp. 45–72. Special Report 12, Center for Archaeological Research, University of Texas at San Antonio.
  1982d Interpretation of Occupation Plane Patterns. In *Eagle Hill: A Late Quaternary Upland Site in Western Louisiana,* edited by Joel D. Gunn and David O. Brown, pp. 318–343. Special Report 12, Center for Archaeological Research, University of Texas at San Antonio.
  1982e Conclusions. In *Eagle Hill: A Late Quaternary Upland Site in Western Louisiana,* edited by Joel D. Gunn and David O. Brown, pp. 344–347. Special Report 12, Center for Archaeological Research, University of Texas at San Antonio.
  1982f High Resolution Environmental Column. In *Eagle Hill: A Late Quaternary Upland Site in Western Louisiana,* edited by Joel D. Gunn and David O. Brown, pp. 143–145. Special Report 12, Center for Archaeological Research, University of Texas at San Antonio.
  1984a Settlement Pattern Model and Analyses. In *Occupation and Settlement in the Uplands of Western Louisiana,* edited by Joel D. Gunn and Anne C. Kerr, pp. 150–174. Special Report 17, Center for Archaeological Research, University of Texas at San Antonio.
  1984b Points from Peason Ridge and Nearby Areas. In *Occupation and Settlement in the Uplands of Western Louisiana,* edited by Joel D. Gunn and Anne C. Kerr, pp. 135–147. Special Report 17, Center for Archaeological Research, University of Texas at San Antonio.
Gunn, Joel D., and David O. Brown (editors)
  1982   *Eagle Hill: A Late Quaternary Upland Site in Western Louisiana.* Special Report 12, Center for Archaeological Research, University of Texas at San Antonio.
Gunn, Joel D., and Anne C. Kerr
  1984a Site Descriptions. In *Occupation and Settlement in the Uplands of Western Louisiana,* edited by Joel D. Gunn and Anne C. Kerr, pp. 41–111. Special Report 17, Center for Archaeological Research, University of Texas at San Antonio.
  1984b Conclusions. In *Occupation and Settlement in the Uplands of Western Louisiana,* edited by Joel D. Gunn and Anne C. Kerr, pp. 171–174. Special Report 17, Center for Archaeological Research, University of Texas at San Antonio.
  1986   The Flake Chronology Study. In *Cultural Resources Investigations in the Proposed Multipurpose Range Complex Area, Fort Polk, Vernon Parish, Louisiana,* by L. Janice Campbell and Carol S. Weed, pp. 7-42 to 7-60. New World Research, Report of Investigations 85-6, Pollock, Louisiana.
Gunn, Joel D., and Anne C. Kerr (editors)
  1984   *Occupation and Settlement in the Uplands of Western Louisiana.* Special Report 17, Center for Archaeological Research, University of Texas at San Antonio.

Gunn, Joel D., and Linda Wootan
  1984   Vertical Distribution of Flake Widths. In *Occupation and Settlement in the Up-lands of Western Louisiana,* edited by Joel D. Gunn and Anne C. Kerr, pp. 129–134. Special Report 17, Center for Archaeological Research, University of Texas at San Antonio.
Gunn, Joel D., Mark Sheehan, and Edward Garner
  1982   Site Catchment and Settlement Pattern. In *Eagle Hill: A Late Quaternary Upland Site in Western Louisiana,* edited by Joel D. Gunn and David O. Brown, pp. 140–143. Special Report 12, Center for Archaeological Research, University of Texas at San Antonio.
Gunn, Joel D., David O. Brown, Jon L. Gibson, and Anne C. Kerr
  n.d.   A Dated Colluvial-Cultural Sequence for West Central Louisiana, Occupation Floor and Settlement Patterns. Ms. on file, Center for Archaeological Research, University of Texas at San Antonio.
Guy, John, and Joel D. Gunn
  1983   Settlement Patterns in the Fort Polk Region. *Louisiana Studies* 4(4):279–323.
Hackett, D. L. A.
  1973   The Social Structure of Jacksonian Louisiana. *Louisiana Studies* 12(1):324–353.
Hadnot, Andrew Jackson, Jr.
  1975   Letter to Mr. Carl A. Brasseaux, Assistant to the Director, Southwestern Archives, University of Southern Louisiana, Lafayette. July 20.
  n.d.a   Vernon Parish History: Notes on Early Settlers and History of Vernon Parish. Bound photostatic copy at Vernon Parish Library, Leesville, Louisiana.
  n.d.b   Hadnot Collection. Microfilm on file, Vernon Parish Library, Leesville.
Haggard, J. V.
  1945a   The Neutral Ground between Louisiana and Texas, 1806–1821. *Louisiana Historical Quarterly* 28(4):1001–1128.
  1945b   The House of Barr and Davenport. *Southwestern Historical Quarterly* 44:66–88.
Haikey, Larry D., Timothy P. Phillips, and Alan W. Dorian
  1991   *Cultural Resources Inventory on the Kisatchie National Forest, Louisiana. FY 1990.* Report on file with the Div. of Archeology, Baton Rouge.
Hair, William Ivy
  1969   *Bourbonism and Agrarian Protest; Louisiana Politics 1877–1900.* Louisiana State University, Baton Rouge.
Hajic, Edwin R., Rolfe D. Mandel, and E. Arthur Bettis III
  2000   Stratigraphic and Paleoenvironmental Investigations. In *The 1999 Excavations at the Big Eddy Site (23CE426),* edited by Neal H. Lopinot, Jack H. Ray, and Michael D. Conner, pp. 26–36. Special Publication No. 3, Center for Archaeological Research, Southwest Missouri State University, Springfield.
Hamilton, Fran E.
  1999   Southeastern Archaic Mounds: Examples of Elaboration in a Temporally Fluctuating Environment? *Journal of Anthropological Archaeology* 18:344–355.
Hardin, J. Fair
  1939   *Northwestern Louisiana: A History of the Watershed of the Red River 1714–1937.* Historical Record Association, Louisville, Kentucky, and Shreveport, Louisiana.
Harris, W. H.
  1881   *Louisiana Products, Resources and Attractions with a Sketch of the Parishes.* New Orleans Democrat Print, New Orleans.
Hart, J. F.
  1977   Land Rotation in Appalachia. *Geographical Review* 67:148–166.

Hartley, Michael O.
1987   *The Ashley River: A Survey of Seventeenth Century Sites.* Research Manuscript Series 192, South Carolina Institute of Archaeology and Anthropology, University of South Carolina, Columbia.

Hartman, George B.
1922   The Calcasieu Pine District of Louisiana. *Ames Forester* (Iowa State College, Ames) 10:63–68.

Haynes, C. Vance, Jr.
1993   Clovis-Folsom Geochronology and Climatic Change. In *From Kostenki to Clovis: Upper Paleolithic Paleo-Indian Adaptations,* edited by Olga Soffer and N. D. Praslov, pp. 219–36. Plenum Press, New York.

Hays, Christopher T., and Richard A. Weinstein
1996   Perspectives on Tchefuncte Cultural Chronology: A View from the Bayou Jasmine Site, St. John the Baptist Parish, Louisiana. *Louisiana Archaeology* 23:49–89.

Heide, Greg
1999a   *An Archeological Survey of 28 Miles of the Enduro Multiple-Use Trail in the Fort Polk Limited Use Area, Kisatchie National Forest, Vernon Parish, Louisiana.* Southeast Archeological Center, NPS, Tallahassee.
1999b   *National Cemetery Land Transfer Archeological Survey of 84 Acres Fort Polk, Vernon Parish, Louisiana.* Southeast Archeological Center, NPS, Tallahassee.

Heinrich, Paul V.
1983   Lithic Resources of Sabine and Vernon Parishes. In *U.S.L. Fort Polk Archaeological Survey and Cultural Resources Management Program,* 2 vols., edited by A. Frank Servello, pp. 552–556. University of Southwestern Louisiana, Lafayette.
1984   Lithic Resources of Western Louisiana. *Louisiana Archaeology* 11:165–190.

Henderson, Harry McCorry
1951   The Magee-Gutiérrez Expedition. *Southwestern Historical Quarterly* 55:43–61.

Henry, D. O., F. E. Kirby, A. E. Justen, and T. R. Hays
1980   *The Prehistory of Hog Creek: An Archaeological Investigation of Bosque and Coryell Counties, Texas.* Laboratory of Archaeology, Dept. of Anthropology, University of Tulsa, Oklahoma.

Hernandez, Mayor F. E.
1959   Letter to Judge James W. Jones, March 2. Jones Collection, Cammie G. Henry Research Center, Watson Memorial Library, Northwestern State University of Louisiana, Natchitoches.

Hickman, Nollie
1962   *Mississippi Harvest: Lumbering in the Longleaf Pine Belt 1840–1915.* University of Mississippi, University.

Hicks, John D.
1961   *The Populist Revolt: A History of the Farmers' Alliance and the People's Party.* University of Nebraska Press, Lincoln.

Hilgard, Eugene W.
1884   *Report of Cotton Production in the United States, Part 1: Mississippi Valley and Southwestern States.* Census Office, U.S. Dept. of the Interior, Washington, D.C.

Hillman, Mitchell M.
1980   Archaeological Survey, Kisatchie National Forest, Summer 1979. Ms. on file, Kisatchie National Forest, Pineville, Louisiana.
1985   Paleoindian Settlement on the Maçon Ridge, Northeastern Louisiana. *Louisiana Archaeology* 12:203–215.

Hodder, Ian, and Clive Orton
  1976   *Spatial Analysis in Archaeology.* Cambridge University Press, New York.
Hofstadter, Richard, William Miller, and Daniel Aaron
  1967   *The United States: The History of a Republic.* 2nd ed. Prentice-Hall, Englewood
          Cliffs, New Jersey.
House, John H.
  1975   A Functional Typology for Cache Project Surface Collections. In *The Cache River
          Archeological Project: An Experiment in Contract Archeology,* edited by Michael
          B. Schiffer and John H. House, pp. 55–73. Research Series 8, Arkansas Archeo-
          logical Society, Fayetteville.
Howard, C. D.
  1990   The Clovis Point: Characteristics and Type Description. *Plains Anthropologist*
          35(129):255–262.
Howard, Edgar B.
  1935   Evidence of Early Man in North America. *Museum Journal, University of Penn-
          sylvania Museum* 24(2–3).
Hudson, Charles
  1985   De Soto in Arkansas: A Brief Synopsis. *Arkansas Archeological Society Field
          Notes* 205:3–12.
Hughen, K. A., J. T. Overpeck, S. J. Lehman, M. Kashgarian, J. Southon, L. C. Peterson,
R. Alley, and D. M. Sigman
  1998   Deglacial Changes in Ocean Circulation from an Extended Radiocarbon Calibra-
          tion. *Nature* 391:65–68.
Hughen, K. A., J. R. Southon, S. J. Lehman, and J. T. Overpeck
  2000   Synchronous Radiocarbon and Climate Shifts during the Last Deglaciation. *Sci-
          ence* 290:1951–1954.
Hughes, Jack T.
  1949   Investigations in Western South Dakota and Northeastern Wyoming. *American
          Antiquity* 14(4):266–277.
Hughes, M. K., and H. F. Diaz
  1994   Was There a "Medieval Warm Period" and If So, When and Where? *Climatic
          Change* 26:109–142.
Hunter, Donald G.
  1994   Their Final Years: The Apalachee and Other Tribes on the Red River, 1763–1834.
          Florida Anthropologist 47(1):3–46.
Husted, Wilfred M.
  1988   *Archeological Survey of a Proposed Recreational Facilities Area, Fort Polk, Vernon
          Parish, Louisiana.* Interagency Archeological Services Div., NPS, Atlanta.
Husted, Wilfred M., and John E. Ehrenhard
  1988   *Archeological Survey and Evaluation of the Mill Creek Road Relocation Project,
          Fort Polk, Vernon Parish, Louisiana.* Interagency Archeological Services Div.,
          NPS, Atlanta.
Jackson, H. Edwin
  1984a   Archaeological Background. In *Cultural Resources Evaluations, Fort Polk, Loui-
          siana,* edited by Charles E. Cantley and John R. Kern, pp. 23–40. Report R-2639,
          Gilbert/Commonwealth, Jackson, Michigan.
  1984b   Previous Research in the Project Area. In *Cultural Resources Evaluations, Fort
          Polk, Louisiana,* edited by Charles E. Cantley and John R. Kern, pp. 71–77. Re-
          port R-2639, Gilbert/Commonwealth, Jackson, Michigan.

Jacobson, George L., Jr., Thompson Webb III, and Eric C. Grimm
    1987   Patterns and Rates of Vegetation Change in Eastern North America from Full
            Glacial to Mid-Holocene Time. In *The Geology of North America,* vol. K-3, *North
            America and Adjacent Oceans during the Last Deglaciation,* edited by W. F.
            Ruddimen and H. E. Wright, Jr., pp. 277–288. Geological Society of America,
            Boulder, Colorado.
Jameson, John H., Jr.
    2000   Public Interpretation, Education and Outreach: The Growing Predominance in
            American Archaeology. In *Cultural Resource Management in Contemporary So-
            ciety, One World Archaeology 33,* edited by Francis P. McManamon and Alf Hatton,
            pp. 288–299. One World Archaeology Series. Routledge, New York.
Jelks, Edward B.
    1962   *The Kyle Site: A Stratified Central Texas Aspect Site in Hill County, Texas.* Ar-
            chaeology Series No. 5, Dept. of Anthropology, University of Texas, Austin.
    1965   *The Archaeology of McGee Bend Reservoir, Texas.* Ph.D. dissertation, University
            of Texas, Austin.
Jeter, Marvin D., and G. Ishmael Williams, Jr.
    1989a   Lithic Horizons and the Early Cultures. In *Archeology and Bioarcheology of the
            Lower Mississippi Valley and Trans-Mississippi South in Arkansas and Louisi-
            ana,* edited by Marvin D. Jeter, Jerome C. Rose, G. Ishmael Williams, Jr., and
            Anna M. Harmon, pp. 77–110. Research Series No. 37, Arkansas Archeological
            Survey, Fayetteville.
    1989b   Ceramic-Using Culture, 600 B.C.–A.D. 700. In *Archeology and Bioarcheology of
            the Lower Mississippi Valley and Trans-Mississippi South in Arkansas and Loui-
            siana,* edited by Marvin D. Jeter, Jerome C. Rose, G. Ishmael Williams, Jr., and
            Anna M. Harmon, pp. 111–170. Research Series No. 37, Arkansas Archeological
            Survey, Fayetteville.
Jeter, Marvin D., Jerome C. Rose, G. Ishmael Williams, Jr., and Anna H. Harmon
    1989   *Archaeology and Bioarchaeology of the Lower Mississippi Valley and Trans-
            Mississippi South in Arkansas and Louisiana.* Research Series No. 37, Arkansas
            Archeological Survey, Fayetteville.
Jetton, Jeanne, and Darrell Sims
    1984   Plant Survey, Peason Ridge, Section 21. In *Occupation and Settlement in the
            Uplands of Western Louisiana,* edited by Joel D. Gunn and Anne C. Kerr, pp. 32–
            40. Special Report 17, Center for Archaeological Research, University of Texas at
            San Antonio.
Jochim, Michael
    1976   *Hunter-Gatherer Subsistence and Settlement Systems: A Predictive Model.* Aca-
            demic Press, New York.
Johnson, David M.
    1983   *Report on the Preliminary Test Excavations at 16VN481—A Ceramic Period Site
            on the Vernon Ranger District of the Kisatchie National Forest, Louisiana.* Pre-
            pared for U.S. Forest Service, Kisatchie National Forest, Pineville, Louisiana.
    1984a   *Cultural Resources Surveys on the Kisatchie National Forest, F.Y. 1983.* Kisatchie
            National Forest, Pineville, Louisiana.
    1984b   *Cultural Resources Surveys on the Kisatchie National Forest, F.Y. 1984.* Kisatchie
            National Forest, Pineville, Louisiana.
Johnson, David M., James R. Morehead, Timothy Phillips, and James P. Whelan, Jr.
    1986   *The Winnfield Tornado: Cultural Resources Survey and Predictive Modeling in*

the Kisatchie National Forest, Winn Parish, Louisiana. Kisatchie National Forest, Pineville, Louisiana.

Johnson, Jay K.

1987   Cahokia Core Technology in Mississippi: The View from the South. In *The Organization of Core Technology,* edited by Jay K. Johnson and Carol A. Morrow, pp. 187–205. Westview Press, Boulder, Colorado.

2000   Beads, Microdrills, and Blades from Watson Brake. *Southeastern Archaeology* 19:95–104.

Johnson, LeRoy, Jr.

1962   The Yarbrough and Miller Sites of Northeastern Texas, With a Preliminary Definition of the LaHarpe Aspect. *Bulletin of the Texas Archeological Society* 32:141–284.

1964   *The Devil's Mouth Site: A Stratified Campsite at Amistad Reservoir, Val Verde County, Texas.* Archaeology Series No. 6, Dept. of Anthropology, University of Texas, Austin.

1989   *Great Plains Interlopers in the Eastern Woodlands during the Late Paleoindian Times.* Report 36, Office of the State Archaeologist, Texas Historical Commission, Austin.

Johnson, Paul

1991   *The Birth of the Modern World Society 1815–1830.* Harper Collins, New York.

Johnson, William C.

1990a   Geomorphological Setting. In *Data Recovery at 16VN791: A Multi-Component Prehistoric Site in the Birds Creek Drainage, Fort Polk Military Reservation, Fort Polk, Louisiana,* by L. Janice Campbell, James R. Morehead, and A. Frank Servello, pp. 32–35. New World Research, Report of Investigations 188, Fort Walton Beach, Florida.

1990b   Stratigraphy. In *Data Recovery at 16VN791 A Multi-Component Prehistoric Site in the Birds Creek Drainage, Fort Polk Military Reservation, Fort Polk, Louisiana,* by L. Janice Campbell, James R. Morehead, and A. Frank Servello, pp. 35–40. New World Research, Report of Investigations 188, Fort Walton Beach, Florida.

Jolly, Kevin

1982   Lithics. In *Eagle Hill: A Late Quaternary Upland Site in Western Louisiana,* edited by Joel D. Gunn and David O. Brown, pp. 290–301. Special Report 12, Center for Archaeological Research, University of Texas at San Antonio.

1984a   Introduction. In *Occupation and Settlement in the Uplands of Western Louisiana,* edited by Joel D. Gunn and Anne C. Kerr, pp. 1–6. Special Report 17, Center for Archaeological Research, University of Texas at San Antonio.

1984b   Research Design for the 1983 Season. In *Occupation and Settlement in the Uplands of Western Louisiana,* edited by Joel D. Gunn and Anne C. Kerr, pp. 7–14. Special Report 17, Center for Archaeological Research, University of Texas at San Antonio.

Jolly, Kevin, and Joel Gunn

1981   *Terrain Analysis and Settlement Pattern Survey: Upper Bayou Zourie, Fort Polk, Louisiana.* Survey Report 1, Environmental and Cultural Services, San Antonio, Texas.

Jones, Dennis C., Malcolm K. Shuman, and Melissa Weidenfeld

1994   *Cultural Resources Survey of Selected Timber Stands in Four Districts of Kisatchie National Forest (Grant, Natchitoches, Rapides, and Winn Parishes), Louisiana.* Surveys Unlimited Research Associates, Baton Rouge, Louisiana.

1995   *Cultural Resources Survey of Selected Timber Stands in Two Districts of Kisatchie*

National Forest (Grant, Natchitoches and Winn Parishes), Louisiana. Surveys Unlimited Research Associates, Baton Rouge, Louisiana.

Jones, Dennis, Malcolm Shuman, Melissa Weidenfeld, and John Lindemuth
1996a *Fort Polk Delivery Order 5: A Cultural Resources Survey of 824 Acres in Peason Ridge Training Area (Vernon Parish), Fort Polk, Louisiana.* Gulf South Research Corporation, Baton Rouge, Louisiana.
1996b *Fort Polk Delivery Order 6: A Cultural Resources Survey of 470 Acres in Peason Ridge Training Area (Vernon Parish), Fort Polk, Louisiana.* Gulf South Research Corporation, Baton Rouge, Louisiana.
1997 *Fort Polk Delivery Order 7: A Cultural Resources Survey of 370 Acres in the Main Fort (Vernon Parish), Fort Polk, Louisiana.* Gulf South Research Corporation, Baton Rouge, Louisiana.

Jones, M. H., J. A. Schiebout, and J. T. Kirkova
1995 *Cores from the Miocene Castor Creek Member of the Fleming Formation, Fort Polk, Louisiana: Relationship to the Outcropping Miocene Terrestrial Vertebrate Fossil-Bearing Beds.* Gulf Coast Association of Geological Societies Transactions, vol. 45, Baton Rouge, Louisiana.

Jones, Reba
1979 News article describing Peason, Louisiana. *Sabine Index,* September. Vertical files, Sabine Parish Library, Many, Louisiana.

Jordan, Terry G.
1981 *Trails to Texas: Southern Roots of Western Cattle Ranching.* University of Nebraska Press, Lincoln.

Jordan, Terry G., and Mattie Kaups
1989 *The American Backwoods Frontier: An Ethnic and Ecological Interpretation.* Johns Hopkins University Press, Baltimore, Maryland.

Joseph, J. W.
1986 Overview of Nineteenth Century Sites. In *Archaeological Testing of the Fort Howard Tract, Effingham County, Georgia,* compiled by Marvin T. Smith, pp. 437–454. Garrow and Assoc., Atlanta.

Joseph, J. W., Mary Beth Reed, and Charles E. Cantley
1991 *Agrarian Life, Romantic Death: Archaeological and Historical Testing and Data Recovery for the I-85 Northern Alternative, Spartanburg County, South Carolina.* New South Associates Technical Report 39, New South Associates, Columbia.

Joyce, Jane Sally
1981 *A Settlement Pattern Study of the War Eagle Creek Region, Madison County, Arkansas, During the Pioneer Period.* Master's thesis, University of Arkansas, Little Rock.

Juneau, Velma
1937 Kurthwood. On file, Works Progress Administration File, Louisiana State Library, Baton Rouge.

Jurney, David H., and Randall W. Moir (editors)
1987 *Historic Buildings, Material Culture, and People of the Prairie Margin: Architecture, Artifacts, and Synthesis of Historic Archaeology.* Richland Creek Technical Series Volume 5, Archaeology Research Program, Institute for the Study of Earth and Man, Southern Methodist University, Dallas.

Jurney, David H., Susan A. Lebo, and Melissa M. Greene
1988 *Ethnoarchaeological Investigations of the Mountain Creek Area, North Central Texas.* Archaeology Research Program, Institute for the Study of Earth and Man, Southern Methodist University, Dallas.

Justice, Noel D.
   1987   *Stone Age Spear and Arrow Points of the Midcontinental and Eastern United
           States.* Indiana University Press, Bloomington.
Kadlecek, Mabell R., and Marion C. Bullard
   1994   *Louisiana's Kisatchie Hills: History, Tradition, Folklore.* Book Craters, Chelsea,
           Michigan.
Keller, John E.
   1984   *Kisatchie National Forest Cultural Resource Overview.* Report on file, Kisatchie
           National Forest, Pineville, Louisiana.
Kelley, David B.
   1998   Protohistoric and Historic Caddoan Occupation of the Red River Valley in North-
           west Louisiana. In *Native History of the Caddo, Their Place in Southeastern Ar-
           chaeology and Ethnohistory,* edited by Timothy K. Perttula and James E. Bruseth,
           pp. 91–112. Studies in Archaeology 30, Texas Archaeological Research Labora-
           tory, University of Texas at Austin.
Kelley, J. Charles
   1947a   The Lehmann Rock Shelter: A Stratified Site of the Toyah, Uvalde, and Round
           Rock Foci. *Bulletin of the Texas Archeological Society* 18.
   1947b   The Cultural Affiliations and Chronological Position of the Clear Fork Focus.
           American Antiquity 13(2):97–109.
Kelley, J. Charles, T. N. Campbell, and Donald Lehmer
   1940   The Association of Archaeological Materials with Geological Deposits in the Big
           Bend Region of Texas. *West Texas Historical and Scientific Society* 10.
Kellogg, Douglas C.
   1987   Statistical Relevance and Site Locational Data. *American Antiquity* 52:143–150.
Kelly, Robert L.
   1983   Hunter-Gatherer Mobility Strategies. *Journal of Anthropological Research*
           39(3):277–306.
   1995   *The Foraging Spectrum.* Smithsonian Institution Press, Washington, D.C.
Kelly, Robert L., and Lawrence C. Todd
   1988   Coming into the Country: Early Paleoindian Hunting and Mobility. *American
           Antiquity* 53:231–244.
Kelly, Thomas C.
   1962   The Crumley Site: A Stratified Burnt Rock Midden, Travis County, Texas. *Bulle-
           tin of the Texas Archeological Society* 31:239–272.
Kern, John R.
   1984a   Historical Background. In *Cultural Resources Evaluations, Fort Polk, Louisi-
           ana,* edited by Charles E. Cantley and John R. Kern, pp. 41–70. Report R-2639,
           Gilbert/Commonwealth, Jackson, Michigan.
   1984b   Landownership in 1940. In *Cultural Resources Evaluations, Fort Polk, Louisi-
           ana,* edited by Charles E. Cantley and John R. Kern, appendix A. Report R-2639,
           Gilbert/Commonwealth, Jackson, Michigan.
Kerr, Anne C.
   1984   Spatial Distribution of Lithic Debris Frequencies. In *Occupation and Settlement
           in the Uplands of Western Louisiana,* edited by Joel D. Gunn and Anne C. Kerr,
           pp. 114–127. Special Report 17, Center for Archaeological Research, University
           of Texas at San Antonio.
Kerr, Ed
   1958   *History of Forestry in Louisiana.* Office of the State Forester, Baton Rouge.

Kidder, Tristram R.
   1990   Ceramic Chronology and Culture History of the Southern Ouachita River Basin:
           Coles Creek to the Early Historic Period. *Midcontinental Journal of Archaeology*
           15:51–99.
   1992   Coles Creek Period Social Organization and Evolution in Northeast Louisiana. In
           *Lords of the Southeast: Social Inequality and the Native Elites of Southeastern
           North America,* edited by Alex Barker and Timothy Pauketat, pp. 145–162. Ar-
           cheological Papers of the American Anthropological Association, No. 3, Arling-
           ton, Virginia.
   2002   Woodland Period Archaeology of the Lower Mississippi Valley. In *The Woodland
           Southeast,* edited by David G. Anderson and Robert C. Mainfort, Jr., pp. 66–90.
           University of Alabama Press, Tuscaloosa.
Kisatchie National Forest
   n.d.   *Kisatchie.* Kisatchie National Forest, U.S. Dept. of Agriculture, Forest Service,
           Southern Region. Vertical files, Natchitoches Parish Library, Natchitoches, Loui-
           siana.
Kitigawa, H., and J. van der Plicht
   1998   Atmospheric Radiocarbon Calibration to 45,000 Yr B.P.: Late Glacial Fluctua-
           tions and Cosmogenic Isotope Production. *Science* 279:1187–1190.
Kneberg, Madeline
   1956   Some Important Projectile Point Types Found in the Tennessee Area. *Tennessee
           Archaeologist* 12(1):17–28.
Kniffen, Fred B.
   1965   Folk Housing: Key to Diffusion. *Annals of the Association of American Geogra-
           phers* 55(4):549–575.
   1968   *Louisiana, Its Land and People.* Louisiana State University Press, Baton Rouge.
Kniffen, Fred B., and Henry Glassie
   1966   Building in Wood in the Eastern United States, A Time-Place Perspective. *Geo-
           graphical Review* 56:40–66.
Kniffen, Fred B., Hiram F. Gregory, and George A. Stokes
   1987   *The Historic Indian Tribes of Louisiana: From 1542 to the Present.* Louisiana
           State University, Baton Rouge.
Knox, J. C.
   1983   Responses of River Systems to Holocene Climate. In *Late Quaternary Environ-
           ments of the United States,* vol. 2, *The Holocene,* edited by H. E. Wright, Jr., pp.
           26–41. University of Minnesota Press, Minneapolis.
Krieger, Alex D.
   1946   *Cultural Complexes and Chronology in Northern Texas.* University of Texas Pub-
           lication No. 4640, Austin.
   1947   Certain Projectile Points of the Early American Hunters. *Bulletin of the Texas
           Archeological and Paleontological Society* 18:7–27.
LaHaye, Paul, Chris Parrish, James R. Morehead, James H. Mathews, Prentice M. Thomas,
Jr., and L. Janice Campbell
   1999a   *Fort Polk 41: The Results of a Forty-First Program of Site Testing at Ten Sites,
           Fort Polk Military Reservation, Vernon Parish, Louisiana.* Prentice Thomas and
           Assoc., Report of Investigations No. 424, Fort Walton Beach, Florida.
LaHaye, Paul, Philip D. Bourgeois, Jr., James R. Morehead, L. Janice Campbell, James H.
Mathews, and Prentice M. Thomas, Jr.
   1999b   *Fort Polk 44: The Results of a Forty-Fourth Program of Site Testing at Ten Sites,*

Fort Polk Military Reservation, Vernon Parish, Louisiana. Prentice Thomas and Assoc., Report of Investigations No. 497, Fort Walton Beach, Florida.

Laney, Rex
  1940   *This Is Louisiana.* State Dept. of Commerce and Industry, Tourist Bureau, Baton Rouge.

Largent, Floyd B., Jr., Paul V. Heinrich, Ralph Draughon, Jr., Jennifer Cohen, and William P. Athens
  1992a   *A Cultural Resources Survey of 80 Acres at Fort Polk, Vernon Parish, Louisiana.* R. Christopher Goodwin and Assoc., Delivery Order Report RCG-1, New Orleans.
  1992b   *A Cultural Resources Survey of Joint Readiness Training Center (JRTC) Project: Fullerton Forward Landing Strip/Drop Zone (FLS/DZ) at Fort Polk, Vernon Parish, Louisiana.* R. Christopher Goodwin and Assoc., Delivery Order Report RCG-2, New Orleans.
  1992c   *A Cultural Resources Survey of 358 Acres at Fort Polk, Vernon Parish, Louisiana.* R. Christopher Goodwin and Assoc., Delivery Order Report RCG-3, New Orleans.
  1992d   *A Cultural Resources Survey of 718 Acres on the Fullerton Training Road Network, Fort Polk, Vernon Parish, Louisiana.* R. Christopher Goodwin and Assoc., Delivery Order Report RCG-4, New Orleans.
  1992e   *A Cultural Resources Survey of 340 Acres in the Vicinity of the Peason Ridge Cantonment Area, Fort Polk, Vernon Parish, Louisiana.* R. Christopher Goodwin and Assoc., Delivery Order Report RCG-5, New Orleans.
  1992f   *A Cultural Resources Survey of 282 Acres along Four Reroutes of the Fullerton Training Road Network, Fort Polk, Vernon Parish, Louisiana.* R. Christopher Goodwin and Assoc., Delivery Order Report RCG-7, New Orleans.
  1993a   *A Cultural Resources Survey of 924 Acres along Peason Ridge Training Road Network, Fort Polk, Vernon, Sabine, and Natchitoches Parishes, Louisiana.* R. Christopher Goodwin and Assoc., Delivery Order Report RCG-6, New Orleans.
  1993b   *A Cultural Resources Survey of 665 Acres on the Peason Ridge and Fort Polk Military Reservation, Fort Polk, Vernon Parish, Louisiana.* R. Christopher Goodwin and Assoc., Delivery Order Report RCG-8/9, New Orleans.

Largent, Floyd B., Jr., Paul V. Heinrich, Luis M. Williams, Jr., Ralph Draughon, Jr., Jennifer Cohen, Thomas Fenn, and William P. Athens
  1993c   *A Cultural Resources Survey of 345 Acres along Contact Lanes for the Joint Readiness Training Center Interim Live Fire Complex, Fort Polk, Vernon Parish, Louisiana.* R. Christopher Goodwin and Assoc., Delivery Order Report RCG-13, New Orleans.

Largent, Floyd B., Jr., Paul V. Heinrich, Ralph Draughon, Jr., Jennifer Cohen, Thomas Fenn, and William P. Athens
  1993d   *A Cultural Resources Survey of 189 Acres along the Peason Ridge Training Road Network, Fort Polk, Vernon and Sabine Parishes, Louisiana.* R. Christopher Goodwin and Assoc., Delivery Order Report RCG-19, New Orleans.
  1994a   *A Cultural Resources Survey of 567 Acres on the Zion Hills Training Road Network, Fort Polk, Vernon Parish, Louisiana.* R. Christopher Goodwin and Assoc., Delivery Order Report RCG-12, New Orleans.

Largent, Floyd B., Jr., Paul V. Heinrich, Luis M. Williams, Jr., Ralph Draughon, Jr., Jennifer Cohen, Thomas Fenn, and William P. Athens
  1994b   *A Cultural Resources Survey of 1,962 Acres of Timber Sales in Compartments 47 and 48, Peason Ridge Military Reservation, Fort Polk, Vernon Parish, Louisi-*

ana. R. Christopher Goodwin and Assoc., Delivery Order Report RCG-10/11, New Orleans.

Larson, Lewis H., Jr.
1980   *Aboriginal Subsistence Technology on the Southeastern Coastal Plain during the Late Prehistoric Period*. Ripley P. Bullen Monographs in Anthropology and History, No. 2. University Presses of Florida, Gainesville.

Lawrence, Bessie
1961   Vernon Parish, Leesville Observing 90th Birthday. *Alexandria Daily Town Talk*, April 11.

Leesville–Vernon Parish Chamber of Commerce
1945   *Dawn of a New Day*. On file, Vernon Parish Library, Leesville.

Lehmann, Geoffrey R.
1994a   *Heritage Resources Management Summary 94-8*. Kisatchie National Forest, Pineville, Louisiana.
1994b   *Heritage Resources Management Summary 94-20*. Kisatchie National Forest, Pineville, Louisiana.
1995   *Heritage Resources Management Summary 95-21*. Kisatchie National Forest, Pineville, Louisiana.

Lenzer, John P.
1982   Geomorphology of the Fort Polk Military Reservation. In *Cultural Resources Investigations at the Fort Polk Military Reservation, Vernon, Sabine and Natchitoches Parishes, Louisiana,* by Prentice M. Thomas, Jr., Steven Shelley, L. Janice Campbell, Mark T. Swanson, Carol S. Weed, and John P. Lenzer, pp. 4-1 to 4-49. New World Research, Report of Investigations 69.

Lepper, Bradley T.
1999   Pleistocene Peoples of Midcontinental North America. In *Ice Age Peoples of North America: Environments, Origins, and Adaptations of the First Americans,* edited by Robson Bonnichsen and Karen L. Turnmire, pp. 362–394. Center for the Study of the First Americans, Oregon State University, Corvallis.

Lewis, Wayne
1956   A History of Simpson, Vernon Parish, Louisiana. Paper submitted to Dr. George Stokes, Social Studies 303, Northwestern State College, Natchitoches. On file, Cammie G. Henry Research Center, Watson Memorial Library, Northwestern State University of Louisiana, Natchitoches.

Lockett, Samuel H.
1969   *Louisiana as It Is: A Geographical and Topographical Description of the State*. Louisiana State University Press, Baton Rouge.

Lopez, Margo
1982   Fine Grained (Sand) Sediment Analysis. In *Eagle Hill: A Late Quaternary Upland Site in Western Louisiana,* edited by Joel D. Gunn and David O. Brown, pp. 150–156. Special Report 12, Center for Archaeological Research, University of Texas at San Antonio.

Lopinot, Neal H., Jack H. Ray, and Michael D. Conner (editors)
1998   *The 1997 Excavations at the Big Eddy Site (23CE426) in Southwest Missouri*. Special Publication No. 2, Center for Archaeological Research, Southeast Missouri State University, Springfield.
2000   *The 1999 Excavations at the Big Eddy Site (23CE426)*. Special Publication No. 3, Center for Archaeological Research, Southwest Missouri State University, Springfield.

Louisiana Department of Agriculture and Immigration
    1920   *Louisiana: Her Agricultural Resources, Her Industrial Developments, Her Opportunities.* Dept. of Agriculture and Immigration, Baton Rouge.
    1924   *Louisiana Today.* Dept. of Agriculture and Immigration, Harry D. Wilson Commissioner, Baton Rouge.
    1928   *Louisiana 1927–1928.* Dept. of Agriculture and Immigration, Baton Rouge.
Louisiana Highway Commission
    1930   Map of Vernon Parish. On file, Louisiana State Archives, Baton Rouge.
Louisiana Historical Records Survey
    1939   *County-Parish Boundaries in Louisiana.* Dept. of Archives, Louisiana State University, Baton Rouge.
    1941   *Transcriptions of Parish Records of Louisiana, No. 58, Vernon Parish (Leesville),* vols. 1, 2, and 3. The Statewide Records Project, Works Progress Administration, New Orleans.
    n.d.a   Historical Sketch of Vernon Parish. On file, Historical Records Survey files, Hill Memorial Library, Louisiana State University, Baton Rouge.
    n.d.b   History of Vernon Parish Court House. On file, Historical Records Survey files, Hill Memorial Library, Louisiana State University, Baton Rouge.
Lynott, Mark J.
    1978   *An Archaeological Assessment of the Bear Creek Shelter, Lake Whitney, Texas.* Research Report 115, Archaeology Research Program, Southern Methodist University, Dallas.
McCain, Byron
    n.d.   History of Neame, Louisiana. Paper on file, Vernon Parish Library, Leesville.
McClurkan, Burney B., William T. Field, and J. Ned Woodall
    1966   *Excavations in Toledo Bend Reservoir 1964–1965.* Papers of the Texas Archaeological Salvage Project, No. 8, Austin.
McClurkan, Burney B., Edward B. Jelks, and H. P. Jenson
    1980   Jonas Short and Coral Snake Mound: A Comparison. *Louisiana Archaeology* 6:173–206.
McCulloh, Richard P., and Paul V. Heinrich
    1999   *Geology of the Fort Polk Region, Sabine, Natchitoches, and Vernon Parishes, Louisiana.* Report prepared for Fort Polk by Louisiana Geological Survey, Baton Rouge, and Prewitt and Assoc., Austin, Texas.
McDaniel, Roy, Jr.
    1983   *Kurthwood, Louisiana: The Sawmill Town That Refused to Die.* Privately published monograph. On file, Vernon Parish Library, Leesville.
McGahey, Samuel
    1996   Paleoindian and Early Archaic Data from Mississippi. In *The Paleoindian and Early Archaic Southeast,* edited by David G. Anderson and Kenneth E. Sassaman, pp. 354–384. University of Alabama Press, Tuscaloosa.
McGimsey, Charles R.
    1996   *Points, Pits and Potholes: Archaeology in Southwestern Louisiana.* Regional Archaeology Program Management Unit III 1995/1996 Annual Report. Dept. of Sociology and Anthropology, University of Southwestern Louisiana, Lafayette.
McGimsey, Charles R., and Josette van der Koogh
    2001   *Louisiana's Archaeological Radiometric Database.* Special Publication 3, Louisiana Archaeological Society, Baton Rouge.
McKern, W. C.
    1939   The Midwestern Taxonomic Method as an Aid to Archaeological Culture Study.

American Antiquity 4:301–313.

McMakin, Todd, Maria Tavvaszi, and Kenneth R. Jones
1994 *Archaeological Survey of 2,745 Acres on the Main Fort (Vernon Parish), Fort Polk, Louisiana.* Earth Search, New Orleans.

McManus, Jane Parker
1989 *1880 Vernon Parish, U.S. Census of Population Schedules.* Parker Enterprises, Pineville, Louisiana.

Mahula, Royce
1982 Lithic Period. In *Eagle Hill: A Late Quaternary Upland Site in Western Louisiana,* edited by Joel D. Gunn and David O. Brown, pp. 190–221. Special Report 12, Center for Archaeological Research, University of Texas at San Antonio.

Majerus, Kim, and Chris Rewerts
1994 *Planning and Resource Integration Stewardship Modules: PRISM Kajun Kaleidoscope for Fort Polk. Final Report and User's Manual.* U.S. Army Construction Engineering Research Laboratory, Champaign, Illinois.

Marckese, Thomas A.
1993 A Clovis Point Found at Cote Blanche Island. *Louisiana Archaeology* 20:165–167.

Marler, Don C.
1994 *Historic Hineston.* Dogwood Press, Woodville, Texas.

Marler, Don C., and Jane P. McManus (editors)
1993 *The Cherry Winche Country: Origin of the Redbones and the Westport Fight.* Dogwood Press, Woodville, Texas.

Mason, Ronald J.
1962 The Paleo-Indian Tradition in Eastern North America. *Current Anthropology* 3:227–283.

Mathews, James H., L. Janice Campbell, Prentice M. Thomas, Jr., James R. Morehead, and Joseph Meyer
1995 *Fort Polk 19: The Results of a Nineteenth Program of Site Testing at Ten Sites, Fort Polk Military Reservation, Natchitoches and Vernon Parishes, Louisiana.* Prentice Thomas and Assoc., Report of Investigations No. 273, Fort Walton Beach, Florida.

Mathews, James H., James R. Morehead, L. Janice Campbell, Joseph Meyer, Prentice M. Thomas, Jr.
1996 *Fort Polk 23: The Results of a Twenty-Third Program of Site Testing at Ten Sites, Fort Polk Military Reservation, Vernon Parish, Louisiana.* Prentice Thomas and Assoc., Report of Investigations No. 303, Fort Walton Beach, Florida.

Mathews, James H., Joseph Meyer, James R. Morehead, L. Janice Campbell, and Prentice M. Thomas, Jr.
1997 *Fort Polk 27: The Results of a Twenty-Seventh Program of Site Testing at Ten Sites, Fort Polk Military Reservation, Vernon Parish, Louisiana.* Prentice Thomas and Assoc., Report of Investigations No. 336, Fort Walton Beach, Florida.

Mathews, James H., Chris Parrish, Paul LaHaye, James R. Morehead, Prentice M. Thomas, Jr., and L. Janice Campbell
1998a *Fort Polk 34: The Results of a Thirty-Fourth Program of Site Testing at Ten Sites, Fort Polk Military Reservation, Vernon Parish, Louisiana.* Prentice Thomas and Assoc., Report of Investigations No. 365, Fort Walton Beach, Florida.
1998b *Fort Polk 36: The Results of a Thirty-Sixth Program of Site Testing at Ten Sites, Fort Polk Military Reservation, Vernon Parish, Louisiana.* Prentice Thomas and Assoc., Report of Investigations No. 392, Fort Walton Beach, Florida.

1998c   *Fort Polk 37: The Results of a Thirty-Seventh Program of Site Testing at Ten Sites, Fort Polk Military Reservation, Vernon Parish, Louisiana.* Prentice Thomas and Assoc., Report of Investigations No. 393, Fort Walton Beach, Florida.

1999   *Fort Polk 39: The Results of a Thirty-Ninth Program of Site Testing at Ten Sites, Fort Polk Military Reservation, Vernon Parish, Louisiana.* Prentice Thomas and Assoc., Report of Investigations No. 400, Fort Walton Beach, Florida.

Maxwell, R. S.
1971   Researching Forest History in the Gulf Southwest: The Unity of the Sabine Valley. *Louisiana Studies* 10(2):109–122.

Maxwell, Robert S., and Robert D. Baker
1983   *Sawdust Empire: The Texas Lumber Industry 1830–1940.* Texas A&M University, College Station.

Meltzer, David J.
1984   *Late Pleistocene Human Adaptations in Eastern North America.* Ph.D. dissertation, Dept. of Anthropology, University of Washington, Seattle.

1988   Late Pleistocene Human Adaptations in Eastern North America. *Journal of World Prehistory* 2:1–53.

1997   Monte Verde and the Pleistocene Peopling of the Americas. *Science* 276:754–755.

Meltzer, David J., and Bruce D. Smith
1986   Paleo-Indian and Early Archaic Subsistence Strategies in Eastern North America. In *Foraging, Collecting, and Harvesting: Archaic Period Subsistence and Settlement in the Eastern Woodlands,* edited by Sarah Neusius, pp. 1–30. Center for Archaeological Investigations, Southern Illinois University, Carbondale.

Meyer, Douglas K.
1975   Diffusion of Upland South Folk Housing to the Shawnee Hills of Southern Illinois. *Pioneer America* 7(2):56–66.

Meyer, Joseph, James R. Morehead, James H. Mathews, Prentice M. Thomas, Jr., and L. Janice Campbell
1995a   *Fort Polk 16: The Results of a Sixteenth Program of Site Testing at Ten Sites, Fort Polk Military Reservation, Vernon Parish, Louisiana.* Prentice Thomas and Assoc., Report of Investigations No. 257, Fort Walton Beach, Florida.

Meyer, Joseph, James R. Morehead, James H. Mathews, Harry Lassiter, Prentice M. Thomas, Jr., and L. Janice Campbell
1995b   *Fort Polk 20: The Results of a Twentieth Program of Site Testing at Ten Sites, Fort Polk Military Reservation, Natchitoches and Vernon Parishes, Louisiana.* Prentice Thomas and Assoc., Report of Investigations No. 274, Fort Walton Beach, Florida.

Meyer, Joseph, James R. Morehead, James H. Mathews, Prentice M. Thomas, Jr., and L. Janice Campbell
1996a   *Fort Polk 18: The Results of an Eighteenth Program of Site Testing at Ten Sites, Fort Polk Military Reservation, Vernon Parish, Louisiana.* Prentice Thomas and Assoc., Report of Investigations No. 272, Fort Walton Beach, Florida.

Meyer, Joseph, James R. Morehead, L. Janice Campbell, James H. Mathews, and Prentice M. Thomas, Jr.
1996b   *Fort Polk 24: The Results of a Twenty-Fourth Program of Site Testing at Ten Sites, Fort Polk Military Reservation, Vernon Parish, Louisiana.* Prentice Thomas and Assoc., Report of Investigations No. 326, Fort Walton Beach, Florida.

Meyer, Joseph, James H. Mathews, James R. Morehead, L. Janice Campbell, and Prentice M. Thomas, Jr.
1997   *Fort Polk 25: The Results of a Twenty-Fifth Program of Site Testing at Ten Sites,*

Fort Polk Military Reservation, Vernon Parish, Louisiana. Prentice Thomas and Assoc., Report of Investigations No. 334, Fort Walton Beach, Florida.

Michie, James L.
1966 The Taylor Point. *Chesopiean* 4(5/6):123–124.
1968a The Brier Creek Lanceolate. *Chesopiean* 6(3):76.
1968b The Edgefield Scraper. *Chesopiean* 6:30–31.
1972 The Edgefield Scraper: A Tool of Inferred Antiquity and Use. *South Carolina Antiquities* 4(1):1–10.

Miller, Christina E.
1997 *Gulf Lumber Company and Fullerton, Louisiana 1907–1927.* Master's thesis, Dept. of Anthropology, Northwestern State University, Natchitoches, Louisiana.

Miller, E. O., and Edward B. Jelks
1952 Archeological Excavations at the Belton Reservoir, Coryell County, Texas. *Bulletin of the Texas Archeological Society* 23:168–217.

Miller, Merle
1987 *Ike the Soldier: As They Knew Him.* G. P. Putnam's Sons, New York.

Milner, George R.
1999 Warfare in Prehistoric and Early Historic North America. *Journal of Archaeological Research* 7:105–151.

Morehead, James R.
1983 Archaeological Investigations along the Lookout Road Tank Trail. In *U.S.L. Fort Polk Archaeological Survey and Cultural Resources Management Program,* 2 vols., edited by A. Frank Servello, pp. 625–718. University of Southwestern Louisiana, Lafayette.

Morehead, James R., and James H. Mathews
1992 Artifact Analyses. In *Site Testing at Ten Sites on Peason Ridge, Fort Polk Military Reservation, Sabine Parish, Louisiana,* by Prentice Thomas and Assoc., pp. 14–33. Prentice Thomas and Assoc., Report of Investigations No. 215, Fort Walton Beach, Florida.

Morehead, James R., Prentice M. Thomas, Jr., L. Janice Campbell, James H. Mathews, and Joseph Meyer
1994 *Fort Polk 14: The Results of a Fourteenth Program of Site Testing at Ten Sites, Fort Polk Military Reservation, Sabine and Vernon Parishes, Louisiana.* Prentice Thomas and Assoc., Report of Investigations No. 253, Fort Walton Beach, Florida.
1995a *Fort Polk 12: The Results of a Twelfth Program of Site Testing at Ten Sites, Fort Polk Military Reservation, Vernon Parish, Louisiana.* Prentice Thomas and Assoc., Report of Investigations No. 249, Fort Walton Beach, Florida.

Morehead, James R., L. Janice Campbell, Prentice M. Thomas, Jr., James H. Mathews, and Joseph Meyer
1995b *Fort Polk 13: The Results of a Thirteenth Program of Site Testing at Ten Sites, Fort Polk Military Reservation, Vernon Parish, Louisiana.* Prentice Thomas and Assoc., Report of Investigations No. 252, Fort Walton Beach, Florida.

Morehead, James R., Joseph Meyer, James H. Mathews, L. Janice Campbell, and Prentice M. Thomas, Jr.
1995c *Fort Polk 15: The Results of a Fifteenth Program of Site Testing at Ten Sites, Fort Polk Military Reservation, Vernon Parish, Louisiana.* Prentice Thomas and Assoc., Report of Investigations No. 254, Fort Walton Beach, Florida.

Morehead, James R., Joseph Meyer, James H. Mathews, Prentice M. Thomas, Jr., and L. Janice Campbell
1995d *Fort Polk 17: The Results of a Seventeenth Program of Site Testing at Ten Sites,*

> *Fort Polk Military Reservation, Vernon Parish, Louisiana.* Prentice Thomas and Assoc., Report of Investigations No. 271, Fort Walton Beach, Florida.

Morehead, James R., L. Janice Campbell, James H. Mathews, Joseph Meyer, and Prentice M. Thomas, Jr.

> 1996a   *Fort Polk 21: The Results of a Twenty-First Program of Site Testing at Ten Sites, Fort Polk Military Reservation, Vernon Parish, Louisiana.* Prentice Thomas and Assoc., Report of Investigations No. 301, Fort Walton Beach, Florida.

> 1996b   *Fort Polk 22: The Results of a Twenty-Second Program of Site Testing at Ten Sites, Fort Polk Military Reservation, Vernon Parish, Louisiana.* Prentice Thomas and Assoc., Report of Investigations No. 302, Fort Walton Beach, Florida.

Morehead, James R., Prentice M. Thomas, Jr., Chris Parrish, Paul LaHaye, L. Janice Campbell, and James H. Mathews

> 1997   *Fort Polk 30: The Results of a Thirtieth Program of Site Testing at Ten Sites, Fort Polk Military Reservation, Vernon Parish, Louisiana.* Prentice Thomas and Assoc., Report of Investigations No. 346, Fort Walton Beach, Florida.

Morehead, James R., Prentice M. Thomas, Jr., L. Janice Campbell, James H. Mathews, Chris Parrish, and Paul LaHaye

> 1999a   *Fort Polk 40: The Results of a Fortieth Program of Site Testing at Ten Sites, Fort Polk Military Reservation, Vernon Parish, Louisiana.* Prentice Thomas and Assoc., Report of Investigations No. 406, Fort Walton Beach, Florida.

Morehead, James R., L. Janice Campbell, Paul LaHaye, Philip D. Bourgeois, Jr., James H. Mathews, and Prentice M. Thomas, Jr.

> 1999b   *Fort Polk 45: The Results of a Forty-Fifth Program of Site Testing at Ten Sites, Fort Polk Military Reservation, Vernon Parish, Louisiana.* Prentice Thomas and Assoc., Report of Investigations No. 498, Fort Walton Beach, Florida.

> 2000a   *Fort Polk 46: The Results of a Forty-Sixth Program of Site Testing at Ten Sites, Fort Polk Military Reservation, Vernon Parish, Louisiana.* Prentice Thomas and Assoc., Report of Investigations No. 517, Fort Walton Beach, Florida.

> 2000b   *Fort Polk 47: The Results of a Forty-Seventh Program of Site Testing at Ten Sites, Fort Polk Military Reservation, Vernon Parish, Louisiana.* Prentice Thomas and Assoc., Report of Investigations No. 518, Fort Walton Beach, Florida.

Morehead, James R., L. Janice Campbell, James H. Mathews, Philip D. Bourgeois, Jr., Carrie Williams, and Prentice M. Thomas, Jr.

> 2002   *Fort Polk 50: The Results of a Fiftieth Program of Site Testing at Ten Sites, Fort Polk Military Reservation, Vernon Parish, Louisiana.* Prentice Thomas and Assoc., Report of Investigations No. 630, Fort Walton Beach, Florida.

Morris, Richard B. (editor)

> 1965   *Encyclopedia of American History.* Harper & Brothers, New York.

Morrison, Samuel Elliot

> 1972   *The Oxford History of the American People.* 3 vols. New American Library, New York.

Morse, Dan F.

> 1973   Dalton Culture in Northeast Arkansas. *Florida Anthropologist* 26:23–38.

> 1975a   Reply to Schiffer. In *The Cache River Archaeological Project: An Experiment in Contract Archaeology,* edited by Michael B. Schiffer and John M. House, pp. 113–119. Research Series No. 8, Arkansas Archeological Survey, Fayetteville.

> 1975b   Paleo-Indian in the Land of Opportunity: Preliminary Report on the Excavations at the Sloan Site (3GE94). In *The Cache River Archaeological Project: An Experiment in Contract Archaeology,* edited by Michael B. Schiffer and John M.

House, pp. 93–113. Research Series No. 8, Arkansas Archeological Survey, Fayetteville.

1977   Dalton Settlement Systems: Reply to Schiffer (2). *Plains Anthropologist* 22:149–158.

1997   An Overview of the Dalton Period in Northeastern Arkansas and in the Southeastern United States. In *Sloan: A Paleoindian Dalton Cemetery in Arkansas,* edited by Dan F. Morse, pp. 123–139. Smithsonian Institution Press, Washington, D.C.

Morse, Dan F., and Phyllis A. Morse

1983   *Archaeology of the Central Mississippi Valley.* Academic Press, New York.

Morse, Dan F., David G. Anderson, and Albert C. Goodyear, III

1996   The Pleistocene-Holocene Transition in the Eastern United States. In *Humans at the End of the Ice Age: The Archaeology of the Pleistocene-Holocene Transition,* edited by Lawrence Guy Straus, Berit Valentin Eriksen, John M. Erlandson, and David R. Yesner, pp. 319–338. Plenum Press, New York.

Munson, Patrick

1990   Folsom Fluted Projectile Points East of the Great Plains and Their Biogeographical Correlates. *North American Archaeologist* 11:255–272.

Nance, Jack D., and Bruce F. Ball

1986   No Surprises? The Reliability and Validity of Test Pit Sampling. *American Antiquity* 51:457–483.

Nardini, Louis Raphael

1961   *No Man's Land: A History of the Camino Real.* Pelican Publishing, New Orleans.

Nassaney, Michael S., and Kendra Pyle

1999   The Adoption of the Bow and Arrow in Eastern North America: A View from Central Arkansas. *American Antiquity* 64(2):243–263.

Neill, Wilfred T.

1958   A Stratified Early Site at Silver Springs, Florida. *Florida Anthropologist* 11:32–52.

1963   Three New Florida Projectile Point Types Believed to Be Early. *Florida Anthropologist* 14(4):99–104.

Neuman, Robert W.

1984   *An Introduction to Louisiana Archaeology.* Louisiana State University Press, Baton Rouge.

Neusius, Sarah W., and Michael D. Wiant

1985   Early Archaic Settlement in the Little Illinois River Valley. Paper presented at the Annual Meeting of the Midwest Archaeological Conference, Lansing, Michigan.

Newell, H. Perry, and Alex D. Krieger

1949   *The George C. Davis Site, Cherokee County, Texas.* Memoirs of the Society for American Archeology. The Society for American Archaeology and the University of Texas, Menasha.

Newton, Milton B., Jr.

1971   The Annual Round in the Upland South: The Synchronization of Man and Nature through Culture. *Pioneer America* 3(2):63–73.

1974   Cultural Preadaptation and the Upland South. In *Man and Cultural Heritage,* edited by H. J. Walker and William G. Haag, pp. 143–154. Geoscience and Man 5. Louisiana State University, Baton Rouge.

Nials, Fred, and Joel D. Gunn

1982   Geomorphology and Soils. In *Eagle Hill: A Late Quaternary Upland Site in Western Louisiana,* edited by Joel D. Gunn and David O. Brown, pp. 126–134. Spe-

cial Report 12, Center for Archaeological Research, University of Texas at San
Antonio.

Novick, Andrea Lee
1984   The Lithic Analysis. In *Cultural Resources Evaluations, Fort Polk, Louisiana,*
        edited by Charles E. Cantley and John R. Kern, pp. 216–243. Report R-2639,
        Gilbert/Commonwealth, Jackson, Michigan.

NOAA (National Ocean and Atmospheric Agency)
1975   Climate of Leesville, Louisiana. *Climatography of the United States* 20.

O'Brien, S. M., P. A. Mayewski, L. D. Meeker, D. A. Meese, M. S. Twickler, and S. I.
Whitlow
1995   Complexity of Holocene Climate as Reconstructed from a Greenland Ice Core.
        Science 270:1962–1964.

Office of the Chief Engineers
1975   Tract Register, Fort Polk. Real Estate Office, Fort Polk.

O'Halloran, John D.
1951–1952   Historical Vernon. Columns in *The Leesville Leader,* Leesville, Louisiana,
        1951 and 1952. William A. Poe Collection, folder 3, Cammie G. Henry Research
        Center, Watson Memorial Library, Northwestern State University of Louisiana,
        Natchitoches.

Olmstead, Frederick Law
1968   *A Journey in the Seaboard Slave States, With Remarks on Their Economy.* Re-
        printed. Negro University Press, New York. Originally published 1856, Dix and
        Edwards.

Orser, Charles E., Jr., and Claudia C. Holland
1984   Let Us Praise Famous Men, Accurately: Toward a More Complete Understanding
        of Postbellum Southern Agricultural Practices. *Southeastern Archaeology* 3:111–
        120.

Orser, Charles E., Jr., and Annette M. Nekola
1985   Plantation Settlement from Slavery to Tenancy: An Example from a Piedmont
        Plantation in South Carolina. In *The Archaeology of Slavery and Plantation Life,*
        edited by Theresa A. Singleton, pp. 67–94. Academic Press, New York.

O'Steen, Lisa D.
1996   Paleoindian and Early Archaic Settlement along the Oconee Drainage. In *The
        Paleoindian and Early Archaic Southeast,* edited by David G. Anderson and Ken-
        neth E. Sassaman, pp. 92–106. University of Alabama Press, Tuscaloosa.

Ostrum, Carl E., and Keith W. Dorman
1945   Gum Naval Stores Industry. *Chemurgic Digest* 29:1–6. Chemurgic Reprint Se-
        ries.

Otto, John Solomon
1985   The Migration of the Southern Plain Folk: An Interdisciplinary Synthesis. *Jour-
        nal of Southern History* 51(2):183–199.

Otto, John Solomon, and Nain Estelle Anderson
1982   The Diffusion of Upland South Folk. *Southeastern Geographer* 22(2):89–98.

Otto, John Solomon, and Augustus Marion Burns III
1981   Traditional Agricultural Practices in the Arkansas Highlands. *Journal of Ameri-
        can Folklore* 94(372):166–187.

Oubre, Claude F.
1976   Forty Acres and a Mule: Louisiana and the Southern Homestead Act. *Louisiana
        History* 17(a):143–157.

Owsley, Frank
    1949   *Plain Folk of the Old South.* Louisiana State University Press, Baton Rouge.
Parrish, Chris, James R. Morehead, Paul LaHaye, L. Janice Campbell, James H. Mathews, and Prentice M. Thomas, Jr.
    1997a   *Fort Polk 29: The Results of a Twenty-Ninth Program of Site Testing at Ten Sites, Fort Polk Military Reservation, Vernon Parish, Louisiana.* Prentice Thomas and Assoc., Report of Investigations No. 345, Fort Walton Beach, Florida.
Parrish, Chris, Paul LaHaye, James R. Morehead, Prentice M. Thomas, Jr., L. Janice Campbell, and James H. Mathews
    1997b   *Fort Polk 31: The Results of a Thirty-First Program of Site Testing at Ten Sites, Fort Polk Military Reservation, Vernon Parish, Louisiana.* Prentice Thomas and Assoc., Report of Investigations No. 350, Fort Walton Beach, Florida.
    1997c   *Fort Polk 32: The Results of a Thirty-Second Program of Site Testing at Ten Sites, Fort Polk Military Reservation, Vernon Parish, Louisiana.* Prentice Thomas and Assoc., Report of Investigations No. 351, Fort Walton Beach, Florida.
    1998   *Fort Polk 33: The Results of a Thirty-Third Program of Site Testing at Ten Sites, Fort Polk Military Reservation, Vernon Parish, Louisiana.* Prentice Thomas and Assoc., Report of Investigations No. 364, Fort Walton Beach, Florida.
Parry, William J., and John E. Clark
    1987   Expedient Core Technology and Sedentism. In *The Organization of Core Technology,* edited by Jay K. Johnson and Carol A. Morrow, pp. 285–304. Westview Press, Boulder, Colorado.
Patterson, Leland W.
    1977   The Catahoula Projectile Point: A Distributional Study. *Louisiana Archaeology* (Lafayette) 3:217–223.
    1982   Initial Employment of the Bow and Arrow in Southern North America. *La Tierra, Journal of the Southern Texas Archaeological Association* 9(2):18–26.
    1987   The Catahoula Perforator: A Possible New Artifact Type. *Houston Archeological Society Journal* 88:19–21.
    1995   The Archeology of Southeast Texas. *Bulletin of the Texas Archeological Society* 66:239–264.
Patton, Robert, and Raymond Ezell
    1999   Results of Survey. In *Archaeological Survey of 6,407 Acres at Peason Ridge, Fort Polk, Vernon, Sabine, and Natchitoches Parishes, Louisiana,* edited by H. Blaine Ensor, Robert Patton, Raymond Ezell, Jeffrey L. Holland, and Lynn Marie Piatak, pp. 49–329. TRC Garrow Associates, Atlanta.
Paxton, W. E.
    1888   *A History of the Baptists of Louisiana.* C. R. Barnes Publishing, St. Louis.
Perino, Gregory
    1968   *Guide to the Identification of Certain American Indian Projectile Points.* Special Bulletin No. 3, Oklahoma Anthropological Society, Oklahoma City.
    1971   *Guide to the Identification of Certain American Indian Projectile Points.* Special Bulletin No. 4, Oklahoma Anthropological Society, Oklahoma City.
    1985   *Selected Preforms, Points and Knives of the North American Indians,* vol. 1. Points and Barbs Press, Idabel, Oklahoma.
    1991   *Selected Preforms, Points and Knives of the North American Indians,* vol. 2. Points and Barbs Press, Idabel, Oklahoma.
Perret, Geoffrey
    1991   *There's a War to Be Won: The United States Army in World War II.* Random House, New York.

Perry, Percival
1947   *The Naval Stores Industry in the Antebellum South, 1789–1861.* Ph.D. dissertation, Duke University, Durham, North Carolina.

Perttula, Timothy K.
1992   *"The Caddo Nation": Archaeological and Ethnohistoric Perspectives.* University of Texas Press, Austin.

Perttula, Timothy K., and James E. Bruseth (editors)
1998   *The Native History of the Caddo, Their Place in Southeastern Archaeology and Ethnohistory.* Studies in Archaeology 30, Texas Archaeological Research Laboratory, University of Texas at Austin.

Perttula, Timothy K., Mykes R. Miller, Robert A. Ricklis, Daniel J. Prikryl, and Christopher Lintz
1995   Prehistoric and Historic Aboriginal Ceramics in Texas. *Bulletin of the Texas Archeological Society* 66:175–235.

Peter, D. E., and D. E. McGregor
1987   Lithic Reduction Systems and Interassemblage Variability: Problems of Recognition. In *Hunter-Gatherer Adaptations along the Prairie Margin: Site Excavations and Synthesis of Prehistoric Archaeology,* edited by D. E. McGregor and James E. Bruseth, pp. 197–228. Richland Creek Technical Series Volume 3, Institute for the Study of Earth and Man, Archaeology Research Program, Southern Methodist University, Dallas.

Peterson, John K., and Ramona Grunden
1998   Material Culture. In *Archaeological Survey of 12,538 Acres Fort Polk, Vernon Parish, Louisiana,* edited by Christopher Ohm Clement, Ramona M. Grunden, John K. Peterson, Jill S. Quattlebaum, and Steven D. Smith, pp. 377–410. South Carolina Institute of Archaeology and Anthropology, University of South Carolina, Columbia.

Phillips, Phillip
1970   *Archaeological Survey in the Lower Yazoo Basin, Mississippi, 1947–1955.* 2 vols. Papers of the Peabody Museum of Archaeology and Ethnology 60, Cambridge, Massachusetts.

Phillips, Phillip, James Ford, and James B. Griffin
1951   *Archaeological Survey in the Lower Mississippi Alluvial Valley, 1940–1947.* Papers of the Peabody Museum of Archaeology and Ethnology 25, Cambridge, Massachusetts.

Phillips, Timothy P., and Larry D. Haikey
1992   *Cultural Resources Inventory on the Kisatchie National Forest, Louisiana. FY 1989.* Report on file with the Div. of Archeology, Baton Rouge.

Phillips, Timothy P., and Greg Wasson
1989   *Cultural Resources Inventory on the Kisatchie National Forest, Louisiana. April–September 1988.* Interim Report No. 2. Report on file with the Div. of Archeology, Baton Rouge.

Phillips, Timothy P., and Charles G. Willingham
1990   *Cultural Resources Survey on the Kisatchie National Forest. FY 1986.* Report on file with the Louisiana Div. of Archeology, Baton Rouge.

Pielou, E. C.
1969   *An Introduction to Mathematical Ecology.* Wiley Interscience, New York.

Pietak, Lynn Marie
1999   Historic Synthesis. In *Archaeological Survey of 6,407 Acres at Peason Ridge,*

Fort Polk, Vernon, Sabine, and Natchitoches Parishes, Louisiana, edited by H. Blaine Ensor, Robert Patton, Raymond Ezell, Jeffrey L. Holland, and Lynn Marie Piatak, pp. 394–398. TRC Garrow Associates, Atlanta.

Pillsbury, Richard
    1983   The Europeanization of the Cherokee Settlement Landscape Prior to the Removal: A Georgia Case Study. In *Historical Archaeology of the Eastern United States,* edited by Robert W. Neuman, pp. 59–69. Geoscience and Man 23. Louisiana State University, Baton Rouge.

Plog, Fred T., and J. N. Hill
    1971   Explaining Variability in the Distribution of Sites. In *The Distribution of Prehistoric Population Aggregates,* edited by George J. Gumerman, pp. 7–36. Prescott College Anthropological Reports No. 1, Prescott, Arizona.

Poche, Felix Pierre
    1972   *A Louisiana Confederate: Diary of Felix Pierre Poche,* edited by Edwin C. Bearss. Louisiana Studies Institute, Natchitoches.

Pollacia, Nick
    1994   *The Third Army Maneuvers, May 1940: The First of the Great Louisiana Maneuvers.* Master's thesis, Northwestern State University of Louisiana, Natchitoches.

Pool, Joe David
    1992   *People of Providence.* Privately published. On file, Vernon Parish Library, Leesville.

Poole, T. W.
    1889   *Some Late Words about Louisiana.* Louisiana Bureau of Immigration, Ernest Marchand State Printer, New Orleans.

Poor's Manual
    1906   *Poor's Manual of Railroads of the United States.* Poor's Railroad Manual Company, New York.
    1915   *Poor's Manual of Railroads of the United States.* Poor's Railroad Manual Company, New York.
    1935   *Poor's Manual of Railroads of the United States.* Poor's Railroad Manual Company, New York.

Poplin, Eric
    1987   *Cultural Resource Survey of the North Fort Polk Family Housing Area, Fort Polk, Vernon Parish, Louisiana.* Submitted to Headquarters, 5th Infantry Div., and Fort Polk. Report on file with the Div. of Archeology, Baton Rouge.

Post Office Department
    1973   Records of Appointments of Postmasters, 1832–Sept. 30, 1971. Record group 28, M841, reels 51, 52. National Archives, Washington, D.C.

Prentice Thomas and Assoc., Inc.
    1992   *Site Testing at Ten Sites on Peason Ridge, Fort Polk Military Reservation, Sabine Parish, Louisiana.* Prentice Thomas and Assoc., Report of Investigations No. 215, Fort Walton Beach, Florida.

Prewitt, E. R.
    1981   Cultural Chronology in Central Texas. *Bulletin of the Texas Archeological Society* 52:65–89.
    1995   Distributions of Typed Projectile Points in Texas. *Bulletin of the Texas Archeological Society* 66:83–173.

Price, Cynthia R., and James E. Price
    1978   Investigation of Settlement and Subsistence Systems in the Ozark Border Region

of Southeast Missouri during the First Half of the Nineteenth Century: The Widow Harris Cabin Project. Paper presented at the Annual Meeting of the Society for Historical Archaeology, San Antonio, Texas.

Price, Dennis
1977   *Archaeological Investigations in the Kisatchie National Forest, Louisiana.* Report prepared for the U.S. Forest Service, Kisatchie National Forest, Louisiana. Ms. on file at the Kisatchie National Forest, Pineville.

Price, James E., and James Krakker
1975   *Dalton Occupation of the Ozark Border.* Museum Briefs 2, University of Missouri, Columbia.

Prieto, Annabella, Susan Steigler, and Joan Exnicios
1978   Archaeological Survey in the Kisatchie National Forest, Louisiana, Summer, 1978. Ms. on file at the Kisatchie National Forest, Pineville.

Pritchard, Walter (editor)
1938   A Tourist's Description of Louisiana in 1860. *Louisiana Historical Quarterly* 21:1157–1214.

Quimby, George
1951   The Medora Site, West Baton Rouge Parish, Louisiana. *Field Museum of Natural History, Anthropological Series* 24(2):81–135.
1957   *The Bayou Goula Site, Iberville Parish, Louisiana.* Chicago Natural History Museum, Fieldiana, Anthropology 47(2).

Rafferty, Milton D.
1980   *The Ozarks Land and Life.* University of Oklahoma Press, Norman.

Ray, Jack H.
1998   Cultural Components. In *The 1997 Excavations at the Big Eddy Site (23CE426) in Southwest Missouri,* edited by Neal H. Lopinot, Jack H. Ray, and Michael D. Conner, pp. 111–220. Special Publication No. 2, Center for Archaeological Research, Southeast Missouri State University, Springfield.

Raymer, Leslie
1993a   Macroplant Analysis. In *Data Recovery at Site 16VN794: Investigations into Site Formation Processes and the Cultural Sequence of West Central Louisiana,* by Charles E. Cantley, Leslie E. Raymer, John S. Foss, C. Stiles, Linda Scott Cummings, J. W. Joseph, and J. Raymer, pp. 138–144. New South Associates, Technical Report 119, Stone Mountain, Georgia.
1993b   Analysis of Cultural Features. In *Data Recovery at Site 16VN794: Investigations into Site Formation Processes and the Cultural Sequence of West Central Louisiana,* by Charles E. Cantley, Leslie E. Raymer, John S. Foss, C. Stiles, Linda Scott Cummings, J. W. Joseph, and J. Raymer, pp. 145–153. New South Associates, Technical Report 119, Stone Mountain, Georgia.
1993c   Ceramic Analysis. In *Data Recovery at Site 16VN794: Investigations into Site Formation Processes and the Cultural Sequence of West Central Louisiana,* edited by Charles E. Cantley, Leslie E. Raymer, John S. Foss, C. Stiles, Linda Scott Cummings, J. W. Joseph, and J. Raymer, pp. 217–249. New South Associates, Technical Report 119, Stone Mountain, Georgia.

Raymer, Leslie, and L. Scott Cummings
1993   Paleoenvironmental and Subsistence Investigations. In *Data Recovery at Site 16VN794: Investigations into Site Formation Processes and the Cultural Sequence of West Central Louisiana,* edited by Charles E. Cantley, Leslie E. Raymer, John S. Foss, C. Stiles, Linda Scott Cummings, J. W. Joseph, and J. Raymer, pp. 131–144. New South Associates, Technical Report 119, Stone Mountain, Georgia.

Resnick, Benjamin
  1988   *The Williams Place: A Scotch-Irish Farmstead in the South Carolina Piedmont.* Volumes in Historical Archaeology III. South Carolina Institute of Archaeology and Anthropology, Columbia.
Richardson, Norman
  1960   Kisatchie: The People's Forest. *Shreveport Times,* November 20.
Richardson, Otis Dunbar
  1983   Fullerton, Louisiana: An American Monument. *Journal of Forest History* 27(4):192–201.
Robertson, Minns Sledge
  1952   *Public Education in Louisiana after 1898.* Bureau of Educational Materials and Research, College of Education, Louisiana State University, Baton Rouge.
Robinson, Kenneth W.
  1988   Archaeology and the North Carolina Naval Stores Industry: A Prospectus. Ms. prepared for the Office of State Archaeology, North Carolina Div. of Archives and History, Dept. of Cultural Resources, Raleigh.
Rolingson, Martha A. (editor)
  1982   *Emerging Patterns of Plum Bayou Culture.* Research Series No. 18, Arkansas Archeological Survey, Fayetteville.
Ruhe, Robert B.
  1974   Holocene Environments and Soil Geomorphology in Midwestern United States. *Quaternary Research* 4:487–495.
  1975   *Geomorphology: Geomorphic Processes and Surficial Geology.* Houghton Mifflin, Boston.
Ruhe, Robert B., and P. H. Walker
  1968   Hillslope Models and Soil Formation. *Transactions of 9th Congress of International Soil Science Society* 4:551–560.
Russo, Michael
  1994   Why We Don't Believe in Archaic Ceremonial Mounds and Why We Should: The Case from Florida. *Southeastern Archaeology* 13:93–109.
  1996   Southeastern Archaic Mounds. In *Archaeology of the Mid-Holocene Southeast,* edited by Kenneth E. Sassaman and David G. Anderson, pp. 259–287. University Presses of Florida, Gainesville.
Saatkamp, Andrew, C. Andrew Buchner, and Jan Gray
  2000   *An Intensive Phase I Cultural Resources Survey of 6,535 Acres within Portions of Training Areas Sixmile Creek 1, 2, & 3, and Slagle 7, 8, 9, 10 & 11 on Fort Polk Military Reservation, Vernon Parish, Louisiana.* Panamerican Consultants, Memphis.
  2001   *A Cultural Resources Survey of 4,212 Acres on Fort Polk Military Reservation and the Limited Use Area, Vernon Parish, Louisiana.* Panamerican Consultants, Memphis.
Sabo, George III
  1990   Historic Europeans and Americans. In *Human Adaptation in the Ozark and Ouachita Mountains,* by George Sabo III, Ann M. Early, Jerome C. Rose, Barbara A. Burnett, Louis Vogele, Jr., and James P. Harcourt, pp. 135–170. Research Series No. 31, Arkansas Archeological Survey, Fayetteville.
Saitta, Dean J.
  1983   On the Evolution of "Tribal" Social Networks. *American Antiquity* 48:820–824.
Sandel, Luther
  1982   *The Free State of Sabine and Western Louisiana.* Jet Publications, Many, Louisiana.

Sandweiss, Daniel H., James B. Richardson III, Elizabeth J. Reitz, Harold B. Rollins, and
Kirk A. Maasch
    1996   Geoarchaeological Evidence from Peru for a 5000 Years B.P. Onset of El Niño.
            Science 273:1531–1533.
Santeford, Lawrence G., William A. Martin, and E. Thomas Hemmings
    1985   *Excavations at Four Sites in the Cypress Creek Basin, Conway County, Arkansas.*
            Research Report No. 24, Arkansas Archeological Survey, Fayetteville.
Sargent, Charles
    1884   *Report of the Forests of North America.* GPO, Washington, D.C.
Sassaman, Kenneth
    1991   Adaptive Flexibility in the Morrow Mountain Phase of the Middle Archaic Pe-
            riod. *South Carolina Antiquities* 23:31–41.
    1993a   *Early Pottery in the Southeast: Tradition and Innovation in Cooking Technology.*
            University of Alabama, Tuscaloosa.
    1993b   Hunter-Gatherer Site Structure at Upland Sites in the South Atlantic Coast Plain.
            Southeastern Archaeology 12(2):117–136.
    1995   The Cultural Diversity of Interactions among Mid-Holocene Societies of the Ameri-
            can Southeast. In *Native American Interactions: Multiscalar Analyses and Inter-
            pretations in the Eastern Woodlands,* edited by Michael Nassaney and Kenneth
            E. Sassaman, pp. 174–204. University of Tennessee Press, Knoxville.
    2001   Hunter Gatherers and Traditions of Resistance. In *The Archaeology of Traditions:
            Agency and History before and after Columbus,* edited by Timothy R. Pauketat,
            pp. 218–236. University Press of Florida, Gainesville.
Sassaman, Kenneth E., and David G. Anderson
    1994   *Middle and Late Archaic Archaeological Records of South Carolina.* Council of
            South Carolina Professional Archaeologists, Columbia.
Sassaman, Kenneth E., and David G. Anderson (editors)
    1996   *The Archaeology of the Mid-Holocene Southeast.* University Press of Florida,
            Gainesville.
Sassaman, Kenneth E., and William Green
    1993   Lithic Artifact Analysis. In *Early Woodland Settlement in the Aiken Plateau: Ar-
            chaeological Investigations at 38AK157, Savannah River Site, Aiken County, South
            Carolina,* edited by Kenneth E. Sassaman, pp. 155–235. Savannah River Archaeo-
            logical Research Papers 3, Savannah River Archaeological Research Program,
            South Carolina Institute of Archaeology and Anthropology, University of South
            Carolina, Columbia.
Saucier, Roger T.
    1994   The Paleoenvironmental Setting of Northeast Louisiana during the Paleo-Indian
            Period. *Louisiana Archaeology* 16:129–146.
Saunders, Joe W., and Thurman Allen
    1997   The Archaic Period. *Louisiana Archaeology* 22:1–30.
Saunders, Joe W., Thurman Allen, and Roger T. Saucier
    1994   Four Archaic? Mound Complexes in Northeast Louisiana. *Southeastern Archae-
            ology* 13:134–153.
Saunders, Joe W., Rolfe D. Mandel, Roger T. Saucier, E. Thurman Allen, C. T. Hallmark,
Jay K. Johnson, Edwin H. Jackson, Charles M. Allen, Gary L. Stringer, Douglas S. Frink,
James K. Feathers, Stephen Williams, Kristen J. Gremillion, Malcolm F. Vidrine, and Reca
Jones
    1997   A Mound Complex in Louisiana at 5400–5000 Years before the Present. *Science*
            277:1796–1799.

Saunders, Joe W., Reca Jones, Kathryn Moorhead, and Brian Davis
    1998   "Watson Brake Objects," an Unusual Artifact Type from Northeast Louisiana and Southwest Mississippi. *Southeastern Archaeology* 17:72–79.

Schambach, Frank B.
    1970   *Pre-Caddoan Cultures in the Trans-Mississippi South: A Beginning Sequence.* Ph.D. dissertation, Dept. of Anthropology, Harvard University.
    1982   An Outline of Fourche Maline Culture in Southwest Arkansas. In *Arkansas Archeology in Review,* edited by Neal L. Trubowitz and Marvin D. Jeter, pp. 132–197. Research Series No. 15, Arkansas Archeological Survey, Fayetteville.
    1990   The Archeology of the Bangs Slough Site. In *Coles Creek and Mississippi Period Foragers in the Felsenthal Region of the Lower Mississippi Valley,* edited by Frank B. Schambach, pp. 113–123. Research Series No. 39, Arkansas Archeological Survey, Fayetteville.
    1996   Mounds, Embankments, and Ceremonialism in the Trans-Mississippi South. In *Mounds, Embankments, and Ceremonialism in the Midsouth,* edited by Robert C. Mainfort, Jr., and Richard Walling, pp. 36–49. Research Series No. 46, Arkansas Archeological Survey, Fayetteville.
    1998   *Pre-Caddoan Cultures in the Trans-Mississippi South.* Research Series No. 53, Arkansas Archeological Survey, Fayetteville.
    2002   Fourche Maline: A Woodland Period Culture of the Trans-Mississippi South. In *The Woodland Southeast,* edited by David G. Anderson and Robert C. Mainfort, Jr., pp. 91–112. University of Alabama Press, Tuscaloosa.

Schambach, Frank B. (editor)
    1990   *Coles Creek and Mississippi Period Foragers in the Felsenthal Region of the Lower Mississippi Valley.* Research Series No. 39, Arkansas Archeological Survey, Fayetteville.

Schambach, Frank B., and Ann M. Early
    1982   Southwest Arkansas. In *A State Plan for the Conservation of Archeological Resources in Arkansas,* edited by Hester A. Davis, pp. SW 1–149. Research Series No. 21, Arkansas Archeological Survey, Fayetteville.

Schambach, Frank B., and David B. Waddell
    1990   The Pottery from the Bangs Slough Site. In *Coles Creek and Mississippi Period Foragers in the Felsenthal Region of the Lower Mississippi Valley,* edited by Frank B. Schambach, pp. 19–62. Research Series No. 39, Arkansas Archeological Survey, Fayetteville.

Schiebout, Judith A.
    1995   *Paleofaunal Survey, Collecting, Processing, and Documentation at Two Locations on Fort Polk, Louisiana.* DACW 63-90-10-0300 final report produced for the U.S. Army Corps of Engineers, Fort Worth District. Louisiana State University Museum of Natural Science, Baton Rouge.

Schiebout, Judith A., and Brett S. Dooley
    1995   *Fossils from Fort Polk, Louisiana.* Louisiana State University Museum of Natural Science, Baton Rouge.

Schiffer, Michael B.
    1975   Some Further Comments on the Dalton Settlement Pattern Hypothesis. In *The Cache River Archaeological Project: An Experiment in Contract Archaeology,* edited by Michael B. Schiffer and John H. House, pp. 103–112. Research Series No. 8, Arkansas Archeological Survey, Fayetteville.

Schuldenrein, Joseph
    1984   Environmental Setting of the Project Area. In *Cultural Resources Evaluations,*

Fort Polk, Louisiana, edited by Charles E. Cantley and John R. Kern, pp. 7–21. Report R-2639, Gilbert/Commonwealth, Jackson, Michigan.

1996   Geoarchaeology and Mid-Holocene Landscape History. In *Archaeology of the Mid-Holocene Southeast,* edited by Kenneth E. Sassaman and David G. Anderson, pp. 3–27. University Press of Florida, Gainesville.

Scoggins, Lynelle Sue

1961   History of Kisatchie. Research report for M.E., Dept. of Social Studies, Northwestern State College of Louisiana. On file, Cammie G. Henry Research Center, Watson Memorial Library, Northwestern State University of Louisiana, Natchitoches.

Sellards, E. H.

1952   *Early Man in North America.* University of Texas Press, Austin.

Sellards, E. H., G. L. Evans, and G. E. Meade

1947   Fossil Bison and Associated Artifacts from Plainview, Texas with Description of Artifacts by A.D.Krieger. *Bulletin of the Geological Society of America* 58:927–954.

Servello, A. Frank

1983   The Generation of a Replicable Stratification System for Upland Slope Geomorphic Surfaces. In *U.S.L. Fort Polk Archaeological Survey and Cultural Resources Management Program,* 2 vols., edited by A. Frank Servello, pp. 205–224. University of Southwestern Louisiana, Lafayette.

1984a   *Cultural Resources Investigations in the Proposed Multi-Purpose Range Complex—Option 2A Area: The Level I Phase 1 and 2 Sampling Survey Results.* Fort Polk CRMP Report No. 7. Kisatchie Regional Environmental Management Group, Anacoco, Louisiana.

1984b   *CRMP Level Ia Cultural Resources Investigations in the Proposed Multi-Purpose Range Complex—Option 2 and Option 3 Areas, Fort Polk Military Reservation.* Fort Polk CRMP Report No. 8. Kisatchie Regional Environmental Management Group, Anacoco, Louisiana.

1985a   *CRMP Level I Cultural Resources Investigations in the Proposed United Gas Transmission Line Corridor at Fort Polk.* Fort Polk CRMP Report No. 10. Kisatchie Regional Environmental Management Group, Anacoco, Louisiana.

1985b   *CRMP Level I Intensive Survey of Two Proposed Firing Positions in the Six Mile Creek 5 Training Area, Fort Polk.* Fort Polk CRMP Report No. 11. Kisatchie Regional Environmental Management Group, Anacoco, Louisiana.

1985c   *CRMP Level I Investigations at the ARF Range Proposed for Range 15 Alpha in the Northeastern Portion of Zion Hills 3, Fort Polk.* Fort Polk CRMP Report No. 12. Kisatchie Regional Environmental Management Group, Anacoco, Louisiana.

1985d   *CRMP Level I Investigations of Proposed Artillery Firing Points and Facility in Slagle 4 Training Area, Fort Polk.* Fort Polk CRMP Report No. 13. Kisatchie Regional Environmental Management Group, Anacoco, Louisiana.

1985e   *CRMP Level I Investigations at the FP-4 Area of Slagle 5, Fort Polk Military Reservation.* Fort Polk CRMP Report No. 15. Kisatchie Regional Environmental Management Group, Anacoco, Louisiana.

1986   *CRMP Level I Investigations at the FP-5 Area of Slagle 6, Fort Polk Military Reservation.* Fort Polk CRMP Report No. 16. Kisatchie Regional Environmental Management Group, Anacoco, Louisiana.

Servello, A. Frank (editor)

1983   *U.S.L. Fort Polk Archaeological Survey and Cultural Resources Management Program.* 2 vols. University of Southwestern Louisiana, Lafayette.

Servello, A. Frank, and Thomas H. Bianchi
  1983   Geomorphology and Cultural Stratigraphy of the Eagle Hill Area of Peason Ridge.
          In *U.S.L. Fort Polk Archaeological Survey and Cultural Resources Management
          Program*, 2 vols., edited by A. Frank Servello, pp. 377–566. University of South-
          western Louisiana, Lafayette.

Servello, A. Frank, and James R. Morehead
  1983   Cultural Stratigraphy in the Castor Creek Erosional Surface. In *U.S.L. Fort Polk
          Archaeological Survey and Cultural Resources Management Program*, 2 vols.,
          edited by A. Frank Servello, pp. 567–623. University of Southwestern Louisiana,
          Lafayette.

Servello, A. Frank, and James D. Morgan
  1983   Intensive Survey Strategies and Initial Stratification Scheme. In *U.S.L. Fort Polk
          Archaeological Survey and Cultural Resources Management Program*, 2 vols.,
          edited by A. Frank Servello, pp. 182–204. University of Southwestern Louisiana,
          Lafayette.

Shafer, Harry J.
  1963   Test Excavations at the Youngsport Site: A Stratified Terrace Site in Bell County,
          Texas. *Bulletin of the Texas Archeological Society* 24:57–81.
  1973   *Lithic Technology at the George C. Davis Site, Cherokee County, Texas*. Ph.D.
          dissertation, Dept. of Anthropology, University of Texas at Austin.

Sharrer, G. Terry
  1981   Naval Stores, 1781–1881. In *Material Culture of the Wooden Age*, edited by Brook
          Hindle. Sleepy Hollow Press, Terrytown, New York.

Sheehan, Mark
  1982   Flora. In *Eagle Hill: A Late Quaternary Upland Site in Western Louisiana*, edited
          by Joel D. Gunn and David O. Brown, pp. 161–163. Special Report 12, Center for
          Archaeological Research, University of Texas at San Antonio.

Sherratt, Andrew
  1997   Climatic Cycles and Behavioral Revolutions: The Emergence of Modern Humans
          and the Beginning of Farming. *Antiquity* 71:271–287.

Shott, Michael J.
  1985   Shovel-Test Sampling as a Site Discovery Technique: A Case Study from Michi-
          gan. *Journal of Field Archaeology* 12:457–468.
  1986   Technological Organization and Settlement Mobility: An Ethnographic Examina-
          tion. *Journal of Anthropological Research* 42:15–51.

Shreve, Lynn
  1994a   *Heritage Resources Management Summary 94-26*. Kisatchie National Forest,
          Pineville, Louisiana.
  1994b   *Heritage Resources Management Summary 94-28*. Kisatchie National Forest,
          Pineville, Louisiana.

Shuman, Malcolm, Dennis Jones, and Melissa Weidenfeld
  1995   *Fort Polk Delivery Order 1: A Cultural Resources Survey of 313 Acres of Pro-
          posed Perimeter Fenceline on Peason Ridge, Fort Polk, Natchitoches, Sabine,
          and Vernon Parishes, Louisiana*. Gulf South Research Corporation, Baton Rouge,
          Louisiana.

Shuman, Malcolm, Dennis Jones, Melissa Weidenfeld, and John Lindemuth
  1996a   *Fort Polk Delivery Order 2: A Cultural Resources Survey of 1,930 Acres in Peason
          Ridge Training Area (Sabine and Vernon Parishes), Fort Polk, Louisiana*. Gulf
          South Research Corporation, Baton Rouge, Louisiana.

1996b   *Fort Polk Delivery Order 3: A Cultural Resources Survey of 319 Acres on the North Boundary of Peason Ridge Training Area, Sabine Parish, Louisiana.* Gulf South Research Corporation, Baton Rouge, Louisiana.

1996c   *Fort Polk Delivery Order 4: A Cultural Resources Survey of 1,002 Acres in the North Fort, Main Fort, Fort Polk, Vernon Parish, Louisiana.* Gulf South Research Corporation, Baton Rouge, Louisiana.

Singleton, Theresa A.

1980   *The Archaeology of Afro-American Slavery in Coastal Georgia: A Regional Perception of Slave Household and Community Patterns.* Ph.D. dissertation, University of Florida, Gainesville.

Sitton, Thad

1995   *Backwoodsmen, Stockmen and Hunters along a Big Thicket River Valley.* University of Oklahoma Press, Norman.

Skinner, S. Alan

1980   Preadaptation for the Southern Cult in the Caddoan Heartland. *Louisiana Archaeology* 6:207–221.

Smith, Bruce D.

1986   The Archaeology of the Southeastern United States: From Dalton to DeSoto. *Advances in World Archaeology* 5:1–88.

1992   *Rivers of Change: Essays on Early Agriculture in Eastern North America.* Smithsonian Institution Press, Washington, D.C.

Smith, E. Kirby (General)

1864   Report of General E. Kirby Smith, June 11. In *War of the Rebellion: The Official Record of the Union and Confederate Armies in the War of the Rebellion,* series 1, part 1, vol. 34:478. GPO, Washington, D.C.

Smith, Marion

1938   *A Sociological Analysis of Rural Education in Louisiana.* Louisiana State University Press, Baton Rouge.

Smith, Rhonda L.

1991   *Archaeological Survey of 15 Acres on the Main Fort (Vernon Parish), Fort Polk, Louisiana (1991).* Report submitted to the National Park Service, Southeast Region, Atlanta.

Smith, Samuel D., and Stephen T. Rogers

1979   *A Survey of Historic Pottery Making in Tennessee.* Div. of Archaeology, Tennessee Dept. of Conservation, Nashville.

Smith, Steven D.

1986   *Bailey's Dam.* Anthropological Study No. 8, Dept. of Culture, Recreation and Tourism, Louisiana Archaeological Survey and Antiquities Commission, Baton Rouge.

1991   *A Comparison of the Documentary Evidence of Material Culture and the Archaeological Record: Store Ledgers and Two Black Tenant Sites, Waverly Plantation, Mississippi.* Volumes in Historical Archaeology XII. South Carolina Institute of Archaeology and Anthropology, Columbia.

1993   *Made It in the Timber: A Historic Overview of the Fort Leonard Wood Region, 1800–1940.* Midwestern Archaeological Research Center, Illinois State University, Normal.

1994   The Transportation Landscape within the Fort Leonard Wood Region of the Missouri Ozarks. In *Settler Communities in the West: Historic Contexts for Cultural Resource Managers of Department of Defense Lands,* edited by Robert Lyon, pp.

75–83. National Park Service, Denver, Dept. of Defense, Legacy Resource Management Program, Washington, D.C.

1999   *A Good Home for a Poor Man: A Historic Overview of the Fort Polk, Louisiana Region 1700–1940.* Southeast Archeological Center, NPS, Tallahassee.

Smith, Steven D., David F. Barton, and Timothy B. Riordan

1982   *Ethnoarchaeology of the Bay Springs Farmsteads: A Study of Rural American Settlement.* National Technical Information Service, Washington, D.C.

Smith, Steven D., Philip G. Rivet, Kathleen Byrd, and Nancy Hawkins

1983   *Louisiana's Comprehensive Archaeological Plan.* Dept. of Culture, Recreation, and Tourism, Div. of Cultural Development, Div. of Archaeology, Baton Rouge.

South, Stanley, and Michael Hartley

1980   *Deep Water and High Ground: Seventeenth Century Lowcountry Settlement.* Research Manuscript Series 166, South Carolina Institute of Archaeology and Anthropology, University of South Carolina, Columbia.

Speh, Carl F.

1921   The Naval Stores Industry in the Western Territory. In *Naval Stores, History, Production, Distribution, and Consumption,* compiled by Thomas Gamble, pp. 109–118. Weekly Naval Stores Review, Review Publishing and Printing Company, Savannah.

Spiess, Arthur E., Deborah Wilson, and James W. Bradley

1998   Paleoindian Occupation in the New England–Maritimes Region: Beyond Cultural Ecology. *Archaeology of Eastern North America* 26:201–264.

Stanford, Dennis

1983   Pre-Clovis Occupation South of the Ice Sheets. In *Early Man in the New World,* edited by Richard Shutler, Jr., pp. 65–72. Sage Publications, Beverly Hills, California.

1999   Paleoindian Archaeology and Late Pleistocene Environments in the Plains and Southwestern United States. In *Ice Age Peoples of North America: Environments, Origins, and Adaptations of the First Americans,* edited by Robson Bonnichsen and Karen L. Turnmire, pp. 281–339. Center for the Study of the First Americans, Oregon State University Press, Corvallis.

Stephenson, Robert L.

1949   Archaeological Survey of Lavon and Garza–Little Elm Reservoirs: A Preliminary Report. *Bulletin of the Texas Archeological and Paleontological Society* 20.

Stephenson, Keith, Judith Bense, and Frankie Snow

2002   Some Aspects of Deptford and Swift Creek of the South Atlantic and Gulf Coastal Plains. In *The Woodland Southeast,* edited by David G. Anderson and Robert C. Mainfort, Jr., pp. 318–351. University of Alabama Press, Tuscaloosa.

Steponaitis, Vincas P., M. James Blackman, and Hector Neff

1996   Large-Scale Patterns in the Chemical Composition of Mississippian Pottery. *American Antiquity* 61:555–572.

Stewart-Abernathy, Leslie C.

1986   *The Moser Farmstead, Independent But Not Isolated: The Archeology of a Late Nineteenth Century Ozark Farmstead.* Research Series No. 26, Arkansas Archeological Survey, Fayetteville.

Stine, Linda France

1989   *Raised Up in Hard Times, Circa 1900–1940.* Ph.D. dissertation, Dept. of Anthropology, University of North Carolina, Chapel Hill.

Stoddard, Major Amos

1812   *Sketches, Historical and Descriptive of Louisiana.* Mathew Carey, Philadelphia.

Stokes, George A.
   1957   Lumbering and Western Louisiana Cultural Landscapes. *Annals of the Associa-tion of American Geographers* 47:250–266.
   1959   Log-Rafting in Louisiana. *Journal of Geography* 58(2):81–89.
Stoltman, James B.
   1978   Temporal Models in Prehistory: An Example from Eastern North America. *Current Anthropology* 19:703–746.
Story, Dee Ann
   1990   Cultural History of the Native Americans. In *The Archaeology and Bioarchaeology of the Gulf Coastal Plain,* vol. 1, edited by Dee Ann Story, Janice A. Guy, Barbara A. Burnett, Martha Doty Freeman, Jerome C. Rose, D. Gentry Steele, Ben W. Olive, and Karl J. Reinhard, pp. 163–366. Research Series No. 38, Arkansas Ar-cheological Survey, Fayetteville.
Story, Dee Ann, Janice A. Guy, Barbara A. Burnett, Martha Doty Freeman, Jerome C. Rose, D. Gentry Steele, Ben W. Olive, and Karl J. Reinhard (editors)
   1990   *The Archeology and Bioarcheology of the Gulf Coastal Plain.* 2 vols. Research Series No. 38, Arkansas Archeological Survey, Fayetteville.
Strahler, Arthur N.
   1957   Quantitative Analysis of Watershed Geomorphology. *Transactions, American Geo-physical Union* 38(6):913–920.
   1964   Quantitative Geomorphology of Drainage Basins and Channel Networks. In *Hand-book of Applied Hydrology,* edited by Ven Te Chow, pp. 439–476. McGraw-Hill, New York.
Stright, Melanie J., Eileen M. Lear, and James F. Bennett
   1999   *Spatial Data Analysis of Artifacts Redeposited by Coastal Erosion: A Case Study of McFaddin Beach, Texas.* U.S. Dept. of the Interior Minerals Management Ser-vice OCS Study MMS 99-0068, Herndon, Virginia.
Struever, Stuart, and Gail L. Houart
   1972   An Analysis of the Hopewell Interaction Sphere. In *Social Exchange and Interac-tion,* edited by Edwin M. Wilmsen, pp. 47–49. Anthropological Papers No. 46, Museum of Anthropology, University of Michigan, Ann Arbor.
Stuiver, Minze, Paula J. Reimer, Edouard Bard, J. Warren Beck, G. S. Burr, Konrad A. Hughen, Bernd Kromer, Gerry McCormac, Johannes van der Plicht, and Marco Spurk
   1998   INTCAL98 Radiocarbon Age Calibration, 24,000–0 cal B.P. *Radiocarbon* 40(3).
Suhm, Dee Ann
   1957   Excavations at the Smith Rockshelter, Travis County, Texas. *Texas Journal of Science* 9(1):26–58.
   1959   The Williams Site and Central Texas Archaeology. *Texas Journal of Science* 11(2):218–250.
Suhm, Dee Ann, and Edward B. Jelks
   1962   *Handbook of Texas Archaeology: Type Descriptions.* Texas Archeological Soci-ety and Texas Memorial Museum, Austin.
Suhm, Dee Ann, Alex D. Krieger, and Edward B. Jelks
   1954   An Introductory Handbook of Texas Archaeology. *Bulletin of the Texas Archeo-logical Society* 25.
Sutherland, Daniel E.
   1980   Looking for a Home: Louisiana Emigrants during the Civil War and Reconstruc-tion. *Louisiana History* 21(4):341–360.
Swanda, Michael
   1982   *Cultural Resources Survey of 680 Acres on the Vernon Ranger District, Kisatchie*

National Forest, Vernon Parish, Louisiana. Archaeological Assessments Report 18, Pineville, Louisiana.

Swanton, John R.
1911 *Indian Tribes of the Lower Mississippi Valley and Adjacent Coast of the Gulf of Mexico.* Bulletin 43, Bureau of American Ethnology, Washington, D.C.
1942 *Source Material on the History and Ethnology of the Caddo Indians.* Bulletin 132, Bureau of American Ethnology, Washington, D.C.
1946 *The Indians of the Southeastern United States.* Bulletin 137, Bureau of American Ethnology, Washington, D.C.

Taylor, Anna J., and Cheryl L. Highley
n.d. Archaeological Investigations at the Loma Sandia Site (41LK28): A Prehistoric Cemetery and Campsite in Live Oak County, Texas. Ms. submitted to the Texas Dept. of Transportation, Austin.

Taylor, R. E., C. Vance Haynes, Jr., and M. Stuiver
1996 Clovis and Folsom Age Estimates: Stratigraphic Context and Radiocarbon Calibration. *Antiquity* 70(269):515–525.

Taylor, Richard (Major General)
1864a Letter to Brigadier General W. P. Boggs, January 31. In *War of the Rebellion: The Official Record of the Union and Confederate Armies in the War of the Rebellion,* series 1, part 2, vol. 34:930. GPO, Washington, D.C.
1864b Report of General Taylor, April 18. In *War of the Rebellion: The Official Record of the Union and Confederate Armies in the War of the Rebellion,* series 1, part 1, vol. 34:571. GPO, Washington, D.C.
1864c Letter to Brigadier General W. P. Boggs, February 26. In *War of the Rebellion: The Official Record of the Union and Confederate Armies in the War of the Rebellion,* series 1, part 2, vol. 34:991. GPO, Washington, D.C.
1879 *Destruction and Reconstruction: Personal Experiences of the Late War.* Appleton and Company, New York.

Thomas, Prentice, Jr., and L. J. Campbell
1978 *A Multicomponent Site in the Harpyville Bend of Little River 16Sa37: The Whatley Site.* New World Research, Report of Investigations 11, Pollock, Louisiana.

Thomas, Prentice M., Jr., Steven Shelley, L. Janice Campbell, Mark T. Swanson, Carol S. Weed, and John P. Lenzer
1982 *Cultural Resources Investigations at the Fort Polk Military Reservation, Vernon, Sabine, and Natchitoches Parishes, Louisiana.* New World Research, Report of Investigations 69, Pollock, Louisiana.

Thomas, Prentice, Jr., James R. Morehead, James H. Mathews, and L. Janice Campbell
1992 *Fort Polk 2: The Results of a Second Program of Site Testing at Ten Sites on Fort Polk Military Reservation, Sabine Parish, Louisiana.* Prentice Thomas and Assoc., Report of Investigations No. 218, Fort Walton Beach, Florida.

Thomas, Prentice M., Jr., Joseph Meyer, James R. Morehead, L. Janice Campbell, and James H. Mathews
1993a *Fort Polk 3: The Results of a Third Program of Site Testing at Ten Sites, Fort Polk Military Reservation, Natchitoches Parish, Louisiana.* Prentice Thomas and Assoc., Report of Investigations No. 221, Fort Walton Beach, Florida.

Thomas, Prentice M., Jr., James R. Morehead, L. Janice Campbell, James H. Mathews, and Joseph Meyer
1993b *Fort Polk 4: The Results of a Fourth Program of Site Testing at Ten Sites, Fort Polk Military Reservation, Natchitoches and Vernon Parishes, Louisiana.* Prentice Thomas and Assoc., Report of Investigations No. 223, Fort Walton Beach, Florida.

Thomas, Prentice M., Jr., L. Janice Campbell, James R. Morehead, James H. Mathews, and Joseph Meyer

1993c   *Fort Polk 5: The Results of a Fifth Program of Site Testing at Ten Sites, Fort Polk Military Reservation, Vernon Parish, Louisiana.* Prentice Thomas and Assoc., Report of Investigations No. 225, Fort Walton Beach, Florida.

Thomas, Prentice M., Jr., L. Janice Campbell, James H. Mathews, James R. Morehead, and Joseph Meyer

1993d   *Fort Polk 6: The Results of a Sixth Program of Site Testing at Ten Sites, Fort Polk Military Reservation, Natchitoches and Vernon Parishes, Louisiana.* Prentice Thomas and Assoc., Report of Investigations No. 227, Fort Walton Beach, Florida.

Thomas, Prentice M., Jr., L. Janice Campbell, James H. Mathews, James R. Morehead, Joseph Meyer, and Mark E. Stanley

1993e   *Fort Polk 8: The Results of an Eighth Program of Site Testing at Ten Sites, Fort Polk Military Reservation, Sabine and Vernon Parishes, Louisiana.* Prentice Thomas and Assoc., Report of Investigations No. 235, Fort Walton Beach, Florida.

Thomas, Prentice M., Jr., L. Janice Campbell, James R. Morehead, James H. Mathews, and Joseph Meyer

1994a   *Fort Polk 10: The Results of a Tenth Program of Site Testing, Fort Polk Military Reservation, Vernon Parish, Louisiana.* Prentice Thomas and Assoc., Report of Investigations No. 244, Fort Walton Beach, Florida.

Thomas, Prentice M., Jr., James R. Morehead, L. Janice Campbell, James H. Mathews, and Joseph Meyer

1994b   *Fort Polk 11: The Results of an Eleventh Program of Site Testing at Ten Sites, Fort Polk Military Reservation, Vernon Parish, Louisiana.* Prentice Thomas and Assoc., Report of Investigations No. 248, Fort Walton Beach, Florida.

Thomas, Prentice M., Jr., James R. Morehead, Joseph Meyer, James H. Mathews, and L. Janice Campbell

1997   *Fort Polk 28: The Results of a Twenty-Eighth Program of Site Testing at Ten Sites, Fort Polk Military Reservation, Natchitoches and Vernon Parishes, Louisiana.* Prentice Thomas and Assoc., Report of Investigations No. 340, Fort Walton Beach, Florida.

Thomas, Prentice M., Jr., Paul LaHaye, Chris Parrish, James R. Morehead, James H. Mathews, L. Janice Campbell, and Alan Saltus

1999a   *Fort Polk 35: The Results of a Thirty-Fifth Program of Site Testing at Ten Sites, Fort Polk Military Reservation, Natchitoches and Vernon Parishes, Louisiana.* Prentice Thomas and Assoc., Report of Investigations No. 391, Fort Walton Beach, Florida.

1999b   *Fort Polk 38: The Results of a Thirty-Eighth Program of Site Testing at Ten Sites, Fort Polk Military Reservation, Natchitoches and Vernon Parishes, Louisiana.* Prentice Thomas and Assoc., Report of Investigations No. 399, Fort Walton Beach, Florida.

1999c   *Fort Polk 42: The Results of a Forty-Second Program of Site Testing at Ten Sites, Fort Polk Military Reservation, Vernon Parish, Louisiana.* Prentice Thomas and Assoc., Report of Investigations No. 442, Fort Walton Beach, Florida.

Thoms, Alston V.

1992   Late Pleistocene and Early Holocene Regional Land Use Patterns: A Perspective from the Preliminary Results of Archaeological Studies at the Richard Beene Site, 41BX831, Lower Medina River, South Texas. In *Late Cenozoic Alluvial Stratigraphy and Prehistory of the Inner Gulf Coastal Plain, South-Central Texas.* Guidebook, 10th Annual Meeting, South-Central Friends of the Pleistocene. Lubbock Lake Quaternary Research Center Series 4, Lubbock, Texas.

Toth, Edwin Alan

1974 *Archaeology and Ceramics at the Marksville Site.* Anthropological Papers No. 56, Museum of Anthropology, University of Michigan, Ann Arbor.

1979 The Marksville Connection. In *Hopewell Archaeology: The Chillicothe Conference,* edited by David S. Brose and N'omi Greber, pp. 188–199. Kent State University Press, Kent, Ohio.

Turner, Ellen Sue, and Thomas R. Hester

1993 *A Field Guide to Stone Artifacts of Texas Indians,* 2nd ed. Texas Monthly Press, Austin.

Turner, Frederick Jackson

1920 *The Frontier in American History.* Henry Holt, New York.

U.S. House of Representatives

1881 *Report of Survey of the Calcasieu River.* House Executive Document 46, 46th Congress, 3rd Session, January 18, 1881.

1892 *Report of a Preliminary Examination of the Sabine River, from Sudduths Bluff, Texas to Logansport, Louisiana.* House Executive Document 139, 52nd Congress, 2nd Session, December 19, 1892.

Van Note, Beverly

1982a Fine Grained (Sand) Sediment Analysis. In *Eagle Hill: A Late Quaternary Upland Site in Western Louisiana,* edited by Joel D. Gunn and David O. Brown, pp. 145–150. Special Report 12, Center for Archaeological Research, University of Texas at San Antonio.

1982b Geochemical Analysis. In *Eagle Hill: A Late Quaternary Upland Site in Western Louisiana,* edited by Joel D. Gunn and David O. Brown, pp. 156–160. Special Report 12, Center for Archaeological Research, University of Texas at San Antonio.

Varner, John, and Jeannette Varner

1951 *The Florida of the Inca.* University of Texas Press, Austin.

Veitch, F. P., and V. E. Grotlisch

1921 What Uncle Sam Does for the Naval Stores Industry. In *Naval Stores, History, Production, Distribution, and Consumption,* compiled by Thomas Gamble, pp. 135–138. Weekly Naval Stores Review, Review Publishing and Printing Company, Savannah.

Vernon News

1900 Historical, Biographical, and Industrial [?] Including Timber Lumber, and Mill Interests of Vernon Parish. Special Edition, May 1. Vertical files, Vernon Parish Library, Leesville.

Vernon Parish Planning Board

1949 *Vernon Parish Resources and Facilities.* Vernon Parish Planning Board, in cooperation with the State of Louisiana, Dept. of Public Works, Planning Div. On file, Watson Library, Northwestern State University, Natchitoches.

Vernon Parish Tourist and Recreation Commission

n.d. *The History, Services, and Points of Interest in Leesville, Vernon Parish and Fort Polk.* Pamphlet. Leesville-Vernon Parish Chamber [of Commerce], Leesville. Copy on file, Louisiana State Archives, Baton Rouge.

Walker, J. G. (Major General)

1864 Report of Major General J. G. Walker, March 19. In *War of the Rebellion: The*

Official Record of the Union and Confederate Armies in the War of the Rebellion, series 1, part 1, vol. 34:600. GPO, Washington, D.C.

Wallace, Patricia
  1982   Paleo-Indian Projectile Point Chronology in Western Louisiana. In *Eagle Hill: A Late Quaternary Upland Site in Western Louisiana,* edited by Joel D. Gunn and David O. Brown, pp. 221–230. Special Report 12, Center for Archaeological Research, University of Texas at San Antonio.

Watts, William A., Eric C. Grimm, and T. C. Hussey
  1996   Mid-Holocene Forest History of Florida and the Coastal Plain of Georgia and South Carolina. In *Archaeology of the Mid-Holocene Southeast,* edited by Kenneth E. Sassaman and David G. Anderson, pp. 28–38. University Press of Florida, Gainesville.

Weaver, David C., and James F. Doster
  1982   *Historical Geography of the Upper Tombigbee Valley.* Center for the Study of Southern History and Culture, University of Alabama, University.

Webb, Clarence H.
  1946   Two Unusual Types of Chipped Stone Artifacts from Northwest Louisiana. *Bulletin of the Texas Archeological and Paleontological Society* 17:9–17.
  1948a   Caddoan Prehistory: The Bossier Focus. *Bulletin of the Texas Archeological and Paleontological Society* 19:100–147.
  1948b   Evidences of Pre-Pottery Cultures in Louisiana. *American Antiquity* 13:227–232.
  1959   *The Belcher Mound, A Stratified Caddoan Site in Caddo Parish, Louisiana.* Memoirs of the Society for American Archaeology No. 16, Menasha, Wisconsin.
  1963   The Smithport Landing Site: An Alto Focus Component in De Soto Parish, Louisiana. *Bulletin of the Texas Archeological Society* 34:143–187.
  1968   The Extent and Content of Poverty Point Culture. *American Antiquity* 33:297–321.
  1981   *Stone Points and Tools of Northwestern Louisiana.* Special Publication of the Louisiana Archaeological Society, No. 1. Lafayette.
  1982   *The Poverty Point Culture.* Revised; originally published 1977. Geoscience and Man 17. Louisiana State University, Baton Rouge.
  1984   The Bellevue Focus: A Marksville-Troyville Manifestation in Northwestern Louisiana. *Louisiana Archaeology* 9:249–274.
  1991   Poverty Point Culture and Site Definitions. In *The Poverty Point Culture: Local Manifestations, Subsistence Practices, and Trade Networks,* edited by Kathleen M. Byrd, pp. 3–6. Geoscience and Man 29. Louisiana State University, Baton Rouge.
  2000   *Stone Points and Tools of Northwestern Louisiana.* Special Publication of the Louisiana Archaeological Society, No. 1, 2nd ed. Lafayette.

Webb, Clarence H., and Monroe Dodd
  1939   Further Excavations of the Gahagan Mound: Connections with a Florida Culture. *Bulletin of the Texas Archeological and Paleontological Society* 11:92–127.

Webb, Clarence H., and Hiram G. Gregory
  1986   *The Caddo Indians of Louisiana.* 2nd ed. Anthropological Study No. 2, Dept. of Culture, Recreation and Tourism, Louisiana Archaeological Survey and Antiquities Commission, Baton Rouge.

Webb, Clarence H., and Ralph R. McKinney
  1975   Mounds Plantation (16CD12), Caddo Parish, Louisiana. *Louisiana Archaeology* 2:39–127.

Webb, Clarence H., Forrest E. Murphy, Wesley G. Ellis, and Roland Green
  1969   The Resch Site, 41Hs16, Harrison County, Texas. *Bulletin of the Texas Archeo-logical Society* 40:3–106.
Webb, Clarence H., J. L. Shiner, and E. W. Roberts
  1971   The John Pearce Site (16CD56): A San Patrice Site in Caddo Parish, Louisiana. *Bulletin of the Texas Archeological Society* 42:1–49.
Webb, Thompson III, Patrick J. Bartlein, Sandy P. Harrison, and Katherine H. Anderson
  1993   Vegetation, Lake Levels, and Climate in Eastern North America for the Past 18,000 Years. In *Global Climate since the Last Glacial Maximum,* edited by H. E. Wright, Jr., J. E. Kutzbach, T. Webb III, W. F. Ruddiman, F. A. Street-Perrott, and P. J. Bartlein, pp. 415–467. University of Minnesota Press, Minneapolis.
Weinstein, Richard A.
  1986   Tchefuncte Occupation in the Lower Mississippi Delta and Adjacent Coastal Zone. In *The Tchula Period in the Mid-South and Lower Mississippi Valley: Proceedings of the 1982 Mid-South Archaeological Conference,* edited by David H. Dye and Ronald C. Brister, pp. 102–127. Archaeological Report 17, Mississippi Dept. of Archives and History, Jackson.
  1995   The Tchula Period in the Lower Mississippi Valley and Adjacent Coastal Zone. In *"An' Stuff Like That There:" In Appreciation of William G. Haag,* edited by Jon L. Gibson and Richard A. Weinstein, pp. 153–187. *Louisiana Archaeology* 18.
Welch, Robert
  1942   *Geology of Vernon Parish.* Geological Bulletin 22, Louisiana Dept. of Conservation, Baton Rouge.
Wendorf, Fred, and Alex D. Krieger
  1959   New Light on the Midland Discovery. *American Antiquity* 25(1):68–78.
Wendorf, Fred, Alex D. Krieger, Claude C. Albritton, and T. D. Stewart
  1955   *The Midland Discovery.* University of Texas Press, Austin.
Werner, H. E., and Margie H. Rowzee
  n.d.   Fact Sheet on Vernon Parish. On file, Vernon Parish Library, Leesville.
Wheaton, Thomas R., Jr., Amy Friedlander, and Patrick H. Garrow
  1983   *Yaughan and Curriboo Plantations: Studies in Afro-American Archaeology.* Soil Systems, Marietta. Report on file, National Park Service, Atlanta.
Whittington, G. P.
  1935   *Rapides Parish, Louisiana: A History.* Reprinted in one volume from *Louisiana Historical Quarterly.* Alexandria Committee of the National Society of the Colonial Dames in the State of Louisiana, Alexandria.
Willey, Gordon R.
  1966   *An Introduction to North American Archaeology.* Vol. I, *North and Middle American Archaeology.* Prentice Hall, Englewood Cliffs, New Jersey.
Williams, Luis M., Jr., Paul V. Heinrich, Ralph Draughon, Jr., and William P. Athens
  1994a   *A Cultural Resources Survey of 985 Acres in the South Fullerton Remote Village and Timber Sale Area, Fort Polk, Vernon Parish, Louisiana.* R. Christopher Goodwin and Assoc., Delivery Order Report RCG-14, New Orleans.
  1995a   *A Cultural Resources Survey of 1,000 Acres in the North Fullerton Maneuver Block, Fort Polk, Vernon Parish, Louisiana.* R. Christopher Goodwin and Assoc., Delivery Order Report RCG-16, New Orleans.
  1995b   *A Cultural Resources Survey of 1,000 Acres in the North Fullerton Maneuver Block, Fort Polk, Vernon Parish, Louisiana.* R. Christopher Goodwin and Assoc., Delivery Order Report RCG-17, New Orleans.

Williams, Luis M., Jr., Paul V. Heinrich, Ralph Draughon, Jr., Thomas Fenn, and William P. Athens
    1994b   *A Cultural Resources Survey of 995 Acres in the East Fullerton Maneuver Block, Fort Polk, Vernon Parish, Louisiana.* R. Christopher Goodwin and Assoc., Delivery Order Report RCG-15, New Orleans.

Williams, Luis M., Jr., Paul V. Heinrich, Ralph Draughon, Jr., Jennifer Cohen, and William P. Athens
    1994c   *A Cultural Resources Survey of 1,000 Acres in the North Fullerton Maneuver Block, Fort Polk, Vernon Parish, Louisiana.* R. Christopher Goodwin and Assoc., Delivery Order Report RCG-18, New Orleans.

Williams, Marie Durr
    1976   Vernon Parish. Fact Sheet, Louisiana Cooperative Extension Service. Vertical files, Vernon Parish Library, Leesville.

Williams, Michael
    1989   *Americans and Their Forests: A Historical Geography.* Cambridge University Press, New York.

Williams, Stephen
    1961   Historic Sites in the Caddoan Area, and Comments Thereon. Proceedings of the Fifth Caddoan Conference. *Bulletin of the Texas Archeological Society* 31:122–130.
    1964   The Aboriginal Location of the Kadohadacho and Related Tribes. In *Explorations in Cultural Anthropology,* edited by Ward H. Goodenough, pp. 545–570. McGraw-Hill, New York.

Williams, Stephen, and Jeffrey P. Brain
    1983   *Excavations at the Lake George Site, Yazoo County, Mississippi, 1958–1960.* Papers of the Peabody Museum of Archaeology and Ethnology 74, Cambridge, Massachusetts.

Williams, Stephen, and James B. Stoltman
    1965   An Outline of Southeastern United States Prehistory with Particular Emphasis on the Paleoindian Era. In *The Quaternary of the United States,* edited by H. E. Wright and D. G. Frey, pp. 669–683. Princeton University Press, Princeton, New Jersey.

Willingham, Charles G., and Timothy P. Phillips
    1987   *Cultural Resources Surveys on the Kisatchie National Forest, Louisiana, FY 1985.* Kisatchie National Forest Report of Investigations No. 2, Kisatchie National Forest, Pineville, Louisiana.

Wilson, Eugene M.
    1974   Form Changes in Folk Houses. In *Man and Cultural Heritage,* edited by H. J. Walker and William G. Haag, pp. 65–71. Geoscience and Man 5. Louisiana State University, Baton Rouge.

Wilson, James R., David G. Anderson, and J. W. Joseph
    1988   *Cultural Resources Planning Manual.* Vol. 2 of *Fort Polk Historic Preservation Plan,* assembled by David G. Anderson and James R. Wilson. Garrow and Assoc., Atlanta.

Winters, Howard
    1967   *An Archaeological Survey of the Wabash Valley in Illinois.* Revised; originally published 1963. Illinois State Museum Reports of Investigation 10, Springfield.

Winters, John D.
    1963   *The Civil War in Louisiana.* Louisiana State University Press, Baton Rouge.

Winters, Robert Kirby, G. B. Ward, and I. F. Eldridge
 1943   *Louisiana Forest Resources and Industries.* Miscellaneous Publication No. 519, U.S. Dept. of Agriculture, Washington, D.C.
Wise, Erbon W.
 1971   *Tall Pines: The Story of Vernon Parish.* West Calcasieu Printers, Sulphur, Louisiana.
 1988   *Tall Pines: The Story of Vernon Parish—The Expanded Edition.* West Calcasieu Printers, Sulphur, Louisiana.
Wise, Erbon W. (editor)
 1977   *Huey P. Long and Vernon Parish.* Louisiana Offset Printers, Alexandria.
Wobst, Martin
 1974   Boundary Conditions for Paleolithic Social Systems: A Simulation Approach. *American Antiquity* 39:147–178.
 1976   Locational Relationships in Paleolithic Society. *Journal of Human Evolution* 5:49–58.
Woodall, J. Ned
 1980   The Caddoan Confederacies: Some Ecological Considerations. *Louisiana Archaeology* 6:127–172.
Woodiel, Deborah Kay
 1993   The St. Gabriel Site: Prehistoric Life on the Mississippi. *Louisiana Archaeology* 20:1–136.
Woofter, Thomas J.
 1936   *Landlord and Tenant on the Cotton Plantation.* Research Monograph 5, Works Progress Administration, Washington, D.C.
Works Progress Administration (WPA)
 1936   Leesville, Louisiana. Works Progress Administration (author's last name may be Isenberg). On file, Louisiana State Library, Drawer 8, No. 61, Baton Rouge.
Wormington, H. Marie
 1957   *Ancient Man in North America,* 4th ed. Denver Museum of Natural History Popular Series No. 4, Denver.
Wright, H. E., Jr.
 1992   Patterns of Holocene Climatic Change in the Midwestern United States. *Quaternary Research* 38:129–134.
Wright, H. E., Jr. (editor)
 1983   *Late Quaternary Environments of the United States.* Vol. 2, *The Holocene.* University of Minnesota Press, Minneapolis.
Wright, Solomon Alexander
 1942   *My Rambles as East Texas Cowboy, Hunter, Fisherman, Tie-Cutter.* Texas Folklore Society, Austin, Texas.
Wyckoff, Donald G.
 1984   The Foragers: Eastern Oklahoma. In *Prehistory of Oklahoma,* edited by Robert E. Bell, pp. 119–160. Academic Press, New York.
Wyckoff, Donald G., and Robert Bartlett
 1995   Living on the Edge: Late Pleistocene–Early Holocene Cultural Interaction along the Southeastern Woodlands–Plains Border. In *Native American Interaction: Multiscalar Analyses and Interpretations in the Eastern Woodlands,* edited by Michael S. Nassaney and Kenneth E. Sassaman, pp. 27–72. University of Tennessee Press, Knoxville.
Yakubik, Jill-Karen, and Herschel A. Franks
 1990   *Archaeological Survey of 65 Acres on the Main Fort, Vernon Parish, Louisiana.*

Including an Assessment of 16VN1076 and Recordation at Cemetery Number Two. Report submitted to the National Park Service, Southeast Region, Atlanta.

Yu, Zicheng, and Ulrich Eicher
   1998   Abrupt Climate Oscillations during the Last Deglaciation in Central North America. *Science* 282:2235–2238.

Zelinsky, Wilbur
   1951   Where the South Begins: The Northern Limits of the Appalachian South in Terms of Settlement Landscapes. *Social Forces* 30:172–178.

Contributors

David G. Anderson is an archaeologist at the Southeast Archeological Center of the National Park Service in Tallahassee, Florida. The author of numerous papers and monographs on prehistoric and historic archaeology in various parts of North America and the Caribbean, in 1990 he received the Southeastern Archaeological Conference's first C. B. Moore award for excellence by a young scholar. In 1991 he received the Society for American Archaeology's dissertation prize for his work on organizational cycling in Mississippian chiefdoms. He also received the SAA's Presidential Recognition Award in 1997 and the Excellence in Cultural Resource Management Award for Research in 1999. Previous books include *The Savannah River Chiefdoms: Political Change in the Late Prehistoric Southeast* (Alabama 1994); with Kenneth B. Sassaman, *The Paleoindian and Early Archaic Southeast* (Alabama 1996) and *The Archaeology of the Mid-Holocene Southeast* (Florida 1996); and, with Robert C. Mainfort, Jr., *The Woodland Southeast* (Alabama 2002).

J. W. Joseph is the President of New South Associates, a cultural resources consulting firm headquartered in Stone Mountain, Georgia. He received his Ph.D. in historical archaeology from the University of Pennsylvania and has directed historical archaeological investigations of a number of sites, including rural farmsteads and plantations, urban sites, and industrial sites of both the eighteenth and nineteenth centuries. He is the editor (with Martha Zierden) of *Another's Country: Archaeological and Historical Perspectives on Cultural Interactions in the Southern Colonies* (Alabama 2002), as well as numerous articles published in edited volumes and journals.

Mary Beth Reed, a public historian with New South Associates in Stone Mountain, Georgia, has written many historical contexts and studies on historical sites throughout the Southeast. A recipient of the Georgia Women in Preservation award, she has recently coauthored an extensive history of the Savannah River Site titled *Savannah River Site at Fifty* (Government Printing Office).

Steven D. Smith is the Head of the Cultural Resources Consulting Division of the South Carolina Institute of Archaeology and Anthropology. He received his Master's degree from the University of Kentucky in 1983. He is the author of *A Good Home for a Poor Man* (National Park Service 1999) and a coeditor (with David C. Crass, Martha Zierden, and Richard Brooks) of *The Southern Colonial Backcountry: Interdisciplinary Perspectives on Frontier Communities* (Tennessee 1998). His research interests include American military history and southern farmsteads of the nineteenth century. He has received many awards and recognitions from the U.S. Army for his writing of African American military history and assistance in cultural resource management at military installations.

Index